Sources for the History of Cyprus

Volume VI

English Texts:
British Period to 1900

Sources for the History of Cyprus

Edited by
Paul W. Wallace and Andreas G. Orphanides

Volume VI

English Texts:
British Period to 1900

Selected and Edited, with Introduction and Notes by
DAVID W. MARTIN
(University at Albany, State University of New York)

Greece and Cyprus Research Center
1999

ISBN: 0-9651704-6-2

ISBN set: 0-9651704-0-3

TABLE OF CONTENTS

INTRODUCTION

In the present volume we continue to present texts of visitors to Cyprus writing in English. The previous volume ended just before the British occupation; we now present the beginnings of the British period, from 1878 to 1900. We chose to end this volume at 1900, because at about that time interest in Cyprus began to diminish, resulting in fewer visitors and fewer publications. Pertinent publications after that date are generally available.

The first selections are from the *Illustrated London News*, which describe, among other things, the arrival of Sir Garnet Wolseley, the first high commissioner of the island. Wolseley is somewhat representative of the type of traveler that appears in Cyprus during these 22 years. Many of these visitors were military people (or their relatives) or government servants, were usually of high social rank, and had a good education. By far the greater number are British, though Americans appear as well. Women travelers now begin to appear in increasing numbers, and they often give refreshingly novel views of matters that were growing stale.

In the selection of texts for this volume, we were guided by the same principles adhered to in the previous volume. The author must have visited Cyprus to be included, and must have made first-hand observations about the island or its people. We also tended to exclude archaeological works, because those works have often had a wide circulation and can be found in many libraries. We have also continued our former practice of presenting the texts exactly as they appeared in the original publications, excepting only obvious errors.

A number of the texts presented here were excerpted from books in which Cyprus was the exclusive topic of study. We chose not to excerpt material that has been superseded, such as summaries of Cypriot history or scientific observations. Sometimes indeed even first-hand observations of places and events were excluded if they seemed to have no value. On the other hand, we have included some of the occasionally outrageous generalizations (such as the difference between the Greeks and the Turks), for they illustrate the attitude held by people who were in a position (by their publications) to influence the world's view of Cyprus.

The quality of life for the Cypriots, Greek and Turk alike, was undoubtedly much improved by the arrival of the British. Maladministration, excessive taxation, corruption, injustice in courts and daily life, abuse and oppression, had been replaced by a humane and competent administration. It was a new world, and both Cypriots and foreigners reveled in the new era. Some of the foreigners saw at first great opportunities for themselves, only to be disappointed. The views of the Cypriots themselves do not much appear in these pages, except for the incipient desire (among the Greek Cypriots) for union with Greece. Cyprus had indeed entered a new era, but the eastern Mediterranean had also recently changed, and Cyprus, as a British possession, was a world unto itself, neither Greek nor Turk.

The Greek war of independence had resulted in many areas of the eastern Mediterranean being returned to the Greeks. Cyprus had not been included in that conflict and had remained under Turkish control until the arrival of the British in 1878. During the

British occupation Greeks and Turks lived together much as they had before, but an increased awareness of the world around them begins to appear in the 22 years of the present volume. The British remained in Cyprus until 1960, when Cyprus became an independent state consisting of Greek-Cypriots and Turkish-Cypriots, thus preserving it for future conflicts involving the two main communities of the island.

The early British period was an exciting time for the island and saw the creation of a number of works which we now need to acknowledge. The journal of Donisthorpe-Donne was published in ΚΥΠΡΙΑΚΑΙ ΣΠΟΥΔΑΙ with notes by Dr. George Georghallides. It is a pleasure to thank Dr. Georghallides and Mr. George Ioannides, President of the Society of Cypriot Studies, for permission to reproduce the text and notes. The unpublished diaries of F. H. H. Guillemard were the property of J. R. Stewart, whose widow, Eve Stewart, donated them to the Cyprus American Archaeological Research Institute in Nicosia in 1983. The Institute's director, Dr. Nancy Serwint, kindly gave us permission to quote from the diaries. For the reproduction of the numerous illustrations from *The Illustrated London News* we wish to acknowledge The Illustrated London News Picture Library and its manager, Miss Elaine Hart. We wish to thank Dr. Stuart Swiny for making available to us the Donne and Guillemard journals and some illustrations from *The Illustrated London News*. We also appreciate the contribution of materials by Dr. Reed Coughlan and Dr. John Overbeck. Dr. Paul W. Wallace continued his invaluable and considerable editorial publishing skills. Technical assistance was rendered by William Spence and Marianne Simon. Fran Martin's constant support is deeply appreciated.

The interest expressed by colleagues, family members and friends, including those in Cyprus, helped to maintain momentum.

ENGLISH TEXTS: BRITISH PERIOD TO 1900

The Illustrated London News 1878, 1879

[Plates 1–47]

With the British government taking over the administration of Cyprus in 1878, there was an intense interest in this little known Mediterranean island. *The Illustrated London News* began to publish articles and drawings of the island, and sent a "Special Artist and Correspondent" to report back with sketches and written reports. He was known by that title and the initials S.P.O.

S.P.O.'s early letters provide description of the arrival of the first British naval and army units and the confusion, uncertainties, and conflict they faced. His comments range from praise of the hard work and leadership of the Duke of Edinburgh to condemnation of the inadequacies of the army commissariat. In a short span of weeks these letters depict the increase of fever from non-existent to the most serious problem for the troops. His later letters devote more space to his observation of the country and its people. Some of the sketches reproduced in *The Illustrated London News*, and in this volume, are by army officers, but those by S.P.O. predominate and complement his written reports.

The editor of the journal frequently comments on the sketches, and sometimes includes comments which must have been written by eye-witnesses to the events. These comments are not elsewhere published in contemporary literature; we therefore give below first the editor's remarks about the engravings, and then S.P.O's letters (which appear only in the earlier volume). All the drawings and comments appear in 1878 (Volume LXXIII) and 1879 (Volume LXXV), and are reproduced here by the kind permission of The Illustrated London News Picture Library. In this volume we present the drawings in the sequence in which they appeared in the original publication. The volumes themselves were made available to us by the Schaffer Library of Union College, Schenectady, New York.

Remarks by the Editor, *The Illustrated London News,* 1878

Plates 1–4

We present a Map of Cyprus [Plate 4], with accompanying smaller maps to show the environs of several of its chief towns—namely, Famagousta or Famagosta, Limasol, Larnaka (Larnaca), and Cerinia (this name is also written Kyrenia); and with a map showing the vicinity of the neighbouring coasts of Syria and Asia Minor . . .

Our views of Cyprus in this week's Number include those [of] Famagosta [Plate 1] and of Larnaca [Plate 2], the ancient monastery of Cozzafani, and the singular rocks, called "the Hundred and One Houses," at the verge of the northern highlands above Cerinia [Plate 3].

(Editor, p. 70)

Plates 5–7

The new British Administrator, Lieutenant-General Sir Garnet Wolseley, arrived at the port of Larnaca on Monday morning in the transport-ship Himalaya, with his staff and a portion of the troops under his command. The British Naval squadron, consisting of the Minotaur, the Black Prince, the Salamis, the Monarch, and the Invincible, saluted his Excellency on entering the harbour. The troops arriving from Malta are mostly encamped beside the aqueduct, near Larnaca, but one battalion is sent to each of the other chief towns—Famagusta, on the east coast, Kydenia (sic) and Limasol, and Nicosia or Levkosia, which is the capital of the island. We have already dispatched a Special Artist to furnish this Journal with Illustrations of the commencement of British rule in Cyprus. The Engravings published in this and last week's Numbers present views of the capital, Nicosia [Plate 5]; the Holy Cross Mountain, or Stavro Vouni [Plate 6], eastward of Larnaca; and the seacoasts at opposite extremities of the island.

The island of Cyprus, now in British possession, will continue for some time, probably, to furnish subjects for our Illustrations. We give this week a panoramic view of the chain of Mount Olympus [Plate 7], in this island, as seen from the village of Kato Dicomo, comprising the summits of Stavro Vouni, or the Holy Cross, Machera, Adelphi, and Troodos, which are here enumerated in the order they appear, from the left hand to the right hand of this view . . .

The *London Gazette* has this week published despatches received at the Admiralty from Vice-Admiral Lord John Hay, giving an account of the transfer of the government of the island of Cyprus to the British Crown and the hoisting of the British flag. When the announcement of the change which had taken place was made to the people the only word that seemed to be understood was "Victoria," which was echoed by the multitude amidst general cheering. We learn further that Sir Garnet Wolseley, with his civil and military staff, arrived on Tuesday last at Nicosia, the capital of the island, where he was met by Mr. Walter Baring, of the Foreign Office, with Captain Rawson, R.N., and by the Turkish and Greek notables of Cyprus. These leading citizens, as well as the officials lately serving under the Turkish Government, and the Greek priests and Bishops, have given the new British High Commissioner a friendly and loyal reception. The Indian troops remain at Larnaca in their encampment, awaiting further orders. A Special Artist of this Journal has been sent to Cyprus.

(Editor, pp. 85, 89)

Plates 8–10

Our front-page Engraving [Plate 8], from a sketch we have been favoured with by an officer of the Mediterranean naval squadron, shows the scene at Nicosia, the chief town of Cyprus, on Friday, the 12th ult., when Admiral Lord John Hay, C.B., formally took possession of that island, and hoisted the British flag, in the name of Queen Victoria. The figure to the left hand is that of the Admiral, who stands with his right hand raised to the peak of his undress cap, in the act of saluting the Union-Jack, which Captain Henry Rawson is engaged in hoisting, with the assistance of another naval officer. A guard consisting of twenty-five men of the Royal Marine Artillery, and Royal Marine Light Infantry from H.M.S.Minotaur, was all the actual British force present upon this important occasion; but the assembled people, both Greeks and Turks, who heard the Admiral's declaration, repeated in their own language by Mr. Walter Baring, of the British Legation at Constantinople, responded with hearty cheers, more especially greeting the name of "Victoria" with vociferous applause . . . It is probable that the natives of Cyprus expect to make high pecuniary profits out of the British political and military establishments in their long neglected and poverty-stricken island. It was the same on Tuesday, the 23rd ult., when Lieutenant-General Sir Garnet Wolseley arrived at Nicosia with his staff, and took charge of the insular government as High Commissioner for her Majesty the Queen. We have now received from our Special Artist and Correspondent, whose first letter, describing his journey and voyage from London to Cyprus, appears in this week's Number of our Journal, sketches of the interesting scenes that have taken place at the landing of the British and Indian troops, with the ships in the harbour of Larnaca, and various Illustrations of the towns, the country, and the people. These will be engraved and published in future Numbers; in the mean time, we present two more views of the coast—one being that of Cape Kormakiti [Plate 9], the ancient Krommyon, on the northern shore of Cyprus, opposite the mainland of Cilicia in Asia Minor; the other, a small seaport town named Kyrenia [Plate 10], situated also on the north coast, some twenty miles east of Cape Kormakiti.

(Editor, p. 123)

Plates 11–14

Our Illustrations published this week include three views of the landing-place [Plate 14] and piers at Larnaca [Plate 12] and the scene of disembarking troop-horses [Plate 13], from the sketches taken by our Special Artist, whose letter, above printed, sufficiently described their subject. We have received also Sketches of the fleet lying at anchor in the harbour or roadstead, and of the British military encampment at Chevlik Pasha, which may appear in our next. The miscellaneous sketches [Plate 11] presented in our front-page Engraving are partly supplied by two officers, Lieutenant G. H. Lane, of the 101st Regiment, and Lieutenant W. J. Eastman, of the Royal Marine Artillery, to whom we have been indebted for similar help before. One shows the Baffo Gate of Nicosia, henceforth to be called the Minotaur Gate, which was first taken possession of by a detachment of Royal Marines from H.M.S.Minotaur, when Admiral Lord John Hay entered that town, on the 12th ult. The Turkish barracks, now occupied by part of the British force, are represented in the sketch beside that which has been mentioned. The British flag hoisted here is constantly guarded by a sentry, and is saluted both morning and evening. One of these sketches is that of the grave of Sergeant M'Gaw, a veteran of the 42nd Highlanders, who obtained the Victoria Cross for valour in the Ashantee War, and who died here of sunstroke.

(Editor, p. 162)

Plates 15–18

The page Engraving in this Supplement [Plate 17], from our Special Artist's Sketch, represents the British Fleet in the roadstead of Larnaca firing the salute on the Duke of Edinburgh's birthday, the 6th inst. The squadron, every ship of which appears dressed in gala colours, consists of H.M.S.Black Prince, shown to the right hand, H.M.S.Minotaur, H.M.S.Monarch, and H.M.S.Raleigh, ironclads, with H.M.S.Salamis, paddle-wheel despatch-boat, a little in advance, between the Monarch and the Minotaur. The Admiralty transport-ships lie nearer to shore, and a number of hired transports are lying beyond. The Duke of Edinburgh has now left Cyprus and joined the Duchess and their children at Malta, having fairly earned his holiday by real hard work. We are glad also to learn that a plateau upon Mount Olympus, four thousand feet above the sea, and at an easy distance from the capital, has been selected as the site of a cantonment for the soldiers. It is very salubrious, abundantly supplied with water, and favoured with the aromatic fragrance of the pine woods.

(Editor, p. 186)

Plates 19, 20

Our Special Artist and Correspondent "S.P.O." furnishes three sketches of Nicosia, the capital of Cyprus [Plate 20], and one of Sir Garnet Wolseley's head-quarters' camp, on the ground adjacent to a Greek monastery outside that town. It was formerly named Leucosia (pronounced Lefkosia), the original Greek name having been Leucotra. It was a place of high consideration under the Byzantine Empire, and afterwards became the residence of the Lusignan family of Princes, who reigned as Kings of Cyprus in the time of the Crusades. The Cathedral Church of St. Sophia [Plate 19], as shown by our Artist's Sketch of its ruins, was a fine Gothic edifice, the nave of which still remains; but the choir was destroyed by the Turks when they converted it, like the St. Sophia of Constantinople, into a mosque for Mohammedan worship, in token of which stand the lofty minarets rising high above the ancient Christian fane. It contains several tombs of the Lusignans, and of later Venetian governors and nobles. There is little else in the town worthy of remark; the streets are narrow, squalid, and wretched in appearance; but the situation, in a fertile plain sheltered by noble mountain ranges, has some natural attractiveness when viewed from outside the walls. The east gate, which is that by which Admiral Lord John Hay, with his staff, escorted by a party of bluejackets and marines from her Majesty's ship Minotaur, made his entry to take possession of Cyprus for her Majesty Queen Victoria, has received the name of "The Channel Squadron Gate." Another gateway, or rather entrance to the town, from the Larnaca road, is shown in the remaining sketch, with a portion of the old city walls.

(Editor, p. 230)

Plate 21

Our Special Artist in Cyprus, "S.P.O.," contributes a sketch of the scene at the door of the Greek Monastery Church at Kiko, two miles from Nicosia, adjacent to the head-quarters' camp of General Sir Garnet Wolseley, on Sunday, the 18th ult., when the Most Reverend Archimandrite, with other Greek clergy, blessed the British flag. This ceremony was preceded by the performance of a high mass within the church. Outside the main door, between the two towers of the sacred edifice, a carpeting of rugs and cloths, variously coloured, was laid down; a gilt chair of state was placed for the English Governor, and a table, with a pair of tall candlesticks, for the clergy. Sir Garnet Wolseley declined to sit in the chair, which looked too much like a throne; but he stood beside it, while Colonel Brackenbury, Captain McCalmont, and Lord Gifford, members of his staff, were behind the chair. The monks and priests, with acolytes bearing the crucifix and censer and vessel of holy water, came out in procession, attired in gorgeous vestments, and chanting a solemn hymn. The flag was hallowed by the Archimandrite with a particular benediction, and was then hoisted, rather clumsily, by one of the church attendants. Three cheers were given for Queen Victoria, for Sir Garnet Wolseley, and for the British nation. There was no parade of military force; indeed, most of the British Indian troops have now departed, and Turkish soldiers are still employed to mount guard, though under British officers, in the capital of Cyprus.

(Editor, p. 275)

Plates 22–25

We have engraved for this Number our Special Artist's Sketch of the south-west city gate of Famagusta [Plate 23], and shall give a few more Sketches of that place, with his letter describing a trip to the east coast of Cyprus. Famagusta was the principal sea-port and fortress of the Venetians, who ruled Cyprus nearly a hundred years after the fall of the Lusignan kingdom. The siege of Famagusta by the Turks in 1571, and the fate of the Governor, Marcantonio Bragadino, who was skinned alive by his captors to revenge his heroic defence of the city, will be remembered by readers of history . . . Our large Engraving [Plate 25] is a Sketch, by the same Artist, of the landing-place at Baffo (the Greek Paphos), at the western extremity of the island, with British and Indian soldiers, a few sailors, Greeks, Maltese, and donkeys, apparently in some confusion. We are indebted to Captain R. Coveney, of the 42nd Regiment, for the sketch [Plate 22] of a large batch of criminal prisoners, removed from the Turkish gaol at Nicosia, under guard of a detachment of the 42nd, with some Turkish troops, arriving at Kyrenia to be there embarked for transportation to Asia Minor. The number thus transported was altogether 266, and it is stated that they were not natives of Cyprus, but Turks from Asia. The officers in charge were Colonel Baker Russell, Major Lorne Macdonald, Captain Lord Gifford, Major Wood, and Captain De Lancey. We also give a view of the castle of St. Hilarion [Plate 24], near Tembros, on the north coast of Cyprus.

(Editor, p. 291)

Plates 26–28

Our Special Correspondent furnishes also the following notes, in explanation of his sketches of the tombs at Larnaca:—

"At the north-west side of the irregular quadrangle of cloisters which surrounds the Greek Church of St. Lazarus, in a remote corner, there is a small parcel of ground railed off, containing the tombs of English, mostly of the seventeenth century. The three shown in the sketch [Plate 28b.] are elaborately carved in marble, the remaining ones are not so elaborate. I transcribe one of the inscriptions, which is as follows:—'Here lieth the body of Ion Ken, eldest son of Mr. Ion Ken, of London, merchant. Who was born the 3 February, 1672, and died the 12 July, 1693.' The second inscription runs thus:—'Heare lyeth interred the body of Capt. Peter Dare, Comr. of the ship Scipio, who departed this life 25 June, 1685, aged 38 years.' I send you another sketch [Plate 28a.], also of a tomb, but far more ancient. A short distance out of Larnaca, and near where the Madras Sappers have their camp, is a ransacked tomb of remote antiquity, probably Phoenician . . .

The Illustration of a rustic scene near Kyrenia [Plate 27], peasant women and a man gathering the fruit of the carob or locust-bean tree, is from a sketch by Captain Coveney, of the 42nd Regiment. This fruitful tree (the Ceratonia siliqua) abounds in some districts of Cyprus.

(Editor, p. 314)

Plates 29–36

The letter from "S.P.O.," our Special Artist and Correspondent in Cyprus, which was printed in last week's paper, narrated his journeys through the Carpas district of Eastern Cyprus, starting on the 2nd ult. from Famagusta, and passing through Trikomo, St. Theodoro, Hepta Khumi, and Khumi Kebir, visiting the decayed Greek Monastery of Kantara, and returning to Trikomo; thence again making an excursion to Cythraea, by way of Syngrassi and Levconico, not to mention several insignificant villages. It was an official tour made by Captain Swaine, the British Commissioner for the district, which gave our Special Artist the opportunity, by kind permission, of accompanying that officer in this round of administrative inspection. Very soon after setting out from Famagusta, proceeding northward along the seacoast, in the neighbourhood of the ancient Greek fort and town of Salamis, our Artist made his two sketches of a remarkable structure called the Church of St. Katharina [Plate 36], and used by the Greek clergy as a church, but which is of remote antiquity, in form a rude vault, built of large stones without mortar or cement, the "Cyclopean" kind of building, and which he considers to have originally been a sepulchre . . . The roof appears to have been formerly covered with a tumulus, or heap of stones, protecting the sepulchral chamber from access . . . There were two other tumuli of similar appearance in sight at this place.

The subject of the next Sketch of Cyprus we have to notice [Plate 35] was mentioned in the letter published last week. It is the scene at the village of Hepta Khumi, when the British Commissioner, who is popularly called by the Turkish official title of Kaimakam, had to sit in magisterial judgment upon a case of assault, in which a peasant girl, or rather her parents, bore the part of complainant. Mr. Parkes, an English gentleman who has taken up his residence in that district, met Captain Swaine and his party at this village. We are assured that the decision pronounced by the British Kaimakam, in this and other cases, gave satisfaction to the local public; but our Special Correspondent, in a previous letter, dated some days before he joined Captain Swaine or visited the eastern part of Cyprus, laments the deficiency of respectable and competent dragomans, or official interpreters. He says:—

"What we want is officials who can not only talk, but read and write, Turkish and understand Turkish accounts. At present matters are at a deadlock in this respect. Mr. Baring is the only one who talks and understands Turkish in the least, and he does not read or write it; at least, so I understand. Mr. Baring's father-in-law, who has been many years in our Consular service, is well fitted for the highest Government employ here; but the terms offered him are such as he could not possibly accept. All officialdom is in the hands of interpreters, and most unsatisfactory interpreters too. Justice and the administration of the government must suffer. A proper staff of Turkish-speaking Foreign Office officials, from Constantinople and Cairo, should be sent here. It is an uphill job for Sir Garnet Wolseley, with a raw staff, utterly ignorant of the requirements of a strange people, to administer the government. The whole administration will fall into disrepute if we are not alive to our interests which suffer now. Our Treasury is robbed with impunity, as no one knows accurately what should be paid in and what the revenues are; and that can never be arrived at as things are carried on at present.

"It may seem presumptuous for me to say so, but I cannot help thinking that the Executive has too much of the military element in it at present. It is all very well to appoint smart young subalterns of crack regiments as Commissioners and Assistant-Commissioners of districts, but a military education is hardly that which is best fitted to train civilian Judges; a staff of experienced Indian civil servants would have been far superior. As it is, all the appointments made to the districts are good as far as energy, hard work, and goodwill may do the utmost in their power."

The above remarks were written so far back as Aug. 28, and must not be taken as bearing reference to anything witnessed subsequently in the Carpas district, but may find their application more properly elsewhere. It could not have been expected that the British civil administration of Cyprus would at once be made perfect; it is nevertheless a vast improvement upon the barbarous Turkish anarchy, by which the island was all but irretrievably ruined. The Greek Christian population, at any rate, seem to be most grateful for the change.

The remaining Sketch presented this week is a view of the jagged summit of Mount Pentedactylon [Plate 34], about 2200 ft. high, looking over the nearer hills above Cythraea, which pleasant little town, with its surrounding groves and gardens, is situated nine miles to the north of Nicosia, the capital of Cyprus. Our Correspondent spoke with pleasure of his brief stay at Cythraea, which is agreeably shaded with trees, and watered with streams from the neighbouring mountains.

(Editor, p. 377)

Plate 37

The First Lord of the Admiralty, Mr. W. H. Smith, and the Secretary of State for War, Colonel Stanley, left England on Monday, to visit the famous island in the Levant, which has lately been taken into British possession. Our Special Artist in Cyprus, "S.P.O.," has been compelled an attack of fever to seek refuge, for a week or two, in the salubrious highlands of the Lebanon, above Beyrout, on the opposite shore of Syria. One of his sketches is engraved for this week's publication. It is a view of the Carpas range of mountains, from the village of Hepta Khumi, which was described in the letter of "S.P.O." published a fortnight ago.

(Editor, p. 397)

Plates 38, 39

The High Commissioner for her Majesty's Government in Cyprus, Lieutenant-General Sir Garnet Wolseley, K.C.B., holds his official receptions in the Konak, the courthouse of the late Turkish Governor, at Nicosia, the capital city. Upon the occasion of the Mohammedan festival of Bairam, which commences with the new moon after the Fast of Ramazan or Moslem Lent, Sir Garnet Wolseley, adopting the custom of his predecessors, received all the notables of the town and island. This visit is the subject of our Illustration [Plate 38], from a sketch with which we are favoured by Lieutenant Allan Gilmore, of the 61st Regiment, Assistant to the Chief Commandant of Military Police in Cyprus, and now commanding the local police at Limasol. His Excellency the High Commissioner, in blue undress uniform, sits on the sofa, his hands resting upon his sword; an interpreter stands at his left hand. The officer who appears standing in the right foreground is Colonel Biddulph, C.B., R.A., Commissioner, with whom are Colonel Greaves, Chief Secretary to the Government of Cyprus, Colonel the Hon. J. Dormer, Assistant Quartermaster-General, Colonel Baker Russell, 13th Hussars, Assistant Military Secretary, also Surgeon-General Jackson, C.B., and Colonel Brackenbury, R.A., Chief Commandant of Military Police. Major the Hon. H. Wood, 12th Lancers, and Captain Hare, 22nd Regiment, members of the staff, with Captain J. De Lancey, 71st Highlanders, commanding the military police of Nicosia, and Lieut. Gilmore, were also present. The Turkish and other native visitors of the High Commissioner appear in the opposite part of the Engraving, to the left hand. The Cadi, or Mussulman Judge, attired in a green robe and turban, is gravely making his bow to Sir Garnet Wolseley. Rifaat Pasha, in a dark blue military uniform, with a red fez on his head, sits in the chair behind, having another Turkish officer on his right hand, and on his left a Mohammedan grandee in a purple robe, with red fez and white turban. The chief of the Dervishes occupies a chair to the extreme left of the view. These visitors, seated around the stone-paved hall, partake of coffee, sweatmeats, and cigarettes handed to them by the Greek servants, and hold quiet converse with each other, or even, by the help of an interpreter, with the English official gentlemen. Another Sketch [Plate 39a.] by Lieutenant Gilmore presents a view of the head-quarters' camp of Sir Garnet Wolseley, at the Greek Monastery, a mile or so outside the Baffo gate of Nicosia. The monastery building is shown to the left hand; the tents pitched for the abode of his Excellency and of the Staff occupy the middle ground, and there are some farm or villa buildings to the right; and a noble range of mountains in the background of this view. We have already given one Illustration of the head-quarters' camp, from a sketch by our Special Artist, "S.P.O." He made an excursion to the western coast of the island, just before he was taken ill of fever, but was unable to go to Baffo, or to inspect the reputed site of the ancient Paphos, renowned in Greek mythology as the abode of Venus. For our Illustration of this locality [Plate 39b.] we are indebted to another correspondent, Mr. Thomson, one of whose sketches is engraved this week. The supposed site of Old Paphos . . . would lie close to the seashore, near the present village of Konklia (sic), which is seen indicated towards the left hand in this view . . . On the hill to the right hand, several miles distant, is the modern town of Baffo, which has superseded another Greek city, called Neopaphos . . . The tents of the English military encampment are shown upon the cliff near the town.

(Editor, p. 408)

Plates 40, 41

Mr. J. Thomson, a photographic artist, who has lately visited Cyprus to obtain views of its scenery, and of the costumes, figures, and dwellings of the people, ascended to the summit of Mount Olympus in pursuit of his interesting vocation . . . There are plenty of clouds, and sometimes mist or rain, upon the high mountain visited six weeks ago by Mr. Thomson, who has favoured us with a couple of Sketches, and with the following note:—

"Accompanied by an Arab dragoman, Habib Kuri, and my muleteer, I rested at Prodromus for the night. It is the village nearest to the summit of Mount Olympus, built on the crest of one of the lower spurs of the range. The temperature fell perceptibly as we made the ascent during the day, and at night could not have exceeded 40 deg. Fahrenheit. In the Olympian district the mountains are clothed with magnificent forests of cedar. A number of the finest trees have been quite recently cut down, but the supply is still unlimited. We made the toilsome ascent of Olympus on our mules in the morning, accompanied by the headman of the village. The accompanying sketch [Plate 41] pictures the apex of the classic mountain as it appeared partially wrapped in a robe of clouds and mist. Our approach to the summit was heralded by an ominous peal of thunder, that made the earth tremble beneath our feet. It sounded like a terrible protest against the sacrilege of photographing, for the first time, the ruins of the ancient shrine. Dismounting, we clambered through stony débris to the summit. The storm increased, and was accompanied by a deluge of rain and hail, such as one can only experience in high regions. Nothing daunted, after an hour's delay, and with a friendly gleam of light, we succeeded in photographing what remains of the ancient shrine. Shelter there was none, save that represented in the sketch. My dragoman, robed in his bed sheet, which he invariably carried in his saddle-bag, tended the camera; and for the details of our position I refer the reader to the sketch [Plate 40]. Worst of all, my umbrella, of thin calico, proved useless; my pith-hat became limp and pasty; while my shoes gave way entirely as I made the descent on foot."

(Editor, p. 434)

Plates 42, 43

The Engraving on our front page [Plate 42] is a view, from a photograph, of the west front of the ruined Gothic Cathedral of Famagusta, which place was the chief seaport town and fortress of Cyprus under the Venetian rule, from 1473 to 1571. It has been described by our Special Artist and Correspondent, "S.P.O.," who was lately in Cyprus on the service of this Journal . . . In striking contrast to this relic of superb medieval lordship on the eastern shore of Cyprus we give the Sketch [Plate 43] of a quiet pastoral scene near Paphos, at the western extremity of the island. The native herdsman there leads his flock of goats to water, like Tityrus and Menalcas and their like in a poem of Virgil or Theocritus, caring little for the decay of proud Empires and Principalities, which have so frequently come and gone upon the sea-girt plains and hills of Cyprus. "Assyria, Greece, Rome, Egypt—what are they?" Or what the Norman, the Venetian, the Ottoman, or the British Imperial power, when a few more generations of mankind have lived and died?

The Cypriote goats and kids will browse and frolic in their pasture when Sir Garnet Wolseley's administration is long forgotten.

(Editor, p. 456)

Plate 44

The visit of the First Lord of the Admiralty and the Secretary of State for War to Cyprus is the subject of one of our Illustrations. Her Majesty's troop-ship Himalaya, with Mr. W. H. Smith, Colonel Stanley, and a numerous party on board, arrived at Larnaca on the 1st inst. They were received by General Sir Garnet Wolseley, the High Commissioner, who had come down to await their arrival at Larnaca. On the next day they proceeded in a body to Nicosia, and remained the guests of his Excellency and the Head-quarter Staff at the Monastery Camp, which was the subject of a sketch we published a few weeks ago. The same afternoon they paid a visit to the town, and saw the principal buildings, the fine old Venetian Cathedral, now converted into the Moslem Mosque of St. Sophia; the Buykhan, or court-house and police station; and the Konak, which is the building used at present for the head-quarters of the military police force. Then, finally, after partaking of the hospitality of the Commissioner and his colleagues, they went in procession round the ramparts, and so back to the camp. An escort of Mounted Zaptiehs, under the local commandant of police, was drawn up outside the Baffo Gate to receive Sir Garnet Wolseley and his guests on their arrival, and followed the party, who were mounted, through the winding bazaars and narrow streets of the town.

The subject of our sketch is the departure of the distinguished guests from Nicosia. Having bidden farewell at the High Commissioner's house, where they went to lunch, they were escorted by him and the chief commandant of military police as far as the Larnaca gate, where they were met by an escort of mounted zaptiehs, under the Lieutenant commanding, drawn up outside the gate according to instructions, and who accompanied the coach or omnibus some way out of the town. This "bus" is used for the daily mail, and was drawn by two horses and two mules. The view of Nicosia from the Larnaca road is most picturesque, comprising the venerable Mosque of St. Sophia, and the numerous minarets of smaller mosques, intermixed with date-palms, and other species of vegetation, inclosed by a fortification of the bastion system; but which, according to modern warfare, would be perfectly useless. The whole is backed by the sharp outlines of the Kyrenia range of hills to the north-west; and to the south of the town is seen the Olympian Range. The Head-Quarters Camp is situated to the west of the town, and is not seen in this View. The Mosque at the southern extremity of the town was erected in memory of the first Turk who scaled the ramparts in the assault and capture of the town from the Venetians. There are numerous graves scattered about, telling the tale where such and such a Moslem fell, especially in the taking of the Konak, and over each is placed a lantern, in respect to his memory. Our Illustration is from a sketch by Lieutenant A. Gilmore, 61st Regiment, Local Commandant of the Military Police for the Nikosia District.

(Editor, p. 522)

Remarks by the Special Artist and Correspondent, S.P.O., 1878

Cyprus, July 25, 1878

A brief interview at 198, Strand, was quickly succeeded by a short drive to Waterloo, whence we were quickly whirled past Winchester by the South-Western Railway to Southampton and the Havre packet. Our thoughts were chiefly bent on reaching as soon as possible England's latest acquisition of territory, which on that day had been formally taken possession of by Mr. Walter Baring and Admiral Lord John Hay . . .

We leave Marseilles basin in one of Messrs. Fraissinet's boats, the Saint Marc. Of the few passengers bound for Malta the larger proportion are for Cyprus. There are English officers recalled from leave of absence but a day or two after their leave had been granted. These are, naturally, grumbling a little at their hard fate, but, at the same time, ardent to enter upon a new sphere of action. There are Greek interpreters from Manchester and Liverpool . . .

Alas! the boat is a slow one, but it is not the slightest use chafing at delay. The foreigners play dominoes, while the English debate over the map of Cyprus, the future plans of Sir Garnet Wolseley, and the respective merits or demerits of his newly appointed staff . . .

The Trinacria is supposed to be a fast steamer, and we are in hopes of catching up the expeditionary fleet, which has the start of us. But our hopes are not realised . . . During the whole of Monday, July 22, we were in sight of the long mountain ranges of Crete. At last, but not till this morning, Thursday, the 25th, we could discern the distant outline of our new dependency. It had taken us a fortnight from the Strand to Cyprus, consequent on unforeseen delays, which could not possibly have been calculated upon. As the dense fog which had enveloped us since two a.m. lifted under the rising sun, the coastline of Cyprus was disclosed within a short distance of us; and ahead were visible, in the roadstead of Larnaca, the ships of the British expeditionary force. By breakfast-time we were anchored, and were soon in a position to know the state of affairs. The larger portion of the army of occupation had arrived the previous day, under Sir Garnet Wolseley, who, with his staff, still has his head-quarters on board the Himalaya.

(S.P.O., p. 123)

Larnaca, July 28.

In my letter of Thursday I related the incidents of my voyage and journey from London, overland from Havre to Marseilles, thence by one of the Fraissenet line of steam-boats to Malta, and from Malta to Cyprus in the hired transport-vessel Tinacria, of the Anchor line, for my passage in which I was indebted to the kind offices of Admiral Luard at Malta. I find the Channel Squadron and the fleet of transports, which have brought General Sir Garnet Wolseley and the military forces to Cyprus, lying here at anchor . . . altogether, the British force presents an imposing appearance in these waters.

The town of Larnaca, or rather the commercial portion of it, called the Marina, stretches along the water's edge, and presents the usual Oriental features of a Levantine seaport, except that it is more sleepy and quiet than most of those towns. The arrival of the expedition alone gives life to the place; and already one end of the town is assuming a business-like look; but the present hurry and bustle is all European; the phlegmatic Turks are as impassive and unconcerned as if it was no business of theirs. The vessels of the expedition, arranged as I have mentioned, are lying between a mile and a mile and a half from the low sandy shore on which the town is built. On one side of the town the coast stretches southward to Point Dades, a dismal dried-up salt-marsh covered with prickly pear (Opuntia vulgaris) and with a few sparsely scattered date-trees. In the other direction, the land trends to the north and east, for some miles away, to Capes Pila and Grego, backed by long, low, flat-topped terraced limestone hills. The mosques of the town are insignificant, and, except for the present of half a dozen minarets, one would almost suppose the population of Larnaca to be Christian, as the Greek churches are more conspicuous with their bell turrets. Behind the town the land extends in a barren plain away into the interior. About five miles away on the plain to the south-west are the camps of the European regiments, at a place called Chevlik Pasha. Beyond rises a mountain of above two thousand feet elevation, on which is a small white structure, probably a chapel, as the mountain is named Oros Stavro, or Mountain of the Cross; and in the distance beyond rise the mountain ranges of Adelphi and Troodos, 6000 ft. high.

The Channel Squadron has not been idle since its arrival in preparing for the occupation of this place by the troops. The Duke of Edinburgh and a large number of sailors have formed a naval camp at the landing-place north of the town and have erected five piers and landing-stages. His Royal Highness is still occupying the old quarantine lazaretto building, close by; while his sailors are in bell-tents and under sail-cloth awnings around his head-quarters, which are marked by his flagstaff and signal, a portable semaphore for telegraphing seaward. His Royal Highness deserves the greatest credit for the way in which all the arrangements for the disembarkation have been carried out by him. Civilians can have little or no idea of all the forethought and care required to land a force of ten thousand men on a sandy beach, where the facilities have hitherto only existed negatively. The Royal Prince, ever active and zealous, burnt as brown as a gipsy with exposure, but looking as hard as nails, personally superintends the landing and clearing of the boats and vessels, as they arrive at the beach. There are no working parties of soldiers here. All the regiments on their arrival march straight to their camping-grounds; and all the unloading is done by the blue-jackets, who seem to enjoy the business amazingly. From four a.m. till dark incessant work of various kinds is proceeding; in all directions are lighters and native craft, horse-boats towed by steam-launches, and pinnaces continually going and returning. A very short time suffices to unload them, and the busy scene at the landing-place can hardly be imagined. The Monarch has started a canteen marquee close by, which is a decidedly good arrangement. A constant throng of camels, mules, donkeys, Indian tats and native cavalry horses, ordinance and commissariat stores, Ghoorkas and Punjaubees, Greeks and Mussulmans, all combine to give a bewildering and constantly changing kaleidoscopic effect of colour and form. Under the blaze of the noonday sun, during the Cyprus dog-days, with all the glare, dust, and heat, the fatigue endured by our sailors and their Captain, the Duke, is no slight work. Already a case or two of sunstroke has been reported, and more are we fear, yet to be expected. Hitherto the health of the force has been excellent; but, of course, there has not yet been time to judge of the effect of the heat and exposure on the European troops. It is possible that malarious fever may be apprehended should the soil be disturbed, as was the case at Hong-Kong at Kowloon . . . The landing of the troops here and unlading of the stores by the bluejackets under the Naval officers were, as I have said, carried out with dispatch and energy. I am sorry to add that I cannot bestow such unqualified praise on the departmental business of the Army Commissariat. The commissariat stores were apparently pitchforked into the various transports at Malta without the slightest method or arrangement, and without tally; so that the commissariat offices, on their arrival here, do not seem to have known what stores were on board any particular vessel; and the consequences are just what might be imagined.

Sir Garnet Wolseley and staff leaves the Himalaya to-day (Sunday), shifting the head-quarters to the Salamis despatch-boat, in which his Excellency has already made trips to the other parts of the island. He will go to Nicosia, the capital of the island, on Tuesday. The troops have been detailed to proceed to different places, and some to stay at Larnaca. That very useful and workman-like body of men, the Bombay Sappers and Miners, are performing good service at Larnaca. Colonel Prendergast is already doing wonders, and the useful will speedily replace the picturesque in this Oriental locality. This invasion of the modern British anticrusaders in aid of the Turk will cause rapid changes in the features both of town and country. The supply of animals for transport service is almost, if not quite, equal to the demand. Camels, mules, donkeys, and small horses seem plentiful, although naturally the price has risen 70 per cent. Beef is more than double what it was in value before the occupation. We have snow-ice, at about 3d. per pound, from the Lebanon Mountains, viâ Beyrout, packed in wooden cases, with chopped straw as a non-conductor of heat. Meantime, the narrow streets and shaded bazaars are crowded with our Indian soldiery, and the red tunics brighten up the dark pokey shops in every direction. The cafés are booths, as usual, on rickety wooden platforms projecting over the water, similar to those at Smyrna, one of which was disastrously precipitated some years since with great loss of life. These cafés are crowded by riff-raff adventurers from the Piraeus, Syra, Zante, and Anatolia. We recognise the faces of rascals we have often seen in Pera and Stamboul; while Port Said and Alexandria also contribute their quota of scoundrelism to this new field of depredations on English pockets. The price asked for a small garret, with a wretched bed or pallet, and without another single piece of furniture, is six shillings a night. An interpreter asked us ten shillings a day, with his keep; and other things are in proportion. The bullock-waggons (arabas) are rough but useful; machines of transport, and the cattle yoked to them seem in good case and well treated. The donkeys are particularly handsome and sleek, though not of large size; they are highly prized, and exported to Egypt for breeding purposes. Their price, consequently, sounds exorbitant; but, like everything else, will soon find its level.

On Saturday evening the minarets were illuminated, which, with the lights in the town and the innumerable lights of the shipping, with their reflections in the glassy sea, rivalled only by those of the brilliant starlit sky above, formed a striking scene. The strains of music from the bands on board the men-of-war and of the regiments on the transports sounded so like England, that, were it not for the heat, we might have imagined ourselves at anchor in Plymouth Sound.

The Himalaya is ordered to return to Malta, and will leave this evening. There is now, it appears, some uncertainty about the stations to be occupied by the different regiments here, as some of the orders have been countermanded, owing to the backward commissariat arrangements. It should be understood that there are marines and bluejackets at Kyrenia, a port on the north coast, which favourably spoken of by the sailor officers who have been there, and at Baffo to the west, as well as at Nicosia, at Limasol, and at Famagosta. This will be, of course, only a temporary measure, and the detachments of marines and seamen will be relieved at an early date. The three English regular battalions are now and will be stationed at the camp at Chevlik Pasha, though yesterday (July 27) a company of the 42nd was ordered to be in readiness to proceed to Limasol, where the 31st Punjaubees were also to be quartered. A battery of the 2nd Brigade of Royal Artillery, and a battery of the 1st Brigade, are to remain at Larnaca, but the latter has not yet arrived from Malta. The destination of the native Indian troops now seems to be uncertain.

(S.P.O., p. 162)

Larnaca, Aug. 7.

Yesterday at eight in the morning the fleet was gay with bunting in honour of the thirty-fourth birthday of Captain the Duke of Edinburgh, while the bands of the different ships could be distinctly heard on shore. At noon the Royal salute was fired by the ships at the anchorage, and the Captains and other officers of the fleet went on board H.M.S.-Black Prince to pay their respects to the Royal Duke. In the evening, at six o'clock, there was a review of the Larnaca division of the troops, and his Royal Highness, in undress uniform as a Naval Aide-de-Camp to the Queen, inspected the parade, which was particularly smart and well turned out, and there was the usual march past. To-day H.M.S.-Salamis leaves for Brindisi and I proceed at once to Nicosia.

Sir Garnet Wolseley has now established the seat of Government at Nicosia, and Commissioners have been appointed at the various ports throughout the island. The arrangements for the moving of the troops have been greatly delayed by contrary orders. At one time the troops were detailed for their respective stations, and were on board their transport and troop ships ready; to proceed when they were suddenly ordered to land. They were accordingly disembarked on Saturday evening and Sunday morning (27th and 28th ult.), and encamped in rear of the Marina. Meantime H.M. ships Himalaya and Orontes were ordered away, the former (viâ Syracuse with mails) en route to Malta, and the Orontes to Malta, presumably for reinforcements of stores. The transport Suez had previously been sent to Beyrout to fetch horses, which were to have been purchased by Captain Bury, of the Royal Artillery. But it was found impossible to obtain any horses of the requisite stamp, and the Suez returned without her cargo after a fruitless visit. It is curious that the Suez should have been sent before the horses were purchased. At all events, information could have been obtained by telegraph as to the state of the horse market in Syria. An idea is current, at Damascus and Beyrout and the neighbouring towns, that the French contemplate an occupation of Syria; and those towns, judging from their fortunate neighbours at Cyprus, look forward to a rich harvest of European gold. The troops which had disembarked on the Sunday were ordered to re-embark on Friday, together with their stores and camp equipage, and sailed the same evening at nine o'clock for their several destinations. H.M.S.Tamar embarked some for Kyrenia, and H.M.S.Simoom some for Baffo; the hired transports Bengal and Goa took others to Famagosta, convoyed by the Tamar troop-ship; while the Madura and Malda left for Limasol, where the Pallas is lying. Brigadier-General Macpherson and his staff rode overland to take command at that port. As for the head-quarters of the British forces, their large camp at

Chevlik Pasha is now well organised, in first-rate order, and, barring the heat, might form a portion of Aldershott. The camp is formed on a sloping plateau, elevated 150 ft. above the sea, and distant about four miles and a half from the Marina of Larnaca. The lines face the north, with the Royal Artillery on the extreme right. A slight interval separates them from the Bengal cavalry, whose camp is next. A larger space and a slight depression separate the cavalry from the British infantry, which are camped with the 101st in the centre, with the 42nd and 71st on the right and left flanks respectively. The ground falls to the front, forming a gradual descent, at the lowest level of which is the aqueduct, which supplies Larnaca with a perennial flow of pure and wholesome water. A portion of this water is diverted for various watering-troughs. As the ground falls away to the eastward, the aqueduct, which is carried across the inequalities of the ground on solid and apparently ancient arches, becomes higher, and here and there forms an important feature in the landscape. The soil is sandy and dusty, but wonderfully fertile; and, wherever any irrigation is possible, the brightest verdure is apparent. Of course, at this time of the year the surface of the ground is burnt up and the vegetation is scorched; but, nevertheless, where the ground is but scratched green crops of various descriptions are to be seen growing. The gardens about the thriving villages are wonderfully productive, as is, indeed, shown in the inexhaustible vegetable supply of the Larnaca bazaars and market. The place can produce anything; the soil is rich and fertile, in spite of its present pulverised, dusty look. The health of the troops at present is reassuring; the percentage of sick in hospital is as small, if not smaller than it would be in England at the same time of year. We hear of no sickness among the inhabitants either of town or country; and it is not possible to see a more healthy lot of country folk than these cheery Cyprians, some very rough-looking but picturesque peasants, with a large predominance of classical features. A great proportion, we notice, have fair complexions and hair.

The Canara transport, which had gone to Malta a week since, returned on Aug. 2, towing a schooner. On the same day the usual sea-breeze increased to nearly half a gale of wind, and put a stop to the disembarkation for a few hours. Some heavy rain also alarmed the commissariat for the shelter of their exposed stores of flour; but no harm was experienced, and the oppressive weather has become decidedly improved in temperature since, as the thermometer, which under a double awning and in a cool situation originally stood from 85 deg.–90 deg. in the day, has fallen to 80 deg.–85 deg. The heat, however, is considerably tempered by the sea breeze, which sets in regularly as the sun gets high. The land breeze at night from off the heated shore is, on the other hand, wonderfully warm and dry.

But no sooner have the troops been disembarked, re-embarked, and again disembarked at the outer stations, than orders are again received by telegraph to prepare the whole of the Indian force for return to Bombay this autumn, and the transports are to be ready for the reception of the troops by the 23rd of this month—i.e., in little more than a fortnight. All this change of front is most provoking to everybody; counter-orders succeed to orders so rapidly that no one, from the Admiral downwards, knows what is to be the next move, and a good deal of discomfort and some discontent is the result. The Indian troops, however, will be glad to return to their own country, their known desire to be back, and the complications likely to result as to troops serving in the same island receiving different rates of pay are among the causes which have led to this decision of the home authorities. By this time the disembarkation of troops and stores has been completed, and things are settling down somewhat on shore; the naval camp on the beach has been broken up, and the Duke has re-embarked with his staff on board his ship, the Black Prince. Saturday, Aug. 3, was the fête day of H.I.H. the Duchess, and the ships of war were dressed in bunting for the occasion. The crew of the Black Prince gave a burlesque entertainment in the evening before the Duke and the officers of the squadron, the Captains of the transports also receiving an invitation to be present.

From Nicosia we hear that his Excellency the High Commissioner, finding the heat, dirt, and general discomfort of the inclosed capital intolerable, has, with his staff, formed his camp a couple of miles to the south-west, without the walls.

As soon as the Salamis despatch-boat has departed with this packet it is our intention to proceed to Nicosia without delay, and thence to Kyrenia, from which our next installment will be dispatched.

(S.P.O., p. 186)

Larnaca, Aug. 8.

The despatch boat Salamis, with his Royal Highness the Duke of Edinburgh, Captain of the Black Prince, on board, sailed yesterday for Brindisi. General Ross, who came to Malta in command of the Indian contingent, also left in the Salamis on a month's leave in England. The absence of his Royal Highness here will be much regretted, as he had made himself very popular both ashore and afloat. The London newspapers which arrived here last contained the speech of Mr. Anderson, of Glasgow, who objected in Parliament to the vote of money for the Duke of Connaught on the plea that the Royal Princes did not work. But if Mr. Anderson could only have been at North Beach, Larnaca, during the last three weeks he would have been rather startled at the amount of work, of real physical labour, gone through zealously and indefatigably by the Royal Duke. From four a.m. till after dark the work was incessantly carried on, Sundays not excepted, and even during the hours of the night his Royal Highness was never free from interruption, as letters, with incessant inquiries or instructions were continually brought to him from the Admiral, who well sustains the character which he bore in the Hector and Odin of old. Lord John Hay has not been fortunate in his relations with the commissariat. Without a great deal of tact on both sides the relations between naval and military heads of departments, during debarkation, are nearly sure to cause friction between clashing interests, and this occasion has been no exception to the rule. On the re-embarkation of the Indian levies for Bombay we may expect to see some of these contests renewed.

The expected malarious fever has at length begun to show itself. Most of the Minotaur's and Monarch's men, who were up at Nicosia, have succumbed to the disease, which only attacked them on their return to their ships at Larnaca. A party of Royal Engineers are reported to have been stopped in their survey by fever, which has stricken down the whole of them. The Highlanders also, and other Europeans at Chevlik, are said to be sending a large proportion of their men into hospital from the same cause. The ride up to Nicosia is through an almost barren plain, and in these sultry days of August the country is quite arid. There is a diligence which traverses the road daily between Nicosia and Larnaca; but it is entirely taken up the Government for official passengers, and after wasting two days we were compelled to ride. Blazing white limestone rocks, with little moisture or vegetation, prevailed for the first half of the journey, and it was needful to rest at Atheno, a village half way. Cyprus may be delightful in the winter, but journeying at mid-day in the island is simply torture. I have experienced Chinese, Indian, and Central American summers; but I never remember to have suffered more from heat and vermin, and I can quite imagine the effect upon the British troops.

The temperature of the atmosphere in the Levant is more variable than that of most parts of the Mediterranean, for it alters with every change of wind. Along the south-eastern coast of Cyprus, from Limasol to here at Larnaca and on to Famagosta, a regular land-and-sea breeze prevails in the absence of strong winds. This land-and-sea breeze is termed the "imbatto." It sets in with a sea breeze from the S.W., and, freshening towards noon, lasts till about three p.m. at this time of year; but sometimes it continues till about sunset, when it dies away. An almost dead calm then ensues when a light air springs up from the land, which continues until about an hour after sunrise. In August the refreshment afforded by the sea breeze, cooled by passing over the sea, is most grateful to the inhabitants of the south coast. Without it, Cyprus would during the dog days be aptly termed "infamis nimio caloro." Admiral Smyth, in his work on "The Mediterranean," considers that the whole island of Cyprus affords an epitome of the usual Levantine weather, for here the action of the breezes is confined to a comparatively circumscribed space.

We reached Nicosia by sunset, and had great difficulty in obtaining a lodging. Hotels are unknown, and one or two extemporised grog-shops do duty for the unexpected travellers. Fortunately, a letter from the Consul at Larnaca procured us a decent lodging at the house of the Governor's dragoman. At Government House discomfort reigned supreme; Colonel Biddulph, R.A., and staff were as badly off as ourselves.

We rode out at once to see Sir Garnet Wolseley, and it is needless to say how genial and kind he always is. He takes a most hopeful view of affairs here, which are to the outsider a hopeless mass of confusion. The amount of work requisite here to be got through by the staff is overpowering. We found Sir Garnet, with Colonel Greaves, Lieutenant-Colonel Brackenbury, R.A., and others of his staff established in a long row of most commodious buildings within the sanctuary precincts of a Greek church. Just as we arrived the body of a murdered man was being taken in, loosely carried in a sheet, previous to its interment in the church. Sir Garnet's flag is to be consecrated in due form shortly; but, as we must be on the move, it is doubtful if I shall be present. Having waited for the mail here, I proceed next to Cythera, of which we hear glowing accounts from Mr. Forbes, of the *Daily News*, and then to Kyrenia.

Now, as to the future of Cyprus, should the present protectorate of Turkey in Asia continue on a firm basis and become permanent. To what practical use could we put it? There is one suggestion which naturally arises—it is that, if we are to protect Turkey, Turkey must be taught how to protect itself; and Cyprus with its wide plains and convenient position, is admirably adapted for a large Turkish camp of instruction. Here young Turkish officers could be schooled in modern warfare; and English officers might learn how to deal with Turkish soldiers. It is proposed to erect cantonments on the western slopes of the Troodo range of mountains near Paphos (Baffo), as soon as a site has been selected for the wooden huts which have been ordered from England, and which, indeed, ought to be on their way out here by this time. Here, in these elevated regions, about

2000 ft. above sea-level, the main body of European troops might be quartered, at all events during the summer months and during the season when fever is prevalent on the lower plains, on the same plan as the troops in Jamaica are mostly kept up at Newcastle, on the high ground. The intended station, in all probability, will be formed in the direction of Melia, Phyti, and Panaia, in the neighbourhood of the large monastery of Grisovoghiatissa. It will form an excellent sanatorium both for soldiers and for the sailors of the Mediterranean squadron, as well as for our garrisons at Malta and Gibraltar, where troops suffer from the insupportable heat from July to September. The change of quarters will be most beneficial after the monotonous routine of garrison duty; and Cyprus will doubtless soon be looked upon as a favourite quarter, as Corfu was once similarly regarded. Game laws are at once to be instituted; the hunting will be first rate across the wide Messarian plains, and we shall see the wooded slopes of west and north Cyprus dotted with villas, and resorted to by invalids during the winter months, in preference to Nice, Monaco, Mentone, or even Algiers. A fashionable watering-place will soon spring up, and with a garrison of three crack regiments, and a numerous English official staff of civilians as well as military, prosperity of a certain description may certainly be predicted for Cyprus . . .

The mail from this place closes almost directly, and therefore we must send off at once, not to lose an opportunity.

(S.P.O., p. 210)

Varoschia (near Famagusta), Sept. 2.

Having closed the mail for England on Thursday, the 29th ult., I lost no time in leaving Larnaca, its dirt, dust, and extortions; and having chartered an open boat, with a crew of three Greeks, I embarked for a trip to the eastern shores of this island. We sailed merrily before the south-west breeze, which blows regularly here at this time of year, so as really to be a trade wind, all day after ten or eleven o'clock till sunset. In about two hours we were off the steep bluff of Cape Pyla, distant from Larnaca thirteen miles as the crow flies. We then passed the lower land, where the Turks are said to have disembarked three centuries ago (1570), previous to the capture of Famagusta. Four o'clock in the afternoon brought us to Cape Greco, the ancient Pedalium Promontory, twenty-six miles from Larnaca. Here there is a bold headland, a miniature Gibraltar, or rather Table Mountain, looking like a Cyclopean citadel cut out in terraced limestone. Doubling the cape, and still with a fair breeze, only wearing the boat, and having the wind on our port beam instead of right aft, as we had hitherto been running before the wind, we coasted within a stone's throw of the low ledge of rocky coast, apparently of coral formation, and passed a fleet of boats off shore engaged in sponge-fishing. The breeze subsided slightly in the afternoon, but we slipped along till dark in smooth water, and anchored, or rather were beached, on the sandy shores of Varoschia, the inhabited suburb or Greek village a mile outside Famagusta, having sailed in all forty miles from Larnaca by sea. Famagusta is a walled city, only inhabited by two hundred and odd Turks, no Greeks being permitted to live there. A lodging was soon procured by the dragoman in a garden of figs and pomegranates, watered by two rude water-wheels, turned by mules, and raising the water from wells some thirty feet deep, cut in the solid rock.

In the morning I accompanied the Commissioner (Captain L. V. Swaine, of the Rifle Brigade) to the Konak or official residence in Famagusta. This place, which probably is destined to be *the* port of Cyprus, is at present quite a city of the dead; Pompeii is hardly more so. Surrounded with high and massive masonry, the large fortress town appears from without as if constructed of lasting masonry, the large fortress town appears from without as if constructed yesterday. The broad ditches and moats, cut out of the solid rock, must have cost an infinity of labour, and were doubtless the work of galley-slaves. They were formed in the twelfth century for mediaeval warfare. The Venetians, and after them the Turks, readily adapted the strong lines for artillery, and even now they are no mean fortification. Within, after traversing the permanent bridge and drawbridge across the moat, one enters a deserted ruin. A few Zaptiehs and a guard of Turkish soldiers at the gate spring up on our approach to salute the Commissioner, and that guard passed we are in solitude. I was at once struck with the anomaly that in a strongly-fortified city such as this, with the union-jack flying over it, there should not be a single English soldier, while at Baffo and other out-of-the-way places in the open country there are companies of infantry with nothing to guard except their precious health. As it is, in Famagusta the united strength of Turkish soldiers, who, by-the-by, are deserting daily, and of Zaptiehs, is barely sufficient to keep up the sentries at the gates of the town. The truth, I suppose, is that Famagusta is reported unhealthy; and, having a bad name, it is shunned accordingly. I do not myself believe Famagusta to be at all more unhealthy than Larnaca, if so unhealthy; but of this we may hear more by-and-by. Leaving the Commissioner at his office, I traversed the walls and ruins of this city of the dead, and naturally bent my steps towards the ruins of the ancient Cathedral Church, now used as a mosque. The west front, although dilapidated, shows traces of great architectural beauty; and it is depressing to see the Moslem disfigurement and desecration. Surely, where the Mohammedans are in such a miserable minority, these ancient churches should be restored to their pristine sanctity, and the ugly traces of Islam removed. Let the ruins be Christian ruins, at least. Although not so large as St. Sophia at Nicosia, the design of the Famagusta Cathedral is lighter and more elegant, especially the apse at the eastern end. The photographs by M. Dumas lately taken will show more fully than pages of description the beauties of the edifice. Various other monastic and conventual buildings, all in a state of desolation, are scattered between the ruins of the streets. Old bronze cannon, in considerable numbers, are lying here; and there are some mounted on the walls, others dismounted and lying inside the gates, especially the water-gate, as if ready for removal. Most of these guns bear the winged lion, or the winged horse, on the chase of the piece; and, as a rule, their cascables are cast flat, without the ornamentation of rings, fillets, and ogees.

Captain Swaine, with his Assistant-Commissioner, Captain J. A. S. Inglis, of the 71st Highlanders, are the only two European residents in Famagusta. Till to-day Lieutenant Eastman, of the Marine Artillery and belonging to the Minotaur, has been acting here in charge of the native police (Zaptiehs); but, as his ship is leaving, he is to proceed home with her. This is another mistake in the semi-military, semi-civilian administration of this unfortunate island. None of the appointments in Cyprus are permanent. None of the officers appointed to civilian posts feel secure; they all know that not only they may be moved at any time, but that they are nearly sure to be ultimately, ere not long either, altogether. In fact, a general feeling of mistrust pervades the community. The policy of the

Government of secrecy keeps everyone from settling into a state of security. Trade—that is to say, legitimate trade—is paralysed, for a state of uncertainty will not tempt the merchant to risk his capital. The unparalleled extortionate demands of the citizens of Larnaca and Nicosia have prevented those cities reaping the full benefits that they might have expected from the British occupation. Larnaca will *not* be the port of the future—in all events, in an official sense. All the available ground there, and the buildings, have been bought up by speculators; whereas at Famagusta all the sea face remains in the hands of the Government. They have only to throw down the sea-face walls, and the materials will construct any amount of quays. The harbour of Famagusta, though considerably full of silt and sand, can easily be dredged, and a mole inexpensively constructed. The route from Famagusta to Nicosia presents far easier gradients, than that from Larnaca, and the district of Famagusta, including the Messarian plain, is the largest corn-growing and richest country. So likewise at Nicosia, the extortionate demand of the house holders for rent has already driven the head-quarter of Sir Garnet Wolseley out of the town, and in all probability the British settlement will be formed on another site without the town. The Government will wait and keep their counsel till the last moment, when I predict all the present speculators will have their eyes opened considerably.

Colonel Prendergast, commanding the Engineers of the Indian contingent, has left with the Indian force for Bombay. He sailed in the Trinacria; and when I last saw him on board that vessel, was very ill with the prevalent Cyprus fever. Lieutenant-Colonel J. Popham Magnay, commanding the Royal Engineers, is most energetic at Nicosia. He is not the man to stick at trifles, and difficulties soon melt before him. He is importing timber from Trieste, and intends placing the huts which are arriving from England upon wood framework of piles, like the ancient lake dwellings. Ultimately these platforms can be filled with concrete, forming solid platforms, like the "stoops" of the South African Dutch houses, over which at a later period, verandahs can be constructed. We have sapper officers in all directions, spying out the nakedness of the land and selecting sites for sanatoria and cantonments. Young Bethell has been through the Troados range, and found good sites, and Lieutenant A. H. Bagnold, R.E., has found a suitable camping ground up in the Carpas Mountains, not far from the Castle of Cantara, which commands a view of the sea on either side of the ridge, as well as of the opposite coasts of Asia Minor.

The 101st and 71st Regiments are by this time at Dali, the ancient Idalium, some ten or twelve miles south of Nicosia, but on higher ground, where it is to be hoped they will be more healthy. I intend to pay them a visit there shortly. The thirty-first company of Royal Engineers at Nicosia have, I regret to learn, lost four men by death from fever and sunstroke, and has other men badly ill. Acclimatised men from Gibraltar and Malta should have been sent. Absurd hurry, utterly uncalled for haste and confusion, has been the predominant feature hitherto of the hasty occupation and rapid partial evacuation of Cyprus. Thousands of tons of hay are arriving for cavalry horses which have departed. This is sold at a loss to speculators who are eagerly buying up forage, which is being stored at Beyrout, it is said on good authority, on French Government account: if so, it is significant. Major Maitland, R.E., is over in the hills near Beyrout suffering from dysentery, an old complaint, which should have prevented his coming out here (at least in the summer) at all. Another blunder is that which I learnt at the Consulate before starting for here. The commissariat here are buying up firewood for fuel in large quantities, at what is considerably above normal market rates. Well, now it appears that this firewood is all obtained from the extensive Government forests and property on the mountains to the north of the island, and so the English Government has actually been buying its own wood at an exorbitant price; and not only that, but the forests, which are valuable, are being destroyed for this purpose, and within the last two months more damage has been done in the way of disforesting and devastating the few remaining woods still existing in the Kyrenia and Carpas districts than had been accomplished in a decade of years. As it is, the island is quite burnt up enough, so that it is distressing to see the enormous piles of firewood along the beach and by the landing-places at Larnaca, and to know that they represent many square miles of wood-land recently destroyed. The wood, too, itself, is not of worthless scrub, only fit to burn, but includes olive and other fruit-producing trees, cypress and various useful woods, which would be valuable to individual owners; but, as it is government property, of course all the contractors care for is to get wood as conveniently near as possible for transport in boats to Larnaca. Of course, all this will be remedied, and promptly, as soon as it is known; but, meantime, it shows us that the task we have set ourselves of ruling Cyprus is far from an easy one: so let us take heed before we are too much entangled in Asia Minor.

(S.P.O., p. 312-314)

Trikomo, District of Carpas, Sept. 6.

On Monday, the 2nd inst., after leaving drawings, photographs, and letters for you with Captain Inglis, the Assistant Commissioner at Famagusta, to be forwarded to Larnaca, we started on our trip into the Carpas district, hitherto looked upon as the wildest of all the country districts. The Commissioner, Captain Swaine or rather the Kaimakam of the district, as he is styled by the natives, with his secretary and interpreter, Mr. Cambettino, and myself, formed the party. We were attended by our baggage-mules and muleteers, and were preceded by an escort of two Turkish zaptiehs, or mounted police, in picturesque costumes—altogether forming a small cavalcade. Having assembled in front of the Konak at Famagusta, we left the town by its mediaeval gates, the guard turning out and saluting the Kaimakam in correct form. Captain Swaine is a strict disciplinarian, and keeps both his zaptiehs and soldiers up to the mark; but I am sorry to say that there are, just now, many deserters. This is not on account of strict discipline; but the Turks feel that their rule is ended in the island, and know that they have given too much cause to fear retaliation from the Greeks. An emigration of the Turks to the coast of Syria has consequently set in.

It began to grow dusk long before we reached our first station, and as the sun sets early it was past dark that we arrived at Trikomo. Here we had been invited to stay with the chief agriculturist and merchant of the neighbourhood, Mr. Michael. At his house, on the outskirts of the village, we alighted after three hours and three quarters in the saddle. We were agreeably surprised with the comfort of our apartment. We were up betimes on Tuesday morning, myself to sketch and the Commissioner to transact business. There was a deputation to be received of two priests and three Greek farmers. One of the farmers spoke well and seemed very intelligent, while the priests were backward and diffident.

Their talk was all of taxation and money advanced to the Turks, who seem to have despoiled the Greek villages prior to their departure by all manner of extortion.

We left Trikomo at three in the afternoon, and did not expect to reach Haghios Theodoro until dark, but we only rode for about two hours and a half. Our track lay eastward, towards the seacoast, through a more undulating country covered with low scrubwood, apparently juniper. We crossed several streams, and went round a rocky point within a few feet of the sea, meeting a train of mules coming in the opposite direction, just where the path was worst. After passing this point, Palaea, we turned northwards, through Gastria, to St. Theodoro, a miserable hamlet, where we were to stay at the house of M. Dingli, half Maltese by birth. He did all he could for us in the way of hospitality. This place is only interesting as being the locality of the custom-house; but I doubt very much if, after the inspection by the English Kaimakam, it will much longer remain the seat of customs.

We were not sorry to get away next morning as soon as we could, after the usual deputation of notables of the neighbourhood, priests and farmers, all of whom seem to have been ground down by taxation and to be very poor. We now followed a track leading towards the hills, leaving the sea at our back. Soon the landscape improved, and the scenery became more rural and less desert. The fields, villages, and farms were more frequent; the watercourses were not entirely dried up, and wherever moisture remained in their beds thickets of lovely oleander bloomed. The flocks of sheep and herds of cattle were larger, and thriving better. The olive-trees, too, were more abundant. Altogether, we had entered a richer district. We crossed the line of telegraph which joins the submarine cable to the eastward. We were almost up to the hocks of our animals in marsh and water in one of the gullies. The mere sight of anything like water, or even moisture and vegetation, is pleasant to the eye after a continued course of desert and sunburnt plains. We passed caravans of camels and riders on mules, which also betokened a thriving district.

Early in the day we reached Hepta-Khumi, a bright looking village on a spur of the southern slopes of the Carpas Mountains. Here we met Mr. Parkes, an Englishman, who, next to the late Consul, Mr. Lang, has the greatest experience of the island. We were amused by the custom of incensing which takes place on the arrival of any important guest or on the occasion of any serious business. The dwelling in which we put up was more quaint and original than any we had yet seen. We were surprised to see a fireplace, and were told that it is really cold here in the winter. As we had no aneroid with us, we could not tell the altitude with any accuracy; but I should judge we were at least 500 ft. above the sea-level. The usual deputation, on a rather large scale, was duly received; and the Mudir from the neighbouring village also paid an official state visit to the English Kaimakam. A case of assault was brought before the Kaimakam, and it was stated that in this rude district abductions were of frequent occurrence. The proceedings were quite peculiar and picturesque; a large amount of incense was burnt. Satisfaction appeared to reign here, as it did everywhere, after Kaimakam's visit. Captain Swaine appeared to be very popular, and generally received what is vulgarly called an ovation.

After mid-day we were escorted by the Mudir to Khumi-Kebir. We had sent on our baggage by a more direct route from St. Theodoro. We were received by all the population of the village, the bells of the Greek church clanging out their best peal to apprise the country-folks of the arrival of the Kaimakam. We were followed to the house prepared for us by a crowd of villagers, who nearly all had to run to keep up with our animals. The reception and durbar here was very similar to all our previous ones, though on a larger scale. We subsequently visited the Mudir at his own house, and accompanied our host to his gardens outside the village. Melons of different kinds, maize, bringals, chilis, and other vegetables were in profusion here, as where-ever water for irrigation is procurable. But the people are too poor to procure the means of digging wells and tanks, or to employ the labour of mules and horses requisite for the machinery of the water-wheel to raise the precious fluid. Outside Khumi Kebir there are plenty of vineyards and quantities of olives; and here was the only place where we observed hedges forming regular lanes. At this village we first came across stone mills for crushing the olives, and the wooden rude screw presses with which the coarse bags of crushed olives are squeezed to make the oil exude—a very crude process. In about a fortnight's time the olives would be ready for picking. I should fancy that the introduction of proper machinery for pressing and refining the oil would pay any enterpising Englishman who turned his attention to this matter. On Thursday we sent our baggage by direct route back to Trikomo. We ourselves obtained the service of a guide to take us over the mountains to the monastery of Kantara. We knew that, according to the map, the monastery was only a few miles beyond the castle of Kantara, which is a conspicuous object for miles round, as it crests the highest mountain-top. Apparently that was all our so-called guide knew. He took us safely enough up within half a mile of the castle, and then was anxious to take us down to Davolo, on the other side of the mountain ridge. But to this we decidedly objected, and consequently made the best of our way as we could to the castle itself, or rather foot of the stupendous crag on which this magnificent Gothic ruin stands,

Like an eagle's nest perched on the crest of lofty Apennine—

And sure enough several splendid eagles were soaring about the ruin, a pair of them occasionally swooping down within a few yards of us. Their tameness showed that few guns find their way up so high as this place. The crests of this range, which hardly anywhere exceed 2000 feet, are remarkable for their jagged forms. We were on the higher ground, and could see the sea on either hand as we rode westward along what was really nothing but a goat's path on the very summit. We diverged here and there, where the precipitous rocks forced us to push through thickets of myrtle, and pines of small, stunted growth (Pinus Laricio), and we often had to find paths for ourselves. The guide was utterly out of his reckoning. I send you a few rough sketches of the really grand scenery. We could see, in front of us, the chain of mountains stretching west till their peaks were lost in the haze of the distance, boldly faced with precipices towards the sea on their northern sides, and descending in smoother slopes towards the Messarian plains to the south. We were delighted to find the monastery in sight, and to learn that the priest from Ilios had arrived there to meet us, well provided with cold chicken and eggs.

The sole actual resident at this tumble-down old monastery is an aged and very ragged monk, who complains that the neighbouring herdboys throw stones at him, and bring their flocks not only into the grounds of the monastery, but actually upon the roofs of the buildings. He pointed out holes in the ceiling of the cloisters, which this obnoxious proceeding had occasioned. We were many feet above the sea, and the solar radiation was intense; we consumed a large amount of cold water. Our Turkish zaptiehs, true to their Mussulman religion, alone refused to drink, merely washing their faces and hands, it being Ramazan this month (from Sept. 28 to Oct. 27), when they are forbidden to touch food or drink or even smoke between sunrise and sunset. The rapture with which they enjoyed their sunset drink of water and subsequent pipe was interesting to witness. Of the monastery of Kantara there is little or nothing to say, as there was nothing to see. Only the chapel building is actually in repair, and its interior is curious to a certain extent from its intense squalor and poverty-stricken appearance. As this monastery owns, I believe, a considerable acreage of property, it would be interesting for economists to inquire into the expenditure. The portly, hospitable priest who came from Ilios lives in affluence. The descent from the monastery into the plains was an ordeal not willingly to be repeated. The series of zigzag paths, which in the rainy season must be simply the beds of torrents filled with boulders and rolling stones, are of such gradients that to ride down is simply impossible. Though fully exposed to the rays of the afternoon sun, these paths are so sheltered from all breezes that to enter them is like entering an earthly purgatory. To lead a refractory mule down such a place is an intense agony. We got cold water about half an hour afterwards at a small village, and coffee at Ilios, in the priest's house; but we were pretty well done up when we arrived here, at Trikomo, last night, after sunset.

(S.P.O., p. 350)

Nicosia, Saturday, Sept. 7.

Yesterday was certainly the hottest day we have yet felt. Leaving Trikomo, we traversed the sandy plain for an hour, reaching the village of Syngrassi, where, after some trouble, we found the head-man. Captain Swaine halted to hold the usual reception of notables; but the heat was so great, as there was not the slightest breath of air, that I rode on quietly with the baggage. We then ascended a limestone plateau, perfectly destitute of vegetation, with little or no depth of soil, but with stony ridges of limestone cropping up, the whiteness of which reflected the blazing rays of the sun in a manner quite painful to the eyes and face. Another hour brought us to Lapatos, where we obtained a few minutes' shelter and a drink of water. The next village was Ipsos. As all these villages are alike, there is little to describe—they are merely a collection of mud huts. If the village is Turkish, there is a miserable building used as a mosque, barely rising above the other houses; and the women are in white, and covered, as to their heads, with yashmaks. Should the village, as is oftener the case, be Greek, there is as miserable and squalid a church, and the women are in colours, with only kerchiefs tied round their hair. Another hour brought us to Levconico, the most important town in the district. A zaptieh had ridden on to announce our approach; and, as we were expected to stay the night, the best house (that of the doctor) was prepared for us. I had hurried on in front, so that I was able to witness Swaine's approach and entry with more advantage than if I had accompanied him. The people were assembling at the entrance of the village, and as soon as the Kaimakam and his escort were observed coming over the plain, the bells of the Greek churches noisily clanged. Many hundreds soon collected together in the street, and also on the roofs of all the houses which commanded a view of the scene. A good many priests and other leading men of the town went out some distance to meet the Kaimakam on his arrival, and a regular triumphal procession was formed; but there was no cheering, no noise of any description, except that of the bells ringing. In front rode the brigand-like zaptiehs, looking as important as possible, and then came Captain Swaine and his interpreter on their ponies, surrounded by a motley crowd of townsfolk, which increased in numbers as they moved along. Under the window from which I surveyed the scene were collected a large number of women, who on the like occasions always keep together, and hold aloof from the men, awaiting the approach of the procession, which came on at a rapid pace. Priests and all were on the trot, kicking up no end of dust, but, as I said before, without noise. This noiseless crowd had a curious effect; it must have numbered at last six or seven hundred, and such a tumultuous running and jostling crowd would in England and most parts of Europe have been accompanied by shouts, hurrahs, and other cries. But all these people were so serious and quiet that the contrast was peculiar. Captain Swaine was taken aback by his reception, but preserved his imperturbable demeanour; in fact, he looked every inch the Kaimakam. The scene would have been almost ludicrous if it had not suggested the painful thought of what these silent, reserved people had suffered under former Kaimakams, and of what they looked forward to under British rulers. On dismounting, Captain Swaine came up to the upper chamber, where I was and the room was quickly filled; not only the room, but the house was full of all the people who could manage to push in, blocking up stairs, windows, and doors, wherever there was a chance of viewing the Kaimakam. The lady of the house approached and presented the usual burning incense in a handsomely worked silver censer, through the fragrant smoke of which you are expected to pass your hand and waft the scent to your face, after which rose-water was poured on our hands from a quaintly fashioned and chased silver-gilt vessel or phial, and then coffee in the usual minute cups was handed round.

Business now commenced, and the customary compliments were exchanged through the medium of the interpreter. Here be it observed that until our officials are able to converse freely and fluently with the people in their own tongue we shall never be able truly to rule them justly or understand their requirements. This place, Levconico, is mostly a Christian town; but there is a small community of Turks. The Kaimakam, in his speech, observed that henceforth Turk and Greek, Mohammedan and Christian, would be treated alike under the Queen's rule. But to show how little these people appreciate toleration, they almost immediately asked that two neighbouring Turkish villages should be destroyed, or rather that the Turks should be driven away from these two villages, because they annoyed them and stole their sheep, and they had never hitherto been able to get redress. There was the old palaver about poverty and the same cry of too hard taxation; and there is little doubt that the Turkish officials ground down these unhappy people whenever they could.

Our travels for the day were not yet over, as we had decided to go on at once to Cythraea. So, mounting our animals at three p.m., we quitted Levconico, and rode over the same flat plains, gradually approaching the foot of the mountains. Leaving on our left hand, to the southward, several populous villages, we rode into the groves and avenues of Cythraea after sunset, delighted to see green leaves, luxuriant vegetation, and hear the sound of many streams, which spring from the abundant sources at the foot of Mount Pentedactylon. We were astonished to see such large buildings rising through the trees by which they are surrounded. In the principal place of the town, where the cafés are, grow plane and sycamore trees of some height and girth, almost large timber, the first umbrageous trees of any respectable size we had yet seen in the island. A large proportion of ground in this neighbourhood is planted also with mulberry, and there are very many acres of cotton and the ubiquitous sesame. This oasis at the foot of craggy Pentedactylon is visible from Nicosia, which is only about nine miles off to the south. We were hospitably entertained in the large roomy house of an Armenian trader, and were thoroughly tired out after our long ride.

Next morning (Saturday) we rode to Nicosia, sorry to leave the verdure of Cythraea. I have omitted to mention that two English agriculturists, Messrs. Sparrow and Bass, have bought a large farm, called Cheftlic Lazara, at Leisata, in Kouklia, not far from the sea. They speak highly of the country, and intend importing good breeds of English sheep, which they have found successful in Australia. These gentlemen are the first English farmers who have become settlers in Cyprus, and it is to be hoped that their experiment will prove remunerative, and thus induce other Europeans to follow their example. I shall endeavour, when I visit that part of the island, to inspect their domain, and to judge for myself of their prospects, when they have had more time to know the capabilities of their property. It would be a good thing if the Government would hold out inducements for men of this sort to embark their capital in land here, as at present the landowners hold such small properties, and larger proprietors could farm at a far less expense.

(S.P.O., p. 350)

Remarks by the Editor, *The Illustrated London News,* 1879

Plate 45

ST. NICHOLAS CHURCH, CYPRUS.

[*the church referred to here is the building now known as the Bedestan*]

The beautiful old Church of St. Nicholas, at Nikosia, in Cyprus, which is said to have been built by the Crusaders, perhaps English, at the end of the twelfth or beginning of the thirteenth century, but which has been desecrated since the storming of the city by the Turks in 1570, is about to be restored for Divine worship according to the rites of the Church of England. This project originated with the Bishop of Gibraltar during his late visit to Cyprus. The Chaplain for the English Residents, the Rev. Josiah Spencer, B.A., has secured, on behalf of the Society for the Propagation of the Gospel, a perpetual lease of the building from the Turkish official corporation of trustees for an annual payment of 6000 piastres (£33.6s.8d.); and he is at present engaged in collecting, in England, the sum necessary to restore the chancel, which portion of the church, having a beautiful vaulted roof, octagonal lantern and dome, will be sufficient for present requirements. We are informed that £500 will be required before the work can be commenced, which ought to be in October. The present floor of the chancel, roughly paved with pebbles, is three feet above the true floor, and it is expected that inscriptions will be found.

In a pastoral letter which the Bishop of Gibraltar has just published we read:—"It is a remarkable fact that at the beginning of the fourteenth century there was at Nikosia a church which went by the name of 'St. Nicholas of the English,' and is so styled in old records. You will find a notice of this church in a lecture delivered last year at Oxford by the Regius Professor of History. As you may not have an opportunity of reading this lecture, I will give you a short account of the church. When Acre, which was the last fortress in Palestine surrendered to the Turks, was in 1291 finally compelled to yield, and the forces of the Cross had withdrawn from the Holy Land, some found a home in Cyprus, and among them the Order of St. Thomas of Acre, a small, semi-religious knightly order of Englishmen. This order had been founded by the sister and the brother-in-law of Becket, and possessed a hospital, built on the site of the house where Becket was born, and a church on the spot where now is the chapel of the Mercers' Company. During the Crusades the order settled at Acre, and devoted themselves to the office of burying the dead. At the siege of Acre the order is represented as leading the 5000 soldiers whom the English King, Edward I., had sent to Palestine. Such members of the order as survived the siege settled at Nikosia, where they possessed a church called 'St. Nicholas of the English.' The story of the appearance of St. Nicholas and St. Thomas to the London Crusaders in a storm at sea in 1189 or 1190, as Professor Stubbs suggests to me, probably had something to do with the establishment of the order; and the connection between St. Nicholas and the English is clearly due to the fact that the English were sailors. Various religious ceremonies are recorded in ancient documents as having been held in this church. It seems to have been the place in which the masters, priors, and custodes of the order were appointed to their offices. The name continually appears in the registered acts of the order. Speaking of one such ceremony, Professor Stubbs thus writes:—'The ceremony was performed in the Church of St. Nicholas of the English, in the city of Nikosia, one of the many churches which formerly, according to Father Stephen of Lusignan, adorned that city, but of which any relic would now, since the Venetians destroyed 130 in the process of fortification, scarcely be looked for.' Whether the desecrated Church of St. Nicholas which I saw in Nikosia was originally built by funds from London, and is that very edifice in which Englishmen worshipped 500 or 600 years ago, I have not yet been able to discover. At any rate, the church bears the same name. The style, moreover, is transitional. Whatever its history, if we make it our church, we shall have in it a bond connecting us, if not with this knightly order of Englishmen who lived in Nikosia in days long past, yet with our English brethren, whose forefathers worshipped in it before it was seized and desecrated by the Turks."

(Editor, p. 346)

Plate 46

SUMMER ENCAMPMENT IN CYPRUS.

In order to avoid the intense heat in the plains of Cyprus, his Excellency Major-General Robert Biddulph, C.B., has been for two months encamped within 400ft. of the summit of Mount Troodos, the ancient Olympus. The ground is a mass of rough rocks and stones covered with stunted pines; and, amongst these, tents were pitched for the High Commissioner of the Island, and his personal staff, consisting of Lieutenant Walter H. Holbech, 60th Rifles, private secretary, and Lieutenant F. Hammersley, 20th Regiment, A.D.C. Even at this altitude, 6000ft. above the sea-level, the heat of the sun at midday was excessive, and the thermometer in the tents frequently reached 90 deg., but sitting outside in the shade was pleasant enough, and the evenings were almost too chilly after the sun set. Within a hundred yards of this camp the officers and men of the 20th Foot had stretched their canvas on a plateau, from which magnificent views are obtained looking northwards. On the other side, the Royal Engineers had set up their tents on a ridge overlooking a deep ravine which runs away eastwards. The scenery is certainly magnificent, and the health of the troops has been excellent, with the exception of a few men who have suffered from eating too much fruit and not wearing sufficient clothing after sunset. Our Illustrations are supplied by a set of photographs which were sent to us on the 16th ult. The photographic artist employed was Mr. Helios, a Greek name which seems highly appropriate to his profession, as we should say "Mr. Sun."

(Editor, p. 366)

Plate 47

GREEK CHURCH AT LARNACA, CYPRUS.

Among the ecclesiastical antiquities of this island, which has so recently passed under British rule, the seaport town of Larnaca, most frequently visited by foreign vessels, contains one that has a certain degree of interest. We give an Illustration of the interior of the Greek Church attached to the Monastery of St. Lazarus, at Larnaca. It stands in the centre of a large square, one side of which is a burial-ground, inclosed by tall iron railings, and the other three sides consist of the cells formerly inhabited by the community of monks, but now let out on hire to common lodgers, while the cemetery has become a boys' playground. The church is reported, by Greek religious tradition, to contain the tomb of Lazarus, who is said to have come from Bethany, long after Our Saviour raised him from the dead there, and to have ended a long life here in Cyprus. They keep tapers ever burning in the vault beneath the altar; there is a descent by a few steps, and in the dim light of the shrine a granite slab is visible, arched at the top, with a little spring of water under it, filling a stone basin. This water has miraculous properties, for the healing of sores, by the application of rags dipped in the water. It would seem that the Lazarus, the poor man who had sores, mentioned in the New Testament parable of Dives and Lazarus, is considered by the Greek clergy to be the same Lazarus that was raised from the dead.

(Editor, p. 474)

Wolseley 1878

After the Congress of Berlin where it was agreed that Great Britain would lease, occupy and administer Cyprus, Lieutenant General Sir Garnet Joseph Wolseley was quickly appointed as Her Majesty's High Commissioner for the Island of Cyprus. He assumed administration of the island July 22, 1878. He remained only until the end of May 1879 when he was assigned to South Africa. A record of the first half of his stay in Cyprus is contained in *Cyprus 1878, The Journal of Sir Garnet Wolseley*, edited by Anne Cavendish, published by the Cyprus Popular Bank Cultural Centre, Nicosia, 1991. Because that source is now so available, the quotations here comprise all the letters from Wolseley to his wife from Cyprus contained in *The Letters of Lord and Lady Wolseley, 1870–1911,* edited by Sir George Arthur, published in New York: Doubleday, Page & Co., and London: William Heinemann, 1922.

LARNAKA, CYPRUS, *23rd July.*

We arrived here yesterday morning. I went ashore in the evening, and swore myself in as Lord High Commissioner and Commander-in-Chief of the Island, the Duke of Edinburgh being amongst the spectators: it was rather curious my sitting in state whilst he stood amongst the officers present.

Whilst I think of it, remember to take in the *Daily News*, for Mr. Forbes of that paper is here and will send home letters describing our doings. Larnaka is not such a bad place as it is generally represented to be. I have ordered a house to be hired at Nicosia (accent on the i), which will put you up very well; I hope soon to see it and will report to you what it looks like.

NICOSIA, CYPRUS, *5th August 1878.*

Minutes to be written upon every subject under heaven—petitions from peasants, declaring they have been beaten and ill-treated by the police, or some one else, and a thousand other things, one after another, until my poor brain goes round like a humming-top. This is a filthy hole, and I am going to clear out and encamp round a small monastery. I am having the island explored to discover a good site for a large cantonment, where I shall establish the three European regiments, and to which I shall remove the seat of Government. I have asked for eight large tents for myself, as a sort of residence; until they are up you cannot possibly come here. Taylor packed our things most disgracefully, and the result is that candles, jams, blacking, and mustard, etc., have come out of some of our cases in one heavy mass. All but one of my cases have turned up; the missing one contains my saddles, very valuable articles in a country like this. The horse-flies drive my old horse nearly wild, and the extreme dryness of the climate, added to the heat, have made his hoofs so brittle that I cannot really use him—large pieces of his hoof break off like shortbread; however, when I get him into camp, I shall make him stand in moist ground to keep his feet soft and cool.

I wish all my staff had half Brackenbury's brains; and when I think of the beautiful regularity with which my books were kept by him, I am sad to think of the scrawling hideousness which will be left to me as my records of Cyprus.

The sanitary arrangements here are dreadful; how the people exist I cannot imagine, and yet they live and have large, healthy families. The wife of the owner of this house said the other day that she had never been outside Nicosia in her life: she has a host of children, all of whom looked healthy. Fleas and bugs abound. I was going over an old building, when some one drew attention to my trousers, which, below the knee, were literally covered with a mass of jumping fleas. I thought how the tapering ankles of a certain lady would have suffered in such a place.

Oh, if you could only see my shirts as they have come home from the wash! Despair would fill your mind: but I hope to import washerwomen—may they be good-looking!!—from Malta, where the art of starching is well understood. A quaint Irish doctor, just from England, says that Cyprus reminds him of maps of the moon which show there is neither water, vegetation, nor even atmosphere in it. Don't allow any one to think I am disappointed with the place—tell them I write most cheerfully. I really like the work: it bristles with difficulties, but they are made to be beaten down: if only I spoke Turkish how quickly I could surmount them. Herbert, my admirable private secretary is worked hard ciphering and deciphering the telegrams.

CAMP NICOSIA, *24th November*

This day month I hope to see you installed in Government House, if all goes well. My next letter I shall address to the Consul at Naples, as Sir Geoffrey Hornby most kindly sends a dispatch boat there for you. It will be a four days' passage from thence to Larnaka, where I shall meet you: I could not leave the island without special leave from the Queen, and I do not want to ask for it at present, for many reasons. I hope you have been able to get the Frenchwoman, for even if she only stays a year it will be a great help in starting the establishment. I shall have no difficulty in finding a couple of Greek women as housemaids for our own private part of the house. I have heard of a cook at Malta who seems to promise well.

Bring some mignonette, some sweet pea, some hop, some wallflower, some heartsease seed, and a few dozen of crocus roots; anything and everything will grow here. Also enough good grass seed to sow an acre. I hope to have a gardener by the time you arrive.

I want a hand magnifying-glass for examining maps, and a set of lawn-tennis things—the best rackets and five dozen of the best covered balls. I have just got the silk for the Queen, and have ordered enough for a dress to be sent to Eyty. I am sending Lady Cowell a chemise like the one I sent the Queen. When you come here, I think we can please friends by sending them gold coins which I can buy for a pound apiece. I am afraid the house will be so unfinished that you will not be as comfortable at first as I could wish you to be: however, I am sure you won't mind that.

CAMP NICOSIA, *2nd December 1878.*

To-day I had a visit suddenly from a Mr. Blunt and his wife, Lady Anne Blunt; she is a daughter of old Lord Lovelace by his first wife and so a granddaughter of Lord Byron. They were *en route* for Damascus and the Desert.

I trust we may not be separated again for some time to come, and that our mountain sanatorium may prove a great success: otherwise I shall have to send you off to France or Switzerland. If Cyprus does not suit you, I shall try and get out of it when I have put it in order. But if I leave this, I don't know what I am to do, for the Commander-in-Chiefship in India will not be vacant until 1881, and then it is not by any means certain I should be given it; I presume it will fall to Sir Neville Chamberlain who has taken Sir E. Johnson's place on the Viceroy's Council, and who is in high favour with Lord Lytton at present. I have just had a letter from Colley, in which he says that if I had gone to Bombay, I should have been employed by Lytton in the war, but that he could not, without giving great offence to the Army in India, have sent for an outsider to take command: to have done so would have been to say there was no one in India fit for the job. I don't see this, of course, in the same light. If he has a man in India as fit as I am, then he is quite right in his reasoning, but if the man he has employed is, in his opinion, inferior in military ability to me then he is altogether wrong. In his place I would insist, in the public interest, on having the ablest General in the service, even if I had to send to Timbuctoo for him.

Brassey 1878

[Plates 48-52]

Baroness Annie Allnott Brassey traveled in Cyprus in 1878 and recorded her observations in *Sunshine and Storm in the East or Cruises to Cyprus and Constantinople*. The following is excerpted from that book published in 1880 by Longmans, Green & Co., London, and reprinted in New York by Henry Holt and Company, 1890.

CHAPTER V.

ISLAND OF CYPRUS.—PORT PAPHO, LIMASOL, LARNAKA.

Thursday, November 7th.—At 6 a.m. I came on deck, to find that we had already made Cape Arnauti, the western point of the island, two hours previously, and were rapidly approaching Cape Drepano, Port Papho, the small town of Ktima above, the ruins of ancient Paphos, where may still be traced the remains of the temple dedicated to the worship of the Paphian Venus. The coast is high, rocky, and at present very brown and bare-looking, though after the winter rains it will probably become green and bright. Both sky and sea were of the most lovely blue, as we crept along the shore before a light breeze, scarcely sufficient to ripple the water or to fill the sails of our own vessel and those of two or three small coasting schooners in our vicinity. Not far off was a large five-masted man-of-war, which proved to be the 'Minotaur,' Lord John Hay's flagship, lying to in order to send some boats on shore. We exchanged names with her, and the admiral then hoisted the signal, 'Will you come on board to breakfast?' to which Tom replied in the same manner, 'Very happy,' and in due time proceeded to avail himself of the invitation.

After our own breakfast we all paid a visit to the mighty monster, though it was not without difficulty that we got on board, as she was then under way. There was, of course, no accommodation-ladder down, and they wanted to lower a chair for me from the yard-arm; but I preferred mounting by the ordinary steps against the ship's side—not a very wonderful feat after all, as there were ropes to hold on to, and the ship was comparatively steady. She is certainly a magnificent vessel, with a charming stern gallery, first-rate officer's quarters, and two splendid decks, well furnished with guns of various sizes, all, it need hardly be said, in perfect order and as bright and clean as possible. She does not, however, show to advantage just at present, as the upper deck is encumbered with large boats inboard and some Indian ponies which are being sent back, while the main deck is curtained off for the invalid officers returning from Cyprus. Yesterday all the big guns on board were fired for practice, and we were told that the vibration stove in the bulkheads in the admiral's cabin. What a treat for the poor invalids, who lie with their heads right against them! . . .

Everyone on board the 'Minotaur' gives a bad account of the climate of Cyprus, and seems thoroughly glad to get away from it. The crew have always drunk distilled water during their stay, and though they have been much on shore they have enjoyed a comparative immunity from fever. Mr. Hepworth Dixon, who is on his way to Malta, after spending over three months in Cyprus, was among those on board the flagship. I was pleased to have the opportunity of meeting a man whose works I have enjoyed so much. We had an interesting conversation, in the course of which he gave us a great deal of valuable information about the island, and the things best worth seeing in it. He specially recommended us to beware of the horses; which are often extremely skittish—a fact of which he himself had had painful experience, having broken his collar-bone by a fall from one of them.

Getting down again into our boat was not quite so easy as getting up had been, for the 'Minotaur's' sides are high and steep; but the sailors carried the children, and we all safely accomplished the descent. After the admiral had returned our call, he steamed away towards Malta, while we approached still closer to the shore, and at last anchored just outside the ruined fort and harbour of Paphos, which looked very pretty from the yacht. Over the square tower of the little fort the flag of old England drooped languidly in the breezeless air. Along the shore grew the trees of what were once the gardens of the Temple of Venus, beyond which was a barren spot, covered by the ruins of the temple itself, with more groves of trees close at hand. On the hills at the back is perched the little village of Ktima, with its mosque and minaret, above which stood the white tents and brown huts of the 71st Regiment; while the background of the whole scene was formed by the more distant mountains, part of the chain to which Mount Olympus belongs . . .

Very little of the ruins of Ktima now remains above ground. A few broken marble columns, sarcophagi, and slabs with inscriptions on them, some standing, some lying down, were all we saw, though even the fields and roads were strewn with fragments of white marble capitals and acanthus-leaf ornaments. Venus's bath still remains, with a stream of pure water flowing into it; and the column to which St. Paul was tied, that he might be scourged for preaching the Gospel in the island, was also pointed out to us.

It was quite a steep climb up the rocks to Ktima, a little Turkish village, surrounded by gardens full of fruit. Wherever there was the least sign of moisture, the ground seemed to produce in abundance. We went to the prison and the court of justice, and then rode through the bazaar, most of the shops in which were already closed, it being nearly the hour of sunset. A very short distance beyond the town is the camp of the 71st. Some of the huts were finished yesterday, and were already occupied. Hitherto the men have been crowded together in tents, without beds, sleeping on the bare ground, with one blanket under and another over them. No wonder, therefore, that out of 105 officers and men, 27 are still down with fever, while many of those who are convalescent show terrible traces of the disease, being hardly able to crawl about, and looking more like ghosts than men. The camp contained an imposing-looking surgery, but unfortunately no supply of proper fever medicine, and the poor doctor was consequently in despair. The site of the camp looks healthy, and the view from it, especially at sunset, when we saw it, is lovely . . .

In the mountains, near at hand, are found the celebrated Paphian diamonds, which are really only a superior kind of rock-crystal, and also that curious incombustible mineral, asbestos.

Some of the officers of the 71st came on board to dinner. We had a cheery evening and plenty of talk about Cyprus, and we were all very sorry when it was time to separate and say good-bye.

Friday, November 8th.

* * * * *

Limasol, where we arrived at about 10 a.m., is a long low white town, stretching along the sea-shore, with domes and minarets interspersed among the houses and palm trees. Never was anything so blue as were the sky and sea this morning; but if the colouring was beautiful, the heat was disagreeably intense. The very small landing-stage was decorated with vines and olive branches, the remains of a triumphal arch prepared two or three days ago on the occasion of the visit of the Governor and the Lords of the Admiralty. The mayor and the whole of the population came down to see us land, thinking probably that we were another party of distinguished English visitors, to whom more addresses ought to be presented. When they found we only wanted some mules for ourselves and the children to ride, their interest abated, though the mayor and a select body of followers accompanied us all round the town to the khan, the place where the market is to be, and to the old semi-Venetian, semi-Turkish fort, from which there is a fine view over the surrounding country.

While we were wandering about, a letter was brought to us from the Commissioner, Colonel Warren, with whom we had travelled some years ago in Russia, asking us to lunch with him. He soon found us out himself, and said that he had just returned from a three days' expedition into the mountains, that he had been much delighted with all he saw, and was amazed at the fertility of the land and the enormous acreage of the vineyards. We went with him to the Government House—which is also the post-office and court-house—where we found that the Assistant Commissioner was very ill with typhoid fever. The doctor, who had been sent for from Larnaka, was in despair, as he had arrived to find his patient almost dying, and he had no medicines to treat him with. Fortunately we were able to supply him with what he wanted, and also with port wine, beef-tea, turtle, and other medical comforts, of all of which he was absolutely destitute.

When it was time to embark the mayor saw us off, and gave me two or three specimens of old glass, of which great quantities are found in the tombs near here. Digging for antiquities is now forbidden, and I believe the Government intend to take the matter into their own hands.

Limasol is now a fairly clean town, without any pretension to a harbour. There are no troops here; but the fever seems to be very bad among both European and native residents. Colonel Warren has been here some time, and takes great interest in his work, which is of the most arduous and varied description, as his jurisdiction extends over several hundred square miles of country.

We had rather an amusing barter with the colonel, exchanging *new* newspapers for *old* pots and earthenware vases, some of beautiful shape, from the tombs; and after a few little delays we finally got under way again and proceeded on our voyage along the coast . . .

For dinner this evening we had some of the beccaficos, or preserved birds, which are so well known in these parts. Delicious fat little morsels they would be; but to my mind they are completely spoilt by being dipped, as soon as they are killed, feathers and all, into the strong vinegar made from the wine of the country, the taste of which spoils their own delicate flavour, though they are considered a great delicacy by most people. They are preserved in bottles for months, and thus sent away to other countries. Even in the classical ages they were famed, and at the time of the Crusades they were specially prized, no doubt owing to their having been preserved to greater perfection in the Commandaria wine made by the Knights of St. John.

About 9 p.m. we were off the port of Larnaka . . .

Saturday, November 9th.—All the ships in port were dressed to-day in honour of the Prince of Wales's birthday. The harbour-master came on board at 6 p.m. to give us *pratique*, and soon afterwards Lord Lilford's agent, to whom he had given instructions, came to see what he could do for us. He gave a very bad account of the health of the place, which, considering the hot and steamy state of the atmosphere at the time, seemed by no means surprising.

A little later on a telegram arrived from Sir Garnet Wolseley, asking us to go up to the Monastery Camp near Nikosia, to stay with him, which we arranged to do as soon as mules and a conveyance could be procured. There was some talk of a diligence, but it ultimately proved to be a small tea-cart drawn by a horse and a mule. Horses for us to ride were also provided, as well as mules to carry the luggage.

While waiting to start, we had an opportunity of seeing something of the town of Larnaka. I believe it has already considerably improved in appearance since the arrival of the English; but it is still a miserable-looking place, with half-a-dozen wretched little jetties and broken-down quays, in course of repair with stones from ancient Salamis, on the sea-shore. The sea itself washes almost up to the house-doors, and in many places it is necessary to make a detour by a back street in order to get into a house. There are some large stores, full of things not now required, the owners of which will, I fear, in many cases be ruined, owing to their having speculated to provide for a larger number of troops than have been sent to the island. The last of the Indian contingent embarked last week. They seem to have left a good impression behind them, as the best-behaved and most docile soldiers ever seen. Their surplus stores were sold off a day or two ago at a fearful loss, horses fetching from seventeen shillings to a pound each, and their provisions for the winter and other things being sold at equally low prices. Truefitt's establishment, of which we have heard so much in England, is rather a large affair, and does a good deal more business than merely haircutting and hairdressing. All the men engaged in it have been down with fever, most of the hairdressers are gone home, and neither the children nor I could have our hair cut by Truefitt in Cyprus, as we had intended doing. Some of the stores are really very well supplied, and almost any reasonable requirement can now be satisfied at Larnaka. But it is quite depressing to go into any of the shops or houses, or to speak to anyone residing here; they all have a more or less invalid look, and agree in giving a terrible account of the fever that has prevailed among them.

About 3 p.m. we started, passing through the narrow dusty streets of mud houses, by a Turkish mosque, where the wet-nurse of the Prophet Mohammed is supposed to have been buried, and a Roman Catholic convent of Oros Stavro, or Mountain of the

Cross, the sisters of mercy belonging to which have behaved like angels all through the recent times of sickness and misery. On leaving the town, the road lies over sunburnt plains and between stony hills, all the way up to Nikosia, not a trace of cultivation being visible except in the gardens just round two or three wretched little villages, and in a few forsaken vineyards and cornfields. The road itself is bad, and we were just an hour and a half going the first eight miles, to the village of Furin, where we changed horses. Here an enterprising English blacksmith and a plumber and glazier, failing to obtain employment in their respective trades, have entered into partnership, and, pending the completion of a stone house they are building, have pitched a tent, which they call the 'Dewdrop Inn,' and from which they supply the thirsty traveller with beer, lemonade, and other refreshments. Another nine miles' ride brought us to Athienu, where we changed again. The proceedings of nearly all our horses and mules, being of a highly erratic character, made our journey occasionally rather a perilous one. Once we were as nearly as possible upset, owing to the horses shying at a dead donkey (a sight said to be as rare as that of a dead post-boy) lying in the middle of the road, which no one had thought it worth while to remove, though, as our driver informed us, it had been there for more than two days. We met the regular diligence during the afternoon, and between the last two stations passed the tents of the Eastern Telegraph Company's employés, who are busy replacing the present temporary wooden poles that support the wires by more substantial iron posts. We also met innumerable trains of heavily laden camels, bringing produce down from the interior, and long lines of empty bullock-carts, returning to fetch more things for the camp.

CHAPTER VI.

NIKOSIA, MATHIATI, AND FAMAGOUSTA.

It was now nearly dark, and the surrounding country was hardly visible. By the time we at last reached the gates of Nikosia we found them closely shut for the night, and it was only after waiting a long time, with much hammering and shouting on our part, that an old Turk made his appearance, with a lantern and the keys, to admit us. The air was rather cold, and we were quite glad of the wraps we had been recommended to bring with us. The walls of the city are high, thick, and machicolated, with many Venetian cannons lying about outside. In the bright moonlight the effect was very fine, and I think the gateway itself, through which we entered, cannot be better described than in the words of Ali Bey, a celebrated traveller between the years 1803 and 1807:

'The city has three gates, Paphos, Chirigua, and Famagousta. The last is magnificent. It is composed of a vast cylindric vault, which covers the whole slope or ascent from the level of the country below to the upper plain on which the city is built; halfway up the ascent there is an elliptical cupola, or a segment of a sphere, in the centre of which there is a circular opening for the admission of the light. The monument is entirely constructed of large hewn stone or rough marble, and the whole edifice is worthy of the ancient inhabitants.'

The narrow, dirty, and tortuous streets were deserted, the dogs howled and barked dismally, and the moonlight shone over the confused mass of Turkish, Greek, and Venetian palaces, mud houses, minarets, churches, and mosques. At last we drew up near what looked like a *café*, our coachman refusing to go any further, and proceeding forthwith to unharness his horses for the night. We were soon surrounded by a gesticulating crowd, who were very polite and brought us chairs to sit upon, but who all appeared to be desirous of taking us off in different directions. Unfortunately not a single word of any language we could speak to them was understood, and their remarks were equally unintelligible to us. 'The Governor,' 'the Pasha,' 'Sir Garnet Wolseley,' 'the Camp,' 'the Monastery,' 'Government House,' were all tried; but as each name was pronounced it seemed to have no other effect than that of puzzling them more and more. At last one man, evidently struck with an idea, flew off, and returned in a few minutes accompanied by the German-speaking landlord of the 'Albert Hotel, Restaurant, and Lodging,' as it was described on the card he gave us, who evidently taking in the situation at a glance, endeavoured to persuade us to pass the night at his hotel, throwing all sorts of difficulties in the way of our proceeding further, and asserting that the camp, our destination, was still a matter of an hour and a half's journey. A waiter or friend who was with him, however, informed us that Government House was not so far off and offered to show us the way. Tom put me on one of the horses, the rest followed on foot through more narrow streets, till at last, to our joy, we beheld the red uniform of a soldier of the Royal Engineers. He had been sent to meet us at a point where there was a short cut into the town, but had somehow missed us, and hence all our difficulty and delay. He told us we had still two miles to go, and at once proceeded to take us out through another gate and across some ground by the side of an aqueduct, over the dry bed of the river, till at last we arrived at the Monastery Camp, Sir Garnet Wolseley's head-quarters. Here we were warmly wlcomed by friends, both old and new, including Sir Garnet himself, Colonel Brackenbury, Colonel Greaves, Çolonel Dormer, Captain Wood, Lord Gifford, Mr. Herbert, and several others. Three huts, opening into one another, and comfortably furnished with impromptu sofas, easy chairs, writing tables, rugs, and mats, for which we learned afterwards that nearly every tent in the camp had been ransacked, were placed at our disposal. We were the first ladies to pass a night in the camp, and as our arrival had taken place rather sooner than was expected, everybody had been busy all the afternoon, after the receipt of our telegram, trying to make things as comfortable as possible for us; and most thoroughly they had succeeded.

* * * * *

The town [*Nicosia*] is disappointing inside, although there are some fine buildings still left. The old cathedral of St. Sophia, now used as a mosque, is superb in the richness of its design and tracery, and the purity of its Gothic architecture. Opposite the cathedral is the church of St. Nicholas, now used as a granary. The three Gothic portals are among the finest I have ever seen. Every house in Nikosia possesses a luxuriant garden, and the bazaars are festooned with vines; but the whole place wears, nothwithstanding, an air of desolation, ruin, and dirt. Government House is one of the best of the old Turkish residences.

From the Turkish prison we passed through a narrow dirty street, with ruined houses and wasted gardens on either side, out into the open country again, when a sharp canter over the plain and through a small village brought us to the place where the new Government House is in course of erection. This spot is called Snake Hill, from two snakes having once been discovered and killed there, a fact which shows how idle are the rumours of the prevalence of poisonous reptiles in the island. It is a rare thing to meet with them, and I have seen one or two collectors who had abandoned in despair the idea of doing so. The site selected for Government House is a commanding one, looking over river, plain, town, mountains, and what were once forests . . .

Monday, November 11th.—The night was again cold, and even at 8 a.m. breakfast, by which time the sun was high and bright, the air was still chilly. About 10 a.m. we started to ride to Kythraea, a village situated in a lovely valley, about ten miles off. Our road at first was by way of the bridge over the river Pedaeus. Close by is a precipice, down which are thrown the carcases of all the animals that die or are killed in the town; consequently there was a pack of hungry half-starved dogs hanging about, who barked at us most vociferously as we disturbed them. We passed a corner of the town, and rode along under the massive walls to the Kyrenia gate, which forms the entrance to a fortress, and is very like the Famagousta gate, already described. Here it was that, on August 25, 1878, a curious scene was enacted. The Turkish prisoners confined at Nikosia were all brought out, bound together in threes, made up into parties of about fifty, and marched in detachments to Kyrenia to embark on board the 'Black Prince' for the opposite coast [Plate 22]. The walls of the town were covered with Turkish women, weeping, howling, and lamenting. Some of the men broke down, others behaved like Stoics; but it must have been a sad sight as they were marched off, and the women were left weeping round the three camel-loads of chains that had been removed from the prisoners. The men had previously been informed of what was going to be done with them; but it seems that they were under the impression that they were to be set free on arriving at their destination, and they therefore marched bravely along to Kyrenia, fifteen miles distant, without one of their number breaking down or attempting to offer the slightest resistance. It was well that this was the case; for the guard in whose charge they were, both English and Indian, were so much affected by the heat of the sun that they kept falling out by the way, and could have done little to resist any attempt of their prisoners to escape, more especially as the latter helped the tired soldiers by carrying their guns. They all reached Kyrenia at 4 p.m., having started at 7 a.m., and were handed over to the care of the commissioner, by whom they were put into the old fort, under the guard of some men of the 42nd regiment. During the night two of them managed to escape through a hole in the wall, but the remainder were safely embarked on board the 'Black Prince' the next morning; and right glad was everybody in the island to be rid of them, for they were a set of desperate ruffians.

Leaving the walls of the city behind, we crossed a sandy stony plain. For about two hours we saw no signs of fertility, but we then began to pass through vineyards, cotton-fields, and pomegranate, olive, and orange-tree plantations, till we reached the house of a rich Armenian, whose brother is one of the interpreters at the camp . . .

After that, we mounted fresh mules, and rode up the valley, by the running water, to the point where it gushes from the hill, or rather mountain, side, a clear stream of considerable power. It rises suddenly from the limestone rock at the foot of Pentadactylon, nearly 3,000 feet high, in the northern range of mountains. No one knows whence it springs; but from the earliest times it has been celebrated, and some writers have asserted that it comes all the way, under the sea, from the mountains of Karamania, in Asia Minor. The effect produced is magical, trees and crops of all kinds flourishing luxuriantly under its fertilising influence. The village of Kythraea itself nestles in fruit-trees and flowering shrubs, and every wall is covered with maidenhair fern, the fronds of which are frequently four and five feet long. The current of the stream is used to turn many mills, some of the most primitive character, but all doing their work well, though the strong waterpower is capable of much fuller development.

* * * * *

The drive from this point to the main road from Nikosia to Larnaka was through a more fertile country, and Larnaka was finally reached at about 7 p.m., the Commissioner and another friend being engaged to dine with us on board at 7.30 p.m. The diligence, due at 4.30 p.m., had not arrived, nor the mules with the baggage. The muleteers, who almost all live at Athienu, halfway between Nikosia and Larnaka, are obliging and honest, but unpunctual and slow. It was 10 p.m. before the first lot of luggage arrived, and 8 a.m. the following day before the remainder reached us.

Colonel White showed us a great many interesting things during our few minutes' stay at his office—talc in large slabs, yellow ochre, lead, gold, copper, plumbago, and other mineral products of the island. Lastly he showed us a room full of vases and glassware, which General Cesnola's brother had dug up, and was taking away when stopped by the English officials. Unfortunately he had already succeeded in smuggling off a good many things before they knew what he was about . . .

Wednesday, November 13t . . . We found ourselves once more on board, really ready for a start, at 10 a.m., and the 'Sunbeam' steamed out of the open roadstead of Larnaka, along the barren coast, past some uninteresting towns and villages to Famagousta, where we arrived at about 2 p.m.

H.M.S. 'Foxhound,' which had anchored shortly before our arrival, hoisted the signal, 'Take care—great caution required;' so we proceeded very slowly, until the officer in command, Lieutenant Noel, kindly came on board and showed us the way in. The channel is not really very intricate, but the mole is all broken down, and it is not easy to see where the reef ends. The walls of the town, from which there is a fine view over the surrounding country, are very massive, though in ruins in many places. The cathedral and churches stand out grandly from amid the surrounding palm-trees, and give the place rather an imposing appearance; but there is an air of desolation about the whole city such as I never saw elsewhere, and the picture of ruin and decay was completed by an adjacent marsh. Famagousta is one of four cities founded by Ptolemy Philadelphus in honour of his sister Arsinoë, whose name it bore until after the battle of Actium, when it was renamed Fama Augusti by the victor, Augustus, in his own honour. The city has been built, rebuilt, and fortified by Lusignans, Genoese, and Venetians, successively, always with stones from the ancient Salamis, four miles distant, across the plain by the sea-shore. The original of Shakespeare's Othello was at one time governor here.

On the way to the shore we met the doctor coming off in his boat to give us *pratique*; he turned round, and we all landed together. The inner harbour was full of small caïques, and on the shore stood a long team of camels, laden with pomegranates in sacks. Some civil but ragged Turks met us, offered the children and me some pomegranates, and showed us the way to the Latin cathedral of St. Nicholas. As in the case of St. Sophia at Nikosia, its Gothic arches are filled in with Turkish wooden tracery, and the building is now used as a mosque.

If Famagousta presents a melancholy appearance from the outside, the spectacle within is still more depressing. In the midst of the dust and ruins of houses and palaces, once containing a population of three hundred thousand souls, are now to be found a few miserable mud huts, the habitations of some three hundred people. Three churches remain standing where once there were two hundred; and in the streets only a few cadaverous looking creatures may be seen gliding about like ghosts.

At the Government House we went to see some officers whose servants are all down with fever, including even the groom, a once celebrated Syrian highwayman, rather in the Dick Turpin style, whose history is decidedly interesting. This man was originally a groom in the employ of a wealthy Turk near Smyrna; but having eloped with his master's daughter, he found it necessary to flee to the mountains, where he became a brigand of the romantic type, robbing only the rich and assisting the poor. It is even said that at various times he gave dowries to as many as two thousand Greek girls. Every effort was made by the Turkish authorities to capture him; but as he had a friend in every peasant, he invariably succeeded in evading the soldiers sent after him. During the Crimean war, some British troops assisted the Turks in one of their expeditions in search of Kattirdji-Janni (which was the brigand's name), but with the same result. On one occasion it is related that he suddenly entered a house near Smyrna at the head of a dozen followers, all armed to the teeth. The family were at supper, and Kattirdji-Janni, quietly seating himself, remarked that as soon as they had finished he and his men would take the opportunity of refreshing themselves. His involuntary hosts at once rose and proceeded to supply him with all that he desired, whereupon, as a proof of his gratitude, he promised them his protection, and assured them that if they should happen to be travelling and to fall in with any of his band, they might rely on not being molested by them. At last, either tiring of his adventurous life, or being hard-pressed, he gave himself up to the Turkish authorities, upon their promise that he should be exiled to Cyprus. He was taken to Constantinople, and would probably have been sent thence to the spot he had chosen, had not a Frenchman connected with the consulate, who had formerly been robbed by Kattirdji-Janni and his followers, demanded that he should be severely punished. Thereupon he was imprisoned and kept closely confined in a small cell, where he was chained to the wall, for seven years. Later on he was removed to Famagousta, still heavily chained; and though the severity of his punishment was somewhat mitigated in 1875, owing to the intercession of Madame Cesnola on his behalf, it is only quite recently that he has entirely regained his liberty, and even now he is not allowed to leave the town of Famagousta.

Captain Bolton lives a little way off, at Varoshia, a thriving village, surrounded by orchards and gardens—not an over-healthy place, I dare say, though the living there is cheap and good. The other three gentlemen live in this fearful town; and most sincerely I pity them. Close at hand is an extensive marsh, which abounds with woodcock, snipe, teal, and wild fowl of every description; but the story goes that should any sportsman venture there to shoot, he is certain to be down with fever before the birds he has killed can be cooked. These officers have not yet tried the experiment themselves, but the 'Foxhound' landed a shooting party to-day, and I shall be anxious to hear the result.

Notwithstanding the fact that the Turks have removed several shiploads of them, many of the fine old Venetian cannon still remain here, with tons of iron and marble shot.

We brought away a specimen of the latter, as a remembrance of the ancient city that has withstood so many attacks from foreign invaders, but which is now left to moulder in silence and solitude in the midst of malaria. If the harbour could ever be restored, and the marshes drained, she might once again rise to comfort and prosperity.

On the way back to the yacht we paid a visit to the 'Foxhound,' a smart little gunboat, to see the officer in command. He gave me some pieces of armour which had formerly belonged to the old Knights of St. John, and which he had found at Famagousta a few months previously. By 6 p.m. we were once more on board the 'Sunbeam,' and continuing our voyage round the island. The visit to Famagousta had depressed us all, and we agreed that we had never been so affected by melancholy at the sight of any place.

CHAPTER VII.

KYRENIA, MORFU, KIKKO, AND KARAVASTASIA.

Thursday, November 14th.—At daybreak the scene was very pretty. The sun, rising to the eastward of the island, right behind us, touched the tops of the northern range of mountains, and caused our old friend Pentadactylon and the beautiful ruins of Buffavento and St. Hilarion to show forth to great advantage.

About 10 a.m. we anchored off Kyrenia . . .

H.M.S. 'Humber' arrived an hour after we did, to embark the 42nd Regiment, and to take them away this evening. She has not come an hour too soon, for the men look terribly white and sickly, and thirteen fresh cases of fever are reported this morning. And yet it is a nice, cool, comfortable day, with a pleasant little breeze blowing, and the place feels to us as healthy as possible.

Mr. Holbech took us to his residence, at Government House, an old Turkish mansion, beautifully situated, with thick walls to keep out the heat of summer and the damp of winter. On one side the view extends over the fort to the bright blue sea beyond, on another over a large garden planted with groves of oranges and lemons—not one or two miserable little trees, but real woods of them, now laden with fruit. Yet even in this delightful spot, sheltered as they have been from the sun, with a pleasant breeze always blowing, and with comparatively light duties to perform, an average of one out of the three men composing the ever-changing guard has been struck down with fever every other day and carried away on a stretcher.

As our steward is still an invalid, I did the marketing to-day, and was surprised at the cheapness of everything. I bought a quantity of spinach, artichokes, capsicums, tomatoes, onions, and grinjals (a kind of egg-plant), amply sufficient for ourselves and the crew (a party of something like forty), for *2s.*! After this business was transacted, we all went to pay a visit to the camp of the 42nd, calling on our way at the Konak, where we were introduced to the Kaimakam, or chief of the district, the Mudir, or head of the village, and the Cadi, or judge. I never saw anything so perfect in the shape of a camp before. It looked quite like a little Paradise. The tents are now nearly all empty for most of the huts have arrived, but they had been pitched beneath large carob-trees, which afford a really thick shelter from the sun, and make it unnecessary for the men to remain altogether beneath the canvas. The officers of the 42nd have hardly used their mess-tent at all, but have breakfasted and lunched under the shade of an enormous carob-tree during the whole of their stay here. Two or three little streets of huts have already been erected; they look comfortable bneneath the shady trees, with a stream of fresh sparkling water gushing from the rocks above, and running close by. We peeped into several huts, built to contain ten men each, and thought they seemed very spacious and snug. In two of the huts we saw two men who had just been struck down with fever. These attacks come on without any apparent cause, and so suddenly that nobody feels safe for a single hour. The order to move was communicated to the regiment only a day or two ago, and it was not until this morning that they knew they were to depart to-day. It seems almost impossible that the arrangement can be carried out; but the confusion and bustle which have been caused by the suddenness of the order can easily be imagined.

After purchasing a nice fat sheep from the 42nd's mess for the sum of 13*s*., we returned to the village, and then went on to the fort, a large and strong structure in a very dilapidated condition, but supposed to be of great antiquity. It is now being repaired, in order to be made use of as a barrack, prison, magazine, storehouse, &c.

It was now luncheon time; and a large, merry, hungry party we were. Afterwards we landed again, and rode across the fertile valley, under big carob and olive trees, up to the convent of La Pais, built by Hugh III., and destroyed by the Turks in 1570. Although all the fine sculpture and tracery of the Gothic cloisters have been defaced, enough still remains to give one some idea of what they have been. One room is nearly 150 feet long by 50 wide, and two stories high; two others are equally large, but not so lofty. Our Engineers had been repairing the floors, and putting windows and shutters into some of the best apartments, in order that they might be made available for the reception of invalids; but after a trial it was found that the place was of no use as a hospital. The men became worse there than even in their hot stuffy huts. It seems altogether unaccountable that a thick stone building like this, surrounded by cloisters, and with a comparatively equable temperature, standing five or six hundred feet above the sea, with plenty of fresh air on every side, should be so unhealthy. But we have been told that even at a height of 3,000 feet above the sea level the fever asserts its sway.

Sir Garnet Wolseley started yesterday on an expedition to the Troödos, to try and find a sanatorium. He was to go by way of Peristerona (the Place of Doves) to Lithodonda (or Stony Tooth) along the side of Mount Adelphi, 5,380 feet high, to Pasha Learthi and the summit of the Troödos, 6,590 feet above the sea, and thence *viâ* Prodromos to Kikko, where we hope to meet him . . .

Friday, November 15th.—We were off and steaming along close to the charming coast soon after 5 a.m., and, having rounded Cape Kormakiti, entered the Bay of Morfu, passed the town of the same name, and anchored off Karavastasia (or Stopping-place for Ships) at 9 a.m. As soon as the interpreter and mules which were to have been sent from the camp at Nikosia to meet us could be distinguished through a telescope, some of the party went ashore. We followed in due course, and found that our little expedition had attracted a crowd of curious villagers, headed by the Mudir, who informed us that he expected Sir Garnet Wolseley to arrive here in the course of the afternoon. The people were, as usual, very polite, offering us chairs during our short detention. At last, about 10 a.m., we effected a start; Captain de Lancey, who could manage to get only a very small donkey, on which he had great difficulty in finding room for all his miscellaneous kit, proceeding to Mathiati, *viâ* Lefka and Tamasos, while the rest of the party, consisting of

Captain M'Calmont, Mr. Herbert, Mr. Bingham, Tom, Mabelle, and myself. with an interpreter, two muleteers, and two boys, were bound for Kikko, *viâ* Kampos. Captain de Lancey had a long ride before him—about fifty miles—but with a zaptieh to lead the way, a Turkish dictionary in one pocket and a Greek dictionary in the other, a packet of sandwiches, a pot of jam, and a bottle of cold tea, he started off as cheery as possible.

Our road, over the stony dusty plain, crossing and recrossing the now dry bed of a river, was not very interesting at first, and was rendered still less agreeable by the heat; but soon we got into a valley among the hills, where the water began to trickle and the forest trees to grow. After rather more than an hour's ride we met Sir Garnet and his staff, on their way down to Morfu. Having found a place where the path was not quite so narrow, we all dismounted, and had a long chat and drank claret and soda-water in the shade. Sir Garnet seems to have been well pleased with his ride and with the country he passed through, though he had come to the conclusion that the forests and the game with which it was said to abound were alike a myth. There are fine trees, but they are few and far between, and in no place do they grow close enough together to form a real forest, or anything more than occasional patches. As for the game, I believe that there is hardly any in the island. The best bag I have heard of was six brace of partridges to two guns, after a hard day's work. There is very little cover, the birds are all redlegs, and they run for miles. In the mountains hares are still to be met with, but we saw only two all the time we were on the island. It has also been said, that horses and ponies, bulls and cows, descended from those let loose by the Venetians in the olden time, are still seen in the interior; but all enquiries on the subject have convinced us that they are now quite extinct.

Sir Garnet told us that the air was delightful early this morning up among the hills—bright, clear, and bracing, with ice half an inch thick on the ground in some places. It sounded very delightful to us after our hot ride in the sun, but by no means improbable, as even where we were the air in the shade was tolerably cool, and it was necessary to be careful to avoid getting a chill.

Having rested and refreshed ourselves, we proceeded on our respective ways, Sir Garnet Wolseley to Lefka and Karavastasia (where he intended to pay a visit to the yacht), and thence by way of the convent of Xeropotamos, to Nikosia, while we continued our course through the valley, climbing gradually higher and higher up the mountain side.

* * * * *

There is not much twilight here, and it soon became dark, when we had to trust to our mules to find their way to the convent [*Kykko*]. Notwithstanding our faith in their powers, however, we were all glad when we saw the hospitable lights shining through the trees. We first alighted at the back door, much to the horror of the subordinate priests, who came out and showed us the way to the proper entrance, to which we scrambled round as best we could. Here more priests met us and led us across the courtyard, up staircases and along passages, to a little room with a beautifully carved cedar-wood ceiling. The head priest, accompanied by his attendants, paid us a visit here, and said that as we had not arrived before sunset they had quite given us up, and dinner could not now be served in less than an hour and a half. This was rather a blow, for we had not lunched at all substantially; but kindly they at once proposed that we should have a little luncheon now, it being past 6 p.m., and promptly produced the usual uneatable sweetmeats, water, and coffee, and then bread, grapes, cheese, mastic, and Cyprus wine. About twelve monks waited on us, watching with great earnestness for the slightest indication of our wishes, though they did not know a word of our language, nor we one of theirs.

Mabelle's and my bed-room was a small vaulted chamber, with walls four feet thick, grated windows, and a silver lamp suspended from the roof. The furniture consisted of two large divans, covered with Turkey rugs, and eight chairs, arranged in two rows against the wall—-absolutely nothing else. When we expressed a wish to wash our hands, one monk appeared with a tin wash-hand basin, another with soap, a third with a towel, while a fourth held a candle. It was with great difficulty that I persuaded them to leave the things for us to perform our ablutions. They politely insisted on holding the basin till we had dipped our faces and hands in it, and then merely waited outside the door till we had completed our toilette.

Saturday, November 16th.—We were up very early, and after a partial toilette Tom, Mabelle, and I went out for a walk, to enjoy the beautiful lights and shades of the early morning on the mountains. But the Archimandrite, who had come up from Nikosia on purpose to receive the Governor and ourselves, was before us, even though he had been suffering from fever the previous evening. He met us as we were going out, and was full of regrets that, owing to our late arrival last night, our reception had been of so informal a character. Had the rules of his order not forbidden his being out after sunset, he would have met us part of the way down the mountain, and would have taken us into a church and blessed us before we entered the convent, and rung peals of bells in our honour. I am not sure that we were sorry to have missed all these attentions, kindly meant as they were.

We climbed up a little hill above the convent, from the summit of which stretches a fine view over the whole length and breadth of the Troödos, and Mounts Adelphi and Olympus. It was rather like looking at one of the raised model maps one sometimes sees, so numerous were the spurs of the mountain, stretching in every direction, and so endless the ramifications of the valleys. Below us were vineyards, now all dry and barren, for the grapes have long since been gathered. We looked over the farm buildings attached to the convent, and saw through the windows the large jars of wine, and the stone press in which the grapes, ripe and unripe, sound and rotten, stalks and leaves, are all crushed together under the feet of the peasants. It is a rough process, but the place seemed cleaner than many others I have seen, where the wine has been kept in a room or storehouse, together with all sorts of nastiness.

We returned to the convent at 8 a.m. to breakfast, after which the Archimandrite again paid us a visit, to conduct us to the church. It is a fine building, much like that at the Nikosia convent, containing an altar screen ornamented with Byzantine pictures, some handsome books and candlesticks, and the same funny little gilt lantern-like pulpit, with its shifting ladder. There is a portrait of the Virgin Mary, said to be by St. Luke; at all events it bears his name. They showed us his signature, which is all anyone is allowed to see, except on one particular day in the year, when thousands of people flock to his shrine.

From the church we went to the Archimandrite's private apartments, and were entertained with sweetmeats, cold water, and coffee. He seemed very ill, poor old man (he is nearly eighty), and could hardly stand, but insisted on showing us round the place, leaning on his staff, or supported by two of his attendant priests. He took us to the library, which contains some choice editions of the old Fathers and of the classics, and afterwards passed through many passages and quaint cloisters. We were shown the piece of wood which used to be struck as a summons to prayer when bells were prohibited by the Turks, and the piece of bronze which was afterwards allowed as a substitute as a special mark of favour. Finally the splendid peal of bells from Moscow, presented by a Russian family, were rung, in order that we might hear their several tones.

The Archimandrite expressed a wish to accompany us to Lefka or Karavastasia; but as the state of his health rendered this absolutely impossible, he sent his private secretary, who carried a gun, rode a good mule, and spoke a few—a very few words of English.

* * * * *

The remainder of the journey to the sea-shore at Karavastasia was completed more quickly and agreably than could have been expected from our previous experience, the temperature being much cooler, and therefore less exhausting. The shadows looked long as we left the narrow valleys and emerged on to the thirsty stony plain, and by the time we had commenced the descent of the last hill, leading to the shore, and caught sight of the 'Sunbeam' lying at anchor, and of the boat putting off from her to fetch us, darkness was fast approaching. Our monkish friend, the Archimandrite's secretary, had been anxious to go on board the yacht with us, and we should much have liked him to see what I am sure would have both pleased and astonished him after his fifteen years' residence in the convents of Cyprus; but unfortunately the sun had set before we reached Karavastasia, and he was constrained to go on to the convent of Xeropotamos, accompanied by the interpreter. Captain M'Calmont and Mr. Herbert went on board with us to dinner before going on to Xeropotamos, where they also are to pass the night . . .

At 8 p.m. we parted from our friends; in half an hour the boat that took them ashore had returned, steam was up, the anchor was hove short, and we soon afterwards bade farewell to Cyprus, where the last ten days have been so agreeably spent.

Butler 1878

Lieutenant-Colonel W. F. Butler, a British traveller, records in his book, *Far Out: Rovings Retold,* a series of world-wide wanderings. The volume was published in 1880 in London by Wm. Isbister, Limited. The first four-fifths of the book tell of his journeys in western Canada, California, Afghanistan, and South Africa. The final fifth tells of his journey in Cyprus apparently in late 1878 and early 1879 shortly after the British take over the administration of the island. A great appreciator of the beauty of the Cypriot landscape, he also has strong opinions about how the British should approach their governance.

[p. 335]

A lonely sea washes the shores of Cyprus. Commerce seems almost to have completely fled the nest in which it first had life. The wanderer who now from the thistle-covered site of Salamis looks east-ward to the sunrise, or he who casts his glance from the shapeless mounds of Paphos, beholds waves almost as destitute of sail-life as though his stand-point had been taken upon some unmapped island in the South Pacific.

To the north and south this characteristic of loneliness is but little changed. Across the bluest blue waters of the Karamanian Gulf the icy summits of many mountains rise above a shipless horizon, and the beauty of the long indented north shore of Cyprus from Kyrenia to far-away Cape Andreas, is saddened by the absence of that sense of human existence and of movement which the white speck of canvas bears upon its glistening wing. To the south commerce is not wholly dead. Between the wide arms of Capes de Gat and Chitti ships and coasting craft are seen at intervals, and the sky-line is sometimes streaked by the long trail of steamer-smoke from some vessel standing in or out of the open roadstead of Larnaca; but even here, although the great highway of the world's commerce is but a day and a half sail away to the south, man's life upon the waters is scant and transient. But the traveller who stands upon the shores of Cyprus will soon cease to marvel at the absence of life upon the waters outspread before him; the aspect of the land around him, the stones that lie in shapeless heaps at his feet, the bare brown ground upon whose withered bosom sere and rustling thistles alone recall the memory of vegetation—all tell plainly enough the endless story of decay; and, as he turns inwards from a sea which at least has hidden all vestiges of wreck beneath its changeless surface, he sees around him a mouldering tomb, which but half conceals the skeleton of two thousand years of time.

Stepping out upon the crazy wooden stage that does duty for a jetty at Larnaca, the traveller from the West becomes suddenly conscious of a new sensation; he has reached the abode of ruin. And yet it is not the scant and dreary look of all things which heretofore, to his mind, had carried in their outward forms the impression of progress. It is not the actual ruin, the absence of settlement, or the mean appearance of everything he looks at, that forces suddenly upon him the consciousness of having reached here in Cyprus a place lying completely outside the pale of European civilisation; it is more the utter degradation of all things—the unwritten story here told of three hundred years of crime; told by filthy house, by rutted pavement and squalid street; spoken by the sea as it sobs through the sewaged shingle, and echoed back from the sun-baked hills and dull, brown, leafless landscape that holds watch over Larnaca.

And yet they tell us that it is all improved—that the streets have been swept, the houses cleaned, the Marina no longer allowed to be a target for rubbish. The men who tell us this are truthful, honorable men, and we are bound to believe them; but the statement is only more hopelessly convincing of unalterable desolation than had Larnaca stood before us in the full midnight of its misery.

As the day draws on towards evening we are taken out to visit the scene of the encampment of troops at Chefflick Pasha, when the island was first occupied. We are in the hands of one of the chief regenerators of the island—Civil Commissioner is the official title—and we are mounted on the back of an animal which enjoys the distinction of having made himself almost as uncomfortable to the First Lord of the Admiralty during a recent official visit to the island, as though that Cabinet Minister had been on the deck of the Admiralty yacht in a gale off the Land's End.

But if the spirit of ruin had been visible in Larnaca, the ride to Chefflick Pasha revealed the full depth of the desolation that brooded over the land—the bare brown land with its patchwork shreds of faded thistles, over which grey owls flitted as the twilight deepened into darkness. As we rode along through this scene, my friend, the assistant regenerator, appeared to regard the whole thing as superlatively hopeful—the earth was to bloom again. What a soil it was for cotton, for tobacco, for vines, for oranges, citrons, olives! Energy was to do it all—energy and Turkish law. He had been studying Turkish law, he said, for seven weeks, and he was convinced that there was no better law on earth. We thought that the East generally had been studying the same law, or codes similar to it, for seven hundred years, and had come to a different conclusion regarding its excellence. "What Cyprus had been in the past it would be again in the future. It only wanted British administration of Turkish law over the island to set everything right. Man had done the harm; man could undo the harm." And so on, as we rode back through the lessening light into Larnaca.

Was it really as our friend had said? Could man thus easily undo what man had done? All evidence answered "No."

For every year of ruin wrought by the Turk another year will not suffice to efface.

The absence of good government may mar a people's progress. The presence of good government can only make a nation when, beneath, the foundation rests upon the solid freedom of the heart of the people. The heart of Cyprus is dead and buried. It was dying ere ever a Turkish galley crossed the Karamanian Gulf, and now it lies entombed beneath three hundred years of crime, no more to be called to life by the spasmodic efforts of half-a-dozen English officials than the glories of the Knights of Malta could be again enacted by the harmless people who to-day dub themselves Knights of St. John, and date the record of their chapters from a lodging-house in the Strand.

The mail-cart running between Larnaca and Nicosia usually left the former place at five a.m., but as the English mail-steamer had arrived from Alexandria at midnight, the hour of the post-cart's departure had been changed to half-past three a.m. A few minutes before that time we had presented ourselves at the point of departure, only to find office, stable, and stable-yard sunk in that profound slumber which usually characterise the world at that early hour. A glow of ruddy light falling across the street from a large open door suggested some one astir, and we bent our steps in its direction. The red light came from a blacksmith's forge. At the anvil beat and blew a swarthy smith, and yet a courteous son of Vulcan too, for he stopped his beating and his blowing as we came up, and put a candle-end in a bottle, and put the bottle on a bench, and placed a rough seat beside it for our service. He hails from Toulon, he says. Simple services all of them, but of great value when it is borne in mind that ten minutes previously we had called at the post-office, and received from the wearied official in charge a packet of English letters and papers just sorted from the mail. So, as the blacksmith beat we read, waiting in the small hours for the mail-cart to Nicosia.

Suddenly there was a clatter of horses and a rush of wheels along the street. The mail-cart had started. We rushed wildly into the still dark street. It was too true, the cart was off! With a roar that ought to have roused Larnaca, we gave chase. The roar failed to arouse the sleeping city, but, doing still better, it halted the flying mail-cart. Ten seconds more and we were beside the vehicle, and beside ourselves with breathless rage. A Greek held the reins, another Greek sat on the back seat. When the driver found that the roar had only proceeded from a passenger who had been left behind, he was about to resume his onward way; but it could not be allowed. A short altercation ensued. The Greek driver, reinforced by the proprietor of the cart, a Frenchman, gesticulated, swore, and threatened the combined penalties of Turkish and English law. We calmly replied that, acting under the direction of the French proprietor, we had presented ourselves at the mail office at half-past three a.m., that for two mortal hours we had waited for the cart, and that now the cart must wait until our bag, still at the forge, could be brought up and placed beside us. The Frenchman declared, "It was impossible; the delay of a minute would be his ruin. The mules must proceed."

"No; not until the bag was brought up."

"Forward!" roared the proprietor. The driver shook his reins and shouted to the mules. There was nothing for it but to seize the reins and stop further progress. The mules, four in number, instantly declared themselves on our side of the controversy; they stopped dead short, and the imprecations of their owner and driver being alike powerless to move them, the bag was brought up, the imprecations ceased, and we jolted out of Larnaca. Day was breaking

Softly came the dawn over the face of the weary land. Over hilltops, over swamps, and shore and sea, touching miserable minaret and wretched mosque and squalid building with all the wondrous beauty that light has shed upon this old earth of ours since two million mornings ago it first kissed its twin children, sea and sky, on the horizon of the creation.

And now, as the sun came flashing up over the eastern hills, Cyprus lay around us, bare, brown, and arid. Watercourses without one drop of water; the surface of the earth the colour of a brown-paper bag; the telegraph poles topped by a small grey owl; a hawk hovering over the thistle-strewn ground; a village, Turkish or Greek, just distinguishable from the plain or the hill by the lighter hue of its mud walls and flat mud roofs—east, west, or north, on each side and in front, such was the prospect.

The owls on the telegraph posts seemed typical of Turkish dominion. The Ottoman throned on the Bosphorus was about as great an anomaly as the blinking night-bird capping the electric wire.

Twenty-five miles from Larnaca the road ascends a slight rise. As the crest is gained the eye rests upon a cluster of minarets—houses thrown together in masses within the angles and behind the lines of a fortification, and one grand dark mass of Gothic architecture towering over house and rampart. Around lies a vast colourless plain. To the north a broken range of rugged mountains lift their highest peaks three thousand feet above the plain. Away to the south-west higher mountains rise, blue and distant.

The houses, ramparts, and minarets are Nicosia; and the Gothic pile, still lofty amid the lowly, still grand amid the little, stands a lonely rock of Crusaders' Faith, rising above the waves of ruin.

If the Turk had marked upon Larnaca the measure of his misrule, upon Nicosia he had stamped his presence in even sharper lines of misery and of filth. People are often in the habit of saying that no words could fitly express the appearance of some scene of wretchedness. It is simply an easy formula for begging the question.

The state of wretchedness in which Nicosia lies is easy enough to express in words—in these matters the Turk is thorough. There is nothing subtle in his power to degrade; there is no refinement in his ruin. The most casual tourist that ever relied on Murray for history, and Cook for food and transport, could mark and digest the havoc of the Ottoman.

* * * * *

[p. 345]

The streets of Nicosia, narrow and tortuous, are just wide enough to allow a man to ride along each side of the gutter which occupies the centre. No view can anywhere be obtained beyond the immediate space in front, and so many blank walls, by-lanes, low doorways, and ruined buildings lie around, without any reference to design or any connection with traffic, that the mind of the stranger soon becomes hopelessly confused in the attempt at exploration, until wandering at random he finds himself suddenly brought up against the rampart that surrounds the city.

It is then that ascending this rampart, and pursuing his way along it, he beholds something of the inner life of Nicosia. The houses abut upon the fortifications, and the wanderer looks down into court-yards or garden plots where mud walls and broken, unpainted lattices are fringed by many an orange-tree thick-clustered with golden fruit.

In the ditch on the outer side lie, broken and destroyed, some grand old Venetian cannon, flung there by the Turk previous to his final departure. His genius for destruction, still "strong in death," he would not give them to us, or sell them, so he defaced and flung them down.

We wander on along the northern face. Looking in upon the city all is the same, mud and wattle in ruin, oranges, narrow streets, brown stone walls, minarets, filth, and the towering mass of the desecrated cathedral.

But as the sunset hour draws nigh, and the wanderer turns his gaze outwards over the plain, he beholds a glorious prospect. It is the sunset-glow upon the northern range.

Beyond the waste that surrounds the ramparts—beyond the wretched cemeteries and the brown mounds, and the weary plain, the rugged range rises in purple and gold. What colours they are!

Pinnacled upon the topmost crags, the gigantic ruins of the Venetian castles of Buffavento and St. Hilarion salute the sunset last of all, and then the cold hand of night blots out plain, mountain, mound, and ruin; the bull-frogs begin to croak from the cemeteries, and night covers in its vast pall the wreck of Time and of Turk . . .

Ten miles north of Nicosia a road or track crosses this north range of hills through a depression about one thousand two hundred feet above the sea-level. A mile or two beyond the foot of the range on the further side from Nicosia, Cyprus, unlike her great goddess, sinks into what she rose from—the sea. Here in this narrow strip between hill and water it would seem as though nature strove to show to man a remnant of what the island once had been. The green of young corn overspreads the ground; the shade of the karoub-tree is seen; myrtle clothes the hillsides, and the dark grey olive-tree is everywhere visible over the landscape.

Looking down from the summit of the pass one sees Kyrenia clustered by the shore, whose gentle indentations can be traced many a long mile away towards Karpos to the east, washed by a blue waveless sea.

But our goal is Kyrenia.

Our companion has been over the ground many times already, and we are late upon our road. As we descend the ridge the north face of the range opens out to the right and left behind us. It is green with foliage. We have left aridity behind us beyond the mountains. A couple of miles away to the right a huge mass of masonry can be seen rising from groves of olives. Towers, turrets, and battlements lift themselves high above the loftiest cypress-tree; but no minaret can be seen. It is the Venetian monastery of Bellapays. We will have a nearer view of it later on.

Kyrenia was the head-quarters of another assistant regenerator, a practical man, who seemed to have already realised the fact that the collection of taxes was by far the most important part of the administration of Turkish laws.

A couple of hours before sunset found us climbing the steep paths that led to Bellapays. Everywhere around spread olive-trees of immense age. Their gnarled trunks, clasped round with great arms and full of boles and cavities, still held aloft a growth as fresh as when Venice ruled the land. The fig-tree and the orange grew amid gardens that had long run wild. Here and there a colossal cypress-tree lifted its dark tapering head high above all other foliage. The path, winding amid dells of myrtle, led right beneath the massive walls of the monastery, where a spring gushing out from a fern-leaved cave formed a dripping fountain of pure cold water.

From the rock above the spring towered the great front of the building; in mass and architecture not unlike the Papal palace at Avignon. Within the walls ruin had scarcely touched. The cloisters had suffered, but the great hall of the building was intact; one hundred feet in length, with high vaulted roof and Gothic windows that looked out over green groves and long lines of shore and longer stretch of sea, from whose blue waters rose the snow-clad peaks of Karamania.

Beautiful Bellapays! while thy great walls rise over the fruit-clad land the loveliness of Cyprus will not be wholly a name. How perfect must thou have been in the olden time, when the winged lions flew over yonder fortress of Kyrenia! Well have they named thee beautiful, whose beauty has outlived the ruin of three hundred years, and defied the Turk in his fury and in his dotage!

Behind the monastery, and nearer to the mountain, a Greek village stood deep in orange gardens. In this village dwelt one of the representative Greeks of the island.

We found Hadgi at the door of his court-yard ready to welcome us to his house. A steep wooden stair led to the upper story. In a large corridor open at both ends, and with apartments at either side, we were made comfortable with many cushions spread upon a large wooden bench. Here a repast was soon served. First, coffee in tiny cups was handed round; then a rich presence of fruits with cold spring water; then oranges of immense size, peeled and sliced into quarters, were produced, together with Commanderia wine, in which the oranges were steeped. A small glass of mastic closed the feast. Many children, servants, and women stood around, and the host did the honours with that natural politeness and ease which characterise the peasant of every land save the "free-born" Briton. Hadgi's experience went far back in Cyprus. His love for the Turk was not strong, nor was it to be wondered at. He could remember one year when thirty thousand of his countrymen fell beneath the bullet, the rope, or the yatagan. And yet he was not an old man. Hadgi saw us into our saddles, and we rode back towards Kyrenia as the sunset shades were gathering over sea and land. We followed a more direct path than the one by which we had come. On both sides the ground in many places was thickly covered with square stones, showing that buildings had once been there. Probably from Kyrenia to Bellapays one long street had once existed. Next to the Turk ranks the goat as a destroyer in Cyprus.

As we drew near Kyrenia a large herd was being driven in for the evening. They were making the most of a lessening opportunity. Here and there a goat could be seen in the gnarled fork of some old olive-tree, stretching forth his head to grasp a leaf. The lower branches of the trees had all been cropped off long ago; but goats were standing on their hind legs vainly trying to reach some pendant branch. One in particular, a little longer than his comrades, did succeed in catching between his teeth the lowermost twigs of a bough. Long experience had doubtless taught him that if he attempted to pull down his prize all would be lost; his efforts were, therefore, directed to maintaining a balance upon two legs and holding on by the bough until assistance came to him. This it quickly did. In an instant twenty goats were ready to lend a helping foot; out of these some half-dozen succeeded in getting their teeth into a twig, then all lent their weight together to the pull, and down came the olive-bough to the ground, to be instantly devoured by the rush of animals which settled upon it.

The advantages of pillage upon co-operative principles were here plainly apparent. Had the goat learned them from the Turk, or was the goat the tutor to the Turk?

Leaving Kyrenia on the morning of January 20, we held our way between the mountains and the coast towards the east.

About six miles from Kyrenia we passed out of cultivated land, and began gradually to ascend the north range.

The country became wild and broken. Great glens, covered with dark green myrtle, led from the range to the sea. The path wound along the edges of these valleys, passing many nasty places where the sure-footed ponies had all their work to do to keep their footing, and where the stones and gravel loosened by the hoof rolled many a yard ere the bottom was gained. There had been a heavy fall of rain during the previous night, making the clayey places even more treacherous than the gravel, and causing the ponies to slide in their thin Turkish shoes as though they must go over. But somehow they never did go over, and when a couple of hours' riding had carried us to the mountains, the track, though rough, became safe. Passing the summit of the depression in the range, where Pentahaclyon lifts his five fingers directly over the path to the left, we began to descend the stony and now arid south side. Below us the great plain of Morphu, and that which lies between Nicosia and Famagusta, spread out under clouds that come drifting up from the Olympian range.

Suddenly a turn in the path brought us in sight of the strangest natural sight to be seen to-day in Cyprus. It was the spring of Kytherea. Out of the sun-baked mountain gushes a stream of pure, cold water.

"No stinted draught, no scanty tide," but a rush that seems to come from an inexhaustible subterranean source, that no neighbouring indication can possibly account for. Above and around nothing can be seen save bare brown hills utterly destitute of water; below the spring a long line of foliage and cultivation runs down the mountain side and spreads out into the plain beneath. Thickly cluster the houses along this life-giving stream. To right and left rills of water are led off along the descending slopes, and the baked and barren hill-sides are made to bloom in many shades of green; for corn and vine, olive and fig, orange and citron, are all springing in luxuriant life around these packed houses, and children's faces peep out of leaf-covered court-yards; and the blacksmith's anvil, the carpenter's bench, and the weaver's shuttle, are busy, all called into life and sustained by that single spring of clear, cold water, whose source in these arid hills no man can tell.

Perhaps in the old days Cyprus possessed a score of such springs. If they or others can again be made to flow, then may the island see her golden age revived, and count her million souls, and her "hundred-streamed cities."

At the lower end of Kytherea, where the lessened stream runs faint, we stopped to rest and lunch in a large Greek house, occupied by two officers of the Royal Engineers, who were employed in the trigonometrical survey of the island.

Then away across the level plain towards Nicosia. A Zaptieh guide, who had accompanied us from Kyrenia, appeared to think that the moment had now arrived when he could exercise to the fullest advantage a cavalry charge after the manner of a Bashi-bazouk. During the earlier part of the journey, while we were yet at the north side of the mountains, he had developed this instinct in a strong degree. Without any visible cause whatever, he would suddenly stint off at full gallop straight ahead along the pathway. His headlong impulse to scatter mud on all sides was apparently only controlled by the duration of his turban in shape around his head. While his turban lasted he was a Bashi-bazouk, when it fell off he became an ordinary Ottoman. One of these headlong flights, however, terminated more disastrously. He was going along at a tremendous pace, stirrups clattering, a bag of coppers jingling at his belt, when his pony, pitching heavily forward, rolled its rider to the earth. The turban flew one way, the bag of brass *caimes* rolled another; never was the spirit of Bashi-bazouk taken more completely out of a hero. During the remainder of the ride to Kytherea he kept a crestfallen position in the rear; but now, on this Nicosian plain the spirit again revived, and he began to gallop furiously at intervals along the track.

As there were no women, or children, or fugitives, he did not pursue his wild career beyond certain limits, and as there was no enemy whatever, he did not retire when his charge had spent itself at the same pace as he had gone.

Darkness had fallen when we reached the walls of Nicosia. Skirting the city by its eastern ramparts, we ascended the ridge of old tombs upon which stands the new Government House, the lights from whose wooden halls formed the only visible objects in the wide circle of surrounding gloom.

At a place called Mathiati, some fifteen miles south of Nicosia, a regiment of infantry was in camp. After many sites had been tried, all more or less unhealthy, this place, Mathiati, had been selected; and huts, sent out from England, had been erected on a level space surrounded by hills. A few olive-trees, a small Greek mud village, and, farther off, the blue ridges of Mount Adelphi, made a prospect not wanting in beauty, but utterly destitute of any other feature that could give an interest to the existence of an English regiment; sport, society, the coming and going of human beings—all were wanting, and except to the tomb-hunter or to the student, Mathiati could vie, in absence of life, with any station in the wide circle of British garrisons round the earth.

The regiment now in camp at Mathiati had only lately arrived from Nova Scotia; and the contrast between the cradle of a new-born civilisation which they had quitted, and the grave of the old world's decay in which they found themselves, was vividly put before them. As may be supposed, their views of the latter were not hopeful. They spoke of

Cyprus as a place of exile, dashed with a kind of humour learned, perhaps, in the New World.

"The medical fellows never knew the use of the spleen until we got to Cyprus," said one of the garrison, "but they've found it now."

"What is it?"

"Two months' sick leave out of this infernal hole," replied the first speaker. "The spleen has been what they call a dormant organ of the human body until we took possession of the island; now its use is clearly understood."

So ran the *badinage* of the mess-hut at Mathiati, and perhaps there was as much corn of sense lying beneath the "chaff" as could have been found among many of the graver reasons elsewhere advanced in favour of the new possession.

As day broke over Nicosia plain, on the 23rd of January, a small party of horsemen crossed the dry bed of the river channel that lies at the base of the rocky ledge on which stands the Government House, holding their way westward towards Peristeromo. They were bound for Mount Olympus, in search of a site for a summer encampment. The experience of the past summer had been sufficient to show that men could not live in health in the Cyprian plains, or along the shore, during the summer months.

Before the sun had again entered the Northern tropic a camp in the mountains must be found.

At the same hour and at the same instant of time (for the line of sunlight through Cyprus and through Zululand are one) that this small party of horsemen rode out to the west from the hill of tombs near Nicosia, a few horsemen, the last of a weary and spent British column, were moving off from a ridge, leaving one thousand dead comrades lying tombless to the vultures that watched on the rock ledges of Isandlana Hill.

High up above the ledges one great frontlet of rock frowned over the ghastly scene—the "Lion's Head" some early traveller had named it. If sermons are spoken by stones and lion ever speaks to lion, surely this stone lion could have spoken that day a curious homily to his brother on the mound at Waterloo. What that homily would be we may not write now, nor would the dawn at Isandlana and the dawn at Nicosia on the 23rd of January meet in these pages if that day's work at the first-named place had not been destined to turn in the future the footsteps of the four men here bound for Mount Olympus towards Zululand.

We reached Peristeromo, fourteen miles, in two hours. Here mules were waiting to carry us farther into the hills. The Greek priest had come out to the river (at last it was a river and not a dry channel) to welcome us into the village. Arrived at his house there was the usual hand-shaking and coffee-sipping, and then the saddles were changed from the ponies to the mules, and all made ready for the onward journey.

Three of the four mules were animals in fair condition; the fourth was, it would be wrong to say skin and bones, for so much of his skin had vanished under the abrasions of pack-saddles and uncouth harness gear that the bones in many places were alone represented. Poor beast! he was a dreadful sight! When the saddles were placed on the mules outside, somehow or other the skinless mule fell to the lot of the writer of these pages. That it was most unconscionable cruelty to ride the beast there can be no doubt; but what was to be done? The halting-place for the evening lay twenty miles distant, high amid the hills. The only alternative was to abandon the expedition. There was nothing for it but to accept the inevitable and mount the lacerated back. Then came fifteen miles of gradually ascending pathway, amid hills scantily covered with small pine-trees. As the track wound along the ridges the air became crisp and fresh, the sound of rushing water arose from deep valleys, and the bright blue vault above rested on the clear-cut edges of the hilltops. How pleasant would it have been to jog along those narrow paths upon an animal of sound skin; but now there was an ever-present sense of pain inflicted to mar the whole scene, and to cause each step of the ascent to be mentally as painful to the rider as it was bodily so to the poor mule.

For many miles of the track a stray raven kept hovering aloft in the blue heaven—was he scenting his prey? At last we reached the mountain-village of Litheronda, which was to be our halting-place for the night. It stood on the southern slope of the hills, at an elevation of about four thousand feet above the sea. The air was keen and frosty, for the sun had gone down behind Olympus, whose white ridge could be seen to the west. The village houses were all of the lowest kind; they projected from the hillside, out of which they had been partly dug, so that the slope of the hill and the roof of the houses formed one continuous line. Thus a person could walk down the hill on to the roof, until reaching the edge of the front wall he looked down six or seven feet upon the door-step. A few of the rudest and most antiquated implements of husbandry lay on the paved space around the door way—a lean pig or a leaner dog grunted or barked at the intruder. The mule had long ago given out; but it was infinitely more pleasant to follow the track on foot, driving the wretched animal in front. The rest of the party had gone on long out of sight, and by the time the mule and his driver drew near Litheronda, camp had already been made on the further side of the village. As we descended the path a Greek, riding a fine young horse, suddenly appeared, coming towards us from the village. With many vehement signs he signified that he had been sent to meet us; the horse was for our especial use, the mule might be trusted to find its own way to the camp. So, mounting the Turkish saddle, and accommodating feet to the slipper stirrups and legs to the short leathers as best one could, we trotted on towards the camp. It stood under some large walnut-trees, now leafless, and by the side of a small stream. A huge fire of dry logs blazed before the tents; at another fire farther off dinner was being prepared. A few villagers stood gaping at the Englishmen—the first without doubt who had penetrated to their remote nook. How they must have speculated upon the reason of one's visit. Did it mean fresh taxation, new law of grape gathering, relief from some of their many loads?

* * * * *

[p. 364]

Meantime, however, while thus we stand before the camp fire at Litheronda, the snow begins to fall through the leafless walnut-trees, and the night wind blows cold over the white shoulder of Mount Olympus. At daybreak next day it blows colder still; the ridge, across which our onward track lies, is white with snow, which holds its own even as the sun climbs higher into the eastern sky, and the guides, who are to lead us across the shoulder of Olympus to Pasha Leva, assert that the route will be impracticable for some days to come; so, striking camp, we held our way for nine miles along a rocky glen that led to the village of Manikito, and then turning westward, and crossing some very rough and broken ground, we reached at three o'clock in the afternoon the hill village of Platris, on the south slope of Olympus.

Behind Platris, to the north, the mountain rose steep and pine-clad; below Platris, to the south, many valleys led the eye downwards to the sea; where the coast beyond Limasol, and the ruins that mark the site of the monastery of the Knights of St. John, built when Acre had fallen to the Saracen, lay twenty miles distant in reality, but seemingly close at hand, seen through the blue and golden light that filled the whole vast vault far out beyond the land into the shipless sea. To-morrow our line would lead us down to that shore, but now—to-day—ere the sun, already far into the west, should reach the sky-line beyond Paphos, we had a chance of scaling the lofty ridge that rose behind the village, and of planting a footprint in the snow of Olympus.

Away on fresh mules up the mountain. There is no time to lose, and anxiously we watch the aneroid to note our upward progress, and the sun to mark the time that yet remains to us. At a point about five thousand five hundred feet above the sea-level the snow becomes too deep for the mules, so we dismount and tie them to pine-trees; then, while two of the party turn off to the right to select a site for the summer encampment, we strike up the hill alone to make a race for Olympus with the sunset. The ridge is very steep, but the snow holds a firm crust, and the air is keen and bracing. The aneroid soon shows another five hundred feet gained, and a hill, which seems to be the summit, appears close at hand. It is won, but at its farther side the ground sinks abruptly only to rise again out of a deep valley into the real Mount Olympus. Better had we kept more to the right and avoided this deep glen that now lies across our line to the summit. There is nothing for it but to retrace our steps to the right, and then take the crest of the curving ridge which runs round almost at our present level to the foot of Troados. But every second is precious. Away we go at topmost speed along the crest, which, though level when looked at from a distance, is broken into many hills and valleys when nearer seen. All is silent around save the quick crunching of the snow beneath rapid footsteps. Lofty pine-trees rise on every side. We are now under the shadow of Olympus, whose white head, bare of pine-trees, has hidden the low-sunk sun. Through the pines to the north the eye catches glimpses of the low country, the north range, and the far-away sheen of snow on the mountains of Asia Minor; but there is no time to note anything save the lessening light and the bare summit that rises above the dark pines. We pass out from the shadows of the trees, and stop a moment to take breath for the last ascent. Looking across the valley, around three sides of which we have just circled, the sunlight is seen still bright upon the crest we started from, but the rays fall level; and already around us, in the shadow of Olympus, the blue light of evening has fallen upon the snow. Nothing but the croak of a solitary raven from a withered pine-branch close at hand breaks the intense silence of the scene. Another four minutes' hard pull and we stand upon the bald crest of Troados. The sun has not yet set. Far out, resting on a ring of immeasurable sky-line, he seems to pause a moment ere he sinks into the sea. There is a faint crescent moon in the western sky. A vast circle spreads around, and within this huge horizon all Cyprus lies islanded beneath the light of sunset.

There is sea beyond the north range, and beyond the sea there is sun on a long line of snow set far above the gathered shades of evening. There is sea in the wide curve of Salamis, and beyond the ruined ramparts of Famagusta; sea where Paphos sinks into a golden haze of sunset in the west; sea where Karpos stretches his long arm into the arch which the earth's shadow has cast upon the Eastern sky, for all Cyprus below this lonely

Troados lies in twilight, and the great circle of the sea is sunless, save where, on the western rim, the blood-red disc sinks slowly from a sky whose lustre pales in lessening hues from horizon to half-zenith. And now the last speck of sun has gone beneath the waves. Olympus is cold and blue, like many a lesser ridge around him; the crescent moon grows clearer cut against the heaven; grey and cold, the sky rim narrows, and the wide bays and long-stretching promontories of the island lie in misty outline upon the darkening sea; far away to the north Karamania still holds aloft one last gleam of sunlight upon his frozen forehead.

We will stay until this "light of Asia" is blotted out. Another moment and the Karamanian range is cold; and then, fading into the night, Cyprus lies in the gloaming—a vague but mighty shadow, from whose forgotten tombs and shattered temples the night wind comes to moan its myriad memories amid the pines of Olympus . . .

Down the snowy side of Troados we ran at top-most speed, ploughing deep into drift, and crushing through crust, doing more in a minute of time than had been done in ten minutes of toil upon the upward road. There was not a moment to lose. Never did night gather her shadows more quickly around her than now as we went plunging down into her depths. Scant is the measure darkness gives in the Mediterranean when once the sun has gone below the horizon; but now we lessened that short interval by each rapid stride, for we were literally descending into darkness.

Some fifteen hundred feet lower down the mule had been left picketed beneath a pine-tree. To that tree there was no track, save the footprints of our upward course in the snow. These were, in many places, only to be observed in the closest scrutiny; in others, where the breeze was drifting the light frozen particles, they had become invisible. It was therefore a matter of moment that we should make the most of the afterglow to get out, at least, from the denser pine-trees and deeper snow of the upper mountain, and set our faces straight in the direction of the mule.

As before it had been a race with the sun up mountain, in which we had won, now it was a race with night, in which we were the loser. Still, enough of light remained to enable us to follow our footprints clear of the broken ground below the summit ridge, and, before darkness had quite fallen, to see that our course was set straight down-hill towards the south.

At the edge of the snow there suddenly appeared right in front two large ears, projected forward in relief against a faint afterglow, that lay along the lower sky from north to south. It was the mule, looking wistfully towards the new comer. His companions had long since been taken away, and the prospect of spending a hungry night on the cold shoulder of Olympus had doubtless convinced the mule that there were worse things in life than his old enemy—a rider. Still, when he realised that he was not to spend the night in cold and hunger, he began at once to manifest his old repugnance to the saddle.

At last the girths were tight, and we began to descend the steep hillside. It was now quite dark. We had got into a maze of rocks, pine-trees, and brush-wood. A general goat-track seemed to pervade the entire mountain, upon which the mule appeared to be now quite content to spend the remainder of the night. At last, amid a labyrinth of rocks, he came to a standstill. Dismounting, we endeavored to lead him; but he would not be led. Passing the halter behind we now tried to drive him before us; he would thus find the right road, and would lead the way into camp. In the new order of things it will be sufficient to say that he at once entered into that part of the programme which had reference to finding the right road; but there appeared to be a vast difference in his mind between finding the road for himself and showing it to his driver, for no sooner had he set his head straight downhill than he determined to set his heels in the opposite direction, with the view of dissolving partnership with his master. Out of the darkness in front there suddenly came two vicious and violent kicks; the Turkish shoes just reached us, but not close enough to do serious damage; a couple of inches nearer would have soon ended the matter of partnership, and left us alone on the shoulder of Olympus. To jump aside amid the rocks and haul vigorously at the halter was only the work of a second. Soon we succeeded in slewing round the animal's head, and the saddle was again occupied, not to be quitted under any pretence until mule and man were safely landed in the camp at Platris.

An hour later lights shone below, and we reached the camp, to find a relief party about to start up the mountain to look for us.

Six hours' ride, next day, carried the party to Limasol, from which port the writer of these pages set out to cross the mountains to the monastery of Kiku and the west shore of the island. An interpreter, a muleteer, and three mules; a Zaptieh riding in front; an order, in Greek and Turkish, to the mudirs of the towns *en route* to board and lodge us; small kit of apparel and slender store of commissariat hastily got together, and we leave with little regret the hot streets of Limasol and the low coast lands of Kolossi. Ruins of temples along the narrow track; at intervals a village, with cultivation and a few orange trees around it; then upwards in a long ascent by arid hills, from which at every turn the eye looks back at bluest sea and buildings cleaned and freshened by sun and distance.

As on we ride an old negro suddenly issues from a cave by the wayside, and invites us to stop a moment and refresh with coffee. His cave is twenty feet deep in the rock, fairly lighted from its large entrance, and with a lean-to hut on one side, forming a porch. He is very black and very garrulous. His name is Billali. Many years before a Turk named Seyd brought him from Upper Egypt to Cyprus. He became free, and took to this cave, where now he cultivates the land around. He had sent his wife away. He was born in Kordofan, in the midst of the desert, and there his name had been Tameroo; that was a long while ago —before the time of Mehemet Ali Pasha. He is very happy up on this hill, for he can look down on the sea and on the houses, and till his land as he likes. His wife used to bother him a good deal; but he sent her away, and now he is quite happy. So spake Billali, once Tameroo of Kordofan, as he blew the embers about his little Turkish coffee-pot, and prepared the tiny cup of real coffee for us. Then we parted from this poor old black Tameroo, and held our course by Shivellas and Everssa towards Mallia.

We reached the latter place in a downpour of rain at sunset. The mudir had a room ready, the Zaptieh having gone on in front to announce us. Dinner soon followed, and then coffee, cigarettes, and much conversation. Mallia was a purely Turkish village, and all the talk was of the Turk. There were one or two present who had been to Mecca. There were many questions asked about the future of the island, about the discovery of gold— "a mountain of gold," they say, in Midian—and about politics, foreign and domestic. There seemed to be an impression amongst them that if this mountain of gold could only be discovered in Cyprus all would be right. I replied through the interpreter that there was plenty of gold lying around, but that it was in the wine, the oil, the wheat, that came yearly from the ground; that the Egyptian, the Roman, the Venetian, and the Greek had left but little of other treasure remaining, but that each returning summer called again to life the riches of which I spoke.

Meantime there is much bringing of coffee and rolling of cigarettes among the cross-legged circle grouped before the large kitchen fire, and finally it is time to lie down for the night.

The wine at Mallia was good, and with generous hands my Turkish hosts filled my glass, declining to join me themselves; but rumour said that they were not always so shy, and that Mallia knew the flavour of a flagon of Commanderia and the smack of mastic as well as any wine-bibbing village of Greek or Maronite persuasions.

Early next day we are again on the track. Rough and stony, it leads to Arsos, and through the mass of ruins called Hy Nicolo into the beautiful valley of the Carissos River. As the mules in single file wind down into the valley two eagles come soaring close above our heads. A large stone-pine slants from the hillside, and beneath his wide-spread branches white Troados is seen ending the upper valley. Then we zigzag down to the river meadows and halt by the oleander-lined banks for the mid-day rest.

On again across the single-arched bridge of Jellalu, up the farther side of the valley. A very old Greek church stands in ruins on the slope, and near it one solitary pine-tree eleven feet in girth. Then the ascent becomes steep, the zigzags are short and severe, and we see above us the pine-clad crest beyond, which is the monastery of Kiku, our destination.

At last we gain the summit. The track now leads along the crest or sides of narrow ridges. Troados lies to the right, rising in long profile out of a very deep glen; innumerable other deep glens sink around on every side. The sides of the hills descend so steeply into these valleys that the stones go rolling from the feet of the mules as we jog along; but the sense of the steepness of the declivity is lessened by the pines and arbutus-trees that grow around—the arbutus only on the north faces of the hills.

The atmosphere is intensely clear; we are about four thousand feet above sea-level, and as the sun draws to the west the valley between us and Troados seems shot with varying hues of light, yet all so clear that every pine-tree on the mountain is visible, and the snowy crest looks but a short mile distant. A turn in the path brings the monastery of Kiku in sight, the road dips a moment along the east side of the crest, which the sun cannot reach, and the ground is hard-bound in frost. As we draw near the monastery a monk comes up the hillside and joins us. He carries a gun and a bag, but no game. Then we dismount at the great doorway,—lead the mules into the court-yard, and presently a portly prior, followed by many Greek monks, come to bid us rest and welcome. A cell is soon got ready, and the portly prior shows us to it. Three little windows in a very deep wall; low-arched ceiling, from the centre of which swings a brass lamp; a brick floor, with carpet slips laid upon it; a brazier of hot charcoal on one side; a sofa, a few chairs, and a wooden table, and our cell is as comfortable a little den to get into at sunset amid these cold Cypriote hills as traveller could wish to find.

A quaint old place this Kiku, set four thousand feet up in the hills. Long arched corridors and passages run round quiet court-yards. Off the corridors open cells, dormitories, and refectories. A great bell hangs at one corner of the quadrangle; it has come all the way from Moscow—for the fame of Kiku's sanctity goes far over the Greek world. How this bell was ever carried up the mountain must remain a mystery. It is of enormous size and weight, and the path is but a narrow mule-track; but there it hangs, all the same, to ring out its deep note in the grey dawn to the misty mountain solitudes, and to wake the mouflon on the hills ere the sun has kissed the frozen forehead of Troados. But the glory of Kiku is the church, and the glory of the church is the silver image of the Virgin and Child, given by Alexis in the tenth century, and hidden, so say the monks, from human vision ever since. "As I am not to see it again," said the Greek emperor, when he sent it to Cyprus, "then let no other human eye ever rest upon it." So the head and upper portion of the figures have been veiled from view. All this and more was poured forth by half a dozen old monks, in whose care we made the circuit of the monastery. Before we began our inspection sweetmeats and coffee were produced; when the inspection was over our dinner was ready. It was an excellent repast, and, after a long day spent in the keen mountain atmosphere, appetites were not wanting to do it justice. Lest they should be, one priest specially attended to see that the guests lacked nothing. The Commanderia wine was the best we had yet tasted, and the mastic was old, lùscious, and plentiful. As the frost grew harder outside the little cell-windows, and boy attendants brought freshly fanned charcoal to the brazier, the cell looked indeed a cheerful billet for a mountain traveller.

The portly prior came and sat with us after dinner, and, among other matters, produced a paper that had caused the worthy brotherhood intense astonishment. It was an official document in English, having reference to a return for taxation. The monks could not make much of it, so they had invoked the aid of a passing traveller, versed in Greek and English. Unfortunately he had rendered the English word "pitch," the resin of the pine-forests, into the Greek word "bitch," and the brethren were amazed at finding themselves taxed for ten thousand okes of bitches. We appeased the afflicted and perplexed mind of the prior, and, redolent of garlic, he thanked us, bade us good-night, and retired.

Early morning at Kiku. How very beautiful it is! The sun peeps over Mount Olympus; the tops of the hills are all alight, and the deep valleys are in shadow; far away there are pale glimpses of distant sea; a vast stillness dwells on all things—stillness deepened by distant murmur of mountain stream and the softest whisper of old pine-trees. Of that wonderful old forest—now nearly gone—that glorious growth which has given decks to Turkish galleys for three hundred years, that forest for whose destruction Greek and Turk have for once joined hands upon the handle of the felling axe. Burned, hacked, slashed at, barked, and wounded, some grand old survivors still stretch forth their gaunt arms, as though they asked for mercy from the destroyer; and still, when the night hides the wreck that man has made, the wind-swept song of their sorrow is wafted in unutterable sadness over the ruined land.

Amid the farewells of the assembled brethren we moved off next morning from Kiku, descending northwards towards Kampo and the Bay of Morphu. It was another day of exquisite views, as, winding down the narrow mule-track, we saw below the curve of the Bay of Morphu the broken north range and the white summits of Karamania far away to the north, over the lonely blue sea.

At the village of Kampo we stopped a few minutes. An old Greek woman brought us raisins, and supplemented her offering with an harangue. Its burden was that she expected many things from the English, and she trusted she would not he disappointed. "Tell her," we replied through the interpreter, "that the English expect much from her.

When we left England they were all full of expectation about this island; all the papers were writing about her and her people." She appeared to be astonished at the information, and we continued downhill towards Levka.

Six hours' ride brought us to Levka. The mudir, engaged at the moment of our arrival in a full court of tax collection, immediately dissolved his court, and became our host, adviser, and director. He soon produced a meal of walnuts steeped in honey, of which it will be sufficient to record that for a condiment of singular indigestibility it would be difficult to parallel it in any conglomeration of sugar and fruit known to Western palates. Perhaps we are taking away the character of this condiment, and that, viewed in the capacity of a conserve, it might be approached with comparative safety; but as a *pièce de résistance* to set before a hungry man, after a six hours' ride, walnuts steeped in honey, plentifully administered, would probably solve for ever the "Eastern question" of any Western traveller's farther progress through the land. No wonder the Turk has been the "sick man " of Europe upon such a regimen.

We were afterwards informed that the mudir of Levka had but recently in his own person exemplified the transitory nature of earthly distinction. He had, in fact, undergone incarceration in prison for two months for misappropriation of taxes. He was still, however, administering the laws in Levka, and, so far as we could judge, his misfortune had in no way tended to withdraw from him the confidence of the inhabitants, while it had apparently left unimpaired his reputation as a high-class government official. He was a Turk.

We spent that night at the monastery farm of Xerapotamiss, by the shore of the Bay of Morphu.

After night fell we wandered down to the sea. In a long wave, that rose its crest only to fall upon the shore, the Mediterranean sobbed against the wide curving bay. The moon was over the sea. We wandered along the shore, keeping on a strip of glistening sand close by where the surf broke.

All lonely now this shore, but thick with memories. On this very spot the Turk landed for the conquest of the island. Hither, two thousand four hundred years ago, came the great lawgiver of the Greeks to end his life. In the farmyard of the monastery hard by, but an hour since, our muleteer tied his mules to the icanthus-leaf of a prostrate Corinthian capital. Yonder, in the moonlight, Pendaia's ruins are still dimly visible. Well may the sea sob upon the withered breast of Cyprus, and the pines sigh over her lonely hilltops.

Two days' ride carried us across the island to the eastern shore, and it was again moonlight when our cavalcade passed the long bridge that crosses the rock-hewn ditch and entered the gate of once famed, now fevered and famished Famagusta.

Within the massive gateway a dead city lay beneath the moonlight. A city so dead and so ruined that even the moonbeams could not hide the wreck or give semblance of life to street or court-yard—and yet, withal, it was modern ruin that lay around. The streets were cleared of stones and rubbish, the massive ramparts were untouched, the roofless houses were not overgrown with creepers. Many of the churches still held portions of roof or window reared aloft against the sky; through lancet window or pointed archway the palm-tree hung motionless against the moonlight. Many owls flitted amid the ruins, and the sole sound was the ring of our hoofs and the roll of the distant surf outside the eastern rampart.

Soon after sunrise next morning we went out to see by clearer light this modern capital of all ruined cities—this skeleton in armour, whose huge ramparts, and deep ditch, and towering cavaliers hid only crumbling streets, squares, churches, and mansions.

We pass out by the grand sea-gate, not a stone of which has been defaced. Above the marble keystone of the arch the winged Lion still holds the open gospel to the deserted wharfs and silent shingle.

The name of the Venetian ruler is still bright in letters that were carved and gilt at the time Columbus was steering his ship to the New World, and when De Gama was about to strike the first blow at Venetian sway by his passage of the Cape of Storms.

A reef of rocks marks the old harbour limits and the area which it is proposed to dredge into a refuge for ironclads. "They may dredge out the mud from the sea," says our informant, "but they won't dredge away the fever from the shore."

He tells us the fever is incessant, that every one gets it, that it is worse than West African fevers, so far as its sensations are concerned; and that it doesn't matter what one eats or drinks, or where one sleeps, that the fever is bound to come all the same. "There are four of us here," he goes on, "and we were all down together with fever only three weeks ago." Then we go in again into the mournful city, and ramble on through more grass-grown streets and ruins. A plover rises from the waste and calls shrilly as he mounts on rapid wing above the ramparts. We ascend the ramparts. From the cavalier looking north the eye ranges over the mounds that have, for sixteen hundred years, marked the site of Salamis, and farther off the hills of Kanfara dropping into the long peninsula of Karpos.

Along the rampart two coaches could drive abreast; beneath the rampart are the arched dungeons wherein Venice held her slaves; ruined churches everywhere within the walls—churches with deep doorways traced in curious patterns of stone-carving, with the frescoes still fresh on their walls, and the floors cumbered with overturned tomb effigies and prostrate crosses. Little patches of wheat grow here and there through the ruins. We try to count these churches, but cannot do it. Tradition says there once stood one hundred Christian temples within the walls of Famagusta.

Towering high above all other ruins, the cathedral raises its lofty Gothic towers, the most mournful of all the relics of this saddest of cities. Amid wreck of flying buttress and lancet window of Northern Gothic art, the feathery palms seem strangely out of place.

Older ruins and wreck of time deeper in the bygone can be met on all the shores of the Mediterranean; but nowhere a city like this one of Famagusta, nowhere else a scene which brings us so closely face to face with the grandeur of Venice and the glory of the Norman crusader both strangled in the grasp of the Turk, and lying yet unburied by the merciful hand of Time.

We may quit Cyprus—no other scene, within her shores, can grave upon our memory a deeper record of her matchless ruin.

It is evening. We have crossed the ridge that divides Famagusta from Larnaca, and are descending towards the sea for embarkation. The sun is going down behind the steep ridge of Santa Croce, whose white monastery looks like a snow-cap on the summit.

The long waves roll in upon a wide curving shore. Far out to sea, one or two ships are standing to the south, and around us the barren soil spreads a weed-grown waste, with ruins at intervals that stand out wondrously white and clear in the level sunlight. The earth rings hollow under our mule hoofs, for the honeycombed rock beneath has been a tomb for three thousand years. No other word tells of Cyprus so exactly. Tomb of Phoenician, of Egyptian, of Hittite, of Greek, Roman, and Jew; tomb of the exile from Lybia, from Athens, from Pontus; tomb of the rich fugitives that fled before the armies of the Pharaohs or the hosts of Babylon; tomb of all those countless waifs and strays of conquest, commerce, and commotion, who in the dim dawn of civilisation found in this island a refuge and a grave.

Tomb, too, of Byzantine, of Norman crusader, of Venetian, and lastly of the Turk, whose grave scraped shallow amid the ruins of empire has blurred the record and scattered the ashes of twenty vanished peoples.

* * * * *

And now what is to be the future of this island? Can it be redeemed from ruin? Yes. By us? No. By its people? Yes. The Turk ruined; the Greek can renew. Let us beware of attempting to lead or to direct a people who, when their first sensation of surprise is past, are bound to hold us in ridicule and in aversion. Already the symptoms of the first are apparent. "What a pity it is," said the people of Limasol, as they watched our road-making operations into the mountains, "what a pity it is that God, who has given these English so much money, should not also have bestowed upon them some brains!"

There is a singular delusion pervading the English mind that we can civilise and improve a people. It is just the one thing we have never been able to do. No nation in history has ever had so many opportunities of imparting Christianity and civilisation to the Gentile. We have been in close contact with the heathen, with the fire-worshipper, with the Buddhist, with the worshippers of the stick, and the stone, and the bone for the better part of two centuries. Yet what has been the sum total of our success?

Have we really Christianised twenty square miles of any continent or island? Have we made any race or people in the whole wide circle of our vast dominion more truthful, more honest, more chaste, or even more happy than they were before they came in contact with us and our civilisation ? Few men will answer, Yes.

The truth is, the Anglo-Saxon race can spread itself, but cannot impart to others its Christianity or its civilisation. We can only do what the Dane, the Saxon, the Frank, or the Goth could do. The work of the Greek or the Roman is beyond our power, and the reason of our incessant failure is obvious. We will not take, as the Romans took, the best strings of native character and play our tune of civilisation and progress on them; but we must invariably take our own mould and proceed to run down into it whatever type of national character we come in contact with.

We cannot train or teach; we can only multiply and spread. If we conquer a nation we must either destroy it or fail to govern it. French Canada is an exception; but French Canada won from our generals, after our defeat at St. Roche, so many national privileges that its laws, language, religion, and territory have remained French.

In fact, French Canada is a lasting proof of what can be done by letting people develop themselves upon their own lines.

One hundred and thirty years ago French Canada had a population of less than one hundred thousand souls. It was the poorest and most inhospitable country in North America. It has to-day one million and a half of French Canadian inhabitants.

In Ireland, on the other hand, we would only develop on the British basis. For seven hundred years we have been busy at this development, and it is only now dawning upon us that it will not do.

But people will say, "Ah, the Greek is different; he is a semi-Asiatic. We really must train and educate this Greek." My dear, good, Mr. Bull, you are in sober truth a mere child to this Greek; even at your own long-practised game of buying and selling, of barter and chaffer, he can beat you hollow. He has taken the trade of the Levant from you; he has penetrated into the heart of your great city and holds his own against your most able money-changers. "Ah, but," I hear you say, "he can't fight." There also you are mistaken. You yourself have never fought against a tenth of the odds that he has contended with. At Scios he performed an exploit in the centre of the Ottoman fleet which, measuring it by the "decorative period" of modern English warfare, all the bronze in the Trafalgar lions could not yield crosses for. When you have fought the tenth part of what this Greek has fought, and suffered the hundredth part of his sufferings in the cause of freedom, then you may talk of teaching him how to fight or how to die.

No; let us endeavour to develop this island for the Greek peasant, and by the Greek peasant; not for the benefit of the usurer as we have done in India, or for the landlord as we have done in Ireland, or for the benefit of the Manchester man, or the Birmingham man, or the London man, or the outside man generally, as we have done in other parts of the world. My friend the sea-captain, who is still doubtless fully prepared to settle the Greek question after his own fashion, would probably urge the rule of thumbscrew and gallows in dealing with Cyprus; but the world has got beyond that stage now.

If our dominion in Cyprus is to escape the fate of our Ionian experiment, we must try to learn Greek before we attempt to teach English.

Kitchener 1878

H. H. (Horatio Herbert) Kitchener (1850–1916) was sent to Cyprus in 1878 to carry out the first methodical survey and mapping of the island. Lack of adequate funds interrupted the work until 1880. After an interruption while Kitchener scouted the route from Alexandria to Cairo disguised as Levantine, the work was virtually complete in 1882 when he was assigned to duty in Egypt. He was involved in the unsuccessful attempt to save Gordon at Khartoum, but later became Governor General of Eastern Sudan, led cavalry in the defeat of the Dervishes and eventually overcame the Mahdis and recovered Khartoum. As second in command in South Africa his planning was instrumental in defeating the Boers. In 1902 he was appointed Commander in Chief of India and in 1914 was named Secretary of State for War. In this role he played a major role in the defeat of the Germans in World War I by expanding the British army from 20 to 70 divisions. He perished aboard the HMS Hampshire when it struck a mine and sank.

This article, "Notes from Cyprus," appeared in *Blackwood's Magazine* in August 1879. It presents a delightful view of Cyprus in the eyes of a surveyor-mapper.

Cyprus is an island of sudden changes. Both climate and landscape are subject to rapid variations. From the glare of an overpowering sun one may enter the cool shade of a tropical garden, with the murmur of water trickling past as it wanders amongst the groves of oranges, figs, and palms. The bare treeless plain may be changed in a very short space for pine-forests of magnificent trees: instead of sand and dust, we trample on brackenfern by the side of rills and torrents running in steep gorges. The climate changes from great heat to chilling cold. We have noted a daily variation of 50° of temperature; after a calm, clear morning, with the distant hills apparently close, suddenly a windy hurricane, accompanied by a thick haze, comes over the island, and shuts out the view. In the landscape it is the same. There are no gentle slopes; the hills all rise steeply from the plains; the water-courses run in deep beds, cut through alluvial soil and rock. These signs show the island to have been visited by heavy tropical rains. After the winter of 1877 the great Messarea plain was a lake of water and slime. This winter there has been barely five inches of rainfall—hardly enough to make the roads muddy for a few hours.

We were not fortunate coming to Cyprus in a year of exceptional heat, after a late season of heavy rain. Fever was more prevalent in the island than it has ever been known to be before, but the crops were good. This year we may expect very little fever, but a great scarcity of provisions. The wheat crop has completely failed, and the barley is very poor in the great cereal-growing plain. The harvests are now being reaped, and it is pitiful to see the poor women pulling up the thin stalks of barley, only nine inches long in most cases, where, in former years, the sickles cut down thick crops. Fortunately this is not the case all over the island. In the many fertile valleys of the hill districts, such as Papho, there has been enough rain to produce good crops; and though the great plain has failed completely, there will probably be sufficient in other districts to keep off absolute want, though prices are already becoming exorbitantly high.

There is no doubt that the resources of the island are great, if properly developed. It possesses a very fertile soil, capable of growing almost anything if carefully cultivated and irrigated; without water, the hot sirocco winds from the east soon dry up any vegetation. Irrigation, however, is not a difficult matter. On the plain, water is found almost everywhere at from 18 to 20 feet below the surface; and along the hillsides there are many springs and rivulets that run to waste through the inertness of the people. They would willingly pay a handsome profit for the water if it was brought to them, but have not the capital or the enterprise to make the required aqueducts themselves. A few windmill-pumps on the plain would irrigate a farm sufficiently to make it independent of lack of rainfall, and for the production of crops and trees that require watering after the rainy season is past. There is no want of wind: a strong breeze springs up every day from the N.W., and very often covers the plain in a thick haze; mirage is seen in every direction,—lakes and cliffs rising picturesquely out of a dead flat. The hill-slopes grow vines in profusion, and these vineyards might be greatly extended. Many beautiful spots exist amongst the hills lying completely waste, grown over with scrub, hiding the old rock-cut wine-presses, that show where in ancient times there were once fruitful vineyards. Had the island been taken over by France instead of England, the French would have soon developed the wine-trade enormously. All that is wanted is capital to clear the scrub and plant the vines. For instance, a large tract of hill country, called the Agamas, was, I believe, offered for sale not long ago—it measures about 40 square miles: only £200 was bid, and it was not sold. A little more, however, would have bought it. This tract extends out to Cape Arnaugti, and has the most beautiful slopes for vines, with a low-lying narrow plain along the shore, watered by several springs, one of which now turns a mill. The sea surrounds the property on all but one side, and the coast is indented with little bays and creeks. The hills rise about 1500 feet above the shore. Old wine-presses testify to its former fruitfulness. The hills are now covered with scrub, and are only used as grazing-ground for flocks of goats. Small portions of the plain are cultivated by a few shepherds, who also collect firewood and ship it from the shore. With capital these slopes might be green with vines, the low plains covered with groves of oranges and fruit-trees. Wine might be produced and shipped on the spot without may transport; and besides these advantages, there is undoubtedly great mineral wealth beneath the soil, capable of paying largely for any outlay.

This is not a single case. There are many places in the island just as good waiting for the hand of the capitalist to change them from barren wastes to their former fruitfulness. Land lies idle that would soon form splendid cotton-fields; wheat, barley, and all cereals grow in profusion. Tobacco of a very superior quality can be produced. All the tobacco consumed is now imported, owing to the heavy taxation formerly imposed upon the grown article by the Turks. Indigo might be grown in the warm valleys. All that is required is enterprise and capital.

Roads are a great want in the development of the island. The natives have no desire to save time,—they follow the same narrow rugged tracks up and down the rocks that their fathers followed before them, and if Government undertook to make roads for them, they would soon be again destroyed; but this would change if a few Englishmen settled in the country. The same thing would happen as has happened in the Lebanon. The English colony goes up from Beyrout to some village in the hills for the summer months: a road where there was none before is soon made by the natives; the houses are improved; rents rise; a hotel is started, and a thriving active community takes the place of a torpid village. The same effect would happen if a few colonists arrived: the natives would soon makes roads where they were needed, and the example of activity would speedily infuse energy into the sleepy inhabitants when they saw the advantages of it before them.

The two races that inhabit the country are very distinct types. The Turks are tall, well-built men, generally spare and active. The great characteristic that distinguishes them from the Greeks is their proud bearing. They all have a certain reserved expression on their faces, evidently thinking well of themselves. They are not at all fanatical about their religion; and though good Moslems, they do not share in the sterner precepts of the law of Mohammed. They work better than the Greeks, are more inclined to take an interest in what is being done, but are also more independent and less submissive under reproof. It is rare to find the Turks inhospitable: they are generally very obliging at first. For instance, I have been told at a village that everything would be provided for nothing; that I must accept their hospitality, not only in words of politeness, but really intending that I should live on them. After refusing such offers, it is strange to be cheated in the price of barley and chickens; but it is Turkish and oriental. They generally have receding foreheads, whereas the Greek forehead is straight; and the dark Nubian and semi-Nubians have domed foreheads. They prefer white-and-red-striped Manchester stuffs for their clothes, whereas the Greeks are almost always dressed in blue indigo-dyed stuffs of home manufacture. They are brave, fearing and looking up to no one, making splendid soldiers, and are peaceful, moderately honest, and industrious.

The Greeks are also fine-made men. They have a mild and humble expression of countenance, and are timid. They hide in the villages as a Government official passes through, without any real cause. They are very religious, generally going to church every evening and keeping a great number of saints' days, and believing every superstitious story. They are stupid, and are bad workers, shirking as much as they can. They like a shilling a-day, but after two or three days they are all inclined to strike with three shillings. They are rich enough to lie in the sun and do nothing for a long time; and they object to working when they become such capitalists. There are bright exceptions to this rule—energetic Greeks, who are better sometimes than stupid Turks; but the great test of stamina, the keeping at continual steady work, breaks them all down. They are not nearly so intelligent or such good workers as the Maronites and Druses of the Lebanon.

The women of both races are not at all prepossessing; it is rare to see a face even tolerably good-looking, and their figures and voices are very objectionable. The Turkish women veil their faces, which is an advantage. The women do a great deal of manual labour,—fetching water, accompanying their lords to the fields to reap the harvest, and thrashing the corn: they help in everything except ploughing and sowing. It is odd to see the parties in the fields, reaping, almost always one man to two women, both Greek and Turkish alike.

The children are pretty, some with flaxen hair and cherub faces. The Turkish children are not nearly so pretty as the Greek.

There are a good many landed proprietors of a superior class, looked up to as rich men by their fellow-townsmen, whose word has generally a great influence in the village. Most well-situated villages have one of these magnates, who owns more land and has a better house than any one else. When Turks, they live very retired lives on their properties, and seem to be inclined to be miserly. They associate freely with their *employés*, and it is difficult to distinguish between them. The natives give them the title of Effendi. The large Greek proprietors very rarely live on their land,—they prefer to live in the largest town of the district, letting the land, or having an agent to farm for them. There are also a few Armenians who have large possessions but live in the towns.

The different monasteries of the Greek Church own a large amount of land derived from different sources. Grants from the Sultan, purchases, and legacies, have made them rich. In many cases the lands owned by monasteries have been allowed to lie idle; others have tilled them without opposition, and have thus obtained a right of possession. Thus the boundaries of church properties are in a very confused state, owing to no trouble being taken by the heads of the different monasteries to keep their boundaries clear. A lawsuit with a rich monastery was not objectionable to a Turkish judge, who was able generally to make it very profitable to himself. Naturally the old monks put off the day when they would be obliged to part with their savings in bribes. The result has been that the properties have gradually been encroached upon by the surrounding proprietors.

Next to the monasteries is the *vakuf* land that has been left to mosques and Mohammedan charities by worthy Moslems. These lands are usually let at a very low rent,—they cannot be sold. To escape from a disputed title, a Turk would make his land *vakuf*, and rent it himself. The remainder of the land is divided up into very small holdings owned by the peasants. These properties are subdivided amongst the sons on the parents' decease, so that a quarter of an acre sometimes belongs to four or five brothers. Women were formerly not allowed to inherit land, and they generally inherited trees. Thus the trees belong to a different proprietor to the land.

There are no hedges and ditches in Cyprus. The different allotments are marked, or supposed to be marked, out by stones; but as these stones have generally disappeared, the holdings are only known approximately.

Each village is a little community of itself. They elect each year a head-man called the Muktar, with a council of elders to assist him. The Muktar is recognised by the Government, and all communications to the village pass through him. He collects taxes, is called upon to answer any questions, to find offenders, and to keep order. In mixed villages of Turks and Greeks, where the division is about equal, they elect two Muktars, one for each sect; but when a large majority is of one creed, one Muktar is deemed sufficient for all. Though Greeks and Turks may live together in the same village all their lives, they associate very little together. Generally the village is divided into quarters,—the Greek houses in one part, and the Turkish houses together in another. A Turk marrying a Greek girl is very rare, though it does occasionally take place. The reverse never happens, differing in this from the case among the inhabitants of Crete.

Next to the Muktar in the social scale of the village is the priest or *papa*. In Turkish villages it is the *hodja* or schoolmaster who keeps the mosque. The priests are married, and till their lands the same as any peasant. They generally have been taught to read and write, and are looked up to by the people as guides in cases of difficulty.

The villages on the plain and low-lying hills are almost entirely built of sun-dried mud-slabs about one foot three inches square by four inches deep. The roof is made of wooden rafters laid flat, covered with reed mats; on this about a foot of earth is placed and rammed hard. This forms a good protection from the sun, but the rain soon washes it away. The better class of houses are of two storeys, with a veranda along the upper one, and a row of arches supporting it below. The upper storey is used for sleeping and living in. In the hills the houses are built of stone, and the churches have pitched roofs covered with tiles. On the plain, the churches are large rectangular buildings, with vaulted or domed roofs coated with cement. There is always an apse at the east end, and generally a small belfry is attached. The interiors arc decorated according to the Greek fashion, with a heavy wooden screen, which is generally well carved and covered with gilding. The Russian eagles frequently figure on the gates of the sanctuary.

The natives, both Turk and Greek, wear high boots with clump soles, loose baggy trousers, a shirt and small jacket, and a fez; a Manchester cotton handkerchief is tied round the fez by the Greeks, and sometimes a white turban, but generally plain by the Turks. On feast-days and at weddings the Greeks dress themselves up in very long baggy trousers of dark-blue cloth or shiny calico, tied round the knee, so as to show a white stocking and shoes with buckles. Their waistcoats are bright with embroidery, and they wear small close-fitting jackets. Turkish Effendis and landed proprietors assume a European dress.

The English rule is undoubtedly popular in Cyprus. The Greeks are naturally more enthusiastic than the Turks in their expression of devotion to the Government of the Queen. For instance, in the village of Kethroea on New-Year's eve, while the clocks were chiming the advent of another year, shouts and cheers for Victoria and the English woke us up. No English were with them, and the shouting was quite spontaneous.

The Turks are also pleased with the new rule. They are not worried by *zabtiehs*, they have no fear of conscription, and they rather like the English.

The Greeks may be partially descendants from an ancient Cypriot race. There are some curious types amongst them,—traces of Egyptian crusading and German blood, with, of course, a strong mixture of the Greek peasant race. In the northwest portion of the island, about Korruachitz, there are several villages of Maronites, settlers from the Lebanon. They appear to have arrived about fifteen years ago, and have maintained their religion, though they have given up their language and taken to speaking Greek.

Flocks of goats and fat-tailed sheep roam all over the country in large herds, picking up a scanty sustenance on dried-up herbage. They give a good supply of milk in the spring, particularly in the mountain districts of Limasol and Papho. A large number of cheeses are made and exported from Limasol every year. The cattle are, as a rule, small, and are used for ploughing and carting. They are not milked or eaten by the natives. Donkeys and mules are the common beasts of burden, and are very numerous. The mules are good, but the natives do not understand loading them properly. They have slight trumpery saddles, and, as a rule, carry very little. Ponies are common, and are ridden and used as pack-animals. There are also a few inferior camels.

A slight description of the country from the northern shore to Troados will give some idea of the topography of the island.

The northern shore is completely cut off from the rest of the island by a range of mountains that only leave a narrow strip of very fertile reddish soil between them and the sea. This plain is covered with carob and olive trees, and is well watered from the hills close by. The dense foliage of the carob gives a delightful shade; and this is one of the pleasantest portions of the island to live in. Unfortunately this plain is very narrow, and the land rises steeply to the northern range of mountains, which stand up in sharp crags and peaks, stretching away east and west the whole length of the island. On some of these peaks and overhanging precipices castles are perched, such as the medieval castle of Hilaricon and the two queens' houses at Buffavento and Kantara. The two latter appear probably to have been used as places to look out for an enemy from the north, and by lighting beacons to warn the island of coming danger. Of both of them a legend relates that they are composed of a hundred rooms, ninety-nine of which are known, and that when the hundredth is discovered it will be full of gold. The masonry is rough-hewn, not dressed, and shows no signs of great age. The stones used are only of moderate dimensions, and the whole has more the appearance of being only three or four hundred years old than that of great antiquity.

Along the northern slopes of these hills there are many charming nooks, cool-shaded valleys with bright streams, the sea breaking in the many little coves and creeks of the shore close by—while beyond, the snow-clad hills of Asia Minor stand out clear.

Ascending the pass that leads to Nicosia, we look down on a broad brown plain without trees, that appears quite flat from the elevation we are at. Villages are dotted about, with their white churches standing out conspicuously. Nicosia is seen in mid-plain, with cathedrals and minarets and patches of green; and beyond are the blue range of Makeras and Troados, with the Mount of the Holy Cross standing out by itself to the east.

Immediately below us is a band of shale hills about three miles wide, perfectly barren, and with very steep slopes: they are cut up by innumerable water-courses. The denudation that has formed them has been arrested by layers of almost vertical strata, sustaining the clayey soil at an angle of almost 45°. To the east, amongst these barren hills, appears a strip of brilliant green running out into the plain: this is Kethroea, one of the gems of Cyprus. Below the cliffs of the Pentadactylon a large spring gushes out of the rocks at an elevation of 850 feet above the sea. The spring is enclosed, in modern masonry, in a covered channel which collects the water from four different heads. The water is bright, clear, and slightly warm—67° Fahr. Rather more than four thousand gallons a minute are constantly supplied both summer and winter. The remains of an ancient aqueduct can be traced that once led the water to Salamis. Rushing down a steep valley in the shale hills, the water changes them up to a certain level into the most fertile banks, clothed with green of every hue, and covered with fruit-trees; above the water-line the hills remain the same barren, glaring, mud-coloured ridges, that seem to set off the green-like brightness of the valley they contain. Passing along innumerable aqueducts, covered with luxuriant fronds of maidenhair fern, turning over a score of mills, the streams find their way through thick groves of oranges, pomegranates, mulberries, and other fruit-trees. Reaching the mouth of the valley the water is carried fanlike out on to the plain, fertilising the soil until every drop is expended. Houses cluster along the banks of the main streams, and as these spread on the plain, they form small villages, gradually becoming more distinct and separated.

Leaving Nicosia to the east, we cross the plain, passing the driedup Pedias river. The plain is not so level as it appeared from above; ridges of flat rocks show a former elevation that has been swept away by the rains of centuries, only leaving islands here and there to show what was once the formation. Where the top crust remains all is bare and uncultivated, but where it is broken away by denudation the land is very fertile. Passing the fertile plain of Morphu on the west, we make straight for the hills below Mount Troados, whose glittering snow-clad top serves as a guide. Here we again come on rushing streams of water, groves of oranges and lemons, that make Leoka the noted orange-growing place in the island. Situated at the mouth of a valley a short distance from the sea, it is one of the most charming spots. The hills around are full of mineral wealth, and clothed with mighty pines; broad and fertile valleys lead from them to the plain below.

Advancing up the valley, with the rushing torrent at our feet, we come across villages perched on the steep slopes, resembling villages in Switzerland. Above, the hills are covered with vineyards. To the west the mountains get wilder, and the pine-forests grow larger and more dense. In this little explored country there is a mass of intricate valleys and steep slopes covered with trees. There are streams of water, and the ground in parts is clothed with luxuriant bracken-fern under the lofty pines. Though much injured by burning for resin, they are still fine trees, and there are a good many young ones growing up to refill the spaces that have been cleared.

The mountaineers are very hospitable. They sprinkle our hands with rose-water, and bring out curious preserves of grapes and other sweets. Sometimes they burn olive branches in a large spoon in front of us, as a preventive from the evil eye. The olive-branches have been hung up in the church for some time.

A narrow and steep path leads up to Troados or Olympus. From here we get a magnificent view of almost the whole island. The plain we have passed looks dim and misty below us. The northern range of mountains are blue, and appear to stretch away to the east beyond out range of sight. To the east and west, ranges of mountain-tops fill the space in the utmost confusion. To the west these tops are more densely wooded with dark pines than those to the east. Looking south over the Limasol and Papho districts, hill and valley seem to fill up the whole of the island. The hills are covered with scrub and sometimes with trees. A marked line can be clearly distinguished where the white chalk gives place to the dark metamorphosed rocks of which Troados is formed; and here the vineyards are seen covering the slopes in all directions. Towards the south-west a large white hill stands out prominently, crowned by a little chapel. This is the Panagia Khrisosogiotessa, a large Greek monastery, rivalling the great monastery of Kiku, which can also be seen in the pine-covered hills to our west. Over the Papho district the white chalky limestone seems to prevail. The valleys are large, and have streams of water in them irrigating the lower slopes of the steep hills. The hills are greener, the grass forming in places a perfect turf. Numbers of horses and cattle are grazing, driven over from the parched plain to the north to feed on the luxuriant slopes of the Papho and Limasol hills.

We have had our eyes on Cyprus as a desirable position for some time. As early as October 1876, it appears something had been decided, for the innumerable and very bad maps of the island issued on linen from the War Office are all stamped with that date. Palestine, no doubt, was the great rival, had war broken out with Russia. We might have occupied the country which we must defend from invasion from the north; we might have constructed the works that would make the passes of the Lebanon inaccessible, and have prepared the position about Mount Carmel, the greatest battle-field of the world, for the final contest.

Directly "Peace with honour" prevailed, Cyprus carried the day. We know the advantages of a seagirt shore. No complications of holy sites and sentimental interests, no religious task of sending the Jew back and placing a king on the throne of Judah, tend to embarrass our occupation of the island.

The position of Cyprus was clearly seen to be almost perfect as a base of operations in Syria, and for influencing the reforms in Asia Minor.

So we have come to Cyprus, and some are horribly disgusted because it is not the seventh heaven promised by Mohammed to true believers. Had we been only looking for a charming climate, a delightful and healthy country, rich and prosperous, capable of paying us well for taking possession of it, there is no doubt we might have chosen something nearer the Garden of Eden; but we should have been no better than freebooters, looting from the weak the richest jewels we could get hold of.

The great reasons for our coming should not be lost sight of—to influence the Turkish rule in Asia Minor for good, and to be capable of resisting any further encroachments from the north. Unless we see reforms carried out in Asia Minor, how can we answer the great Christian deliverer when he advances to lift the yoke from suffering Christians? We may know that the Muscovite yoke is twice as heavy as the Ottoman; still, fanatical Christians, as all Christians are in the East, will prefer a heavy yoke, put on by a master of their own faith, rather than a lighter burden imposed by the infidel Moslem.

The army of those who are to be our future allies should also be attended to. We know what splendid fighting material there is in the Turkish soldier. We also know their wants—good officers, discipline, and commissariats. By raising and maintaining a Turkish regiment in Cyprus, we could find out by experience the reforms necessary. It would become the training school for officers, who would be capable of carrying out the same reforms in Asia Minor; and in case of war, we should have men able to raise troops amongst the many warlike tribes of Syria and Asia Minor who would follow an English leader to the death.

By thus employing Cyprus we should make its possession politically of the vastest importance, and we should really possess the key of the East.

McCalmont 1878–1879

Hugh McCalmont, born in Ireland and educated at Eton, joined the British army and had an early connection with what was known in the military world at the time as the "Wolseley Gang," a group of officers associated in numerous campaigns with Sir Garnet Wolseley. McCalmont served in Canada, India, Natal, Egypt and Sudan where he led the unsuccessful Nile Expeditionary Force to save Gordon and his troops at Khartoum.

The segment here deals with his service as ADC (aide-de-camp) to General Wolseley during the latter's time as first British High Commissioner of Cyprus in 1878-1879.

After his extensive military service McCalmont served in the British parliament. He started *The Memoirs of Major-General Sir Hugh McCalmont*" which was completed and edited by Major-General Sir C. E. Caldwell and published in London: Hutchinson & Co., 1924.

The consequence of this trip to England was that I found myself in London just at the time when the arrangement between our government and the Sublime Porte was come to under which Cyprus was temporarily made over to us, and when Sir G. Wolseley was appointed High Commissioner and Commander-in-Chief of the acquisition. I was staying for a day or two in Jermyn Street, when I got a note from Sir Garnet offering me the post of A.D.C. on his staff. He was staying in Portland Square at the time, and when I went to call there he was out; but I saw Lady Wolseley and accepted the appointment to her. Even at the time one felt a little doubtful about it, the more so in view of Sir A. Layard's promise; but all this Cyprus business was started with a great flourish of trumpets, and Wolseley being accompanied by many of his old staff comrades of Ashanti days—Colonel (afterwards General Sir G.) Greaves, who had succeeded McNeill as chief of the staff out there, Brackenbury, Baker Russell, Maurice, etc.

I did not start on my way to the Levant until a week after His Excellency and the bulk of the staff had taken their departure, and I then proceeded overland to Marseilles, and got a passage in a French boat to Smyrna. "The first night out we had a bit of a summer gale," I wrote home from Syra, "which was not pleasant. Just like Frenchmen, though the ship was rolling any amount, they left the ports open and a sea came in about 9 p.m. which completely drenched everything in the cabins and flooded the saloon." Another ship took me on after some delay from Smyrna to Larnaka in Cyprus, where we arrived on the 6th of August, and that night I rode over from there to Nicosia, the capital—a distance of twenty-five miles—on a mule, to find the chief and the staff housed in a fine old building in the town.

It must be confessed that one's first impressions of the island were far from favourable, for it was extremely hot down in the plains around Nicosia. There was a large assemblage of troops encamped round about, who had come from Malta, and who formed part of that "Indian Contingent" which Beaconsfield had brought to Europe some months before at the time when our relations with Russia had been so precarious. Although the days were intensely hot, the nights were cool, and this caused a good deal of malaria and of other forms of sickness in the camps, the Ghurkas suffering especially; these splendid little soldiers never seem to do well in low ground when it is warm weather. The H.Q. Staff in the meantime more or less lived on champagne, and they were consequently right as rain. But, if they were well in health, they were very far from being well contented, for it speedily became apparent to us that we had been right well sold. The Congress of Berlin put an end to all prospect of an Anglo-Russian conflict—of what use to us Cyprus would have been supposing that such a conflict had occurred, neither I nor anybody else has ever been able to make out. The whole thing was just a "gesture" on the part of Lord Beaconsfield, with which to bluff his bewildered countrymen for the time being. Nor did I find my job of A.D.C. in peace-time at all to my taste. "I am an upper servant one minute and a clerk the next," I wrote soon after arrival. "Quantities of letters come in by every mail from lunatics thirsting for employment—a better word would be drudgery in one case and ennui in another—and all these letters are answered to the effect that H. E. regrets that he can hold out no hopes of furthering the wishes of the applicant." One had all sorts of odd jobs to perform. One day, for instance, I had the pleasure of convoying some sixty malefactors from the jail at Nicosia to Kyrenia, on the coast sixteen miles off, to be embarked. A ruffianly lot of murderers they were; all tied together. The escort consisted of twenty Ghurkas and ten Turkish soldiers, but nine of the Ghurkas succumbed to the heat, and the remainder were utterly beat by the time we reached our destination.

There had been a question of Sir Garnet going out to India as Commander of the Bombay army, and although he never complained we knew that he was bitterly disappointed at having been let in for this Cyprus tomfoolery. He made the best of it, however. "Whatsoever thy hand findeth to do, do it with thy might" was his motto, so he devoted himself wholeheartedly to abstruse administrative questions in connection with improving the conditions in the island, and to manifold projects for developing its resources—such as they were. The communications leading from place to place were wretched. It was almost as much as your life was worth to take a drive along these so-called roads; and the sanitary state of the towns was perfectly deplorable, so much so that we speedily moved out of our big house in Nicosia and encamped a short distance from the outskirts of the place. Although tent life had its drawbacks, owing to heat and dust, it was upon the whole preferable to being indoors. I managed to bring off a pleasant trip up Mount Olympus in September. One found it quite cool as soon as one got fairly high up; and shortly after that Lord Brassey arrived in his yacht, the "Sunbeam." He took me for a pleasant cruise in her round part of the island, starting from Kyrenia and proceeding to Limasol.

I had brought out a good mare from home, and one day an officer of the garrison who possessed an arab which he greatly fancied was boasting that this animal of his would beat any other one in Cyprus. Baker Russell promptly took him up, borrowed my mare, and they made short work between them of the arab. It was about the first sporting event to take place, but two or three race meetings were held afterwards. The groom who had come out with the mare from home was a youth of Hibernian extraction named Walsh, who had originally been a stable-boy, but who had caught my eye as a likely fellow and one who could uncommonly well take care of himself. He was something of a character, and I had him with me later on in South Africa during various adventures, the fact of his being a civilian and not a soldier sometimes proving a disadvantage, but at other times proving to be a point in his favour. He will be referred to again in later pages.

The news of the breach with the Amir of Afghanistan, which occurred at this time, and of the subsequent outbreak of hostilities in that quarter, did not tend to make one any the better satisfied with being planted down in this back-water where prospects of active service had become absolutely nil. The trouble on the north-west frontier of India made one speculate whether it had not been a mistake to exchange out of the 9th Lancers when they went abroad. They were, I knew, stationed up country, and before long it transpired that they were to take part in the campaign. Had I stuck to them, I should now have been second-in-command, and I should, moreover, in all probability have led them before many months were out, for their colonel, Cleland, was severely wounded at Kabul, in December, 1879. My mother, moreover, had a great idea of my going into Parliament, and, on my learning during the winter months that there was a likelihood of a vacancy occurring in the representation of the County Antrim, I seriously debated the question of standing. My brother Jimmy, who had left the Army some years before and who was now an A.D.C. to the Lord Lieutenant of Ireland, had come to be a very well-known figure in Ulster, and his influence would undoubtedly have helped me when the matter of selection cropped up. But the anticipated vacancy did not occur as soon as had been expected at the time. Aware that I had been recommended for a brevet-majority on account of the Armenian campaign, I was somewhat disappointed at hearing nothing official on the subject, but the announcement in the "Gazette" at last appeared, and I found myself promoted as from the 30th of November, 1878, together with Ardagh and Trotter.

The winter climate was pleasant enough, although there was still a certain amount of sickness amongst the troops "One fellow died of fever in camp a couple of days ago," I wrote on the 6th of December, "and at the funeral one of his 'firing party' managed to shoot another fellow in the eye. So we are getting on pretty well in our small community."

The Bairam Festival had just come off, on which occasion His Excellency and the rest of us for the first time appeared in full dress; and we presented a most imposing appearance, mounted on ponies, and attended by a swarm of Turkish, Greek and nigger rag-tag and bob-tail in all sorts of garments, by way of escort. Sweets, coffee and cigarettes were dished out to the notables at the konak, under the direction of Sir Garnet's head butler, and that evening we had a special guest to dinner, Rifaat Pasha, a Turk of light and leading, hailing from Constantinople. On leaving the table, the Chief offered the gentleman a cigar, who promptly helped himself to fifty and rolled them up in his napkin which he likewise purloined. "That's the sort of man I am," he appeared to think, and one hoped that we should not be called upon to entertain many more specimens of this acquisitive type of guest, or there would be nothing to smoke and no table-linen left in the place.

His Excellency was always trying to make out that there was nothing wrong with the island. "Who takes quinine? Never heard of such a thing! Splendid climate!" That was his line; but we knew perfectly well that he took quinine himself every day. A good many visitors began to arrive, most of whom His Excellency hospitably entertained. The Bishop of Gibraltar came on an inspection of this addition to his diocese, and Sir Samuel and Lady Baker turned up; as was only to be expected of such seasoned travellers in impossible countries, they thought fit to live in a sort of caravan, gipsy fashion—"a drawing-room on wheels" they called it—which must have jolted them up a bit when they got on the move along the Cyprus highways. A proper "Government House," a great big wooden barrack of a place, had been run up, and Lady Wolseley arrived on Christmas Eve, bringing with her her little daughter Frances, who is now Viscountess Wolseley. Some other officers' wives also made their appearance.

"She is quite the Queen of Cyprus," I wrote home about Lady Wolseley, "receiving deputations of Turks and Greeks, who go in for worshipping the ground she treads on. In the meantime the unfortunate A.D.C. is engaged in showing these brutes to their chairs, ordering cigarettes and coffee, doing everything, in fact, except handing these delicacies to them..... It was an utter mistake leaving Constantinople in every way. I don't know, however, that I should care to go back there, especially as not knowing languages the very devil for a Military Attaché, but on the whole it was a great pity to have left the place..... There have been two cases of diphtheria in camp. The second was Walsh, but he is much better. I had a row with the doctors about him—they refused to take him to hospital, saying that he would 'infect' the place. Then I said: 'I suppose you want to turn the camp into an infected hospital.' The upshot of it all was that Walsh remained in camp for two days and was then removed to hospital—almost as good a way of infecting two places as could be devised." There was quite a successful race meeting early in January, but my two crocks Erzerum and Cyprus, failed to carry anything off.

The fact of my now being a Field Officer tended to make me more dissatisfied than ever with being an aide-de-camp under the existing conditions. We, moreover, learnt from the newspapers that a struggle with the Zulus was about to take place, and it was evident that this would be, by a good deal, a more serious business than had been the operations against the Transkei and other Kaffirs which had been going on for many months past, and in which Evelyn Wood and Buller, comrades who had gone out with me to Cape Coast Castle in the "Ambriz," had been making their mark. I determined, therefore, to make an effort to get out to South Africa, should it prove at all possible. In the meantime I described the routine of the day in a letter home, as follows "Breakfast at 9 a.m. Then bullyrag the servants, at whom the English butler is the chief and the cheekiest scoundrel in creation, a fellow that neither His nor Her Excellency can get on without, so they say. The chief butler, therefore, occupies a position only second to the Lord High Commissioner in Cyprus. I then order the dinner and send the cook to market. As he cannot understand any of the many languages that I speak the operation is carried out under difficulties and doesn't conduce to good temper in this trying climate. I then have a row with some Greek or Turk about the place. Then copy some letters or argue with Lady Wolseley. Luncheon comes round about 2 o'clock—punctuality is enforced by the chief butler's watch, the most erratic timepiece I have come across and, therefore, my *bête noire*. It is exceedingly difficult to get through the afternoon, but one does somehow or other with the assistance of sherry, brandy and soda, tea and siesta—cigarettes too. The cigars are unsmokable. Dinner is also a punctual meal at 7-30, regulated by the above-mentioned chronometer, and we go to bed, thank God, immediately after it. So you see what a day we're having!"

The more I saw of it the less I felt cut out for the responsibilities of an A.D.C. ship. "What with the lady's maids, housemaids, butlers, soldier servants and *their* wives, and the Greeks and Turks, the place is a sort of pandemonium," I wrote a few days later. "One thing enrages me is the amount they eat. Always guzzling—five times a day. We got over a soldier and his wife from the 20th Regiment to do servants. I suppose they were the best that could be sent, but the wife got awfully drunk and had to be sent back.... The sooner this sort of game is ended the better, although nothing could be kinder than Sir Garnet and Lady Wolseley are to me. Nobody but a born idiot would stop in such a place if he could live out of it."

The news of Isandlwhana made me more than ever keen to get out to Natal, and although Sir Garnet never said a word about it I knew that he also was pining to be at this new seat of war. . . His Excellency naturally felt that this Cyprus appointment was cutting him out of the work that he was best fitted to perform.

In so far as my own chances of getting out to the Zulu business were concerned, I hoped to enlist the sympathies of Lord Cairns, who had always been ready to help me in the past; and I took the necessary steps in that directions. As the weeks passed, I became more and more anxious for the change, and so, I could see, did the Chief. "*Entre nous*," I wrote on the 26th of March: "Sir Garnet has been living on the hope for the last few days of being sent to Natal, and I think the anxiety is almost too much for him sometimes. As nothing has transpired, he is completely down on his luck, though he takes care that strangers don't observe it..... As I write, Herbert has just returned. The mules ran away with the trap, and the invalid and Walsh, who was driving, were pitched out; the carriage wheel went over the latter. Both have got a good shaking, but no bones broken." (St. Leger Herbert, private secretary to His Excellency, had been very seriously ill and was proceeding home, invalided.)

A most sporting event was brought off one day, in the shape of a lawn-tennis match between His Excellency and myself, for 100 best cigars. I have never been an enthusiast for ball games, nor have I ever manifested any marked aptitude for pastimes of that sort, and Sir Garnet was always chaffing me for not being able to shine in this, then new-fangled, form of amusement. So I made a match with him, and, to the great astonishment of H. E., and the spectators, and somewhat to my own surprise, I beat him seven games out of twelve, amid tense excitement. The betting was about four to one against me. It was a few days after this notable triumph that I gave a great week-end picnic out at a magnificent abbey in the hills, at which I entertained the High Commissioner and Lady Wolseley, Sir S. and Lady Baker, and a total of twelve guests. It meant sending tents, servants, food, wine, a cooking-stove, etc., over the mountains, and it required quite a lot of organization. We had our meals in a noble banqueting hall, 40 feet high and 120 feet long, with a fine stone roof, while the camp was pitched in the cloisters. The whole affair passed off very well. "The butler has returned here in a state of semi-consciousness after his work," I wrote from Nicosia.

Earlier in the year I had been robbed of my watch and chain, seals, etc., but had not been able to lay my hands on the thief. Shortly after that picnic I, however, found myself robbed again, on this occasion of money. "This time I think I have nailed the delinquent," I wrote home. "The chief interpreter here, a fellow in receipt of some £200 a year, and quite the confidential man of the establishment. I suspected him of having stolen the watch and chain, but there was no evidence. In this instance there is plenty of evidence, but, unfortunately one of my witnesses has sworn to an impossibility, and if his evidence is to be believed that of the most important witness is contradicted, so I am afraid the housebreaker may get off by a fluke. The witness who is playing the fool is, of course, an old soldier of the 'Mines' type, ready to swear to anything that bears out his idea of the case... We had a visit this week from four M.P.'s ———, ———,——— and ———, all oldish fellows, quite demoralized by the luxury in which they have passed, at any rate, the last decade of their useless existence. One thing rather amused me. I got them a Turkish non-commissioned officer to accompany them in Nicosia. After being with them three hours, the four legislators dismissed the man with a *douceur* of a shilling! The Turk tried ineffectually to explain that it was quite against the rules of the Service to receive remuneration for duty (though I dare say ten shillings might have changed or modified his views on the subject). However, he handed the shilling back to the Officer Commanding on his return to barracks, who forwarded it to me. I am sending it to the House of Commons."

My connection with Cyprus was now at last drawing to a close, for Sir Garnet had the happy thought of going home on two months' leave. It did not take long to make satisfactory arrangements for the conveyance of His Excellency and Lady Wolseley, with select representatives of his retinue including myself attended by Mr. Walsh, to Brindisi by the naval dispatch boat "Surprise." We arrived at that stuffy little Italian port after a pleasant run, and when we were put ashore on the jetty I happened to notice that Walsh was devoting most especial attention to an abandoned-looking package. "What the devil's that," says I. "It's cigars, sir, as I've brought along from the island," says he. " How many," says I. "There'd maybe be a thousand, sir," says he. " Good Lord, man!" says I; "we can't bring all that stuff along with us. I'd be in the workhouse, paying duty on them here, and at Modane, and at Dover." "Sure them divils'd never be after opening His Excellency's luggage," says he. "I wouldn't warrant them," says I, "and, anyhow, you're cigars aren't His Excellency's luggage." "What'll I be doing with them at all," says he. He had evidently been sacking Government House or the Headquarters' Mess at Nicosia; and then I had a sort of brain-wave. I packed him off in a boat to go back to the "Surprise" with my compliments, and the cigars as a present to the wardroom officers. He went near missing the train in consequence; but, had he been left behind, he would have turned up all right, smiling, in England, for he was one of those kind of people who always contrive to fall on their feet.

Vizetelly 1878–1882

Although Edward Vizetelly (Bertie Clere) describes himself as a journalist, he appears as more of an adventurer/opportunist who upon hearing of Britain taking over the administration of Cyprus in 1878, left Greece within two months to arrive in time to describe the other opportunists and government officials. After numerous attempts to make a living, he left Cyprus in mid-February 1882 for further adventurers in Egypt. He records this in his volume *Cyprus to Zanzibar*, London: C. Arthur Pearson, Limited, 1901.

CHAPTER I

CYPRUS AT THE OCCUPATION

The flutter of sensation that exercised Europe when it became known that the Sultan of Turkey had ceded the island of Cyprus to England, flurried as sharply in the Near East as anywhere. Had a report gained credence that a rich gold mine had been discovered in the ancient classic isle, which shares with Cythera the distinction of having given the Mother of Love to Greek mythology, the excitement could hardly have been greater.

Indeed, one smart man from the Near East, a certain Mr. Zealous Zachariah Williamson, residing at the time in London, actually did advance something of the kind, in two or three letters he indited to a morning paper, which the editor naïvely, and apparently without any inquiry or research, printed in bold type immediately after the leading articles. In these delusive effusion, above the name of "Cyprus," the writer, who pretended he had been a consul in the island, boldly declared, among other equally astounding statements, that the proof of gold existing in the place was to be found in the fact that "large pieces of the precious metal" were daily washed down from the hills by the mountain streams.

My faith is too great in the intelligence of my fellow-countrymen, notwithstanding the opinion expressed on that subject by Carlyle, to suppose that either this glittering story, or those of precious stones being picked up in the groves of Paphos, or the tales of coal mines waiting for development, were generally believed. But, none the less, it is a fact that at the time of the occupation of Cyprus, every one in England imagined that the island under British rule would have a great future; and swarms of our fellow-countrymen packed up their traps and flew to the new possession. As a matter of fact we had simply recovered the self-same territory that Richard the lion-hearted had wrested from the power of an usurper in retaliation for discourtesy shown to his betrothed wife; and, with all the commercial instinct of an Englishman, had then sold to the Knights Templars, who dissatisfied with their acquisition, passed it on to Guy de Lusignan, neither of whom, by the way, ever completed the payment of the purchase money.

In the Near East, at that time, but one opinion found expression: this occupation of Cyprus was another link in that chain of British footholds in the Mediterranean, which many then believed might eventually extend to Gallipoli, there to resist Russian designs on Constantinople, and the advance of a Muscovite fleet into Western waters. Cyprus, affirmed these little Near Eastern politicians, would become a big place, a stronghold, a great naval station, after the fashion of Malta and Gibraltar. Fortifications would be raised, docks sunk, barracks and public buildings erected. Whilst friends of England applauded the astute diplomacy of our Foreign Office, and the wonderful perspicacity of the Earl of Beaconsfield and Lord Salisbury, every one agreed that there was evidently money to be made in this new British territory; and a multitude of adventuresome spirits in Near Eastern seaports, particularly such as possessed a knowledge of the English language—Maltese, Greeks, Armenians, Syrians, Hebrews, along with a few Frenchmen, Germans, and Englishmen—hurried off to the exciting centre of attraction, just as our fellow-countrymen did at home.

I was at Athens when the telegraph brought the news of the result of the Berlin Conference and the cession of Cyprus to England. I had been up in the Othrys mountains some time before, dabbling in an abortive insurrection against the Turks; and, regaining the capital when the movement collapsed, had lingered in the classic city to recuperate and enjoy the antiquities.

Two months' delightful repose at the foot of the Acropolis, in the simple home of a hoary-headed palikari, where the branches of a lemon-tree loaded with juicy, golden fruit shaded the windows of my apartment, had proved sufficient. Notwithstanding the charm of the surroundings I parted with them without an effort. In fact, the message announcing the news came as a godsend; and, with the rest, I buckled my portmanteau and set out for the new British possession, with a commission to send letters to the *Glasgow Herald*.

I reached Larnaca, the principal roadstead of the island, which has no ports, early one summer morning, on board the *Ceres* of the Austro-Hungarian Lloyd's line, after a round-about voyage *via* Constantinople and Smyrna. During a brief run ashore at the latter place to stretch our limbs, we learned that the Greek Consul had delivered 1200 passports for Cyprus in the course of a week. When Dr. Heïdenstam, the health officer and mayor, who boarded the vessel at Larnaca to give pratique, inquired how many passengers would disembark, and was told 120, he cast his eyes up to heaven and shrugged his shoulders.

Nothing daunted, this fresh swarm of immigrants eagerly set about getting ashore. Scrambling into the boats plying for hire around the ship, and reaching land, they there encountered a small multitude quite as eager to quit the place and gain the steamer, as they had been to leave the steamer and attain the island. These people told a tale of woe. They had parted with nearly all their spare cash, had done no good, and fared badly. In fact, there was nothing to do, no opening of any kind. Moreover, the place had become so overcrowded with strangers of all sorts and conditions that the cost of provisions had trebled, and to find a lodging was almost an impossibility. Happy the man who had the luck to secure a vacant bed at an exorbitant price amongst three or four others that were occupied, in a dismal room with bare, unplastered rubble walls, on a ground floor.

And those who unfolded this doleful tale of disappointment, who had rushed to the island among the first, to better their fortunes, and were among the first to leave it in disgust, earnestly advised the newcomers to take to sea again and get home as fast as they could. Some were wise enough to follow this counsel; some elected to remain and see for themselves. They went away afterwards, lighter in pocket, and chewing the cud of bitter discontent.

In spite of the congested state of the Larnaca population, I and a fellow-countryman succeeded, after diligent search, in securing an empty room in a house boasting only of a ground floor, and looking more like a stable than a human habitation. We had both brought our bedding with us, and having purchased a couple of iron bedsteads and a few other simple articles of furniture, were able to make ourselves as comfortable as the dismal aspect of the dwelling would permit. This accommodation, though rough and wanting in cheerfulness, was not costly, according to English ideas, for all we paid, between us, was one Turkish lira a month; but, just to give an idea of the value of household property in Cyprus, I will mention that this amount was double what the entire premises could have been rented for, per month, previous to the occupation.

Rents had certainly gone up at a bound, a circumstance partly due to a speculation in which M. Zaraffi, the well-known Greek banker at Constantinople, had engaged, and one that, in the end, proved utterly disastrous. This gentleman having heard at Yildez Kiosk that Cyprus was about to be handed over to England, had promptly dispatched an agent to the island with £20,000, and instructions to buy as much freehold property as he could. Many of the impoverished Cypriots were only too pleased to convert their real estate into hard cash, but when the British warships arrived off Larnaca, along with a fleet of transports, they saw which way the cat jumped, as the saying is, and several of the vendors refused to give up possession, with the result that the judicial authorities had a nice little batch of lawsuits to try, as soon as they settled down to work.

In the meantime Zaraffi had received delivery of a good many of his purchases, and amongst them of a corner house on the Strand facing the sea, usually let at an annual rental of £12, but which had been vacant for three years. To secure this property £300 had been paid. After my arrival at Larnaca these premises were let to a muscular and wiry old Welshman, named Williams, from Constantinople, who took them for three years at a rental of £300 for the first, £320 for the second, and £320 for the third year; so that the freehold was paid for with the first year's rent. But Zaraffi's other investments were not all so successful. In the end, when the excitement was over, and it was found that England did not intend to make Cyprus a naval station, and when practically all newcomers except Government servants and one or two merchants had left the place, rents fell to little over what they had been before the British fleet was sighted.

Although I arrived rather late in the field, Larnaca was still humming with activity, and swarming with Europeans, chiefly our own countrymen, who were all in white,—bodies in white suits, feet in white canvas shoes, heads capped with white helmets or white pulp hats of many different shapes and dimensions. A fleet rode at anchor in the offing, an Anglo-Indian army of 10,000 men was encamped under canvas ashore, Sir Garnet Wolseley was acting as the Queen's High Commissioner and Commander-in-Chief, and the British flag floated serenely from all the public buildings on the island.

My first attempt at business was made the day after I put foot on land, when at dawn, along with a French baker from Alexandria, I set out on mule-back for the camp at Chiflik Pasha, five miles away. This baker, who seemed intelligent enough in other respects, was beset with the inane idea of persuading the Commissary-General to feed Tommy Atkins on French puffy bread. Acting as interpreter I had a long talk with the gentleman responsible for what enters Tommy's inside; but although he admired and gratefully accepted for his own breakfast the samples of crusty *petits pains* that my companion presented to him, he explained that they were not the sort of aliment suitable to the British soldier, who required bread of a much heavier and more compact nature; and he held out no hope that my friend would secure the bread contract, which for that matter was in the hands of an English Smyrniot.

A stroll through the camp and a chat with the soldiers revealed the fact that there was ample room for improvement in the quality of Mr. Atkins's loaf. He complained most bitterly about it, alleging that it was made of indifferent flour, that it was full of sand and only half baked. His beef, he growled, was ill-fed and dirty, and there was no convenience for washing it. As to the potatoes they were all eyes, and quantities were diseased. But, as a set-off against these statements I must place on record that Tommy looked well-fed and rosy, whilst the impression I took away with me was that he appeared too fat.

On returning to town with my disappointed champion of the dough-trough, I happened to get into conversation with an intelligent Greek named Christofides, who could speak several languages fluently, but was unable to write any of them. This amiable son of Hellas lost no time in pointing out to me that a mint of money could be made out of the Cypriots by writing petitions for them to the Government. A vast number of people, he assured me, had something to say to those in authority, some grievance to bring to their notice, some favour to ask, and did not know how to make themselves understood. Under the Turks they went to a Turkish or Armenian scribe, who drew out petitions for them, to which they affixed their seals, and they proposed proceeding in the same way with their new masters.

After some discussion we arranged a partnership. Christofides was to ferret out the petitioners, I to draw up the petitions in my best English, and the proceeds were to be shared every evening, in equal parts. I remembered the ancient formula: "The humble petition of so and so respectfully showeth," etc., and winding up with the words, "and your petitioner will ever pray." So we set to work at once. Our stock-in-trade did not occasion any very great outlay. A small deal table and common chair were procured, and placed in the open air on the Strand, facing the sea, within a strip of shade afforded by some adjoining buildings. There sat I, sipping sweet coffee, smoking cigarettes, waiting patiently for clients; before me a quire of foolscap, a penny bottle of Stephens's Blue Black Ink, a penholder fitted with a J pen, some sand to dry the writing in lieu of blotting-paper, and a few English postage stamps to give an additional air of importance to the documents, which I drew up in as bold a fist as I could command.

Christofides, in the meanwhile, scoured the town in search of customers. His system, if slow, was thorough. Commencing work at six in the morning, he would go from coffee-house to coffee-house, from store to store, courting discourse with all whom he met; and as Cypriots, like other peoples in the Near East, have no lack of spare time and are fond of gossiping, he got through a vast amount of conversation before lunch-time, and found out all that was going on. In this manner he secured clients whom, ever and anon, he brought to me, and whilst he explained their cases I wrote out their petitions. The question of the fee invariably occasioned a lot of haggling. We endeavoured to secure a sovereign for each petition, but this was rarely forthcoming, and rather than allow the client to go away to some rival, willing to work at any price, we sometimes had to be content with a dollar. Still the business paid very well for a time; until, indeed, the Larnaca Cypriots had got over the mania for petitioning the authorities.

The Strand was the great centre of activity: a long, straggling esplanade flanked on one side by the sea, broken here and there by tottering landing-stages propped up with sticks half eaten away by the action of the salt water; on the other by rough stone houses, no more than a story high, with massive Roman-arched entrances and ground-floor windows barred with iron. Here were located the Post-office, the Port-office, the Eastern Telegraph Company, the residence of the District Commissioner, the Municipal Building, the Konak, with its Jail and Court-House, the Custom-House, the places of business of the principal English firms who had rushed off to Cyprus to make fortunes,— Henry S. King and Co., F. O. Harvey and Co., Truefitt from Bond Street, Williams from Constantinople, Janion from Liverpool, and Zealous Zachariah Williamson, a smart, up-to-date Constantinopolitan Jew, the same as had written to the morning paper about the nuggets of gold being washed down by the mountain torrents.

Here also were the principal Greek and Turkish coffee-houses, the French café, the English bars, and the Club, conducted by a couple of broken-down English gentlemen. One of them disappeared from the scene, discontented, at a very early stage. The other struggled on for a long time, relying in the end on his luck at whist and billiards to assist him in joining the two ends. Eventually he had to make a run from his creditors, and got clean off by arranging with the captain of the steamer trading between Egypt, Syria, and Cyprus to slow down and pick him up at sea after she had left the roadstead.

The largest firm attracted to Cyprus by the occupation was Henry S. King and Co. They arrived with a great flourish of trumpets, representing a number of good manufacturing houses, and consigners of general merchandise. Mr. Killerby, a quiet, shrewd, amiable gentleman who is still giving his services to the firm in Cornhill, directed the fortunes of the branch, and enjoyed a full measure of well-deserved popularity. His right-hand man, for a time, was the late Mr. James Bell, the brother of that same Mr. C. F. Moberly Bell who is now a shining light at Printing House Square. Henry S. King and Co. displayed unbounded enterprise and energy, backed up with capital, in the effort to establish themselves in the island, and were one of the last to leave it. But in the end, convinced that the game was not worth the cost of the candle, even this powerful firm considered it wise to take themselves off, handing their business over to one of their clerks, who struggled on in a small way until he died, supplying the few troops and Government servants in the place with such articles as they required from Europe.

In the very early days of the occupation the importation of goods from home was as varied as it was enormous; for the average Englishman on his travels pays slight attention to the musty old saying, "When in Rome, do as the Romans." Arrived at Rome, or anywhere else for that matter, the Englishman's habits and customs undergo little change. When he dashed off to Cyprus to make his fortune he was accompanied by tons upon tons of tinned provisions, bacon, and hams; by thousands upon thousands of cases of jam, marmalade, condensed milk, tea, cocoa, coffee, chicory, spirits, wine, and beer; by hundreds of barrels of soda water and other non-intoxicants; by parcels without number of British cutlery, glass, and crockery, hardware, paraffin lamps, iron bedsteads, pipes, tobacco, patent medicines, agricultural implements, and most of the other articles that he is accustomed to have within reach in his own country.

He had not forgotten his round sponge bath, and every morning when he left his bed it was to get out of his pajamas into his tub. These daily matinal ablutions from tip to toe, in a land where the Christian inhabitants make but small use of water externally, although they take a good deal inwardly, and where soap is regarded in the light of a luxury, caused a singular misconception.

"How dirty these English people must be," one Cypriot lady who let lodgings was heard to remark to another; "they are always washing themselves!"

Far from living like the Cypriots on goat and pillaf, salt anchovies and olives, tomatoes and stringy cheese, cucumbers and fig-peckers—those beccaficos whereon Byron tells us he delighted to feed—onions and garlic, water melons and purple grapes, mastic and thick black wine, the British immigrant chiefly relied for nutriment on the hundred and one different kinds of preserved foods, from Liebig's Extract to bully beef, which had accompanied him across the seas. The consumption of these articles at the commencement of the occupation was prodigious, and only equalled by the absorption of whisky and beer.

But there was a good deal of excuse for the copious libations poured out at the shrine of Bacchus. The swarm of nondescripts attracted to the island by the occupation found on their arrival naught to do. No appointments to be obtained, no business to transact; and so, in the daytime, they strolled from bar to bar and talked and drank. In the evening they went to the Music Hall, just started in the Bazaar by some Frenchwoman of easy virtue from Alexandria, or they met at the Club; or, packed together in the parlours of the one or two apologies for hotels that had sprung into existence, they played nap, poker, brag; toasted the Queen, God bless her! and "Dizzy"; screeched that famous Jingo song about the dogs of war being loose, along with variations of "The Elephant walks around."

"If," as my Uncle Toby affirms, "they swore terribly in Flanders," they drank as well as swore in no small degree in Cyprus. Abuse of alcohol in the intense heat, with the sky like lead and the earth like brass, as young Perks, a correspondent of the *Daily News*, borrowing from Scripture, aptly described the situation in a telegram to his newspaper, was in many instances attended with baneful results. A chief accountant to Government, of all persons in the world, shut himself up with two or three cases of champagne to assist him to get his balance right, but only succeeded in making his head as wrong as his figures, and in creating such a frightful scandal that he had to go home and relinquish his post to his first assistant. An intelligent youth, an orphan son of a former British Consul, on his way to bed one night at Larnaca, reeled over the low railing round the landing at the top of an outside staircase, and was picked up next morning with a broken neck.

But perhaps the worst example of tippling to excess was that of a young man employed as salesman and barman. Part of this assistant's duty consisted in opening the store early in the morning; and it was ascertained afterwards that during the interval which elapsed before the arrival of his employer he habitually treated himself to many more nips from the bottle than were good for him. This foolish habit, coupled with what he took with customers in the course of the day, had in the end completely unhinged a brain that by nature, perhaps, was not particularly robust.

One afternoon a report ran along the Strand that Harvey's assistant was in a state of collapse. Rushing to the store with the others to see what was the matter, I found the young fellow lying on the stone-flagged floor in shirt and trousers, apparently in a fit, panting and contorting himself as if in great pain. His moist, fever-stricken eyes, dilated and starting from their sockets, wore a wild, fiery, inhuman look, enhanced by the thin, bubbling, brownish froth oozing from between his lips. All at once, rearing up, with one hand on the ground and the other outstretched, pointing to the wall, he screamed—

"Do you see that spider? There, there he goes! Take him away! Kill him! There! There—!"

And with extended forefinger he followed the course of the tarantula, which in the insane imagination of a disordered brain he saw creeping up the wall. Some of the onlookers laughed a brutal laugh. There was no spider. In the hope of relieving the poor wretch, we turned him over on his side to make him look in another direction. But it was all the same. Wheresoever his glance alighted, there he saw the tarantula. The fanciful vision of that venomous insect scaling the wall clung to him, look where he would. When Dr. Heïdenstam arrived he pronounced the writhing figure on the flagstones to be a raging lunatic. There was nothing to be done for him, said the medicine man; he was suffering from an acute attack of delirium tremens; and so it proved. The young fellow expired, exhausted, in the evening, after most atrocious agony, amidst the tins of lobster and bully beef, the beer and whisky, the rum and gin, still raving of that imaginary spider which had struck terror into his being.

The only bottled beer one saw at the commencement of the occupation bore the familiar label Bass and Co., which I have come across in all kinds of outlandish places. The charge for an ordinary quart was 1s. 6d., whilst 6d. was asked for a glass of lager beer; but an enterprising man soon posted a notice outside his store announcing that he intended retailing Bass at 4d. the glass, and he was as good as his word. Eventually the price of a glass of beer went down to 2½d., above which it should never have risen, for the extra ½d. amply provided for carriage and duty. All provisions had gone up threefold; and yet a good fowl, one of the descendants of those brought out by the followers of the lion-hearted Richard, could be bought for a little over 1s., while the best meat, which was not good, cost 4d. per lb. Bread was dearer than it should have been, but all kinds of vegetables might be had for a trifle. A lad would sell you twelve Barbary figs, and peel them, so that you should not prick your fingers, for ld., and while Cyprus wine was 2d. a bottle, the price of great bunches of purple grapes did not exceed l½d. the pound.

In the intensely hot summer months those who were wise ate considerably less meat at their meals than they would have done in a more temperate clime. I well remember a capital salad that often formed my lunch, and which I recommend to my readers. Take half a dozen salt anchovies, wash and fillet them; five or six tomatoes cut in fours; as many onions sliced, and two or three hard-boiled eggs. Mix the whole in a bowl along with a dressing of oil, lemon juice in place of vinegar, pepper, and salt, and then sprinkle some chopped chervil over the top.

Henry S. King and Co. brought out the first printing press, and issued the first newspaper, *Cyprus*, a sort of double-headed enterprise, half English and half Greek, but the latter was not a translation of the former, nor the former of the latter. This curious news-sheet had two editors, absolutely independent of one another, a certain Mr. Palmer, who I believe also contributed to the *Times*, being responsible for the English, and a M. Constantinides for the Greek. But the Greek editor knew not a word of our language, nor did the English editor understand the tongue of the modern Hellene, and it was not long before the pair had a nice game together.

The Cypriots are a discontented lot of people, ever on the growl. Before the occupation was six weeks old they imagined that they had some cause for complaint against the new order of things, and Constantinides promptly took up the cudgels for them in that half of Henry S. King and Co.'s Anglo-Greek newspaper which no Englishman could understand. But one day a Government interpreter revealed what was going on to Mr. Killerby, who lost no time in instructing Palmer to take the offensive on behalf of the British. This Palmer did with vigour, and thereby drew down upon his head the wrath of the indignant Greek. The controversy thus commenced, continued week by week with ever-increasing violence, to the amazement of the few who could read both languages; and an example was provided, unique perhaps in the annals of journalism, of two editors abusing one another in different languages in the columns of the same print.

At length Constantinides had to leave the office, and *Cyprus* thenceforth became all English. But the Greek editor did not long remain out of collar. An Italian named Mascalchi, financed by a Catholic Cypriot, having imported some printing plant, including both Greek and Roman characters, Constantinides found shelter at this new establishment, where he started a newspaper of his own called the *Néon Kition*, which for some years was the mouthpiece of Cypriot discontent. But as the paper was set up entirely in Greek, the editor and the Cypriots had all the fun to themselves.

Palmer was a remarkably tall, lean man, with a face as red as a boiled lobster, a neck like that of a crane, and quite as crimson as his visage. He dressed in a suit of white duck having a button-up-to-the-throat jacket. The absence of a high collar which, owing to the heat, would have been uncomfortable, made his neck look all the longer; whilst the immaculate whiteness of his attire gave additional warmth to the fiery ruddiness of both neck and visage, and a tall bell-shaped helmet increased his height.

This scribe, in the end, got himself into trouble over some exceedingly ungallant remarks that he ventured to print in *Cyprus* concerning a couple of very handsome and smart young ladies from Smyrna, who had come to the island with their father, an English merchant of high position in those parts, just then engaged in some contract business with the Government.

Maybe Palmer held similar views in regard to ladies' attire to those of Viscountess Harberton; perhaps he also considered it more decorous for our revolted daughters to cover up their shoulders and expose their legs, in bloomers, to the public gaze, than the reverse. Anyhow, he took exception to the height of the frocks worn at an evening party by the two pretty young ladies, and made comments on the subject that were considered quite unwarranted. A few days afterwards, strolling down White Street, he was surprised to receive a perfect avalanche of blows on the back of the head, dealt with a big stick; and, turning round, found himself face to face with the cousin of the young girls. The whole affair was threshed out in the Police Court at the Konak, and ended in the assailant being fined £5 and costs. Shortly after this rumpus Palmer left the island, more on account of the newspaper venture proving a failure, like almost every other commercial undertaking in our luckless new possession, than for any other reason.

Mr. Killerby now added the editorship of *Cyprus* to his other duties, but it was not long before he found that editing even this small print occupied much more time than he could afford to give. It was then that he approached me with the suggestion that I should take over the work, but under his supervision, because, as Henry S. King and Co. were Government agents, and I a sort of firebrand, he was anxious that nothing likely to offend those in authority should by any chance creep into the paper.

I accepted the offer, and at once went into harness. I found an Armenian gentleman, a M. Alexander Sarafian, in charge at the *Cyprus Press* in Printing House Street, with two or three compositors under him. Sarafian had edited a paper in Turkish at Constantinople, but, having had the temerity to criticise the Government, had got into trouble with the Censor. Being a Turkish subject they did not mince matters with him. Banished first of all to Tunis, he had, after a lapse of time, returned to Stamboul; but falling again into the clutches of the Turkish authorities he had been shipped off to Syria. It was while there that news reached him of the British occupation of Cyprus; and, managing to evade the vigilance of the police, he had embarked on board a steamer for Larnaca to seek fortune under our rule.

We had now settled down in the island. The fleet had left us; almost the whole of the troops had been withdrawn, after being terribly racked by fever; nearly all the immigrants had gone, many selling their effects to help to pay their voyage home; several merchants had closed their doors, and to the general relief most of the boozing dens, along with the Music Hall in the Bazaar, had shut up shop. The rush to Cyprus had been a spree, a beanfeast over the water, a spree that had run riot while it lasted, among soldiers and sailors and the five or six hundred nondescripts walking about the streets with cash in hand and naught to do. We had had race meetings, gymkhana meetings, horse sales, cricket, gambling, drinking, swearing, dancing, singing, and all the fun of the fair. When it was over, Larnaca, save that a slight increase in population rendered the place a trifle more lively, practically resumed its normal aspect before the act of occupation, which events proved to have been a mere squib in the air.

I had long since given over drawing up petitions, for want of petitioners, and my series of letters to the *Glasgow Herald* had also reached an end. Previous to my arrangement with Mr. Killerby I had been sending occasional telegrams to the *Daily News*, and living on my savings. I had caught the fever, which had clung to me for several months, and reduced me to such a skeleton that most people thought I should leave my bones in the island. This bad state of health was in no small measure due to my own obstinacy in rejecting quinine, and endeavouring to set myself right with infusions made from the young leaves of the lemon-tree, which, nevertheless, did have a beneficial if slow effect, and is the fever remedy invariably resorted to by the Cypriot peasants.

With the fever already on me, I had the unhappy idea of taking a two-roomed cottage out at a village near Larnaca, called Livadia, which I afterwards ascertained to be one of the most unhealthy in the district. Purchasing the useful, simple furniture in the place, from an English overseer on the Famagousta Road, where the culverts were under repair, I settled down to breed poultry, which are remarkably fine in Cyprus. My rustic abode stood in the centre of a plot of rough ground swarming in the spring with daffodils. The swallows came through the open door and window, and built in the corners of the living room. Sometimes, at eventide, when by accident they had been shut out, they would make a rare noise chirping and beating against the woodwork until they were let in. Two or three great rugged-coated lizards, a foot or more long, lived in the eaves, and would occasionally show themselves basking in the sun. The corn-chandler's account was trifling. The poultry roamed hither and thither, picking up what they required. When the harvest had fallen to the reaper's hook and was gathered in, roosters and hens would take themselves off in the early morning, half a mile or more away to glean the grain scattered about the fields, never failing to return at sundown with the master rooster leading the van.

My stay at Livadia, attended as it was by fever and ague, very nearly knocked the life out of me. I shall never forget an event that occurred one day when I lay in dim obscurity, sick almost to death in my bedroom, the shutters closed, but the front door, as well as the one communicating with my bedroom, wide open. I had managed to crawl out early in the morning, but, being overtaken by one of those sharp attacks of fever which visited me daily at the same hour with strange punctuality, I had gone in and slid between the blankets again, there to remain until the access had passed away. All of a sudden my light slumber was disturbed. My landlord, a rough Cypriot peasant, the father of a large family, who came to see me every morning, arrived with a visitor, the village priest, a dark, handsome man, with black beard, delicate skin, classic head and features, but, as I ascertained afterwards, as ignorant and narrow-minded a creature as most of the Greek village clergy are wherever one may chance to come across them. The new arrivals seated themselves, one on either side of my bed, and asked me how I felt. They thought I was going to die. I could hear them saying as much, one to the other in Greek. All at once, as they were talking, I felt the long filbert-nailed fingers of the priest stealthily creeping beneath my bolster. Though fever-stricken and weak, I had all my faculties about me. I was lying on my right side, my left hand close to the pillow. It went under and clutched a sock containing all my worldly wealth, a matter of £18. I drew my property slowly towards me; the priest's hand went slowly back to his sombre garb. No one said anything, and a few minutes later, after an interchange of civilities, my visitors left me.

A day or two later, feeling better, I packed the fowls in baskets, and placing baskets and furniture into one of my landlord's carts, made my way back to Larnaca. I often saw that classic-featured priest afterwards, when I strolled out Livadia way looking for quail or a partridge; and although he always sought to avoid my society, I invariably insisted on dragging him to the village coffee-house, to treat him and enjoy his embarrassment. We never once alluded, at any time, to that sock, heavy with sovereigns and dollars, but he knew very well that I knew, and could never look me straight in the face.

CHARTER II

A CIVIL SERVANT ON SIXPENCE A DAY

When the Anglo-Indian army landed at Larnaca and ran up the Union Jack the Turkish authorities were allowed forty-five days to settle their affairs and clear out of the island; but no modification occurred in the system of government, which was considered excellent in theory, although badly applied.

The High Commissioner found Cyprus divided into six districts, and so he left it; only the Turkish governors and assistant governors were removed, and English officers put in their places as civil commissioners and assistant civil commissioners. Colonel White, of the Royal Scots, the civil commissioner for Larnaca, will always be remembered on account of his unflagging energy. He set to work with a will to clean out the Augean stable. Caring not a straw for existing laws and regulations, he issued edicts of his own which had to be obeyed. No more offal in the Bazaar, no more rubbish-heaps in the streets, which must be repaired as well as lighted with petroleum lamps, and swept and watered day by day. Moreover, they must be named, and an illiterate Maltese painter, who appeared on the scene with brush and paint-pot at the right moment, was engaged to do the work. This poor fellow could hardly read or write; but being proof against ridicule, and possessed of a full measure of perseverance and self-confidence, he gaily took the contract, which afforded him an opportunity to learn how to make big Latin letters at a remunerative rate of pay. Although his efforts were somewhat childlike, they answered the purpose, which, after all, was the chief thing. It was thus that the thoroughfares of Larnaca were decked with such names as Victoria Street, Wolseley Street, Beaconsfield Street, White Street, the Strand, and so on, which they retain to this day. Paddy O'Shea, the special correspondent of the *Standard*, true to the colours of his newspaper, was responsible, I believe, for having "Beaconsfield Chambers" painted in huge black letters on the front of the house where he happened to have a room.

Colonel White was guilty of all sorts of illegalities, for the public weal, which he left to the Government as a legacy to legalise in the best way they were able. Larnaca had no proper slaughter-house. The Colonel decided it must have one promptly. On the beach, a mile from the town, an appropriate site was marked by the skulls of a swarm of Circassians,—men, women and children,—wrecked in an Austro-Hungarian Lloyd's steamer that had gone ashore some time before, and whom the Cypriots, with guns in their hands, had prevented from landing, and had thus doomed to perish in the waves before their eyes. Two French contractors from Egypt, named Thial and Jean, who had worked at the Suez Canal, were at hand. They were ready to build anything, from a slaughter-house to a church or a Government residence. A French butcher named Beynet had arrived from Marseilles. He secured a concession from Colonel White and contracted with the French builders to erect the slaughter-house. Neither of the latter had much cash, but the Anglo-Egyptian Bank was there. They had sent out an agent named Küss, an Alsatian, son of that same Küss, Mayor of Strasbourg, who so distinguished himself during the siege of the fortress in '70. This gentleman's coffers were bursting with gold. Anxious to do business, he opened them to the builders, whom he, moreover, employed to erect premises for the Bank; but in the end the builders got the better of the banker, or rather the buildings did, for the two contractors ultimately left the island poorer than when they came, and the bank lost money. Küss, while acting throughout in an honourable spirit, only succeeded in wasting the funds of the Bank. At last he was superseded by Mr. George Goussio, a remarkable man, who subsequently for many years acted as general manager of the Anglo-Egyptian Bank in the Near East. Küss died prematurely at Marseilles, not long after leaving the island, utterly broken down with disappointment.

But Colonel White got his slaughter-house. To pay for his other improvements he levied taxes on the townsfolk, which was absolutely illegal, but that did not trouble him. He probably foresaw that when the legality of his acts came to be discussed he would be far away, as in fact happened.

When the Colonel became Commissioner of Larnaca, he found a Headman, assisted by a Council of Elders, in charge of municipal affairs. Unable to get along with these worthy people, whose ideas were not in keeping with European notions of urban government, he dismissed them in a body, and in their place appointed Dr. Heïdenstam, whom he invested with the functions of Mayor and Police Magistrate, having authority to levy rates and taxes in the former capacity, and to fine those who neglected to cash up in the latter. In this manner every one in business was made to pay an annual tax of £10, £5, or £2, according to the trade he happened to be engaged in.

A Dane by sire and country, English by his mother—the daughter of one of our Bishops—Heïdenstam had qualified for the medical profession at Paris, and marrying a remarkably pretty Greek girl from the Ionian Islands, had settled down to enjoy connubial felicity in Cyprus, where, at the time of the occupation, he held the position of Health Officer at Larnaca under the Turks. At the moment we landed, being one of the only people able to speak English, Greek, and Turkish, he had proved a perfect treasure to our authorities; and, having an eye to business, had wisely taken advantage of his position to secure the transport contract. This, within a very short space, had yielded a profit of some few thousand pounds, which had enabled "the Doctor," as he was always called, to build a substantial private residence in the European style on the Nicosia road. The balance he invested in mortgages on house property, and practically lost it all; for the Cypriots indebted to him paid neither interest nor principal, and when at length he foreclosed, no one appeared to buy the properties on which his money was secured.

Heïdenstam could speak six languages besides his own, but could not write them all correctly, and among those in which he showed some weakness was English. He required a secretary, and found one in the person of a pleasant, gentlemanly young Jew named Raphael, who had come out from Portsmouth, where his friends followed the trade of tailors.

There were no Israelites in Cyprus previous to the occupation, and it is perhaps not generally known that there are practically none in Greece, or in the Greek Islands. The Jew cannot live among Greeks, they are far too smart for him, just as an Armenian is too clever for a Greek. A good many Jews went to the new British possession in the Mediterranean in the general rush, and those who understood the languages of the Near East easily found employment as interpreters or in the police. One who came from England intending to engage in business died very shortly after his arrival, and the utmost difficulty was experienced in finding him a sepulchre. The orthodox Greeks, who made no difficulty about burying Protestants in their graveyards, would not have him, nor would the Mohammedans, nor the Roman Catholics established in the island since the days of the Lusignans; and the Protestants, at that early period of the occupation, had neither clergy, churches, nor cemeteries. At length one or two co-religionists of the deceased took the body and interred it somewhere near the seashore, where it was half devoured during the night by pariah dogs.

When Raphael persuaded a cousin to emigrate from Portsmouth and open a tailor's shop on the Strand, he resigned his position as clerk to the Municipality and private secretary to the Mayor of Larnaca, and I stepped into his shoes, retiring from the newspaper *Cyprus*, which, my readers will perhaps hardly credit, had been yielding me a weekly wage of no more than ten shillings. Everything went on well so long as the townsfolk continued to pay Colonel White's imposts. When it at last dawned upon them that these exactions were illegal, and, not having been confirmed by any of those Ordinances of the High Commissioner by which the island was governed, could not be enforced, the inhabitants refused to pay any longer, and a general break-up followed.

My post, while it lasted, proved a comfortable one. My pay was £10 a month, as good as £20 at home, and my chief a charming man who met the troubles of life with all the equanimity of a philosopher. I worked with him constantly for three years, writing all his medical and medico-legal reports from his dictation, as well as those on the cattle plague in the island, which were issued to Parliament in the form of Blue Books. I also transacted the business of the Municipality that had to be done in English, whilst exercising a general supervision over everything that took place there, and attending to the

Doctor's English correspondence. Not once during the whole of that period did we have a hasty word, and my connection with Dr. Heïdenstam is one of my most pleasant recollections of a long residence in the Near East. Frequently we were overwhelmed with work; for, apart from the position the Doctor held as Mayor and Police Magistrate, he acted as Medical Officer of the district, and Health Officer of the port. When the cattle disease broke out it became his duty to enforce the regulations, and on quarantine being established against the cholera, he had to see it maintained.

One day, long after the townsfolk had given up paying taxes, Dr. Heïdenstam mentioned to me that a vacancy had occurred in the office of the District Commissioner, which I could fill if I pleased. My salary was several months in arrears, and there appeared no prospect of its being paid. So the Doctor advised me to take this post, and while frankly telling me that it was not worth much, he pointed out that it would be something coming in, pending the settlement of the municipal question. As a matter of fact this question never was settled so long as I remained in the island, although it has been since. Even then the Town Council never had the decency to pay my arrears of salary, although they were perfectly well aware of my whereabouts in Egypt. But no matter, I followed Dr. Heïdenstam's advice, and it was arranged between us that I should give half my time to the District Commissioner and half to the business of the town, which the Doctor continued to direct, although in an inefficient manner, owing to lack of money.

I not unnaturally imagined, when I came to this understanding, that my services under Government would at all events be recompensed with sufficient remuneration to enable me to live and pay for a modest lodging. What was my amazement when, looking over the *Official Gazette* one day, my eye alighted on the announcement that Sir Robert Biddulph, the High Commissioner, who was receiving, with allowances, £6000 a year for administering this wretched little island, three-quarters of which are a barren, uncultivable waste, had been pleased to award me pay at the rate of 6d. a day. I was staggered. Nevertheless I continued to discharge my duties, which, it is only fair to add, were neither arduous nor important, consisting chiefly in entering a summary of the correspondence we received and dispatched in two portly folio registers and making a few copies. I drew, without a murmur, my 3s. a week from Government, and nothing from the Municipality, hoping for an improvement that never came.

The Commissioner for Larnaca at that time was Mr. Claude Delaval Cobham, M.A. He had succeeded Colonel White, and was a much more cautious and law-observing party than his predecessor. Formerly, I believe, he had been a clergyman. Although a very clever man, and a hardworking, painstaking public servant, he was not popular. Having had the misfortune, at some previous time of life, to meet with an accident on a staircase, attended with results similar to those that not very long ago laid the Prince of Wales on a bed of pain, but unable to command the same skillful treatment as was bestowed on the heir to the throne, his knee had remained stiff and bent, so that he walked lame.

No sooner did he show his face at Larnaca than some wag, with a flash of brutal wit, forthwith dubbed him " Dot and carry one." When Mr. Brown, who had played an important part in building the famous breakwater at Alexandria, arrived in Cyprus, with one leg shorter than the other, to take over the duties of Director of Public Works, and was perceived walking along the Strand with Mr. Cobham, the same individual blurted out: "Hulloa ! Dot and carry two."

It was while I was working in the office of the Commissioner for Larnaca that we had the first public execution in the island, an event vividly impressed on my mind. The Cypriots are deft handlers of the knife, which they all carry concealed in the sash girded about their loins, and use indifferently to cut their victuals or disembowel an enemy. At times this ugly weapon is whipped out and plunged into the victim in a mere drunken brawl. At others it plays a fatal part in a cold-blooded assassination at a street corner, in the dead of night—the last act in a love tragedy; an outraged husband buries his blade in Lothario; a brother avenges a dishonoured and abandoned sister. It is never used for mercenary motives. Frequently the corpse alone remains in the road to tell the tale. No one can find out how it came there.

At a wedding feast one Mavro Sava, a Cypriot Greek, taunted by a Turkish Zaptieh about his alleged prowess, proved himself the bravo he was reputed to be, by drawing his knife and laying his tormentor dead at his feet. He was a bad character, half smuggler, half brigand, the chief actor in more than one ensanguined exploit in Greece and Asia Minor. The murder of the Zaptieh was not his first crime, but he was a Cypriot Greek who had killed a Turk, and all Greeks were with him. A rough-looking customer himself, swarthy as an Arab—hence his name Mavro Sava, the Black Sava—he had two delightfully pretty sisters at service with Richard Mattei, a large Italian landowner, who had the mortification to see all his property, which an uncle had wrung from the Cypriots by usury, swallowed up by the Ottoman Bank, to which he had become deeply indebted. Macro Sava bolted after slaying the Zaptieh, and for three weeks hid in a sort of cavern at the bottom of somebody's garden. At last friends were detected taking him food. Captured, tried, and convicted, he was sentenced by Judge Phillips to be hanged. But the Cypriots made such a stir in the matter, petitioning the Queen, the High Commissioner, Lady Biddulph, that in the end the sentence was commuted to one of penal servitude for life.

At Limassol one autumn evening at dusk, an officer in the police, a Jew, had a knife plunged into his back as he walked along the esplanades. The blow must have been dexterously dealt, for the blade found the victim's heart. He had just time to stagger to a drinking saloon, kept by an Englishman named Craddock, where he dropped down dead in the bar before he could utter a word. This crime was set down as a husband's vengeance, but although the police made every effort to bring the author to justice, they never succeeded.

There were other similar cases equally mysterious; for the Cypriots know how to keep their own counsel in such matters. But a singularly horrible affair, attended by no mystery whatever, was that of two brothers who had been together to the market at Larnaca, where they had drunk more deeply than wisely of the thick potent black wine of the country, and of that maddening mastic. I knew them well. They lived at a village about a couple of miles from the cottage I had occupied at Livadia. Both had wives and families. Returning late at night to their village, after the drinking bout in town, they quarrelled on the road, and one did the other to death with his knife. The murderer, an inoffensive peasant under ordinary circumstances, was tried, convicted, and sentenced to the extreme penalty. No power on earth could save him, for the authorities, exasperated at the frequent use of the knife, had determined to make an example.

I shall never forget the scene at the public execution in one of the courtyards of the Konak. A lofty scaffold with a cross beam on two perpendicular poles had been erected in a corner, and made to come on a level with a first floor window for the convenience of the authorities. The public had been admitted to the courtyard, and when the place allotted them was filled, the great ponderous gates were swung to and bolted.

At the bottom of the yard stood a row of low black huts, and on the door of one these being opened by Paul Blattner, the police lieutenant from Nicosia, the poor manacled wretch, and the priest who had been comforting him in his last moments, emerged upon the scene. Without assistance, with the awful gallows whereon he was about to dangle facing him, this Cain who had slain his Abel in a fit of drunken aberration, shuffled along in his high boots and baggy breeches, as fast as ever he could go to his doom, bellowing for mercy at every step, and with a flood of burning tears streaming down his face. It was as much as Blattner with his two Zaptiehs, and the priest in black gown, stove pipe hat, long beard and flowing hair, who followed at his heels, could do to keep up with him without breaking into a trot. The condemned man had to ascend a lofty flight of stairs to reach the noose at the end of the journey, but even that effort he accomplished without assistance, still bellowing as he took one step after another, and approached nearer and nearer to eternity. A Welshman named Phillipson, a ganger on the roads, acted as executioner for the nonce, and Cobham, who had superintended all the arrangements with minute care, performed the duties of Sheriff.

When the hideous drama was at an end, and the gates thrown open to let out the crowd had closed again; when the sun had set, and Cain had been cut down, there came wailing and gnashing of teeth outside the jail, and a hammering at the wicket for admission. It was a poor old hag, a forlorn mother, poverty-stricken and wretched, who had lost her two boys by violent deaths within so short a space, clamouring, for the hanged man's clothes.

The Cypriots are an excitable people, ever ready to join in manifestations when their leaders persuade them they have a grievance calling for redress. In the early years of British occupation they were prone to send home petitions direct to the Secretary of State, the Prime Minister, even to Her Majesty the Queen, until made to understand that such communications must be forwarded through the High Commissioner; and they would often subscribe together to defray the expense of a long telegram, embodying what they had to say, so that their complaint might reach its destination with the utmost speed.

On one occasion when I happened to be in the Bazaar at Larnaca in the early afternoon, I was amazed to witness all the shopkeepers, apart from the Maltese, suddenly putting up their shutters, as if panic-stricken, but without any apparent cause. Inquiring the reason, it was only vouchsafed to me that some one had shaved off a priest's beard.

Shutters up and shops secured, the townsfolk gathered in their hundreds, and along with their leaders, some pettifogging lawyers educated in France, proceeded to the residence of the District Commissioner to protest. On a deputation being received by Mr. Cobham, it transpired that Captain Scott-Stevenson, of the Black Watch, was the cause of all this hubbub. Captain Scott-Stevenson, one of the best and most popular of our District Commissioners, had been placed in charge of Kyrenia. He resembled Colonel White, in so far as energy went, and I do not think either that he cared very much about the too scrupulous legality of his acts, so long as he put things straight in his district, which was one of the most picturesque in the island.

At the time we took Cyprus over from the Turks a wiseacre had succeeded in convincing the authorities that the place had formerly been covered with forests, which the ruthless Turk, for the purpose of greedy gain, had cut to the ground. As a fact Cyprus was never covered with forests. Sir Samuel Baker and other authorities have settled that point beyond question. But under the erroneous belief that a vast range of forests had formerly existed, and that owing to their destruction the island annually became a prey to drought just at the time when it should have rained, the Government enacted an Ordinance absolutely forbidding the felling of all trees whatsoever, whether private or public property. So that no one might cut down a tree, even in his own garden, without exposing himself to prosecution.

In face of this rather Draconian law, an obstinate Cypriot priest, with the usual unkempt beard and dirty greasy locks falling about his shoulders, deliberately, after repeated warnings to desist, felled a tree standing on his own property. Brought before the Commissioner, he had no defence save that he maintained he had a right to do as he pleased with what belonged to him, and was sentenced to a short term of imprisonment. So far nothing could be said; but when Scott-Stevenson got the recalcitrant priest into jail, and had his unclean hair and beard shorn off, in accordance with prison regulations then in force, unaware that the hirsute adornment of a priest of the orthodox Catholic faith is practically sacred, he fairly roused Cypriot ire; and to appease it, the High Commissioner had to issue special orders that if any more priests got locked up, their hair and beards were to be left alone.

I had been working for some little time in the office of the Commissioner for Larnaca when that gentleman took himself off on a three months' holiday to Europe, and I found myself transferred to the Assistant-Commissioner, Mr. Robert Fisher, barrister-at-law, at the Konak, where I became clerk to the Larnaca division of the High Court of Justice, whilst continuing to inscribe an epitome of the correspondence with the Chief Secretary to Government into the two big folio registers, and to draw no more than 6d. a day.

This Mr. Fisher was a quiet, inoffensive gentleman, who never uttered one word more than was necessary. He had formerly been a captain in the London Scottish Rifle Volunteers. It was Zealous Zachariah Williamson who dubbed him Balukchi Pasha, a Turkish word signifying fisherman, and this nick-name clung to him. Fisher had brought out a fox-terrier, which became as fat as a sucking-pig. This canine pet followed his master everywhere,—to the office, where he curled himself under his writing-table and snored; to the Tamiz Court, where he was provided with a chair beside his owner, who solemnly sat in justice, flanked by the Turkish Cadi on one side, and by his dog and a Greek Cypriot judge on the other.

I had nothing to do with the Tamiz Court, which under the Turks had been the Court of the Cadi, but I sometimes peeped in there to enjoy the fun. Fisher, who understood neither Turkish nor Greek, was equally ignorant of the Ottoman law. But anxious to do his best, he insisted on all the proceedings being translated to him by his Armenian interpreter. Whilst he and the Armenian conversed together in English the case under investigation went on, the Cadi speaking Turkish, the Cypriot judge Greek, the lawyers addressing the Court together in the language of the Ottomans, and wrangling one with the other in that of Hellas, the litigants ever and anon bursting into angry protestations, the witnesses and audience keeping up a constant chatter in English, French, Italian, German, Greek, Arabic, Turkish, and Armenian. Suddenly, amidst this babel of tongues the piebald dog, disturbed in his sleep, would give three or four sharp snappish barks. Then rising and having a good shake before seating himself on his haunches, he would emphasise his canine expression of discontent by a loud peal of barking which he interspersed with playful growls, and not until his master had several times ordered him to lie down would he curl himself up on his chair and resume his slumber. Amidst such entertaining surroundings was meted out some of that " substantial justice," against which I have naught to say, that Sir Garnet Wolseley on leaving the island proudly proclaimed the Cypriots had enjoyed during his term of administration.

Fisher acted as Registrar to the Larnaca Division of the High Court of Justice, which gave us both a fair share of work. Collier, the representative of a Liverpool firm, proved one of our most troublesome litigants. He was well known in the Near East. At the time of the Crimean war, being in business at Smyrna as sardine packer, he had taken a contract from the British Government to supply our forces with some thousands of tins of these dainty fish in oil. But the firm had not much capital and less credit. Without cash no oil could be had. At one moment, having run out of money and oil alike, and it being necessary to dispatch a rather large parcel of sardines to the seat of war, Collier found himself in a fix. But, equal to the occasion, he had the tins of fish soldered up without their unctuous bath, and shipped them to the Crimea, where they arrived in a very lively condition. Collier, after this, was not likely to be forgotten in those parts, and the story of his sardines deprived of oil was still a standing joke among English residents in Smyrna at the time he resided in Cyprus.

Collier was an Irishman who had never been able to free himself of the brogue. Of middle height, spare in figure, he had white hair, white moustache, and a countenance as florid as that of Palmer, the editor. Notwithstanding his advanced age, which must have been over sixty, he still possessed a vast measure of vitality. He had some knowledge of music, was very poetical, and in society proved himself an amiable, urbane man. Not so in the High Court of Justice.

On and off he would burst into our office like the blast of the blizzard; and, apparently beside himself with indignation at something that had occurred in connection with a case he had in hand, would threaten to address the Chief Secretary to Government, the Judicial Commissioner, the High Commissioner, to petition even Her Majesty the Queen, and in that respect he resembled the Cypriots. But he did not get much change out of Fisher, on whom his bombastic irritability took no effect. Fisher hardly spoke, never turned a hair, but sat still and listened with imperturbable countenance. I, over in my corner among the registers, did the same. When this rampant litigant at the end of his gas had retired, Fisher, calm as a cucumber, would simply look at me and smile, and without exchanging a word we resumed our work.

The last I heard of Collier came from a mutual friend, later on, in Egypt, who had met him aboard a steamer bound for the Levant. He was then accompanied by a young wife, whom he was taking out to Smyrna "to begin life afresh!" said he. What, oh!

Another pleader, whose wrongs afforded some diversions, was a gentleman with a name that escapes me, but who was always known by the motto "Carpe Diem," which figured at the top of his notepaper. Led away by Zealous Zachariah Williamson's glowing accounts of the island, of the nuggets of gold washed down by the mountain torrents, the groves of Paphos strewn with precious stones, the coal mines awaiting only pickaxe and shovel to yield untold wealth, this enterprising speculator, in a moment of imprudent enthusiasm, had consigned to the author of these fairy tales a quantity of goods that were to sell at a hundred per cent or more profit. But when the long-delayed day of reckoning at length arrived, it was to find, to his amazement, a balance on the wrong side of his account, the outcome of expenses wherein that conveniently elastic item "storage" played no unimportant part. If Carpe Diem failed on this occasion to act up to his motto and enjoy the present himself, he placed it within the reach of his agent to do so.

The unfortunate speculator's advent in Cyprus to thresh the matter out only resulted in good money going after bad, and in causing a deal of commotion that very unjustly amused the gallery at his expense. Every one sided with Zealous Zachariah, which no doubt was very wrong. A public meeting, attended by many Cypriots ever ready for an opportunity to protest, even passed a resolution condemning the undue interference of Mr. Commissioner Cobham in the matter, and a telegram was dispatched to England proclaiming what had happened. Judgment none the less went for the plaintiff, which proved poor satisfaction, for he could not recover. Zealous Zachariah had sold his business, and a steamer arriving just about the time the court gave its decision, he considered it convenient to sail by her for some other shore.

When Mr. Cobham returned from leave, he wanted to know what had been going on in his absence. Without a word to me, a Zaptieh was sent down to the office at the Konak, after I had left for the day, to fetch the registers. I resented this off-hand treatment. I was beginning to think I had seen quite enough of the Government service on 6d. a day, as also of Mr. Dot-and-Carry-One, Balukchi Pasha, and the Piebald Dog. So on arriving at the office in the morning, and finding under what circumstances the registers entrusted to my care had been removed, I simply put on my hat again and, without a word to any one, walked off to the Municipality Building, and thus severed my connection with the government of Cyprus.

CHAPTER III

"THE CYPRUS TIMES"

A few days after leaving the Government service at the Konak, I and a Cypriot named Nicolas Rossos started a tiny news-sheet, on which we had the courage to bestow the name of *Cyprus Times*. This Nicolas Rossos, whose father had just died, was a man of some small means. A naturalized Frenchman, he had studied the Code Napoléon in France, and at Aix had passed his examination as advocate. But the French, although pleased enough to confer degrees on properly qualified foreigners, entitling them to practise as doctors, advocates, chemists, veterinary surgeons, and so forth, are the reverse of anxious that these gentlemen should set up in business in the country that has thus befriended them. When they receive their diplomas they are generally politely informed that it is understood to be a matter of courtesy for them to go and exert their talent elsewhere.

So Nicolas Rossos had returned to the land of his fore-fathers to follow his profession and make a position. In that view he sought, first of all, to wrest the mantle of Mayor from the shoulders of Dr. Heïdenstam and clothe himself therewith, intending afterwards to court election as native member of the Legislative Council, and I believe he ultimately succeeded in both these aims, although long after I left the island. To further his ends he considered he required a newspaper in which to set forth his ideas in English, so that the authorities might read them and thus be made aware of the existence of his interesting personality. Unfortunately the only languages he understood were Greek and French; but when he imparted his ideas to me and persuaded me to join him the difficulty was solved, and the *Cyprus Times* saw the light of day.

I did not get on very well with Rossos. He proved conceited, pettifogging. He would dictate long-winded articles to me in French which I had to write down in English, wherein the few points were so involved in verbosity as to be practically lost. But he particularly tried my patience when commenting on some judgment delivered in one of the courts, he would expatiate on his respect for the *chose jugée*, just like the partisans of the military party in the Dreyfus case.

The *Cyprus Times* was a weekly sheet, printed at the office of Henry S. King and Co., like *Cyprus*. We had not brought out more than a few numbers of the new venture when it came to my knowledge that my partner was in treaty for the purchase of *Cyprus*, which, I ascertained, could be secured for £50. I made a bid to that amount, and arranged with Heïdenstam to advance me the cash, but there was some delay, and when I finally took the money down to the late Mr. Turner, who had succeeded Henry S. King and Co. and Mr. Killerby, and started on his own account as Turner and Co., it was to ascertain that paper and printing-office had been sold to Mr. Nicholas Rossos and paid for. When asked, a few days later, what I would take a week to express the views of M. Nicholas Rossos in English in the *Cyprus* and see them through the press, I declined to entertain the idea at any price; and the former arrangement between that gentleman and myself having by now been brought to an end, I took the *Cyprus Times* to Mascalchi's printing-office, where Constantinides had found hospitality with his *Néon Kition*, and started on my own account.

I was now a newspaper proprietor as well as editor, and I went frankly into opposition. As it was necessary to have a policy, mine became—government by civilians, and military men back to their regiments. This policy, not very long afterwards, was the one adopted by the Home Government when the island was placed under the Colonial Office. My paper was entirely dependent on its subscribers; but although I worked in the interests of the Cypriots, comparatively few gave me their support. All Cypriots are poor, and not unnaturally careful of the little money they possess. Deeming it extravagant to subscribe to more than one paper, they had to choose between Constantinides, Rossos, and me, with the result that they showed a preference for the *Néon Kition*, which they could read themselves but their rulers failed to understand, to either of the two English sheets, which were double Dutch to most of the Cypriots, although intelligible enough to those placed in authority over them—a distinction that these simple people did not seem to perceive.

To meet the deficit on the newspaper and earn a living I conducted small cases in the High Court, and when Dr. Heïdenstam received orders from the District Commissioner to dispense with my services at the Municipality as punishment for the tone I had adopted in the *Cyprus Times*, I set up as a schoolmaster and taught English, while continuing to act as the doctor's private secretary at his house. I had several youths who came to me three days a week to take private lessons of an hour, and I held a class twice a week for those not sufficiently well off to pay the fee of private pupils. One of the young gentlemen to whom I thus imparted a knowledge of the English language bore the historic patronymic of Dandolo. His father always maintained that the family was descended from that illustrious Venetian stock, which had given four Doges to the famous Republic on the Adriatic, and his one ambition was to see his son raise the fallen fortunes of the house. With that object in view he worked and slaved. An adroit bookmaker, he paid me for his offspring's English instruction in shoe-leather, an arrangement that never gave me cause for dissatisfaction. Another of my pupils was Mr. George Goussio, who had superseded Mr. Küss at the Anglo-Egyptian Bank. I gave Goussio lessons at his office, and we formed a friendship that continued later on in Egypt. A Greek of Chalcis, famous for its roses, he had joined the insurrection of '78, and had lost an eye fighting round Volo, at the same time as I was in the Othrys mountains.

The house in which I rented two unfurnished rooms was a good one, although somewhat dilapidated, owing to the owner's poverty. The worst part of the building proved to be the flat roof, emerald in spring, with an abundance of green barley and grass that afforded pleasant pasture to some goats and an Easter lamb, which were hoisted up there every morning and taken down at night. This roof, in autumn and winter, as is not uncommon in Cypriot houses until they get thoroughly soaked, after the scorching summer, sometimes, but not always (happily for me) let in rain. Frequently have I been aroused from sleep by a thin stream of water falling through my mosquito curtain on to my face or bed-clothes, and on some occasions have had to move my bed more than once during the night before finding a weather-tight corner.

Sir Robert Biddulph, the High Commissioner, lately governor-general of Gibraltar, enjoyed no greater popularity than Mr. Cobham. He had done nothing. His appointment was entirely due to Court influence; but in order to place some gilt on the gingerbread it was pointed out that Sir Robert was a first-class financier; although where his ability in finance appeared I was never able to discover.

To saddle this wretched, impoverished island with a governor who drew £6000 from its exchequer was placing it on a level with Malta and Gibraltar, without giving it even a shadow of the same advantages in naval and military establishments; for while the former was entirely wanting, the latter consisted merely of some companies of infantry and a few details. It had no fortifications and no naval port.

Why we ever took possession of Cyprus has always been a mystery, unless it was to prevent the French going there. But can it be possible that our pet, practical statesman, the Earl of Beaconsfield, was influenced in his action by some poetic idea to restore to these realms that territory which our bold warrior King Richard, of the lion heart, conquered by the sword, and for which he only actually encashed one-third of the sum he agreed to sell it for, so that the purchase was really never completed? The island could not be made a naval station; for apart from having no port, it has no natural inlet that could be converted into a port, where disabled warships might enter and refit in security. Famagousta, the ancient Salamis, named after the famous island on the southern coast of Attica, though great under the Venetians, has been useless since powerful artillery was invented. Even if the old harbour, good enough for Venetian galleys, were cleaned out and placed in an efficient state, a hostile fleet appearing in the offing could still shell and burn every vessel that sought refuge there, without the least trouble, since the only protection seawards is a low ridge of rocks. Gibraltar, Malta, Suda Bay, are very different places. Had we planted our flag on the heights of Suda, and left Cyprus alone, we should have had a white elephant the less, and gained a splendid harbour and a strategic point in the Mediterranean of inestimable value, commanding the entrance to the Aegean Sea.

As to the vaunted fertility of Cyprus, three-quarters of the island are an arid waste where practically nothing grows. In the remaining quarter the vine flourishes among other produce, and if more extensively cultivated, the thick, black, heavy Cyprus wine which finds a ready sale at Marseilles and Montpellier would bring wealth to the husbandman. The corn crop invariably fails, owing to want of rain at the proper moment; for while it pours in torrents in autumn and winter, spring and summer are accompanied by prolonged drought, so that the grain rarely attains sufficient weight to make it a marketable produce. I remember negotiations at one time being opened with a firm at Liverpool for the sale of a quantity of barley, which it was proposed to give to the tramway horses in place of oats, but the affair fell through because the sample proved far too light, and this was no exceptional instance. All Cypriot grain is light. The farmer, to his dismay, can grow naught else. Moreover, the cotton is as bad as the grain. If Cyprus was one of the granaries of Rome, as we are asked to believe, it must have been under very different circumstances from those that at present prevail. Two things are essential to bring prosperity to the place: a much more extensive cultivation of the vine, and storage of water as in India and elsewhere, so as to permit artificial irrigation when required. A further advantage would be reaped by sinking wells, and using the Egyptian water-wheel as suggested by Sir Samuel Baker, for the island has no rivers, and in summer its few water-courses are practically dry. Cyprus exports carobs, cocoons, sponges, antiquities, terra umbra, and a few good mules which are useful in our little wars, and it is a pity they are not more extensively bred. It also produces remarkable Queen bees, famous throughout the universe.

No doubt Cyprus has profited by British rule. Roads have been made and kept in repair, an efficient postal service exists; and while the various towns are connected by telegraph, the island is in communication with Europe by cable. Public security has been maintained and justice distributed with an impartial hand. The inhabitants have free Municipalities as well as a voice in legislation. But they are not content. Possibly the root of dissatisfaction lies in their poverty, and in their disappointment at England not having filled their pockets with untold gold. To improve their position would involve the outlay of a very large sum of money in irrigation works, which long since should have been undertaken; for Cyprus, deprived of the water-can, will ever remain in its present deplorable state. A standing grievance is the heavy expenditure on administration; but as the island costs the British Exchequer £30,000 a year to govern, without any advantage whatsoever being derived from the enjoyment of that responsibility, it may fairly be said that Great Britain herself bears any extravagance that may be shown in remunerating an efficient staff of Government servants.

A more just complaint, and one that has always been a sore point with the Cypriots, is the enormous tribute of £93,000 paid annually to Turkey. Up till now it has cost them nearly two millions sterling to be free of Turkish misrule. To put the matter plainly, they are paying £93,000 a year for their liberty, which they ought to think cheap at the price. True, the burden is heavy, particularly when one thinks of all that might have been done with those bagful of sovereigns in improving the island, but it must be borne. A thing the Cypriots cannot be made to understand, in regard to this item, is that these £93,000 do not actually go into the pocket of the Turk, but into the coffers of the Bank of England, where they help to make up the interest due on the loan contracted by Turkey at the time of the Crimean War, and guaranteed by France and England. Should this amount fail to find its way into the hands of the old lady in Threadneedle Street, City, we should have to make it good, and Cyprus would then be costing us something like £123,000 a year, which would be rather an expensive luxury.

I had not been conducting the *Cyprus Times* very long before I had gathered round me several contributors, one a brilliant, charming lady whose portrait I give here. Some of these good people, out of sheer deviltry, kept me supplied with tit-bits of information that delighted my readers. I thus ascertained that Sir Robert Biddulph's nickname at college was *Foxey*, "because he was so sly," added my informant. Some one else wrote, under ban of the strictest secrecy, that part of the duties of Sir Robert's aide-de-camp, Lieu. George Wisely, R.E., consisted in going down into the kitchen at Government House every Monday morning to weigh out the week's tea and sugar for the cook. This Lieutenant Wisely was a very goody-goody young man, the son of an English parson at Malta. He was also handsome, and having made the acquaintance of one of the Miss Curries, when she visited the island along with her father, Sir Donald, aboard their yacht, he had the good fortune to captivate and marry her.

An invaluable contributor was Mr. H. P. Roach of Lincoln's Inn, Barrister-at-law. He was engaged in an action against the Government to recover a very large sum of money as damages for the non-performance of a contract entered into with an Italian to supply them with a quantity of eucalyptus trees, and eventually he won his case. Roach was a poet and a victim to dyspepsia. Once at Cairo, later on, when I asked him to dinner, he astounded the waiters and every one else at the restaurant by calling for a crust of bread and a glass of water, and to my dismay confined himself to that frugal fare. Dyspepsia was not the only thing that troubled him. He was in love, but his fond passion failed to meet with reward. On one occasion, perhaps exasperated with the unrelenting creature, he brought me these cruel lines with the request that they might be printed in the *Cyprus Times*, and I complied—

To——

On Sunday afternoon you're fair,
And who could then be scorning,
Your wealth of powder and false hair,
Rouge, paint, and such adorning?
But what a disappointment rare,
Awaits on Monday morning!

One week the paper, quite in keeping with the cry for civilian government by civilians, came out with some extracts from an imaginary burlesque, which it was gravely announced would shortly be produced by amateurs at Larnaca. The curtain rose, it was explained, to discover the Government House at Nicosia surrounded by a few dead eucalyptus stumps. A number of officers in uniform advance to the footlights, all in a row and arm in arm, and there sing the following chorus to the tune of the popular Jingo song of the day—

We don't want to go, by Jingo! if we do,
We like the work,
We love the Turk,
But more we like the screw,
We might have been at Candahar, Basuto, or Zulu,
But we all prefer to bungle on in Cyprus!

Just about that time great fuss was being made over a new baby at Government House. So the scene changed to the drawing-room at the High Commissioner's residence.

Colonel Falk. Warren, R.A., Chief Secretary to Government, has called to see Sir Robert, who enters the apartment with the new baby in his arms. Colonel Warren, brother to Sir Charles Warren, in those days wore a monocle, which rarely left the orbit of his right eye. The Colonel advances and pats the baby's cheeks, but the little pet, instead of laughing, is frightened at the strange countenance, and bursts out screaming. Thereupon Sir Robert sways the infant to and fro, singing the while—

Hush-a-by,
Do not cry,
Baby, baby rare.

He won't bite,
Though a fright,
With his perspicacious stare.

These playful skits, though received at the Government Residence in high dudgeon, brought down the house. I sold out and had to reprint. If the *Cyprus Times* still cost me money, the pupils increased in number, so that the paper served as a sort of advertisement for the classes. My plan was to endeavour to interest the young idea in what he was learning. To break the dull monotony of grammar I set him to read aloud from books likely to amuse him. All were intensely patriotic, so I put Dandolo on the history of Venice, and Demetrius on that of ancient Greece, and thus made them look forward to their English class as a pleasure rather than a task.

When an immense multitude of locusts swooped down on the island the High Commissioner, while endeavouring to exterminate the invaders by means of ingenious traps invented by the late M. Richard Mattei, had the unhappy idea of supplementing his efforts in this direction by putting into force an old Turkish law compelling every inhabitant to deposit in the hands of receivers appointed by the authorities, a specified quota of locusts and locusts' eggs, and an Ordinance was promulgated accordingly.

Roach and I at once took the matter in hand, and pointed out in the *Cyprus Times* that this Ordinance, in so far as British subjects were concerned, was illegal; for the reason that it compelled them to perform forced labour against their will and subjected them to the corvée system; and we maintained that whilst we could be obliged by Ordinance of the High Commissioner, acting with the advice of the Legislative Council, to pay taxes to meet the expense of exterminating the locusts, we could not legally be made to go out into the highways and byways to collect locusts and their eggs.

This contention on our part gave rise to a good deal of discussion and amusement. Many persons at first adopted our view, but all gave way in the end and supplied their quota of the enemy. Not so Roach and I. We would neither collect nor would we purchase the locusts and their eggs, which for that matter were on sale in the Bazaar at so much per measure, the price fluctuating in accordance with the supply and demand. Finally we were summoned and fined after having a field-day at the Konak. Refusing to pay the fines and costs, our goods were seized. When visited by that genial officer of Police, Paul Blattner, who courteously left it to us to say what article we would prefer to have taken in satisfaction of the judgment, we both spontaneously indicated our dress suits, which caused some hilarity. Swallow-tails, waistcoats, and pants were sold by the Greek auctioneer in the Bazaar; and two Cypriots, who had the meanness to acquire the garments, afterwards had the courage to strut about in them, as proud as peacocks, at evening parties in Larnaca and Nicosia.

I forget exactly how it happened that I entered into correspondence with that highly capable and hard-working public servant, Colonel Falk. Warren, Chief Secretary to Government, who is now in Vancouver's Island. I think I approached him with inquiries concerning the extermination of the locusts, and I know he supplied me with some very interesting statistics. When we had exchanged a few letters, the Colonel mentioned that he was moving to Trōōdos for the summer, and that if I happened, at any time, to be that way, he would be pleased to see me.

Not very long afterwards I paid a visit to the monastery of Trōōditissa, where Sir Samuel Baker put up to write his interesting book on the island, and I called on the Colonel on my way back to Limassol. I passed the night at his house, and in a long chat we had together, he urged me to moderate the tone of the *Cyprus Times*; promising me, if I would do so, that on the return from England of the High Commissioner then imminent, he would talk the matter over with him, and endeavour to obtain some support for me, from the Government of the island. I confess I was becoming tired of fighting, and I undertook to do as the Colonel wished.

Next morning, after breakfast, when Colonel Warren had taken himself off to his office under canvas in a pine grove hard by, I was buttonholed by his good wife. We were seated in easy chairs on the terrace, a rugged ledge of rock overlooking forest, mountain, and ravine.

"Listen!" said she. "My husband is perfectly sincere in what he has been saying to you, but do not put too much faith in his hopes. I know as a positive fact, and I tell you, that if Sir Robert Biddulph, or Mr. Cobham, could work you some terrible harm, ruin you irretrievably, neither of them would hesitate to do so."

"Well, Mrs. Warren," I replied, "I am not a bit surprised. Give and take, you know." And whilst thanking her for the warning, I told her I intended, all the same, to act on her husband's suggestion and see what came of it.

Returning to Larnaca I published a conciliatory article in the ensuing issue of the *Cyprus Times*, and was forthwith denounced by Constantinides in the *Néon Kition* as a traitor who had gone over to the Government, some very harsh remarks being made anent my visit to the Chief Secretary at Trōōdos by this mouthpiece of a public that had given me no tangible support. I answered never a word, but in the next number of the *Cyprus Times* printed this doggerel—

Know'st thou the land where the cholera morbus
Will take a man off in a very short time?
Know'st thou the land where the price is enormous
Of soap, and the use of fresh water a crime?
Know'st thou the land where the fever's sublime?
Where there's always a jumble 'twixt old and new time;
Where the damsels are fair as their own terra umbra,
And powderless, false-hairless, only in slumber;
Where the European Levantine's a glorious brute,
And the voice of the slanderer never is mute;
Where the Consuls are gods in a very small way,
Where you die in the night and are buried next day,
Where the people won't work for their masters' small pay?
'Tis the island of Cyprus, the land of the sun,
The hardest baked pie crust he ever beamed on.
Oh! false as the sapphires in Paphos' sweet dell,
Are the vows its maids make and the fables they tell.

These lines raised quite a hornets' nest about my ears. The Cypriots went mad. I was privately informed that a select party of palikaris would waylay and give me a beating, but nothing came of it. Just at that time I had to run down to Limassol to be present at the opening of a new iron jetty by the High Commissioner, who had returned to the island from England. No sooner did I arrive there than I was challenged to fight a duel by the choleric editor of the Limassol Greek newspaper, the *Alethia*. I was unable to oblige him, because, as I pointed out, if I killed him, as I might do, it would be murder, according to English law, and I should be hanged, which was much too great a risk to incur. The same evening I was very nearly mobbed by a band of a hundred rascals, ready for anything, got together by the leaders of public opinion. These ruffians marched up to the coffee-house beside the sea where I had been sitting with Dr. Heïdenstam, to hoot and perhaps lynch me, for all I know. But the police were on the alert. A young lieutenant named De Jongh had come, in great anxiety, to warn me of what was going on, and to entreat me, in order to avoid a disturbance, to quit the coffee-house ere it was too late. I reluctantly consented to beat a retreat and, accompanied by Dr. Heïdenstam, passed through the mob without recognition, on my way down the road, as they advanced up it to find me. That night I was constrained to accept the hospitality of Mr. Brayshaw, the popular manager of the Eastern Telegraph Company in Cyprus, who had a bed made up for me on a divan at the office.

When I returned to Larnaca, my printer, the Italian Mascalchi, influenced by his Cypriot partner, peremptorily demanded a settlement of his account, notifying me that the next number of the paper would not appear unless the amount due was at once forthcoming.

For some time previous to all this, I had been watching events in the Valley of the Nile, where the Arabist movement appeared to be making steady progress. A recent mail from Egypt had brought me a letter from a Mr. Andrew Victor Philip, the Editor of the *Egyptian Gazette*, with which I had been exchanging. This small English news-sheet, then appearing twice a week at Alexandria, was owned by a trio of Englishmen—Mr. Philip, who had previously been in business as a stationer; Mr. Charles Royle, an able barrister, author of *The Egyptian Campaigns*, now Judge at the Native Court of Appeal at Cairo; and Mr. C. F. Moberly Bell, an insurance agent and correspondent of the *Times*, who has since become well known as manager of that paper.

Mr. Philip's letter contained the MS. of a lampoon on Arabi Pasha in French doggerel, with the request that I would have it printed and forwarded with all secrecy to an address he gave me at Alexandria. The copies had been struck off, and were lying there, on my table, awaiting the mail. When I received my printer's ultimatum I determined to deliver them myself. I had then had quite enough of Cyprus one way and another.

CHAPTER IV
THE HOME OF MIRACLES

When I had made up my mind to turn my back on Cyprus, it did not take me very long to prepare for my departure. I was able to take passage on board the first steamer that left for Egypt after the *Cyprus Times* had ceased to appear, and reached Alexandria at the end of a few hours' run. We were then about the middle of February '82.

Baker 1879

Sir Samuel White Baker, a well-traveled author of numerous books on Africa and Ceylon passed winter, spring, and summer completing a trip through every district of Cyprus. He was accompanied by Lady Baker, his hunting dogs and rifles, and cook and drivers hired in Cyprus. Two gypsy vans were shipped from England and specially rigged for comfortable sleeping quarters around the island. After difficulty negotiating the narrow streets of towns and the rugged countryside, they were left in Nicosia and their oxen replaced by mules and camels.

In his 479-page volume, *Cyprus as I saw it in 1879*, London: Macmillan and Co., 1879, he provides observations of each district and of the people, climate, geography, villages and cities. He remarks on irrigation, taxation, wages and agriculture. The appendix includes meteorological data, census data, and extensive revenue and expenditure estimates. Of interest are his observations of his lengthy stay on the monastery grounds at Trooditissa.

CHAPTER I.
ARRIVAL AT LARNACA.

. . . The left flank of Larnaca was bounded by a small Turkish fort, absolutely useless against modern artillery; upon the walls the British flag was floating. We landed upon the quay. This formed a street, the sea upon one side, faced by a row of houses. As with all Turkish possessions, decay had stamped the town: the masonry of the quay was in many places broken down, the waves had undermined certain houses, and in the holes thus washed out by the action of water were accumulations of recent filth. Nevertheless, enormous improvements had taken place since the English occupation. An engineer was already employed in repairing the quay, and large blocks of carefully faced stone (a sedimentary limestone rock of very recent formation) were being laid upon a bed of concrete to form a permanent sea-wall. The houses which lined the quay were for the most part stores, warehouses, and liquor-shops. Among these the Custom House, the Club, Post Office, and Chief Commissioner's were prominent as superior buildings. There was a peculiar character in the interior economy of nearly all houses in Larnaca; it appeared that heavy timber must have been scarce before the town was built, as the upper floor was invariably supported by stone arches of considerable magnitude, which sprang from the ground-floor level. These arches were uniform throughout the town, and the base of the arch was the actual ground, without any pillar or columnar support; so that in the absence of a powerful beam of timber, the top of the one-span arch formed a support for the joists of each floor above. In large houses numerous arches gave an imposing appearance to the architecture of the ground floors, which were generally used as warehouses. Even the wooden joists were imported poles of fir, thus proving the scarcity of natural forests. The roofs of the houses were for the most part flat, and covered with tempered clay and chopped straw for the thickness of about ten inches. Some buildings of greater pretensions were gaudy in bright red tiles, but all were alike in the general waste of rain-water, which was simply allowed to pour into the narrow streets through innumerable wooden shoots projecting about six feet beyond the eaves. These gutters would be a serious obstacle to wheeled conveyances, such as lofty waggons, which would be unable in many cases to pass beneath. The streets are paved, but being devoid of subterranean drains, a heavy shower would convert them into pools. Foot passengers are protected from such accidents by a stone footway about sixteen inches high upon either side of the narrow street. Before the English occupation these hollow lanes were merely heaps of filth, which caused great unhealthiness; they were now tolerably clean; but in most cases the pavement was full of holes that would have tested the springs and wheels of modern vehicles.

I had heard, prior to leaving England, that hotels, inns, &c., were unknown in Larnaca; I was, therefore, agreeably surprised on landing, to find a new hotel (Craddock's) which was scrupulously clean, the rooms neatly whitewashed, and everything simple and in accordance with the requirements of the country.

The miserable reports in England respecting the want of accommodation, and the unhealthiness of Cyprus, had determined me to render myself independent; I had therefore arranged a gipsy travelling-van while in London, which would, as a hut upon wheels, enable us to select a desirable resting-place in any portion of the island, where the route should be practicable for wheeled conveyances. This van was furnished with a permanent bed; shelves or wardrobe beneath; a chest of drawers; table to fall against the wall when not in use, lockers for glass and crockery, stove and chimney, and in fact it resembled a ship's cabin, nine feet six inches long, by five feet eight inches wide.

I had another excellent light four-wheeled van constructed by Messrs. Glover Brothers, of Dean Street, Soho: both these vehicles had broad and thick iron tires to the wheels, which projected 5/8 inch upon either side beyond the felloes, in order to afford a wide surface to deep soil or sandy ground without necessitating a too massive wheel.

The vans with all my effects had left London by steamer direct for Cyprus, I therefore found them, upon my arrival from Egypt, in the charge of Mr. Z. Z. Williamson, a most active agent and perfect polyglot; the latter gift being an extreme advantage in this country of Babel-like confusion of tongues.

I was now prepared to investigate Cyprus thoroughly, and to form my own opinion of its present and future value.

The day after my arrival I strolled outside the town and exercised my three spaniels which had come out direct from England. The dogs searched for game which they did not find, while I examined the general features of the country. About three-quarters of a mile from the present town or port are the remains of old Larnaca. This is a mere village, but possesses a large Greek church. The tomb of Lazarus, who is believed to have settled in Cyprus to avoid persecution after his miraculous resurrection from the grave, is to be seen in the church of St. George within the principal town.

* * * * *

In ancient days the shallow harbour of Cittium existed on the east side of modern Larnaca; whether from a silting of the port, or from the gradual alteration in the level of the Mediterranean, the old harbour no longer exists, but is converted into a miserable swamp, bordered by a raised beach of shingles upon the seaboard. The earth has been swept down by the rains, and the sand driven in by the sea, while man stood idly by, allowing Nature to destroy a former industry. All the original harbours of the country have suffered from the same neglect.

There was little to be seen in the neighbourhood. The site was pointed out where the troops were encamped in the tremendous heat of July in the close vicinity of the swampy ground, upon pestiferous soil, and the usual tales of commissariat blunders were recounted. Close to the borders of this unhealthy spot, but about twenty feet above the level of the lowest morass, stands the convent belonging to the Sisters of Charity, which includes a school, in addition to a hospital. Great kindness was shown by these excellent ladies to many English sufferers, and their establishment deserves a liberal support from public contributions.

I walked through the bazaar of Larnaca; this is situated at the west end of the town near the fort, close to which there is a public fountain supplied by the aqueduct to which I have already alluded. Brass taps were arranged around the covered stone reservoir, but I remarked a distressing waste of water, as a continual flow escaped from an uncontrolled shoot which poured in a large volume uselessly into the street. Within a few yards of the reservoir was a solitary old banian tree (*ficus religiosa*), around which a crowd of donkeys waited, laden with panniers containing large earthen jars, which in their turn were to be filled with the pure water of the Arpera springs.

Although the crowd was large, and all were busied in filling their jars and loading their respective animals, there was no jostling or quarrelling for precedence, but every individual was a pattern of patience and good humour. Mohammedans and Cypriotes thronged together in the same employment, and the orderly behaviour in the absence of police supervision formed a strong contrast to the crowds in England.

The Mosque being within a few feet of them, the Mussulmans could perform their ablutions at the threshold. Around the font, women were intermingled with a crowd of men and boys. The girls and lads were regular in features and good-looking, though dirt and torn clothing of various gaudy colours gave a picturesque, but hardly an attractive, appearance to the group. The bazaar was entered at right angles with the quay; the streets were paved with stones of irregular size, sloping from both sides towards the centre, which formed the gutter. Camels, mules, bullock-carts and the omnipresent donkeys thronged the narrow streets, either laden with produce for the quay, or returning after having delivered their heavy loads. The donkeys were very large and were mostly dark brown with considerable length of hair. In like manner with the camels, they were carefully protected by thick and well stuffed packs, or saddles, and were accordingly free from sores. They appeared to be exceedingly docile and intelligent, and did not require the incessant belabouring to which the ass of other countries is the victim. Large droves of these animals, each laden with three heavy squared stones for building, picked their way through the narrow streets, and seemed to know exactly the space required for their panniers, as they never collided with either carts or passengers.

The shops of the bazaar were all open, and contained the supplies usually seen in Turkish markets—vegetables, meat, and a predominance of native sweets and confectionery, in addition to stores of groceries, and of copper and brass utensils. An absence of fish proved the general indolence of the people; there is abundance in the sea, but there are few fishermen.

An hour's stroll was quite sufficient for one to form an opinion of Larnaca. A good roadstead and safe anchorage offer great advantages, but until some protection shall be afforded that will enable boats to land in all weathers Larnaca can never be accepted as a port. There is shoal water for a distance of about two hundred yards from the shore, which causes a violent surf even in a moderate breeze, and frequently prevents all communication with the shipping. The quay was in many places undermined by the action of the waves, and it would be necessary to create an entirely new front by sinking a foundation for a sea-wall some yards in advance of the present face. There would be no engineering difficulty in the formation of a boat-harbour, to combine by extensive pile-jetties the facility of landing in all weathers. A very cursory view of Larnaca exhibited a true picture of its miserable financial position. The numerous stores kept by Europeans were the result of a spasmodic impulse. There was no wholesome trade; those who represented the commercial element were for the most part unfortunates who had rushed to Cyprus at the first intelligence of the British occupation, strong in expectations of a golden harvest. The sudden withdrawal of the large military force left Larnaca in the condition of streets full of sellers, but denuded of buyers. The stores were supplied with the usual amount of liquors, and tins of preserved provisions; none of the imported articles were adapted for native requirements; an utter stagnation of trade was the consequence, and prices fell below the cost of home production. The preceding year had been exceptionally sickly; many of the storekeepers were suffering from the effects of fever, which, combined with the depression of spirits caused by ruined prospects, produced a condition of total collapse, from which there was only one relief—that of writing to the newspapers and abusing the Government and the island generally.

CHAPTER II.

THE GIPSY-VANS ENCOUNTER DIFICULTIES.

My gipsy-van was not of doubtful character. I had purchased it direct from the gypsies in England, and it had been specially arranged for the Cyprus journey by Messrs. Glover Bros. of Dean Street, Soho, London. It had been painted and varnished with many coats both inside and out, and nobody, unless an experienced gipsy, would have known that it was not newly born from the maker's yard. Originally it had been constructed for shafts, as one horse was considered sufficient upon the roads of England, but when it arrived in Cyprus it appeared to have grown during the voyage about two sizes larger than when it was last seen. As the small animals of Larnaca passed by, where my lovely van blocked up the entire street, and forced the little creatures upon the footpath, they looked in comparison as though they had just been disembarked upon Mount Ararat from the original Noah's ark, represented by the gipsy-van! The Cypriotes are polite, therefore I heard no rude remarks. The Cypriote boys are like all other boys, therefore they climbed to the top of the van, and endeavoured by escalade to enter the windows. On one occasion I captured *half a boy* (the posterior half) who was hanging with legs dangling out of the window, his "forlorn-hope" or advance half vainly endeavouring to obtain a resting-place upon vacuity within (as the fall slab-table was down). I had no stick; but the toes of his boots had imprinted first impressions upon the faultless varnish. What became of that young Cypriote was never known.

Even in Cyprus there are municipal laws, and now that the English are there they are enforced; therefore my huge van could not remain like a wad in a gun-barrel, and entirely block the street. A London policeman would have desired it to "move on" but—this was the real grievance that I had against Larnaca —the van *could not "move on*," owing to its extreme height, which interfered with the wooden water-spouts from the low roofs of the flat-topped houses. This was a case of " real distress." My van represented civilisation: the water-spouts represented barbarism. If a London omnibus crowded with outside passengers had attempted to drive through Larnaca, both driver and passengers would have been swept into—I have not the slightest notion where; and my van was two feet higher than an omnibus!

I determined that I would avoid all inferior thorough-fares, and that the van should pass down Wolseley Street, drawn by a number of men who would be superior in intelligence to the Cypriote mules and be careful in turning the corners.

I did not see the start, as a person with an "excess of zeal" had started it with a crowd of madmen without orders, and I was only a late spectator some hours after its arrival opposite Craddock's Hotel. It rather resembled a ship that had been in bad weather and in collision with a few steamers. How many water-spouts it had carried away I never heard. The fore-axle was broken, as it appeared that in rounding a corner it had been dragged by main force upon the curbstone about sixteen inches high, from which it had bumped violently down. It had then been backed against a water-spout, which had gone completely through what sailors would term the "stern." One shutter was split in two pieces, and one window smashed. Altogether, what with bruises, scratches, broken axle, and other damages, my van looked ten years older since the morning.

Fortunately among the Europeans who had flocked to Cyprus since the British occupation was a French blacksmith, whose forge was only a few yards from Craddock's Hotel, where my wrecked vessel blocked the way. I had a new fore axle-tree made, and strengthened the hinder axle. I also fitted a bullock-pole, instead of shafts, for a pair of oxen; the springs I bound up with iron wire shrunk on while red-hot. I took out the stove, as it was not necessary, and its absence increased the space; and I inserted a ventilator in the roof in place of the chimney. When repaired, the van looked as good as new, and was much stronger, and well adapted for rough travel. The only thing it now wanted was a *road*!

The highways of Cyprus were mere mule-tracks. The only legitimate road in existence was of most recent construction, which represented the new birth of British enterprise, from Larnaca to the capital, Nicosia (or Lefkosia), about twenty-eight miles. The regrettable paucity of stone-hammers rendered it impossible to prepare the metal, therefore huge rounded blocks, bigger than a man's head, had been thrown down for a foundation, upon which some roughly broken and a quantity of unbroken smaller stones had been spread. Of course there was only one method of travelling upon this route with the gipsy-van: this was to avoid it altogether, but to keep upon the natural soil on the side of the newly-made level.

My second van was most satisfactory, and was light in proportion to its strength and capacity. This was arranged specially for luggage, and was entirely closed by doors at either end, which were secured by bolts and locks. Above the luggage, and about two feet six inches below the roof, a sliding deck formed of movable planks afforded a comfortable sleeping-berth for a servant. In the front a projecting roof sheltered the driving seat, which was wide enough to accommodate four persons. I had fitted a pole instead of shafts, as public opinion decided against mules, and it was agreed that oxen were steadier and more powerful for draught purposes. After a careful selection, I obtained two pairs of very beautiful animals, quite equal in size to ordinary English oxen, for which I paid twelve shillings *per diem*, including the drivers and all expenses of fodder. I also engaged the necessary riding mules, as the vans were not intended for personal travelling, but merely for luggage and for a home at night. Our servants consisted of Amarn (my Abyssinian, who had been with me eight years, since he was a boy of nine years old in Africa), a Greek cook named Christo, who had served in a similar capacity upon numerous steamers, and a young man named Georgi, of about twenty-one, who was to be made into a servant. This young fellow had appeared one day suddenly, and solicited employment, while we were staying at Craddock's Hotel; he was short, thickset, and possessed a head of hair that would have raised the envy of Absalom: in dense tangle it would have defied a mane-comb. George had a pleasant expression of countenance which did not harmonise with his exterior, as his clothes were in a ragged and filthy condition, his shoes were in tatters, and trodden down at the heel to a degree that resembled boats in the act of capsizing; these exposed the remnants of socks, through the gaps of which the skin of his feet was exhibited in anything but flesh-colour. It is dangerous to pick up a "waif and stray," as such objects of philanthropy frequently disappear at the same time as the forks and spoons. In reply to my questions, I discovered that Georgi was in fact the "prodigal son;" he had not been leading the fast life of that historical character, but he had left his home in Mersine (on the coast of Asia Minor) owing to an unfortunate disagreement with his father. In such domestic estrangements, rightly or wrongly, the fathers generally have the best of the situation, and Georgi, having left a comfortable home (his father being what is called "well to do"), had taken ship, and, like many others, had steered for Cyprus, where he arrived unknown, and quickly experienced the desolation of an utter stranger in a foreign town. Georgi became hungry; whether he had sold his good clothes to provide for the coats of his stomach I cannot say, but the rags in which he first appeared to me were utterly unsaleable, and few people would have ventured upon an engagement with so disreputable a person. However, I liked his face; he could speak Turkish and Arabic fluently: Greek was his mother-tongue, and he had a smattering of French. I sent for the tailor, and had him measured for a suit of clothes to match those of Amarn—a tunic, waistcoat, knickerbockers, and gaiters of navy-blue serge. In a few days Georgi was transformed into a respectable-looking servant, with his hair cut.

We left Larnaca on the 29th of January. A native two-wheeled cart conveyed the tents and superabundant baggage. The oxen made no difficulty, and the gipsy-van rolled easily along. An enterprising photographer, having posted himself in a certain position near the highway, suddenly stopped our party, and subsequently produced a facsimile, although my dogs, who were in movement, came out with phantom-like shadows. These useful companions were three spaniels—"Merry," "Wise," and "Shot;" the latter had a broken foreleg through an accident in the previous year, but he was an excellent retriever and could work slowly. The others were younger dogs, whose characters were well represented by their names; the first was an untiring, determined animal, and Wise was a steady hunter that would face the worst thorns, and was a good retriever.

This party was now in movement, and I intended to make a preliminary *détour* from the Nicosia route to visit the springs of Arpera, about eight miles distant, which supply the town of Larnaca.

* * * * *

After a short march of three miles we arrived at the steep banks of the river a mile above the village of Arpera. The bed of this river was about forty feet below the level of the country, and here our first real difficulty commenced in descending a rugged and precipitous track, which at first sight appeared destructive to any springs. The gipsy-van was conducted by the owner of the fine pair of bullocks; but this fellow (Theodoris) was an obstinate and utterly reckless character, and instead of obeying orders to go steadily with the drag on the wheels, he put his animals into a gallop down the steep descent, with the intention of gaining sufficient momentum to cross the sandy bottom and to ascend the other side. If the original gipsy proprietor could have seen his van leaping and tossing like a ship in a heavy sea, with the frantic driver shouting and yelling at his bullocks while he accelerated their gallop by a sharp application of the needle-pointed driving prick, he would have considered it the last moment of his movable home. I did the same; but, to my astonishment, the vehicle, after bounding madly about, simply turned the insane driver head over heels into the river's bed, and the bullocks found themselves anchored in the sand on the opposite side. Glover Brothers' blue van was driven by a fine fellow, Georgi, who was of a steady disposition; and this very handy and well constructed carriage made nothing of the difficulty. Georgi was a handsome and exceedingly powerful man, upwards of six feet high, of a most amiable disposition, who always tried to do his best; but the truth must be told, he was stupid: he became a slave to the superior intellect of the hare-brained rascal of the gipsy-van. Why amiable people should so frequently be stupid I cannot conceive: perhaps a few are sharp; but Georgi, poor fellow, had all in bone and muscle, and not in brain . . .

CHAPTER III.

ROUTE TO NICOSIA.

Having proved that any further progress west was quite impracticable by vans, I returned to the new main road from Larnaca, and carefully avoiding it, we kept upon the natural surface by the side drain, and travelled towards Dali, the ancient Idalium.

The thermometer at 8:00 A.M. showed 37°, and the wind was keen. The road lay through a most desolate country of chalk hills completely barren, diversified occasionally by the ice-like crystals of gypsum cropping out in huge masses. In one of the most dreary spots that can be imagined the eye was relieved by a little flat-topped hut on the right hand, which exhibited a sign, "The Dewdrop Inn." The name was hardly appropriate, as the earth appeared as though neither dew nor rain had blessed the surface; but I believe that whisky was represented by the "Dewdrop," and that the word was intended to imply an invitation, "Do-drop-in." Of course we dropped in, being about an hour in advance of our vans, and I found the landlord most obliging, and a bottle of Bass's pale ale most refreshing in this horrible-looking desert of chalk and thistles that had become a quasi-British colony. This unfortunate man and one or two partners were among those deluded victims who had sacrificed themselves to the impulse of our first occupation, upon the principle that "the early bird gets the worm." Instead of getting on, the partners went off, and left the representative of the "Dewdrop" in a physical state of weakness from attacks of fever, and the good industrious man with little hope of a golden future . . .

On the following morning, after a slight shower, we started for Dali. The narrow valleys were more or less cultivated with vines, and about three miles from the halting-place we entered the fertile plain of Dali. This is about six miles long, by one in width, highly cultivated, with the river flowing through the midst. As far as we could see in a direct line groves of olives, vineyards, and ploughed land, diversified by villages, exhibited the power of water in converting sterility into wealth.

I always make a rule that the halting-place shall be at a considerable distance from a village or town for sanitary reasons, as the environs are generally unclean. All travellers are well aware that their servants and general *entourage* delight in towns or villages, as they discover friends, or make acquaintances, and relieve the tedium of the journey; therefore an antagonistic influence invariably exists upon the question of a camping-ground. It is accordingly most difficult to believe the statements of your interpreter: he may have old friends in a town to which you believe him to be a stranger; he may have the remains of an old love, and a wish to meet again; or he may have a still more powerful attraction in the remembrance of an agreeable *café* where he can refresh himself with liquor, revel in cigarettes, and play at dominoes. It is therefore necessary to be upon your guard when approaching a town, which should be looked upon as the enemy's camp.

My amiable bullock-driver, the big Georgi, had always assured me that "game abounded in the immediate neighbourhood of Dali;" of course I knew that the happy hunting-ground contained some special interest for himself. Upon arrival on the outskirts

I ordered the vans to pass on the outside of the town, and I would seek a camping-place up-stream. Instead of this I was assured that we should pass through the town, and find a lovely grove of olive-trees by the river-side, the perfection of a halting-place. For the first time I now discovered that Georgi's wife and family lived in Dali, and that he was not such a fool as he looked.

In a few minutes we were descending a lane so narrow that the gipsy van only cleared the walls of the houses on either side by three or four inches. This lane had been paved centuries ago with stones of all sizes, from a moderate grindstone to that of a foot-ball. When people had wished to build a new house, they had taken up a few stones to make a foundation; the street was a series of pitfalls filled with mud and filth, including miniature ponds of manure-coloured water. The surface appeared impassable; the projecting water-spouts from the low roofs stuck out like the gnarled boughs of trees. Here was a pretty mess!—all because Georgi's wife was in town. It was impossible for anything larger than a perambulator to turn, and as the springs yielded to the uneven ground, the van bumped against the walls of the houses and threatened destruction. "Halt!" was the only word, and as the drag-shoe was on the wheel, we stopped. At this moment of difficulty a priest and some old women appeared with earthen vessels smoking with burning olive-leaves; they immediately passed the smoke beneath the nostrils of the oxen, then around the van, and lastly ourselves. At the same time some good young women threw orange-flower water over my wife and myself from pretty glass vases with narrow necks as a sign of welcome. The incense of the priests was supposed to avert the "evil-eye" from the gipsy van and our party. I felt much obliged for the good intention, but I did not mind the "evil eye" so much as the water-spouts. In my experience of travelling I never met with such kind and courteous people as the inhabitants of Cyprus. The Dali population had already blocked the narrow streets from curiosity at our arrival, and soon understanding the cause of our dilemma, they mounted the house-tops and tore off the obstructing water-spouts; where these projections were too strong, they sawed them off close to the eaves. A crowd of men pushed the van from behind, and guided the oxen, while others assisted by digging up the large paving-stones that would have tilted it against the house-walls. In this manner we arrived without serious accident upon the bank of the river which ran through the town. There was an open space here which was crowded with women and girls, who, with feminine curiosity, had assembled to see the English lady. Among these was the prettiest young woman I have seen in Cyprus, with a child in her arms. Her large blue eyes and perfect Grecian features were enhanced by a sweet gentle expression of countenance. She seemed more than others delighted at our arrival. This was Georgi's wife!—and I at once forgave him for deceiving us and yielding to the natural attraction of his home.

We were not quite out of our difficulty. Several hundred people had assembled, and all spoke at once, raising their voices in the hope that we should understand their Greek better than if spoken in a moderate tone: (why people will speak loud if you do not know their language I cannot understand:) but as we were utterly ignorant of their meaning we were not confused by their differences of opinion respecting our direction. It ended in our crossing the stony bed of the river, through which a reduced stream only a few inches deep flowed in the centre, and having with difficulty gained the opposite bank a hundred yards distant, we soon arrived in a sort of natural eel-trap formed by a narrow avenue of gigantic olive-trees, the branches of which effectually barred our progress and prevented the vans from turning.

A temporary loss of temper was a natural consequence, and having ridden in advance for about half a mile, I returned and ordered a retreat. We took the bullocks out, and by hand backed the wheels, until by shovels and picks we could clear a space for turning. We then recrossed the river, and disregarding all native advice, struck into the country, and halted near a small grove of olives close to the new English road to the military station "Mattiati."

* * * * *

There was no object in prolonging my visit to Dali; the tombs of ancient Idalium had already been ransacked by the consuls of various nations; and had I felt disposed to disturb the repose of the dead, nominally in the interests of science, but at the same time to turn an honest penny by the sale of their remains, I should have been unable to follow the example of the burrowing antiquarians who had preceded me; a prohibition having been placed upon all such enterprises by the English government.

It is supposed that Idalium is one of the largest and richest treasuries of the dead in Cyprus. For several centuries the tombs had been excavated and pillaged in the hopes of discovering objects of value. The first robbers were those who were simply influenced by the gold and other precious ornaments which were accompaniments of the corpse; the modern despoilers were resurrectionists who worked with the object of supplying any museums that would purchase the funeral spoil.

It is a curious contradiction in our ideas of propriety, which are measured apparently by uncertain intervals of time, that we regard as felonious a man who disinters a body and steals a ring from the fingers of the corpse a few days after burial in an English churchyard, but we honour and admire an individual who upon a wholesale scale digs up old cemeteries and scatters the bones of ancient kings and queens, princes, priests, and warriors, and having collected the jewellery, arms, and objects of vanity that were buried with them, neglects the once honoured bones, but sells the gold and pottery to the highest bidder. Sentiment is measured and weighed by periods, and as grief is mitigated by time, so also is our respect for the dead, even until we barter their ashes for gold as an honourable transaction.

The most important object of antiquity that has been recently discovered by excavations at Dali is the statue of Sargon, king of Assyria, 707 B.C., to whom the Cypriote kings paid tribute. This was sent to the Berlin Museum by Mr. Hamilton Lang, and is described in his interesting work upon Cyprus during the term of several years' consulship.

The ruins of ancient cities offer no attraction to the traveller in this island, as nothing is to be seen upon the surface except disjointed stones and a few fallen columns of the commonest description. The destruction has been complete, and if we wish to make discoveries, it is necessary to excavate to a considerable depth; but as all such explorations are prohibited, the subject remains fruitless. General di Cesnola, whose work upon the antiquities of Cyprus must remain unrivalled, describes the tombs as from forty to fifty-five feet beneath the present surface, and even those great depths had not secured them from disturbance, as many that he opened had already been ransacked by former explorers.

On the 7th of February the thermometer at eight A.M. was only 40°. The oxen were put into their yokes, and after a discussion concerning the best route to Lefkosia, it was agreed that Georgi should be the responsible guide, as he was a native of the country . . . Georgi had assured us that no difficulty would delay us between Dali and the high road from Larnaca to Lefkosia, which we should intersect about half-way between the two termini . . .

We passed on our left a large farm that exhibited a wonderful contrast to the general barrenness of the country. The fields were green with young wheat and barley, and numerous *sakyeeahs* or cattle-wheels for raising water supplied the means of unfailing irrigation. I believe this property belonged to Mr. Mattei, and there could be no stronger example of the power that should be developed throughout this island to render it independent of precarious seasons . . .

At about six miles from Dali we struck the road between Larnaca and Lefkosia (or Nicosia). The newly-established mail-coach with four horses passed us, with only one passenger. We met it again on the following day, with a solitary unit; and it appeared that the four horses on many occasions had no other weight behind them than the driver and the letters. With this instance of inertia before our eyes, certain lunatics (or *wise contractors*) suggested the necessity of a railway for twenty-eight miles to connect the two capitals! The mail had an ephemeral existence, and after running fruitlessly to and fro for a few months, it withdrew altogether, leaving an abundant space in Cyprus for my two vans, without the slightest chance of a collision upon the new highway, as there were no other carriages on the roads, excepting the few native two-wheeled carts.

We halted five miles from Lefkosia, where a new stone bridge was in process of construction and was nearly completed . . . We halted for the night at the new stone bridge, which, as usual in Cyprus, spanned a channel perfectly devoid of water. On the following morning we marched to Lefkosia, and passing to the left of the walled town, we reached the newly-erected Government House, about a mile and a half distant, where we received a kind and hospitable welcome from the High Commissioner, Sir Garnet, and Lady Wolseley . . .

The Government House was erected upon one of these flat-topped hills in a direct line about 1900 yards from the nearest portion of Lefkosia. It was a wooden construction forming three sides of a quadrangle. The quarters for the military staff were wooden huts, and the line of heights thus occupied could not fail to attract the eye of a soldier as a splendid strategical position, completely commanding Lefkosia and the surrounding country. From this point an admirable view was presented upon all sides. The river Pedias (the largest in Cyprus), when it possessed water, would flow for about 270° of a circle around the base of the position, the sides of the hill rising abruptly from the stream. The dry shingly bed was about 120 yards in width, and although destitute of water at this point, sufficient was obtained some miles higher up the river to irrigate a portion of the magnificent plain which bordered either side. Sir Garnet Wolseley was endeavouring to put a new face on the treeless surface, and had already planted several acres of the *Eucalyptus globulus* and other varieties on the lower ground, while date-palms of full growth had been conveyed bodily to the natural terrace around the Government House and carefully transplanted into pits. This change was a considerable relief to the eye, and the trees, if well supplied with water, will in a few years create a grove where all was barrenness.

The position of Lefkosia has been badly chosen, as it lies in the flat, and must always have been exposed to a plunging fire from an enemy posted upon the heights. It was fortified in the time of Constantine the Great, but in 1570 the Venetians demolished the old works and constructed the present elaborate fortfications. Although the walls are in several places crumbling into ruins, they are still imposing in appearance, and present a clean front of masonry flanked by eleven bastions, and entered by three gates, those of Baffo, Famagousta, and Kyrenia. The original ditch can be traced in various places, but the counterscarp and glacis have been destroyed; therefore the soil has washed in during the rainy seasons, and to an unpractised eye has obliterated all traces of the former important work. On the other hand, the disappearance of the glacis renders the height of the walls still more imposing, as they rise for thirty or forty feet abruptly from the level base, and at a distance maintain the appearance of good condition.

It is difficult to imagine the reason which induced the Venetians to reproduce Lefkosia after they had demolished the original fortifications; but it is probable that they had already erected the cathedral before the expected Turkish invasion rendered the improved defences necessary. Although in the early days of artillery shell-fire was unknown, both the Turks and Venetians possessed guns of heavy calibre far exceeding any that were used in Great Britain until recent years. The marble shot which are still to be seen in Famagousta are the same which served in the defence of that fortress in 1571. These are nearly eleven inches in diameter, while in the fort of Kyrenia the stone shot are still existing, nineteen inches in diameter, composed of an exceedingly hard and heavy metamorphic rock. The long bronze guns which threw the smaller stone shot of from six to eleven inches, would command a far more extensive range than the interval of the heights which dominate Lefkosia; and even should battering have been ineffective at that distance against walls of masonry, the plunging fire would have destroyed the town and rendered it untenable. Traces are still visible of the Turkish approaches when the town was successfully carried by storm on the 9th of September, 1570, after a siege of only forty-five days. The short duration of the attack compared to the length of time required in the siege of Famagousta, which at length succumbed to famine, and not to direct assaults, is a proof of the faulty strategical position of the fortress of Lefkosia.

Most Turkish towns are supplied with water by aqueducts from a considerable distance, which would naturally be cut by an enemy as the first operations. The water is brought to Lefkosia from the hills at some miles' distance, and is of excellent quality; but the wells of the town must be contaminated by sewage, as there is no means of effective drainage upon the dead level of the town, unless the original ditch is turned into a pestilential cesspool. The filth of centuries must have been imbibed by the soil, and during the process of infiltration must in successive rainy seasons have found its way to the wells. In case of invasion, Lefkosia could never have resisted a prolonged siege, as in the absence of the aqueduct a garrison would quickly have succumbed to disease when dependent for a water-supply upon the wells alone. When the Turks captured the city by assault, the population far exceeded that of the present time (16,000), and the greater portion were massacred during several days of sack and pillage. Some thousands of girls and boys were transported to Constantinople. Richard I. of England occupied Lefkosia without resistance, after his victory over Isaac Comnenus.

Although experienced in the illusion of Turkish towns, I was more than disappointed when I visited the interior of Lefkosia. The new Chief Commissioner, Colonel Biddulph R.A., C.B., had already improved certain streets, and the eye was immediately attracted to points which bore the unmistakable stamp of a British occupation; but nothing can be effected in the arrangement of such a town without an unlimited purse and a despotic power. It is almost as hopeless as London in the incongruity of architecture, and the individual indulgence of independent taste, which absolutely dismays a stranger. The beautiful Gothic cathedral of the Venetians has been converted into a mosque by the conquerors, and two exceedingly lofty and thin minarets have added an absurd embellishment, resembling two gigantic candles capped by extinguishers, as though the altar-tapers had been taken for the models. The neighbouring church of St. Nicholas has been converted into a granary. In all Turkish towns the bazaars are the most interesting portion, as they illustrate the commercial and agricultural industries of the country. Those of Lefkosia formed a labyrinth of the usual narrow streets, and resembled each other so closely that it was difficult to find the way. The preparation of leather from the first process of tanning is exhibited on an extensive scale, which does not add to the natural sweetness of the air. Native manufactures for which the town is celebrated, that are more agreeable, may be purchased at a moderate price in the shape of silk stuffs: and a variety of mule-harness, pack-saddles, and the capacious double bags of hair and wool that, slung across the animal, are almost indispensable to the traveller. There were a few shops devoted to European articles which were hardly adapted to the country, and were expensive in a ridiculous degree. The narrow streets were muddy from the recent rain, and the temperature was at 55°, but the inhabitants were sitting at the various *cafés* in the open air smoking and drinking their steaming coffee as though in summer. From natural politeness they invariably rose as we passed by, and at one place I was immediately furnished with a string that I might measure a large vine-stem which during summer must afford a dense shade. I found the main stem of this unusual specimen was twenty-two inches in circumference.

The only agreeable walk in Lefkosia is the circuit of the ramparts, as the high elevation admits of fresh air and an extensive view. From this we looked down upon numerous gardens well irrigated by the surplus water of the aqueduct, and the remarkably healthy orange and lemon trees were crowded with their loads of ripe fruit. There are many good and roomy houses in the town, each furnished with a considerable garden, but as they are surrounded with high walls, it is difficult to form an opinion of their actual dimensions. The house occupied by the Chief Commissioner is large and well constructed, the staircase and landing airy and capacious, with an entrance-hall open at the extreme end and well arranged for the burning climate during summer. All houses are paved with slabs of gypsum, which abound in many parts of the island, and are sold at a remarkably low price, as the blocks laminate, and are divided into sheets of the required thickness with a minimum of labour.

The Turkish Pacha (Rifat) still remained at Lefkosia, as he was responsible for the transfer of various movable property to Constantinople. The interesting Venetian cannon of bronze that were utterly valueless as modern weapons had been conveyed away both from Lefkosia and Famagousta. One of these was a double octagon, or sixteen-sided, and would have been a valuable specimen in the collection at the Tower of London. Many of the curious old Venetian cannon had recently been burst into fragments with dynamite, to save the trouble of moving the heavy guns entire.

There can be little doubt that the prime object in selecting a central position for the capital of Cyprus was a regard for safety from any sudden attack; but upon any other grounds I cannot conceive a greater absurdity. The capital should be Limasol, which will become the Liverpool of Cyprus. Lefkosia is completely out of the commercial route; it is valueless as a military position, and it offers no climatic advantage, but, on the contrary, it is frightfully hot in the summer months, and is secluded from the more active portions of the island. It *is*, simply because it *was*; but it should remain as a vestige of the past, and no longer represent the capital.

There is no position throughout the plain of Messaria adapted for a permanent government establishment as head-quarters. The depressing effect of that horrible landscape, embracing the extensive area from Trichomo and Famagousta to Larnaca, Lefkosia, and Morphu, is most demoralizing, and few Europeans would be able to resist the deleterious climate of summer, and the general heart-sinking that results in a nervous despondency when the dreary and treeless plain is ever present to the view. There is no reason why officials should be condemned to the purgatory of such a station when Cyprus possesses superior positions where the great business of the future will be conducted. The new road already completed from Larnaca to Lefkosia must be carried on to Morphu, and thus connect the north and south extremities of the plain; Kyrenia, sixteen miles distant, must be connected with Lefkosia; branches must then be extended to Kythrea and to Famagousta; and subsequently, from the latter town a direct road must be continued parallel with the south coast to Larnaca. Such roads may be constructed for about £350 per mile at the low rate of labour in Cyprus, considering the presence of stone throughout the district, and their completion will open the entire plain of Messaria to wheeled communication with four ports, to north and south.

CHAPTER IV.

THE MESSARIA.

Having passed a week with our kind hosts, Sir Garnet and Lady Wolseley, at Government House, which formed a most agreeable contrast to the friendless life that we had been leading, the vans once more started *en route* for Kythrea, Famagousta, and the Carpas district. I had hired a good, sure-footed pony for my wife and a powerful mule for myself, and, having given the vans a start of several hours, we followed in the afternoon.

* * * * *

The delay had been great, and the evening was drawing near: we were about seven miles from the upper portion of Kythrea, where we had proposed to camp, and the route was partly across country, to avoid layers of natural rock which in successive ridges made it impossible for the vans to keep the track. Several deep watercourses intervened, which required the spade and pickaxe, and it was quite dark when we were obliged to halt about a mile from Kythrea.

On the following morning Mr. Kitchener, Lieutenant of the Royal Engineers, called at out camp, and was kind enough to pilot us to the celebrated springs about three miles above the village. This able and energetic officer was engaged, together with Mr. Hippersly of the same corps, in making the trigonometrical survey of the Island, and they were quartered in a comfortable house on the outskirts of the town. With this excellent guide, who could explain every inch of the surrounding country, we started upon a most interesting ride.

* * * * *

On the 16th February a painful conviction was established that Cyprus was unfitted for wheeled carriages and springs. Although the plain appeared flat and without natural obstacles, the ground had been completely traversed by deep trenches for the purpose of checking and conducting surface water to the fields in the event of a heavy shower. Our course should have been directly across the plain to intersect the road from Lefkosia to Famagousta, but a glance at the intervening country showed the impossibility of moving the vans through the miles of green crops which were nourished by innumerable watercourses, each of which must be levelled before we could advance. It was therefore necessary to retrace our steps to within a mile and a half of Lefkosia, to the point where the main route branched to Famagousta. This was a great waste of time, but there was no other way of avoiding the difficulty.

* * * * *

The 17th February was a day of considerable bodily exercise, as we arrived at a series of watercourses as deep and broad as military trenches for sapping up to fortress. We had no sooner levelled an embankment, and with great difficulty dragged the vans across, than we encountered a new and similar obstruction. At length we arrived within half a mile of the large village Arshia, which, being well irrigated, opposed a perfect network of barriers in the shape of artificial water-channels. The oxen became disheartened, and the pair which drew the blue van driven by our favourite Georgi determined to strike work just as he was applying the sharp driving prick to their posteriors in ascending a steep bank, through which we had cut a passage from the deep water-course beneath. Instead of keeping a straight course, these pig-headed bullocks made a sharp turn to the right up the incline. Down went one upon its knees in rage and dispair! while round went the other in an opposite direction; crash went the pole in two pieces! and the blue van, having vainly endeavoured to right itself like a lady about to faint when no one is at hand to save her, tottered for a moment, and turned over with a crash that betokened general destruction . . .

On the following morning at daybreak I made a few alterations in the work of the preceding night, and having thoroughly secured the new pole, we started for Kuklia, about thirteen miles distant . . . This was Kuklia, our halting-place, the property of Monsieur Richard Mattei.

Upon arrival at the village we selected a pretty spot upon elevated ground which overlooked the entire country, and from which we could faintly distinguish Famagousta, twelve miles distant.

* * * * *

Having examined the neighbourhood thoroughly, I changed the position of our camp and halted a mile and a half up the aqueduct on the higher side of the village, at a point where the water first issued from its subterranean channel into the conduit of masonry and cement. We thus secured a supply in its original purity, before it should be contaminated by any washing of clothes in passing through the village in an open channel, which from its convenience offered an irresistible invitation. Such a tempting stream, running through a canal upon a broad wall of masonry open to all comers would, in any European country, have been the natural resort of boys, who would have revelled in the freedom of nakedness and the delight of bathing in forbidden waters; but in Cyprus I have never once seen a person washing himself in public. This is not from any sense of indecent exposure, but from their absolute dislike to the operation. I had subsequently in my service a remarkably fine man who was always carefully dressed, and in fact was quite a dandy in exterior, but during the hot weather when he on one occasion saw my Abyssinian Amarn swimming in the sea, he declared that, "rather than bathe, he would prefer to cut his throat."

CHAPTER VII.

KYRENIA AND THE NORTH COAST.

. . . Our camp was daily visited by the women of both Turks and Cypriotes, who came to indulge their curiosity, and my wife had some difficulty in receiving the increasing circle of acquaintance. The want of a female interpreter was at first acutely felt, as the conversation was much restricted when Georgi was the only medium. After a few days this shyness on the part of the Turkish ladies wore off, and Georgi, who was a good, painstaking young fellow, became a favourite; some of these ladies were exceedingly gracious, and took off their veils when in the tent with Lady Baker and myself, and conversed upon various subjects with much intelligence. A few were decidedly pretty; all were studiously clean and well dressed, and they formed a marked contrast in appearance and general style to the Cypriote women; the breed was superior, their hands were delicate and well cared for, but disfigured by the prevalent habit of staining the nails and palms with henna. This plant is called *shenna* by all Turks and Cypriotes, and it is imported from Syria for the purpose of dyeing the hair, and also the feet and hands of Turkish women. It is not a production of Cyprus, as has been erroneously stated by some authors; I made particular inquiries in all portions of the island, and of all classes, upon this subject. The henna, or shenna, is only to be met with in some few gardens, where it is cultivated as an ornamental shrub, in the same manner that the arbutus may be seen in the shrubberies of England. The Turkish women are very particular in dyeing their hair, and use various preparations. The shenna produces a glossy red, which some years ago was the fashionable tinge in England. There is also a small seed of a plant which is prepared by roasting until burnt, like coffee, and then reducing to powder, which is formed into a paste with oil; this is a well-known dye, which turns the hair into a deep black. There was a sudden rush for information when the British occupation of Cyprus was announced to the startled public, and books were rather hurriedly put together, compiled from various authorities, which, although yielding valuable information upon many points, unfortunately perpetuated errors by reproducing erroneous statements. The asserted existence of henna as "an indigenous shrub which originated the name of Cyprus," is an instance of such mistakes, similar to the descriptions of "*heath*-covered surface," when no such plant exists upon the island . . .

On 6th April the general *rendezvous* was the monastery of Bellapais, three and a half miles distant from Kyrenia, in response to the invitation of Major McCalmont, 7th Hussars, on the staff of Sir Garnet Wolseley, who had taken immense trouble for the gratification of his guests by sending tents, baggage, and sleeping accommodation for two nights, in addition to every kind of necessary refreshments.

The route from Kyrenia lay through a country of the brightest shades of green, parallel with the sea, about a mile and a half distant, towards which a succession of deep ravines, which formed river-beds in the rainy season, drained from the mountains at right angles with the path. This side of the Carpas range formed a strong contrast with the parched southern slopes, as every garden and farm was irrigated by water conducted from the mountains in artificial channels, which would otherwise have been absorbed and lost in the wide and stony stream-beds if left to its natural course. We passed through sombre groves of very ancient olives of immense girth; then through villages concealed among a luxuriant growth of fruit-trees, the almonds being already large, and eaten eagerly by the inhabitants, although still unripe. The oranges in heavy crops weighed down the dark green branches, the deep yellow fruit contrasting brightly with the foliage, and the fields of barley that had benefited by artificial irrigation looked like green carpets spread between the neighbouring villages and gardens. Having crossed several deep and wide stream-beds, in one of which the water still trickled in a clear but narrow channel, we commenced a steep ascent among scattered but numerous caroub-trees, which gave a park-like appearance to the country, and upon gaining an eminence we came suddenly upon the view of Bellapais. The monastery was not more than 600 yards distant, but a deep hollow intervened between the opposing heights, which necessitated a circuit of more than a mile before we could reach the village. It would be impossible to select a more beautiful position for a house than the flat summit of the height upon which we stood. The valley at our feet nursed a rippling stream deep in the bottom of a precipitous gorge, the rough sides clothed with myrtles, which now occupied basket-makers who were completing their work upon the spot where they cut their wands of this tough wood in lieu of willow. The fine old Gothic building stood before us on the opposite height upon the extreme edge, surrounded by trees of various kinds, including tall poplars which unfortunately were not yet in leaf. This grand old pile was an impressive contrast to the scene around; there were neat villages with flat-topped roofs of clay, down in the vale far beneath, with the intense blue sea washing the rocky shore: there was also the adjoining village at the rear, occupying the same plateau as the monastery, with its rich gardens and groves of orange-trees; the ruined walls and towers of Buffavento upon the highest crags dominated our position by more than 2,500 feet, and the castle of St. Hilarion stood upon a still higher elevation on the western sky-line behind Kyrenia. There was nothing modern that appeared compatible with the style and grandeur of Bellapais. When this monastery was erected, Cyprus must have been a flourishing and populous country worthy of such architecture, but the present surroundings, although harmonizing in colouring, and in a quiet passiveness of scene, in no way suggested a connection with a past that gave birth either to the Gothic building or to the important castles of Buffavento and St. Hilarion.

Having skirted the amphitheatre upon the monastery level, we passed through an orange-garden and entered the courtyard. The church occupies the right side, and the wall is fronted by cloisters which, supported upon arches, form a quadrangle. A stone staircase ascends from the cloisters to the refectory upon the left; this is in considerable ruin, but must originally have formed an imposing hall. Upon the flat roof of the cloisters, which is perfect for three sides of the quadrangle, a magnificent view is obtained through the fine old Gothic open window, which looks down sheer to the great depth below, and commands the entire country seaward. Descending into the courtyard to the northern cloister we pass two large sarcophagi of white marble. One of these has been elaborately worked in rich garlands of flowers and very grand bulls' heads, together with nude figures, all of which have been much damaged. These sarcophagi have been used as cisterns for containing water, as the tap is still visible. Immediately opposite is the entrance to the great hall, which is in good repair, as a new cement floor was added by the British authorities, with the intention of converting it into a temporary hospital when the troops were suffering from fever at Kyrenia. This hall is 102 feet long and 33 feet wide, with a height of upwards of 30 feet. Nothing can exceed the beauty of the view from the windows of this grand entrance, and in the deep recesses we found Sir Garnet and Lady Wolseley enjoying the scene, while our host, Major McCalmont, welcomed his guests in this splendid vestige of the Knights Templars.

* * * * *

In a ride from our camp to St. Hilarion I carefully remarked throughout the extremely rugged nature of the route that no plot, however minute, had been neglected. In one rocky nook buried among the cliffs was a little cottage, with hanging gardens all terraced by exceedingly high walls, yet affording the smallest superficial area for cultivation. This is discernible with a powerful telescope from the base of the mountains, although to the naked eye it appears like a cluster of barren rocks, tinged with the green of fruit-trees growing from the clefts. If such labour had been expended to produce a picturesque effect the object might be appreciated, but that it should be profitable is beyond belief.

The summit of St. Hilarion is 3340 feet above the sea, from which, in a direct line, it is not three miles distant. The cliffs are quite perpendicular in some places for several hundred feet, and the greatest care has been taken to perch the towers and walls upon the extreme verge. Although from the base of the mountains at Kyrenia the castle appears to occupy an impregnable position, it can be easily approached by one of those rough paths in the rear which can be scrambled over by the Cyprian mules. I am afraid that my willing animal grumbled somewhat at my weight, as it was obliged to halt for breath seven or eight times before we reached a secluded little dell among the mountain tops, from which the path ascended by steep zigzags, directly through the entrance of the old fortification. This narrow dell, hidden among the surrounding crags about 2800 feet above the sea, was entirely cropped with barley, and the people who owned the plot resided in a cave that had been arranged for a habitation for themselves and animals.

On the ridge before we descended into this vale the view was magnificent, as two lofty crags formed a natural frame for the picture within. Between these rugged peaks of silvery grey limestone, tinted by ferruginous rocks with various shades of red and brown, we looked down a precipice beneath our feet upon the blue sea, the snowcapped mountains of Caramania in the distance, and the rich border of our own shores covered with green trees, gardens, fields, and clustering villages: in the centre of which was the fort and harbour of Kyrenia. I could just distinguish our white tents among the caroub-trees far beneath. To complete this superb landscape there should have been a few sails upon the sea; but all was blue and barren, without signs of life. The castle of St. Hilarion stood before us on the left as we faced the sea, and the towers occupied the peaks within less than a quarter of a mile of our position. Continuing along the narrow vale, a mountain-top upon our left hand, which sloped to the path upon which we rode, appeared slightly higher than the extreme summit of the castle peak; the sides of this steep slope were covered with dwarf-cypress and occasional young pines, and it was clear that St. Hilarion would be commanded by a battery upon these heights, or even by the fire of modern rifles. Ascending the zigzag path among blocks of fallen stone, which had rolled from the partially dismantled walls, we entered the gateway, and at once perceived the great extent of the old fortress. The entire mountain-top is encircled by a high wall, flanked at intervals by towers, and crenellated for archers or cross-bowmen. Although the opposite mountain would by artillery fire completely command the inner and lower portion of the works, which we had now entered, the distance would have been far beyond the range of catapults or arrows at the time when the defences were erected. The error appeared to have been in the great area of the fortifications, which would have necessitated a garrison of at least 4000 men, entailing a large supply of provisions and water. There was no trace of a well throughout the works, but I observed the remains of water-pipes in numerous directions, which appeared to have conducted the rainfall into reservoirs. The nearest water was by the caves, occupied by the peasants in the glen, about a quarter of a mile distant. Nothing would have been easier than an investment, which would sooner or later have reduced the garrison to starvation, as the precipices upon the north, west, and east, which rendered the position impregnable from those directions, at the same time prevented an exit, and effectually barred all egress either for sorties or escape. The first court upon entering the gateway comprised several acres, but there was no level ground, and the natural slope of the mountain was inclosed by walls and parapets upon all sides, until at convenient places the earth had been scarped out for the erection of buildings, which had either been barracks or magazines. These were all of stone and hard cement, and were now used as stables for various animals by the few peasants of this wild neighbourhood. Passing through galleries, from which an occasional window showed a deep chasm of many hundred feet beneath, and continuing until we entered a tower which terminated the passage upon a perpendicular peak that enfiladed the outer line of defence, and at the same time from its great height commanded the main approach, we descended a rude flight of steps, and presently entered a grand hall supported upon numerous arches which appeared to connect two peaks of the mountain. Descending from this solid work, we entered upon a plot of grass which sloped towards a precipice of rock that completely closed this side of the fortress. Several cypress-trees grew among the stones, which assisted us in ascending from this steep and dangerous slope, until by a passage which led into a quadrangular courtyard of grass we emerged into an imposing portion of the ruin which commanded the west face. This was a wall built upon the extreme edge of a precipice, which looked down a giddy depth, and afforded a lovely view lengthways of the narrow strip of caroub-forest and verdure along the mountain range to the margin of the sea. The guide knew every inch of these labyrinth-like works, and upon my expressing a desire to ascend to the earth on the summit, he commenced a scramble over loose stones, large rocks, and occasional slippery grass, holding on to the now numerous dwarf-cypress, until we reached a narrow saddle of the peak, over which a man could sit astride and look down to the right and left into the depth below. It was necessary to cross this saddle for about ten or twelve feet to gain the wider pathway formed by the natural rock, which was terminated after a few yards by the castle tower. This, as may be imagined, was built upon the verge, and formed an artificial peak to the precipices upon all sides. The view was superb, as it commanded a panorama of mountains, valleys, the sea, precipices, and all that could make a perfect landscape.

Sitting down to rest upon the solid rock upon the left of this castle entrance, I observed that it was composed of white marble. The exterior had a greyish coating from the action of the weather, but this could be scraped off with a knife, which exposed the white marble beneath. I remarked that the cement of the masonry was mixed with small fragments of the same material, and subsequently I discovered blocks of this substance in the immediate neighbourhood of Kyrenia.

There was a peculiarity in the walls and towers of the fortress of St. Hilarion: the stones were of such small dimensions that few exceeded forty or fifty pounds in weight, except those which formed the principal halls or other buildings upon the secure plateaux within the outer works. The masons had apparently depended upon the extreme tenacity and hardness of their cement, which bound the mass into a solid block. Upon a close examination I discovered the reason. As the towers and many of the walls were built upon the extreme edge of various precipices, it would have been impossible to have erected a scaffolding on the outside, in the absence of which it would have been difficult to have raised heavy weights; the builders were therefore obliged to limit the size of stones to the power of individuals, who would be obliged to supply the material by the simple handing of single stones as the work proceeded. By this crude system the mason would stand upon his own wall and receive the stones as his work grew in height.

The origin and date of this interesting fortress are uncertain, but it is known that, like other eagle-nests upon this craggy range, it formed a place of refuge to some of the Latin kings of Cyprus. As in ancient times the port of Kyrenia had been an object of frequent attacks, the lofty fortresses of St. Hilarion and Buffavento offered immediate asylums in the event of a retreat from the invaded harbour. In close proximity to the sea these elevated posts commanded an extended view, and the approach of an enemy could be discerned at a distance that would afford ample warning for preparing a defence. Both St. Hilarion and other mountain strongholds upon this range were dismantled by the Venetian Admiral Prioli about A.D. 1490, shortly after the annexation of the island by Venice.

CHAPTER IX.

FROM BAFFO TO LIMASOL.

. . . While all hands were pitching the tent upon a sandy turf within a few yards of the sea-beach I took the dogs for a ramble up the thickly-wooded valley along the banks of the stream, as I had observed a number of blue-rock pigeons among the white cliffs, and I thought I might perhaps find a hare for the evening stew. I killed some pigeons, but did not move a hare, although the dogs worked through most promising ground, where green crops upon the flat bottom surrounded by thick coverts afford both food and shelter. We were returning to camp when I suddenly heard Merry and Shot barking savagely in some thick bushes upon the steep bank of the stream. At first I thought they had found a hedge-hog, which was always Shot's amusement, as he constantly brought them into camp after he had managed to obtain a hold of their prickly bodies. The barking continued, and as I could not penetrate the bush, I called the dogs off. They joined me almost immediately, looking rather scared. It now occurred to me that they might have found a snake, as a few days ago I had heard Merry barking in a similar manner, and upon joining him I had discovered a snake coiled up with head erect in an attitude of defence. I had killed the snake and scolded the dog, as I feared he would come to an untimely end, should he commence snake-hunting in so prolific a field as Cyprus. Since that time all the dogs hunted the countless lizards which ran across the path during the march, and Shot was most determined in his endeavours to scratch them out of their holes.

I had called my three dogs together, and we were walking across a field of green wheat, when I suddenly missed Shot, and he was discovered lying down about fifty paces in our rear. Merry, who usually was pluck and energy itself, was following at my heels and looking stupid and subdued. This dog was indomitable, and his fault was wildness at the commencement of the day; I could not now induce him to hunt, and his eyes had a peculiar expression, as though his system had suffered some severe shock. Shot came slowly when I called him, but he walked with difficulty, and his jaws were swollen. I now felt sure that the dogs were bitten by a snake, which they had been baying when I heard them in the bush about five minutes before. We were very near the camp, and the dogs crept home slowly at my heels. Upon examination there was no doubt of the cause; Shot had wounds of a snake's fangs upon his lip, under the eye, and upon one ear; he must have been the first bitten, as he had evidently received the greatest discharge of poison. Merry was bitten in the mouth and in one ear, both of which were already swollen, but not to the same degree as Shot, who, within an hour, had a head as large as a small calf's, and his eyes were completely closed. I had not the slightest hope of his recovery, as his throat had swollen to an enormous size, which threatened suffocation. I could do nothing for the poor dogs but oil their mouths, although I knew that the poison would assuredly spread throughout the system. The dogs had been bitten at about 3.40 P.M. At 8 P.M. (our dinner-hour) Shot was a shapeless mass, and his limbs were stiff; the skin of his throat and fore-part of his body beneath his curly white and liver-coloured hair was perfectly black; his jowl, which now hung three inches below his jaws, was also inky black, as were his swollen tongue and palate. Merry's head and throat were swollen badly, and he lay by the blazing fire of logs half stupefied and devoid of observation.

On the following morning Shot was evidently dying; he did not appear to suffer pain, but was in a state of coma and swelled to such a degree that he resembled the skin of an animal that had been badly stuffed with hay. Merry was worse than on the preceding night, and lay in a state of stupor. I carried him to the sea and dipped him several times beneath the water; this appeared slightly to revive him, and he was placed in a large saddle-bag to be carried on a mule for the day's march. Shot had been quite unconscious, and when the men prepared an animal to carry him, it was found that he was already dead. This was a little after 8 A.M., and he had been bitten at about 3.40 P.M.: about 16 1/2 hours had elapsed. My men dug a grave and buried the poor animal, who had been a faithful dog and an excellent retriever. From Merry's appearance I expected that we should have to attend to his remains in the same manner before the evening.

Snakes are very numerous in Cyprus, but I cannot believe in any great danger if these generally hated creatures should be avoided. If dogs will insist upon hunting and attacking them, they must be bitten as a natural consequence; in this fatal case there can be no doubt that the dog Shot was the first to discover and attack the snake, and Merry, upon hearing him bark, joined in the fight. It is quite unnatural for any of the serpent tribe to attack, except for the purpose of devouring their natural prey. As a general rule, the food of snakes consists of rats, mice, frogs, or toads, beetles, and other insects; the pythons and larger serpents feed upon such animals as hares, birds, and the young of either antelopes, deer, pigs, &c. Although a snake if trodden upon might by a spasmodic impulse inflict a bite, it would nine times out of ten endeavour to escape. The idea of any snake wilfully and maliciously premeditating an attack upon a man is quite out of the question, unless it has been either teased or excited by a dog when hunting. The same principle will hold good in the case of animals. No snake that feeds only upon rats, mice, and such small animals would seek to attack a dog, or any creature that was not its natural prey, and the actual danger from such reptiles is quite insignificant. The stories that are circulated of accidents are mostly exaggerated, or are perpetuated by constant repetition. I have been in snake countries such as Ceylon and Africa during many years, the greater portion of which has been passed in practical explorations, and I can safely say that I never thought of snakes until they met my eye, and no person that I ever knew was killed by a poisonous bite. In Cyprus there are several varieties. I have only seen three, a black species which is harmless, a mottled variety also non-poisonous, and a grey snake that is supposed to be deadly; there may be more, but I have never met with them. The stony nature of the country, and the bush-covered surface of the hills, together with the dryness of the climate, are all favourable to the development of snakes and lizards. The latter are exceedingly numerous, and are most valuable destroyers of insects; there are several varieties, but the most common is the bright copper-coloured species with a smooth skin. The chameleon also exists.

* * * * *

The dog Merry, that had been bitten by the snake, had lain for days in a state of stupor, black and swollen; I had poured quantities of olive oil down his throat, as he could not eat, and at length I gave him a dose of two grains of calomel, with three grains of emetic tartar. After this he slowly recovered; the ear that was bitten mortified, and was cut off, but the dog was sufficiently restored to accompany us upon the march, together with his companion Wise.

CHAPTER XII.

THE MONASTERY OF TROODITISSA.

The monastery of Trooditissa had no architectural pretensions; it looked like a family of English barns that had been crossed with a Swiss châlet. The roofs of six separate buildings of considerable dimensions were arranged to form a quadrangle, which included the chapel, a long building at right angles with the quadrangle, which had an upper balcony beneath the roof, so as to form a covered protection to a similar arrangement below, and an indescribable building which was used by the monks as their store for winter provisions. The staircases were outside, as in Switzerland, and entered upon the open-air landings or balconies; these were obscure galleries, from which doors led to each separate apartment, occupied by the monks and fleas. The obscurity may appear strange, as the balconies were on the outside, but the eaves of the roof at an angle of about 48° projected some feet as a protection from the winter's snow, and occasioned a darkness added to the gloom of blueish gray gneiss which formed the walls and the deep brownish red of the tiled roof.

The great walnut-tree overshadowed a portion of the mule stables that formed a continuation of the building, and faced the exterior courtyard, which was inclosed upon two sides of the square, in the centre of which was an arched entrance to the inner court. This doorway was beneath a covered gallery, and the ground floor formed a well-protected verandah, from which a magnificent view was commanded down the great gorge towards Phyni, overlooking the lower mountain tops to a sea horizon beyond the peninsula of Akrotiri and the salt lake of Limasol.

The covered gallery above this verandah was supported by stone pillars with exceedingly rude capitals, upon which long beams of the native pines, laid horizontally, supported the joists and floors. It was a dull and dirty abode, and at first sight I was disappointed. The angle of the mountain in which the monastery stood was formed by a ravine which intercepted the principal gorge at almost a right angle, thus a path which continued at the same level from the courtyard to the other side of the ravine, represented the letter V laid horizontally. From the walnut-tree across the broad base of the letter would be about a hundred yards, to a series of cultivated terraces upon an equal level.

This might have been made a lovely station, as no less than three springs of water issued from the mountain side in various positions: the first already mentioned; the second on the further side of the letter V beneath another splendid walnut-tree; and the third upon the same level beyond, which fell into a trough beneath a large trellis, upon which some vines were trained to produce a shade.

The terraces formed an angular amphitheatre, the outer courtyard of the monastery being the highest level, looking down upon tree-tops of planes and pines throughout the dark gorge to Phyni. The gardens appeared much neglected; they were overcrowded with fruit-trees, including filberts, mulberry, pears, apples, figs, walnuts, plums; the only grape-vine was represented upon the trellis; the position was too high for apricots.

An Englishman's first idea is improvement, and I believe that upon entering heaven itself he would suggest some alteration. This was not heaven, but, as a monastery, it was the first step, and a very high one for this world, being 4340 feet above the sea. We began by cleaning, and I should have liked to have engaged Hercules, at the maximum of agricultural wages, to have cleaned the long line of mule stables, a dignified employment for which the hero-god was famous; the Augean were a joke to them. Piles of manure and filth of every description concealed the pavement of the capacious outer yard of the monastery. The narrow path by which we had arrived from the spring was a mere dung-heap, from which the noxious weeds called *docks*, of Brobdignagian proportions, issued in such dense masses that an agricultural meeting of British farmers would have been completely hidden by their great enemy. The priests or monks had filthy habits; it would have been impossible for civilised people to have existed in this accumulation of impurities, therefore we at once set to work. I had a spade and pickaxe, and we borrowed some other tools from the monks, among which were strong grubbers (which combined the hoe and the pick). There were a number of people belonging to the monastery, including some young embryo priests, that we might accept as deacons; these I set to work with the pickaxe at one shilling a day wages. The boys who were being educated for the Church I employed in removing all the loose stones which choked the surface of the ground, and subsequently in sweeping and scraping the courtyard. I gave them six pence a day if they worked from early morning, or three-pence if they came at noon after their lessons. There was a shepherd's family, upon the hill about 250 feet above the monastery, of seven handsome children, two boys of nineteen and seventeen, and five girls. These were hard at work, even to a pretty little child of four years old, who carried her stones, and swept with a little broom with all her heart (this was little Athena). Of course they were all paid in the evening with bright new threepenny pieces which they had never seen before. Even the priests worked after a few days, when the spirit of industry and new shillings moved them, and in the history of the monastery there could never have been such a stirring picture and such a dust as we made in cleansing and alterations. Nearly a month was occupied in this necessary work, by which time the place was entirely changed. I had made a good road as an approach from the spring, with a covered drain, dignified by the name of an "aqueduct," which led the water when required to a little garden that I had constructed close to the tent, where a nondescript slope had become a receptacle for filth. I had cut this down from the road, and mixed the earth with the accumulated dirt and manure, which I levelled off in successive layers, so that the stream led from the spring would irrigate my beds in succession. This garden was carefully fenced against the intrusion of goats and donkeys, to say nothing of pigs, and it was already sown with tomatoes, cucumbers, melon, barmia, and beet-root. The priests had a grand bed of onions upon a terrace, which was usually occupied by the pigs, goats, and donkeys, as they had been too lazy to arrange a fence.

The docks in the monastery gardens were at least six feet high; I had these cut and collected to thatch the sides of a peculiar shed (in which I am writing at this moment), which was a great comfort and formed a very original retreat, combining a seat in an amphitheatre with a modern summer-house. This was an oblong, of fifteen feet by twelve, erected within three feet of the tent beneath the walnut-tree upon the extreme verge of the abrupt incline. I laid a foundation of stones, which I covered with pounded earth and water, to produce a level with the tent. I then placed horizontally a beam of wood, secured from slipping with stakes driven to the heads into the bank upon the edge of the incline. Upon this a row of large stones was cemented together with mud to form a margin level with the floor, from which the abrupt inclination at once leapt to the lower terraces and the deep gorge, continuing for upwards of 4000 feet to the sea; this was visible beyond the inferior mountain tops.

There was nothing pretty in the arrangement of this "rachkooba," as it would be called in Africa; it was a simple square of upright poles, connected with canes secured across, thatched inside with ferns, and upon the outside with docks, fastened down with the peeled willow-like shoots of mulberry-trees. The mulberry-trees for silkworms are always pollarded annually, and they throw out shoots about seven or nine feet in length every season; the wood is exceedingly tough, and the bark of these wands when stripped is serviceable for tying plants or securing fences in lieu of cord. For lack of silkworms the monastery mulberry-trees had several seasons of growth, and the shoots were serviceable for our work. The ceiling of our opera-box was cloth, with a curtain of about three feet suspended along the front, which broke the morning sun as it topped the high ridge of the mountain on the other side of the gorge, about a thousand feet above us. The shed was carpeted with mats and furnished roughly with a table and chairs; hat-pegs were suspended around, made from the red-barked wood of the arbutus, simply cut so that by inverting the branch with the stem attached to a cord, the twigs, cut at proper lengths, would form convenient hooks.

From this cool hermitage we looked down upon the dense foliage of rounded mulberry-tops and the fruit-trees of the gardens within the gorge, while exactly in our front, a hundred yards across the deep ravine, was the rocky steep of the mountain side, densely clothed with ilex and arbutus, until the still higher altitudes banished all underwood, and the upper ranges of Troodos exhibited a surface of barren rocks clothed with tall pines and cypress, 2000 feet above us.

By the time we had completed our permanent camp a certain degree of improvement had taken place in the people, as well as in the actual cleanliness of the locality. Everybody washed his, or her, face and hands. The customs of the monks had so far reformed that the immediate neighbourhood was no longer offensive. When strangers with mules arrived the road was immediately swept, and upon Saturday evenings a general embellishment took place in honour of the approaching Sunday. The young clergy were remarkably good and active; they worked in my little garden at a shilling a day, went on errands to Platraes and the camp at Troodos, and made themselves generally useful for a most moderate consideration. I can strongly recommend all young curates who are waiting in vain for livings to come and work upon the holy soil of Trooditissa at one shilling *per diem*; and should they (as curates frequently are) be poor in this world's goods, but nevertheless strong in amorous propensities, and accordingly desirous of matrimony, they will find a refuge within the walls of this monastery from all the temptations of the outer world, far from garden-parties, balls, picnics, church-decorations assisted by young ladies, and all those snares of the Evil One; and the wholesome diet of the monks including a course of soaked broad-beans and barley bread, with repeated fastings upon innumerable saints' days, will affect them sensibly, both morally and physically; under this discipline they will come to the conclusion that a wife and large family upon an income of £500 a year in England would not confer the same happiness as one shilling a day with the pickaxe, broad-beans and independence, at Trooditissa, which is true "muscular Christianity."

It was extraordinary to see the result of a life-long diet of beans and barley-bread in the persons of the monks, who very seldom indulged in flesh. The actual head of the monastery was a handsome man of seventy, perfectly erect in figure, as though fresh from military drill, and as strong and active as most men of fifty. The younger priests were all good-looking, active, healthy men, who thought nothing of a morning's walk over the fatiguing rocky paths to Troodos and back (twelve miles), to be refreshed on their return by an afternoon's work in their gardens. The head of the Church was an especial friend of ours, and was a dear old fellow of about seventy, with a handsome face, a pair of greasy brass spectacles bound with some substance to retain them that was long since past recognition, and swelled feet that prevented him from walking beyond the precincts of the monastery, which he had never quitted for twelve years. The feet looked uncommonly like the gout, but I can hardly believe in the co-existence of that complaint with dry beans and barley-bread, although the truth must be confessed, that the monks are fond of commanderia, or any other production of the vineyard. There was one exceedingly disagreeable monk with whom we held a most remote acquaintance, and whose name I willingly conceal; he has been seen upon several occasions to sit down upon an imaginary chair, the real article of furniture being eighteen inches distant, and the stunning effect of arriving suddenly in a sitting posture upon the hard stones of the courtyard disabled him from rising; and even when assisted his legs were evidently affected by the shock. His enemies declared (as they always do) that he was the victim to an over-indulgence in the raki and wine of Phyni. We generally knew him by the alias of " Roger," in memory of the *Ingoldsby Legends*, where

> "Roger the Monk
> Got excessively drunk,
>   So they put him to bed,
>   And tucked him in."

There was no friend to bestow such care upon our Roger, he therefore lay helplessly upon the bare stones until refreshing sleep restored his eyesight and his perpendicular.

Our particular friend the head of the Church was a very different character, and was a most simple-minded and really good religious man. I employed a photographer of the Royal Engineers (kindly permitted by Major Maitland, R.E.) specially to take his picture, as he sat every morning knitting stockings, with a little boy by his side reading the Greek Testament aloud, in the archway of the monastery. This was his daily occupation, varied only when he exchanged the work of knitting either for spinning cotton, or carving wooden spoons from the arbutus: these he manufactured in great numbers as return presents to those poor people who brought little offerings from the low country. Never having mixed with the world, the old man was very original and primitive in his ideas, which were limited to the monastery duties and to the extreme trouble occasioned by the numerous goats which trespassed upon the unfenced gardens, and inflicted serious damage. The chapel, which was under his control, was of the usual kind, and at the same time rough and exceedingly gaudy, the pulpit being gilded throughout its surface, and the reredos glittering with gold and tawdry pictures of the lowest style of art, representing the various saints, including a very fat St. George and the meekest possible dragon. Our old friend had never seen a British sovereign with the St. George, and was vastly pleased when he discovered that his saint and ours were the same person, only differing in symmetry of figures and in ferocity of dragons.

There was one very extraordinary effigy in bas-relief upon silver-gilt about two feet six inches high, of the Virgin Mary, to which peculiar miraculous properties were attributed. The possession of this relic formed the principal attraction of the monastery. About a quarter of a mile above the present establishment there is a small cave concealed among the ragged masses of rock that crust the mountain side; this has been formed by one rock which leans across another, and each end has been walled up artificially, so as to form a stone chamber of about twelve feet in length by seven in width, with a small entrance. According to the account given by the old monk, this cave was the origin of the present monastery through the following accident. Among these wild mountains, where no dwelling of any kind exists, it has always been the custom after the melting of the snows in early spring to pasture the numerous flocks of goats, which are at that season driven up from the parched herbage of the low country to the fresh herbs of the cooler altitudes. Three or four hundred years ago a shepherd, having lost his goats at night, was surprised at the appearance of a light among the rocks high up on the mountain, and with superstitious awe he related his discovery to his fellows. For some time the mysterious light was observed nightly, and various conjectures were on foot as to its origin, but no one dared to venture upon an examination.

At length, the authorities of the Church having been consulted, it was resolved that a priest should accompany the party of investigation and the matter should be thoroughly cleared up.

It was a difficult climb to the pathless crags at night, but the light was glimmering like "the star that the wise men saw in the east," and though occasionally lost at intervals, it guided the party on their way. Upon arrival at the cave, there was no inhabitant. A lamp burnt before a small effigy of the Virgin Mary suspended against the wall of rock, but no trace of human foot or hand could be discovered.

Such is the legend; and the inexplicable mystery caused much excitement and agitation in the minds of the Church authorities. At length it was determined that, as the apparition of the light was miraculous, it was incumbent upon the people to erect a monastery upon the site of the appearance, contiguous to the now sacred cave.

This was an extreme difficulty, as the inclination formed an angle of about 60°, and the mountain was hard gneiss that could only have been scarped by expensive blasting. However, it was hoped that a blessing would attend the good work; therefore, in spite of all obstacles, it was commenced, and masons were engaged from the village of Phyni to arrange a foundation.

There was no water nearer than the torrent in the deep hollow half a mile below, therefore extreme labour was required in mixing the mortar for the walls; the jars in which the necessary water was conveyed upon men's shoulders up the precipitous rocks appeared to be influenced by some adverse but unseen, agency, as they constantly slipped from their hold and broke. During the night the work which the masons had accomplished in the days fell down, and was discovered every morning as a heap of ruin; the building could not proceed. In this perplexity the Church was relieved by a supernatural interposition. Early one morning a jar of pure water was discovered in the sharp angle of the hollow between the hills, exactly below the rachkooba, where I am now writing. It was evident to the priestly mind that an angel had placed this jar of water to denote the spot where some hidden spring might be developed, which would be a favourable site for the new monastery. They dug, and shortly discovered the expected source.

It was therefore resolved that instead of erecting the monastery close to the effigy in the cave, where bad luck had hitherto attended their efforts, it would be more advisable to commence the building upon a favourable spot, where a level already existed, in the angle between two mountain slopes within a few yards of the spring; it would be easier to convey the small effigy to the new building than to erect the monastery close to the effigy. Accordingly the work was commenced: the walls no longer fell during the night, and the unseen agency was evidently propitious.

Upon completion of the monastery the original effigy was enshrined, and Trooditissa became famous as a holy site. Years passed away, and the reputation of the establishment was enhanced by the arrival of a lady of high position from Beyrout, together with her husband, as pilgrims to the now celebrated mountain cave. The lady was childless, and having presented a handsome offering, and kissed the rock entrance of the cave, in addition to the effigy within the monastery, she waited in the neighbourhood for a certain number of months, at the expiration of which she gave birth to a son. The monks claimed this boy as their lawful prize, and he was brought up as a priest; but there is some discrepancy in the accounts which I could not well understand, as it appears that his parents insisted upon his restoration, and that an angelic interposition at length prevented litigation. It may be well imagined that the result of the lady's pilgrimage spread far and wide; the reputation of the monastery reached its zenith, and all the unfruitful women flocked to the shrine to kiss the cave and the picture of the Virgin within the church; at the same time offering a certain sum for the benefit of the establishment. The friction of constant and oft-repeated kissing at length began to tell upon the sacred effigy, and it became almost worn out; it was therefore determined that a beautiful silver-gilt Virgin and Child should be supplied by a first-rate artist which should cover the original relic within. This was remarkably well executed by Cornaro, and a small aperture like a keyhole of a door has been left, which is covered by a slide; this is moved upon one side when required, and enables the pilgrim to kiss through the hole a piece of rather brown-looking wood, which is the present exhausted surface of the effigy.

Although decayed by time and use, the miraculous property remains unchanged. This was exhibited a few years ago in a remarkable manner, where a childless lady had become old in barren expectation; but a visit to Trooditissa produced the desired result, and conferred much happiness upon the once despairing wife, who now became a mother. In addition to a monetary offering, this lady had presented the Virgin with a handsome belt with massive silver-gilt buckles, which she had worn during pregnancy. This offering is now suspended around the present effigy, and for a small consideration any lady applicant is allowed to fasten it round her waist. The effect is infallible, and quite equals that of the rock and silver Virgin. This remarkable inductive power may perhaps be some day explained by philosophers, but it is now exceedingly dangerous, and unfortunate results have occurred, when in a sudden impulse of devotion young maidens have kissed the rock entrance to the cave, or imprudently pressed their lips upon the sacred effigy.

During my sojourn at Trooditissa no arrivals of despairing wives occurred, but in the exhausted conditions of the finance throughout the island, it would have been the height of folly to have desired an increase of family, and thereby multiply expenses; possibly the uncertainty respecting the permanence of the English occupation may deter the ladies, who may postpone their pilgrimage to the monastery until their offspring should be born with the rights of British subjects.

I have described the origin of the ecclesiastical retreat at Trooditissa as nearly as possible according to the *viva-voce* history related by the monks. It is impossible to gauge the opinions of the world, as individuals differ as much in nervous structure and in theological creeds as they do in personal appearance; some may accept the monks' belief implicitly, while others may suggest that the original occupant of the cave was some unknown hermit secluded from the world, whose solitary lamp burning before the Virgin had attracted the attention of the shepherds from the mountain opposite. The old man may have fallen down a precipice and died, leaving his lamp still alight; but it would be unfair to interfere with the original legend, which must remain with the usual clouds and uncertainties that obscure the tales of centuries.

About 250 feet above the monastery the ridge of a spur afforded a level space beneath some tall pines which threw a welcome shade, and would have been a convenient camping-ground. This spot was occupied by the roughest of log-huts, which had been erected by a shepherd as his summer residence when the goats should be driven from the low ground to the mountain pasture. This man was originally a Turk, and formed one of a peculiar sect known in Cyprus as Linobambaki (linen and cotton). These people are said to be converts to Christianity, but in reality they have never been troubled with any religious scruples, and accordingly never accommodate their principles to the society of their neighbourhood. In a Turkish village the Linobambaki would call himself by a Turkish name, as Mahomet, or Hassan, &c., while in a Christian community he would pass as Michael or Georgy, or by other Greek appellation. The name "linen and cotton" applied to them is expressive of their lukewarmness and time-serving, their religious professions fluctuating according to the dictates not of conscience, but personal interest. It is supposed that about 1500 of these people exist in various parts of Cyprus; they are baptised in the Greek Church, and can thus escape conscription for military service according to Turkish law. The goatherd upon our mountain had been a Turkish servant (shepherd) in a Greek family, and had succeeded in gaining the heart of his master's daughter, whom he was permitted to marry after many difficulties. This woman must have been very beautiful when young, as, in spite of hard work and exposure, she was handsome at forty, with a pair of eyes that in youth might have been more attractive than the mysterious light in the hermit's cave. It is one of the blessings of fine eyes that they are almost certain to descend to the children. Property may vanish, litigation may destroy the substance of an inheritance; but the eyes, large, soft, and gentle, which can occasionally startle you by their power and subdue you by a tear, are the children's entail that nothing can disestablish. Even when time has trampled upon complexion, the eyes of beauty last till death.

The children of this Linobambaki and his handsome wife were seven—two boys of about nineteen and seventeen, and five girls from fourteen to one and a half—all of whom had the eyes of the mother developed most favourably. I cannot well describe every individual of a family: there were the two handsome shepherd youths who would have made level ground of mountain steeps, through their power and activity.

> "Right up Ben Lomond could he press,
> And not a sob his toil confess."

These young fellows matched the goats in clambering up the rocks and following their wayward flocks throughout the summits of the Troodos range; and their sisters the little shepherdesses were in their way equally surprising, in hunting runaway goats from the deepest chasm to the sharpest mountain-peak.

I hardly know who was our greatest favourite. There was "Katterina " (about fourteen) too old to make a pet of, but a gentle-charactered girl, always willing to please and never out of temper, and even in the big, hateful, beauty-destroying, high hobnailed boots she could run up the mountain soil and clamber like a monkey. Then came, I believe, our best favourite, the bright, large-eyed, sparkling child "Vathoo," who was the real beauty of the family, about ten years old; she was full of life and vigour, a perfect goat upon the mountains, with a most lovely face that would have charmed Murillo as a subject, with an extreme perfection of features, a bronzed complexion, but hardly the soft expression required for a sacred picture; in fact Vathoo was a perfect little gipsy beauty, with perhaps more devil than angel in her impulsive character.

Then came the real gentle little face with gazelle-like eyes, "Baraksu," about eight years old: followed by a minimum shepherdess, "Athena," of nearly five years old, who climbed the rocks, shouted, and threw stones at her refractory flock, as though an experienced goat-herd of forty. The youngest was just able to stand; with a pair of the biggest black eyes, and a natural instinct for gorging itself with unripe fruits and hard nuts, which, added to its maternal sustenance that it was still enjoying, proved the mill-like character of its infantine digestion. For two months we thought this young Hercules was a promising boy, until by an accident we discovered it was a "young lady" Linobambaki! When we arrived at Trooditissa these children were in rags and filth, but under the tutelage of my wife they quickly changed, and the never-failing fountain, assisted by a cake of soap supplied occasionally, effected a marked improvement in all complexions.

They were remarkably well-mannered after the first natural shyness had worn away, and formed a contrast to children of a low class in England in never misbehaving when intimate. All these little creatures were employed in cleaning and improving the place; even the minute Athena might be seen carrying a great stone upon her small shoulder, adding her mite to the work, and rubbing the galled spot as she threw down her load. The bright threepenny pieces were in great favor, and the children invariably hastened to their mother with their earnings at the close of the afternoon. When the camp and monastery surroundings were in perfect order there was no longer any remunerative employment for the family, except the uncertain and occasional work of collecting wild flowers for the tent and table. The myrtles bloomed in early July, and in the deep ravine by the waterfall the oleanders were then still in blossom. Several plants which were strange to me were added to the collection; the days were generally passed by the children in minding the numerous goats until the evening, when each child brought some simple offering of flowers. We bought sheep from the low country at about six or seven shillings each, and Vathoo was the special shepherdess of our small flock, for which she was responsible; they were invariably driven out at 4 A.M. and brought home at 8 to avoid the sun, and again taken out from 4 P.M. till 7.

In this simple manner we passed our time at Trooditissa; my amusements were my small garden, writing an account of Cyprus, and strolling over the mountains.

CHAPTER XV.

LIFE AT THE MONASTERY OF TROODITISSA.

The life at our quiet camp at Trooditissa was a complete calm: there could not be a more secluded spot, as no human habitation was near, except the invisible village of Phyni two miles deep beneath, at the mountain's base. The good old monk Néophitos knitted, and taught his boys always in the same daily spot: the swallows built their nests under the eaves of the monastery roof and beneath the arch which covered in the spring, and sat in domestic flocks upon the over-hanging boughs within a few feet of our breakfast-table, when their young could fly. Nightingales sally before sunset, and birds of many varieties occupied the great walnut-tree above our camp, and made the early morning cheerful with a chorus of different songs. There was no change from day to day, except in the progress of the gardens; the plums grew large: the mulberries ripened in the last week of July, and the shepherd's pretty children and the monastery boys were covered with red stains, as though from a battlefield, as they descended from the attractive boughs. It was a very peaceful existence, and I shall often look back with pleasure to our hermitage by the walls of the old monastery, which afforded a moral haven from all the storms and troubles that embitter life. On Sundays we sent a messenger for the post to the military camp at Troodos, about five and a half miles distant, and the arrival of letters and newspapers restored us for a couple of days to the outer world: after which we relapsed once more into the local quiescent state of complete rest. It must not be supposed that we were idle; there were always occupations which by degrees I hope improved the place, and to a certain degree the people. Occasionally I asked the old monks to sit and smoke their cigarettes in our "rachkooba," when they sipped their hot coffee, and explained difficult theological questions to my intense edification; of course I always listened, but never argued. My particular friend old Néophitos treated me to long stories which he imagined must be new and interesting, especially the history of Joseph and his brethren, which he several times recounted from beginning to end with tears of sympathy in his eyes at Joseph's love for the youngest brother Benjamin. The Garden of Edèn, the Deluge, including the account of Noah's Ark, and several equally modern and entertaining stories, I always listened to with commendable attention. Yet even in this solitude, where the chapel-bell on Saturday night, and at daybreak upon Sunday mornings, was in harmony with the external peaceful surroundings, and it appeared as though discord could never enter the walls of Trooditissa, the old monks had their cares and difficulties.

The principal cause of trouble was "servants!" I was quite surprised, as I thought we were nearer heaven in this spot than in any earthly locality I had ever visited; but even here the question of "servants" was an irritation to the nerves of the patient monks. My own servants were excellent, and never quarrelled or complained; they appeared to have been mesmerized by the placid character of their position, and to have become angelic; especially in not fatiguing themselves through over-exertion. With the monks the case was different. In this quiet retreat, where man reigned alone, as Adam in the Garden of Eden; where the cares and anxieties of married life were unknown within the sacred walls of celibacy, a single representative of the other sex existed in the ubiquitous shape of a "maid of all work;" and as Eve caused the first trouble in the world, so the monastery "maid" disturbed the otherwise peaceful existence of Néophitos.

This maid's name was "Christina," and she received the munificent sum of one hundred piastres per annum as wages, which in English money would be fifteen shillings and six pence every year. The world is full of ingratitude, and strange to say, Christina was dissatisfied, which naturally wounded the feelings of the good monks, as in addition to this large sum of money she received her food and clothes; the latter consisting of full trousers, and a confusion of light material, which, having no shape whatever, I could not describe. Christina, though young, was not pretty, and she was always either crying or scolding, which would of course spoil any beauty; while at the same time she was either washing all the clothes belonging to the whole establishment of monks (a very disagreeable business), or hanging them out to dry near the spring; or she was sweeping the monastery; or arranging the very dirty rooms of the establishment; or baking all the bread that was required; or cooking the dinner; or repairing all the old clothes which the monks wore when they were only fit for a paper-mill. As there was no special accommodation in the shape of a laundry, Christina had to collect sticks, and make a huge fire beneath a copper cauldron in the open air, into which she plunged all the different vestments of the monks and priests, and stewed them before washing. This was a Cyprian "maid of all work," whose gross ingratitude troubled the minds of her " pastors and masters;" and one day a peculiar mental disturbance pervaded the whole priestly establishment and caused a monasterial commotion, as, after a violent fit of temper attended by crying, Christina had declared solemnly that she "would stand it no longer," and "she wished *to better herself!*"

Whenever there was a difficulty the monks came to me; why, I cannot imagine. If the shepherd's goats invaded their gardens and destroyed the onions and the beet-root crops, they applied to me. Of course I advised them to "fence their gardens," and they went away satisfied, but did not carry out the suggestion; so in due time their crops were devoured. They now told me that *they always had a difficulty with women!* This new theory startled me almost as much as the novelty of the old monks' stories. They explained that *young women wouldn't work, and old women couldn't work.* It had not occurred to them that a middle-aged woman might have combined all that they desired. Knowing their strict moral principles, I had suggested an "old woman" as the successor of Christina; as I explained to them that, to be in harmony with the establishment, a woman of a "certain age" as general servant would not detract from the religious character of the place. However I might argue, the old monk hesitated; but while the monk wavered, Christina's "monkey was up," and, taking her child in her arms, she started off without giving a "month's notice," and fairly left the monastery, with monks, priests, deacons, servants and the dogs all aghast and barking. There was nobody to wash the linen, to bake the bread, to sweep the rooms, to cook the dinner, to mend the clothes! Christina was gone, and the gentle sex was no longer represented in the monastery of Trooditissa.

I was sorry for Christina, but I was glad the child was gone; although I pitied the poor abandoned and neglected little creature with all my heart. As a rule, "maids of all work" should not be mothers, but if they are, they should endeavour to care for the unfortunate child. This wretched little thing was about two years old—a girl; its eyes were nearly closed with inflammation caused by dirt and neglect; it was naked, with the exception of a filthy rag that hung in tatters scarcely below its hips; and as its ill-tempered and over-worked mother alternately raved, or cried, the child, which even at this age depended mainly upon her nursing for its food, joined in a perpetual yell, which at length terminated in a faint and wearied moan, until it laid itself down upon the bare, hard stones, and fell asleep. It was a sad picture of neglect and misery; the shepherd's pretty children shunned it, and in its abandoned solitude the little creature had to amuse itself. The face looked like that of an old careworn person who had lost all pleasure in the world, and the child wandered about alone and uncared for; its only plaything was my good-tempered dog Wise, who allowed himself to be pulled about and teased in the most patient manner. I cured the child's eyes after some days' attention, and my wife had it washed, and made it decent clothes. This little unusual care, with a few kind words in a strange language only interpreted by a smile, attracted the poor thing to the tent, where it would sit for hours, until it at length found solace in the child's great refuge, sleep. It would always follow Lady Baker to and fro along the only level walk we had, from the tent to the running spring, and would sit down by her side directly she arrived at our favourite seat—a large flat rock looking down upon a precipitous descent to the ravine some 500 feet below, and commanding a view of the low country and the distant sea. It was an obstinate and perverse little creature, and it insisted upon climbing upon rocks and standing upon the extreme edge overhanging a precipice. If it had been the loved and only offspring of fond parents, heiress to a large estate, it would of course have tumbled over, in the absence of nurses and a throng of careful attendants, but never having been cared for since its birth, it possessed an instinctive knowledge of self-preservation, and declined to relieve its mother of an extra anxiety. It was an agreeable change to lose the sound of a child's constant wailing, and I suggested to the monks that its presence was hardly in accordance with the severe aspect of the establishment. There was some mystery connected with it of which I am still ignorant, as I never ask questions; but it is at the least ill judged and thoughtless on the part of "maids of all work" to engage themselves to any situation where the kissing of a rock, or a holy effigy, may lead to complications. It was of no use to moralise; Christina was gone, together with the child; there was absolute quiet in the monastery; neither the scolding of the mother, nor the crying of an infant, was heard. The monks looked more austere than ever, and remained in unwashed linen, until they at length succeeded in engaging a charming substitute in a middle-aged maid of all work of seventy-five!

About the 20th July the swallows disappeared, and I have no idea to what portion of the world they would migrate at this season. In the low country the heat is excessive, and even at the altitude of Trooditissa the average, since the 1st of the month, had been at 7 A.M. 70 7/10°—3 P.M. 77 3/10°.

The birds that had sung so cheerfully upon our arrival had become silent. There was a general absence of the feathered tribe, but occasionally a considerable number of hoopoes and jays had appeared for a few days, and had again departed, as though changing their migrations, and resting for a time upon the cool mountains.

I frequently rambled among the highest summits with my dogs, but there was a distressing and unaccountable absence of game; in addition to which there was no scent, as the barren rocks were heated in the sun like bricks taken from the kiln. The undergrowth up to 4500 feet afforded both food and covert for hares, but they were very scarce. A peculiar species of dwarf prickly broom covers the ground in some places, and the young shoots are eagerly devoured by goats; this spreads horizontally, and grows in such dense masses about one foot from the surface that it will support the weight of a man.

When grubbed up by the root it forms an impervious mat about three or four feet in diameter, and supplies an excellent door to the entrance of a garden, to prevent the incursions of goats or fowls. The Berberris grew in large quantities, which, together with the foliage of the dwarf ilex, is the goat's favourite food. Not far from the village of Prodomos, upon the neighbouring heights, I found, for the first time in Cyprus, the juniper, which appeared to be kept low by the constant grazing of the numerous herds.

The walking over the mountains is most fatiguing, and utterly destructive to boots, owing to the interminable masses of sharp rocks and stones of all sizes, which quite destroy the pleasure of a lengthened stroll. The views from the various elevated ridges are exceedingly beautiful, and exhibit the numerous villages surrounded by vineyards snugly clustered in obscure dells among the mountains at great elevations above the sea. Prodomos is about 4300 feet above the level, and can be easily distinguished by the foliage of numerous spreading walnut-trees and the large amount of cultivation by which it is surrounded.

There was no difficulty in gaining the highest point of the island from our camp, as a zigzag rocky path led to the top of a ridge about 600 feet directly above the monastery, which ascended with varying inclinations to the summit of Troodos, about 2100 feet above Trooditissa; by the maps 6590 feet above the sea, but hardly so much by recent measurement.

The moufflon, or wild sheep, exists in Cyprus, but in the absence of protection they have been harassed at all seasons by the natives, who have no idea of sparing animals during the breeding season. The present government have protected them by a total prohibition, under a penalty of ten pounds to be inflicted upon any person discovered in killing them. In the absence of all keepers or guardians of the forests, it would be difficult to prove a case, and I have no doubt that the natives still attempt the sport, although from the extreme wariness of the animals they are most difficult to approach. The authorities should employ some dependable sportsman to shoot a certain number of rams which are now in undue proportion, as the ewes with young lambs have been an easier prey to the unsparing Cypriotes.

Absurd opinions have been expressed concerning the numbers of moufflon now remaining upon the island, and it would be quite impossible to venture upon a conjecture, as there is a very large area of the mountains perfectly wild and unoccupied to the west of Kyka monastery, extending to Poli-ton-Khrysokus, upon which the animals are said to be tolerably numerous. There are some upon the Troodos range, but from all accounts they do not exceed fifteen.

On 2nd July I started at 4 A.M. with a shepherd lad for the highest point of Troodos, hoping by walking carefully to see moufflon among some of the numerous ravines near the summit, which are seldom evaded by the flocks of goats and their attendants. I took a small rifle with me as a companion which is seldom absent in my walks, and although I should have rigidly respected the government prohibition in the case of ewes, or even of rams at a long shot that might have been uncertain and hazardous, I should at the same time have regarded a moufflon with good horns at a range under 150 yards, in the Abrahamic light of "a ram caught in a thicket" that had been placed in my way for the purpose of affording me a specimen.

On arrival at the top of the ridge above the monastery the view was superb. We looked down a couple of thousand feet into deep and narrow valleys rich in vineyards; the mountains rose in dark masses upon the western side, covered with pine forests, which at this distance did not exhibit the mutilations of the axe. At this early hour the sea was blue and clear, as the sun had not yet heated the air and produced the usual haze which destroys the distant views: and the tops of the lower mountains above Omodos and Chilani appeared almost close beneath upon the south, their vine-covered surface producing a rich contrast to the glaring white marls that were cleared for next year's planting. The top of Troodos was not visible, as we continued the ascent along the ridge, with the great depths of ravines and pine-covered steeps upon either side, but several imposing heights in front, and upon the right, seemed to closely rival the true highest point.

As we ascended, the surface vegetation became scanty; the rocks in many places had been thickly clothed with the common fern growing in dense masses from the soil among the interstices; the white cistus and the purple variety had formed a gummy bed of plants which, together with several aromatic herbs, emitted a peculiar perfume in the cool morning air. These now gave place to the hardy berberris which grew in thick prickly bushes at long intervals, leaving a bare surface of rocks between them devoid of vegetation. There was little of geological interest; gneiss and syenite predominated, with extremely large crystals of hornblende in the latter rock, that would have afforded handsome slabs had not the prevailing defect throughout Cyprus rendered all blocks imperfect through innumerable cracks and fissures. A peculiar greenish and greasy-looking rock resembling soapstone was occasionally met with in veins, and upon close examination I discovered it to be the base of asbestos. The surface of this green substance was like polished horn, which gradually became fibrous, and in some specimens developed towards the extremity into the true white hairy condition of the well-known mineral cotton.

We were near the summit of the mountain, and arrived at an ancient camp that had been arranged with considerable judgment by a series of stone walls with flanking defenses for the protection of each front. This was many centuries ago the summer retreat of the Venetian government, and it had formed a sanatorium. This extends to the summit of the mountain, where fragments of tiles denote the former existence of houses. In the absence of water it would have been impossible to adopt the usual custom of mud-covered roofs, therefore tiles had been carried from the low country. It is supposed that the stations fell into decay at about the period of the Turkish conquest.

A rattle of loose stones upon the opposite side of a ravine suddenly attracted my attention; and two moving objects at about 230 yards halted, and faced us in the usual manner of inquiry when wild animals are disturbed to windward of their enemy. The rocks were bare, and their *café-au-lait* colour exactly harmonised with that of the two moufflon, which I now made out to be fine rams with large and peculiar heads. Motioning to my shepherd lad to sit quietly upon the ground, upon which I was already stretched, I examined them carefully with my glass. Had they not been moving when first observed I should not have discovered them, so precisely did their skins match the rocky surface of the steep inclination upon which they stood. They remained still for about two minutes, affording me an excellent opportunity of examination. The horns were thick, and rose from the base like those of the ibex, turning backwards, but they twisted forward from the first bend, and the points came round towards the front in the ordinary manner of the sheep. Like all the wild sheep of India and other countries, the coat was devoid of wool, but appeared to be a perfectly smooth surface of dense texture. It was too far for a certain shot, especially as the animals were facing me, which is always an unsatisfactory position even when at a close range.

I put up the 200 yards sight, and raised the rifle to my shoulder, merely to try the view; but when sighted I could not clearly distinguish the animal from the rocks, and I would not fire to wound. My shepherd lad at this moment drew his whistle, and, without orders, began to pipe in a wild fashion, which he subsequently informed me should have induced the moufflon to come forward towards the sound; instead of which, they cantered off, then stopped again, as we had the wind, and at length they disappeared among the rocks and pines. It would be almost impossible to obtain a shot at these wary creatures by approaching from below, as they are generally upon high positions from which they look *down* for expected enemies, and the noise of the loose rocks beneath the feet of a man walking up the mountains would be sure to attract attention. The only chance of success would be to pass the night on the summit of Troodos, and at daybreak to work downwards.

I made a long circuit in the hope of again meeting the two rams, during which I found many fresh tracks of the past night, but nothing more.

The summit of the mountain was disappointing, as the haze occasioned by the heat in the low country obscured the distant view. It was 8.10. A.M., and the air was still deliciously cool and fresh upon the highest point of Cyprus, which affords a complete panorama that in the month of October or during early spring must be very beautiful. Even now I could distinguish Larnaca, Limasol, Morphu, all in opposite directions, in addition to the sea surrounding the island upon every point except the east. The lofty coast of Caramania, which had formed a prominent object in the landscape when at Kyrenia, was now unfortunately hidden within the haze.

From this elevated position I could faintly hear the military band practicing at the camp of the 20th Regiment, invisible, about a mile distant among the pine-forests, at a lower level of 700 feet. There were no trees upon the rounded knoll which forms the highest point of Cyprus: these must have been cleared away and rooted out when the ancient camp was formed, and the pines have not re-grown, for the simple reason that no higher ground exists from which the rains could have washed the cones to root upon a lower level.

I now examined every ravine with the greatest caution in the hopes of meeting either the two rams, or other moufflon, but I only came across a solitary ewe with a lamb about four months old; which I saw twice during my walk round the mountain tops. Upon arriving during my descent at the highest spring of Troodos, where the cold water dripped into a narrow stream bed, I lay down beneath a fine shady cypress, and having eaten two hard-boiled eggs and drunk a cupful of the pure icy water mixed with a tinge of Geneva from my flask, I watched till after noon in the hope that my two rams might arrive to drink. Nothing came except a few tame goats without a goatherd; therefore I descended the abominable stones which rattled down the mountain side, and by the time that I arrived at our camp at Trooditissa, my best shooting boots of quagga hide, that were as dear to me as my rifle, were almost cut to pieces.

There was a terrible picture of destruction throughout the forests of Troodos. Near the summit, the pines and cypress were of large growth, but excepting the cypress, there were scarcely any trees unscathed, and the ground was covered by magnificent spars that were felled only to rot upon the surface.

I was not sorry to arrive at the shepherd's hut upon the ridge overhanging the monastery upon my return. The good wife was as usual busy in making cheeses from the goat's milk, which is a very important occupation throughout Cyprus. The curd was pressed into tiny baskets made of myrtle wands, which produced a cheese not quite so large as a man's fist. I think these dry and tasteless productions of the original Cyprian dairy uneatable, unless grated when old and hard; but among the natives they are highly esteemed, and form a considerable article of trade and export. Cesnola mentions that 2,000,000 (two million) cheeses per annum are made in Cyprus of this small kind, which weigh from half a pound to three-quarters. I have frequently met droves of donkeys heavily laden with panniers filled with these small cheeses, which, although representing important numbers, become insignificant when computed by weight.

During our stay at Trooditissa we occasionally obtained eels from a man who caught them in the stream at the base of the mountains; this is the only fresh-water fish in Cyprus that is indigenous. Some persons have averred that the gold-fish dates its origin from this island; this is a mistake, as it is not found elsewhere than in ornamental ponds and cisterns in the principal towns. It is most probable that it was introduced by the Venetians who traded with the far East, and it may have arrived from China.

The streams below the mountains contain numerous crabs of a small species seldom larger than two inches and a half across the shell, to a maximum of three inches; these are in season until the middle of June, after which they become light and empty. When alive they are a brownish green, but when boiled they are the colour of the ordinary crab, and are exceedingly full in flesh, and delicate. The shell is extremely hard compared to the small size, and the claws must be broken by a sharp blow with the back of a knife upon a block.

We frequently had them first boiled and then pounded in a mortar to a paste, then mixed with boiling water and strained through a sieve; after which cream should be added, together with the required seasonings for a soup. I imagine that the common green crabs of the English coasts, which are caught in such numbers and thrown away by the fishermen, would be almost as good if treated in the same manner for *potage*.

The calm monotony of a life at Trooditissa was disturbed every now and then at distant intervals by trifling events which only served to prove that peculiar characters existed in the otherwise heavenly atmosphere which showed our connection with the world below.

One night a burglar attempted an entrance; but the man (who was a carpenter) having been previously suspected, was watched, and having been seen in the middle of the night to place a ladder against the outer gallery, by which he ascended, and with false keys opened a door that led to the store-room of the monastery, he was suddenly pounced upon by two strong young priests and fairly captured. On the following morning the monks applied to me, and as usual I vainly pleaded my unofficial position. I was either to do or to say something. If the man was sent to Limasol, thirty-five miles distant, the monks would have the trouble and expense of appearing as prosecutors; the robber would be imprisoned for perhaps a couple of years, during which his family would starve. I could offer no advice. I simply told them that if any robber should attempt to enter my tent I should not send him to Limasol, but I should endeavour to make the tent so disagreeable to him that he would never be tempted to revisit the premises from the attraction of pleasing associations. I explained to the monks that although a severe thrashing with stout mulberry sticks would, if laid on by two stout fellows, have a most beneficial effect upon the burglar, and save all the trouble of a reference to Limasol, at the same time that the innocent wife and family would not be thrown upon their relatives, they must not accept my views of punishment as any suggestion under the present circumstances.

About half an hour after this conversation I heard a sound of well-inflicted blows, accompanied by cries which certainly denoted a disagreeable physical sensation, within the courtyard of the monastery, and to my astonishment I found that my interpreter and willing cook Christo had volunteered as one of the executioners, and the burglar, having been severely thrashed, was turned out of the monastery and thrust down the path towards the depths of Phyni. Christo was a very good fellow, and he sometimes reminded me of a terrier ready to obey or take a hint from his master upon any active subject, while at others, in his calmer moments, he resembled King Henry's knights, who interpreted their monarch's wishes respecting Thomas à-Becket.

On 6th June we had been somewhat startled by the sudden appearance in the afternoon of a man perfectly naked, who marched down the approach from the spring and entered the monastery-yard in a dignified and stage-like attitude as though he had the sole right of *entrée*. At first sight I thought he was mad, but on reference to the monks I discovered he was perfectly sane. It appeared that he was a Greek about forty-five years of age, who was a native of Kyrenia, and for some offence twenty years ago he had been ordered by the priests to do penance in this extraordinary manner. His body, originally white, had become quite as brown as that of an Arab of the desert; he possessed no clothing nor property of any kind, not even a blanket during winter; but he wandered about the mountains and visited monasteries and certain villages, where he obtained food as charity. He would never accept money (probably from the absence of pockets), neither would he venture near Turkish villages, as he had several times received a thrashing from the men for thus presenting himself before their women, and it is to be regretted that the Cypriotes had not followed the Turkish example, which would have quickly cured his eccentricity. He was a strong, well-built man, with good muscular development; his head was bald with the exception of a little hair upon either side, and he was interesting to a certain extent as an example of what a European can endure when totally exposed to the sun and weather. Sometimes he slept like a wild animal beneath a rock among the mountains, or in a cave, when such a luxurious retreat might offer a refuge; at other times he was received and sheltered by the priests or people. This individual's name was Christodilos, and according to my notes taken at the time, he is described as "originally a labourer of Kyrenia; parents dead: one brother and two sisters living."

CHAPTER XVIII.
ON POLICE, FOOD, CLIMATE, &C.

. . . At some future time Cyprus will become the resort of delicate persons to escape the winter and spring of England, as the climate of the southern portion of the island is most enjoyable during the cool season. In the neighbourhood of Limasol there are many excellent sites for building, in picturesque spots within two or three miles of the town. At present there is no adequate comfort for invalids, and the hotels are hardly adapted for persons who are accustomed to luxury. The commencement is attended with risk, and it would be dangerous under the existing conditions of the island to build and furnish an hotel with grounds and gardens sufficiently attractive for English visitors. There is no direct communication from England, which effectually debars Cyprus from an influx of travellers. It is necessary to land at Alexandria either from Marseilles or Brindisi, and thence to re-ship in small and uncomfortable steamers, which are by no means suitable for ladies or invalids. The extra expense, and above all the trouble and delay of landing in Egypt and again embarking, together with the cost of hotel charges at Alexandria, are quite sufficient to deter strangers from visiting Cyprus. The first necessary step will be the establishment of direct communication from Marseilles and Brindisi, or from Trieste. In that case, a commencement might be made by a small company of friends who determine to visit Cyprus annually, and to arrange an hotel upon some favourable site near Limasol, which they will themselves occupy, and which can be extended according to future requirements. English people are somewhat like sheep in following each other, and a quiet beginning in this simple but convenient form would quickly develop, and Cyprus would be linked with the beaten paths of tourists. The neighbourhood of Kyrenia is the most beautiful, but during winter it is exposed to severe north winds from the snowy mountains.

CHAPTER XX.
CONCLUSION.

TROODITISSA MONASTERY, CYPRUS.

It is the 22nd August, and the manuscript of *Cyprus as I saw it in* 1879 has already been forwarded to England. In another month we shall be *en route* for the Euphrates *viâ* Alexandretta, and through Bagdad to India by the Persian Gulf. I shall therefore be placed at the serious disadvantage of an exclusion from the proofs, which may require alterations and corrections; this will I trust excuse me should any repetitions be apparent that would otherwise have been detected before publication. There is little to add to the description I have given that would be of public interest, therefore the few additional details are consigned to a short Appendix.

The seclusion of the monastery has been an agreeable interval that has formed a moral harbour from the uncertain seas of busy life, and we shall leave the quiet spot and the good old monks with some regret. A great change has been effected since our arrival in early May. The heaps of filth have given place to extreme cleanliness; the monks wash their hands and faces; even the monastery yard is swept. No atom of impurity is allowed to deface the walk from the cold spring to the great walnut-tree. My little garden has flourished and produced largely; the melons were of excellent flavour; the tomatoes and other vegetables were good, including a species of esculent amaranthus which is a substitute for spinach. I employed a man and his son to open the path for 2¾ miles, from the monastery to the military route to Troodos, which much improved the communication, and somewhat relieved our solitude by increasing the visits of our friends. If any stranger should now arrive from England at Trooditissa he would appreciate the calm and cool asylum contrasting with the heat of the lower country; but should he arrive even one short month after our departure, I fear the picture will have changed. Throngs of mules will have defiled our clean courtyard, and will be stabled within our shady retreat beneath the walnut-tree, which will remain unswept. The filthy habits of the people, now restrained only by strong remonstrance, will be too apparent. The old monks, Néophitos and Woomonos, (who are dear old people when clean) will cease to wash, and the place and people will certainly relapse into the primaeval state of dirt and holiness in which we first discovered it.

We leave in friendship with all, and during our sojourn at Trooditissa of more than three months, no quarrels, or even trifling disagreements, have occurred between the servants or the people. The temporary storm occasioned by the abrupt departure of Christina was quickly lulled by the arrival of the middle-aged-maid of all work of seventy-five, who has performed all her arduous duties with admirable patience. Our own servants have been most satisfactory since their first engagement upon our arrival in Cyprus in January last; Georgi the "prodigal son," has been of much service as interpreter, and is an honest and willing young man, but there is a peculiarity in his physical constitution exhibited in the mutual want of attachment between his person and his buttons. These small but necessary friends continually desert him; and his shoes appear to walk a few inches faster than his feet, leaving him in a chronic state of down-at-heel. Collars will not assimilate with his neck; whether they are tied with strings, or fastened with buttons, the result is the same, and Georgi's exterior when all or three parts of his buttons have deserted him, exhibits a looseness which I am glad to say by no means applies to his character. The cook Christo is an excellent fellow, always willing to please, and good in his profession; added to which, he assumes a demeanour of importance which is irresistible, and makes all paths smooth. My Abyssinian, Amarn, is always the same quiet, steady character, who performs his daily work with the calm regularity of the stream that turns a mill-wheel, and can always be depended on. It is a pleasure to me that our party does not dissolve upon leaving Cyprus, but the servants accompany us on the Asiatic shore.

Dixon 1879

[Plate 52]

British Cyprus is W. Hepworth Dixon's very personal reflections on Cyprus at the time of the first arrival of the British in 1878, published by Chapman and Hall, London, 1879. Although positive about some of the attributes of Cyprus, his florid style clouds his observation and results in presumptuous generalizations and predictions. Some of his reflections are excerpted here.

Dixon records his meetings with Sir Garnet Wolseley, High Commissioner for Cyprus and other British officials as conversations into which he injects himself, lecturing them on history, prompting court-room procedures and generally making himself sound important. These dialogs are suspect as Wolseley recorded in his *Memoirs* that he found Dixon unbearable.

CHAPTER VI.
OUR ARRIVAL.

Our act of taking over Cyprus from the Sultan to the Queen without a voice being heard—a hand being raised—against the change of flag, has classical and humorous features, like the rape of some fair mortal by one of the elder race of gods or demigods. A bag of sixpences played a part in the affair, as in so many other Eastern stories. We have taken Cyprus very much on the method known in ancient law-books as 'marriage by force.'

At five o'clock on Monday afternoon, July the first, 1878, a telegram arrived at Suda Bay, in Crete, addressed to Vice-Admiral Lord John Hay, commanding the Channel Squadron in those seas. That telegram was in cipher, and was dated from the Admiralty, near Charing-cross.

Lord John was lying with his ships in Turkish waters, waiting on events. A lull had come; the war having ended for the moment in a truce which might or might not lead to peace. Sir Geoffry Hornby's squadron covered the waterways of Constantinople, and a Russian army under General Todleben, stood within striking distance of the walls which guard Seraglio Point. Lord Beaconsfield and Prince Gortschakoff were at Berlin, wrangling with high-bred courtesy, at Prince Bismark's board. Opinions ran on peace; yet Russian agents were intriguing against us on a line of country from Cairo to Cabul. We had to free our arms and stand in readiness to strike at distant and decisive points. One angry word, one accidental shot, might plunge all Europe into war.

If peace were signed, the Channel Squadron would retire to Malta on her way towards Portsmouth, but if war blazed out, she might advance into the Dardanelles and occupy the Boulair lines. For either purpose, Suda Bay was a convenient starting point.

Some of our ships were out at sea, and many of our officers were ashore on leave. For days past every one had been talking of the homeward voyage; but British admirals are never at a loss. The fleet was ready for a cruise, and no less ready for a fight; to go anywhere that ships can sail, to do anything that men can do. Few words sufficed. A signal sped from poop to poop, and every vessel on the station throbbed with life. They were to sail! Despatch boats ran to sea, with orders for the absent ships to join. Officers were called from shore; quick eyes were cast on bunk and magazine. All hands were mustered, and the names read out; each sailor and marine responding smartly to his name. That cipher was the Admiral's secret, but a sense of change—the press and presence of a duty to be done—ran through the squadron like the stream from a galvanic battery through the body of a man.

At daybreak, fires were got up and anchors hauled in. Orders for the day then passed from ship to ship, and the great ironclads began to move. At ten, the flag-ship *Minotaur*, headed from the bay, followed by the *Monarch* and *Defence*, and having cleared the islet, turned her ram due east. What now? Malta lies due west, Boulair due north, of

Suda Bay; so that, on turning eastward, every one saw that they were going to neither Portsmouth nor the Dardanelles. Where, then? Port Saïd—Acre—Scandaroun? Some guessed the first, and more, the last. Some had a theory about our Indian troops at Malta; they had been at Port Saïd when those troops came through, and were prepared to carry them to the Syrian coasts. It was no secret that ground for five or six camps had been taken up, at points to give us easy access to the Jordan Valley and the passes of the Lebanon. Was the Channel Squadron moving on those points? All day they hugged the coast, and in the evening hailed the *Black Prince* off Retymo, where she was engaged in gun-practice, and ordered her to join. The *Pallas* and the *Bittern* were also picked up on the way, and word was left for the *Foxhound* to follow in their wake. Wednesday was spent at sea. Daybreak of Thursday showed them land; a mountain mass higher than any other crest or cone in the Archipelago. That mass was Mount Olympus. Out from the shore stood reefs and rocks; unpleasant objects in a sailors sight; especially when they differ from the dots and soundings on his sailing-charts. Behind these reefs lay a tiny town and port—the port of Papho. Marking those rocks and reefs for future use, the Admiral steamed on, passing Cape Gatta and the coast of Limasol, to Cape Kiti, on rounding which he entered the Bay of Larnaca. Here he found the *Raleigh* and *Invincible*. These vessels, which had crossed from Port Saïd, were signalled to raise their anchors and join the fleet. By sun-down, the whole squadron was in line, holding the bay from Cape Kiti to Cape Pyla, in a ring of fire.

With what intent? No one as yet could say.

That a Convention, giving us a right of entry into Cyprus under certain terms, for certain purposes, was being arranged at Constantinople, was known to many; but the nature of our right of entry and the object of our presence in the island were as yet unknown. The signatures to the final articles of that Convention were hardly dry, for they were written only on the day when Lord John got his secret telegram in Crete. No copy of these articles had reached the *Minotaur*. The Admiral had to grope his way, guided only by his mother-wit, his long experience of affairs in office and out of office, and the sailor's faculty for seeing in the dark.

Next morning, Friday, the *Foxhound* came from Crete with news; on which the *Raleigh* was sent into the bay. Little was known of Larnaca; but a fort, a konak, and other public buildings were visible from the poop. What guns they mounted, and what troops defended them, no one could tell. The *Raleigh* dropped her anchor opposite to the fort; and the *Foxhound*, acting as 'beef-boat,' communicated with the shore and with the fleet. On Saturday information reached the fleet that Cyprus was to be 'taken over' from the Sultan to the Queen. By the same messenger came from the Admiralty a six weeks' 'leave of absence' for the Duke of Edinburgh, captain of the *Black Prince*. This 'leave' the high-spirited young sailor resolutely declined.

The Admiral had never been in Cyprus; no one in the flag-ship spoke the native tongue; no officer of his staff had ever landed on the shore. No proper maps existed; only sham maps, got up in the ministries of foreign states; French maps, German maps, Italian maps; all more or less spotted with the lights that lead astray. Except his sailing charts, he had no key to the intricacies of reef and roadstead, yet he knew that sailors of the greatest eminence differed as to the site of sunken rocks. Nothing was known about the people. Were they likely to approve his orders to take them over? If not, were they to be feared?

How many troops were kept in garrison? How many ports were armed? How many inland towns were walled? Who was the acting governor—who was the military chief? Were they instructed to fall back as we advanced? If not, were we to treat them as enemies, and drive them back by force? Had we the right to lower the Sultan's flag and hoist our own? If the Sultan's troops resisted that proceeding, were we authorized to shoot them down? No one could say.

Doubts hung on every point; yet he was bound to act and act at once. One feeble hour, and we might have to fight from port to port, from ridge to ridge, and blur our passage through the land with blood and fire.

The first thing was to surround the island by his ships, to seal up all the ports, and to prevent the landing of foreign troops. First, the *Bittern* was sent round the island to Cerinia, with orders to close that port and watch the northern coast as far as Cape Andreas; next, the *Pallas* was sent to cruise between Cape Kiti and Papho, so as to hold in blockade all the southern coast; then the *Raleigh* was directed to the west, with orders to cruise between the *Bittern* and the *Pallas*, while the *Black Prince* stood off the island, guarding the approaches from the west and north. These vessels were commanded to watch the coast, to warn intruders from the harbours, and to sink any craft that might attempt, in face of this warning, to throw any troops on shore. By sunrise on Monday mornings, Cyprus was embraced by ironclads.

Early in the day, the *Minotaur* steamed in to Larnaca Bay, and dropped her anchor half a mile from shore. Little was known about the people; nothings at all of their political sentiments. Who was governor of the town, and who commander of the fort? What guns were in position, and were they likely to be used? Captain Rawson, of the *Minotaur*, was sent on shore. This officer has a faculty for picking up intelligence like that of his chief for seeing in the dark. In China and in Egypt his talent had been put to proof. On shore, he saw the consul, and learned that the town was governed by a caimacan, the harbour defended by a small fort, armed with old Venetian guns, and garrisoned by a hundred men. The caimacan—that is to say the lieutenant-governor—was a man of mild and indolent nature, living in the konak with his wives, and seldom came into the town. On Rawson's return to the *Minotaur*, the Admiral went on shore, visited the caimacan, and took his measure of the place. A rumour, as he heard, was current on the quay and in the bazaar, that Cyprus was being turned over to the English, but the caimacan was without instructions on that point. Our speed from Crete had outrun the Sultan's messengers from the Bosphorus. But the Admiral was bound to act.

Next morning, Rawson went on shore again, to learn what could be learnt; and in the afternoon he laid a brief report before the Admiral on all the leading points, not only as to Larnaca, but as to every corner of the island. The town-folk he described as 'quiet and sociable, very lazy, and given to pleasures of every sort;' but they were not 'fanatical,' that is to say, they would not fight. 'Drunkenness was not uncommon,' amongst the Orthodox; but on the other hand, 'robberies, assassinations, and brigandage were nearly unknown.' They were a tame and feeble folk, unlikely to resist. What more could Admiral wish to know?

Parties of blue jackets were put in boats and sent on shore, with orders to land above the town and build a pier. They were to ask no leave, and make no fuss; but set to work and do the job as they were told; acting as they might do on the fore-shore of an

English port. On seeing these sailors land, some of the natives sidled up and stared at them. When they set up a spar, and hoisted the English flag, those natives stared still more; but no one interfered to stop their work. No one knew what to do or what to think. The caimacan and the Quarantine master, were as much in the dark as other people; but while the caimacan sat still in his konak, the Quarantine master, being a foreigner, came on board the flag-ship to see how matters stood, and after glancing at the big guns, offered his humble services to the Queen.

Taking no notice of the fort, we raised our flag and built our pier; taking no heed of the caimacan, we made our consul governor of the town. On Tuesday afternoon our occupation was complete by sea and land.

CHAPTER VII.

TAKEN OVER.

A foothold in the country being secured, might we not now advance from Larnaca to Nicosia? We were to take the island over, not merely to obtain a footing on the shore. How was this order to be carried out? Larnaca is an open port, and in the province of a fleet to seize and hold. Nicosia is an inland capital, lying beyond the passes through a range of hills. Ironclads are useless when the place to be attacked is separated from the sea by mountain walls. To reach Nicosia, the Admiral must go by land.

In Rawson's brief report, the people of Nicosia, being chiefly 'Turks,' were set down as 'fanatical'; men devoted to their religion and faithful to their caliph; in other words, men who might possibly turn out and fight. Their city was a fortress, armed with both English and Venetian guns. The walls were thick, the bastions strong. A Turkish flag was floating from Papho gate. A pasha who had seen service in the field was governor of the island, with a lodging in the konak. A garrison of a hundred and twenty soldiers held the gates, backed by a Mohammedan population counting no less than three thousand fighting-men. On coming to Nicosia, we should have to lower their flag and hoist our own. Would they stand by and see their flag hauled down? Nations are jealous of their flags; the visible expression of themselves. On coming, to Nicosia, we must take possession of the gates and public offices; that is to say, disarm the soldiery and depose the governor. Would they submit to be disarmed, deposed, and swept away? If not, how many guns and men would be required to shoot them down? Our Admiral, who had served with Ottomans by sea and land, knew how those men can fight behind stone walls. He had no need to think of Plevna; he had seen with his own eyes Silistria, Eupatoria, and other battle-grounds. Our new governor of Larnaca, a man of great experience in the island, hinted that he ought to wait for the arrival of British troops. Sir Garnet Wolseley was coming out as High Commissioner, and the Indian regiments then at Malta, stood in readiness to embark. In four or five weeks they might arrive.

How many men, this resident was asked, could venture to go up to Nicosia ?

'Fifteen thousand men, certainly not less.' From Larnaca to Nicosia is twenty-seven miles, more or less, according to the pass through which one rides. By way of Dali, it is rather more; by way of Athieno, it is rather less. Both tracks run over ridges, through a parched and stony waste. The heat was near a hundred in the shade. No water, save at one poor hamlet standing on the river Idalia, was to be expected on the road.

Suppose the Admiral had his fifteen thousand men on parade at Larnaca? How was he to march them—cavalry, infantry, siege-gun, commissariat, hospitals, and ammunition train—across that burning waste?

That night, the Admiral formed his plan; a subtle and a humorous plan. Our entry should be made at once, but in a friendly and civilian spirit; taking our right to occupy the soil for granted, and our welcome by all classes of the islanders as a thing of course. That welcome was to be assured by visible means. All salaries were in arrear. Just as the villagers were in arrear to the Crown, the Crown was in arrear to all its officers. Nothing is so welcome to the eyes of Orientals as a little coin, especially newly-minted coin. The Admiral proposed to enter Cyprus with some sacks of newly-minted sixpences, and to send before him news that he was going to pay off all arrears. He was to go at once, without a guard; to hire a wagonette, the only one in Cyprus; and to drive up quietly to Nicosia with his secretary, and a couple of mules laden with English sixpences. He would enter Nicosia as the minister of a Queen who never falls into arrears, and let the people understand that he was ready to pay the Sultan's debts. Was any man, from pasha to zaptieh, likely to repulse an ally of the Sultan who proposed to hand him over his arrears of pay?

On Wednesday, the *Salamis* arrived, having on board the Ottoman agent, Samih Pasha, and the English agent, Secretary Baring. Samih brought a firman, or 'handwriting of the Sultan,' for the transfer of his island to the English queen. Baring brought a copy of the articles which had just been signed in Constantinople. The firman was addresses to Pessim Pasha, governor of the island; the articles to Lord John Hay, Commander of the Channel Fleet. So far as written words could go, the thing seemed done; and yet, for practical purposes, the problem was unsolved. We had a legal right to march into Nicosia, to depose the Sultan's officer, and disarm the Sultan's troops. Whether these officers and troops would bow their heads was far from being sure. Some facts in Bosnia and Albania raised a doubt as to the prompt obedience of all Ottoman officers to the Sultan's sacred name. Samih was ready to go up. He thought the governor would yield; Baring agreed with him; but neither Samih nor Baring knew the governor and people of Nicosia.

Next morning, Thursday, they set out—Rawson at their side. Rawson was instructed by the Admiral to mark all tracks and rivulets, to observe the townsfolk and the garrison, and to sketch the city walls and gates. Most of all, he was to search the ramparts, and to find the weakest part of the defensive lines. If force had to be used, the Admiral wished to see how the capital could be taken by assault.

Never was officer employed with more success. While Samih and Baring were at the konak, smoking their pipes, sipping their coffee, and listening to the scruples of Pessim Pasha, Rawson was threading his way from khan to mosque, from gateway to bazaar; diving at Famagosta gate into the magazines, climbing the staircase of the minaret, and marking with a sailor's eye the amount of 'fight' in troops and citizens. The men, he thought, were stiff, and full of 'fight.' He made a circuit of the walls, inside and out; noting each trench and angle with a view to an assault. One bastion in the circuit struck his eye; Zechra, an outwork standing in rear of the Serai. There, should the matter come to blows, he saw his chance of leading a column of blue jackets against the scarp.

At dusk he took his road back to Larnaca, leaving Samih and Baring in the capital. He arrived at half-past ten. On hearing his report, the Admiral's impulse was to start at once; he and his secretary in the wagonette. But there were difficulties in his way about the flag. In taking Cyprus over, he was forced to hoist the Union-Jack in Nicosia, and the fixed rule in the service is, that the flag shall never go without a guard. Since the flag must go, men must go with it, in sufficient numbers to impose respect. Rawson was appointed to carry up the flag; and telling off a company, fifty of Captain Kelly's marines, and fifty blue jackets, he returned with them to shore. The night was hot, the country rough, but having set his men in order, he was ready to advance by four o'clock. Then, riding round his little band, he gave the word—'Quick, march.'

At five the admiral started in his wagonette; crawling and bumping over the white and blinding earth. At seven, he overtook and passed his troop, and took up Rawson into his wagonette. Choking with dust, thrown up by his wagon wheels, he pushed on rapidly, grinding over ridge after ridge, until he sighted the palms and campaniles of Nicosia from a crest not more than a mile from the city walls. Curling round a disused cemetery, he entered Nicosia by Famagosta gate at eleven o'clock.

It was the hour of prayer, and all Nicosia seemed asleep. Driving through an oblique tunnel, he curved by way of Thata Kale Mosque into Treboti Lane, a street and water-passage leading through the town from east to west. At Ali Effendi Khan, his wagonette drew up; the farther portion of this lane, by way of Locanda della Speranza, and the Balik bazaar, being only passable for mules and camels. Friday being sabbath, and eleven o'clock the hour of prayer, no visit could be paid, no business done, till after noon; but with a temperature at ninety-nine in shade, a little rest and cover were not unwelcome, even to a sailor bronzed by tropical suns. At three, the Admiral mounted and set out. His mules, gaily attired, rode on in front of him, groaning under their weight of silver coin. To right and left the news ran out among the crowds, that this great English lordo, sent to them by the noble Queen, was going to pay off all arrears of debt. Every one was to get his own; from zaptieh to cadi, from caimacan to pasha, every one was invited to send in his bill. All that was owing, would be paid; not in the dirty caimés of the country, but in solid English sixpences. Such news was strange enough to take men's breath. A governor bring in money to their town! The Golden Age had come again. Could any old man recollect a time when pashas came to give and not to take? Not one. Pashas had always come in lean and gone out fat. Never before had a Nicosian seen a pasha bring in money. The effect was instant—magical. All eyes were strained after those sumpter-mules; all heads were bent before that officer in blue and gold. Even a 'fanatic' with his salary in arrear six months, saw in a moment that this English pasha was the man for him.

Meantime Kelly and his column had arrived at Famagosta gate by three o'clock, after a march of twenty-six miles. Not a man had fallen out of rank. Two marines had suffered from sunstroke, but had kept their places, and the column had only once been halted for half an hour. Out ran the Ottoman troops with cups of coffee and jars of water for the men. These excellent fellows helped in every way; unloading our baggage-carts and getting out the things. In eighty minutes, both the red-coats and blue-jackets mustered on parade. Rawson, after much palaver, got the garrison to retire from Famagosta gate, and left some thirty bluejackets to hold that post, which, sailor-like, they at once inscribed with the legend, 'Channel Squadron Gate.'

What followed in the konak was a form—a bagatelle—a cigarette. Pessim gave up his chair of office, and the English admiral took his seat.

At five the Ottoman flag was lowered with military honours. Kelly's marines presented arms, and in the Admiral's presence, Rawson ran up the British flag. All government debts were ordered to be verified and paid. No voice was raised except to cheer. Victoria spoke to her new children from the silver coins. What caimacan, what zaptieh could resist a lady whose minister's first act was not to tax them but to pay their debts?

Long before Sir Garnet Wolseley and his regiments arrived at Larnaca the work of taking over Cyprus from the Sultan to the Queen was done. To the High Commissioner was left the task, more arduous, perhaps, but less pictorial, of quickening a torpid Oriental body like these Cypriotes into an active and progressive state of life.

CHAPTER VIII.

THE NEW RULE.

No one can say that we have put a satrap over Larnaca to eat and sleep, and earn his Paradise by leaving things alone. Colonel White, of the Royal Scots, our new Commissioner, has no respect for dogs, nor for the vested rights of dogs. In his sight, dogs are nuisances, to be whipped away like other nuisances. Why his horsehair whip? Not satisfied with hustling off the caimacan, pushing his harem from the konak, hurling his old Venetian guns from the castle-wall—where they are lying now, poor relics of a vanished reign—he has ventured to lay his hand on rights and liberties, older in date than our own great charter, older in date than our Anglo-Saxon laws.

Like other communes, Larnaca is a small republic; governed through officers elected by herself. She has a Head-Man, corresponding to an English mayor, who is assisted by a Council of Elders, corresponding to an English Common Council. These officers are chosen once a year by the whole body of citizens. Head-Man and Elders rule the town; lay rates, or don't lay them; clean streets and roads, or don't clean them; build piers and jetties, or don't build them. Chosen by their townsmen, they must please the town or lose their places. Larnaca is a pure democracy, ruling herself by immemorial rights. These local rights are in our way, and we arc treating them, as we have treated the Venetian guns.

A new Head-Man has just been elected by public vote; but he is not the kind of man we want; so we have snuffed him out and put another in his place: one Heidestan, that quarantine-master, who so quickly put himself on the side of the biggest guns. He is a stranger in the town, and we have called him mayor.

Head-Man and Elders are no doubt, old fogies; willing to let everything alone. 'Dimani' is their motto, as of other Oriental folk. What, if the streets are choked by dust? What, if the khans are foul with dung? What if the quays are channelled by tide and surf? Nobody cares. They have no money to expend. To lay a rate is only to excite the public wrath. Why should the Head-man and his Elders vex their souls about improvements for which no one cares? The Head-Man, like the caimacan, finds his peace in leaving things alone.

To do what must be done, we want new men; to put in force what must be put in force, we want new rules.

Our satrap gives us lots of rules.

'Don't go on shore, Sir,' says the youngster of the Howling Wilderness, laughing with a boy's enjoyment of his fun. 'Don't go on shore, Sir; it's *too* dangerous.'

'Dangerous? What's too dangerous? You don't mean to say the gig will upset, and the pier break down?'

'No, Sir; the gig's all right, and the pier's all right; no fear of them. What's dangerous is the new rules, made by the big bashaw.'

'New rules and big bashaw! What do you mean? What are the new rules, and who is the big bashaw?'

'English rules—they are the new rules—Colonel White—that is the big bashaw.'

'You call the new Commissioner a big bashaw? How will he prove dangerous to *me*, if I go on shore?'

'Down on you like a shot, Sir. He is more peremptory than a pasha of twenty tails.'

'And how does he come down on you like a shot?'

'Fines, sir, fines. Five shillings to two pounds, Sir; not less than five shillings, not more than two pounds. That's the big bashaw. Mostly ten bob, Sir. Some men are unlucky. That sub-lieutenant hardly ever gets off shore under fifteen bob.'

'What does he fine you for?'

'Anything—nothing; spitting in the street, smoking on the pier, blowing your nose on the quay, winking your eye at a ghost.'

A ghost, I find, is English for a veiled Mohammedan woman.

'Why, Sir,' laughs the youngster, 'I got fifteen bob for only just having a lark with a ghost in the bazaar.'

'My friend, if you will have larks with ghosts in howling wildernesses you must pay for them.'

'It's getting beyond a joke, Sir. Why, his fines—not less than five shillings, not more than two pounds—have all but stopped our leave. Fellows can't afford to go on shore, when it's ten bob for kicking up a bit of a dust.'

Larnaca is the chief place in the province, or Caimacanate of that name; but for the sake of cooler air and better water, head quarters have been fixed at La Scala—the port. Here stand the konak, the castle, and the town-hall. Here we have taken up our ground.

The province starts from Yeni Kale, in the centre of the bay; skirts the ochre-pits near Mavro Vouni, crosses the limestone ridges under Santa Anna; climbs the heights of Machera, and running along the summit of that mountain, drops by way of Calavasso to the sea. Much of this country is rocky waste; sacred and classical, no doubt; but of an unproductive soil. Carobs and prickly pears abound; but mulberries, oranges and palms are scarce. A headland bears the name of Carob Point, and a small bay, called Zu, is frequented by tiny craft for those locust beans which Greeks and Russians eat as John the Baptist's bread. But, Larnaca and Leucara excepted, this province cannot boast of having a single town. The villages are small; the best amongst them, such as Kellia and Aradippo, being no more than little groups of cottages. In England even Leucara and Larnaca would hardly rank as towns: the first having less than eighteen hundred souls, the second less than two thousand souls. The soil is thin; the peasants living on that soil are poor. Few taxes can be raised. Not many trades are carried on, and some of those who profit by the business of La Scala pay their taxes into other public chests. To wit, the muleteers who carry goods from Larnaca to Nicosia and other inland towns, live in Athieno, a village in the province of Famagosta; so that the profit of their enterprise goes into the public chest of Famagosta, not into that of Larnaca.

Our Commissioner at Larnaca has pressing and ungrateful duties to perform, and should be judged, in fairness, by results. To some, his treatment of the ancient laws will seem offensive and unjust; not to be excused by any evidence he may show of cleaner streets and better paved quays. Others may think his improvements worth the price, including his suspension of rights and liberties which the Ottomans have respected for three hundred years.

Larnaca has a good deal of dust to lay; a good deal of spitting in the streets to stop. A Levantine port, it has the ordinary—and something more than the ordinary—rubbish of a Levantine port. Larnaca is a holy place, sacred to more than one race of saints; drawing to her mosques and churches pilgrims from many sides. Arabs and Egyptians come over sea to pray at the Sultana's tomb above the town; Copts and Maronites come over sea to pray at the shrine of Lazarus within the town. These shrines are of peculiar sanctity. The mosque of the Sultana is supposed to cover the ashes of Omm Haram, Mohammed's cousin. The shrine of Lazarus is supposed to cover the grave of him who was once before entombed at Bethany, and was afterwards restored to life. Pilgrims come in shoals. Unhappily, all towns of pilgrimage are dirty, for the pilgrims, whether 'Turk' or 'Greek,' or only black earth, all come from a low, improvident and superstitious class.

Larnaca cannot boast of being the one exception to a general rule. Before our new Commissioner entered on his task, the streets were choked with dust, and the bazaars with filth. Dogs, mules and camels fouled the roads, arid every suburb stank with dead and unburied animals. Beasts were slaughtered in the street, and the offal left to fry and rot. A ledge of broken stones was called the quay. In and out among these stones the waters washed and frothed, drenching the passer-by, tearing out the boulders, and stopping up the road. The shores were cesspools, and the public khans no more than heaps of dung. Four or five good houses, tenanted by consuls, tried to keep the enemy at bay. Their fight was stout, but they were always beaten in the end; for the Caimacan, living in the Turkish quarter, was untouched in his own harem, and what cause had he to rouse the head-men and his set of elders from their trance? What to him were the woes of strangers? Men must sleep under the trees they plant. So the Caimacan smoked his pipe, and left the hucksters of the port to perish in the filth they made.

But with our advent things are changed. We make these vagrants decent whether they will or no. Once dirtier than Beyrout or Jaffa, Larnaca is becoming as clean as Folkestone or Holyhead. Of course, this work is up-hill work. Men who never swept their doors before, don't like to sweep them now; men who were never made to clean their khans object to paying fines. We force all persons in the town, even those who land for a few hours only, to observe the decencies of life. These rules are hard for Levantines to learn; but then a fine, from five shillings up to forty, is still harder for a Levantine to pay. Colonel White's scheme is strict. No nuisances are allowed, and no offences are condoned. Every man must either do or pay his duty. A butcher in the bazaar shall keep no offal near his stall; a stable-keeper shall not throw his refuse on the street. No idler shall 'kick up a dust,' annoy a ghost, or misbehave in a public place.

Under rules so strict, and so unusual, comic incidents of course arise; your engineers, we know, are sometimes 'hoist on their own petards,' and magistrates, we hear, are sometimes fined in Larnaca under their own rules. Even the big bashaw has not escaped.

In going about the port with Colonel White, and still more frequently without him, I compare the present with the past. I am surprised to see how much has been achieved, and at so slight a cost. White has no public chest to draw from: yet he has changed La Scala so completely that a native, absent from the town for ten or twelve weeks, would hardly know his place again. Houses are being cleaned and whitewashed, and the windows paned with glass. Holes in the ground are filled up, and angles in the buildings cut away. The streets are named—White Street, Wolseley Street, Bank Street—and the quays are being widened and aligned. Parts of the camel-ground are being enclosed; dead animals are buried out of sight. Only in one suburb have I seen a skeleton battened on by kites and crows.

CHAPTER XI.

OUR VILLAGE.

'No milk to be got, Hassan?'

'No, Effendi, not a drop; nothing but milk in tins; sweet stuff, that no one cares to drink.'

'Why so?'

'I don't know why, Effendi; but we have none, that is certain.'

'You have lots of cows. Yesterday, when I was out, I met a dozen herds—sheep, goats, and cattle. Many of the cows had calves. No milk?'

'These people never milk their cows, Effendi.'

'Never milk their cows!'

Taking up my whip, I walk into the lane, meaning to inquire from some one why they have no milk. On looking down the road, I see a herd of cattle on the hill; among that herd trot three or four calves. Why, then, is milk not to be had?

Ormidia lies in the Caimacanate of Famagosta. Our village boasts of some special gifts. Lying near the sea, and in a dip between two hills, we have a fresh breeze blowing through the lane by day and night. Even when it drops by day, it never fails to rise again at sunset. But our chief felicity is water; more than all else the spring that rivals Zemzem. Other sources send their blessings to our door,—water for the bath and kitchen, water for the mill and field; this spring is for the lips, and one might almost say, the souls of men. Lying nine or ten miles from the main camel-track, we arc rarely visited by satraps and their satellites. A bye-path runs along the shore, leading in old time to a temple of Apollo, and in later ages to a chapel of St. George; but god and saint have long since vanished from these shrines. Thus, we are left alone, closed in by limestone downs, forgotten by the world.

Our village has some twenty cabins, sprinkled over a rough and tangled surface. Cypriotes, whether 'Turk' or 'Greek,' prefer to dwell apart, each man on his own patch of ground. A 'Turk,' keeping closer to the traditions of shepherd life, prefers a wider sweep; but his 'Greek' neighbour likes to have his homestead covered by a fence, and entered only by a private gate. Within that gate he lodges, he and his wife, his man-servant and his maid-servant, his ox, his ass, and anything else that may be his, together with the stranger who may happen to be his guest. If rich, he sinks a well; however poor, he plants a tree. Under that tree and near that well he loves to sit and smoke; watching his females raise the pitcher, and his little folk gather in the fruit.

The cabins, one and all, are built of earth cakes, kneaded with stubble and baked in the sun; a cross between the mud hovel on the Nile and the adobe ranch on the Rio Grande. No chimney breaks the outline, for all fires are lighted, as in Egypt, in the open air. Thus, in the waning light, both roof and fence appear to sink into the earth. In colour they are all alike, and all are lost within the shadow of adjacent hills. So we are lost to sight; and to escape from notice is a gain. No villager wants to hear the crack of a Caimacan's whip.

Though poor, these Cypriote rustics are not wretched in the sense in which the words poverty and wretchedness describe an Egyptian fellah, a Spanish galego, and an Irish kerne. Nearly every one owns his patch of ground. The commune means equality; liberty implies possession of the land.

Meeting a herdsman driving in his cattle from the hills, I ask him why he never milks his cows. He stares, perplexed. Milk his cows ? Twiddling at his beard, he stops to think, and looks at Hassan, with a puzzled stare. At length he says, 'Tell the Effendi that we never milk our cows. Why not? The Effendi wants to know why not ? Well . . . . I don't know; because . . . . we never milk our cows.'

That is the only reason he can give. I try him once again:

'Tell him, Hassan, that is the fact. What I want to know is the reason for that fact. Why do they never milk their cows?'

Vain, all vain; the herdsman cannot see my point. To him fact and reason are the same. When told that we milk cows in England, and drink the milk for our daily food, he drops his eyes, and says, it must be right, because it is our custom; but . . . perhaps the head-man can tell us. He can read and write, and comes from foreign parts. Perhaps the head-man can tell.

I have no mind to seek the head-man; yet this personage from foreign parts is worth a moment's notice; his rise and progress showing a weak side of these village democracies.

Born in a busy port, and nursed in the petty arts of trade, this man, whose name is Heracles, settled in our village with a few piastres in his pouch. Squatting on a piece of dry heath, lying outside the commune towards the sea, he raised a mud cabin and began to ply his trade. Instead of scratching his barren earth for food, he looked about to see how he could cheat the ignorant and shiftless peasants out of their better lands. These rustics were as babies in his clutch. To them he seemed a nice and neighbourly fellow, with a little money in his pocket, and a heart to feel for people in distress. When money can be borrowed easily, people are always in distress. Heracles found many customers for his loans. Of course, he took securities; and he only lent his money where either lands or water-rights could be got in pledge. When he saw fit to close, he closed with sudden snap. The law against non-paying persons is severe; thus, bit by bit, a good deal of the land, and still more of the water-right, have passed into this stranger's hands. A field, presented by him to the Archbishop of Nicosia, is supposed to have secured for him a friend at court. No one can stand against him now. Already he is said to be the richest person in our village. In a little while he may succeed in getting every rood of ground and every spring of water, into his own hands.

For my part I shall grudge him the monopoly of Zem-zem and the apricots.

Our landing in the island has alarmed him, and at present he is trying to face about. Nothing suited him so well as having a satrap in Famagosta who only ate and slept; leaving the kids and lambkins to the dogs. In India we know this class of men, and I have seen them playing their game on the Pacific slope.

For good and bad, we have these small republics on our hands. Living under many rulers, and in every case rejecting konak laws, these village democracies have known but little change. The first comers from Syria brought the communes with them, and the latest comers from England find these communes in their ancient force. These things are rooted in the soil. Judges and elders ruled in Israel before the people in their vanity and weakness chose for themselves a king.

At times, the outer rule may have been mild and fatherly, at other times harsh and brutal; but the rustic seldom felt much difference in that outer rule. Once, it is said, the rustics of a village tried to gain the ear of a compassionate governor. The pasha used to ride about the country, and to ask from each caimacan about the happiness of his district. Lodging with his lieutenant-governor, he heard reports, and being a good man, smoked his pipe in peace. Of the inhabitants he saw but little; for the peasants and the camel-drivers knelt to him in their roads, but never followed him into their towns. He was too great for them to face—their fancies dwelling chiefly on his horsehair whip. One of his caimacans being a bad man, the elders of several villages put their jowls together and resolved to march on the konak, see the kind pasha, and complain of their local tyrant. On the day appointed, they assembled in his court-yard as the pasha was about to leave.

'Who are these people, and what do they want?' the pasha asked.

'Men of the place, your highness; honest folk; not very clean and wholesome; but extremely good. I gave them leave to come and thank your highness for their happiness.'

'Ugh! Happy, say you; that is pleasant, caimacan. I wish to see my people happy and content. But dirty in their persons! When I am gone convey to them my thanks—ugh!'

The villagers marched home.

In fact, these small republics usually escape all notice from the great. They keep their head-men, their village elders, and their patriarchal rule. Haroun and Amurath are to them the same. Dwelling apart, they live their life; a noble or ignoble life as may be, but in keeping with the wants and wishes of a shepherd race.

CHAPTER XIII.

IN CAMP.

'What do you think of Cyprus?' asks Sir Garnet Wolseley, High Commissioner for Queen Victoria in Cyprus, much as Sir Philip Sydney was High Commissioner for Queen Elizabeth in Walcheren.

'Think of Cyprus! I have always liked the island, and I see no reason to change my mind.'

Our camp is called Monastery Camp, from the monastic building near our tent; a small dependency of Kikko, the famous convent on the slope of Mount Olympus, where the picture of Panayia, the All-holy, painted by St. Luke, is kept. Our camp is pitched about a mile from Nicosia, outside Papho Gate. A priest and two or three monks retain their cells; otherwise, the monastery is given up to Sir Garnet and his staff.

Sir Garnet has the refectory for a saloon; near him, in their cells, sit Colonel Graves, secretary, and Colonel Dormer, adjutant. A third cell is the telegraph station, and a leather bag, nailed to the outer wall, serves as a post-office for the camp. These are the working rooms; the dining-tables and the beds are in the open under canvas. We are still, as one may say, a-field. Some of the men are hutted, but the officers are still in tents.

Between the city and the monastery flows the Pedia, usually a rapid river, though at present it is dry. In summer-time this obstacle is nothing; but in winter, after rain has fallen, it must isolate the camp. Sir Garnet is preparing for a move. At first the convent offered us not only the convenience of a stone building for our books and papers, but the shade of several well-grown trees, with level ground about, and good supplies of water. Yet the natural site for a camp is on the southern bank, in free communication with the capital by Papho Gate.

'This plain,' I venture to remark, 'was once a paradise of the earth, and under English rule, it should be so again. Suburbs used to run up higher than this convent, covering both banks of the river with kiosks and gardens. That was before the Venetian came.'

'In riding up and down,' returns Sir Garnet, 'I have often come on walls in ruins; portions of the ancient city walls. I'll point them out to you when we ride out.'

'Under the Venetian rule, the population shrank so much—for they were always fighting over their religious dogmas—Greeks driving out Latins, Latins driving out Greeks—that the city became more than half garden.'

'Yes, all this open ground might be cultivated. Look at the bluff out there, beyond the river bed.'

'Yes, I know that bluff—King Richard's camp.'

'King Richard's camp! That is the spot where I am laying out my house—in future, government house. Just now, it looks no better than a limestone waste. I mean to lay it out in shrubberies, and in a little time, my roof will be protected from the sun.'

'It's a question, I suppose, of water. Have you a well up there?'

'Not yet; but I am sinking a deep shaft. When I touch water half my trouble will be over.'

'Yes; and when you find water, other men will try; the example in the camp, may act in every part of Cyprus.'

'Well, we rather count on that—but, for the moment, everything is new,' replies Sir Garnet.

CHAPTER XIV.

OUR RIGHT IN CYPRUS.

'One thing, you will find, Sir Garnet, in Mas Latrie's books—Guy de Lusignan was French. King Richard, as you know, considered him an Anglo-Norman count. Beyond all question he was Richard's vassal; but you find no mention of that fact in M. de Mas Latrie's text. First, the Lusignans are Franks; after a hundred pages they are French; hence forward they are always French.'

'Yes, I have noticed that.'

'One need not push these ancient rights too far,' I venture to remark; 'still, truth is truth; if any vestige of a right attaches to the Lusignans, that right descends to us.'

* * * * *

Cyprus, in the view of English king and English council, had never ceased to be an English fief—had never passed legitimately from the jurisdiction of the English crown.

Our policy, Sir Garnet, should connect our ancient occupation with the new. Whether we will or not, the facts of our former visit stare us in the face. There, for example, you are building your new quarters on the ground once occupied by Lion Heart's men.'

'A good idea! I will call that place King Richard's camp.'

Richard—Victoria! By these great names we link our second advent with our first. A chain from Richard to Victoria seems long; but England is an ancient country, and her sovereigns are connected with each other by unbroken lines.

CHAPTER XV.

NICOSIA.

'What say you to Nicosia from King Richard's camp?'

Standing on the bluff among the lines of our new position, we face the mosques and gardens of the capital. A low wall, broken on the scarp by bastions, stretches and turns to right and left. A gate, from which depends a British flag, opens in our front; flanked on one side by the kisla, or barrack, on the other side by a military hospital. Above the wall and gate spring minarets, campaniles and trees; the minarets tapering into points, each capped by crescent moons; the campaniles, square in form, with open fretwork, capped with iron crosses; the trees of many kinds and colours, ranging from willows and cypresses to oranges, figs and palms.

'Say to Nicosia? A little sister of Damascus.'

'You venture to say that?' asks the High Commissioner.

'I venture to say that. Of course, Nicosia is much smaller than Damascus; but these minarets and trees remind one of the Syrian capital.'

This little sister of Damascus is a labyrinth of lanes and alleys; winding under minarets, towers and fruit-trees; round about khans, kiosques, and fountains; in and out among brown walls, running waters and broken grounds. Only a native of the town can find his way from gate to mosque, from coffee-house to khan. A clever engineer, whose tents are pitched near Papho gate, tells me that he took twelve days to learn the shortest way from his camp outside the gate to the archbishop's palace and the mosque. Fancy the stranger of a day in such a place—and more than all, the stranger of a night!

Each alley is own brother to the rest; a gut between blank walls, through which a camel and her load can hardly squeeze. Triboti Lane, running from west to east—from Papho gate to Famagosta gate—is hardly more than an open trench, or sewer; the water in the bed being crossed on stepping-stones. The walls are built of sun-dried cakes of earth, threaded with straw or stubble, such as the Syrians learnt to bake in Egypt, and to use when giving up their tents for a more settled life. The few stone houses—chiefly in St. John's Lane, and near the cathedral church—are built of rough and undressed stones, filled in with mud and lime. Stone that will bear a mason's tool is scarce. Good clay is dear, and marble is unknown. A hundred of such lanes and alleys make the labyrinth of Nicosia—little sister of the Syrian capital.

One thing separates Nicosia from the city on the slope of Lebanon; the want of any street, which, even by the courtesy of Orientals, can be called the Straight.

CHAPTER XVII.

HIS BEATITUDE.

'How do you get on with his Beatitude of St. John's?' I ask our High Commissioner.

'Pretty well. He is a kindly sort of man. Some of the old archbishops, I have heard, were great oppressors of their people; but the present man appears to be a good exception to that rule.'

'He has an excellent character for piety and charity amongst the town folk,' I reply.

'Yes and he deserves it, I believe. We get on pretty well, and might get on much better, only that he wants me to do things for him which we cannot undertake. Example: he asks me, as Governor of Cyprus, to collect his dimes.'

'Of course, you have heard that the Pashas used to help him in that way?'

'Yes, so he says; and I believe they did so. That was a fault in them—one of their many faults. Anything that anybody asked them to do, those Pashas did; never stopping to inquire whether what they were asked to do was right or wrong. They only wanted a quiet life. We stand on other ground; we try to find out what is right, and cause it to be done. What has the State to do with bishops' dimes ? The dime is not a public tax. Why should the public pay the cost of getting in a clerical rate? Enough for us the public service. If you lay a church-rate, you must get it in yourself, not send for the police.'

CHAPTER XVIII.

BRITISH RULE.

'I came out,' says our High Commissioner, 'under the impression that I might have to change the whole system of government; brushing aside, not only the fiscal system, but the legal courts and the executive bodies.'

'You were rather anti-Turk at first, I think you said?'

'Certainly. When we first came out, myself and staff were of the same opinion. We expected nothing good in Cyprus; nothing better in the usages than in the men.'

'And you have not been forced to sweep them out?'

'Fortunately, not. You see it is much easier to get on with laws to which people are accustomed than with foreign codes. Luckily, we find these laws are very good. All that is wanted is to put them into force. When you apply them properly you find they serve you very well. All of us have changed our first opinions; no one more so than myself. In truth, the more I master the whole body of these Turkish laws, the more I am surprised at their humanity and justice.'

'Some of our folks at home, you are aware, imagine that these laws are nothing but a hotch-potch from the Koran, framed by cunning mufti, to support a race of tyrants ruling over concubines and slaves.'

'Well, that was partly what I thought myself. But facts are otherwise. The laws in vogue are founded on the code Napoléon; they are very clear and full; and are well adapted to an Oriental people. When I came to Nicosia, we thought of setting up a few plain rules, founded on English law and practice, and of working outward from these rules. But I soon saw my error, and withdrew my scheme. The local laws are just; even the administrative rules are good. In theory, I regard these laws and rules as perfect.'

'Perfect is a strong expression?'

'But I mean it. Many of the officials were, no doubt, to blame. Offenders offered bribes, and some of the judges took those bribes. Sometimes—but not always—justice failed. But here the men, and not the methods, were in fault. If you were to ask me what is the main fault of these Ottoman laws, I should answer that they are too lenient towards vagabonds and criminals. They give a rogue too many chances of escape. A Turkish judge is slow to act. A murderer, with the blood of two victims on his hands, is now lying at Papho, waiting an order for his execution. No one gives that order, and the wretch remains unhung.'

'Is it not the case, that under Ottoman law nobody in this island has power to put a man to death? Is not the Governor bound to lay his case before the Governor-general of Rhodes, and is not that Governor-general of Rhodes bound to lay his case before the Grand Vizier at Constantinople?'

'Yes, that was so. Turks are so slow to shed blood coldly, that they can never make up their minds to carry out their sentences. Until a criminal chooses to confess his crime, they never hang him. Here is where these people need us most; nobody in this island has the courage to do right.'

'Ah, that is one of the rarest qualities in the world.'

'Still one has to do it, and to stand to it when done. If not, where is the use of law? We mean to see all sentences carried out, not caring who is hurt. In no long time, people will begin to feel that law must be obeyed.'

Thus, in taking Cyprus over from the Sultan to the Queen, we keep the local laws intact, but pay no heed to usages, which, even when they are old, have grown up outside the law. 'Show me the code, point out the article,'—this is our method, this our means. Looking to nothing but the end, we take the straight course, letting people see that what is written in the book is no dead letter, but a living and protecting spirit.

Not only have we left the laws in force, but we have kept the boundaries and offices intact.

CHAPTER XIX.
PUBLIC JUSTICE.

'No, there is not much crime in Nicosia; not much, that is to say, for an Oriental town,' says Colonel Biddulph, our Civil Commissioner, as we sit at breakfast in his cool apartments in the Levantine quarter. Government House is built of stone, with gardens in the rear and palm-trees on the flank. Close by are two fine fountains, and the upper windows overlook the ramparts and command the range of Mount Olympus. Our Commissioner's rooms are cool.

'No, there is not much crime among these people. Vices they have in plenty—drunkenness and debauchery without end; but they are not often guilty of the deeper and blacker sorts of crime.'

'My court will open at ten o'clock,' interposes Lieutenant Seager, an officer of marines, who has the great advantage of having been called to the bar; 'If you like to come and see us, though we don't allow barristers to plead, we never mind seeing them in court. I shall be glad to show you what we do and how we do it.'

'Lawyers may be present to advise?'

'Yes, to advise their clients; but they are not allowed to address the bench. We are a simple people, and we hold a patriarchal court. Counsel for the prosecution, answered by counsel for the defence, are out of our line. We want to get our business done.

'Not, one hopes, like the hungry judge who hung his men right off in order that he might go home and dine?'

'Oh, no! The forms, you'll see, are long enough. We run no risk of being too curt.'

'Nor of giving a wrong sentence, like that fox in the fable who condemned his crony, the guilty shark, to be thrown into the sea ?'

'No, we have law enough for that.'

At ten o'clock, we enter the Medjalis Davi, now removed from Cythrea to the capital. The bench, as under Ottoman rule, is occupied by two Christian judges and by two Mohammedan judges; all of the four elected by the people to their posts by popular vote. A cadi presides; and Lieutenant Seager sits as Sama, 'listener'—as we should say, 'assessor.' His duties are, to hear the pleas, to sift the evidence, and to sign the judgment. He is not supposed to meddle with the law; but, since no sentence is good without his signature, he is obliged to satisfy himself about the law. In practice, Lieutenant Seager is the court.

The room is small, with wooden floor, and paper peeling from the walls. A chair is placed for the 'listener,' and a second chair for myself. Natives squat and lean on the divan. The cadi and his Mohammedan brethren sit on their calves; the Orthodox members dangle their legs about, pushing their slippers on and off. A clerk, a zaptieh, and a dragoman, assist the court. Loafers in taboosh and turban represent the citizens. In every sense, the room is open; for neither rope nor rail divides the culprit from the bench. No dock exists. In Ottoman eyes, an untried person is an innocent man. Not till sentence is accorded, is he in the hands of justice. Neither have we a witness-box; the Ottoman system not allowing a man to be pilloried merely for standing up to speak the truth.

First case is called:

Constantinos Janni steps into the room, and bowing to the judges, makes his charge. Certain persons, he alleges, owe him sums of money. A list is handed to the bench, containing twenty or twenty-five names, with sums set down against them, from ten or twelve piastres up to fifteen or twenty medjedés.

'Who is this man, a money-lender?' I ask Lieutenant Seager.

'No, a dealer in the bazaar.'

'Have these debts been made in the ordinary way of trade?'

'Yes, precisely.'

'Well, and what does he expect the court to do for him?'

'Collect these debts. He wants us to send out zaptiehs and compel his customers to pay.'

'I suppose he used to get that sort of thing done for him in the Pasha's time?'

'Yes; the man is well off, and a great spouter. Listen to him; he is better than a play.'

The man is loud and voluble, even for a Greek. He says he wants justice, and no more than justice. He wants his money, and no more than his money. Why is he refused his zaptieh? He always had a zaptieh before. What has he done? Why is he now denied? Seager asks him whether he thinks it right to send a public officer twenty miles to collect a sum of twenty pence? Yes, he certainly thinks it right; it is the law; it is the custom of his country; it was always done.

After glancing down his list, I ask Lieutenant Seager if the items have been proved?

'No, not at all; they stand on his bare word. The thing is like a farce. None of the alleged debtors are present; and no evidence of debt has been produced.'

'Ask him whether he has sent his debtors any notice of this charge?'

Being asked this question by the dragoman, Constantinos answers that he has done nothing of the sort. How could he send them notice? He has nobody to send; he has no zaptiehs in his house.

'Ask him whether he has taken pains to collect his money.'

'No,' reports the dragoman, 'he says they live in different places; some a long way off. Unless the cadi lends him zaptiehs, how is he to gather in his debts?'

Case remanded for a week; Lieutenant Seager telling him he better make some effort to collect his money for himself.

Exit Constantinos; clouded in face, and evidently confused in brain. For him, justice is postponed, if not denied.

Second case called.

Kerides Janni strides into the room, salutes the judge, and asks for justice in the customary form. A man of vile expression, with a hanjar in his belt, he glares around the court, passing the four elected judges with a kind of sneer, and fixing an inquisitive and beseeching eye on the English 'listener.' Then he makes his charge. A neighbour in his quarter of the city owes him, he alleges, one hundred piastres. He has asked him for the money times on times. The fellow will not pay, and now he has the impudence to deny his debt.

One of the Christian judges lifts his hand; the zaptieh orders silence: 'This case,' says the Christian judge, 'has been already heard; I recollect it well. It was about a year ago.'

The clerk remembers it, and turns his record over. 'Yes, here it is. Case heard, and judgment given.'

'What was the verdict?' I inquire.

'That the accusation was untrue.'

'And made for purposes of fraud?'

'Yes, that was the opinion of the bench.'

'Was nothing done to punish him?'

'No; the charge was treated as a mistake. Nobody wished to press him hard. He was dismissed.'

'Ask him why he comes again and makes this charge a second time.'

My question being put to him by the dragoman, Kerides answers that he is an injured man, and thought the English Effendis would do him justice. It is true that he was heard twelve months ago, but he was badly heard and falsely judged. It was under another cadi, and his enemy bribed the court. A few words pass between Lieutenant Seager and the Chief Justice. Then the cadi says: 'This case has been already judged. No man can be tried twice on the same charge. This is no court of appeal. Next case.'

Kerides backs out with a vicious look.

Anki Christopher steps in. Anki desires to have summons granted by the bench against his neighbour in a case of petty trespass. It is an ordinary application, made and granted every day. On payment of a fee of one piastre the summons is made out. Then comes the question: At whose expense shall it be served? Nicosia is the chief town of a Caimacanate extending from the heights above Cythrea to the summits of Mount Machera. Anki's adversary lives some sixteen miles from Nicosia, and Anki expects the State to send a zaptieh with his summons to that distant part. A 'listener,' representing public thrift, raises objections on the point of cost. Zaptiehs mean expense. To send a zaptieh on a ride of sixteen miles is to employ a man and horse two days. A man and horse are worth from thirty to thirty-five piastres a day; from sixty to seventy for two days. Fine profits for the State! One piastre received for granting a summons, and seventy piastres spent in serving it!

The matter has a second face, no less objectionable to a 'listener' bent on doing what is right. A trader, having no costs to pay beyond his two penny summons, can afford to gratify his petty spites. Here are two men who have a quarrel. One of them lives in Nicosia; the other on his distant farm. The citizen, eager to annoy the rustic, comes into court, and on the pretext that the rustic owes him five piastres, gets a summons. To him the cost is twopence. His enemy must appear in person at Nicosia. Say the charge is heard, the case dismissed. The rustic loses time and money, while the citizen, sitting at his stall in the bazaar, enjoys his joke. That fancy costs him twopence; for the main expense is thrown by custom on the public purse. Under such easy rule, what wonder that the courts are busy, the officials always in arrears of pay?

But here comes our embarrassment in the affair. As with the Primate's dimes, so with the huckster's summons. In the Pasha's time zaptiehs were always sent. Our cadi has, in fact, no choice. His summons must be served, and Anki's zaptieh is allowed, but under protest from the 'listener,' as a vicious custom, costly to the State, and tending to encourage personal spite. A new rule should be made.

A female, breaking from a zaptieh, who is mildly trying to prevent her entrance, steps with a flush and frown into the room. A tall and handsome creature, with a ruddy cheek lit up by burning eyes, and clothed in heaps of parti-coloured garments, she neither curtsies to the bench nor prays that the judge's feet may be prevented from straying into crooked ways. The cadi starts a little, as he might do at the spring of a leopardess. He has evidently seen her face before, and was clearly not expecting her in court to-day. Throwing her head back, and looking proudly at the bench, she says: ' Name, Cosora Mariam; nationality, Greek; age, forty-five."

'Who is this woman?'

'Curious case, this,' replies Lieutenant Seager. She was present yesterday, and we adjourned the matter till Saturday next. I want to master the accounts. She is reported to be rich; but all her property is in land; that is the case with many people here. Money is scarce, and farmers mostly pay their debts in kind—a sheep for a coat or turban, and a basket of onions for a pair of shoes. Accounts are rather hard to keep. Cosora is said to own six hundred acres; one of her neighbours, I believe a money-lender, is pursuing her for a balance or pretended balance of account. According to her tale it is the other way; he owes her money. Anyhow there is bad blood; the man is pushing her to the wall; by hook or crook he means to get her land.'

'That is a common case in Cyprus, I suspect?'

'Quite true; those money-lenders are our greatest curse.'

'You have adjourned the hearing: why is she in court to-day?'

By this time something of her fury is relaxed! On being asked what she requires, the fury darkens on her face again:

'Justice! I want to go home. Till I get justice I cannot go home.'

The cadi answers mildly: 'Your hearing, Cosora Mariam, is adjourned to Saturday next.'

'I cannot wait till Saturday next.'

Her voice—deep, proud, yet tender—touches every one, and most of all, I think, the cadi:

'Why not, good woman?'

With a haughty gesture, such as Rachel might have envied in an actress, she replies:

'Effendis! I live a long way off. I have no food, no house, no money in this place. I came here yesterday. You sent for me; I came. I walked the whole way. I have no husband and no son. That man is trying to bear me down. My land is there, my garden there. I have no money. Tell me to wait—you kill me. Saturday! Where shall I eat—where shall I sleep—till then? My persecutor knows all that. Saturday! On Saturday I shall be dead!'

The cadi winces; but the bench can give her no help. Kind words are used; the cadi asking her to remember that accounts take time. At last his explanations seem to settle on her mind. Turning to the door, she neither bows nor smiles, but goes away in a proud anguish very sad to see.

CHAPTER XX.

THE KONAK.

Leaving the cadi and his court, we turn into the gallery; here, as in every other house, an open walk, with arches on the shady side. This gallery is old and quaint, with bits of finery here and there; relics of Venetian times and even of Crusading times. Here are some Latin letters graven on a stone, recording that in such a year So-and-so was prefect of this place. Yonder stands a Gothic window, with heraldic lions sculptured in the wall. Here again, under our feet, lies a slab of foreign marble, taken from some chapel, and employed to mend the floor. Here paced those Anglo-Norman kings who owed their lordships to English valour, and their sceptres to imperial greed and guile. Here, in her robe and diadem, walked the Queen of Cyprus, long before the art of Titian had endowed her with a more lasting crown. Venetian prefects, one of them, that Moor of Venice who is best known to us as Othello, trod this gallery, looking on the ‘ lads of Cyprus' in his court below. Here, if anywhere beyond a poet's dream, the scenery of Desdemona's passion must be sought.

Zaptiehs, suitors, witnesses, and idlers crowd the gallery and impede the stair. Some one is coming, and these idlers want to see the show. A noise is heard; a scuffle, as of horse's hoofs; a rattle, as of swords and spurs. Though nothing can be seen, the noise being still far off, the crowd shrinks backs as though the caftans and tarbooshes were melting into the wall.

Pushing through this crowd, Cosora gains the great stair, now clearing fast, and drops down slowly step by step, as if in pain and doubt. Once on the ground, she staggers towards a tree, puts out her hand, and leans against the trunk. That tree! One wonders whether this poor creature knows that tree or not. That trunk is death; the Tyburn of Nicosia; the hanging-tree on which the blackest criminals are swung. One fears that trunk is an unlucky staff to lean on. Heedless of the crowd, Cosora turns a little on her heel and lifts her eyes to the door from which she stole just now in her proud pain. Her heart is evidently coming back; refusing to accept that verdict from the bench. To her, poor thing—houseless and penniless—justice must seem not only blind but lame.

That noise without draws nearer to the gate. At length, in clouds of dust, our High Commissioner and his staff ride in. Cosora turns her eyes. In boots and helmet that High Commissioner looks more like a knight of chivalry than the cadi, in tarboosh and slippers, sitting cross-legged on his divan. It seems within her mind to speak; if so, she lets her chance go by. Slipping from his horse, our High Commissioner moves on rapidly to the stair. Saluted and saluting in his turn, he passes down the gallery to his room. The Council waits him, and the door is closed. Taking no notice of the woman, a zaptieh hitches the High Commissioner's horse to that ill-omened tree. Watching the man, Cosora seems to recognize the hanging-place—starts back a little—stiffens up her frame, crosses the courtyard with a martial stride, and passing through the gateway, disappears from sight.

An officer on the staff, provided with a pass-key to the harem, wanders with me up and down the konak. Hassan follows in our wake; no less jealous for his master's dignity than ready with an answer on all points of local detail. Passing from gateway to garden, from stable to seraglio, we notice every part in turn; guard-room and jail, conduit and fountain, council-house and court of justice, with the range of private chambers, from the Pasha's bedroom to the cabinets of that Pasha's wives and concubines.

Taken as a palace, the konak in Nicosia is one of the queerest piles on earth; the first floor, a prison; the second floor, a palace; and the whole so bare and rickety that the planks spring under your feet, and the window sashes when you touch them crumble in your hands. Yet all about lie ample gardens, groves and walks, with jets of water making music everywhere.

We enter by a gate that seems to be the nave or crypt of a Venetian church; a cool and shady passage, serving as a guard-room and a lounge. Three ancient plantains grow outside. A cadi used to sit in this shady nook, practicing his trade on such as came to him for law. His mat lay on the ground, and there he sat, crossed-legged and slippered, waiting 'in the gate'; reading his book of prayers when he was not engaged in 'making peace.' Men came to him with their griefs from farmsteads in the hills and villages in the plains. They came to him about their blood-feuds, disputed bargains, third divorces, and projected re-marriages. Standing before the learned man, the disputants and rivals said: 'We come to thee, O judge, for justice. May the seventy-two prophets keep thy feet from straying into crooked ways; so that thy field may prosper under thee, and joy may sit on the face of thy favourite son.' Settling their disputes, he took such presents as they gave him for his pains. A learned man, upright, and faithful to his text, his rulings were received by high and low as final.

The inner court is large and square. One angle is divided from the rest by a mud-wall. This angle forms the prison-yard, opening from the jail, the Newgate of Nicosia. Near the mud-wall stands the hanging-tree. Men and women are passing in and out of that prison-yard. A zaptieh dawdles by the door, twisting his cigarette, and flirting with the girls as they go in and out. Ten or twelve criminals are in the yard, walking about in pairs, eating the fruit brought in to them, or lying in the shady nooks. Others, within the jail, are peering through the iron grates. Some of these fellows in the yard are fettered. One fellow has a cannonball fastened to his leg. He seems accustomed to his burden, for when he wants to move about, he lifts the weight deftly, poises it against his shoulder, and takes his exercise like any other man.

Some of these wretches, I am told, have taken life; not in our time, or they would not be here; but in that golden age when no one in Nicosia held the power of life and death. Here is a fellow talking to two women; ankle and wrist are chained. He had a near escape. Not long ago (but still before our time) he quarrelled with a neighbour in the coffee-house outside Papho gate; their swelling spirits excited by mastic, dominoes, and dancing girls. He drew his knife and drove it through his neighbour's ribs. The victim dropped down dead, and he was taken on the spot. Once lodged in jail, his way to the hanging-tree seemed open; but the times were ticklish, and the Pasha was afraid of a conviction that would send his case to Rhodes. Trouble might come of it. Suppose the murderer were condemned to die? The papers must be sent to Rhodes, and the proceedings overhauled. Then all the evidence would be forwarded from Rhodes to Constantinople. More inquiries would take place. A grand vizier, already overwhelmed with work, would have new labours cast on him. The Governor of Nicosia would be blamed, if not removed. So he resolved to try the man for homicide. For homicide he could give the wretch ten years, and so escape that reference to his Vali and his Grand Vizier. Thus the murderer escaped with life. Feeling that the sense of justice was unsatisfied, the Pasha looked what more could be safely done. He closed the city gate at sunset. At other times, he might have closed the coffee-house where all the deviltry had been done, and not condemn the innocent city gate. But then, to close the coffee-house was to rouse a private foe, on which another question might be sent to Rhodes. And so the gate was closed at sun-down, and the innocent citizens of Nicosia were punished for that wretch's crime.

The konak is two stories high. One story is devoted to the prison, offices, and stables; the second, to the Treasury, Court of Justice, Hall of Audience, Transfer Office, Council Chamber and Governor's House. Inside and out, above and below, the edifice is worn and broken. Hardly any of the rooms are fit to live in, but are excellent quarters for rats and mice. Some of the rooms are showy, but the floors are rotting into dust. Hassan, a native, has to walk with wary feet.

Though all the rooms are shabby and the corridors out of order, one perceives on coming to the harem that the female quarters are the best; the best in size, in situation, and in light. One wing of the upper story was devoted to the Pasha's family. As in other houses, this wing stands on the garden side; so that the inmates look from their windows into shady groves, and catch the play of fantastic water-jets. Balconies hang over the gardens, luring into the tenement every breath of air.

In other times this harem was the Hall of State, in which Venetian prefects held their feasts and revelries in imitation of the Doge and Signory. Four rooms are built in the four angles of this hall, one room for each of the four wives allowed by law to a True Believer. Each room looks into gardens, but has no other outlet than the common hall. Thus, privacy was secured for each, with the convenience of a general room for exercise and gossip, and for giving audience to female visitors, chap-women and story-tellers.

Two or three smaller rooms stand in a corridor. These rooms are darker than the others.

'What were these little rooms used for by the Pasha?' I inquire. 'Servants and slaves?'

Hassan smiles: 'Perhaps so, Effendi.'

'What are you smiling at? You mean something else? These were the chambers of his concubines?'

'Perhaps so, Effendi.'

'That is what we hear from every one about,' adds the staff-officer; 'but I believe it was some time ago.'

The rooms have certainly no appearance of having been lately used.

'Anyhow, captain, you must feel glad that you are not expected to carry out this portion of the Turkish law.'

Among these time-worn chambers, one room is of deeper interest to us English than the rest; that in which our Admiral took over Cyprus from the Sultan to the Queen. Fancy may play about the edifice in various parts. You can figure Cassio and Iago parleying on this stair, and Desdemona passing down this gallery from her chapel to her cabinet. You can imagine Catarina Cornaro whispering in this archway to her brother Georgio the terms of her surrender of the island to the Doge. No effort is required to paint the room in which Pessim, last of the long line of Ottoman pashas, sat in this chair of state when handing his province over to the English Queen. A large and lofty room, with showy ceiling, to which clings the gold and paint of Italian decorators, it is furnished in the simple Ottoman taste with a divan, a table, and a row of chairs. Windows give on gardens and on minarets; a fountain plays below, and cedars tempt you to accept their shade. A wasted, but luxuriant paradise of greenery lies below. Here, Pessim heard the firman read; here, Pessim learned the story of those laden mules. A man with four fat wives, and salary in arrear, lay open to the blandishment of solid silver coin. Not one piastre lined the public chest. His tenure of the post was insecure, and Kiamil's fate might any day become his own. Living in a world of dreams, one thing alone was safe and sound—the silver on those laden mules. Giving up his chair to the English Admiral, the Pasha took his pay, rolled up his bed, set his fat wives on mules, and rode out of the city by the Famagosta gate, leaving the konak to an English officer, and the Papho gate under an English flag.

The departing pasha carried off his harem, but he could not take away with him things he had not introduced—the sentiment and practice of harem-life.

CHAPTER XXIV.

ST. NICOLAS OF THE ENGLISH.

'Betestan!' I say. 'Is that the quaint old building at our feet, divided from us only by this narrow lane?'

In passing the Cafe Speranza, I have more than once noticed, behind a row of fruit-stalls, some stone arches, old-looking, and of great beauty; but the place in front of them is a market, thronged at all times by mules and camels, from whose teeth and hoofs one is but too glad to get away. But I have always meant to give an hour to them some day. Just now, in winding up the minaret stair, I caught, through slits in the wall, glimpses of a structure unlike any of the other mosques and chapels in Nicosia. It seemed to wear an English face; reminding one of bits of Westminster Abbey and the Tower. 'What is that place, Hassan?' I asked my servant in the rear. 'That, Effendi, is the Betestan.' There my queries ended. Betestan brought no meaning in the sound.

Emin Bey looks down on the quaint edifice; a long, low stack of masonry, covering some open ground—half-garden, and half-cemetery; which might be the relic of a Carmelite convent or an ancient London inn.

'The building at our feet? That is the Emerghi mosque.'

'And not the Betestan?'

'One and both. It was a mosque; it is a granary. That is one of the places we contrived to save. Like Santa Catarina, we saved it from the Orthodox torch by calling it a mosque. We put it under guard; but, as you see, it stands too near for a religious house, being only nine or ten feet from the wall of our chief mosque.'

'It is vacouf—mosque property—I suppose?'

'Of course, and only to be used for pious objects. You can dig a well with mosque property; you can buy a cemetery with mosque property; you can dig a water-course with mosque property; you can build a granary with mosque property. All acts of mercy can be done with sacred funds. So, we have turned a useless mosque into a useful granary. Is that good, according to your custom?'

'H'm. It seems an old place?'

'One of the oldest in Nicosia. Famagosta gate is not so old.'

'What was the place in ancient time?'

'A sacred house, church, cloister . . . . how should we barbarians know?'

'Orthodox or Catholic?'

'Catholic. Otherwise the Venetians would have blown it down. Those corsairs rifled and destroyed a hundred places—more than half this capital, and the whole of Lion Mount, Cantara, and St. Hilarion. There are grave-yards, as you see, about the Betestan; but I suppose no saints were buried there, or the Venetians would have stolen them. They were fine grabbers, those Venetians; especially fond of stealing saints.'

'Yes, true enough, O Bey! An old priest told me the other day, that the Venetians stole the ashes of St. Lazarus from Larnaca, just as they had previously stolen the ashes of St. Mark from Alexandria.'

'So these Orthodox people say. That comes of being civilized, and wearing boots instead of slippers. When you are civilized you can do—anything you like. What you can carry off is all your own.'

'The old name of Haidar Pasha mosque has been preserved. Is the old name of Emerghi lost?'

'Not at all. The old name of the Betestan was St. Nicolas; just as the old name of Haida Pasha Mosque was Santa Catarina.'

St. Nicolas and St. Catharine! That union has an English sound. Had we not a famous hospital in Canterbury dedicated to these saints, in connexion with St. Thomas? Were not St. Nicolas and St. Catharine the martyr's favourite saints? A 'brotherhood of St. Catharine' was founded in the church at which St. Thomas had been baptized. An English sound—decidedly an English sound. If the masonry of the Betestan be English, as it seems, there must be some connexion of these buildings with our English trilogy of saints. A key may perhaps be found in the Turkish name.

'Pray what is Betestan? Not a granary, I suppose?'

'No . . . not a granary . . . I think. But who am I to find out mysteries for a Frank?'

'Come, we are not so proud as that. Help me a little—we shall perhaps be able to find our way. '*Bete*, no doubt, is house. One knows that *beth* in Hebrew, and *beit* in Arabic, mean house. *Bete* must be the same. But what is s*tan*?'

'*Stan, estan, istan*, means a place or province of some people. *Betestan* means the house of some nation or of some brotherhood.'

A light breaks through his words. House of some nation or some brotherhood? An English structure of the middle ages, dated by every stone-course in the reign of Henry the Third, and dedicated to St. Nicolas? A church of St. Catharine close to a fraternity of St. Nicolas? One turns back on the memory of that old hospital in Canterbury, which bore the triple shield of St. Nicolas, St. Catharine, and St. Thomas. Also on that brotherhood of St. Catharine near Cheapside, in London, founded in honour of St. Thomas, at his baptismal shrine. House of some brotherhood? House?

We know that in the middle ages all crusading brotherhoods called their lodgings 'houses;' not convents, cloisters, priories, cells, retreats, or monasteries. Those of Spanish origin were casas; those of Italian origin albergoes; those of French origin aubergues; those of English origin houses or inns. Such names were long in use; and were all translated by the Arabic *beit*. If the Betestan in Nicosia be English, it was neither church nor cloister, but the house of some knightly order. Of what order? Not the Templars, one is sure. These knights held property in Cyprus, but their settlements were at Colossi, on the farther slope of Mount Olympus, five or six miles from Limasol. Templars affected Oriental tastes. Instead of bringing Gothic forms into the East, they carried Oriental forms into the West. Our Temple church is one of their Oriental forms. A round church built on the mode of the Holy Sepulchre, was their type; but this English edifice in Nicosia is in the purest Gothic style.

Was there any English order of crusading knights, existing in the reign of Henry the Third, who might have lodged in Nicosia, and built this chapel of St. Nicolas, and the other structures in the Betestan?

Yes, certainly; an order which connects the cycle of these saintly names—that order of St. Thomas of Acre, founded in the reign of Lion Heart, which gave a lasting form to the great impulse out of which the Crusade sprang.

The tale of this order is one of the dropt chapters in English history. Templars and Hospitallers were recruited from all countries, Rome being anxious to put the Cross above the sceptre, and to sink the minor differences of race in the absorbing unity of creed. But Rome was beaten on her chosen line. The instinct of nationality revolted. A Spanish order of Alacantara was created by Alfonzo the Seventh; a Portuguese order of Evora by Alfonzo the First; a German order of Teutonic Knights by the companions of Kaiser Friedrich. After these examples an English order of St. Thomas was created in the reign of Lion Heart.

Acre was to be their home until the Holy Sepulchre should be won. Acre was the Christian place of arms. Templars, Hospitallers, Teutons—all had homes in Acre, and were commonly called Knights of Acre. Our English knights wore the dress and carried the arms of St. George; a shirt and cloak, with red cross on white ground, and a sword and shield, with red cross on white ground. Lands were given to them in Nicosia, and here, they built a house and chapel, and inclosed their gardens and their lodgings by a wall. St. Nicolas was the martyr's saint. But Nicolas is a Greek saint also; and the Knights of St. Thomas named him with a difference, as 'St. Nicolas of the English,'—S. Nikolai Anglicorum. When Acre fell, the Knights of St. Thomas came to live at Nicosia, while the Templars and Hospitallers settled down near Limasol. They had 'houses' in Sicily, in Calabria, in Flanders, in Scotland, and elsewhere; but the Master, or Preceptor, lodged in Nicosia, in the pile now called the Betestan.

Our Knights of St. Thomas outlived the Templars. In the reign of Edward the Third, Sir Hugh Curteys was Preceptor in Nicosia. When Cyprus fell to the Genoese, our knights were driven from Nicosia, and their 'house' appropriated by the conquerors. After that time, their principal 'house' was in Cheapside.

Here, then, we have in this Betestan, a piece of English work, that has outlasted Lusignan kings, Genoese governors, Egyptian satraps, Venetian prefects, and Turkish pashas.

We ought to get possession of our house again; a garrison hospital, and a garrison church.

'That is our property; stolen from us by the Genoese,' I observe to Emin Bey. 'We ought to have that place again. Could it be sold to us?'

Emin shakes his head:

'It is vacouf. Mosque property is never sold; once given to God, is always given to God.'

'But then, mosque property may be hired?'

'Yes, certainly. Even now, the Betestan is hired; but only to a man of trust, who will not suffer the place to be abused.'

'Then you might hire it out to us? An English chapel, you may feel assured, will never be defiled by us.'

Emin whispers to the sheikh before he answers me; and then he says no more than this:

'Well, God is great, and orders things according to his will.'

CHAPTER XXVI.

A VILLAGE PRIEST.

'Any milk to he obtained in Piroi?'

'No, Effendi,' answers Hassan, with a shrug: 'it is the same in Piroi as in Ormidia. No one milks his cow.'

'Nowhere in Cyprus?'

'That is so, Effendi. In Cyprus, no one ever milks his cow.'

'Why not, Hassan? Do you think it is religion?'

'I am not sure of that; but sometimes think so.'

'You have nothing in your Koran against milking cows, and these Greeks have nothing in their Gospel against milking cows.'

Near the village water-wheel, we met a herdsman driving in his cattle for the night. 'A knowing fellow,' Hassan whispers me: 'a fellow up to things, who can give a reason for what he does.' After some talk, I put my query, which he answers quickly.

'Object to milk my cows? No, not a bit.'

'Still, as a fact, you do not milk them?'

'No, Effendi, no. Why should I?'

'To get milk and butter.'

'Well, I don't care much for milk; but of the two, I prefer camel's milk to cow's milk.'

'But you like fresh butter on your bread?'

'Not when I can get date-jam and honey; no, I very much prefer date-jam.'

'But you might sell your milk and butter, and put piastres in your pocket. You would find a ready market for such articles on board our ships.'

'Well, one has to think of that. I don't like putting back piastres. But my women would object.'

'Your women! Do you mean that your wife and daughter object to milking cows?'

'They would be sure to make a fuss, and I should have to show my stick.'

'Now, that is what I wish to learn. Why would your wife and daughter make a fuss?'

'All-holy Mother! how can I tell that? Women are such fools. But why not ask the pope? Nobody knows so much of women as the pope; for he is always with them, and they tell him everything.'

We wander towards the church, dedicated to Panayia—the All-holy Mother—a pile of ancient type, yet modern date . . .

Pedros, the pope, comes out to us. He is an old, but not imposing personage. By birth a peasant, he is a man just like his neighbours on the right and left. He owns a little farm, abutting on the lane, and breaks the bit of field behind his house with his own plough. His wife (a village pope *must* be a married man) assists him in the kitchen, at the mill, and on the farm; cooking his meals, coaxing the water to his wheel, and gathering in his sugar-canes. He owns some sheep and cows, and is a man of substance in the place. Besides his office of pope, Pedros is miller of the village, for his plot of ground contains the water-wheel, at which he grinds his neighbour's grain at so many paras the sack. He is reported to be rich . . .

Nothing in his dress marks Pedros off as of another class to the villager whose grain he mills at so much a sack,—except his cap. That cap is curious, and no other person in the village wears the like:—a relic of an ancient world, denoting priesthood and a sacerdotal caste. Pedros, though a 'learned' man, is unaware that his cap was worn by persons of his calling in this island more than a thousand years before the birth of Christ. Yet, in the tombs about his feet, lie proof on proof, that the priests of Astarte wore this kind of cap. Astarte passed into Aphrodite, Aphrodite into Venus—but her priests continued to wear that cap. The cap is conical in shape; and every one knows, that the cone is an emblem of Astarte, Aphrodite, and Venus.

Here, then, is a relic of a time long past; and Astarte yet has her share in our village pope.

On leaving the village church, I ask his reverence why the farmers in Cyprus never milk their cows.

'They dare not,' he replies, with the austerity of a priest of Isis or Astarte.

'So I understand. But why?'

'No woman dares to milk a cow. My wife would rather thrust her hand into fire than touch the udder of a cow.'

'Indeed! Yet women milk goats and camels. Why not cows?'

'It is a sin; it is profane; their hands would wither and drop off, like a leper's flesh.'

Wither and drop off! What can he mean? Is this the voice of some deep-lying superstition older than the memory of man? Pedros wears the cap of Astarte. May not his wife's repugnance to milking cows be a relic of some ancient form of worship? Cyprus is the land of goddesses. One of the oldest of these female deities was Isis. Cows were sacred to Isis. Isis passed into the form of a cow—Athor, mother of the sun was suckled at her teat. Hence, the cow was sacred, and the udder of a cow was seven times sacred. Isis had many shrines in Cyprus, and at all these shrines her emblem was a cow. May not that ancient form of worship live—nameless and unsuspected—in this stern reluctance of the Cyprian female to touch the udder of a cow?

Pedros inherits something from Astarte. Why may not Pedros' wife inherit something from Isis?

CHAPTER XXVIII.

FAMAGOSTA.

. . . In the earliest known form, Famagosta is Amtikhadasta; an Assyrian word in the days of Esarhaddon: 'place of the goddess' or *high*-place of the goddess—in accordance with the site. The natives, an Aryan, not a Semitic people, called the name Amagosta. Greek traders wrote the name Ammochostos. Famagosta is a modern form; modern as compared with the times of Esarhaddon; but the native name has never changed on native lips, Amagosta in the reign of Esarhaddon is Amagosta in the reign of Queen Victoria. It clings alike to sea and land. The great bay, stretching from Cape Grego to Cape Elia, is Amagosta Bay, and the main headland on that curving line is Amagosta Point.

Here, then, is evidence that the city now called Famagosta, was a port and stronghold—high-place of an Assyrian goddess, long before the swamps at Salamis were occupied by Greeks.

Looking at the marshes and the ruins, I am led to think that Amagosta and Salamis were names of one and the same place, very much as Devonport and Plymouth are names of one and the same place. The site marked on maps as Salamis, lies at the northern entrance of the reef. If any strong force were on that point, the traders in the upper city must have been entirely at their mercy. No one could have put to sea—no one returned to port, without their leave. Under such conditions, neither Greeks nor Syrians could have lived in peace. Strife must have broken out, and one or other have gone down. Two hostile cities never could have stood on such a site.

My notion is that Amagosta was a strong place, seized by the first-comers from the Syrian coast; and that Salamis was an open station at the entrance of the reef, occupied by trading Greeks. On the shore we see the ruins of ancient piers, and in the swamp, we trace an ancient causeway, built on piles. That pier and cause-way were erected in the Greek suburb. The Greeks, I think, grew stronger than their neighbours, and in time got hold of both their port and bluff. The rising ground became their citadel, and was at length included in the bounds, and covered by the name of Salamis.

Famagosta is a heap of sand and dust; not a city of the dead, and yet a city without life; a middle-age Pompeii, riven and rent by one disaster, and then shut up from human sight. Seen from the bay, the city wears a winning and pictorial face. Her walls and parapets are all intact. Over these walls and parapets spring towers and pinnacles, broken arches and ruined aisles, with here and there a date-tree, shooting from the side of flying buttress and marble shaft. Enter the gate. In front of you stands an ancient lion, vast in bulk and crude in art; the genius of the city and the island; which has outlived twenty dynasties and a dozen creeds. Look round; you are in a lifeless place, more striking than ruins like Petra and Pompeii, since the courts and lanes, though silent as the grave, are not abandoned to the dead. Some ghostly forms still haunt the earth, making the silence and the desolation more complete; much as a Bedouin tent, pitched in the desert, makes the loneliness and terror of that desert more complete. A female figure clothed in white shrinks timidly round a corner. At the sound of human foot, she draws the yashmak round her eyes, as though she were afraid lest you might cross her path, ask her to stop, and let you gaze on one come back again from the dead. A turbaned brow puts out from a half-open door in a garden-wall. That garden occupies the fore-court of a ruined chapel; and the tenant looks as though he had been left among this wreck of sacred things on guard. A pair of sorrowing eyes appear to say, as you glide up: 'Peace be with you and yours. What may our brother lack? What turns his feet this way? Comes he to find sweet water, and to taste his servants' fruit?'

As you salute and smile, he seems to feel that he has done his duty, and he drops behind his garden-wall.

Few things are to be seen on earth so strange as these Venetian walls, with pomegranates on their slopes—these Gothic towers, with mulberries under every arch. Choking with dust, you trudge through the deserted streets. Stones are piled up on every side. Stones, great and small—stones, dressed and rough—fry, blister, bake in the hot sun, and dropping to the earth feed the dry lane with still more heaps of sand and dust. Old stories say that more than three hundred churches stood within these walls. Three hundred is a magic number; Rome boasts of three hundred churches; York and Norwich used to boast of three hundred churches; and Nicosia, like Famagosta, used to boast of having three hundred churches. All depends on what you call a church. A niche, containing an icon of the virgin, with a lamp, may be called a church. One church of the first rank in Famagosta has been saved and turned into a mosque. This, as in Nicosia, is the cathedral of Santa Sofia.

Passing through a narrow chink in the outer wall, you find yourself in an open court, fronting the sacred edifice with the purifying fountain on your right. Drawing the curtain you step in. The imaun is at prayer; kneeling on a bit of mat, his turban bowed in reverence to the ground. Most of the floor is bare, and on that portion of the mosque you tread without offence. Round you lie tombs of knights; the slabs still rich in names and shields. Some of these stones bear English names; one slab is carved with the arms of Raleigh, and is probably the gravestone of a crusading ancestor of the famous knight.

Mounting a wall, and looking to north and south across the wreck and waste, you see that the destroying agency has been that of man rather than that of time. Some buildings have been struck by shot; others have been mined and blown into the air. These blocks were Latin churches, schools and cloisters, and as such, were sinks of heresy and abomination in the eyes of Cypriotes following the Oriental rite. Once the Venetians were expelled, the Orthodox natives rushed into the town. Three hundred shrines—some large and lofty like the churches of St. Nicolas and Santa Sofia, some small and humble, like the niches at street corners and at public fountains—offered themselves for desecration and destruction. Religious hate was glutted. What the siege had left untouched, religious passion rent and razed. Wall and tower, gateway and citadel, were kept intact, for these were occupied by the conquerors. Some portion of the cathedral was preserved, for this was needed as a mosque; but all the rest of the great city was delivered over to Orthodox avenging bands.

Their reign was short, for when the fight was over, Mustafa drove them from the town, and shut the gates. No Cypriote was allowed to live within the walls. Outside the landward gate, Varossia and other villages were free to him, and there he raised his temple, ploughed his field, and sowed his crop. The city was regarded by the conqueror as a fortress, and was occupied solely by the Sultan's troops. A Cypriote might come into the town to buy and sell, to ask for justice from a court of law, and pay his share of the redemption-tax, but he was not allowed to build a shed, open a magazine, or take possession of a ruined church.

Peace settled down on the great wreck. Years, ages, of repose came after; smoothing with a tender touch the jagged outline and the blackened arch. Such lines of beauty as the ruined chancel and the broken shaft still show, is the redeeming gift of time.

CHAPTER XXX.

CERINIA.

An Indian troop-ship rides at anchor in a broad and noble strait. Two mountain ranges sentinel this strait; that on our left hand being the northern wall of Cyprus; that on our right hand being the southern curtain of the Bulghar-dagh. We anchor off a tiny port; a swell is on the sea, and the strong vessel, lifted from below, heaves in her seat and drags uneasily at her chain. Before us lies a little port, emerging from the shadow of that mountain wall. From water edge to summit, rising three thousand feet, that ridge of wall is green; not thick and dark with leafage, like an English wood; but pricked and tattoed into pictures like a Spanish mountain side. Along the shore, a fruitful and abounding plain, you notice palms, pomegranates, limes, and oranges. A little up the slope, grow olives, vines, and fig-trees; higher still, ascending to the sky-line, you have clumps of pines and firs. Above these clumps, again, start peaks and pinnacles of rock, sharp as the needles of an Alpine gorge. Yet these bare points are capped by weird and massive ruins; remnants of old forts and castles built by Byzantine dukes and catapans. When Lion Heart came to Cyprus, these forts were in Duke Isaac's hands. The castle on our left hand bore the name of Lion Mount. A lion was the badge of Cyprus, and Lion Mount was the strongest fortress in the land. The castle on our right then bore the name of St. Hilarion, a local saint of great celebrity, whose ashes lay in the convent near that lofty peak. These castles fell into Richard's power. Under our Anglo-Norman rule, we changed the name of Lion Mount into Chateau de la Reine, and that of St. Hilarion into Chateau du Dieu d'Amour. One of these names remains. Venetian had no objection to a god of love; but, as republicans, they abhorred the name of queen. Under their rule the name of Chateau de la Reine was changed for the more ancient form of Buffamente—Temple of the Winds.

CHAPTER XXXI.

PAPHO.

. . . Yet the future of Papho may lie in mines and minerals rather than in gardens and in sheep-walks. Agates, and other stones, are picked up on the coast and in the gullies of the mountain range. One of these stones is that variety of adamar known as the blue diamond. This stone, which bears the name of either Cyprian diamond or Paphian diamond, is now, I understand, regarded as a sapphire; but the matter is not clear, the principal diamond merchants being divided on the point. In ancient times that stone was sacred, not to the priests of Venus only, but to those of Jehovah. Epiphanius tells us that the diamonds found near Papho were the Urim and Thumim of the Jewish priests; worn on the breastplate when they entered the sanctuary, and showing by their change of colour the acceptance or rejection of their prayers and sacrifices. Epiphanius was the best authority on such a point, being himself a Cypriote, a bishop, and a saint.

Two miles from Papho lie these diamond fields. Among the hills lie veins and lumps of malachite. Malachite is the green carbonate of copper; where malachite is found copper may be sought with hopes of good success. Papho used to export enormous quantities of copper ore. Old mines should be explored afresh; the science of our day being equal to finding profit in a mine which worshippers of Venus may have abandoned in despair. Iron was also found near Papho in great abundance, and the royal priest, who ruled the country and the temple, is supposed to have invented anvil and hammer, lever and tongs. Metal more precious than iron or copper may be found. As long since as the days of Pliny it was known that the presence of diamonds is an index of the neighbourhood of gold. Among the diamond fields at Papho gold has been already found. No thorough search has yet been made; but there is just a chance that an experienced miner from Australia might discover gold-flakes in these long-neglected diamond-fields.

Greaves 1879

Beginning with his cadet days at Sandhurst and assignments in India, Africa and New Zealand Greaves spent his life in the British military. In *Memoirs of General Sir George Greaves*, London: John Murray, 1924, he describes those military adventures up to his retirement in Wales. In 1879 he saw brief duty in Cyprus as "Chief of Staff and Chief Secretary to Government" under Sir Garnet Wolseley, the first British high commissioner on the island. He appears to have felt very negatively about Cyprus and his time there, and dwelt on getting away. He served as Acting High Commissioner for less than two months after the departure of Wolseley for Africa and before the arrival of Sir Robert Biddulph and his own return to India.

CHAPTER XIV

APPOINTED CHIEF OF THE STAFF, CYPRUS

In July 1879 I went to Cyprus with Sir Garnet Wolseley as Chief of the Staff and Chief Secretary to Government. After a pleasant voyage we arrived at Larnake early one morning, landed at 3 p.m. in full dress, and the Governor, Sir Garnet Wolseley, swore himself in. I read the Queen's Commission, and Sir Garnet Wolseley's proclamation; this last, having been previously translated into Greek and Turkish, was read in these languages. The people cheered, and Sir Garnet Wolseley was Governor of Cyprus.

The heat was intense, and on riding inland with Brackenbury we found the country most desolate, and the smells and dirt were indescribable. I set to work as usual to make myself acquainted once more with the duties of Chief of the Staff. It was very pleasant meeting so many old friends; among them Jim Dormer, Baker-Russell, Wauchope, Brackenbury, and others.

One night Sir Garnet and I dined at a place called Nisso, ten miles from our headquarters, with a Mr. Mattee, who was an Italian and had lived in Cyprus for thirty-five years. He tried to cheer us up about the island which we thought so hopeless, and said: "It is a good place." The roads were very bad. However, riding out one day we found a very pretty place called 'Bella Pacase,' an old monastery turned into a barracks by Lieutenant Morgan, R.E., who was quite the best of the Royal Engineer officers out there.

After a short time Sir Samuel and Lady Baker arrived; Sir Samuel always keen to explore fresh places. He had sent a very fine caravan out by steamship to live in while exploring, but to their intense disgust found there were no roads, only bridle-paths; so they pitched their caravan close to Government House, and we saw a great deal of them. Such interesting people! He was a thorough sportsman and a good shot, and most entertaining.

Lady Wolseley and her sweet little daughter, Frances, arrived about this time, and brightened up the place for us, but was as disappointed in Cyprus as we all were; it was so absolutely uninteresting and the climate horrible. I took great pleasure in teaching little Frances to ride, and found her very clever. She was only six and could speak French fluently. Lady Baker-Russell also arrived to join her husband, with very beautiful clothes which were wasted on the desert air. Mrs. Scott-Stevenson was also at Nicosia, where her husband's regiment was stationed; and the only idea we all had was to get out of Cyprus as soon as we decently could.

When Sir Garnet left for England *en route* for South Africa, I officiated as High Commissioner. At that time I received a letter from Lord Beaconsfield saying he was glad to see me in a position where he might help me, having heard from Sir Garnet Wolseley how well I had done as Chief Secretary, etc. etc. He added: "Of course you agree as to the value of Cyprus to us as a place of arms. For instance, for any force required for service in Turkey or Egypt, and as a sanatorium, which could be formed on Mount Olympus. Then there is the harbour of Famagusta, which in old days used to be one of the finest harbours in the Mediterranean, and could now, with a little dredging, be made available for our fleet."

I wrote, after compliments, as they say in India, that I was very sorry I could not agree about the value of the island, as it was a very unhealthy place for British troops, and the sides of Olympus were so steep that a tent could not be pitched on it without digging out a foundation. As to Famagusta, it might have been a harbour for rowing-boats in the old days, but in the opinion of the Engineers it could only be made use of for our ships now by such dredging as would either cover the present island with silt or make another island out at sea! I never heard from him again, and yet it was all quite true.

I had my troubles as High Commissioner of Cyprus. The Greek Archbishop came to see me in a great state of excitement. Two of his priests had had their hair cut and their beards shaved off, and had been imprisoned in the jail at Famagusta, and he required their instant release. I asked him not to be in such a hurry; the priests had been imprisoned on conviction of stealing, and the attention to their hair and beards was in accordance with prison regulations, which had come from the English Government. He was not at all appeased and went off in anger. Late that evening I received a telegram from England, to know why I was mutilating and imprisoning the Greek priests!

Before this event, a Turkish colonel had arrived from Constantinople with orders to remove the cannon in the island belonging to the Turks, on which they set a great value. He was entertained at mess and asked Sir Garnet Wolseley how soon he expected to fill his portmanteau, meaning how soon would he get enough money to get out of the place. The Turk was very sketchy about the guns and said his orders were to take them away; so we told him to carry on. On inspecting them ourselves, we found none fit for service, but among them were some beautiful old pieces of sorts. After a time, our friend, who professed to be in communication with his own Government, said his orders were to destroy them. There was a telegraph wire to Constantinople, and talking the matter over with my interpreter, a Greek, he told me I had only to go to the telegraph office to find out what instructions the colonel was receiving; or he would go himself with orders from me. The clerk in charge showed him all the telegrams the colonel had received. First, he was to bring the guns away; next, if he proposed to destroy them, the English would surely buy them; if not, he was to destroy one and come back at once. So we destroyed one old rubbishy thing, and the colonel went on his way rejoicing.

On Friday, 30th May, 1879, I got a wire from Wolseley, saying: "I am going to the Cape; wish you were coming. Sell my horses," and on the same date wrote me the following letter:

ON BOARD THE "EDINBURGH CASTLE,"
DARTMOUTH, 30*th May*, 1879.

MY DEAR GREAVES,

Here I am, on board for Natal, and I look round at those who accompany me and miss your cheery face. Indeed it is true that feeling I have left you in Cyprus and that you are not with me, or to be with me in this new venture, is the drop of gall in the cup of my happiness at present.

I have had a rough time of it at the Horse Guards. . . . For peace's sake I had to be conciliatory. . . .

I am so glad you are to have India, and I hope we may meet there, if I succeed in South Africa. Ellice told me plainly that the Horse Guards had had nothing to do with your appointment, but that H.R.H. could not say 'No' when Haines asked for you, as he had previously told him that he should have whoever he asked for. You are not, therefore, in any way indebted to H.R.H. for what you are to have.

Please give my kindest remembrances to the Judge.

I called on Mrs. Phillips when passing through Paris, but unfortunately missed seeing her. How I wish, for my sake, that he was to be my legal guide in Natal. He would be worth a brigade to me.

I wish I might send all the major-generals now there to Cyprus in exchange for him.

I am so glad I am not burdened with the government of Cape Colony, and my only dread is that old Frere may resign. If he does, I have begged the Colonial Office to send out a successor to him as soon as possible. I shall then be quite free to return home as soon as I have settled the Zulu and Transvaal affairs. Indeed, I do not see why I should not eat my Christmas dinner in England this year.

McNeill was fishing in America, so I could not take him with me, and as all military operations must be over by the 31st August, every day was of consequence.

I have telegraphed to Colley, who goes with the rank of Brigadier-General as Chief of the Staff.

Good-bye. My kindest remembrances to all my old friends in Cyprus. My wife, I know, intends writing to you at length about all sorts of small matters.

Please sell all the wine and stores that may reach Cyprus to my address whilst you are there, except a case of cigars, which was in the Custom House when I came away. Please send it home with my baggage, which I believe my wife has arranged to be transported by King & Co.

Always most sincerely yours,

G. J. WOLSELEY.

On 12th May, 1879, I was sworn in as Administrator of the Government of Cyprus in the absence of Sir Garnet Wolseley. So I continued to work away, with no end to do, till June, when I heard that on my departure from Cyprus Sir Robert Biddulph would succeed me and I was to be appointed 'Adjutant-General in India,' and had to take up my appointment in October.

After my return to England I was glad to get a month's leave and proceed at once to Vichy, to get rid of any Cyprus malaria that might still be lurking in my blood; which I did after a course of bathing in the waters of Vichy.

In July I received the following from Lord Salisbury, who was then Secretary for Foreign Affairs:

FOREIGN OFFICE,

11*th July*, 1879.

SIR,

I have received your dispatch No. 219 of the 18th ultimo, informing me that you were about to leave the island of Cyprus, after handing over the government to Colonel Biddulph, and have much pleasure in conveying to you, on the part of Her Majesty's Government, their thanks for your services in Cyprus, and their approval of your conduct as Acting High Commissioner.

I am, sir,

Your most obedient humble Servant,

SALISBURY.

Donisthorpe Donne 1880

The following extract from the journal of Donisthorpe Donne is included in this volume by the kind permission of the Society of Cypriot Studies, which published Donne's remarks about Cyprus in its journal ΚΥΠΡΙΑΚΑΙ ΣΠΟΥΔΑΙ in 1963, pp. 1-50, edited with notes by George Georghallides, Ph.D. Donne's journals, letters, and paintings were also published by Alan Harfield in *The Life and Times of a Victorian Officer*, The Wincanton Press, 1986. Georghallides' text was compared with Harfield's text and is here printed in full, with only a few minor orthographic corrections. We also include Georghallides' notes and essays.

THE PRIVATE JOURNAL OF LIEUTENANT DONISTHORPE DONNE CYPRUS 1880-1882

Introductory Note

The material in Lieutenant Donisthorpe Donne's journal of his Cyprus experiences is in many ways similar to the published accounts of British travellers and officials who visited Cyprus in the first few years of the British occupation.[1] From them it is possible to get an idea of the condition of the island and of its people at the end of three centuries of Turkish rule. Donne, like many of the British visitors to Cyprus, quickly became an enthusiastic admirer of the island's landscape and an amateur student of its past. In his keen pursuit of places of scenic beauty and archaeological interest, he showed himself an indefatigable traveller, never discouraged by the difficult, and sometimes atrocious, terrain over which he had to ride. His love of nature, his robustness, his horsemanship and his dashing temperament appear from the journal to have been Donne's most appealing qualities. These were put to good use in the service of the Cyprus Police. His first appointment was that of officer commanding a Pioneer detachment which had been detailed to carry out relief work following the disastrous floods at Limassol on December 24, 1880. He commanded the men from January 8 to March 18, 1881, when, in accordance with the Gladstone Government's decision, the Cyprus Pioneer Corps was abolished and amalgamated with the Cyprus Military Police.[2] He subsequently served as Chief Commandant of Military Police in Limassol from August 24, 1881, to February 3, 1882; as temporary Local Commandant of Military Police in Nicosia from February 7 to June 14, 1882; and again as Chief Commandant of Military Police in Limassol[3] from June 18 to September 4, 1882, when he resigned his post and rejoined his regiment which had been ordered to Egypt to take part in the suppression of Orabi Pasha's rebellion.

In the exercise of his Police duties Donne had constantly to travel around the countryside to investigate crimes and seek out wanted men. This part of his job was obviously something that he greatly enjoyed and the journal is rich in long descriptive passages of travels and adventures. As a policeman Donne was effective: he showed forcefulness and determination and it is not to be wondered that, with such keen British army officers as commanders, the old Turkish zaptiehs soon ceased to be lazy and indisci-

---

[1] See generally: W. Hepworth Dixon, *British Cyprus*, London, 1879; Sir S. Baker, *Cyprus as I saw it*, London, 1879; Mrs Scott-Stevenson, *Our Home in Cyprus*, London, 1880; H. M. Sinclair, *Camp and Society*, London, 1926.

[2] In 1879 the Disraeli Government, which wanted to reduce the British garrison stationed in Cyprus, paid for the raising of a Police and Pioneer Corps whose duties were of a semi-military nature ('The Cyprus Police Augmentation Ordinance, 1879'). In 1880 there were two separate Police Forces: first, the Cyprus Military Police which though expanded in numbers and reformed was substantially the old Force of Turkish zaptiehs; secondly, the Police and Pioneer Corps which consisted of one third Greek and two thirds Turkish Cypriot recruits (*Report by Her Majesty's High Commissioner for 1880* (C. 3092), London, 1881, Biddulph to Kimberley, June 7, 1881, pp. 5-6; *Correspondence Respecting the Affairs of Cyprus* (C. 2930), London, 1881, Report by the Chief Commandant of Police, February 24, 1881, p. 100).

[3] None of Lieutenant Donne's appointments in the Pioneer and Police Force appear to be recorded in the 'Cyprus Gazette'. This may indicate that his appointments were in the nature of temporary secondment from his regiment during its stay in Cyprus.

plined[4] and the habitual oppressors of the peasantry.[5] It is also true, however, that the early British officials in their endeavour to establish law and order and respect for the Government were not entirely free from arbitrariness and sometimes harshness in their treatment of the Cypriots. In 1879 the Commissioners of Limassol and Famagusta (both of them officers) involved themselves in serious wrangles with the Greek Cypriots who protested at their high-handed actions.[6] Something of that same impatience and irritation at what Englishmen considered as the natives' procrastination or malignancy can be seen in Donne's journal where he confesses that on one occasion he nearly beat an old peasant who could not explain why his son had suddenly run away from a Police patrol.

For the historian of this period it is disappointing that Donne passes over in silence his administrative duties, his relations with the Limassol and Nicosia municipal authorities and the state of the Police Force and Prisons. The journal is almost equally devoid of any revealing references concerning the character of the officials and other people that he met on the island. One significant fact does, however, emerge from his meticulous listing of the names of Government officials: of the thirty-four officials mentioned whose appointments can be traced in the 'Cyprus Gazette' eighteen were, like Donne, officers of the British army. This figure bears out the strong military presence in the early British administration of Cyprus.

In the postscript to the journal, written during a later visit to Cyprus in 1893, Donne recorded his impressions of the island's 'dormant condition'. This condition, he reckoned, was likely to persist since Britain, after her acquisition of Egypt, had lost interest in Cyprus; moreover, the Government of Cyprus had been forced to subordinate the development of the country to the payment of the Turkish Tribute. Donne concluded that the island's value, both as a trading centre and as a 'place d' armes', would remain insignificant so long as British sea-power was supreme in the Mediterranean. These views, from one of Queen Victoria's loyal officers of above average distinction, are not without importance.

THE PRIVATE JOURNAL OF LIEUTENANT DONISTHORPE DONNE CYPRUS 1880-1882[1]

Malta

. . . [1880] our time in Malta was also drawing to a close. [Sept. 7] On the 7th we were placed under orders to go to Cyprus, our new possession. Head-Quarters and 5 Companies were ordered, the rest to stop at Malta. Nothing particular happened before our departure. . . [Sept. 9] Having packed up I slept at the Club that night and next morning we paraded on the French Curtain and marched through Valetta and the old Strada Reale for the last time, played out by the pipers of the 26 Cameronians. The splendid discipline in which Colonel Hackett[2] had the Regiment was evinced by the way the men marched out. It was like a Floriana parade, not a move in the ranks, not a wave of the hand to show the

[4] Cyprus (C, 2930), *op. cit.*, Report by the Chief Commandant of Police, February 24, 1881, p. 100.

[5] Cyprus (C. 3092), *op. cit.*, Report by the Chief Commandant of Military Police for 1880, p. 49.

[6] See below notes 20 and 37.

bystanders that the Royal Sussex was off. We embarked from the Marina on board the Troopship "Tamar" and at 3 p.m. rounded Ricasoli point on route to Cyprus, not sorry to see the last of Malta.

The 1st two days was the usual hellish experience of redcoats afloat, the sea running pretty high, but on 3rd when off Crete it cooled down. [Oct. 3] We coasted along the fine high mountains of Crete and sighted Cyprus on the 5th and rounded Cape Gatto, dropping anchor off Limassol in the evening.

Cyprus

[Oct. 6] The morning we landed in Cyprus was a dead calm and the process of shifting baggage ashore by means of native lighters was begun early. *We were the first English troops to land at this place* and our destination, Polymedia Camp, which was in sight in the hills a few miles out of the town. The background was mountainous crowned by Mount Troodos 6000 feet, a long ugly mountain not looking nearly its own height. The town straggled along the shore of the bay. In slinging the chargers overboard Sapte's charger was killed through the sling slipping and breaking. Several pieces of baggage including the Armourers' forge also fell through the pier into the sea.

Cyprus had only been occupied by England since August 1878 and of all the big occupation force sent there at the time the troops were now reduced to our half Battalion and some Engineers. The country looked very much parched up after the long hot summer when it never rains. We marched straight up to the Camp on landing, and many men fell out from the excessive heat. We took over Quarters in tents, Indian Sepoy ones left by the Indian troops, and remained under canvas all the winter.

[Oct. 7] I marched down to Limassol with a fatigue party in a.m. to land baggage and out again. The 20th Regiment whom we relieved had sailed overnight in the "Tamar". In the afternoon Sir R. Biddulph,[3] the High Commissioner rode out and inspected the Half Battalion on parade, and was entertained in our temporary mess hut.

Once having shaken down to our new camp life, the monotony of life was not much varied. [Oct. 8] Sunday Church parade was conducted in the open by a remarkable looking Armenian Chaplain, the Reverend Galboushian whom we christened the 'Missionary'. Walks and rides about the country and up the Troodos road, the only one in the district, were our principal afternoon employments. There was little or no attraction in Limassol.

[Oct. 25] The rains began today, the forerunners of what was in store for us during the winter, and on the 26th we had a heavy storm in the a.m. which introduced itself through my canvas.

[Oct. 28] Walked into Limassol and called on Royal Engineers fellows and Mrs. Hackett.

[Nov. 1] Tremendous thunderstorm which soaked everyone and washed down many houses in Limassol.

[Nov. 6] Walked into Limassol to see Gilmore[4] at the Konak.

[Nov. 19] With Chapman, Sapte and Ashurst on our first shooting expedition to the Salt Lake, lunching at a place we called Bleak House.

[Nov. 22] Commenced the old signalling game again, which went on till the end of the year. I established regular communication with Limassol.

[Dec. 4] Nearly all the English of Limassol and Polymedia met at a picnic at Kolossi where there is a fine old Venetian Tower, now turned into a farmhouse, about 6 miles out.

I had now purchased Thornton's pony. Cyprus was certainly far preferable to Malta. A fine mountainous country with lots of interest historical and natural and any amount of riding. [Oct. 11] On the 11th it blew a gale which made the tents very wretched and blew down several, besides driving one or two craft ashore in Limassol Bay. On Christmas Eve the worst storm I ever remember came over us. Coming up from the west it continued for 3 hours with great fury in huge hail stones, which literally darkened the air and deluged the country. Had there been any wind not a vestige of the camp could have remained. The ground was covered by inches of hail and when it abated the country round Limassol was a vast lake and the destruction in the town tremendous. 10 lives were lost[5] and 96 houses washed down. The river overflowed and communication with the town was cut off. In 3 hours 6 inches of rain was gauged!

[Dec. 25] In spite however of our damp and uncomfortable condition and the impossibility of a plum pudding we spent a very jovial evening in the mess hut. [Dec. 28] I went down to see the destruction in Limassol on 28th, whole streets being washed away. The High Commissioner came down to see it on the 30th and inspected the Regiment at the same time. [Dec. 31] The Sergeants held their usual dance on the last day of the year after which we let the old year out and the new one in at the mess hut.

Exit MDCCCLXXX

[Jan. 1, 1881] 1881 begins in Cyprus and likely enough will end there too and will contain sufficient body matter in between to fill many pages—the Levant is a big field and I saw a good deal of it. [Jan. 3] HMS "Monarch" arrived at Limassol on the 3rd January bringing Sir A. Cunningham, late C.O.[6] at the Cape. [Jan. 4] Colonel Hackett had an inspection parade in his honour on the 4th and we gave the officers a big lunch. Marriott, R.M.A.,[7] came and I meet an old 'Simoon' friend Chamberlain, Sub-Lieutenant on board. Having got leave to go to Larnaca with her I squared up my accounts and prepared for a trip to see something of the Island.

[Jan. 5] I went on board early on the 5th and had a capital trip down the coast as Marriott's guest. Strangely enough I stumbled across another whilom friend Tufnell, Sub-Lieutenant of the "Cygnet" a brother of my companion at N. Sachwerfen in 1874. By him I learn he was married and in India. We had a rattling Gun-Room lunch on the strength of it. Arrived in Larnaca roads we landed in the Cutter and the middy getting us broadside on in the surf, we got no small ducking including the old veteran Sir A. Cunningham.

Tufnell dined with me in the Club and I put up at Quesley's Army and Navy Hotel, if such it could be called being a relic of the occupation 2 years before but now of the past.

On landing I was handed a telegram from Colonel Hackett offering me the Command of a Pioneer Detachment at Limassol if I liked to return forthwith. Although this knocked my trip on the head I naturally jumped at it and wired back 'yes'. [Jan.6] So I started off back the next morning at 8 a.m. arriving at Limassol about 7 p.m. having done the nearly 50 mile ride on a small mule. I naturally saw little of Larnaca but much of the country between it and Limassol. It is a monotonous journey skirting the coast most of the way and passing through only one village Zee (Zyyi), about half way where I lunched. It is here that the Telegraph wire from Alexandria lands. The country is flat all round Larnaca the road passing the Salt Lakes, which make the place very unhealthy in summer. Monte Stavro Vouni, or "the Sacred Cross" stands out by itself inland, and having once passed Zee (Zyyi) the country becomes more mountainous. Limassol is first sighted about 10 miles off from a gap. Commanding a good view of the bay. One then rides down to the plains of Paleo Limassol, past the site of ancient Amathus and through a flat thickly treed and cultivated plain into Limassol.

I took over my command next morning from Gilmore, Local Commandant which consisted of two native officers and 100 NCOs[8] and men of the Cyprus Pioneer Force, who had been sent down from Nicosia to work on the improvements for the prevention of further flood destruction in the town. I had command of them until the end of March and rode into Limassol every morning from Polymedia. The weather was very wet and nasty but during this time the men worked well and cut a canal into the river to draw the water off from the town. At some times there was considerable discontent among them owing to their little pay and hard work. They were a mixed force of Greek and Turks and I had to do everything through an interpreter, which of course handicapped me very much.

[Jan. 16] Owing to a row in the Greek Quarter of the town 6 men deserted on 16th but they were all brought back at different periods and sent to prison. I conducted my office work in Gilmore's office. The men also, principally the Greeks, took to malingering to get off the works but having made a good example of one man, it stopped the rest.

[Feb. 19] On the 19th I rode out to Episkopi village with Gilmore and in trying to ford the river, which was very high, was nearly washed down and we had to cross higher up by the bridge. Episkopi is one of the prettiest villages in the Island, surrounded by orange gardens etc. The Turkish Mulshtar[9] was very hospitable and entertained us. Then we rode on to see the ancient ruins of Curium, on a promontory commanding a fine view. The place was noted in the ancient history of the Island and was probably a large town when St. Paul passed that way on his journey from Salamis to Paphos. It was here that De Chesnola found his great Treasure in 1875 underneath the ruins of a temple. Large mounds of ruins and heaps of rubbish were strewn about and marble and fluted columns were plentiful; we also found some fine fragments of tesselated pavement. The Cyclamen was growing in great abundance and we took some roots back with us. [Mar. 1] The men were afterwards employed in clearing the course of the river out. Captain Chetwynd[10] 61st Regiment, Second-in-Command of Military Police came down and inspected the men at the Konak.

[Mar. 2] On the 2nd I struck the camp at the Konak and marched to Hiafila (Ay Phyla) 3 miles out to cut a quarry road, on which they were employed till the 14th [Mar. 14] having shifted the camp back to Limassol again on 11th. [Mar. 15] On the 15th, having received orders to march the men back to Nicosia the camp was finally struck on the 16th and I set out for Nicosia with the party. [Mar. 17] The first night we stopped at Jochni[11] a village in the Larnaca District and slept in a native house where I was almost eaten alive. Started at 7 a.m. on 17th across the mountains to north of Stavro Vouni mountain through a fine country and arrived at Viso[12] in the Messaria plain in the evening. I preferred to sleep out in a tent here and passed a very cold night on the ground. [Mar. 18] Left early the next a.m. and after a very cold ride marched into Nicosia the capital of the Island. We entered by the Famagusta Gate and I handed over the force to Captain Croker[13] Adjudant 93d Regiment and put up with Chetwynd and Gordon[14] the Commissioner. Nicosia is a beautifully situated town in the middle of the Messaria plain one of the richest granaries in the world, and at this time looking its best. It is unique in one respect as being perhaps the only city in the East where Mahomedan and Christian religions are tolerated side by side. The old Cathedral of Santa Sophia is now a mosque and above the walls of the town Greek Church spires rise up side by side with Moslem minarets, and in the busy and picturesque bazaars Greek and Turk are freely mixed. A grand view is obtained of the Northern Range and distant Carpas, and altogether I was immensely pleased with Nicosia.

I dined with H.E. the High Commissioner one night and at Mr. King-Harman's[15] another, and met most of the English officials of the Capital.

[Mar. 22] I started on the 22nd for Kyrenia on the North Coast. The road takes one over the northern Range and the view from the top of the pass is very grand, the peaks of St. Hilarion rising perpendicularly to the right, the lonely plains of Kyrenia spread out like a map below, with the small town and its big fort in the centre. It looked altogether like a sort of small fairyland shut out as it is from the rest of the Island and bursting on one's view in such an unexpected and delightful manner. The coast of Karamania and Asia Minor is very plainly visible to the North.

I put up with the Scott-Stevensons in their charming house close to the fort and looking over the little harbour.

[Mar. 23] I went over the old fort and castle with Scott-Stevenson,[16] Commissioner. I had a long day of it the 23rd starting early with a zaptieh as guide for the Monastery of Bella Pais. This is one of the most lovely spots imaginable—a fine old ruin with a grand view looking north. I stopped an hour to sketch it, then rode on up the side of the mountains to a place in the pass I had come over the day before, and met Houston a Scotsman settled *pro tem* at Kyrenia, who had brought out lunch. So we feasted on 'foi gras' and then rode up to St. Hilarion.

The glorious view from the craggy heights of the splendid ruins of the old castle, built as it is on almost inaccessible points of rock 3000 feet above Kyrenia I cannot adequately describe. I should like to have camped there a week, but could barely spare more than an hour as I had to get back to the pass again, and then a long ride to Nicosia. I could only hope to visit it again some day—I parted from Houston in the pass, who returned to Kyrenia, and after a farewell glimpse at that bright little fairyland from the top, rode off to Nicosia and got in just in time for dinner.

[Mar. 24] I dined with Nicolle[17] next evening and left Nicosia on the 25th for Limasol. [Mar. 25] I slept that night at Cofinu (Kophinou) and got into Limassol next day after a capital ride through the country. After taking over my old company from Powell I started another signalling class: but this one I never completed having got leave of absence for four and half months before its completion. Having made my arrangements to go home by Constantinople and see as much as possible of the Levant while out there I left by the SS. "Fortuna" on the 17th, [Apr. 17] Grattan and Trafford going by the same boat, the latter for Malta.

(Here follows an account of the author's journey to England via Egypt. the Greek Islands, Athens, Smyrna, Constantinople and thence by Danube Steamer to Vienna and by rail through Austria and Germany).

The Journal continues in Interlaken Switzerland.

[Jul. 6] On the 1st July there was a great Gazette. The 107th was incorporated with the 35th, and numbers ceased to exist in the British Infantry. I was now 4th Senior Subaltern of the new two-Battalion Regiment with liability to be promoted into either Battalion.

[Jul. 29] A letter arrived from Colonel Gordon,[18] C.C.M.P. Cyprus, offering me the post of Local Commandant Military Police at Larnaca which was about to become vacant so I determined to throw up the remainder of my leave and return to Cyprus forthwith, and I went down to Lauterbrunnen and wired that I should be in Larnaca on the 12th prox.

(Lieutenant Donne describes his journey back to Cyprus via Brindisi, Corfu, Crete and Alexandria)

[Aug. 12] 1 p.m. next day we were off Cyprus once more and soon at anchor off Limassol after having been just twelve days out from Wengen Alp. I went on to Larnaca in the "Elpitha" and happily met Colonel Gordon at the Club who informed me that I was destined to take the Limassol police and not the Larnaca as I had thought, and Gilmore was to come to Larnaca instead. This change of course suited me well. [Aug. 13] I therefore remained at Larnaca, dining with Cobham*[19] the Commissioner on the 13th inst. and returned to Limassol with the Colonel on the 14th inst. [Aug. 14] per SS. "Cymiote".

Limassol—Being unable to take over the duties for some days, until orders were received, [Aug. 15] I started off for the Camp on Mount Troodos about 5 p.m. Having nothing but a miserable screw to ride the result was disastrous for I spent most of the night on the road, only arriving dead tired out at the Platres hotel at 1 a.m. After a nap and a 'cooler' I rode on to the camp on the top, my wretched screw more dead than alive, and which I vowed I would never ride down again.

[Aug. 16] Mount Troodos—After the scorching heat of the plains the air was delightfully refreshing and cool, and the water like ice. I rode over in the afternoon to call on the Warrens[20] at their house above Platres. I stayed on the hill till the 18th living at our mess "in civilian", Colonel Hackett at the time being Acting High Commissioner of Cyprus.

[Aug. 18] On my way down to Platres I called at Colonel Warren's, the Chief Secretary, for orders (this time on a good mule) and got into Limassol again at 7.30 [Aug. 19] and put up at the Club.

---

* Author of Excerpta Cypria

[Aug. 20] On the 20th orders came for me to take over the duties of Local Commandant of Military Police from Gilmore, and the next four days we were busy taking and handing over the many and laborious duties of the Command. [Aug. 24] On the 24th I found myself properly installed as L.C.M.P. and Governor of Limassol Prison with 60 jail birds to be responsible for inside. It took me some time to get into the swing of the work which embraced all police duties in the Town and District of Limassol, the management of the Prison, and prosecutions at the Daavi Court,[21] to say nothing of payments and accounts and book keeping. There were about 100 zaptiehs all told, of which 30 were mounted (including prison warders). Lieutenant Mustafa Shafki was native officer to the force, Dayan interpreter and De Yough police Inspector.

[Aug. 26] On the 26th I took over Gilmore's Quarters in Albert St. at Hedji Nicola's house, and engaged John Houlihun a Coyfu lad as servant and groom. A short time after I bought Lieutenant Mustafa's pony, a nice looking grey, and which suited me very well, for £19-. During the last week in August the heat was very trying. Bairam Festival was on and the men as usual had a holiday. Mitchell[22] the Commissioner was away on leave in the Lebanon, Thompson doing the work.[23] The most disagreeable part of my work was visiting the Prison and town at night.

[Sep. 5] Colonel Gordon came down on quarterly inspection and inspected the Detachment and Prison: and again on the 9th Sir R. Biddulph the High Commissioner returned from England and I had a zaptieh Guard of Honour on the pier.

Police Adventures near Episkopi

[Sep. 10] Started off on my first district tour with Dayan and 3 zaptiehs and rode up to Selico[24] and investigated a peculiar case of theft. Then over the hills to Kilani the chief village of the Nahieh[25] and put up there for the night. The next a.m. we went on to Malia the centre of a very lawless district near the Papho boundary. Chiefly Turkish inhabitants and much given to raiding and cattle lifting it being my special object to try and capture some of the men who had been long wanted by the Authorities. However although many complaints of theft were brought forward no information was obtainable, the people being very unwilling or unable to give information. So after waiting till dark I rode on to Pahna to try and capture a man named Andoni Nicola, a notorious ruffian who with several others was the Scourge of the district. He however had flown having apparently got wind of our being in the neighbourhood, and as I afterwards found out had been warned from Malia by his confederates and had ridden off that evening, armed, on a donkey, no one professed to know where.

So this expedition was so far a failure, and we put up for the night in the best house we could find, a wretched Greek hotel, full of wine chatties and dirt, but the inmates did their best and cleared out for our reception. I have often since had to put up in as bad, and even worse places. The next morning we left Pahna at daybreak and set out for Limassol over the mountains, Pahna being in the midst of very rough country on the top of a hill. We rode back through Khandu and other villages and got into Limassol again about midday, after a very hot ride.

[Sep. 15] A few days afterwards a report came down that a soldier had been shot at on Mount Troodos so I hastened off along the long and dusty road to Platres to find that case had been settled by De Yough who had gone up the day before. So I slept at Letts Hotel at Platres and came back the next day.

[Sep. 18] HMS "Hecla" came in and curiously enough I found a connection on board, Naval Lieutenant Bradley, who knew that I was in Cyprus.

[Oct. 6] Today the new pier (at Limassol) was opened by the High Commissioner with great festivities. A guard of honor of the Regiment and most of the Officers and Island officials were present, and the ceremony was followed by a Banquet to everyone and much speech making. About 70 persons sat down in the new Konak buildings.

[Oct. 10] Left Limassol on a round of Inspection in the District in the Limassol Nahieh, riding to Gelagi (Kellaki) village and on to Heftagonia (Eptagonia) for the night. The scenery in the valleys and mountains round was very fine, and this part of the Island had been little visited before by anyone. We rode on up a very fine valley to Aracapa (Aracapas), Atracko (Athrakos)[26] and Collochaco (Kalokhorio) to Zobie (Zoopiyi) where we rested. The Bishop of Kition was also here inspecting but I did not see his holiness as he was taking his siesta. The village was in gala, and the little church was flying the white church flag in honor of the occasion.

After a short rest for ourselves and the ponies we had to be up and off over the long and very mountainous road to Agro (Agros). We passed over a very breakneck road and had to lead our ponies most of the way to Ayayanni (Ayios Ioannis) a picturesque little vine-growing village in a dell, and at last arrived at Agro the highest village in the mountains of Limassol. There is a Monastery[27] here which is disused apparently, as we could find none at home but a decrepid old monk, who informed us that there was no bedding or food to be got, and that we had better go to the village the other side of the ravine. I shall always remember Agro village as being the worst place I have ever found Quarters in. It would be difficult indeed to find a place more primitive or more cut off from the outer world. But there are many such in Cyprus high up in the mountains, where one would least expect to find them.

[Oct. 12] Leaving early the following morning we arrested a man in his vineyard who had been reported by the Muchtar as a villain of the deepest dye. He drew a knife and ran at first, but the zaptieh appearing over the crest of the hill with a rifle, he was brought to his senses and surrendered to the call. He was soon in tow of the zaptieh and we proceeded down the valley and passed through Potamnitza (Potamitissa) and then crossed over a mountain range to Palendria[28] a large vine-growing village. Here I released the man thinking the lesson would be a warning to him, and seeing the impossibility of getting back that night if we kept him with us. The vintage was in full swing here as everywhere else and we lunched accordingly on some magnificent bunches of grapes, the finest I recollect having ever seen. From here we rode over hill and dale to Hia Mania (Ayios Mamas), an incident occurring on the way which I at first thought was going to be a great catch. A man sitting down at the bend of the road a short distance in front suddenly sprang up when he saw me and bolted out of sight, a companion who was with him remaining. I immediately thought of the men who were 'wanted' and followed hard. Not until the interpreter came up however could I gain any information from the old man, whom in my eagerness I had seized and was about to beat to make him speak. It turned out however, instead of the runaway being a murderer or such like as I suspected, he had run away from fear, and looking up we saw him standing on a hill above. He came down on his father's summons and we could then see that the poor boy was shaking from some imaginable fear and was too much afraid to speak. Having therefore assured ourselves that their errand was an honest one and having searched them, we proceeded, thinking the boy at least to be crazy.

At Hia Mania a murder had been committed a short time before, so after having collected some necessary evidence and lunched in a very clean little house, owned by the muchtar's son, we rode back to Limassol through Gabellu (Kapilio) and Corfi (Korphi). Passing Corfi we were caught in a heavy shower the 1st of the season, and a prelude of the coming winter weather, or I should say the 'break up' of the hot weather.

[Oct. 25] Rode out round the Salt Lake to see the ruins of an old Monastery[29] from whence a picturesque view of the Salt Lake and hills beyond. The next day the "Tyne" (troopship) came in with a large draft for the Regiment under Campbell and Ramus, and the latter who was evidently very ill with consumption put up with me for a week.

[Nov. 3] The 3rd Nov. being a Bairam holiday for the men, I issued the new police clothing to the whole force in the afternoon the old red jacket being discarded for a blue uniform with red braid. [Nov. 6] On the 6th Colonel Gordon came down and inspected the Detachment again, heavy rain falling overnight and Troodos being covered with snow for the 1st time this winter. The Zaptiehs and Troopers were paraded next day.

[Nov. 11] Left again for the district of Evdimu (Evdhimou), acts of violence becoming more numerous every day. I rode out with 5 troopers along the coast through Episcopi arriving at Evdimu at dusk. After a long rest we started again up country for Pahna (Pakna) to try and surprise Andoni by night this time. We surprised some donkey stealers on the road who, seeing the party coming along left the path and fled to the bush. After a wild scurry through the bush by moonlight over rocks stones and bushes, it ended by the principal thief getting away; however we got one man, and the stolen convoy and took them on to Prassiu (Prastio) with us where they were identified by the village priest as his property. So we bound the captured culprit up, and sent him back to the Konak at Evdimu.

We arrived before Pahna about 3 a.m. and after picqueting the horses separated into two parties for the attack. With two Zaptiehs I crept up to the suspected man's house, the other making a detour to prevent his possible escape in the other direction. Placing one man on the roof with a Martini Rifle ready loaded, I went to the door with revolver ready cocked but we eventually found he was not 'at home' that night, his Lady Love being the only occupant. After searching several other houses we were forced to give up the search and, having gathered the villagers together and warned them on the subject of harbouring the criminal, we rode back again to Evdimu in the morning.

[Nov. 12] After the fatigues of the night we were glad to stop at Evdimu and in the evening I rode down to the shore and had a dip.

[Nov. 13] On my way back to Limassol next day I found the ruins of the Temple of Apollo Hylates near Curium. It occupied a commanding position not far from the promontory and a few 100 yards from the road to Paphos. There is a jumble of ruins and fallen columns and the foundations can all be traced and in one place I observed a fine piece of Greek inscription bearing the word 'Apollo' on it. At Episkopi the black Muchtar gave me a very good dinner à la Turk: after which I summoned the principal villagers to a meeting on the subject of theft, etc. We also called on the Lord of Colossi Tower[30] on our way back.

Gilmore arrived in the evening on board the Mail en route to England, and after dining at the Hackett's, I bade him farewell from the pier. He had worked hard in the police for more than 3 years.

[Nov. 24] I made another excursion into the Evdimu Nahieh sleeping as usual at the Mudir's[31] house. [Nov. 25] And the next day visited Prassiu, Platanissia (Plataniskia) and Electora (Alekhtora) riding through a fine country with charming views seaward. We put up for the night at Pissouri and had a long discussion with the native magnates on the subject of theft in general, but like all Cypriots they were free enough to complain, but not to assist the police in the apprehension of offenders.

[Nov. 26] The next a.m. the sky was black and rain coming down hard, making it impossible for us to proceed as Pissouri is on top of a high hill with steep roads leading to the plain. From Cape Blanko near there is a splendid view along the coast. It cleared up about midday however, and as the roads were in consequence execrable, we did not get into Limassol before evening.

[Nov. 27] HMS "Superb" came in next day and lunches and cricket: matches were enlivening topics of the day, and also an inspection of the ship.

The Kitchener Episode

[Dec. 7] Today I started on a very memorable excursion to my usual hunting ground, a report having come in overnight that Kitchener,*[32] the Government Surveyor, who was surveying round Pissouri had been shot at near Platanissia by a man unknown. We saddled early the next morning and rode off to Pissouri with a force of Troopers and arriving there in the afternoon I had the time to ride over to Platanissia with Kitchener himself, and examine the ground. We also examined the natives in the village but could get no information of the man in particular. Having therefore returned to Pissouri I put up for the night. After having retired to bed, my servant Yanni came in with a shepherd, who volunteered information against a man who he stated was in hiding in a mandra (sheep fold) a little distance off. Having therefore got two Troopers together with their rifles and borrowing Kitchener's shotgun myself, we proceeded to the place on foot with the shepherd as guide and Yanni as interpreter. After an hour's walk we were indicated the fold by the shepherd, who however refused to go further not relishing the chances of being 'potted' as he informed us the man was armed.

The Capture of Salih Bobi

Having made my disposals to surround the place as well as possible, and guided by the moonlight, and the barking of the sheepdogs, who had already taken the alarm, we advanced to the Attack at a smart pace in order if possible to get up before the dogs woke the inmates. I missed the entrance myself and before I was aware found myself looking

---

* Afterwards Lord Kitchener of Khartoum

down on the sheepfold from some rocks above, and the two Zaptiehs creeping outside with their rifles ready. I soon discovered my error and was down in a minute beside them and clearing the fence outside with as little noise as possible, got at the entrance of the cave inside the fold. At the further end a fire was smouldering beside which sat a shepherd, who had apparently just roused himself to the fact someone was at the entrance. The nearest Zaptieh and myself then ran in and saw at the same time that another man was also lying on the ground near, with a pile of arms near him. Before we had time to do anything or to take in the situation, he leapt up with a howl and attempted to catch the arms near him. The Zaptieh and myself however were on him in a moment, and after a struggle that lasted for a few seconds, pinioned him on the ground. The other Zaptieh who was guarding the entrance then came in, and after a short time, we soon had both men securely bound up.

On searching the cave which was a spacious one, and ran back some way, we found a considerable store of arms. consisting of 2 large knives or yatagans, carried by the Turks in their belts, two flintlock pistols loaded with ball, and two double barrel fowling pieces, also loaded with shot and slugs. One of the knives we found drawn in the shepherd's bed. One of the men also wore a large sporting belt well stocked with powder, ball, shot and slugs. In fact had we not surprised them in time, they might have kept any number of men at bay at the narrow entrance to their cave. Having secured the arms and the men, and ransacked the cave, we marched them back to Pissouri about 1 a.m.

[Dec. 8] Instead of being a murderer, however as I had expected, I found that the younger man was one Salih Bobi a notorious ruffian and an escaped convict from Nicosia, who had long defied the Paphos police and been fired at in that district once by the L.C.M.P. It was also clearly established that he was actually the man who had fired at Lieutenant Kitchener. So thus far our raid was an entire success.

The other man was a Shepherd who had knowingly harboured the convict and was in consequence sentenced to Limassol jail for 6 months. Salih Bobi was sent in the next a.m. to Limassol.

I rode to the cave again next a.m. to examine it by daylight but could gain no information of the murderer, whom I afterwards ascertained from my informant, had actually been there in Salih's company that night! But by some accident or other he had left the cave a short time before we entered it. (This was proved by the fact that one of the guns was his, also that he had but one boot on, we having found the other odd one in the cave). His brother was there in the morning but would vouchsafe no information. I rode on to Platanissia again and back to Pissouri, dining with Kitchener and on to Evdimu to sleep at the Konak. (see Press Comment at Appendix 'A').

The death of Molla Tahir

[Dec. 9] I prepared next morning to ride up country to Pahna and Malia and try and gain some news of the wanted Andoni who had again been heard of in the vicinity. We started for Pahna accordingly but getting scanty news pushed on to visit a village called Chissousa (Kissousa) en route to Malta. Having entered the village and perceiving a large mandra just above it, I called for the commission, to enquire for my 'wanted' friends, but as usual no information was forthcoming. They know nothing of any of them. Retracing our steps therefore I was in the act of riding up to the mandra where several men were loitering, when my leading Zaptieh Mouslu Osman, shouted out loudly that Molla Tahir, a notorious ruffian and long wanted by the police, was in a ruin in front. Almost at the same moment I saw him running across the front of the Zaptieh, down the steep hill towards the river. He carried a gun and a long knife in his belt. Another moment and he would have disappeared, so, in the excitement and fear that the man would escape us, I shouted down to Mouslu to fire. Mouslu carried one of the fowling pieces we had captured the day before, and which was loaded, but no one knew precisely with what sort of ammunition. Mouslu turned his horse and raising the gun, fired at the man about 20 paces off, who was running across him. Molla Tahir then disappeared behind a wall and was lost to our view, no one knowing at the moment whether he was hit or not. I fancied he had made for the river bed and would escape on the opposite side, so in great anxiety lest he should after all elude us, I rode as fast as the ground would allow down to the river directing Dayan the interpreter and the other Zaptieh to ride through the village and cut him off. Mouslu rode to the other side of the river where the ground was rough and rocky.

Finding no traces of the man in the river bed, about 5 minutes later as I was turning my pony to ride towards the village again I saw him emerge from a house facing the river and run towards the Zaptieh on the opposite side with his gun raised to fire. Mouslu, who from his position had seen the man in the house before me, was shouting wildly to the other Zaptieh, who was now standing on the flat roof of one of the houses close by. At the same moment he raised his rifle and fired at Molla Tahir, 20 or 30 paces off. I thought that the bullet had again missed its mark as Tahir ran on, and disappeared again round some walls.

I rushed up and dismounted taking the rifle from the Zaptieh who was very excited, and followed in the direction I had seen the man go. Blood marks on the ground a little further on however soon told me that the ball had told but too truly, and meeting the interpreter at the entrance of the village, I asked him hurriedly where the man had gone. "He's lying round the corner of the road there, Sir, and must be dying" was his answer. Dayan was trembling with evident fear, and excitement. When I came up with this ill-fated highwayman, robber and thief, one could see at a glance that he was fast dying. He was lying in the arms of a villager, his life blood ebbing out on the stones, and the palor of death on his rough countenance. His unhappy wife, a Turkishwoman with her white yashmak all bathed in blood, was hanging round his neck uttering wild exclamations of anguish, terror and vengeance against the Zaptieh who had shot her husband, and several other Turkish women who had gathered round joined in the dismal wail making a scene I shall not soon forget. Molla's gun, yatagan and belt were lying round dripping with blood and we could do nothing but stand round as spectators to the scene, the women being far too frantic and violent to permit anyone to interfere.

Turning my back therefore on this terrible picture I took out my pocket book to make the necessary entries and to note the names of those standing round. These craven-hearted fellows (for they were the ones who had been in the mandra with the deceased, and whom I had questioned before in the village as to Molla's whereabouts) tried to slip away seeing my object, and I had even to send the Zaptiehs for some in their houses.

Molla Tahir breathed his last about 10 minutes after I came up, having been shot right through the body; he had gone a considerable distance after receiving the fatal bullet, and had even attempted to shoot the interpreter, the latter (being unarmed) having taken refuge in the nearest place, and barred himself in.

Molla was a man notorious throughout the Island as a desperate ruffian and the terror of the country round for years past. He was a great cattle stealer, as well as having committed many highway robberies and rapes.

I flattered myself on having done a great stroke of business in having rid the district of such a pest, and congratulated the Zaptieh Ahmet warmly on having shot the poor fellow, Ahmet being in a great state of mind from fear of the consequences, and the execrations heaped on him by the wailing women. Nothing would comfort him, so I sent him straight off to Limassol, where he arrived I believe the same night without stopping a moment on the way such was the man's terror of vengeance from Molla's relatives.

Nothing more remaining to be done at Chissusa, I rode on to Malia to inform the man's relatives of his death, and also to show the villagers here that the police meant work, and to hold up Molla's fate as a warning to his confederates. Having accordingly gathered the villagers together in the Square, I informed them that Molla Tahir, one of their own number, had been shot dead at Chissusa for refusing to surrender himself to me when called on, and added that I meant to hunt out the rest of his associates and treat them in the same way if they did not give themselves up. This had an astonishing effect on the hitherto indifferent crowd, amongst whom were two of Molla's brothers, and many relations, and men women and children all set out for Chissusa as fast as they could go to verify with their own eyes if the astonishing news was really true.

It being necessary for me to return forthwith again to Limassol to report these circumstances and to send the Doctor out to make a post-mortem examination, we lost no time in turning our backs on Malia to get over the long ride back to Evdimu before nightfall, where we arrived about 6 p.m.

[Dec. 10] I got into Limassol again next midday where I found greatly exaggerated accounts of the case had proceeded us. The Konak was besieged, and when we arrived with such an array of knives, pistols and guns etc. stuck about us, everyone thought that at least we had had a desperate fight for it. I telegraphed the circumstances to the C.C.M.P. at Nicosia who in his turn hardly knew how H.E. the "Vali"[33] would take it. However all's well that ends well, and when my detailed report in writing went in, it was generally accepted at Head-Quarters that nothing better could have happened. Many of the villagers who had suffered by this man's depredations afterwards came in to thank me for the service that had been rendered them and to express their joy at his death. As the result of this energy on the part of the police, Molla's brother, one of the gang, gave himself up shortly after, and the notorious Andoni of Pahna who had all along evaded all attempts to capture him, was taken by the Zaptiehs at Nicosia (Press extracts at Appendix A).

[Dec. 13] *Postscript for* 1881. The French gunvessel "Voltigeur" paid us a visit and we entertained the officers at the Club. Fairfield[34] of the Colonial office came down to overhaul government affairs.

[Dec. 23] Olive,[35] I.C.M.P. Papho, came up and next night being Christmas Eve, we entertained the English married people at the Club at dinner with a very small hop afterwards.

[Dec. 25] Being Christmas Day I had my Parade of the Zaptiehs and visited the prison in the morning, and in the afternoon entertained Hedji Emmanueli's family and some of Papa's friends at my lodgings and rode out to Polymedia to dine with the Regiment in the evening. It was a warm fine day.

1881 being well nigh run out I may safely say that I have seen and done more during the last twelve months than in any previous year.

"Non numero horas nisi serenas"

and I cannot resist this little quotation, dedicated respectfully to the year passing away:—

"yet I leave, as waves leave their Treasures
of coral and shell,
a gift passing sorrows and pleasures,
our friendship to tell".

[Jan. 1, 1882] Limassol. Most of my time during the 1st half of January was occupied in making up the Annual Police and Prison reports. I had but little time to go into the district myself. To my disgust Andrea the Corfi (Korphi) murderer was again captured by Zaptiehs but succeeded in escaping from them, and the loss of a rifle by one of the Zaptiehs on duty at Pahna led to an enquiry on the subject.

[Jan. 20] About the 20th the weather became unusually severe, and the hills round Silico (Silikhou) were covered with snow. [Jan. 27] On the 27th I rode round to Fassoula (Phasoula), Palodia (Palodhia) and several other villages within a day's ride to inspect.

Transfer to Nicosia

[Feb. 3] About this time I was ordered to relieve Bor,[36] L.C.M.P. at Nicosia whilst he was employed superintending the Locust Destruction. I accordingly handed over the Limassol Command and Prison to Powell, 35th, as a temporary measure during my absence at Nicosia, and [Feb. 5] started for the Capital on the 5th. Having packed up my traps and sent them on ahead, I said goodbye to Hedji Emmanueli's family (amongst whom were not a few moist eyes) and left Limassol on a very cold morning for Cofinu (Kophinou). Later on it commenced snowing and when I arrived at Cofinu under the shadow of the great Stavrovouni Mount I was not sorry to take shelter in the little house of—Effendi, a very hospitable old Turkish gentleman.

[Feb. 6] Continuing the road next morning I covered 25 miles in time for lunch with Bor and Inglis[37] at the Commissioner's house Nicosia, after which I went out to stop with Colonel Gordon at his new house outside the walls—until I could find lodgings in town. The country all round was looking very fine and wintry with the Troodos Mountains completely wrapped in snow away in the distance and the fine Northern Range looking strangely near in its covering of snow. [Feb. 7] The next day I took over command of the Nicosia Police from Lieutenant Bor—a large force of over 300 men of which 70 were Suwaris, or mounted men.

[Feb. 8] Having found suitable rooms in town in the Bashmahallak Quarter[38] I shifted into them and settled down for a few months. I also got over several calls on the English of Nicosia and H.E. the Governor at the Tepe.[39] Harden was commanding a Detachment of 50 men of the Regiment at the staff huts with Thornton and . . . . A burst of gaiety seemed to have possessed Nicosia, at this time, a farewell dance to Mr. and Mrs. Marsh,[40] the retiring Auditor General, and several others of minor importance among the smaller officials. [Feb. 12] I dined with Seager,[41] an old Wellingtonian, and Deputy Commissioner on the 12th, the cold still continuing and even running up to 7 degrees of frost. [Feb. 15] The Nicosia Harriers[42] were also in full swing and the season ended by a big field on the 15th in the Larnaka direction, but unfortunately I was too late to take part in the run.

Nicosia life was exceedingly pleasant, albeit quiet, and to my liking. Numerous dinner parties were the order of the Day. It was impossible to be living in Nicosia without enjoying the lovely scenery of the surroundings, and the innumerable picturesque bits which every turn and corner of this old Turkish Capital afforded.

[Feb. 21] Parsons[43] and I rode out together on the 21st to a village called Kaimakli to take sworn evidence on a murder case which he followed up by riding on to Voni and from there home through the pretty village of Kitherea (Kythrea), under the Pentadactylon Mountain. Without a doubt a murder under peculiar circumstances had taken place some time since at Chrisostomo Monastery and the monks had heavily bribed those cognizant of the facts to keep what they knew to themselves. The case however when brought to court fell through. It was a mystery that will never be solved now, and when I think of Chrisostomo and its monks I cannot help bracketing them with the murder mystery.

[Feb. 22] The Molla Tahir shooting case was heard by Themez Court[44] on the 22nd which ended, as I have already recorded, in the police being honourably, acquitted of all blame in the man's death. [Mar. 4] Colonel Gordon came down to inspect the force which was drawn up in the Courtyard of the Buyuk Hahn[45] about 200 strong.

[Mar. 8] Today I took a holiday and made one of those rare excursions which one is not always in a hurry to forget. Harden, Dr. Johnstone[46] and myself started off early for Chrisostomo Monastery and the Castle of Buffavento, perched on one of the highest peaks of the Northern Range. We galloped away through the Kyrenia Gate with a Zaptieh to show us the way and were soon across the Messaria plain and among the Hummucks (Sic). After another hour's scrambling we arrived at Chrisostomo Monastery (alias the White Monastery) most picturesquely situated at the foot of the mountains. The monks received us with great hospitality as usual and as we were picknicing I did not introduce myself as the Commandant of the District which in fact is not in Nicosia but Kyrenia, so I actually had no jurisdiction there, although the murder mystery rather tempted me to have a look round.

We left our ponies behind here and scrambled up to the summit on foot and I seldom recollect having been up a more breakneck place. When we arrived at the fork of the hill just below the summit, a most glorious panorama burst on our view. The Northern shore lay at our feet 3000 feet below and behind us the whole of the Messaria Plains with the Troodos range like a massive wall in the blue distance topped with snow, and away to the North across the deep blue straits that intervened were the Taurus Mountains with a similar night cap on. I have always considered it to be one of the finest panoramic views in Cyprus. The beautiful soft colouring of the hills with the azure sky above and intense blue of the sea at one's feet combine to produce a lovely effect. We scrambled about and explored our mountain eyrie which indeed must have been a strong place in the days of King Richard of England who reduced it.[47]

Away in the midst of the great brown Messaria Plain was Nicosia like a round spot in the distance with its minarets sticking up like slender sticks in the hazy distance. I was glad to have time to get a sketch as a memento of this most wonderful view, as well as another small one from Chrisostomo.

The Ayios Ermolaos Affair

[Mar. 10] Revenant à nos mouton, however, the alarming news came in from Kyrenia on the 10th that 5 convicts had broken loose from there, having taken with them rifles and ammunition. This demanded immediate measures being taken for their recapture, and in an hour's time I was galloping out of the Kyrenia Gate with a Detachment of 8 armed Troopers. In two hours' time we were at the foot of the Agurda Pass leading over to Kyrenia and, detaching 4 of them to watch the pass and the village of Pano Dicomo (Pano Dhikamo) near there and two others to watch another mountain path I took the remainder with me along the Northern slope of the mountains to see if I could gain any intelligence of the runaways.

After riding a considerable distance and passing several villages the evening began to draw on, so we made for a large village named Hia Mola (Ay Ermolaos) a short distance ahead. An extraordinary scene presented itself on my arrival. A number of villagers rushed up to us, shouting and crying and gesticulating in every imaginable tone, and one man was bleeding profusely from a wound in the head. Further on were lying what appeared to be dead or dying corpses, some moaning and howling in a piteous way. I first of all imagined that the convicts had been there and sacked the village, and that we had arrived in the nick of time, and I instinctively drew my revolver as a precautionery measure. We were soon however undeceived for when something like order had been restored and we could hear each other speak my interpreter extracted the truth from the villagers.

It appears there had been a free fight between the villagers and a band of strange gipsies who were from "across the sea" and the latter having been followed up from Morfou (Morphou) and other villages by their creditors, the minds of the peaceable men of Hia Mola had been prejudiced against the intruders, and Hia Mola had in consequence become the theatre of a desultory warfare which had thus far been going on all day. Our opportune arrival happily put an end to hostilities, and we therefore set to work to collect the casualties.

There they lay like so many logs in the street, who seemed incapable of moving, but after a bit we managed to drag them all into the nearest "Caffeeniss", and set about to patch up their wounds. The men were nothing like as bad as they appeared to be at 1st sight: their wounds consisted mostly of cuts, bruises and contusions, which my interpreter, Theodore Mavrogordato[48] very cleverly overhauled. The only serious cases appeared to be two women one of whom appeared to have a broken thigh and the other a fractured skull—I therefore dispatched a messenger across the mountains to Kyrenia for a surgeon, and a report of the case to the Commissioner of the District. We then set to work to take evidence as to the causus belli which occupied us till midnight when we went to roost in the most decent looking hut we could find.

Scott-Stevenson with his Medical officer, Interpreter and Prison Sergeant turned up about 4 a.m. having been out all night, and in a short time the casualties were again overhauled and the whole gang of gipsies bundled off to Kyrenia, some as prisoners, some as patients, and I have seldom seen a motley utterly miserable looking troop in my life as they collected their wretched traps and decamped, leaving the villagers once more to resume the even tenor of their every day life.

During this little bit of excitement, we had almost forgotten the convicts of whom Stevenson informed me 3 had been already recaptured, it being most probable that the remaining two had got well away over night. It was therefore hardly necessary for me to remain in the Kyrenia District any longer, so after a hearty laugh with Stevenson over the amusing little incident, my party saddled up and rode back to Nicosia in the afternoon.

[Mar. 11] I was called up to a fire that night which soon burnt itself out, fires in Cypriot towns being of rare occurrence owing to the mud and stone construction of the houses.

Nicosia Race Week

[Mar 12] Several of our fellows and the band came up from Polymedia for the Race Week and during the week the townspeople were treated to some good music. [Mar. 17] The race meeting was a great success. [Mar. 18] The numbers of Turkish women and harems who turned out to see the fun, and settled themselves down in a great cluster opposite the Stand all clothed in their picturesque dress and white yashmaks, gave the prettily situated course a most unusual and oriental appearance. Nicosia was very gay all the week and the festivities wound up with a bachelors' ball at the Government offices outside the town. Morton won the handsome cup given by the Regiment.

[Mar. 14] I rode over to Kyrenia on the 14th with Campbell and Ashurst where we had a look round the fort and lunch at the Stevensons.

Expedition to Kykko

[Mar. 22] Being anxious to make a more extended tour of the Nicosia District whilst the weather seemed favourable, I started with my interpreter on 22nd to inspect the Morfou and Lefka Nahiehs.[49] The locusts had begun to appear in large quantities and most of the traps for their destruction were already in working order. In order to visit them therefore, we rode cross country via Gonelli (Geunyely) and found Naim Eff, the Lefka Mudir and Chief Superintendent Locust Destruction at work there. We joined the road again to the north of Yerollaka (Yerrolakkos) and shortly before sunset arrived in sight of Morfu (Morphou). The Bay of Morfu was beyond with the bold Troodos Range and Lefka hills springing up from the sea in fine cliffs, and Cape Kokkino the west point of the bay, jutting out into the sea, was growing very dark with the sea glittering all round it as the sun went down.

Morfou itself is a mile or so from the sea in the midst of the great plain. It is essentially a Greek town, just as Lefka is Turkish. We put up at the Monastery[50] which in the matter of interior economy and hospitality is rather behind most of the Cypriot Ecclesiastical Establishments of the sort. However as long as I was in the Nicosia District I always took care to steer for one of them if within a Sabbath day's journey.

[Mar. 23] Lefka is situated at the foot of one of the finest valleys of Troodos and is one of the happy lands of Cyprus watered by unfailing streams from the great Mount, as Sir S. Baker says.[51] The valley is filled with innumerable fruit trees, and the houses are almost hidden by the luxurious foliage that surrounds them. It is a great place for lemons. The little mosque with its minaret, surrounded by fruit olives and caroub trees, makes a very pretty picture with the snowy tops of Troodos for a background.

[Mar. 25] Having inspected the Police Detachment and slept at the little Konak, we started next a.m. for the Marathasa valley. It is a good eight hours' ride to Ghikko (Kykko) Monastery but through some of the finest and wildest scenery in Cyprus. The bridlepath is rough and steep continually crossing and recrossing the stream until one at length arrives at the quaint old village of Kampos (Kambos). Lunching here at a very clean and respectable little dwelling where our hostess was busy weaving, we continued our journey up the steep hill sides to Ghikko and after innumerable twistings and turnings round the hilltops, at length sited this greatest and most important of Cyprian Monasteries. It was a massive looking building under the brow of a hill to protect it from the west, with a fine view of Troodos opposite.

The Monastery is very rich with a staff of about 80 monks so needless to state we were regally entertained. The Agumenos[52] was a grand old veteran and showed us all over the curious and unique old Chapel. I also tasted the Ghikko "red mastic" for the 1st time.

My excuse for coming to Ghikko was to try and find a murderer who was supposed to frequent the place at times, but our errand was fruitless. There was still snow lying about the vicinity in patches and the nights were very cold at this altitude so early in the year. Having written our names in the visitors' book which Sir R. Biddulph had given to the Monastery the summer before we said Goodbye to our kind hosts and got on our way to Everico (Evrykhou) It was over one of the most abominable tracks I know in the Island and we had to dismount and lead our ponies down most of the steep descents. It was a wild and lonely part of the Island, and the haunt of the Moufflon as some say, but I never saw any of those "spectre animals". After riding down a steep and difficult gorge we reached Kalapaniotissa (Kalopanayiotis) one of the largest and certainly the most curious of Cypriot village I had seen. The houses were built in tiers in the side of the hill, one above the other, and one had to ride over the flat mud roofs to reach beyond. This is likewise a Greek colony and we lunched at the little 'Jack of all trades' shop. [Mar. 26] The villagers had their usual complaints to make and after noting them, we got on our journey again down the valley, and did not arrive at Everico until after sundown at 7 p.m., having been nearly 10 hours in the saddle. Everico is an important place in the fertile

Everico Valley and, like Lefka, rejoicing in a bounteous supply of water from Troodos which renders its valley nearly the most prolific in the Island.

We put up in a very superior 2 Storeyed house rejoicing in a superior iron bedstead to have a good sleep on, but although our hostess emphatically denied their absence (Sic) I was nevertheless able to undeceive her the next a.m. by showing a goodly number of slaughtered 'bugbears' which, thanks to Keating, I had netted.

A deputation awaited me in the morning on the subject of the never-ending water disputes, so we did not get on our homeward road to Nicosia before 10.30. It is a long journey across the plains. We arrived in the afternoon at Peristerona where owing to the indisposition of my interpreter we were delayed an hour or two. Calling at Akakie and Tremitia (Trimithia) on our way in we finally passed through the Baffo (Sic) Gate at 7 p.m. after 5 days' hard riding.

More praise of Kyrenia

[Apr. 16] On the 16th I rode over to Kyrenia to see Houston the Stevensons being away at the time. I was induced by Houston to remain overnight, and such has always been my admiration of this fairy land that the more I saw of it the more it stamped its rare beauties in my mind. Can it be wondered that a man like Houston, possessing an independant property as he did of his own in Scotland, and having travelled all over the World should in visiting Kyrenia last of all, determine to buy land there and settle. He too no doubt saw its exceptional beauty and advantages.

After trying to sketch the harbour and hills we dined together at Law's,[53] the Assistant Commissioner's and an old Wellingtonian friend of mine, and had a good talk over Cypriot affairs in general, Dr Carlotti[54] the D.M.O.[55] also joining us.

I don't think any poet has ever yet visited this out of the way spot otherwise we should have heard its praise chronicled in verse before now. I got back to Nicosia early next a.m. and luckily in time to install myself in office, as the High Commissioner inspected the Buyuk Hahn and Prison that morning.

Plague of locusts

[Apr. 5] I was ordered to Morfu again a few days afterwards on Locust Inspection. After zig-zagging across country visiting the different Traps and Screens[56] about Gonelli, Yerollako and Akakie we were caught in a regular Cyprus downpour before reaching Morfou and it rained hard most of the night, the roof of the old Monastery over our heads being little better than a seive. In the morning it brightened up, so crossing the limestone hills and sand ridges to the East, we rode to Aya Marina and visited all the traps on the way back to Nicosia by Aya Vasili (Ay Vasilios) and Gonelli, reaching home at even.

[Apr. 19] Being Easter Sunday and the great Greek festival of the year, feasting and holiday-making was the order of the day with the Greeks.

[Apr. 21] The locust campaign was now fairly well started and these pestivorous insects were now appearing in alarming quantities and every day increasing in size and developing their destructive qualities I was ordered out again on the 21st by the Commissioner on a round of inspection embracing all the Traps in the Nicosia District which took me a week riding round.

Throughout the Messaria plains stretching from the Carpas to Morfou on the north there were altogether in use upwards of 140 miles of Traps and Screens! This astonishing length will give some idea of the work in hand. The Screens were of canvas bound with oil cloth at the top, and about 3 ft high, the oil cloth over which the animals could not crawl obliging them to crawl along the canvas until they hopped into the pits dug for their reception. These pits were dug at right angles to the Screens at intervals of about 20 yds, being likewise lined with zinc, preventing the locusts from climbing out again. In whatever direction the locusts appeared to be advancing therefore, were the Traps and Screens erected to intercept them. In this manner vast multitudes were destroyed, so many labourers being detailed to watch a certain length of trapping. The whole of the Messaria was in this manner spread over with long lines of Screens, sometimes a mile or more in length, according as they were more or less required in any particular locality.

I started in the Kyrenia direction and after a hard day's riding visited all the traps in that direction, and put up for the night at a very comfortable little place in Kitherea (Kythrea). [Apr. 22] We were off again early next a.m. in a westerly direction passing by Timbo (Tymbou), Margo, and Piroi. Here the locusts were passing the Larnaca road in countless myriads, filling the traps to overflowing. The streams were all full of them; the country was all black with them, such an extraordinary sight did they present.

The labour and the Screens seemed indeed utterly inadequate to entrap a hundredth part of their number. Here I met Colonel Gordon on his way to Nicosia by Diligence with a friend fresh arrived from England, and they were looking in amazement at the extraordinary procession of these insects—all treading in one direction, and hopping into the traps as if despising the puny efforts of men to diminish their numbers.

Wedding in Dhali

We continued our ride to Dali the ancient Delium, where Chesnola excavated so successfully, and put up for the night. Dali is the chief town of the Mudirate,[57] and an important one for Cyprus. It has a Christian and a Mussulman population and we found a very intelligent schoolmaster there, with a considerable flock under his command. Close by there to the little Greek church is the grave of an English Soldier who belonged to the 71st Highland Regiment in the days of the occupation. A curious place quoth I, to find a British Grave, but then British soldiers never can reckon where their mortal clay will rest—the whole of this wide world is his burial ground.

In the village great matrimonial preparations were going forward; the belle of the village was about to be given in marriage and it was amusing to watch all the buxom females of the place, Turk and Greek alike, busily beating up the nuptial bed to the sound of Dance music. It was a curious Levantine scene. As I desired to see the bride, she was in due course brought forth and presented to me, and, indeed, for a Cypriot woman very good looking in truth she was. On the strength of my arrival in the Town the musicians came down and serenaded us at meal time. The accommodation at Dali was exceptionally good.

[Apr. 23] We left for Latchia (Laxia) next a.m. and were drenched by a heavy hail storm on the road. We continued cross country to Deftera (Dheftera) and the sun which had again appeared, soon dried us off. The Mudir of the Dagh Nahieh gave us a feed at

Deftera and hungry enough we were. On the road across the hills to Yerollako we passed large quantities of locusts moving in the Deftera direction. At Yerollako we arranged to stop for the night at the Muchtar's house, tempted by its clean and neat appearance from proceeding further that day. The Muchtar and his family (and he had two pretty daughters) served us with a most excellent supper.

[Apr. 24] From Yerollako to Peristerona is not a heavy day's journey but as we moved about in all manner of directions to inspect the various traps we did not get to our night's resting place till evening. Passing through Acachie (Akaki) and Tremithia we rode to Meniko in which direction the locusts were marching in hosts, and the river was brown with them. They made no difficulty of crossing it, taking their chance of being washed up on the opposite side and then proceeding to attack the crops. Naim Eff, the energetic Mudir of Lefka, was here running up Screens in all directions to intercept their march. Meniko is a quaint little Greek village, after the usual pattern. We got down to Peristerona towards evening and I took a drawing of the extremely curious Greek church[58] which is of great antiquity and has three or four domes springing from the roof. Being on the high road to Troodos, Peristerona is accustomed to see strangers passing through and an old Turkish lady offers excellent accommodation in a superior 2d story old house with a well furnished divaned room for travellers. The wall there which was scratched over with the names of those who had found shelter there, acted as a visitor's book.

[Apr. 25] Next day, Tuesday, we crossed the Messaria to Panteleimon Monastery in the Kyrenia District near Cape Kormakiti. We rode through Potamie and Astromeriti where the locusts were in millions, and the work of destruction progressing well. Then on to Gira, Chrisoliou (Khrysiliou) and Capouti where we got some food at the Priest's miserable little den. Two hours' ride over a rugged uncultivated succession of rocky hills and valleys zig-zagging up and down over a surface of white marl overgrown with stunted myrtle bushes, we at length arrived at Myrtu village, close to which is Panteleimon Monastery. The Bishop was here at the time and everything about the place betokened an unusual advance in civilisation one is hardly accustomed to find outside the big towns. In the little house I put up in at Myrtu village everything was as clean and comfortable as one could wish for a week's stay, and my kind hosts and their grown up daughters were as kind as they could be, refusing to let me pay anything for my board when I left next morning.

From just beyond the Monastery on the brink of a steep precipice looking down a 1000 ft into the sea is a splendid view across to Asia Minor, a reminiscence of which I managed to secure before it was too dark to draw. [Apr. 26] We rode in next day along the Northern Range to Aya Marina, Shillura (Skylloura), Ay Vasili (Ay Vasilios) and Gonelli (Geunyely) visiting traps all the way, and got home at 4 p.m. having had six day's continuous riding.

[May 10] Colonel Gordon inspected my detachment again on the 10th May at which I had but about 70 men—and having a day or two's leave, I started on the 11th May for Famagusta.

Visit to Famagusta and Salamis

[May 11] I broke the long and monotonous journey across the parched up Messaria plain at Eshia (Asha) where there is a very decent resting place, and got into Varosia, a large village outside Famagusta walls where the officials and most of the inhabitants live. Famagusta itself is a wonderful mass of ruined churches and palaces and I walked through the town with Buchan, an architect, and brother-in-law of Colonel Gordon who was staying there. There is nothing in Cyprus that impresses me more vividly than this once important fortress. The old Cathedral of St. Nicholas, now a Mosque, is a grand specimen of a Gothic church and presents a much finer appearance than even Santa Sophia at Nicosia.

Inside the great walls which are for the most part dug out of the solid rock all is abomination and ruin, with the exception of the Government offices, a small bazaar and the Zaptieh Konak. It has remained in this ruined state ever since it was sacked and ruined by the Turks after the memorable siege of 1571. The walls are still in almost perfect condition, which illustrates the massive construction of the Venetians. The Venetian Lion and Coat of Arms is still affixed to all the principal bastions. The subterranean works and magazines would from the massiveness and durability of their construction, have afforded an admirable lesson to many an architect. I made several sketches of these interesting and picturesque old ruins with the silted up harbour and Carpas Mountains beyond running out until they lost themselves in the regions of Cape Saint Andrea.

Young[59] the Commissioner being away with his family on a tour to Cape Saint Andrea, I put up with Captain Gordon,[60] the Assistant Commissioner who also had the Bishop of Gibraltar as a guest, and Mr. Spencer,[61] our Nicosia Chaplain. [May 13] I rode out to the site of ancient Salamis on the 13th where many of the foundations of this ancient Capital can be traced. Excavations for the London Museums were being carried on, and a fine piece of mosaic pavement just brought to light. In the days of St. Paul's visit this was the most important town, and the place where he landed. A mile and a half inland is the Church of St. Barnabas, supposed to mark the site where the Saint's body was found, with the Gospel of St. Mathew. An ancient Cyclopean Mausoleum called the Tomb of St. Catherine is almost the only ancient monument now visible of the Necropolis of Salamis.

[May 14] I rode back to Nicosia on Sunday the 14th, Gordon keeping me company for a few miles, but he was driven back by a heavy storm that overtook us. I took a different route as far as Esher[62] and after a long and lonely ride of 35 miles entered the old familiar Larnaka Gate of Nicosia at sundown.

[May 20] A man having stabbed another at Ay Vasili we had an exciting chase after him but he had too good a start of us to come up with him, so I secured his house with a Zaptieh guard, as well as some weapons we found in his house. One was a fine long yatagan which I annexed, as also a remarkable old blunderbuss bearing the date 1765 with a muzzle as big as a railway bell.

We did not get back to Nicosia till after midnight. The gentleman in question was brought in a few days after.

The Queen's Birthday

[May 24] The next great event at Nicosia was the Queen's Birthday, for which the Zaptiehs and Troopers had to be drilled up a day or two in advance. I had about 30 Troopers as escort to the Vali, and 2 Companies of Infantry as a guard in front of the Konak. I rode out with the Commissioner and Bor in full uniform to meet H.E. outside the Papho Gate, and quite a procession was formed to the Konak. After a reception of the Greeks and Turks the proceedings terminated. I dined with Bor and rode out afterwards to the Reception at Government House which like most of its kind was a very stiff affair.

[May 27] I rode over to Kyrenia on the 27th to spend Sunday with Law, spending a few hours at St. Hillarion on the way. As I was entering the stable at Law's house I was kicked in the face by one of the ponies, which knocked me over insensible, nor did I recover till next a.m. [May 28] when I found my head tied up in a bundle. Happily the consequences were no worse than a severe headache for the rest of the day, and a plaster patch over my left eye for a fortnight after. [May 29] I got back to Nicosia midday on Monday meeting Barry[63] and Colonel Melville who had come over to have a sniff at the Kyrenia Scenery.

Return to Limassol

Nothing much else happened until the time came for me to hand over my stewardship to Bor again, the locust campaign being now over. [Jun. 14] It was getting very hot and stifling inside the walls of Nicosia, so after bidding adieu to many kind friends there I started for Limassol again on the 14th June. It was a terribly hot day the sun glaring down on the parched-brown plains like a furnace. I struck out a new route from the ordinary road by Cofinu in order to cross the Machearas[64] Mountains. We rode through Somiloff (Psomolopheu) and struck up the Mountains to Machearas Monastery, arriving there in the afternoon.

It is without exception the most curious old place in Cyprus and well worth seeing, seldom however visited owing to its out of the way situation. There were a goodly no of monks, and they kept a visitors' book in which however there were but few English names. But every entry testified in warm terms to the hospitality of Macheara. The old Agoumenos and his mirmidons danced continual attendance on me and I had an excellent appartment to sleep in. Even up here in this mountain retreat it was very hot and I found afterwards the glass had registered 103 in the shade that day at Nicosia.

[Jun. 15] The good monks complained much of the Common Enemy, the Locust, which eat up everything in their well stocked garden.

[Jun. 16] The old court and the buildings round offered a heap of picturesque study, but I had to be off at 5.30 a.m. next morning on our long journey to Limassol.

After missing the way once or twice (for in many places there was no road at all) and riding up and down innumerable hills and valleys, we arrived at last on the highest ridge, saw the Southern Coast down below like a map and commenced the precipitous descent Oron (Ora) in the Larnaka District—and from there on to Heftagonia (Ephtagonia) and had a good rest. I was so thirsty that I drank the whole contents of a pannikin of cocoa. We got into Limassol at 6 p.m. that evening.

Holiday in Troodos

[Jun. 24] I took a run up to Troodos on the 24th for a day or two holiday. Starting at Daybreak I rode up to Platres in 5 hours and from there on to the camp at the top, finding a rest in Keay's tent. What a glorious place Troodos is to enjoy a few days' cool rest after the hot plains, and who could describe the wonderful panorama view from the top! It is second only in extent to Etna that I have seen in the Mediterranean. The sea vanishes into the sky all round except in the Karamanian (Taurus) direction, where the opposite Mountains stand out grander and bolder than ever as if disputing the sovereignty of the seas with old Olympus. The rocky ridges of Troodos spring up all round and away in the west is Chrisofou (Khrysokhou) Bay and the fine promontory of Arnauti. Limassol can be seen with a glass and on a fine day even the Towers of the Cathedral at Famagusta.

It is the favourite promenade of Troodos Society to walk to the Summit of an evening.

[Jun. 28] I rode down again on the 28th in time for dinner.

Rebellion in Egypt

[Jun. 15] Limassol—Refugees were pouring in from Alexandria in numbers, every sailing and steam ship being full of them, and, until the Bombardment of Alexandria on the 11th July, they continued to arrive every day in large numbers. [Jun. 18] So after taking over the police again from Powell we had our work considerably increased in registering their names and nationalities.

[July] Events were now rapidly culminating in Egypt and numbers of refugees continued to arrive in port. One ship had left so hastily that she had been two days without water, and on board another from Damietta two of the crew had been killed by the mutineers before leaving harbour there.

. . . [Jul. 11] on the 11th Alexandria was bombarded and given over to fire and pillage, the telegrams causing immense sensation in Limassol. The rebellion[65] had commenced and Troops were already on the move from Malta and Gibraltar, and our own men were itching up in Troodos to be off to the scene of operations. [Jul. 13-14] Part of the Channel Squadron arrived on the 13th and 14th with General Sir A. Allison and troops for the front, who sailed again the next morning.

After this Limassol became a very active little base of operations, ship after ship with either troops or stores arriving for the war. Our own half Battalion at Malta under Colonel Vandeleur was also on its way to Egypt, the Head-Quarters being also placed under orders of readiness. But although they were every inch ready to march down from Troodos and equipped for the campaign, for nearly two months had they to remain in this state of expectancy and excitement, without being allowed to go, nor was it until the whole army of Sir G. Wolseley had been concentrated in Egypt that our unfortunate selves were given final orders to march.

About this time I was obliged to prosecute my Greek servant Yanni Holihun for stealing a cheque. He had been behaving very unsatisfactorily of late and it ended in his being convicted and sentenced to Limassol jail for a year. I was sorry for the boy, because he was very smart and intelligent. I replaced him by another Greek from Papho.

Archaeological Interlude

[Jul. 26] Hake*,[66] having come down from Salamis was excavating near Curium for the S. Kensington Museum about now, and some highly interesting tombs were opened near the road between the old acropolis and Episkopi. I rode out on the 26th and was present when the best find of all was opened. It was Phoenician, and its contents were as they had been left some two thousand old years before. Mixed up with the crumbling bones of the deceased were a fine collection of glass and pottery—the irridescence of the glass being unusually brilliant. They had to be taken great care of as the action of the air speedily impaired them. Some of the vases too were fine, with the usual description of ring ornamentation on them. As the deposit was carefully brought to light and sifted several gold earrings, rings etc. were found. This tomb was about 18 ft. under the present level of the road and, unlike many others had never been despoiled.

We lunched under the shade of some fine caroub trees with the glass and pottery lying around us—the spoils of the dead. I wonder what aspect that bit of country with Curium and the sea for a background, presented so many years ago, when the dead were brought there for interment! In those days Curium must have been a flourishing little city.

The results of the excavations were afterwards collected at the Limassol Konak, to be packed up for transport to South Kensington, and a goodly collection they made.

I still held on in the Police Force but had signified my intention to Headquarters of rejoining my Regiment when ordered away, in order to take my chance of active service with the rest.

[Aug. 6] Campbell came down on the 6th and put up with me, and Hadfield[67] of the Commandant also did the same on many occasions when down from Troodos. Ponies and mules were being collected at Limassol for the Egyptian campaign and I had the care and shipping of a good many of them.

[Aug. 19] I was appointed Acting Staff Officer (D.A. and Q.M.G.[68]) on the 19th for the Superintendance of Embarkations etc. pending the arrival of an officer from England. [Aug. 21] Law who was doing duty from Kyrenia vice Thompson rode with me to the Quarantine ground and the next evening I took a farewell ride round the Akrotiri Bay (which proved my last). [Aug. 25] Croker came down to inspect my Detachment on the 25th and Colonel Gordon returned off leave by the mail the same day.

Farewell to Cyprus

[Aug. 26] The next day definite orders at length arrived from England for the Royal Sussex to Embark on board the "Navarino" expected on the 6th prox. for Ismailia, the new base of operations.

So at last our suspence was likely to be at an end, and our hopes of active service realised.

I sold my old pony "Sali Bobi" to Tolson who intended to take him to Egypt.

[Sept. 4] On the 4th Sept I handed over Command of the Police and Prison to Thompson, Assistant Commissioner, on which my brief period of Civil Service in Cyprus ended, and I again became a soldier. [Sept. 9] Between that and the 9th, on which day we

* future brother-in-law

embarked, I was employed on Transport duty at the Wharf. Having packed up and bid adieu to the scene of my labours, the Regiment marched on to the pier in the evening from Troodos in Service marching order, and I found my old (H) Company there under Captain Kelly. Ammunition was here served out and we got on board the Steam Tug "Cephalonia" to put us on board the Transport. Crowds had assembled to bid us Goodbye and God Speed on our warlike errand.

As the Tug cast off the band struck up "Old Lang Syne" and hearty cheers were raised from the crowds on the pier and responded to by all on the Tug. It was almost dark when we got on board, so we soon lost to sight the Shores of old Cyprus.

"Though lost to sight, to Memory dear"

and although there were not a few among us who were not heartily glad to be under weigh at last, yet I must own to a pang of regret on my own part to be cast adrift from the old place which I had learnt to like like a second Jamaica, and only those who have had an interest in the Island can know how to appreciate its best qualities and resources. Hard work and occupation for the mind is more conducive to happiness than life in a mess-room, where one cannot but reflect on the amount of one's time lost in idleness and good living.

So we sailed away from the Isle of Venus, and the next morning were off Port Said and the entrance to the Canal . . . steaming past the Fleet of British Ironclads . . . and the double line of Foreign Men-of-War, attracted like vultures to the scene of action.

(The Royal Sussex having arrived too late to take part in the Battle of Tel-El Kebir on 12th September, joined the 4th Brigade in Cairo on 29th).

POSTSCRIPT

CYPRUS REVISITED—MAY 1893

Before Dawn the next morning, the "Niger" was already off Cape St. Andreas the extreme point of the Carpas promontory and by the time dawn broke was pointing her bows across the Bay of Salamis. Bit by bit, as the rising sun began to illumine them, I could make out familiar points in the landscape, and as we glided onward across a glassy sea towards Cape Greco, I could make out, in the distance, the walls of famous Famagusta. Then the proud outline of Buffavento and the Pentidactilon Mountain appeared in the far distance, and as the bay of Larnaka opened, the long white outline of the low lying town came in view, mirroring itself in the glorious expanse of tranquil waters. Larnaca is by no means an attractive place, or at all calculated to favourably impress new arrivals with the Island, but the lovely morning light showed her at all events in her best array. The first boat was seen alongside as we dropped anchor as near inshore as possible, bearing the blue ensign, the only visible token of English occupants.

There was little or no change in the place since my former visit some 12 years previously. Not a house seemed to have been altered. There was the same Commissioner's house on the Scala occupied indeed by the same official who has reigned there ever since. But a new iron pier jutted out from the shallow shore to make a landing easier than it was in 1881. Landing on that occasion in one of the ship's boats of H.M.S. "Monarch", the Midshipman in charge got her broadside on to the surf and we all got a severe ducking—including General Sir A. Cunningham, who was a passenger on board. But now we disembarked on this fine new jetty, and were assisted up by a Zaptieh in the old familiar garb I had seen introduced in 1881. Not a stitch of their uniform had evidently been altered since my time. After the easy formalities of the trim little Custom house had been submitted to,—it seemed a veritable pleasure after the horrors of the Syrian Ports—I had leisure to stroll through the town. Although still early, there were few signs of life about. The old cobble-paved bazaar street was just the same as formerly but all the English established Mercantile houses had gone. Larnaca that boasted a race-meeting and a club in 1881 had dwindled again into the insignificant seaport of Turkish times—with but its three English officials to add to its importance and population. Before proceeding to Nicosia, I went to seek and breakfast with my old friend Major Chetwynd, the Police Commandant and acting Commissioner of the District, and I found him in much the same place, and indeed occupation, as I had left him many years before, and living with Mr. Morton, now promoted to the Head of the Island Customs. Besides the pleasure at being once more in this "Enchanted Island', a hearty welcome, and a chat over the many chances and changes that years carry with them, soon passed the time, as I had to be on the Nicosia road by 9 oclock. With 3 Cyprus ponies harnessed to an old chaise, the 28 miles is now covered in 4 hours.[69] Fortunately for me a very heavy thunderstorm the previous day had deluged the country and rendered the usually dusty road pleasant to travel over. Passing through the uninteresting plains of Larnaka and the bare white chalk hills, hardly a living creature or peasant's hut is seen until a small inn is reached some 13 miles inland. Here the ponies rested from their hard trot or hard canter which they had maintained nearly the whole of this dreary way. On the telegraph wires that follow the road I counted some 15 or 20 of the small Cypriot owls perched at various intervals. These were the only creatures I saw and seemed emblematic of the dormant condition that Cyprus exists in. Resuming our way, the Messaria plain began to open before us and the craggy peak of Buffavento and the Carpas range made the landscape more deserving of Cyprus. Then we passed the Village of Piroi, but not until the last of the undulating hills was topped and we had passed the Leper Farm on the opposite side of a small ravine, did the tall minarets of Nicosia come in sight. All seemed so familiar, yet so novel, to me for the trees and eucalypti planted 12 years before had grown up and almost hidden the old Turkish ramparts and now formed pleasant avenues of approach. Villas too had sprung up on the West of the town mostly occupied by the English officials, and formed a pleasing addition to the scene with their gardens and trees. Away in the distance the long low building of Government House was almost hidden amid the trees that had grown up around it—what 15 years ago when Sir Garnet Wolseley pitched his camp there was only a barren eminence. Beyond again Mount Troodos, in the dim mid-day distance, still showed a few lingering streaks of the Winter's snow, and already seemed to invite to its cool plateaux those who were fortunate enough to escape from the scorching plains beneath. I was lucky enough to arrive at Nicosia before the annual Troodos migration takes place, and found a kindly welcome under the roof of an old friend and Wellingtonian—

Law, who, once Commissioner of Kyrenia, was now Queen's Advocate of the Island. It was in the very same villa where I had years ago lodged soon after my Chief, Colonel Gordon, had built it. Now it was enlarged, improved, and hedged round with shrubbery and garden and other new villas had cropped up around it.

Let me take the reader for a stroll through the interesting old town. At first all the streets and houses, even the ramparts, seemed smaller to me than years ago, but it was only the mirage that time and busier and more important scenes doubtless reflected on my imagination. I found my way exactly through the confusing narrow little streets that seem to lead to nowhere; but all the houses, pleasant courtyards, overhanging windows, Greek ladies, even the stones and bazaar shops were identically as I had last seen them. Even the Zaptiehs of my whilom Police hung about the same places as before. If the town had been in a state of Rip Van Winkleism for the last 12 years, the reproduction could not have been more complete. I looked into a Greek "Caffeniss" (coffee house) in the Bazaar and saw sitting there in the same uniform, the very energetic police official who had formerly served under my orders. I addressed him by name and said I wished him to come at once with me to the Buyuk Khan—he rose and joined me with a sort of wondering look and I could easily see that he was puzzled. My conversation evidently still more perplexed him. Reluctant as a police officer to confess ignorance of someone who was evidently well acquainted with the place, he was driven at last to ask me who I was.

"Surely" I said, "you know the Commandant of Eleven years back?"

"But I can well excuse you if you do not, for I may have changed and you have not".

How interesting it was to see again the old gate of the Lusignan Cathedral—Santa Sophia, with its white washed portals and old Turks sauntering in and out to prayer, all looking so solemn and deserted, yet so calm and peaceful. Those weather-worn walls and buttresses that have seen the Christian ousted and again reassert himself, seemed to endure for all time amid the even tenor of the tranquil, mouldering old town.

Of old friends and fellow-officials there were many left serving on in the Island, some in the same, a few in higher service. But many had left and still more who had laboured hard in the regeneration of the Island and done grand service to the flag, had passed away, leaving their tracks in the sands of time to be filled by others. Foremost amongst them I may mention:

Mr. Samuel Brown,[70] Chief Island Engineer, to whom Cyprus is indebted for its roads, bridges and piers—who died in Hong Kong.

Colonel (Major-General) A. H. A. Gordon, the reorganizer of the Cyprus Military Police who died on his way home from China in 1893.

Lieutenant-Colonel Gordon, the first energetic Commissioner of Nicosia who died at Suez after the Suakin Campaign of 1885.

Mr. Olive, the Commandant of Police of Paphos.

Colonel Scott-Stephenson, the well known popular Commissioner and Commandant of Kyrenia.

Captain Gordon, Assistant Commissioner of Famagusta, lost in the Bayuda Desert 1885, and never heard of again.

Captain Croker, Adjudant of Police and Cyprus Pioneers, accidentally killed at Chicago 1893.

Sir Elliot Bovill,[71] Chief Justice and universally esteemed who was carried away by cholera in the Straits Settlements 1893.

Mr. Langdon Rees, of Smyrna, who started the first Island Journal called the Cyprus Herald in 1881 and liberally supported the Turf. He died in Cairo in 1891, as respected there as he was mourned in Cyprus and the English Levant.

Captain Inglis, Commissioner of Famagusta who died at Nicosia in 1882.

To these I may add, although not officially connected with this Island, Sir Samuel Baker, whose work on Cyprus—"Cyprus as I saw it in 1879"—is a well known and standard book, and Mr Greville Chester a frequent visitor and well known in Egyptian and archaeological circles.

Colonel Bowlby,[72] 20th Foot (1893).

No one knows the work of an English official in Cyprus unless he has been there to see. The Public Works, the Law, the Police, the Customs, Education —all are admirably worked, and with wonderful economy, and it is uphill work too, with two antagonistic races and two foreign languages to combat; and yet there seems to be a brand of ineffectiveness laying its heavy hand upon the whole, which damps all ardour and exposes a restiveness not to be surprised at—and why?

It is because its light has gone out, and illumined another more fortunate locality. Its trade may yet increase and bear better fruit, its wine trade and customs may show better results, and law and crime improve in future years as education and communications improve, but stagnation and debt will for ever cloud it as long as Egypt overshadows it in importance and the burden of the Tribute (payable to Turkey) is unremoved.

Some talk of Cyprus becoming the trade Emporium of the Levant. Some of the facilities of making a port at Famagusta—others the Euphrates Valley Railway to India and the East affecting its importance and making it a 'place d' armes' of the Mediterranean. It is inconceivable that anything of the sort will be effected in our time—if even in the time of our great grandsons. It has no attractions to make it a trading centre—as witness the failure in 1878.

There is no harbour in the Island, and to convert the long-deserted, unhealthy Famagusta—that a Greek cannot even live in—into a harbour of the necessary size could cost millions that no mad-man even would think of flinging away, in the face of the many fine ready-made ports along the Asia Minor Coast and Skenderoon Bay (Iskanderun). Let us even suppose the Euphrates Valley railway to be an accomplished fact, and Famagusta capable of accommodating and docking steamers, the real trade outlet and mail route is much more likely to be the Bosphorous or Smyrna—and indeed is already rapidly tending that way, by the rail to Angora now opened.

Whatever the views held by the Island officials on the future prospects of their—or rather our—Island, it would be treading too much in the sphere of Politics and Strategy to pursue the subject further with any advantage to myself or the reader—But certain it is that our possession of Cyprus, as of all our other interests in the Inland Sea—whether they tend towards the Euphrates Valley, the Suez Canal, or a grand port at Famagusta capable of floating a 15000 ton ironclad—must depend entirely on sea power. As long as our Naval power is adequate in that sea, Cyprus has no superior value to us than many other Islands would in the Levant.

Footnote: the final part of this somewhat disjointed essay was probably destined to be included in a Study of Mediterranean Sea power on which the writer was engaged at the time of his death in 1907.

APPENDICES
TO THE PRIVATE JOURNAL OF LIEUT. DONISTHORPE DONNE
CYPRUS 1880-1882

A. SOLDIER OF THE QUEEN

Colonel Benjamin Donisthorpe Alsop Donne. C.B.[73] (1856-1907) was the elder son of B. J. M. Donne Esq. of Crewekerne, Somerset. Educated at Wellington College and Sandhurst, he was commissioned in the 35th (Royal Sussex) Regiment in 1875, became Captain in 1884, Major in 1892 and Lieutenant-Colonel commanding the 1st Battalion in 1898. After being stationed in Jamaica, Barbados, Malta and Cyprus he first saw Active Service in the Egyptian War of 1882. During a 10 year secondment to the Egyptian Army he commanded the Camel Corps in 1883 and the 3rd Egyptian Battalion during the Nile Campaign of 1884/85. In 1887 he raised the 10th Sudanese Battalion at Luxor and commanded it during the Nile Frontier and Red Sea Operations of 1888/89. The 10th on two occasions marched from the Nile to the Red Sea to reinforce the garrison of Suakin during its investment by the dervish forces of the Khalifa under Osman Digna.

The Battalion also distinguished itself in the actions at Gemaizeh in December 1888 and on the Nile at Arghin and Toski in August 1889, being highly commended by Generals Sir Evelyn Wood, Sir Francis Grenfell and Kitchener.

After a spell on the Staff Major Donne went to India in 1896 as Second-in-Command of the 2nd Royal Sussex. He took part in the North West Frontier Campaign of 1897/98 including the Tirah and Bazar Valley expeditions and the occupation of the Khyber Pass.

During the South African War Lieutenant-Colonel Donne commanded the 1st Royal Sussex during the march from Bloemfontein to Pretoria, including the engagements at Welkom Farm, Zand River—where his horse was shot under him—, Doornkop, the occupation of Johannesburg and Pretoria, and the action at Diamond Hill. During the subsequent advance into the Orange River Colony he commanded a detached column in the operations round Bethlehem, in the Caledon Valley, and at Retief's Nek; and he was present at the surrender of the Boer forces at Golden Gate in August, 1900. Later on he was engaged in the operations round Thabanchu, Winburg; commanded the garrison at Lindley during the investment by the Boers from September 1900 to January 1901; and took part in several engagements during the investment. Subsequently he commanded the Centre Sector, Orange River Colony.

For these services Colonel Donne was mentioned in dispatches on numerous occasions, awarded the Nile Medal and bronze star with clasps, the Frontier Medal with two clasps, the South African Medal with four clasps, the King's Medal with two clasps, and the C.B.

Colonel Donne was married in 1886 to Cecil Frances Grace, daughter of the late Reverend Robert Edgar Hughes, by whom he had two daughters. He died in 1907, at the age of 51, whilst in charge of the Home Counties Infantry Records at Hounslow.

At the time of his death he was working on the manuscript of a book on "the Mediterranean" which was to have included an account of his journeys in the footsteps of St. Paul and his studies of the sieges by the Turks of the Great Venetian fortresses in Crete, Rhodes, and Cyprus. His book entitled "The Conquest of Cyprus by the Turks", which incorporated a "guide and Directory to Cyprus" appeared in 1885 being the first English book to be printed and published in Cyprus.

In addition to being a soldier, traveller and writer of some merit Donisthorpe Donne was an outstanding watercolour artist. He shared this distinction with his father, brother and three sisters and passed his talent on to his daughters and to some of his grandchildren. Unlike his brother—the late Colonel Beadon Donne C.B., Royal Norfolk Regiment—Donisthorpe's painting enthusiasm embraced military subjects, battle scenes, regimental colours, studies of ships. Much of his work is therefore of historical value. Some fifty of his finest paintings, ranging from Jamaica to India and South Africa, together with his medals, swords, papers and Sudanese battle trophies are at present on display in the Donne Room at the Army Commissions Board at Westbury in Wiltshire.

(Colonel Donne's Journal from 1873-1885, together with a selection of watercolours painted in Cyprus, Egypt and the Levant are now in Cyprus where his grandson Lieutenant—Colonel (Retired) W. Donisthorpe—Shaw is staying).

B. EXTRACTS FROM THE "CYPRUS HERALD" 1881

December 7th. "Information was received in Limassol yesterday evening to the effect that Lieutenant Kitchener, R.E., Director of Survey, had been shot at near the village of Pissouri: it appears that seeing a man near where he was at work, Mr. Kitchener approached him to ask for some information, when the man levelled a gun at him, and kept moving about still keeping the gun in a threatening position. Mr. Kitchener then went some distance to fetch a native to interpret for him, and on returning to the spot the man again levelled his piece, and eventually fired a shot at Mr. Kitchener, but fortunately without hitting him. The native with him bolted, and Mr. Kitchener was unable to capture the miscreant. Lieutenant Donne with two of the police started for Pissouri this morning".

December 14th. "Following the outrage attempted on Lieutenant Kitchener, R.E. which was reported by us last week, the police have had a very busy time of it in the district, resulting in the capture of an escaped convict named Salih Bobi, who is supposed to be the man who fired at Lieutenant Kitchener, and in the death of another named Molla Tahir, who was shot by a Zaptieh while in the act of levelling his gun at another Zaptieh".

"Considering the arsenal with which Salih Bobi had surrounded himself, his character and the state of the neighbourhood, we think that Mr. Donne deserves high praise and commendation for the energy, zeal and courage displayed by him in the capture of one who for so long had been able to defy the law".

"The man Molla Tahir whom we have already alluded to as having been shot by a zaptieh, is said to have been the terror of the district; and was wanted by the police as an escaped prisoner on charges of rape, theft and highway robbery: the police were in reality searching for one Andoni an escaped prisoner . . ."

"Since writing the above we learn from different sources that the inhabitants of Episcopi and the Circassian Village near the Salt-Lake, have expressed their satisfaction at the death of Molla Tahir of whom they have been in constant terror: several of his late comrades have fled from the district, in the direction of Papho, with the intention of embarking from thence in a caroub ship".

December 21st. "From every village in the neighbourhood, we hear nothing but expressions of satisfaction at the death of Molla Tahir, who has been a terror to all the inhabitants of the district . . ."

December 11th. "We have received news of the capture of Andoni Nicola, an inhabitant of Pahna, near Nicosia where he had gone with several members of his family with the intention it is said, of treating with the authorities for his surrender. It appears that for some months past Lieutenant Donne, our energetic L.C.M.P. has so harrassed Andoni and kept him on the move, that he at last came to the conclusion that liberty under such circumstances was scarcely worth having, - - -".

NOTES

1. The original manuscript of Lieutenant Donne's journal has not been made available for publication. The foregoing extracts and appendices are based on a type-written copy of the journal. It has not been possible to determine whether apparent spelling mistakes occurred during the typing of the text or whether they were part of the journal. With the exception of all place-names such spelling mistakes have been corrected.

I am graceful to Mr Th. Papadopoullos, Mr C. Kyrris, Mr M. Christodoulou, Mr C. Hadjipsaltis and Mr K. Keshishian for their kind assistance.

2. Colonel Simpson Hackett, 35th Regiment. Senior Officer in Command of Her Majesty's troops stationed in Cyprus. Member of the Executive Council, October 6, 1880 (*Cyprus Gazette*—hereafter cited C.G.—No. 60, October 25, 1880). Officer Administering the Government of Cyprus in Sir R. Biddulph's absence from July 11 to September 9, 1881 (C.G. Extraordinary, July 11, 1881, and, C.G. No. 77, October 19, 1881). Left Cyprus in September 1882 (C.G. No. 91. October 17, 1882).

3. Major-General Sir Robert Biddulph. Commissioner Nicosia, August 7, 1878 (C.G. No. 1, November 5, 1878). Served as High Commissioner of Cyprus from June 23, 1879 to March 9, 1886.

4. Lieutenant A. Gilmore, 61st Foot Regiment. Local Commandant Military Police Nicosia, August 28, 1878 (C.G. No. 1, November 5, 1878). Local Commandant Military Police Limassol, August 8, 1879 (C.G. No. 33, August 8, 1879).

5. Mitchell, the Commissioner of Limassol, in his annual report for 1880, put the number of deaths at six. See, C. 3092, *op. cit.*, Report by the Commissioner of Limassol, p. 29.

6. Commanding Officer.

7. Royal Military Academy (Sandhurst).

8. Non Commissioned Officers.

9. Mukhtar or Mouktar. After the Tanzimat of 1839 a popularly elected mukhtar (head-man) was appointed in all the villages of Cyprus. His duties were administrative and fiscal (Sir George Hill, *A History of Cyprus*, vol. IV, Cambridge, 1952, p.8.). The British authorities preserved the mukhtar's office ('Administrative Divisions Ordinance, 1878') and successive laws assigned to the mukhtar increasing responsibility for the conduct, welfare and health of the villagers. See, *The Mukhtar's Handbook*, Nicosia, 1911.

10. Captain the Hon. E. J. Chetwynd, 61st Regiment. Local Commandant Military Police Larnaca, December 6, 1879 (C.G. No. 41, December 30, 1879). Adjudant in the Police and Pioneer Force, January 1, 1880 (C.G. No. 42, January 13, 1880). Second-in-Command and Paymaster in the Police and Pioneer

Force, April 18, 1880 (C.G. No. 52, May 20, 1880). In addition to existing duties Second-in-Command and Paymaster in the Military Police, December 1, 1880 (C.G. No. 63, December 8, 1880). Resigned September 1, 1881. Assistant Commissioner Nicosia, September 1, 1881 (C.G. No. 78, November 8, 1881).

11. Tochni, a mixed Greek and Turkish village.

12. He evidently means the Greek village of Lysi.

13. Captain E. W. D. Croker, 93rd Highlanders. Adjudant and Quartermaster in the Police and Pioneer Force, April 18, 1880 (C.G. No. 52, May 20, 1880). In addition to existing duties Adjudant and Quartermaster in the Military Police, December 1, 1880 (C.G. No. 63, December 8, 1880). Second-in-Command in addition to existing duties, September 1, 1881 (C.G. No. 78, November 8, 1881).

14. Major R. W. Gordon, 93rd Highlanders. Commissioner Nicosia, November 10, 1879 (C.G. No. 38, November 13, 1879). Resigned January 1, 1882 (C.G. No. 81, January 31, 1882).

15. Charles Anthony King-Harman. Private Secretary to the High Commissioner and Clerk of the Executive and Legislative Councils, December 1, 1879 (C.G. No. 40, December 8, 1879). In addition to existing duties Assistant Commissioner on the Establishment, December 1, 1879 (C.G. No. 58, September 11, 1880). In addition to existing duties Assistant to the Chief Secretary, April 1, 1881 (C.G. No. 68, April 2, 1881). Served as High Commissioner of Cyprus from October 17, 1904 to October 12, 1911.

16. Lieutenant Andrew Scott-Stevenson, 42nd Highlanders. Assistant Commissioner and Local Commandant of Police Kyrenia, November 19, 1878 (C.G. No. 3, January 1, 1879). Registrar of the High Court of Justice, February 25, 1879 (C.G. No. 11, February 25, 1879). Commissioner Kyrenia, February 27, 1880 (C.G. No. 46, March 1, 1880). His wife was the author of the book *Our Home in Cyprus*, London, 1880.

17. Hilgrove C. Nicolle. Assistant Auditor, February 17, 1880 (C.G. No. 47, March 15, 1880).

18. Major A. H. A. Gordon, 65th Regiment. First Commandant of the Cyprus Police and Pioneer Force, November 29, 1879 (C.G. No. 39, November 29, 1879). Promoted Lieutenant-Colonel and appointed Chief Commandant of Military Police, to hold the combined command of the two existing Police Corps (i.e. the Military Police and the Police and Pioneer Force) under the provisions of 'The Cyprus Police Ordinance, 1880'. December 1, 1880 (C.G. No. 62. November 26, 1880).

19. C. D. Cobham. Assistant Commissioner Larnaca, October 1, 1878 (C.G. No. 1, November 5, 1878). Registrar of the High Court of Justice, February 25, 1879 (C.G. No. 11, February 25, 1879). Commissioner Larnaca, March 18, 1879 (C.G. No. 15, March 18, 1879). Provisionally member of the Legislative Council, February 7, 1880 (C.G. No. 45, February 7, 1880).

20. Lieutenant-Colonel F. G. E. Warren, Royal Artillery. Commissioner Limassol, October 1, 1878 (C.G. No. 1, November 5, 1878). Chief Secretary to Government; member of the Executive and provisionally member of the Legislative Council, August 1, 1879 (C.G. No. 32, July 31, 1879). When serving as Commissioner of Limassol Warren had quarrelled with Kyprianos the Bishop of Kition concerning the rights of the Church and other questions of local administration. The Bishop accused Warren of an arbitrary and oppressive management of public affairs and of prejudice against both the Church and the Greek Cypriots (*Further Correspondence Respecting Complaints made against the Government of Cyprus* (C. 2355), London, 1879)

21. 'At the time of the British occupation the Nizam (i.e. Law) Courts in existence were—a Daavi ('Pleas') Court in each of the six Qazas (districts), and a Temyiz (Appeal) Court in Nicosia and a Tijaret (Commercial) Court at Larnaca; and there were also tribunals called the Mahkemeh-i-sheri, which had jurisdiction in religious and domestic matters between Moslems . . . But all the above Courts, except the Mahkemeh-i-sheri, have been superseded by the Courts constituted by the 'Cyprus Courts of Justice Order, 1882' (Sir J. T. Hutchinson and C. D. Cobham, *A Handbook of Cyprus*, London, 1904, p.26).

22. Ronald L. N. Mitchell. Commissioner Limassol, August 1, 1879 (C.G. No. 34, August 21, 1879).

23. H. L. Thompson, Assistant Paymaster, Army Pay Department. Civil Treasurer, August 31, 1878 (C.G. No. 1, November 5, 1878). Assistant Commissioner Paphos, September 1, 1879 (C.G. No. 36, September 6, 1879). Assistant Commissioner Limassol, March 10, 1881 (C.G. No. 69, April 18, 1881). Acting Commissioner during the absence on leave of R. L. N. Mitchell. June 21, 1881 (C.G. No. 76, August 20, 1881).

24. He is evidently referring to the mixed Greek and Turkish village of Silikou.

25. The casa (district) of Limassol comprised the following nahiehs (sub-districts): Limassol, Episcopi, Evdim (Evdimou), Kilani (C.G. No. 82, March 3, 1882).

26. A small hamlet whose inhabitants have now emigrated to neighbouring villages and only a few dilapidated houses are occupied during the summer months.

27. This is the Great Monastery of Agros, a ninth century foundation which after the 1770's was overcome by debts. By the nineteenth century it was practically derelict (N. Κληρίδης, Συμβολὴ στὴν 'Ιστορία τῆς Πιτσιλιᾶς, 'Η Μονὴ τοῦ Μεγάλου 'Αγροῦ, Λευκωσία, 1948; C. P. Kyrris, ''Αγροῦ Μεγάλου, Μονή'', Θρησκευτικὴ καὶ 'Ηθικὴ 'Εγκυκλοπαιδεία, 1ος τόμος, 'Αθῆναι, 1962, columns 323-329).

28. He means the Greek village of Pelendria.

29. 'St. Nicolas of the Cats', one of the earliest monasteries founded in Cyprus. According to legend it was built by the rebel Calogaerus in the reign of Constantine the Great; it was he who introduced cats in order to destroy the large number of serpents in the Akrotiri area (Κυπριανός, 'Ιστορία Χρονολογικὴ τῆς Νήσου Κύπρου, 'Ενετία, 1788, pp. 142-143; I. Χάκκετт, 'Ιστορία τῆς 'Ορθοδόξου 'Εκκλησίας τῆς Κύπρου, τόμος Β', μετάφρασις Χ. Ι. Παπαϊωάννου, Πειραιεύς, 1927, pp. 150-153).

30. Colossi Castle was built in 1454 by the Knights of St. John of Jerusalem and in the sixteenth century it passed to the Cornaro family (R. Gunnis, *Historic Cyprus*, London, 1936, pp. 276-279). After the Turkish occupation the ownership of the Castle is obscure. It is merely known that a certain Mazhar Effendi turned the Castle and the land around it into a *Vakf* in *Idjaretin* (G. Jeffery, *Cyprus Monuments, Historical and Architectural Buildings, New Illustrated Series*—No. 5, Nicosia, 1933, p.9). Various travellers mention that the Castle was rented or owned by private individuals (L. Ross, *A Journey to Cyprus (February and March 1845)*, translated by C. D. Cobham, Nicosia, 1910, p. 83; F. von Löher, *Cyprus, Historical and Descriptive*, London, 1878, pp. 184-186; A. Smith, *Through Cyprus*, London, 1887, p. 237). It appears that after 1878 the Castle changed hands frequently. Research in the Evkaf archives is needed to identify the tenant or owner of the Castle in 1881 (from the travellers' accounts he must have been a substantial farmer of education and good manners). Sir Harry Luke in his *Cyprus, A Portrait and an Appreciation*, London 1957, pp. 160-161, recounts that in 1913 the British Order of St. John bought 55 out of a total of 256 shares of the ownership of the Castle from about ninety Moslem peasants. The principal owner of the Castle from the beginning of the twentieth century until about 1926, when he sold it to the Government, was one Syrian Sidarus Pischara.

31. After the Tanzimat of 1839 Cyprus was divided into cazas administered by a kaimmakam and into nahiehs administered by a mudir (Hill, *op. cit.*, vol. IV, pp. 4-10).

32. Lieutenant H. H. Kitchener, Royal Engineers. Director of Revenue Survey, March 15, 1880 (C.G. No. 47, March 15, 1880).

33. A Turkish administrative rank roughly equivalent to Governor-General. Before the British occupation the Mütessarif (Governor) of Cyprus was under the authority of the Vali of the Vilayet of Rhodes. In the present context Donne is making a facetious reference to the High Commissioner who, under the provisions of the 'Administrative Divisions Ordinance, 1878', had assumed all the powers formerly exercised by both the Vali of Rhodes and the Mütessarif of the Sanjak of Cyprus.

34. His Report on the island's administration was published in *Finance and Administration (Mr. Fairfield's Mission), (C.* 3661*)*, London, 1883.

35. Laurence Olive. Adjudant Military Police, October 1, 1878 (C.G. No. 1, November 5, 1878). Acting Assistant Commissioner Nicosia, August 21, 1879 (C.G. No. 34, August 21, 1879). Registrar of the High Court of Justice, September 6, 1879 (C.G. No. 36, September 6, 1879). Acting Police Magistrate Larnaca, December 8, 1879 (C.G. No. 40, December 8, 1879). Local Commandant of Military Police Paphos, April 23, 1880 (C.G. No. 49, April 23, 1880).

36. Lieutenant James Henry Bor, R.M.A. Local Commandant Police Paphos, August 28, 1878 (C.G. No. 1, November 5, 1878). Local Commandant Military Police and Governor of the Prison at Nicosia, August 8, 1879 (C.G. No. 33, August 8, 1879).

37. Captain J. A. S. Inglis, 31st Foot Regiment. Assistant Commissioner Famagusta, August 1, 1878 (C.G. No. 1, November 5, 1878). Commissioner Famagusta, October 13, 1878 (C.G. No. 6, February 11, 1879). Acting Commissioner Nicosia from 4 to 31 December 1881 (C.G. No. 80, December 19, 1881). Commissioner Nicosia, January 1, 1882 (C.G. No. 81, January 31, 1882). In May 1879 Inglis, the Commissioner of Famagusta, ordered the shaving of the heads and beards of two Orthodox priests who, for

some minor breaches of the law, had been sentenced to one week's and one month's imprisonment respectively. The Greek Cypriots protested at the humiliation suffered by the unfortunate priests and Inglis earned the rebuke of Lord Salisbury, the British Foreign Secretary. See, *Correspondence Respecting the Treatment of Prisoners at Famagusta (C.2398),* London, 1879.

38. The principal quarter of the town, around the present Atatürk Square.

39. It refers to the low hill on which Government House was built.

40. W. H. Marsh. Acting Auditor and Accountant-General; member of the Executive Council and provisionally of the Legislative Council, September 1, 1880 (C.G. No. 59, October 13, 1880). Resigned February 14, 1882 (C.G. No 82, March 3, 1882).

41. Lieutenant M. B. Seager, R.M.L.I. Assistant Commissioner Nicosia, August 7, 1878 (C.G. No. l, November 5, 1878). Registrar of the High Court of Justice, February 25, 1879 (C.G. No. 11, February 25, 1879). Commissioner Kyrenia, July 1, 1879 (C.G. No. 31, June 28, 1879). Acting Commissioner Nicosia from August 19 to November 10, 1879, (C.G. No. 38, November 13, 1879). Police Magistrate and a Deputy Commissioner Nicosia, February 27, 1880 (C.G. No. 46, March 1, 1880).

42. The British officials in Cyprus had organised a pack of harriers for hunting hare; the master of the hunt was Major Luttman-Johnstone (Sinclair, *op. cit.*, p. 141).

43. John Parsons. Inspector of Police, August 1, 1881 (C.G. No 79, November 26, 1881).

44. See above note 21.

45. The Great Khan (inn) of Nicosia built soon after the Turkish conquest of Cyprus (Hill, *op. cit.*, vol. IV, p.2, note 3). The Khan and the Konak of Nicosia were used by the British authorities as prisons (C.G. No 21, May 3, 1879).

46. He is probably referring to Surgeon W. M. Johnston M.D. Civil Surgeon Kyrenia from December 30, 1879 to April 2, 1880 (C.G. No. 41, December 30, 1879, and, C.G. No. 56, July 7, 1880).

47. King Richard did not take Buffavento Castle by assault; it surrendered to him when Isaac himself surrendered to Richard and before the crusader armies had attacked it.

48. Theodore E. Mavrogordato. Interpreter to the Police, February 1, 1882 (C.G. No. 85, May 23, 1882).

49. The nahiehs (sub-districts) of the caza of Nicosia were: Nicosia, Dagh (Orini), Morfou and Lefka (C.G. No. 82, March 3, 1882). On December 8, 1880, the High Commissioner, exercising the authority granted him by the 'Administrative Divisions Ordinance, 1878', abolished the old Turkish caza of Deyrmanlik and replaced it with the caza of Nicosia. (C.G. No. 63, December 8, 1880).

50. This is the Monastery of Ayios Mamas, founded at the end of the twelfth century, I. Χάκκετ, Ἱστορία, *op. cit.*, τόμος Β', pp. 147-148; N. Κληρίδης, Ὁ Μεγαλομάρτυς Ἅγιος Μάμας, Μόρφου, 1963.

51. Sir S. Baker author of *Cyprus as I saw it*, London, 1879.

52. Hegoumenos, the abbot.

53. Archibald FitzGerald Law. An Assistant Commissioner Nicosia, February 4, 1880 (C. G. No. 45, February 7, 1880). Assistant Commissioner Kyrenia, March 1, 1880 (C.G. No 46, March 1, 1880). Registrar of the High Court of Justice, September 11, 1880 (C.G. No 58, September 11, 1880).

54. Dr. Clement Carletti, Officier de Santé (Constantinople). Civil Surgeon and Health Officer Kyrenia, April 2, 1880 (C.G. No. 56, July 7, 1880).

55. District Medical Officer.

56. Richard Mattei, an Italian landowner long resident in Cyprus, had in Turkish times devised the traps and screens (Hill, *op. cit.*, vol. IV, p. 250, note 1). This system proved effective but the British Government of Cyprus reintroduced it on a small scale only in March 1880 (C. 3092, *op. cit.*, Report by the Commissioner of Nicosia, p. 10). In 1881 the first Locust Ordinance was enacted ('The Locust Destruction Ordinance, 1881') and a massive campaign against the pest was organised. By 1883 the number of locusts caught and destroyed reached about 200,000 millions (Hutchinson and Cobham, *op. cit.*, p. 51).

57. Before December 8, 1880, Dali belonged to the old nahieh of Deyrmanlik (De Mas Latrie, *L'Ile de Chypre*, Paris 1879, pp. 36-38; C.G. No. 63, December 8, 1880). It subsequently came under the nahieh of Nicosia of which Dali and Kythrea were the most important villages (C. 3092, *op. cit.*, Report by the Commissioner of Nicosia, p. 8).

58. This is the Church of St. Barnabas and St. Hilarion (built in the early eleventh century).

59. Lieutenant Arthur Henderson Young, 27th Foot Regiment. Local Commandant Military Police Kyrenia, August 28, 1878 (C.G. No. 1, November 5, 1878). Assistant Commissioner Paphos, November 20, 1878 (C.G. No. 3, January 1, 1879, Registrar of the High Court of Justice, February 25, 1879 (C.G. No. 11, February 25, 1879). Commissioner Paphos, September 1, 1879 (C.G. No. 36, September 6, 1879). Commissioner Famagusta, January 1, 1882 (C.G. No. 81, January 31, 1882).

60. Captain W. H. Gordon, Suffolk Artillery Militia. An Assistant Commissioner, January 5, 1879 (C.G. No. 6. February 11, 1879). Registrar of the High Court of Justice, February 25, 1879 (C.G. No. 11, February 25, 1879). Assistant Commissioner Famagusta, June 2, 1880 (C.G. No. 53, June 4, 1880).

61. The Reverend Josiah Spencer B.A. Director of Education, December 3, 1880 (C.G. No. 64, December 24, 1879).

62. He probably means Asha.

63. F. W. Barry M.D. Sanitary Commissioner of Cyprus, April 23, 1880 (C.G. No. 49, April 23, 1880). Resigned July 10, 1882 (C. G.. No. 90, September 16, 1882).

64. Macheras.

65. For a recent account of Orabi Pasha's anti-European nationalist movement and British intervention in Egypt see: P. J. Vatikiotis, *The Modern History of Egypt,* London, 1969, pp. 144-158.

66. George Gordon Hake. Chief Clerk in Chief Secretary's Office, April 24, 1879 (C.G. No. 26, May 20, 1879).

67. Lieutenant Charles Arthur Hadfield, 98th Regiment. Lieutenant in the Police and Pioneer Force and Acting Local Commandant Military Police Famagusta, March 1, 1880 (C.G. No. 46, March 1, 1880).

68. Deputy Adjudant and Quarter-master-General.

69. On July 20, 1878, the road from Larnaca to Nicosia had been described by Lord John Hay as follows: 'There is a only one road (in Cyprus) that can be dignified by that name, and is the one which connects Larnaca with Nicosia; its condition is as bad as possible' (cited in C. V. Bellamy, *A monograph of the main roads of Cyprus,* Nicosia, 1903, p.1). Over the next decade, by annual improvements, the Public Works Department thoroughly repaired the road.

70. Samuel Brown. Government Engineer, August 13, 1880 (C.G. No. 58, September 11, 1880).

71. Elliot Charles Bovill. Assistant Legal Adviser and Assistant Judicial Commissioner, December 30, 1879 (C.G. No. 41, December 30, 1879). Acting Judicial Commissioner, June 1, 1880 (C.G. No. 53, June 4, 1880). Judicial Commissioner of the Queen's High Court of Justice for Cyprus, November 26, 1881 (C.G. No. 80, December 19, 1881). President of the Court of Temyiz, June 12, 1882 (C.G. No. 87, June 17, 1882).

72. Major H. R. Bowlby, 20th Regiment. Chief Commandant of Military Police and Inspector of Prisons, April 1, 1879 (C.G. No. 17, April 2, 1879). His services terminated on the amalgamation of the two Police Forces, December 1, 1880 (C.G. No. 62, November 26, 1880).

73. Companion of the Bath.

Scott-Stevenson 1880

Mrs. Esmé Scott-Stevenson accompanied her husband, Captain Andrew Scott-Stevenson, to Cyprus, where he was posted with the Forty-Second Royal Highlanders (the Black Watch), as Assistant Commissioner under High Commissioner Sir Garnet Wolseley. He was subsequently appointed, by Wolseley's successor General Biddulph, as Commissioner of Kyrenia, where they made their home after a series of temporary encampments around the island.

Mrs. Scott-Stevenson traveled the island with her husband and wrote of their life in Cyprus in her book *Our Life in Cyprus*, London: Chapman and Hall, 1880. She was a keen observer with a refreshingly positive view of the island. She avoided military and political issues in her account.

INTRODUCTION.

. . . I began this book when Andrew was made Assistant Commissioner of this place by Sir Garnet Wolseley, the late High Commissioner of the island, who has been succeeded by General Biddulph, C.B. The latter has the satisfaction of seeing Cyprus, under his government, growing healthier, happier, and richer day after day. Every one seems contented and satisfied. There are no complaints of injustice or individual hardships made by Turk, Greek, or English officials; and General Biddulph has certainly succeeded in gaining the love and esteem of all those who have come in contact with him personally, or who have had anything to do with his wise and considerate government. I cannot close my letter without telling you that Andrew has now been appointed Commissioner of Kyrenia; so the interest he takes in his district, and the eagerness with which he watches the increasing prosperity, is only in accordance with his greater responsibility and higher position.

CHAPTER I.
LARNACA.

I left Alexandria for Cyprus on the evening of the 28th of September, 1878, in one of the "Asia Minor" line of steamers. My only fellow-travellers—if a few French and Greek merchants visiting Larnaca in hope of doing business be excepted—were Mr. Hepworth Dixon and two officers of the Royal Engineers, Mr. Kitchener and Mr. Hippisley, sent out to survey the island by the Foreign Office. We sighted the mountains of Cyprus at four P.M. next day, and at two A.M. on the following morning got into the roadstead of Larnaca. I slept on deck all night, as the cabins were unbearably hot, and was awakened by the barking of many dogs, a sound I have got well accustomed to since.

* * * * *

It was very alarming, on our route [*to Nicosia*], to meet the half-wild dogs, which would fly savagely at us from every corner we passed. Sometimes they would spring almost as high as my saddle; and as this naturally caused my horse to plunge about, I had great difficulty in holding my own little dog, which I had in my arms. My husband's hunting crop was the only thing that kept them at a distance. Indeed, in one solitary spot he had to fire his pistol two or three times among them before they would take alarm. These poor homeless creatures are the scavengers of the towns, living on the dead carcases and offal lying about; and, as they have their uses in this way, the Cypriotes never think of destroying them; consequently the suburbs of nearly all the towns swarm with hundreds of the half-starved animals. The belated traveller, as he approaches, is met by a chorus which is not only perfectly deafening for the time, but, being unmusical and unceasing, effectually rouses the inhabitants, and keeps them awake half the night.

CHAPTER II.
NICOSIA.

. . . The town is surrounded by a moat, with well-built ramparts, and towering above them may be seen many a Turkish mosque and Christian church, with steeples, domes, and minarets of infinite variety. The graceful palms and datetrees, and the rich foliage around the larger houses, make a striking contrast to the glistening white of some of the buildings. Here and there a red-tiled roof relieves the monotony of the flat mud roofs or the zinc covering of the Greek churches. There are four entrances to Nicosia: the Famagusta, the Larnaca, the Baffo, and the Kyrenia Gates, which are all closed at night by drawbridges, and guarded inside by zaptiehs, and at that time could not be passed without a special permission, although I understand this annoyance is done away with, it being only necessary now to summon the sentry.

* * * * *

On our return to the hotel, we found an invitation from Lord Gifford, asking us to dine that evening with Sir Garnet Wolseley. Sir Garnet, with his staff, had taken up quarters near a monastery about a mile from Nicosia. A small encampment had been made on a little elevation, later called "Snake's Hill," from the number of the reptiles seen by the Engineers when erecting the huts on the spot.

I rode out in my habit: it was too far to walk, and of course not a carriage of any kind was to be had in Cyprus. In fact, with the exception of a diligence started later, the only vehicle approaching such a thing in the island, was a two-wheeled go-cart that my husband brought with him from Malta; and this, as there is no road over the Kyrenia mountains, had to be shipped with our other things in the *Raleigh*.

We found Sir Garnet in a large hospital hut, not only famously ventilated, but most cool and comfortable, being lined with dark green felt like the Indian tents. He was surrounded by a brilliant and distinguished staff; but, except himself, one and all seemed wofully disappointed with Cyprus. Even plucky Lord Gifford had no good word to say for it. Sir Garnet had not lost heart, and was as cheerful and genial as if in the midst of the London season . . .

As Sir Garnet goes to bed early, we said "good bye" shortly after ten o'clock. It was then quite dark,—so much so that we could see scarcely a yard before us, and after groping our way, all at once found ourselves amongst the loose stones and jagged pieces of wood of a Moslem cemetery. The way out was more difficult to find than the way in, but ultimately we safely reached the Baffo Gate, alas! to find it closed against us for the night, for my husband had forgotten to have the guard warned of our return.

My husband hammered and kicked until, I regret to say, the varnish came off his boots, and shouted till he was hoarse,—all to no purpose. At length he took to shying stones at the only speck of light in the mass of masonry before us, presumably a window, for it was too dark to distinguish anything. These had the desired effect. A few words of Turkish were heard. My husband called in reply, "Gate—open—friend—English!" whilst continuing to shy the largest stones he could find. The woodwork was moved a few inches, when, quick as lightning, my husband shoved against it with all his strength, and the gate flew back. But as we had been kept outside for nearly an hour, we were too ruffled even to vouchsafe a "good night" to the half-awakened guard.

CHAPTER IV.

"CYPRUS FEVER."

. . . It should be noted that the fever was seldom fatal; for although one-fourth of the men were in hospital at one time, only three deaths occurred in the whole regiment. The remains of these poor fellows lie in a little graveyard situated just above the site of the encampment, shaded by olives and carob-trees. After the Forty-Second left, my husband asked permission to have the land and trees bought, which was readily granted, and a neat wall and gate were put round the enclosure. Some opposition was shown to this by the acting commissioner, but on asking Colonel Greaves my husband gained his point.

It had a good effect in showing the Cypriotes that the English not only could be just to the living, but respected and cared for the remains of their dead. Besides, my husband took another view of the case. As a soldier himself, he knew that these poor men's lives had been just as much sacrificed for their country as if they had been killed in battle; and the English army would surely think very little of those who govern their country if, for a saving of a few pounds to the treasury, the bodies of their dead comrades were allowed to lie on a waste spot, to be disentombed by dogs, or ploughed over by oxen.

I should add that amongst the troops there were occasionally slight cases of typhoid, and a few, but very few, of dysentery. I noticed that amongst the natives the most frequent diseases were fever, not reckoned by them fatal or even dangerous, and an affection of the spleen or liver,—both, it is said, the result of residence in a malarious climate. The effects of the latter complaint were distressing to see. Often, when later I visited the poorer villages, I have seen little children from three years upwards so swollen as hardly to be able to walk, and women looking exactly like the pictures of natives in India when extended almost to bursting, after eating an inordinate quantity of rice. They have a sallow unhealthy look, but seem quite fit for their ordinary avocations. Diseases of the eyes are very frequent. It was simply frightful to see the number of blind or partially blind people one meets. One village (Agirda) that I visited frequently with my husband when on duty, was unpleasantly remarkable not only in this way, but for the signs of the ravages of small-pox. Diseases of the chest are very rare; bronchitis and consumption almost unknown, although, in spite of what some of the newspapers say, rheumatism is not unfrequent. But the diseases of Cyprus, if numerous, are seldom fatal. As a rule the people live to very old age; more than once, old men, said to be over a hundred, have been pointed out to me . . .

It was during this stay in camp that Mr. and Mrs. Brassey and their little girl were also Sir Garnet's guests. They had ridden over from Larnaca, where the *Sunbeam* was anchored.

CHAPTER V.

BELLAPAÏS AND LAPITHOS.

. . . On the other side of the mountains is "Larnaca" of Lapithos, a small village of stone-built houses, and probably the necropolis of ancient Lapithos, which was one of the most important towns on the north coast. This is very likely, not only because "Larnaca" signifies a rock-cut tomb, but because large burying-grounds were distinguishing marks of all Phoenician or Greek cities, whilst there are no tombs whatever on the other side of the mountain.

This "Larnaca" is reached by two roads,—one that passes over the hill to Ciscalip; the other, and preferable because prettier, past Vassilio, with its picturesque little monastery perched on the rocks above. The ride this way ascends by a rugged pass, through gorge after gorge, crossing small streams, through little forests of olive and fir, pushing a way at times between the thick brushwood of chiniah and sagerose plants.

It is a road that is impossible to describe, for it winds perpetually, first to the right, then to the left, with glorious views of sea and land at every turn, leads down into a small valley a few feet wide, but still sown with corn, then up a precipitous pass over boulders and roots of trees. Its variety makes it almost the finest of the different roads across the northern mountains, and when the brow of the hill on the southern side is reached, the labour of the ascent is well repaid by the delightful view.

The Troädos range is much more distinctly seen from this than from Kyrenia. Every village on the Messarian Plain, from Morphou to Nicosia, lies at one's feet; whilst pretty little embowered Larnaca below looks a most inviting resting-place.

On one occasion I went with my husband to visit the tombs, the Commissioner of Kyrenia having obtained permission to open a few. We pitched our tents just above the village, at the foot of the huge boulders and crags that beetle above, looking as if every moment they must fall and crush to atoms the little town they helped to build.

The rocks here are very fine. Only an earthquake could have hurled such huge masses on to the slopes below. Just above these are the tombs, many of them already opened. You enter, crawling on hands and knees, by a narrow passage the size of a man's body, and most frequently find yourself in a large compartment, with a shelf or ledge of stone at one end. Occasionally there are three of these shelves round the three sides of the tomb. Frequently niches for lamps or statuettes are cut in the wall, and the ground is covered with fine soil.

There are many hundreds of these rock-cut tombs; but Cesnola and a French consul opened most of them. My husband saw two inscriptions in ancient Greek on some huge stones that had been dug up, but too heavy to be moved. These he copied, hoping some one may later decipher them for us.

CHAPTER VII.

THE NEW ADMINISTRATION.

. . . The duties of my husband's appointment were, first, to assist the Commissioner in superintending the administration of justice in the district Court. Four days a week he had to sit from ten till one, and from two till five, listening to cases, and settling knotty questions of law, with the Cadi, of course, to help. There were also an interpreter, and a Greek and a Turkish secretary.

Occasionally when the Commissioner took the Court business, my husband used to start off on horseback, escorted by one or more mounted zaptiehs, to the different villages, to see if all was quiet in the district, and settle any disputes not brought into the Court. In the rare cases of murder or of violent outrages, he had to go to the village, accompanied by the doctor, to take down the evidence of those present, and decide which witnesses were to appear.

Sometimes he would make a regular progress through the district, taking servants and tents, staying away several days. I always accompanied him on these occasions, and used thoroughly to enjoy the change.

As governor of the prison, his work was much the same as that of a gentleman in the same position in England—the daily inspection of the prison. Its inmates I thought well off for prisoners. They are well fed: bread, cheese, and vegetables to the extent of fourpence halfpenny per diem, increased to sixpence when at hard labour by the addition of meat. Amongst the vegetables were colocasses, a sort of potato, the root of a plant with large arrow-shaped leaves, cultivated all over Cyprus, and when either boiled or fried most nutritious. The prisoners were confined in the fort. Thus comfortably housed, wholesomely fed, and working in the open air (they are employed on the public buildings and roads), they enjoy excellent health; and my own opinion is, they rather prefer being in prison than out of it.

My husband considered as his principal appointment the post of Local Commandant of Police, and took great pride in perfecting his zaptiehs in all soldierly attainments.

One of the first acts of the new administration was to form a new police force, raised in great part from such of the Turkish zaptiehs as were left in the island by the Ottoman Government.

The corps is now called the "Cyprus Military Police," and is composed almost entirely of Mussulmans. It is a fine soldierly body, with a strength of two hundred cavalry and four hundred infantry, and most popular with the people.

When my husband first got his command, the men were in a most picturesque state of raggedness. Some still clung to the remnants of the old Turkish uniform served out to them at least half a dozen years ago. Composed of Lincoln green cloth braided with red, gaiters, baggy trousers, and short Turkish jacket all to match, while at the ankles, knees, and waist the snow-white under-garments were allowed to protrude, with a crimson fez as head-gear, it was much more effective than the hideous blue serge suits with red jackets now given them. Some of them had the good taste to object to this costume, as making them too like the Indian troops, and wanted a regular British uniform. The Greeks objected to wearing a white turban round their fez, declaring that it turned them into Turks! With the former my husband reasoned, but with the latter he had no patience. "They might wear it, or be dismissed."

In fact, the Greeks turned out unsatisfactory. It was intended that they should form one half the force. But they were found so utterly incapable of learning their drill, and were of such dirty habits, and so entirely without an idea of discipline or respect for their officers, that my husband would not allow them to join his force, every zaptieh under his command to-day (with one exception) being a Mussulman.

The Turks are fine, brave, obedient fellows, most loyal and devoted to their commanders. The infantry drill just as steadily as the best British regiment, but the movements of the cavalry are rather erratic and eccentric at times. On one occasion, at an inspection, the Local Commandant had to stand in the centre with a long whip, and make his cavalry revolve round like the horses in a circus! This I heard. Certainly my husband's men are not so bad as this, some of them being fair horsemen; but it is impossible they should have the same smartness as regular cavalry, for the Government does not provide their equipment. Their ponies are most hardy, but not fast. It was sometimes rather a trial to our patience with one of them in front of us during our riding tours. But their company was a necessity, not only as guides, but to ride on to turn out of the way the strings of mules and donkeys, which otherwise would have blocked up the narrow roads.

Many of the zaptiehs come from Asia Minor, where probably they were brigands. Some of them still retain their curious old guns and daggers, inlaid with mother-of-pearl and Damascene work. In becoming zaptiehs, they seem to make it a point of honour to lay aside all bad practices, and I would trust any of my husband's men with every valuable I possess. I liked them all, from the dignified Chawush (sergeant), and dear fat Sucri the corporal; down to poor little Niccola the Greek, who had only a shilling a day to support himself, his wife, and six children.

One shilling a day for the infantry and two shillings for the cavalry (who supply their own horses) seems very small pay. It might have been ample in the time of the Turks, but now the price of house rent and food is trebled, the poor chiefly suffering from the change. Both horse and foot are exercised with the Henry-Martini rifle, with which the latter are armed, and are capital shots, some of them making better practice, my husband says, than he would have expected from regular soldiers; possibly from their habits, for they are extremely sober, many of them drinking water only.

So different from English recruits, they are positively *anxious* to become proficient in drill. The non-commissioned officers are perfect in it, can give the word of command in English distinctly, and can number off the ranks like British soldiers, and have become independent of either the English drill instructor and his interpreter attached to my husband's command. Being Mussulmans, they have no fear of death or danger. I have often heard my husband say they would, to a man, follow him devotedly into action, and nothing would give them greater pleasure than to be let loose amongst the Muscovite hordes.

Their hatred of the Russians is very remarkable: they look upon them as their inveterate and deadly foes. Every man amongst them has some separate deed of the butchery and treachery of their detested enemies to relate. It is curious to watch the quiet, sleepy Turk rouse up when Russia is spoken of; to see his eyes flash and his hands tremble with rage; the intense excitement that pervades his whole body at the idea of being led against them. It is impossible to live in the East and not entirely to sympathize with their feelings; for the nearer one lives to Russia, the more home to one comes the cruelty of her acts and the treachery of her Government.

CHAPTER IX.
OUR CYPRIOTE HOUSE.

Our house in Kyrenia was the quaintest little dwelling imaginable. It was only one story high, and built in the shape of a hollow square. In the centre was a court filled with orange, lemon, quince, and mulberry-trees. The roof was flat and covered with mud, and became, in the springtime, a perfect garden, full of iris and anemones, grown from seeds sown by the birds and the wind.

All the mud roofs become green in the spring. Viewed from the top of one of them, Kyrenia has the look of a garden floating in mid-air. As the sun dries up the verdure and the flowers wither, the inhabitants set fire to the roofs, which they declare prevents them letting in the rain during the winter. After the fire has burnt itself out, the roofs are well soaked with water and flattened by a wooden roller, which invariably lies in the corner of one of them, and belongs as much to the furniture of the roof as the big red chatty serving as a chimney.

CHAPTER X.

MOUNT HILARION.

. . . There are snakes, as I have said. Some of them are most venomous, and the natives are very much afraid of them. But I never heard of death resulting from a bite, although it produces swelling and acute suffering. I feared more for my dogs than for myself, as I always wore high boots. Sir Samuel Baker lost one of his favourite spaniels through the bite of one.

I have seen three distinct kinds since my arrival here, but as the natives call them all "Kufi" (asp), I cannot say which is the most poisonous. One of them my husband shot on Mount Hilarion. It was about three feet long and almost as thick as his wrist, extraordinarily thick in proportion to its length. The head was flat and not very pointed, more in the shape of a heart than a dart. It narrowed suddenly, not gradually, at the tail. In colour it was a greyish-brown. The strangest part about the reptile was its fierceness. Instead of wriggling away on seeing a man approach, it actually *made at him*, hissing loudly. The serpent was about three yards off when my husband first observed it. In a moment it uncoiled itself and came gliding straight towards him, with head erect. When within a yard, he fired, and blew its head off. The beaters were so afraid that even when dead they did not like to touch it; so my husband skinned it himself.

I have also repeatedly come across a black snake. It is jet black all over, with a pointed head, and though a long snake, does not exceed three inches round the thickest part of its body. The smallest I ever saw was four feet long, and one my husband killed just outside the house measured six feet one inch, the longest snake I have seen out of the Zoological Gardens. Lying across the road, it might readily be taken for a burnt stick, were it not for its glistening skin. The last one we saw was on a journey to Nicosia, when I noticed the spirited young mule on which my husband, who was a little ahead of me and cantering pretty fast, was mounted, give a tremendous swerve. This was followed by bucking and turning round and round like a dancing dervish. The saddle unfortunately being loose, my husband was thrown, and off went the mule so frightened that it took us nearly an hour to catch it again. As my husband fell, I saw the tail of a snake disappearing amidst the bushes. It had, as it appeared, crossed the road in front of him, and lifting its head, had darted at the mule's feet. This snake is said to live in trees. An officer of the Forty-Second saw one coiled round the branch of a carob-tree near Bellapaïs.

The third kind, a spotted snake, has a greyish-brown back dotted with black spots, which grow fainter on its light grey stomach. I believe it to be harmless, for we killed several near the stable and poultry-yard. The first we saw was found crawling over the window-sill of my husband's dressing-room; another was discovered beneath a servant's bed; and a third we found had changed its skin during the night in the verandah close to the kitchen door. In fact, they were constantly found, and always as promptly dispatched.

CHAPTER XI.

THE COURT-HOUSE.

The Court was forbidden ground to me; but one day, knowing the Commissioner was away, and that my husband was sitting with his back to the light, I summoned courage to peep in at the window.

I saw a large whitewashed room, with a divan at one end, at which my husband was sitting, with the table in front of him covered with papers and law books. He looked very stern, but, had I been a prisoner, I would have felt much consoled at the sight of his favourite meerschaum, which I noticed he was smoking. Close to him sat the "members" of the Court: Hadji Savas, from Bellapaïs, with his blue spectacles on his hooked nose, looking very like an old owl; fat old Abdullah, who keeps THE shop at the corner near the Konak (or court-house), and who offers me a spoonful of jam every time I pass; another fat and old member from Casaphani, so rotund he had to have a special chair made to fit him; the Cadi, in his long yellow robe, bordered with wolf fur from Russia, of which he is so proud, rolling cigarettes, and politely offering them to every one; the Kamaikan beside him, a fine-looking Turk, but who at that moment was busily occupied in the not very elegant occupation of catching fleas inside the breast of his coat. I was so fascinated watching the latter curious performance that, unconsciously, I had raised myself up till I was almost sitting on the sill of the window, and only became aware of my position by seeing the keen eye of Sucri, the zaptieh corporal, fixed on me with a stern look.

He was standing opposite, in front of the "bar," beside a prisoner, who had the chawush (sergeant) on the other side. I made a face at dear old Sucri, and raised my finger to tell him he was to take no notice of me. He took the hint, and discreetly fixed his eyes in another direction.

It was most amusing to watch him. If a prisoner dared put his dirty paw on the sacred "bar," down came Sucri's fist on it in no light manner. If he bent a knee to rest himself, Sucri, who always stood at "attention," would immediately stoop down and straighten the offending joint, as if he were teaching a new recruit. Should the prisoner so far forget himself as to venture to speak before he was spoken to, in one second Sucri's outspread hand was clapped over his face, and his own round little mouth formed a long "hush." He was backed up in everything by the chawush, who, on this latter breach of Court etiquette, invariably pushed the offender tight against the wall, and with his shoulder held him steadily there till the case was over.

The grave expression, the important air of the two men, the ludicrously punctilious performance of their duties, were too much for me, and an involuntary laugh, on my part, electrified the whole Court. The grave Turks were immeasurably scandalized, the secretaries, interpreters, and clerks highly delighted; and my husband—well, he evidently felt bound to look shocked at the indecorum of my proceedings; but, before any one of them had time to recover from the surprise, I had slipped off the window-sill, and disappeared round the corner, with "Souris" and the collie dog after me.

When my husband returned to lunch, I expected a great scolding; but, as he had not to keep up appearances, he only laughed at my exploit, confessing that he had had the greatest difficulty to maintain his gravity. He made me promise, however, not to repeat the performance, and having had my own way, and seen what I wanted to see, I readily agreed not to do so.

* * * * *

Certain educated (?) Christians of the well-to-do classes have tried, without much success, save among their own particular circles, to create a feeling in the island in favour of its cession to Greece. They are encouraged in this foolish agitation by sundry Greek professors and Athenian agitators, who profess to look upon the Cypriote Christian as a brother Hellene. They tell him he is as much oppressed under the English rule as under the Turkish one, and generally endeavour to make him as discontented and disloyal as possible.

The centre and mainspring of the so-called "feeling" is a society named "The Cypriote Brotherhood," with head-quarters at Alexandria, and branches at Larnaca, Limassol, and Nicosia. The Brotherhood is said to have collected a large sum of money for the purpose of outbidding the British Government when the time shall come for the final and complete purchase of the island from the Turks. One member of the fraternity declared that if the English Government gave over one hundred and ten thousand pounds per annum, he and his fellow-patriots would subscribe one hundred and twenty thousand pounds!

But if these characteristic intrigues should not be entirely ignored lest they gain some hold on an imaginative people, still the "Brotherhood" have gained little.

CHAPTER XIII.

THE LEPER VILLAGE.

In Cyprus there is a "leper village,"—a small colony of those afflicted with the terrible disease. The miserable beings are compelled to live on a kind of farm provided by Government, situated about a mile and a half from Nicosia. During one of our visits to the latter place, we learned that strangers were permitted to visit the spot, and, curious to see it, my husband and I started one morning for the village.

Leprosy, I am told, is not very common in Cyprus, and yet during this year, from one village (Morphou) alone, six lepers were banished to this place.

We left on horseback by the Larnaca Gate, and following the road for about a mile, turned off to the left, by a pathway leading through fields of corn, to what seemed a large one-storied mud house, built in the shape of a square. It had a prison-like appearance, for the few windows looking outwards were closed with strong wooden bars. There was only one entrance, with a small house in front of it, where the keeper lived. A few trees, destitute of leaves at that time of the year, which surrounded the building, their branches covered with hundreds of hoodie, or carrion crows, did not help to dispel the melancholy of the scene.

We saw a man, a little way in front of us, riding upon a donkey laden with panniers filled with small loaves. He had also some poultry fastened in front of him. Our guide told us this was the "guardian" of the lepers, who would show us all over the building.

On questioning him, the man told us he had lived for twenty years in the small house we had observed, that he was in daily contact with the lepers, and was the sole means of intercourse between them and the outside world, as they are never allowed now to leave the place allotted to them by Government.

He was a gaunt, pale, haggard-looking man, with a care-worn expression that even a big "backsheesh" could not enliven. He had the same appearance about the lips that I noticed afterwards in many of the lepers. They were tightly drawn back, displaying two rows of strong yellow teeth. He reminded me painfully of many a dried monk I had seen hanging in the fearful catacombs of Palermo, having the same wizened look.

On dismounting, he tied our horses up for us to some of the trees. My husband armed himself with a strong cigar, and I tied my pocket-handkerchief over my mouth and nose, in case of any unpleasant perfume. We followed our guide, with the interpreter, through a large doorway into the interior of the building, and found ourselves in a sort of farmyard, with dogs and poultry in plenty, and everything tidy and clean.

There were several ovens for baking bread, and a large well. We saw nothing to make us think that the colony differed from others in any respect. On calling out something in Greek, a crowd of men and women poured out from different doorways. They seemed well and comfortably clothed in the usual outdoor costume of the natives. It was only after a few minutes' scrutiny that I could perceive the appalling nature of their complaint.

There seemed to be here two distinct classes of leprosy: the paler, or rather yellow sufferer, and the bloated and purple one. Of the white leprosy one reads of in the Bible there was none. And I daresay that is why at first I could hardly believe that the people around me were afflicted with any disease; for I expected to see them "as white as snow."

The skin of the first class of sufferer had a parched withered look. It was drawn over the bones of the face, so as to look like a piece of brown parchment. The nose had sharpened till it stood out like a bone. In some the features were drawn so much to one side, that it gave the appearance of a senile smile, a ghastly contrast to the reality of the suffering. This horrible grin affected me more than anything else. I tried to look away from it; but it was useless, my eyes kept turning back with a painful fascination.

The majority of the sufferers were those with a bloated appearance. In this case the skin had changed to a deep purple colour, with an unnaturally smooth and shiny surface. The face and head in one or two cases were swollen to such a size that no features at all were discernible: the eyes had shrunk and closed up, the cheeks were puffed over the distended nose, and the mouth was represented by a small hole.

It seems the hands are generally first affected, especially about the wrist. A small white spot is first visible, then pain and stiffness is felt in the various joints of the hands and feet, and in a short time the fingers become club-shaped, the hand assuming the appearance of a claw. The extremities become much swollen, and the hair and eyelashes fall off. Ulceration sets in, and slowly, but surely, the destruction of the bones and cartilages goes on, till the state is such that the unfortunate being is unrecognizable by his nearest relations. The voices sounded harsh and husky; and this, I was told, is caused in nearly every case by ulceration of the throat. The fingers and toes of many had dropped off, the stumps only remaining. To glance at one of the latter, one would think it impossible that extremities had ever been attached to it, for there was not the faintest indication left of the existence of a joint.

The loss of sensibility is very curious. One man told us that even fire applied to his arm did not cause him pain. The guardian pinched one of the lepers to show this was a fact. A woman who was as black as a negress said that this special change of colour had only taken place a few months previously; and it is rather remarkable that in her case sensibility was not destroyed. This numbness to pain is a great mercy, and accounted a little for the seeming cheerfulness under the suffering they must surely undergo.

My husband requested that the two worst cases should be pointed out to us. We were brought to a doorway, through which we peeped, and were shown a man who lay moaning on a wooden trestle. Two women who were attending on him turned him towards the light. I could only take a single glance and no more. Not a feature of any kind was discernible; and only by the inflated movements, at regular intervals, of the cheeks could we tell a living being lay before us. We could only trust he was unconscious; that his condition was more appalling to the onlooker than the actual suffering to himself. It was believed that he was quite an idiot; but as he could neither speak, nor see, nor smell, nor taste, nor even hear distinctly, it must have been hard to tell whether the brain was still conscious or not. Food was administered by pouring liquids down his throat; but every day even this was mercifully becoming more impossible. So we could only hope that death would soon release him.

They seemed kind to each other, those who were the least afflicted helping and nursing the sick, or guiding the steps of the blind. On the whole, both men and women appeared to be tolerably contented. On asking several if they would like to return to their homes and villages, they all answered in the affirmative; but immediately added, with a dreamy look, they knew it was impossible, and had made up their minds to be contented.

To lessen their misery, the men had in many cases taken the women as their wives. These served as their attendants and companions, doing the cooking, and nursing them when ill, and acted as helpmates generally. Children are *never* born in the village; such a thing, the guardian assured us, was unknown; and we certainly saw no child there of any sort. I have been told, though, that within the last month the wife of a *priest* has been sent there, with her little daughter, aged thirteen. The child is a pretty engaging little thing; and the fatal mark, as yet, has only placed its seal on one of her arms. I am glad she was not there during our visit, for it was harrowing enough without the memory of a childish face and voice to add to the deep impression made upon me. There were forty-six patients, including every one in the "home." They all belonged to the poorer classes. Indeed, it is said that the disease is more frequent in years of famine and distress than in what are called "good years." Men get the disease oftener than women. It generally shows between the ages of eighteen and forty, and is hardly ever known to attack children.

The question of contagion is disputed, but of course there is strong evidence against it, or strangers would never be allowed to visit the village. I have been told that the disease is incurable, as no medicine has been known to have stopped its progress; and though change of climate is recommended, it is very doubtful if even that would have a good result. The lepers are unfit for any laborious work, and take no part in cultivating the adjoining fields. In fact, they seem to do nothing all day but feebly cook their food, and herd together in sunny corners in one indiscriminate mass.

On the whole, they seemed in a more prosperous state than I was led to expect. Government allows them three small loaves and twenty paras (a penny) a day. People who visit them always distribute a small sum amongst them before leaving. We had provided ourselves with a bag of piastres. These, on our departure, we threw at their feet (the guide telling us that this is the custom), and they all scrambled to pick up the pieces. At each house we looked into we also left a little remembrance, which was most gratefully received.

The entire absence of *comfort* in the houses struck me forcibly, the sick having to lie on wooden boards, with a coverlet of quilted cotton, that must have weighed like lead on the aching limbs. To make matters worse, even the dying, and those who seemed to us almost dead already, had their stiff uncomfortable every-day clothes fastened round them, making it impossible, I should say, ever to dress their sores.

The pitifulness of the sight almost overcame the horror, the natural result of the whole scene. It seemed so deadly sad that these unfortunate creatures, for no fault of their own, should be so terribly afflicted. They are torn away from their happy homes, and isolated completely from all friends and family ties. They are banished there to endure a living death, and the apparently well and strong are huddled side by side with those for whom the grave can have no terror, as they endure from day to day the corruption that should only come when breath has ceased.

I saw one man, a fine strong young fellow, with a face that will haunt me as long as I live. The fresh air of the fields seemed still to surround him; the memories of a happy home, and the pleasures of living in a beautiful world, could not yet have departed from his thoughts. He looked the picture of health and strength, and had I met him anywhere else, I would have noticed him as a fine specimen of the Cypriote peasant. On inquiry, I was told he had only been there six days, and that as yet the curse had only fallen on one spot. He seemed pained on our noticing him, and it was hard to credit the reality that he was already buried in a living tomb till mercifully released by death.

When a man is first suspected of leprosy, the people go to the Mukhtar of his village and accuse him of the plague. A council is held, and the case examined. He is then torn from his family, who as a rule are his deadliest enemies; his goods are divided amongst his relatives, and he is banished from their presence for ever. His clothes and a cotton quilt are given him, and a guard of his fellow-citizens conducts him to this place, and here he is left to live or to perish.

A short distance from the colony is their burying-ground, and when dead, their bodies are thrust in the earth without ceremony of any kind.

CHAPTER XVIII.

LARNACA REVISITED.

To say that it was a lovely morning when we started, in the middle of March, on our next journey, is to describe our departure on each occasion; for it seems to me that every morning in Cyprus is fine. This time we were bound for Larnaca and Limassol, and home through the Troädos Mountains; not entirely on pleasure, for official business took my husband to Larnaca, and I, as usual, accompanied him.

We decided to ride the whole distance. To have made use of the diligence which runs daily between Nicosia and Larnaca would have necessitated leaving the horses at the former place . . . We galloped all the way to Nicosia.

The ramparts, green with young grass, the drooping willows hanging gracefully over the battlements, and the palms among the domes and minarets, make it the most picturesque-looking city imaginable; but for my husband the place has associations which cause a painful reminiscence whenever he passes it,—that of the scene he witnessed on the first occasion of his leaving it.

A few days after his arrival in Cyprus, he, with several other officers, was ordered to escort three hundred prisoners to Kyrenia, where they were to embark for Asia Minor [Plate 22]. They were Turkish convicts, criminals of the deepest dye, whom the English Government refused to harbour.

As far as the gate, their mothers, wives, and sweethearts were permitted to accompany them, but here the sentries stopped them. So the wretched women rushed to the ramparts for a last view of those they would probably never see again. The wailing, the anguish, the sobbing, the wringing of hands, and the desperate gestures, made a scene indescribably painful. And if that sight my husband could not forget, the history of the following eight hours' march is too harrowing to think of.

These wretched prisoners, who had been shut up between four walls, some of them for twenty years, were suddenly ordered to make this long journey. They were fastened two and two, and had no protection for their heads except the tattered remains of any old fez they happened to possess. The officers in charge were all mounted, and some of the Ghoorkas were told off as escort; whilst four donkeys were allowed by our generous Government in case any of the prisoners should give in.

Through mismanagement, the miserable cavalcade did not start until past eight A.M., and this under an August sun, along a road which for twelve miles does not offer the shelter of a bush the size of a cabbage-plant. As might be expected, before three miles were traversed, the stiffened joints of these unfortunates refused to support them, and one after another they began to stagger. But the power of the sun, growing fierce at every moment, made it only cruel kindness to allow them to lag, and officers and soldiers had to force them to go on, although, when half-way was reached, the Ghoorkas themselves gave in, lying panting on the ground; so that, had the prisoners any energy left, every one of them might have escaped.

The sight, at this point, my husband describes as sickening. One poor wretch threw himself on the ground, tearing up the earth with his teeth in his agony. Another, an old, old man, appeared dead—his face blue, his eyes glazed and sightless, his head hanging on one side. He could only be got along by being tied to two others, who dragged him between them; for the donkeys were already laden three deep. Indeed, at this time my husband, worn out himself, his head almost bursting with the heat, could not see how he was to get forward with his batch; when, fortunately, a company of the Forty-Second, with my brother at their head, was seen advancing over the brow of the hill. In moments of intense feeling, as I may call it, anything new or sudden seems a rest, and the sight of these fellow-creatures, Giaours though they were, seemed to revive the poor stricken men.

My husband was greatly touched by one incident of this terrible march. One of the prisoners had been allowed the companionship of two dogs in prison, and now brought them with him. So exhausted that they could go no farther, the wretched animals gave in in turn. But the man, though so weak himself that he could scarce drag one leg after the other, would not desert his faithful friends, and essayed to carry both as best he could, until my husband, compassionating him, took one in front of his saddle. The look of gratitude in the man's face, he said, was unspeakable.

I do not know, but I think, had I been in my husband's place, I should have been tempted to allow this prisoner to escape, to give him one chance to prove he was not altogether bad; for be he murderer or thief, a man who, suffering as he was, thinks first of his dumb companions, must have some good in him. As it was, my husband did not lose sight of him when Kyrenia was reached,—obtaining leave from the English authorities for the convict to keep his dogs, and when the ship came round to take him to Turkey, arranging with the captain that the dogs should go also.

For several days my husband suffered bodily from the effects of that ride, but little in comparison to the mental torment which the remembrance of the sufferings of the prisoners would cause.

We did not go into Nicosia. Turning to the left, passing the lepers' village at a distance, we gained the Larnaca road, and stopped at a little inn where we knew there was stabling. Whilst pulling our horses up, a very disagreeable-looking old man approached, offering us a tumbler of muddy water to drink. We told Theodore to inquire if he was a leper. The old wretch was terribly insulted, and hobbled off, muttering very unpolite language. We had reason, though, for the inquiry, as before the English came here the lepers were allowed to sit by a pool of water near the roadside, and beg of the passers-by, offering them glasses of water to excite their charity.

One morning soon after Sir Garnet Wolseley's arrival, some of his staff, on entering the monastery where he lived, found, to their horror, that every leper who could crawl had left his bed and village, and formed one of a body, now standing against the wall, waiting to see the Governor, to complain personally of their grievances. But Sir Garnet was spared the unpleasant sight, the petitioners being all sent back whence they came with the assurance that their complaints would all be inquired into at the proper time and place.

* * * * *

In the afternoon we visited the church of St. Jorghios, some three-quarters of a mile from the old town. The Greek priests attached to it are reported very rich. In the churchyard several Englishmen have been buried, by permission of the Greek ecclesiastical authorities. I suppose that in time an English cemetery will be built. Close to these new graves I discovered a broken marble tablet, half buried in the ground, with the following inscription:—

H İNTERRED
OF PİTER DELAU
NDON MERCHANT
O DEPARTED THIS LYF
Y^R 2^D MAY. 1692

a skull and cross-bones being carved below. The interior of the church is profusely decorated with gilt dragons, in honour of St. George.

* * * * *

On leaving the garden we went to see the "Phaneromene," a curious tomb built by the Phoenicians. It is composed of four huge stones, so perfectly cemented as to make it almost impossible to detect the joints. The stone forming the roof is slightly hollowed out in the form of an arch, and the men who succeeded in so evenly placing such enormous blocks must either have had wonderful appliances, or been a race of giants.

The Greeks used to retire there to pray to the Panaghia, and light tapers or lamps in the interior to her honour. But the Hundred and First, when quartered near, with English matter-of-factness, did away with all this, I am sorry to say, and filled up nearly the whole of the tomb with the refuse of the regiment. We cannot expect the British soldier to have much regard for Phoenician relics, no matter how ancient or marvellous; but I think the officers might have had sufficient taste and respect for the only monument of these ages in Larnaca to have found a more appropriate place for the camp rubbish . . .

Cesnola also gives the history of the old tombs he discovered round Larnaca, and an account of how he excavated them and appropriated their contents. These excavations are now strictly forbidden. Major Cesnola, the Consul's brother, was summoned before the Court at Larnaca for continuing them. His discoveries were confiscated, and are lying under lock and key in a room in the Commissioner's house.

Colonel White allowed me to see some of the treasures. The floor was covered with hundreds of earthenware vases, some with designs in black drawn on them, others similar in shape to those discovered by Dr. Schliemann at Hissarlik. I counted fourteen large basketsful of pieces of glass, and these of course form the most valuable part of the collection. I believe it is a matter of consideration at present with the home Government what to do with these treasures.

Before leaving the town, I visited the most important Greek church in it, that of St. Lazarus. It stands in the centre of a large square, three sides of which are formed of the buildings where at one time the ecclesiastics lived, the fourth by the burial-ground, enclosed by tall iron railings. The buildings are now let as lodging-houses to natives, and presented a most untidy appearance. The cemetery, to which a dilapidated gateway, seemingly always open, gave access, had been turned into a play-ground by the boys from the school close by. I thought it such a pity to see these little urchins leaping and running over the finest tombs, and drawing figures on them with a piece of slate.

Some of the inscriptions were very interesting. I counted sixteen bearing English names, all of black and white marble, bordered with delicate raised scrollwork, and often having a coat of arms. I copied a few, but others were so defaced as to be illegible. Here is one:

HERE LYETH THE BODY OF
İON KEN. ELDEST SON OF
MR İON KEN OF LONDON
MERCHANT. WHO WAS
BORN THE THIRD FEB
1672 DIED THE 12TH
İULY 1693.

There was also the tomb of a Mr. William Ken, "merchant of Cyprus," who died in 1707; another of the wife of a Mr. Samuel Palmer, who died in 1820; and again of Captain Peter Dare, Commander of the ship *Scipio*, who died in 1685.

CHAPTER XX.
EN ROUTE FOR THE MOUNTAINS.

. . . In the village [*Pano Platres*] Major Maitland (commanding Royal Engineers) has a house in which he occasionally passes the night, and had kindly given us permission to use it, giving us a letter to the woman in charge. The inhabitants of Platrus are proverbially morose and inhospitable; and therefore we should not perhaps have been surprised when the landlady, on hearing of our coming, decamped with the key.

My husband, thoroughly indignant, resolved to rouse the whole village. He at once sent for the Mukhtars and one of the commission men; but these declared they could not help us. They did not know where the woman was gone, and they added impressively that the village was too poor to give us anything—no chopped straw or barley for the horses, no eggs or bread, and even water they declared was scarce.

But my husband saw through this. It was the will, not the means, that was wanting. He told them, through the interpreter, that he was a Pasha, and would have them all sent to Nicosia, where, if needful, the Governor would deport them to another country. This had its effect. We had left our zaptieh at Zie, and they had probably taken us for nobodies. Now a great hubbub arose. They all began to talk, to whimper, and finally to quarrel amongst themselves, as we found, because each was trying to make his neighbour responsible for our accommodation.

We waited patiently for half an hour. Then my husband would stand it no longer, and seizing a number of lighted pinebranches, here used as torches, and distributing them amongst our people, began to explore the place. First, stables were found for the horses; then we came upon a pile of wood; next, in a recess, chatties full of water. When they found we were in earnest, one of them climbed on to a roof, and, in dead silence, commenced a long oration in Greek at the top of his voice, to the effect that the woman must be brought from the house where she was hiding, at the risk of the Pasha's wrath.

It was the strangest scene. The brigand-looking men in high boots, strange garments, with big knives in their waist scarves; the flickering light of the pine-torches; the figure of the orator on the roof; and my husband standing erect, with flashing eyes, alone amongst these wild people. Presently, a tramping of feet, and a number of villagers appeared pushing before them a virago, in whose face extreme fright predominated over her evident rage. The key was taken from her pocket, and then my husband handed Major

Maitland's letter to the Commissioner; but, as none of them could read, I may be allowed to doubt its use.

After I had been made tolerably comfortable, my husband went out to ascertain for himself the truth, if any, of the reported extreme poverty of the village. He unceremoniously entered each house he came to, and found a plentiful supply of everything. The truth is, as he discovered, in expectation that when the soldiers should come they might ask and get their own prices, the villagers were hoarding their belongings; and, in the meantime, strangers were to be treated in the barbarous fashion in which we had been received—a very different reception, I must say, to any of our previous experiences. I have named the almost universal hospitality which never *asks* for payment. Indeed, the Cypriotes are so *nice* in this way, that even, when gratefully accepting whatsoever we have chosen to proffer, the ignorant peasant has received the money as a thoroughbred gentleman might do, slipping the little remuneration into his pocket without even glancing at it.

In my husband's absence I had been arranging our abode for the night. A wood fire was kindled on the low hearth, our camp beds unpacked, and little travelling lamp lighted. I then discovered a cupboard in one corner, on the door of which was written—"God helps him who helps himself," and on opening it found tea and preserved meat, with all sorts of good things. I was too hungry to resist the temptation or to pause for a moment to reflect that I was robbing Major Maitland's store. So when my husband came back to tell me the result of his inspection, having, as he informed me, ordered the commission man to bring everything we wanted in the morning, I had quite a tempting repast ready for him. In the result we spent a very cosy evening, and before bedtime were in a frame of mind so happy as to be able to laugh over our past difficulties.

CHAPTER XXII.

A JOURNEY DUE EAST—ACCATOU.

. . . Passing Casaphani and Bellapaïs, keeping along the seashore, we came to the prosperous little village, St. Epictitus, most picturesquely situated on the side of a rock. The grey boulders covered with yellow lichen, and the verdure around caused by the overflow of an icy-cold spring, near which we rested, added an unusual beauty to the scene.

A little farther on we came upon a gipsy encampment: three women, four men, and a number of children, with strange beasts of burden in the shape of two lean oxen with native saddles; an apparition not liked by our animals, which only with difficulty could be made to pass them. The copper-coloured skins of these wanderers were freely displayed through their rags. Their hut was ingeniously built of branches placed upright in the ground, with the tops interwoven so as to make a framework in form like a beehive, interlaced with dried grass and shrubs, with a small hole for exit and entrance. The people were squatted inside, round a fireplace built of stones, intent on the stewing of a kid with colocasses.

One often meets gypsies in Cyprus, to which they come from all parts,—Asia Minor, Egypt, and Syria. They bear, I regret to say, no better character than our own in respect to the rights of property; and, though they profess to live by mending pots and pans, their appearance is as much dreaded by the peasants as that of the locusts.

CHAPTER XXIII.
KANTARA AND SALAMIS.

. . . An hour's further ride brought us to the monastery of Kantara.

I had heard so much of the beauty of the scenery here that I confess I was rather disappointed; and we were still more disagreeably surprised to find some half-dozen Greek priests and a bishop duly established here to celebrate Easter. They come up the mountain once a year from St. Elia on the plain, and hold service in the little chapel dedicated to the Virgin.

The Archbishop of Cyprus lives in Nicosia. He and the Archimandrite, who never leaves Constantinople, are the only authorities in the Greek Church allowed to write their name in red ink. The Archbishop must by law be a Cypriote, and no priest can become a bishop unless he is married and has become a widower. Priests may marry, but monks never, which does not detract from the great scandal of the constant presence in the convents of women and children. They are frequently full of them; but on this point I have already animadverted.

At other times the only occupant of the so-called "monastery" is an old hermit, Simeon. I should think he is nearly a hundred years old, and his long white hair and beard give him a most venerable appearance. I was rather astonished later to see with what *gusto* he drank the sherry we gave him at luncheon-time. I believe he originally came from Constantinople, but getting into trouble there, went to the Convent of Mount Sinai, in Palestine, where he lived for forty years, and about twenty years ago came over to Cyprus and established himself near the Kantara church, living on the presents received from the few visitors who occasionally came to pay their devotions in this lonely spot. By degrees, however, he has managed to plant a little garden round his mud hut, and the Bishop has had three additional rooms built, to serve as a dwelling for stray visitors.

Though professing to be very poor, we heard that old Simeon has amassed quite a comfortable little fortune, and report says that most of it has been made by harbouring robbers and evildoers, who, when hiding from the law, took refuge in the rocks round the neighbourhood; Simeon from his perch on the edge of the mountain being able to give them friendly warning of the approach of any zaptiehs sent after them. Nevertheless, some years ago he was nearly killed by a few of these very men, who broke into the little church and stole everything valuable it possessed. They then ransacked the old man's hovel, and on finding no hidden treasure, beat him senseless, in which state he was found by some wandering shepherds, and with difficulty brought to consciousness again. He has no companion, neither man nor beast, save the foxes and the fowls of the air; and except a grass mat on the heap of leaves which forms his bed and a few cooking utensils, his room is utterly destitute of furniture.

In the church we thought we had a treasure trove. The Bishop, with the usual Cypriote courtesy, had invited us to have coffee with him, and in return we had offered him some of our English wine. Afterwards he showed us through the church; a building without a tower, lately repaired and whitewashed, and quite without interest except for the number of small china plates encased in the plaster by way of ornament. I counted fourteen on the roof, five over the door, and four on the apse behind the screen. Those on the roof looked like old majolica, and, as the church is several centuries old, must be very valuable. Of five small saucers originally over the south door, one had been taken by Cesnola, one by a member of Sir Garnet Wolseley's staff, and a third by some one else, and I asked Simeon to let me have the other two, which he promised to do when the Bishop were not there; but in the meantime my husband had asked his lordship (or his reverence: I am not quite clear as to the title of a Cypriote head priest) for the two in the window of the apse, the holy man's hesitation vanishing at the sight of half a sovereign in the church plate.

A ladder was procured, and my husband mounted. As he carefully cut away the plaster with his knife, for they were deeply embedded and difficult to remove, my heart beat with excitement; but great was my disappointment, when the treasures were handed down, to find the majolica one very coarse and inferior in design, and the other a complete imposition. In fact, the original plates had doubtless been taken away, and these more modern ones put in their place; and we had no chance, as I should have liked, to compare them with those in the ceiling; the ladder was much too short . . .

The site of our tents, by the side of a well in the outskirts of the village, swarmed with locusts. Thousands and thousands kept hopping round us, until our people lighted a large fire, and procuring some brooms, swept them into it.

Cyprus has suffered from the "plague of locusts" for many hundreds of years, the ravages sometimes resulting in the entire destruction of the crops.

This year they made their first appearance in the beginning of March, when orders were sent to the Commissioners and Commandants of each district to set to work to have them destroyed. I have accompanied my husband from village to village whilst he made inquiries and took the necessary measures for the destruction of the pest.

The Cyprus locust is, I believe, different from that of the mainland; it is an inch and a half in length (sometimes I have seen them much larger), and of a dull brown colour, and it is said to be indigenous to the island. The female lays about fifty eggs in a sort of bag, like peas in a pod, just under the earth. Over this she places a shining secretion, which used to serve as a guide to those who sought their destruction by gathering the eggs. By the end of March the young insect is the size of a fly, and begins to crawl or hop all over the ground, even thus early doing much damage to the gardens and young crops. In May they are able to fly, and pass in flights to the best feeding-grounds, eating up every blade of green food on their way. About June, when the eggs are laid, both male and female die, and at the end of the month are utterly extinct.

There are several ways of killing them: the easiest is to collect a gang of men from the nearest village, and to make them sweep the ground with strong twig brooms in semicircles till they reach a row of fires which have been previously lighted. The richer villages employ a professional locust-killer. This man ascertains the line of march of the insects, which is invariably straight. Then he sets a number of men to dig a series of deep ditches about twenty yards apart, a mile or two in advance of the spot where the flights may be, the tops of these trenches being lined with zinc, and on the farther side a piece of waxed cloth is stretched upright, the bottom carefully pegged to the ground to prevent the insects passing underneath. The flight travels at the rate of about half a mile a day, devouring every green thing on their route; and when they reach the cloth they immediately attempt to climb over it, but, having no foothold, fall into the trench below, in such vast quantities that those above smother those below, the whole gradually becoming a sticky mass, which has to be covered with earth or destroyed by fires lighted on top, to prevent the smell infecting the neighbourhood. In this way millions are destroyed in a day. Under Turkish rule the natives were forced to do this work without pay; now they receive a shilling a day for work not so efficiently done.

While waiting for dinner we paid a visit to Mr. McLaughlan, a Scotchman, who has lived fifteen years at Trikomo, and has a large farm there. We were received by his kind French wife, who showed us all over their house. It is a two-storied building, with mud walls, and surrounded by a verandah. Attached to the house is a farm-yard, containing every kind of poultry and some fine cattle. Mr. McLaughlan told us his cows and bulls came from Damascus, as for both eating and breeding purposes those bred there are superior to other kinds in the East. He assured us he had never enjoyed better health than in Cyprus, and during his residence in the island had only had one touch of fever, and that, strange to say, last year. He is making quite a fortune, I was told, by his farm, and he informed us himself that he only employed Greek tools and Greek labourers. However, he has a steam machine for grinding corn, which is worked by a Frenchman. Before saying goodbye, Mrs. McLaughlan asked us to taste some of her jams and liqueurs, and I must say they were delicious; our own seemed quite tasteless after hers. She also insisted on a servant accompanying us with a tray of the farm produce —*cow's* milk, which we had almost forgotten the taste of; likewise *fresh* butter, the first we had seen since leaving England, not to mention home-made bread and new-laid eggs,—all showing what care and industry can produce, and what fine farms might be made in Cyprus if only somebody energetic enough would buy the land.

CHAPTER XXIV.
FAMAGUSTA.

. . . The cathedral of St. Sophia is a magnificent remnant of its former splendour, and a grand example of the Tudor style of architecture. The entrance strikes one at once from its resemblance to Nôtre Dame at Paris. The exterior is far finer than the interior, which, being used now as a Turkish mosque, has been whitewashed all over. The old pavement has been pulled up in places, and the marble slabs above the tombs of many French and Venetian heroes have been utterly destroyed and defaced by Moslem fanaticism. The fine windows have been broken in bits, lattice-work of wood and plaster taking the place of the rare old coloured glass of Venice; of which, in many corners, small pieces still adhere to the framework, to give a glimpse of what was once there.

Nothing can exceed the delicacy and lightness of the outside decorations. There still exist two exterior supports or flying buttresses, which were untouched by the Turks. And it is the strangest study to compare them with the barbarous imitations that the Osmanlis have built, to take the place of those so wantonly destroyed during the siege of 1571. The coronals round the higher windows in the apse are the most wonderful bits of floral sculpture I ever beheld; each wreath separate and of a different design. I have heard of artists returning again and again to study them. Certainly, I have seen no stone-carving so beautiful.

The old historians say there used to be a church in Famagusta for every day in the year; but we could only trace the ruins of twenty-five. In the masonry over the arches, in many places, we observed circular earthenware pots, which, Captain Gordon told me, were placed there by the workmen, to prevent the pressure of the enormous weight above going through the arches. The masons could build over and round these light circular pots without the pressure destroying them. It is the first time I have heard of such means being employed to lessen the weight of a mass of masonry.

These five and twenty churches are all fine examples of mediaeval art. Of course there is a great deal of mutilation; but in some of them the frescoes are as bright and distinct as if painted yesterday, and in one we saw a life-size picture of Our Saviour on the Cross, uninjured, to our surprise, by the fanaticism of the Moslem population.

The interior of the Lusignan palace, near the cathedral, is at present the parade-ground of the zaptiehs. At the entrance are four marble columns taken from Salamis. By the mosque is a seat formed of a marble slab, also brought from the ruins, finely sculptured with a representation of Diana hunting the stag and the bear.

Having thoroughly examined all the ruins, we walked to the ramparts to see the grave of "The Destroyer," the ferocious Mustapha Pasha. Over the "Noah's-ark"-shaped tomb a huge fig-tree spreads its branches, which barely reached the ramparts where we stood, the steps giving access to it being sixty feet in depth . . .

Before the English occupation, the State prison was here, and to it and to Nicosia the worst criminals in the empire were sent. But if most of them have been removed, there yet remains one very famous exception; I mean Katerdji Janni, the Robin Hood of the Levant, the famous Smyrniote bandit. During the Crimean War, Sir Henry Storks did his utmost to capture him, but without success, as the mountains and woods in the neighbourhood of Smyrna and Ephesus are full of hiding-places known only to the robber chief and his gang. Several years afterwards, tired of his wandering life, he gave himself up to the Turkish authorities, on condition he should be exiled to Cyprus, and not otherwise punished. On his arrival at Constantinople, he was put into prison at the instance of the French Ambassador, who had heard of the ill treatment of some Frenchmen by Janni's band. For seven years he was chained to the wall of his cell, and afterwards sent to the fortress of Famagusta, where, later, he was leniently treated and allowed a small pension. Captain Inglis has since made him his groom, and the last I heard of him was as riding down to Larnaca with this master.

I had hoped to see him, but unfortunately at the time he was at Derignia; though, before we left, a Greek arrived at our encampment with some lettuces and a lovely bouquet of orangeblossom, surrounded with a wreath of pomegranates, from Katerdji Janni, and a prayer that the "lady would have a safe journey." I was amused and surprised at his politeness, and it proves that prison life has not killed all the chivalrous and gallant nature which made him the most famous of the robbers of the East.

CHAPTER XXVI.

CONCLUSION.

There is decidedly a strong feeling in favour of the Turks among the English officials in the island; though, of course, justice is dealt impartially to Christian and Osmanli alike. This feeling is the result of actual experience in dealing with the two nationalities. The Turk is found to be truthful, sober, abstemious, honest, brave, simple, and devout in his forms and practices of worship, having a child-like faith in his superiors; docile, kind to animals, and remarkable for cleanly habits and customs.

If cleanliness be next to godliness, most assuredly the Turk is the holiest of mankind, for since I have lived in Cyprus I have never seen what I may call "a dirty Turk." The poorest Moslem beggar, though dressed in rags only held together by the merest shred, is still clean; whilst nothing can exceed the scrupulous cleanliness of the well-to-do classes. Even the zaptiehs, who have only a shilling a day to live on, are clothed in spotless white from head to foot, under the garments given them by the English Government. One day, without a moment's warning, my husband ordered the members of his force to take off their uniforms, so that the medical officer should judge if they were fit for active service or not. He was as surprised as delighted with the appearance presented, and I have heard him since express strong opinions as to the character and nature of a religion which, in its teaching, so forcibly insists upon the maxim of godliness and cleanliness.

Another characteristic of the Turk is his hospitality to strangers. Wherever we went on our many expeditions, we were always offered the best the house contained. If we refused to alight, women would come out offering us refreshment and water; the last sometimes costing them more trouble to obtain than wine, and would never dream of asking for any remuneration. I once remarked to a gentleman how singularly nice the Cypriotes were in this latter respect. He replied by asking me "if I had never observed the difference in the hospitality of a Greek and of a Turkish village; how the former only gave from fear, whilst the latter offered you their all from an innate feeling of hospitality?" I confessed I had never noticed the difference, but I suspect there is a great deal of truth in the remark.

The Turks like us; they trust and believe in us, in the justice of our Courts, and in our wish to befriend them; whilst the Greeks, on the other hand, seem to have an instinctive though unspoken dislike to us. They are invariably antagonistic; they look upon us with jealousy mingled with fear, and never fail to try and compare us disadvantageously with the Russians.

At the same time, one ought not to confuse the Cypriotes with the true Hellenes, for in many characteristics the two people are essentially different, almost, indeed, forming a distinct race. The Cypriotes are dull and lazy, they have no ambition, nor the patriotic longings of the Greeks. They are frugal and careful in their habits, sober, and fond of hoarding their money; they do not care about making it, but like saving what they have. As I have said before, they are good parents, and devoted to their homes and villages. They are docile and extremely easily governed. Bad cases of murder or brigandage have been rarely tried before the Courts; though I may mention one instance of the former, told me by Mr. Seager, when at Nicosia.

It seems the Cadi called his attention to a man called Themistocles, living at Baffo, who was *known* to have committed thirteen murders in the island. This man was called the "Greek Avenger." He was an assassin, hired by the Greeks to punish those who had injured them, and whom they thought had not been sufficiently chastised by the law. Mr. Seager did all in his power to prove a case against him; the spots where the murders had taken place were actually pointed out to him. He was shown the murderer, and the men who had instigated the crimes; but he was quite unable to get up evidence in one single case to prove the man to be the actual assassin. So the fellow is at present at large, but narrowly watched by the authorities in the village where he lives.

Since the English occupation, there have only been two cases of murder in the island, and in each case the culprit was hung. The Turks have a great horror of "taking life." They have a superstition about taking the breath from anything animate; and to this day, a murderer is never executed, if, at the last moment, the person most injured by the crime comes and begs the criminal's life, and forgives him the offence.

I have often been struck by the submission displayed by the Cypriote when told to comply with any order or command. Several times, riding about the country with my husband, he has discovered a peasant committing some unlawful act, such as burning brushwood, or cutting down a tree. On being remonstrated with, and desired to appear before the Court at a certain time, the man has just bowed his head and laid down his load, going off in the most touchingly submissive manner, and appearing before the Court at the very hour mentioned. They never resist, or become violent, like so many of the inhabitants of our other colonies.

As another instance of this extreme docility, I may mention an incident that happened lately at Myrtou.

I have already described the convent of Pantalemnon under the peak of Koudounos, with the belt of fir and pine-trees near it. As the grass began to fail on the southern portion of the island, this wood became the place of an encampment of a migratory herd of bullocks, with their owners, who had to leave their own district of Famagusta lest their cattle should starve. On the arrival of the Commissioner to inspect this part of the district, the Mukhtar came to object to the immigration, and begged that the strangers might be removed, stating that he represented the local feeling on the subject. The Commissioner and civil surgeon went at once to inspect the encampment. They found it consisted of forty souls, about eighty bullocks, and twenty donkeys.

The men all gathered round, anxious to hear their fate. They bowed in the usual manner, as much as to say that their heads, hands, and heart were at the disposal of the Commissioner, and then the ordinary attitude of respectful attention was assumed. They were first asked:

"Who are you?"

"Graziers from Famagusta," was the reply.

"What has brought you to Kyrenia?"

"To seek for the roots which form the only sustenance for our dying cattle."

"Were there no roots in Famagusta for the cattle to eat?"

"No. Famagusta is not a good locality for these roots; and what there were had all been eaten long ago. We have either to change our feeding-ground, or see our cattle die. In the time of the Turk, it had been the custom to distribute grain during seasons of drought; but since the English came, none had been given."

"What sort of root is it you give the cattle?"

Here one of the men advanced, and showed the root of the wild artichoke, a species of thistle, the unripe blossoms of which we had eaten ourselves in February. The root is long, like that of the dock plant, cutting like fresh liquorice root, tasting and smelling something like a potato. The questions were then continued as follows.—

"Are you able to pay a small sum per head for the feeding of your cattle?"

"Not a single piastre, for we are penniless."

"Then how do you live?"

"We drink water and eat bread."

The same man who had before advanced again came forward with a specimen to prove the statement; and this time made very clear the meaning of the expression "staff of life." The article consisted of long thin bars of sweet smelling, well made, dark coloured bread, very much harder than the ordinary wood of the island. This had been made in large quantities six months before, and kept for these occasions.

They were again asked if they lived entirely on this.

In reply, the man pointed to a pot stewing on the fire, and on looking into it, it was found to be a stew of snails. It looked rich and nutritious, and *they said* tasted like chicken broth. This he insisted was their only food.

"What will you do if you are ordered away?"

"God is good," they answered. "If the Kaimakan makes us go away, we will go. But we must then starve."

Not a symptom of anger or resentment in the voice of the poor creature as he spoke; only a wistful earnestness, and a patient endurance which was painfully touching—the result seemingly of much crushing and misery.

Their conduct during all the time of their stay had been exemplary; not a twig had been broken off the trees, and not a single complaint by the villagers could be brought against them, except the fact of their wanting the roots. So I am happy to say the Commissioner at once gave them permission to stop, on a promise of their continued good behaviour. These men were true types of the Cypriote peasant, and surely much latent good and strength may be brought forth from people whose only wish is to obey their superiors, and have enough food to support life.

I confess I have a strong feeling of sympathy for these poor people, and a great love of their island, and I earnestly hope this little book will not have been written in vain, and that next year it may be the means of tempting some few to judge for themselves if my descriptions have been correct, or if I have exaggerated in telling of the beauties of the part of Cyprus that my husband has been appointed to govern.

Before closing, I will add a few words on the antagonism shown to the English by a few Greek Cypriotes. This feeling can undoubtedly be traced, to a great extent, to the influence of the priests and monks. They are taught to look on Russia as the actual head of their Church. Russian agents and spies are always coming to and fro amongst them, threatening some, flattering and bribing others. Double eagles have been presented by the Czar to almost every monastery or convent, to be placed over the portals. Constant communication is kept up between the ecclesiastics of both countries. In the heat of an argument, once or twice the priests have let me see their true feelings, and unwisely disclosed their ideas on the power of England and that of Russia, and shown with which country their sympathies lie.

These Russian secret agents seem slowly but surely making their way and influencing the people, distilling the poison of jealousy and discontent into their nature, urging them on to have imaginary grievances, and pointing out that we favour the Osmanli more than the Christian. The schoolmasters even have been known to have these sympathies, and I remember Mr. Ellis, the artist, telling me how, when sketching in a remote part of Cyprus, he heard one evening an altercation going on between his dragoman and the schoolmaster. On inquiring what it was about, the interpreter told him the schoolmaster had just been saying, "The English were dogs (skilos), and the slaves of the Russians, who would soon come and liberate Cyprus and the Holy Church." Mr. Ellis told the man it was most disgraceful for one holding his position to speak in this way, and reproved him in the strongest manner. Next day he came humbly to apologize for his language. But he had spoken out what he felt, and the later retractation was only from fear of the consequences.

All this may only be a beginning, but it would be better not quite to ignore the feeling any more than to take no notice of the "Brotherhood." We ought to remember that forewarned is forearmed, and it is just as well to nip all these little petty treasons in the bud before they rise to become recognized facts . . .

Besides the Christians, Mahomedans, Maronites, and Armenians, there is another sect in Cyprus, the members of which go by the name of "Linobambaki," or "linen and cotton." They are thus called from belonging neither to the Christian nor Moslem faith; though in outward appearance they resemble Turks. They are in reality members of the Greek Church, whose ancestors were forced to declare themselves Mussulmans after the Turkish conquest in 1571. They number about twelve hundred, and live chiefly in a village called Leo-Petro, situated south of Lake Paralimni, and between Cape Pyla and Cape Greco. They are poor and industrious, but not held in much respect by either Turk or Christian.

* * * * *

My little book is finished; yet I feel loth to cease writing of the place and people I have grown to love so dearly. And, indeed, it may well be so, for scarcely ever a day passes without some subject of interest finding a place in my diary. One event of recent occurrence I cannot forbear to relate, it being no less than the unravelment of the mystery surrounding "The Wild Man of Kyrenia."

All over the island startling and improbable stories were current concerning this individual. The soldiers declared they had seen him. The natives assured us such a being often visited them. But as we had never seen him ourselves, we looked upon him as a myth.

However, we were to be undeceived. One day, whilst walking a mile or so from the town, we heard most melancholy and unearthly cries from a distance; and on looking in the direction from which they came, we saw the figure of a tall brick-coloured man, perfectly naked, with a long stick in his hand, walking amongst the trees. He seemed to be coming in our direction; so my husband stepped up firmly, but quickly, towards him, and stood in front of him, never taking his eyes off the madman's face.

He seemed a man about fifty, prematurely old, with a completely bald head. His figure was tall and powerful; the muscles showed plainly through the lean flesh. He walked on towards the town, my husband beside him, step by step. His pace suddenly changed to a run, and he darted into the first house they came to. On following him, he was found sitting in a chair, a number of women crowded up in the farthest corner. One of them threw him a sack, which he fastened round his waist, showing he was not altogether an idiot, and knew that his costume, or rather his *want* of one, was against the law. On the arrival of some zaptiehs, he was taken to the Konak.

The first thing decided on was that he *must* wear some garments. This he sternly and violently refused to do. The Cadi, Kaimakan, and a number of notables were sent for, and a consultation took place. A relation, who lived in the town, volunteered the information that the man's name was Touli; that thirty years ago he had committed a terrible crime, and had been condemned by the Archbishop to wander about like a wild beast. He was forbidden to enter the houses, or hold any intercourse with man. He was condemned to live on the roots and herbs that grew wild in the fields. To confirm his degradation, he was forbidden during the space of ten years to wear any clothes on his body or covering for his head. He had become so wedded to this life, that instead of ten, he had lived it for thirty years; and no one now could induce him to conform to the usages of civilization. It seems that through his madness shone many glimmerings of a shrewd spirit; for though wandering from place to place, he would visit each district at the season most famous for the special fruit of the locality: Varosshia when the cucumbers were ripe; Machera at the time of the grape-picking; Limassol for the olives; or Kyrenia for the carobs. This fact accounted for our never having seen him before, as he had only arrived that day; for the carob-beans were just beginning to ripen.

My husband had some trouble with him at first, but exercised great patience and gentleness combined with firmness. It was indeed curious to see how the wild animal, under the influence of kindness and superior strength of will, gradually grew tame.

For three days he refused all food or drink, though every kind of fruit and vegetable was placed before him; till at last, driven by hunger, he devoured the cheese and bread beside him. Then, from lying on the stone floor, he took to reclining on the divan in the room where he was confined; and at the end of the week he was persuaded for the first time, after so many years, to put on civilized garments.

It was curious how fond he grew of my husband, knowing his step from all others. If he heard a stranger coming, he would instantly rush to the door and barricade the inside, only opening it on hearing my husband's "Come, come, Touli, none of your nonsense; open the door at once."

He would follow him backwards and forwards to the well for drink, and speak quite reasonably, though refusing to answer or acknowledge the presence of all others. But he never could be made to *promise* to wear clothes. He was curiously firm on this point; he was told that if he only wore *one* garment he would be let out at once. But though longing for liberty, no one could persuade him to say he would do so after he returned to his wild life.

One day, after a fortnight's confinement, a zaptieh rushed to our house to say Touli had escaped, and had made for the mountains before any one could overtake him. He had been allowed to walk about the Konak latterly, no one suspecting he thought of running away as long as he had clothes on; but that morning, seeing the guard some few hundred yards off, he bounded forward, and was lost to sight in a few minutes among the trees. He left his costume later by the roadside, and wanders still through the island as the "Wild Man of Kyrenia." And now I have done.

Smith 1887

[Plates 53–54]

Agnes Smith (later Mrs. Lewis) bravely traveled across Cyprus by mule in the middle 1880s with her companion Violet, several comfortable tents, and a retinue of helpers. She fortunately had command of several languages, including Greek, and had written of her earlier travels in Greece in *Glimpses of Greek Life and Scenery*. In this book, *Through Cyprus*, London: Hurst and Blackett, 1887, she describes the difficulties she and Violet experienced on the train across France and their time spent in the Levant on the way to Cyprus. Her trip around the island is portrayed in detail without much historical interest. Her historical chapters and references all derive from other sources.

CHAPTER VI.
BEYROUT TO CYPRUS.

. . .We soon made the acquaintance of Mr. Cobham, the Commissioner, and of Mr. Watkins, who has succeeded Mr. Hamilton Lang in the management of the Imperial Ottoman Bank. Both gentlemen were cordial in their offers of help; and Mr. Watkins kindly took our heavy luggage into his premises until we should have completed our tour.

I asked Mr. Watkins if he thought that the Cypriots are contented under British rule.

'Undoubtedly,' he replied. 'Before the cession they never could call their lives their own. It is only a few hot heads who wish for annexation to Greece. One thing is certain, the island will never go back to Turkey. The great curse of the population is the bad feeling between Moslem and Christian.'

CHAPTER XI.
FROM LEFKA TO KYKKO.

. . . After winding round numberless hill-sides, we came in sight of the monastery [*Kykko*], a two-storied building, partly of grey stone, and partly white-washed. I was far in advance, Violet having dismounted, and, as I turned the last corner, I saw quite an array of monks at the door. The bells rang a merry peal; and I knew this was to welcome us, a letter from the Bishop of Kyrenia having preceded us. I rode up to the door, dismounted, and shook hands with all the reverend fathers.

'Where was the other lady ?' they asked.

I felt that the dignity of our approach was somewhat marred by Violet's absence, but I put the best face I could on it, and said that she was very cautious and liked to walk at every steep place, having been much frightened since she fell off her mule near Lefkoniko. I had then to relate all the circumstances of that accident. One of the monks preceded me into the convent.

The moment I placed my foot on its threshold a great bell added its voice to that of the other bells, and went boom, boom as I ascended a flight of stairs, all scrupulously clean, into a long room with white-washed walls, a book-case at one end, and a lovely blue and gilt candelabra depending from the ceiling. A large bronze church candlestick displayed a solitary lighted candle. At the end of the room opposite the book-case was a raised divan, and all along the side walls a row of cane-chairs. I was asked to seat myself on the divan, and place my feet on the rail of a chair, whilst twelve monks seated themselves on the other chairs. I asked for the Hegoumenos, and was told that he lives at Leucosia, being too old to come up here. I talked with them for about half-an-hour, and young boy servants with long hair and tall caps presented me with sweets and coffee. There were not many monks in the convent at that season, most of them being scattered over the country superintending the harvest. Every Cypriot comes here once at least in his life, on the Virgin's fête day, and he is then considered a Hagi.

None of the monks had ever been in Greece. They thought it more likely that the English residents will learn Greek than that the Cypriots will learn English, an opinion which they are by no means alone in holding. They asked me if there was war between Greece and Turkey, and I replied that they were much more likely to know than I was. Just then the little bells began to sound, and I knew that Violet had arrived, the boom of the great bell announcing her entrance into the monastery. She was in very good spirits, and the chief monk set all his brethren laughing by saying 'Good morning' to her in English. We invited two of them to dinner; but, as it was Friday, they could not come. They promised, however, to take tea in our tents in the afternoon. They showed us their guest-chamber, which was, of course, at our disposal, but we declined to occupy it, on the plea that we had got accustomed to our tents. These were pitched in a most romantic spot on the brow of a cliff close behind the convent, looking down a precipice into a deep wooded valley. We both agreed that we never saw anything quite so charming. We should have liked to stay for a few days, but that was impossible, as we did not wish to lose the French steamer at Larnaca.

The monks accompanied us to the tent door, and asked if there was anything we should like. Violet suggested wine, and accordingly there appeared on our luncheon-table one bottle of black wine, one bottle of Commanderia, and one of a sweet liqueur, like curaçoa. Violet gave a glass to each of our servants, Mustapha alone declining to take it. The only drawback to our pleasure was the high wind.

About four p.m. two of the monks came and had a cup of tea. We had a long talk about Greece and Turkey, and they were much interested by our descriptions of Thessaly. They took us into the monastery, and showed us two deep wells which they have for rain-water, which are filled by means of conduits in winter time. Their spring would soon fail were all the pilgrims who come in September to drink from it. We were then taken into the church, which is a small building in the interior of the monastery, but on a lower level, the ground being uneven. It contains some fine old paintings, and is in the same state as when built in the time of the Byzantine emperor, Alexius Comnenus. There are many curious paintings on wood, representing saints whose hands, faces, halos, crowns, etc., are of silver. But the chief glory of the church is a portrait of the Virgin, said to be the work of St. Luke. The original is, unfortunately, not to be seen. It was already covered up with silver gilt, and with uncut gems when it was sent hither from Constantinople by Alexius Comnenus. But perhaps this is not to be regretted, for the black image of the Virgin by St. Luke, which is exhibited in the Convent of Megaspelion in the Peloponnesus, is really very ugly.

The canopy round this picture is exquisite. It is of some kind of precious wood, inlaid with ivory. There is also a picture of the Virgin looking at her own portrait after St. Luke has finished it.

Violet returned to the tents, but I said that, if they would kindly furnish me with a prayer-book, I should like to be present at evening prayers. I accordingly placed myself in one of the stalls. A young man with long hair began by repeating prayers of which the first words were Κύριε ἐλέησον, Δόξα Θεῷ and Χριστὸς ἀνέστη very often and very fast, until I gave up in despair the attempt to follow him. I employed myself in reading about the resurrection of the Virgin; how it took place three days after she was buried, how she appeared to the disciples, who, when they looked into her grave, found that it was empty, and how after that they were in the habit of saying, 'Μήτηρ Θεοῦ βοήθησον ἡμῖν' ('Mother of God, help us').

The monks then chanted what was supposed to be the 83rd Psalm, but it was in tones more nasal than those of the Arabs. Then the folding-doors of the screen were opened, and two priest, robed in white silk brocade studded with bunches of red roses and green leaves, with long curls of hair hanging down below their high black caps, marched round the shrine in the inner sanctuary, then came out and went round the church swinging a censer with which they incensed every picture and every person, bowing to the pictures, and occasionally chanting in unison with the priests. Each of our muleteers came in, crossed himself, and bowed before the pictures until his head touched the ground.

Whilst this was going on, George, our dragoman, appeared without any head-covering, and, walking up to me, began showing me a photograph which Violet had sent him with for the benefit of the monks. In vain did I remonstrate with him for this irreverent conduct during a religious ceremony. It was a thing, he said, that was quite usual here.

The service ended by some of the monks repeating prayers, and a little boy repeating others with great rapidity.

It seemed as if I had witnessed a scene of the Middle-Ages, and indeed I fear that the spirit of these times is not yet exorcised from Cyprus. It required a great stretch of charity to believe that there was any trace of spiritual worship in these hurried prayers, or that they had nothing to do with the vain repetitions which our Lord reproved. Whilst the old monk explained the various pictures to us, I not only thought that he and his brethren were making the Word of God of none effect by their traditions, but that they are open to the suspicion of enriching themselves not a little by making people believe a lie, there being no doubt that the votaries who flock to the place attribute miraculous powers to the Virgin's portrait. Let us hope that they are themselves deceived.

Salim showed us a short reaper's scythe with a very heavy handle, something like that of a gymnast's club, and furnished with three bells, which made a dreadful clatter whenever the scythe was used, in order to frighten away the serpents.

CHAPTER XV.

LAST DAYS IN CYPRUS.

. . . Mr. Blattner came in the evening. He told us that all the pine-trees which we had seen in the Troados district have been planted by the English. Their age certainly corresponds to that of our occupation of the island. The penalty for cutting down one of them is Draconic. A man had just been sentenced to three months' imprisonment and a fine of sixteen pounds for destroying three of them.

Next morning we rose at six o'clock, and removed our baggage down to the 'Royal Hotel,' a small establishment on the Marina, kept by a retired sea-captain named Gauci. He has not secured as much custom as he deserves, and this owing to the way in which the Levantines persist in misrepresenting everything about Cyprus. Whilst at Beyrout, we met several English families, who were anxious to spend a fortnight in the island, and were deterred from doing so by the false report that Captain Gauci had become bankrupt, and that all the visitors in the hotel had been obliged to hurry out of it, for fear of their luggage being seized by the bailiff. There was not a vestige of truth in the whole story; and I sincerely hope that our countrymen have not introduced into Cyprus the unjust law of distraint, a law which we have inherited from the Dark Ages, and which is, unfortunately, still permitted to blot our statute-book.

English residents in Cyprus were, at the period of our visit, suffering under an intolerable grievance, the abolition of the weekly mail, which had till then been brought by a Government steamer, and the establishment of a fortnightly one, brought by the Austrian Lloyd's from Trieste, by way of Alexandria and Beyrout. The inconvenience was aggravated by the departure of the fortnightly mail-steamer on the day of its arrival; so that letters must be answered within a few hours after their receipt. What this means to bankers and merchants may be imagined. One young man, who had been two years in the island, said to me that the inconvenience of keeping up a correspondence was now so great that his friends, finding that their questions could not be answered in less than a month's time, got one by one disheartened, and ceased to write to him. They would, he supposed, in time forget his existence.

British soldiers who come to Cyprus from Egypt are apt to dislike the island, solely on account of the difficulty they experience of hearing from home during their stay. Postal facilities are curtailed for the sake of economy; but whether this policy be wise, or even just, towards our fellow-subjects, and towards men in the service of Her Majesty, we will not undertake to say.

Our Arab servants sailed on the day after our arrival. George went with them, as we did not wish to detain him for a fortnight after we had gone. We were hospitably entertained to luncheon next day by Mr. Cobham, Commissioner of Larnaca; one of those English rulers who have secured the respect and good-will of the natives, and who adds to his other accomplishments an intimate acquaintance with their language.

We embarked on board the French steamer *Alphée*, taking a rather hasty farewell of our poor faithful muleteers, and brought away with us an intense interest in the future of an island which yields to none of our other British possessions in beauty, in fertility, or in importance.

CHAPTER XVIII.

CONCLUSION.

. . . Mrs. Scott Stevenson tells us that English officials greatly prefer the Turk to the Greek, especially as a member of the zaptieh force; the Turk, she says, is more truthful, sober, honest, brave, simple, and devout, and, above all, more cleanly in his habits and customs.

There must be some truth in this, for all residents in the East agree in praising the Turk for these very qualities, although, they generally add, more stupid. One cannot help respecting a man who, in obedience to the precepts of his religion, practices self-denial in abstaining from wine whilst he sees others enjoying it. At the same time one must never forget that he is virtuous only whilst he remains poor. Let him rise in the world, and take to himself several wives, then the harem system will come into play, and his children will be educated to every kind self-indulgence, drunkenness perhaps not excepted. Many of the precepts of the Kuran are excellent; but we have to bring against that book the charge not only of degrading women, but of guiding the human mind into a groove out of which it cannot raise itself, and of thus limiting human progress.

The Greek peasant is quite as devout as the Turk, according to his lights, and we maintain that he, being a Christian, is capable of more, because the Book he believes in speaks of a spiritual heaven, not of a paradise of running streams, shady groves, embroidered couches, and houris. Educate him, and he will throw away his idols. We write about what we know; for we are often deeply touched by the moral and religious exhortations which we meet with in Greek periodicals. If Englishmen will not give themselves the trouble to understand the Greeks, they will, of course prefer the dog-like docility of the Turks. We submit that Captain Scott Stevenson did not act with an Englishman's wonted impartiality when he dismissed his Greek zaptiehs because they objected to wear the turban, lest they should be mistaken for adherents of a faith which their fathers had refused to embrace at the peril of their lives. Did he reflect on what would have been the consequences had he asked the Turkish zaptiehs to wear a cross?

Toof 1887

The Reverend John Thomas Toof (1846-1896) was an American clergyman who undertook with his wife, Leda Malvina Fox Toof, a journey through Europe and the Holy Lands typical of the 1800s. Their trip in 1886-1887 is recorded in six manuscript volumes at the University of Virginia. The first five volumes are Reverend Toof's diaries, and the sixth is that of Mrs. Toof. Although illness prevented their going ashore, they passed Cyprus in March 1887 and anchored off Larnaca the next month.

[Volume 3, pp 568-569:]

Lordsday March 6, 1887

CYPRUS. We are off for Cyprus, unto which island (Acts11:19), upon the occasion of the "persecution that arose about Stephen," disciples, being scattered abroad, came— "preaching the word to none but unto the Jews only." This seems to be the most western point reached by these pilgrims forced from home & friends & country by their loyalty to their Redeemer.

Hither also came Paul & Barnabas (Acts 13:1-4) being sent forth by the Holy Spirit from Antioch unto a special work for the Lord. It was in Salamis, on the east coast of Cyprus, that they preached the word of God in the synagogue of the Jews, "They also had John to their minister." It was also on this island, at Papho, at western extremity, that Sergius Paulus desired to hear the word of God, but was troubled in accomplishing it by Elymas the sorcerer, who sought to turn away the deputy from the faith. Paul struck him with blindness for a season & by this miracle he saved the deputy & brought many in the island to embrace the truth. I have always regarded this as a singularly philosophical miracle from the reasons:

1. Paul himself was struck blind, that he might see the truth. The glory of Jesus, appearing to him on the way, threw scales over his eyes so that he had to be led, instead of leading others as before, but this very thing was his recovery from error & [*illegible*] in the way of righteousness.

2. This was Paul's first miracle—one like that which he had himself experienced, and a beautiful representation of the world needing salvation, but which boasted of its sight, & which needed to be struck blind universally, that it might see the truth & embrace it.

3. Paul was saved by his affliction, accepting it as from the hand of God, and thereby showed that all others supernaturally stricken into blindness were inexcusable, if they should not accept it as evidence of God's dealing with them, & surrender themselves wholly to his will.

[Volume 3, p. 715:]

Tuesday, April 19, 1887

Arose early 5:30, to see if Cyprus had appeared. Took some tea & bread on my way to deck, & it resulted disastrously. The sea had been very rough nearly all the night through, or was growing rougher almost continually. Many on board were complaining, & some were sick. Leda did not rise at all until we anchored off Lanarkia, ancient Citium, of great antiquity & importance, with a history connected with the most eminent characters & events of the ancient world. The ruins here & throughout the island of Cyprus are set down as among the finest of the entire pre-Christian period. Many of our parties went ashore, but we remained & enjoyed the sea breeze and the fine views of the Cyprian Olympus Mt., the adjacent peaks & ranges & the town of Lanarka. Those who went ashore say but little of interest was to be seen, and that the heat was considerable. It was here that Lazarus is said to have died the second time; and now there is a Church of St. Lazarus to commemorate that event. They also claim to have the cloak that Paul left at Troas. Paul took this island in his route to Rome when he was shipwrecked & a description of this island itself, as for my "Notes" will be found under the date of March 6, 1887. We remained anchored off Larnaca until 8 p.m. - 12 hrs. in this port. Then pushed out into the sea rather thinking we would have a fair sail through the nights but prepared for the opposite without special surprise. The situation of Lanarka is a good one, & her Bay is one of uniform outline. All vessels anchored 1 mile from shore.

The sunset was beautiful—directly over the city from our ship indicating that home was just a sight (*sic*) angle away from where it seemed to be, judging by the decreasing trend of the Mediterranean. Had Bro. S & I gone in the direction we both said home seemed to be, we should have gone just through the Cape of Good Hope!

We enjoyed a full meal at Table d'Hote.

[Volume 6, p. 164:]

Cyprus, Tuesday, Apr 19, 1887 Beautiful

When I made a final attempt to arise this morning the ship was pitching violently and I felt a little sick; so I concluded to remain in bed until she stopped which she did about 8 o'clock. We are anchored about a mile from the town of Laranaca which with the mountains for a background, its white houses, minarets and palms, blue Mediterranean sea, and ships for a foreground makes a pretty picture. Mr. Toof has been about sick all day.

Guillemard 1887–1888

F. H. H. Guillemard (1852-1933) travelled widely to Lapland, South Africa, New Guinea, Malaya as well as Europe and Cyprus. His two visits in Cyprus in 1887 and 1888 were spent primarily in ornithology. His unpublished *Transcript of Four Diaries* was owned by J. R. Stewart and in 1983 was donated to the Cyprus American Archaeological Research Institute, which granted permission for the publication of the following extracts. Much of the diaries records his acquisition of birds and their eggs by his own hunting and that of hired hunters and the skinning and preservation of the many varieties they collected in Cyprus. Guillemard was a medical doctor who was often approached by the people of Cyprus for assistance. He comments, without much evidence, that "syphillis is said be very prevalent" and that "it is probable that abortion is often practised." Along the way he comments on visible ruins and tombs and occasionally purchases coins and other small antiquities. He published *Cruise of the Marchesa* (1889), *Life of Magellan* (1890), an article "Monoliths of Cyprus," and he initiated the Cyprus Exploration Fund in Great Britain. We have inflated most of his abbreviations.

Tuesday, Feb. 22nd. [1887]

. . . Arrived Larnaca about 4 p.m. Fought Miss Burke into a boat, and fought myself and luggage into another. Passed the customs and paid £3 for my guns. Then having found the tout of the Hôtel, I went with him to call upon the Commissioner, one C. D. Cobham, to whom Ward had given me a letter. He was fairly affable, but Oxford, and a bit stiff. Here I found Thomas chief of police, a very good fellow and very much the reverse of stiff. He went round with me to Hotel, and finding no bed (the Mitchells having just returned from Europe with children). Said "you will have to stay with the Walpoles." Went round there and did so, finding Walpole was the same man I had known in old Pembroke Lodge days, and his wife was Miss Forde of Lexden Terrace, Tenby whom I also recollected, and who used to be a friend of Maddies'. Also a queer nice Irish girl with a delicious brogue on to her was there. The Walpoles had to go out to dinner, but their place was taken by Mr. and Mrs. Mitchell and we had a pleasant dinner.

Friday, May 27th. [*Kykko*]

. . . Came home very hot: it is hot now in the sun—and labelled yesterday's birds. Then lunch. I have sent a messenger to a village 3 hours away to get the keradji as soon as possible (he was to come on Monday) as this place is only a waste of time, in spite of my having got another P. lugubris this morn. Tried to get another in afternoon but failed. Wrote diary, and skinned before an audience of monks. Dinner and Shakespeare as usual, then skinned again and so to bed.

Saturday, May 28th. [*Kykko*]

Mules haven't come so I suppose the keradji must be away. Hope they will come tonight, for there is that about this place that is enough to make one cut one's throat. The life these monks must lead makes one shudder. Happily they are as ignorant as cattle and do not drink or smoke. What they do it is hard to say, for there is little cultivation round the monastery. Their day appears to be—3 a.m.–5 a.m. church. Then coffee in the coffee room and library. Breakfast—bread and meat at 9 a.m. Dinner at 12 noon—then every-one—every mother's son of them—goes to sleep and wakes up at 5 p.m. or thereabouts. Then after a loaf they have supper at 7, and so to bed. The gates are shut about 9 p.m.

Wednesday, April 25th. [1888]

. . . The baggage went on ahead, but Joseph, H[*eathcote*] and I started at 10:30, and arrived Kuklia 2 p.m. Saw 5 golden orioles, and after passing Souskiru (a beautiful view looking back on it from the small pass above it) found pretty Gladiolus.

Found Hogarth alone. Elsey Smith gone away. His method of living is more untidy than anything I ever saw. The temple digging has been most successful: 150 inscriptions, and the plan quite complete. It is of a quite unclassic shape. All inscriptions are to Aphrodite. Over the temple was originally a monastery. H. thinks he has found Stadium, and is also opening a tumulus. Both of these are to east of the village.

Thursday, April 26th.

Went down in morning with H[*eathcote*]. to the two "Phallic Stones" by the sea. One is certainly enormous but my faith in my theory is not affected by it. Collected scolopendra and found no birds of any interest but the Little Egret. Both the White Egrets are in Cyprus apparently. We passed what is a mediaeval aqueduct on our way. In the afternoon visited with Hogarth the tumulus digging. Had tea in tent; a Mr. and Mrs. Fulton turned up, en route for England. No birds, but the shoot-man brought a Golden Oriole.

Fyler 1890s

Colonel Fyler, about whom little is known, apparently visited Cyprus in the late 1890s as he quotes reports up to 1896-97. His book, *The Development of Cyprus and Rambles in the Island*, of 137 pages, was published in London by Percy Lund, Humphries & Co. Ltd. but carries no date of publication.

Like many travelers to Cyprus, Fyler begins with a history of the island from the Phoenicians through the British take-over in 1878. He describes the financial arrangements with Turkey, alternatives to

British occupation, and a suggestion for acquiring the island. He compares Cyprus to Crete, Corsica and Ceylon, and like others before him attempts to characterize the differences between Greeks and Turks after brief observation.

He details the historic and contemporary naval and military position of the island and costs of improvement. His description of Cyprus commerce deals almost wholly with agriculture with some attention to hotels in the Troodos mountains. His brief tours of the island included the cities of Famagusta, Larnaca, Nicosia, Kyrenia, Limassol, Paphos, Chrysoko, and the castles and ruins of St. Hilarion, Kantara, Bella Pais, Salamis, and Colossi.

He describes below the destruction of a hemp crop, but notes as well its potential as an income product.

A valuable crop of Hemp (Cannabis Sativa) was grown in the Kolossi district many years ago, but was totally destroyed as an illegal crop by the colonial secretary, who caused it to be set on fire in several places; it burnt fiercely, and, the wind being toward Limasol, the smoke of it is said to have carried a slight stupefying effect even as far as that town, which is about seven miles off.

The medicinal properties of this plant are stimulating and intoxicating: it seems to combine some of the properties of both tobacco and opium; the sun-dried leaf is sometimes smoked, and portions of the plant when dried are called Bhang, in which state it is used by the natives of India and other places, both for chewing and when pounded and mixed with water as a drink. Its more powerful form, however, appears to be that of Churrus or resin, of the properties of which Maunders' Treasury of Botany gives the following account: "In small quantities it produces pleasant excitement, which passes into delirium and catalepsy if the quantities be increased: if still continued a peculiar form of insanity is produced."

The use of Hemp and Hemp seed as an article of commerce is well known. It will grow on almost any soil, the poorest producing the finest quality.

The crop is an extremely valuable one, for commercial purposes alone, and its growth should be sanctioned under strict supervision. It is used in this country for the manufacture of sails, cordage, linen, etc. and should prove a valuable export from Cyprus to England.

The annual report shows the value of £394 for hemp manufacture imported. There is no export.

An experimental growth of Sisal Hemp was reported from Nicosia in 1895-6, when nearly 4,000 young plants were planted out. Perhaps this may lead to its introduction into the Island.

Bulwer 1892

Sir Henry E. G. Bulwer, Her Majesty's High Commissioner For Cyprus, presented to both Houses of Parliament in June 1892 his report for the years 1889-90 and 1890-91 summarized below.

A harvest failure in Cyprus in 1887 and an only fair harvest in 1888 led to depression that lasted until far into 1889.

The major agricultural industries are vine and wine, carob, and cotton. The lesser ones are wool, olives, silk, flax, aniseed, sesame, fruit, vegetables, cheese, livestock, hides and skins, wheat, barley, vetches, and oats.

Wine is exported to France and Egypt where Cyprus has a monopoly, but the French are instituting a duty and Italy is beginning to export cheap wine to Egypt. There has been a steady increase in production since the British takeover of the island.

The carob harvest for the years 1871 to 1880 averaged 13,793 tons per year. For the years 1881 to 1891 the yearly average rose to 21,981 tons per year.

Under the Venetians it was reported that Cyprus produced 850 cantars or 33,000 gallons of olive oil. Drummond in his visits to Cyprus in 1745 and 1750 does not even mention it among the products or exports. However, there was a tremendous growth in production from 98,000 gallons in 1877 to 479,910 gallons in 1890-91. At the same time silk production tripled in okes from 10,459 in 1879 to 32,781 in 1890-91.

In 1745 Drummond reported a production of 500 tons of terra umber. By 1890 production had grown to 2314 tons. In 1889 the sponge fisheries gathered 14,543 okes of sponge.

The major manufactured goods were cotton, coarse calico, hand loom silk, tanning, boots and shoes. (Consul White noted in 1863 that Cyprus manufactured red, yellow, and blue leather slippers for Turkey.)

By 1890 total annual exports reached a value of 399,648 pounds, while imports were valued at 274,123 pounds. Imports without bread stuffs to compensate for the bad harvest, however, reached 259,800 pounds. Revenues for the island in that year were higher than expenses at 194,936 pounds compared to 107,589 pounds.

By 1891 the population had increased to 209,291 from the 1881 level of 185,350. Mahomedans numbered 48,044 and non-Mahomedans numbered 161,247.

Health officials reported influenza in 1889 and some diphtheria and typhoid. In 1890-91 the hospitals handled 579 inpatients and 11,918 outpatients. The leper farm had 74 patients and the lunatic asylum had 15.

The educational system of the island was divided into 225 Christian schools with 10,342 school children and 94 Moslem schools with 3,516 children.

Legislation was passed concerning mukhtars, village field-watchmen, isolation of lepers, regulation of import of firearms, sponge fisheries, and mortgages.

Crime statistics for 1890-91 included the reporting to police of 5,849 offenses, 2,752 summary convictions, and 1,981 acquittals.

The state owns 515 square miles of forests part of which has been designated a forest preserve. To encourage reforestation 6,826 seedlings were issued to private landowners. Rainfall was reported as varying from an annual fall of 16.35 inches at Larnaca to 31.16 inches at Kyrenia. The temperature on the island ranged from 108.2° down to 29.8°.

The major public works carried out by the government included a hospital in Nicosia, the metalling of many roads, and an irrigation project at Kiti.

Mallock 1887

[Plate 55]

In the years shortly after Great Britain had assumed the administration of Cyprus there was considerable curiosity about a land of which little was known. William Hurrell Mallock (1849-1923) was driven by that curiosity to visit Cyprus and secondarily by stories of valuable *Verde antique* lying on the ground in the Kyrenia mountains told to him by a neighbor. The latter, which he disproved, was not terribly disappointing for he discovered so much of Cyprus.

Mallock apparently visited Cyprus in the winter of 1887-1888 and published his 407-page account of his visit: *In an Enchanted Isle or a Winter's Retreat in Cyprus,* London, R. Bentley & Son, 1892. A travel writer, he felt his readers would be interested in his observations, philosophy, and anecdotes. Unfortunately he fails to name many of the villages, monasteries and other places visited. In addition to the selections here, he visited Kythrea, St. Hilarion, Kyrenia castle, Bellapais, and Famagusta. These selections include one of Ayia Napa, not visited or described by fellow travelers writing in English.

CHAPTER IX
A CHARMED LIFE

. . . If anything in Nicosia was like the old world and a story-book, I found that amongst these things the bazaar was to be reckoned foremost; and amongst these things it was in one way wholly singular. The rest of the town, with its mouldering ramparts, its cathedral, its mosques, and its secret tortuous streets, had shown me the past, embalmed or asleep or ruinous. In the bazaar I found it full of animation and movement.

Having threaded with Mrs. Falkland a labyrinth of silent alleys, we emerged suddenly, through an aperture between an old house and a minaret, into a wide street, lined with low-vaulted warehouses, their arched doors being all of them wide open, and showing within a row of shadowy caverns. In the middle of the roadway donkeys were pattering to and fro; and we almost ran against a bare-legged itinerant tinker, who was about to set up his shop at the foot of a blank wall. On either side in front of the warehouse doors the ground was littered with primitive bales of goods; and amongst these, being laden or unladen, groups of camels stood patiently in the sunlight, with red caps and turbans moving and glancing round them. At the end of this street, which seemed like a *cul-de-sac*, was a large fig tree having a Turkish tomb under its branches; but passing round this we were faced by a covered passage, flickering with lights and shadows, which ran away into a wilderness of old stone buildings, and into and out of which, like ants at the entrance of their nest, men and women, with a sort of busy dilatoriness, were constantly coming and going. This was the entrance of the bazaar proper; or rather one of the entrances, for the passage now before us was only one out of many. The bazaar was a spider's web of them.

Externally the view was of no architectural interest; but the moment one entered one was in a world of the curious and picturesque. This particular passage or street happened to be that of the silversmiths. As I looked round me and began to realise the scene, I felt that we were back again at the beginnings of civilisation. The little shops were a succession of open rooms or cells, black with shadow through which the rude walls glimmered, and on the walls a shelf or two and some implements hanging by nails: and at the mouth of each cell, on a wooden stool, sat the proprietor industriously working at his craft, with a charcoal forge making a dim glow at his elbow. Some were fashioning candlesticks, some buckles; and one was finishing the crook of a bishop's crosier.

At the end of this street was the meeting-place of several others. They were all covered in one way or another, some with tattered awnings of canvas or coarse matting, which made stripes above one of blackness and blinding sky, some with stone vaulting, and some with a trellis-work of vines. One was the street of drapers, and this we entered first. It seemed, as one looked down it, to flutter from end to end with gay-coloured triumphal flags, which were really stuffs for sale—veils, gorgeous handkerchiefs, and beautiful native silks. The shops themselves were for the most part vaulted, and looked like a series of chapels with one wall wanting. The dark interiors of some were piled high with goods; others revealed in operation the processes of primitive manufacture. Here would be three men stitching the shaggy capotes of the shepherds; here another, shaping red fez caps over gleaming copper moulds; and here on a low platform, jutting a little into the roadway, a Nubian boy lying almost flat on his stomach, and quilting a coverlet of brilliant white and purple. And at the entrance of every shop was—I was going to say the shopkeeper, but the name sounds far too modern—it is better to say the merchant. Here was an almond-eyed Greek twitching with grimaces and vivacity; there an old Turk squatting superbly calm, like a wax figure moving to slow clockwork, alternately sucking at the amber mouthpiece of his chibouk and stretching a hand with a huge turquoise ring on it over a chafing-dish of live charcoal, looking as if, for him, customers had no existence.

One mentions all this quickly, and then one passes on. But the eye lingered as words cannot linger, as if it would feed on everything and never could have enough—on the masses of quaint detail shining and glimmering in the foreground, on the dimmer objects swimming slowly into sight out of the shadow, on the clear shadows melting into impenetrable darkness, and on all the luminous colours in movement or hanging stationary. Had I only been an artist, I should have longed to be painting everything, and thus to seize it and make its beauty my own.

Passing from this street into another, the longing grew even keener. I felt as if I were in a gallery of living Rembrandts or Van Ostades. What we had entered was the street of the grocers. Here the subdued light flickered on bunches of yellow candles, destined for burning at Christian or Moslem shrines, on huge oil-jars in which the Forty Thieves might have hidden, and on piles of globular cheeses with madder-coloured rinds. They all caught the eye, painted on deep shadow. Then from this street we passed into that of the fruiterers and the sweetmeat-sellers. The change was like that of passing to the works of some other Dutchman. Here in shadow that was browner and more translucent was the fresh greenness of vegetables. There were the wrinkled leaves of cabbages and the faces of creamy cauliflowers, and here and there the whole place was illuminated by piles of pale gold lemons, of fiery-red tomatoes, and rose-coloured stacks of radishes. Farther on one came upon trays of comfits, on gelatinous strips of *nougat,* and great masses of a peculiar pallid sweetmeat, of the colour and the texture of putty, with the large knives sticking in it, that were ready to cut it into slices.

In another street we came upon the shops of the barbers, bare to the public eye as the interior of a doll's house; and not far off were rows upon rows of cafés—deep vaulted rooms, entirely open to the roadway, and showing within, dark in the swarthy twilight, long groups carousing at wooden tables. Not far from these was the more squalid quarter of the shoemakers, where all down an inky alley busy hands were glancing, and boots brown and black, and slippers crimson and yellow, dangled in front of what were less like shops than sheds. Somewhere too in the same neighbourhood a sharp turn brought one amongst the smiths and the iron-workers, where black puffs of vapour floated faintly amongst the awnings, and far away in the gloom forges spat and sparkled.

And through these shadowy ways, from early morning to dusk, the most motley throng kept moving. Greeks and Armenians, in dark, tight-fitting clothing, jostled their way amongst turbans and flowing robes, amongst blue and green and orange colour. Old crones, with silvery hair and faces creased like medlars, tottered along with baskets on their feeble heads; by them went girls, tall and with heads erect, on which were supported jars brimming with water; and slowly gliding in and out of the crowd were veiled Turkish women, muffled in white like ghosts, showing nothing but the gleam of their dark eyes, and attended sometimes by a negro black as ebony. Occasionally the mass would be pressed together and parted by a patriarch with a beard of snow solemnly enthroned on a donkey between coloured saddlebags; and occasionally through the reluctantly formed opening a cart would come, drawn by bullocks, with their huge horns swaying. Then, as one watched and waited, other sights would reveal themselves. Little brown-legged boys would skip by with trays of coffee, which the cafés sent out to the shops; and bakers' men would appear, going more circumspectly, carrying on their heads long trays like planks, each with its row of loaves smelling fresh from the oven.

Of Oriental bazaars that at Cairo is commonly supposed to be the most interesting, and of course in scale and in value and variety of merchandise this of Nicosia cannot for an instance be compared to it. But if the two are judged by the impressions they produce on the mind the advantage is the other way. In the bazaar at Cairo the stranger perforce wanders, accompanied by a *banal* consciousness of the neighbourhood of Shepheard's Hotel, or else at every corner he encounters the inhabitants of it. Cockney and Yankee accents clash in the air close to him, and hands in every direction are red with "Murray's" and "Bädeker's." The existence of the modern world is in no way eclipsed in his mind: the scene seems rather by contrast to bring it into jarring prominence. But in the bazaar of Nicosia everything conspired to make the modern world forgotten. In every sight, in every sound, in the very air itself, there was the flavour of another civilisation and of other centuries—one might almost say of another world. The men who passed were every one of them men who might have seen djins or effreets, have been wrecked on the Loadstone Mountain, or done wonders with talismans. There was not a face that might not have seen marvels, and probably not a heart that did not implicitly believe in them; and the knowledge that this was so, through the quick action of sympathy, wrapped me round myself with the same mysterious atmosphere.

Cairo, again, cannot, nor can any other town that I know of, offer anything comparable to the following experience, with which my first day's visit to the Nicosia bazaar concluded. After wandering about with me for a considerable time, Mrs. Falkland paused before a low squalid-looking arch, which divided two shops, and said, "We will come this way." Plunging through the arch, we emerged under the open sky amongst some outhouses, in a passage which seemed to lead only to somebody's back door. At the end, however, it took a sudden turn. We advanced a few paces, we passed through another arch, and we found ourselves under the shadows of the flying buttresses of the cathedral. It seemed as if in a moment we had travelled three thousand miles. We were surrounded by a vision of silent mediaeval Europe. The pinnacles soared above us and the coats of arms looked down on us.

To both these scenes I again and again returned, the imagination each time taking a fresh draught from them as from a well, and colouring my thoughts afterwards as I sat in my host's cloisters and watched his orange leaves tremble and heard his fountain splash.

Another of the sights of Nicosia—of the sights which the tourist would call such—was a ruinous pile of buildings, which is now called the Konak—that is to say, the Turkish Government offices—but which was once a palace of the kings of the House of Lusignan, and earlier still of the Byzantine Dukes of Cyprus. Its principal entrance opened on a large irregular *place*, and the external view of it was not impressive or interesting. It consisted simply of a long blind wall, patched with mud and ragged at the top, in the middle of which was a tower with a Gothic doorway. The dilapidated doors were not fastened, and Colonel Falkland, who was my guide, unceremoniously pushed them open. Inside was a guard-room with a heavy groined roof, beyond this was another, and then came a long court, surrounded by crumbling buildings that had been used by the Turks as barracks. Of these a part was modern, and consequently already in ruins; but amongst this, and under this, were many parts that were ancient—solid stone staircases climbing to roofless chambers, and halls with ponderous vaulting, of which some were Byzantine. Nothing, however, retained any marked architectural character. All beauties of form and proportion had been lost, most likely for centuries. But the extent still remained of the labyrinthine structure—chamber after chamber, chapels, baths, and banquet halls, faintly and plaintively proclaiming to the eye what they had been, and reminding one by their silence of the life that had for ever left them. Oranges laid their cheeks against walls where had once been frescoes, and the long roofless corridors were carpeted now with violets. I said that the place had no architectural feature. As I was turning to leave it, however, I found that it had one. This was the inner side of the entrance tower. Over the door was a magnificent coat of arms—that of the Lusignans—surmounted by a crown and a helmet; and over this was a window which, the moment I set eyes on it, gave to the whole scene a new soul and sentiment. The lower part was defaced, battered, and broken, choked with bricks and ragged Venetian shutters, but its upper part was as perfect as in the days of its glory—a great Gothic arch filled with exquisite tracery.

The impression I took away with me was one of confused sadness. I little knew what sadness, of a very definite kind, had been near me all the while amongst that desolation and silence, and that I should see it face to face on the occasion of my second visit.

And now that I have mentioned the Konak, the ramparts, the bazaar, and the cathedral, the tourist's sights of Nicosia have, I think, all been enumerated. But the other sights—sights that slowly showed themselves and gave the place its character by a series of delicate touches, each dependent for its force on its surroundings as much as on itself—these were innumerable, and can be described only by specimens. They were, in fact, not so much sights as experiences; and every day yielded a fresh crop of them.

One afternoon, for instance, in a street that was then strange to me I caught, through an open doorway, a glimpse of a long cloister. Slanting sunlight was coming in through its arches, together with some orange boughs and banana trees, out of an unseen garden. I ventured in, with the feeling of a timid trespasser. Directly within the entrance, dim in the vaulted shadow, was a door, surmounted by a mass of intricate carving. At each extremity of the device was a quaint heraldic lion, and in the middle I detected the heads and the wings of angels. I advanced into the cloister. The sleepy garden revealed itself, and on the other side a series of whitewashed cells, each with a bed, a chair, and a bare wooden table. I now realised that I was in some Greek monastic establishment. Presently an old priest, having a long silvery beard and wearing a cassock and a high brimless hat, came towards me, and asked me by smiles and signs if I should like to visit the interior of the church. I assented. He took me to the door with the carvings over it. He pushed it open and I entered. I started. The incense-smelling twilight in which I found myself was a-glimmer with gold and paintings! The actual structure was severely simple. It consisted of three aisles, of which the middle one was lit by a low dome, and the plain-cut stone-work was bare of all ornamentation. But the pulpit stood upon shafts of brilliant gilding, and blue and crimson saints looked down from its sides. There were rows of stalls, with fantastic gilded canopies; and before the unseen altar was a great towering screen, gilt also, and gorgeous with the whole army of martyrs. Overhead from the roof depended antique crystal chandeliers, and on an illuminated reading-desk were the Gospels, bound in embossed silver. The priest had remained outside. There was a profound stillness round me, and my first impression was that I was alone. Presently a faint sound called my attention to the chancel, and I perceived that before the screen were innumerable hanging lamps, and that a silent acolyte was lighting them one by one. I felt a longing to linger; an influence in the stillness detained me. The faint smell of incense, in the strange way peculiar to it, filled the air with a sense of contrition and sorrow and aspiration, of burdens taken away, and of hopes set free to rise again. Are there no burdens borne by the modern world? And if it has them where will it lay them down?

CHAPTER XI

THE ETERNAL COMEDY

That evening I was somewhat late for dinner. Scotty having been absent with me, nothing was prepared for my dressing, and when I came to look for a white tie I was unable to find one anywhere. At last, after a desperate turning over of everything, I came on a collection of them in the strangest place in the world—in the corner of a cupboard, beneath my photographic camera; and near them was another surprise, a number of my silk socks carefully sandwiched between some boxes of photographic plates. When I explained to Mrs. Falkland this mysterious incident, both she and her daughter at once broke into a laugh, exclaiming together, "That must have been Metaphora!"

"And who is Metaphora?" I asked.

"Ah," they said, "she is a specimen of a native Cypriote. She is one of our servants. You are quite sure to have seen her."

Then I too joined in the laugh; for Metaphora, as I now divined, was none other than the curious bouncing creature whose grin and whose movements had already caught my attention. There are some people who are born to excite a smile. I at once seemed to recognise, by a flash of instantaneous insight, that Metaphora was a member of this class; and the accounts I was presently given of her showed me I was not mistaken. Her manners, her English, and her impulses were all equally entertaining. I was gratified to find that, quite unconsciously, I had already aroused in her the liveliest interest in myself, that she had described me to Mrs. Falkland as being a "very pretty gentleman," that she had actually added, "He all the same as Vahly Pasha"—Vahly Pasha being the Governor, the most magnificent human being she knew—and that that evening she had given special attention to my room, "because the poor gentleman would be tired, having been all day on the roses." In Metaphora's language " the roses," I found, meant "roads."

I asked why her idea of making me more comfortable should have shown itself in hiding whatever I was most likely to want. "Ah," said Mrs. Falkland, "she is really almost half-witted. If I tell her to look for a thing she will often start off before she has heard what it is, and then she will come back to me saying, 'I not find it.' I say to her, 'How can you if you will not stay to hear what it is?' and then she answers, not so much to me as to herself, 'Fool Metaphora. She very fool girl. Poor nowti [naughty] Metaphora!'"

The following day I discovered the truth of this description for myself. Looking for some of my letters, which had been placed under a weight on my dressing-table, I found that they all were missing. At last, protruding from a packing-case, which, with an open end against the wall, was supporting a military chest, I espied the tips of foolscap paper and of a torn copy of an old *Evening Standard.* A near examination showed me that all my letters, my envelopes, and the waste paper used for my packing had been rolled up together into a tight ball and stuffed into this hiding-place. I asked Metaphora that evening what had induced her to do this. "Ah," she exclaimed with a long meditative breath; then her eyes shone as if she had solved a problem. "Nowti Metaphora!" she exclaimed. "Me nowti—me very fool girl!" And then putting her head down and giving a sort of caper like a colt, she bounded out of the room and rustled down the stairs like an avalanche.

The servants, Mrs. Falkland told me, were as much amused at her as anybody. One of her peculiarities was a horror of beef, or, as she called it, "bullock meat." It was a favourite practical joke with the Scotch cook, Fraser, to give her beef with some chicken bones stuck amongst the slices, when, thinking the meat chicken, she would swallow it all with gusto, exclaiming, "Good! oh! good! Metaphora, she like that."

Poor Metaphora! Though her mistress thought her half-witted she still was blest with illusions which for her made life beautiful. Her waist was like that of a barrel; her smiling mouth went literally from ear to ear; yet she was firmly persuaded that one of Colonel Falkland's secretaries—a good-looking young Englishman who was quite unconscious of her existence—had fallen in love with her one day when she opened the door for him. She was also persuaded that whilst *he* was in love with *her*, Fraser, the cook of fifty, was equally in love with *him*; and whenever Fraser thwarted any one of her wishes she set it down to the angry jealousy of a rival—or, as she herself expressed it, "Fraser, she jelly me."

She had also her aspirations, which are even better things than illusions, her "devotion to something afar from the sphere of our sorrow." The longing of her life was for a tight-fitting velvet dress like one made for the Princess of Wales as she had seen it in the pages of a fashion-book.

I have lingered over Metaphora not for her sake only, but because from my introduction to her manifold excellences I date my insight into the comedy of Cyprian life. Colonel Falkland, whose sense of humour was keen, by what seemed to me an exceedingly natural transition, went on from Metaphora to something even more naïve and ridiculous; and that is the something which passes for the political life of the island. I had arrived, I believe from a study of *Whitaker's Almanac*, at what Cardinal Newman would call a "notional assent" to the fact that Cyprus possessed an elected legislative council; but I never vividly realised before that evening that this council, to me hitherto merely the shadow of a name, implied all the horrors of a modern popular franchise. At first this discovery terribly shocked and disappointed me. I felt as if suddenly I had fallen out of the clouds to the ground. Good heavens! I thought, and are all these enchanted creatures—these wild shepherds, these mysterious turbaned merchants, who move through an air that seems charged at once with wonder and simplicity —are they really nothing but modern voters in disguise, with beliefs in the people, in the vices of the governing classes, in the popular conscience, and in the mandates of the constituencies? But, as I listened to my host a little longer, I found that my fears were needless. The blight of a constitution which was only inflicted on the islanders—I believe I speak correctly—as a sop to our English Radicals, has fallen on most of them like snow on a summer sea. With the exception of a small minority, drawn principally from the Greek shopkeepers, the glorious privilege of taking part in their own government touches them only as an occasional vague annoyance, which the moment it is over fades away from their consciousness. When the elections take place for the Legislative Council the difficulty is to persuade them to vote at all. The peasants indeed, even during the heat of a contest, are rarely aware of the names of either of the rival candidates. They have been constantly known to ask the returning officer to take their papers and do just what he liked with them. It frequently happens also that the head man of a village is begged by his fellow villagers to go and vote instead of them, and let one piece of meaningless trouble do duty for them all.

No doubt it may be said that though this is true of the majority there is still a minority which understands its political privileges and uses them. There certainly is, and it uses them too with a vengeance, but it uses them in a way so delightfully simple and childish that, instead of infecting the air with the prose of modern Europe, as a corporate body it merely seems to the imagination to be playing the part of Bottom in *A Midsummer Night's Dream*. This minority is composed of perhaps a couple of hundred people, all of them professional Radicals, and the greater part of them Greeks. In almost every respect they are ludicrously faithful imitations of their engaging brethren in the West; only the imitation has this great advantage over the original, that it can hardly be called mischievous and is infinitely more amusing. The professional Cyprian patriot in the effect he produces on the mind is very much like a monkey and a parrot imitating Mr. William O'Brien, the parrot supplying the voice and the monkey supplying the gestures. Almost every device distinctive of the Western agitator is employed by the Cyprian also, from flattery of the people to abuse of the existing order; and his political arguments and exhortations have the same wide range, beginning with lowly exaggeration, then rising to misrepresentation, and finally soaring into the thunders of absolute fiction.

The *Daily News,* or even the *Pall Mall Gazette* itself, might have envied the success with which, shortly before my arrival, the patriots had collected a few hundred women and children, had sent them with a petition from Nicosia to Government House—a pleasant stroll of little more than a mile—and contrived to get the event described in the English journals as a magnificent demonstration composed of ten thousand persons.

I am going here to indulge in a half-minute's digression. To the sober reason few things can seem sillier than the proposal of professional religion-makers to worship idealised humanity; and yet occasionally one can almost detect a meaning in it. For in humanity as a whole there is under the changing surface a persistence, an august immutability, which at odd moments is brought home to us, and is like nothing else in the world. What, for instance, can be more striking than this characteristic, the same always and everywhere: that the men who take the trouble to say they despise rank are men who inwardly grovel and cringe before it, and would wear it themselves, if they could, with the most arrogant vanity? Of this Cypriote patriotism afforded me a very pleasant illustration, and that is the reason why I have thus paused to moralise. During the first years of the British occupation one of the persons whom the Government found most troublesome, was a certain individual who rejoiced in the name of Palaeologus. He was consumed with a passion for the people and for popular freedom. Every *demos*, he held, should manage its own affairs, nor submit its majestic self to any oppression but its own. The Turks, according to him, were indeed vile usurpers, but the English were viler still. Cyprus was a Greek island; it ought to belong to Greece. As for himself, he declared with the eloquence of a Demosthenes he had in his own veins the blood of the Greek emperors, and he appealed to his compatriots to side with him as their natural leader; and under his name as a banner to protest against the oppressions of England. As often happens to agitators, his agitation landed him in a libel, making him amenable to the law, which the oppressors now administered. No sooner had this happened than he triumphantly established the fact that he was not a Cypriote subject, that he was not even a Greek, but that his domicile was at Smyrna, and that his father was a Turkish tailor at Constantinople.

This story suggested to me a very natural question. I asked what the oppressions were of which the English were alleged to be guilty. What a Radical calls oppression is generally some necessary act misrepresented, but still there must generally be something to misrepresent. The most definite something in this case was, so I learned, taxation. It is the only political question which the people at large appreciate, and a reduction of taxes is the cry that most quickly appeals to them. That this should be so is certainly not surprising. They are most of them very poor, and they feel the slightest burden. It would, however, by no means suit the Radicals to make the existing taxes their only or even their principal grievance, for if these taxes were reduced the business of the Radicals would be gone. They are obliged, therefore, to supplement this one definite grievance with a number of others which are at once indefinite and imaginary, which being indefinite cannot be disproved, and which, as they do not exist, cannot be taken away.

Their success in this line is remarkable. I found, from what I was told, that they almost equalled the Irish leaders in what may be called the patriot's vision—that peculiar faculty by which benefits are seen under the aspect of injuries—and also in that faculty, peculiar to the professional patriot also, of frenzied indignation at events that have never happened at all. Thus I asked what the Radicals said about this fact: that the English had conferred on them one blessing at all events, by extirpating the locusts which once ravaged the island.

"Yes," I was answered, "that is a blessing undoubtedly, but the Cyprian patriots have been quite equal to dealing with it. True," they say, "the English have done this. Of course they have; but they ought to have done it sooner. Instead of thanking them for what they have done we have every cause to complain of them for taking so long in doing it, and, after all, who has paid for it? We have! Greece would have done the same thing, but have done it years ago; and Greece would have borne half, if not all, the expense of it."

This is good. Could a Mr. O'Brien, a Mr. Dillon, or a Mr. Davitt have done better? It is, however, outdone by the following burning sentence, with which one of the Cyprian patriots strove to arouse his countrymen: "Under the Turks," he said, "you were merely poor people. Under the English you are helots!" All the logic of modern agitation breathes in those few syllables, which would have absolutely no connection with facts whatever if they did not happen to contain a vague inversion of them.

Let me, however, do the patriots justice. If they are not very honest in the matter of means they are perfectly sincere so far as regards their ends. They do, no doubt, desire the substitution of Greek rule for English, for the definite and intelligible, if not well-founded, reason that they see in it an unlimited prospect of Government places for themselves. It would be cynical also, and perhaps even disingenuous, with the knowledge which I happen to possess, to deny that in some cases their political animosity towards ourselves may be due to feelings of a warmer and less calculating kind. In one case at least this was so. One patriot's wrath—I tell this for the honour of patriotism—was almost epic and heroic in its origin. The hero was a man renowned for his probity, especially for the severity of what would be called his moral character; and entering one night a certain house in Nicosia, the fame of which was hardly equal to his own, he was met at the door by a British soldier emerging, who, brimming over with zeal for the honour of England, hit him in the eye out of a sense of pure superiority, exclaiming as he did so, "You b——y Greek take that!" The Greek's character was far too spotless to enable him to explain his grievance against the soldier, so he avenged his outraged dignity by opposing the British Government.

So much moral modesty will be thought doubly remarkable when the surrounding state of society and of opinion is considered. Though the temples of Aphrodite are overthrown and her altars flameless, though shy professors grub in the dust of her scandalous courts and her very name is appropriate to alien Christian uses, the influence of the goddess is still immortal in the air, and the Bishop of———, when I was in the island, was about, with a curious appropriateness, to figure as the co-respondent in a divorce case. That, no doubt, was a scandal, but a mild scandal only. Another prelate, not very long ago, was said to have a child in every village of his diocese. Another was thought a model of decorum and discipline because he asked leave, instead of taking it, to keep a couple of mistresses; and the present Archbishop of Nicosia who is really a respectable man, is regarded as an absolute saint because no such romances are connected with him.

The behaviour of the Turks is in many ways superior to that of the Greeks; but with regard to the point to which we are now alluding I am not quite sure that their superiority is very decided. The following story makes me feel doubtful. During the early years of the British occupation it fell, Colonel Falkland told me, to the lot of a friend of his to superintend the collection of taxes in certain parts of the island. One day the person in question had been up betimes in the morning, and having visited already two Turkish villages, arrived about noon at a third. Here he was given breakfast at the house of the principal inhabitant, and while the meal was in progress an official report was brought to him of the taxes that still were owing there. Half the people, it seemed, had that year paid nothing. He asked why. He was told that the people were poor. “Who,” he asked, “are the richest?” The names of the richest were read to him. “Have these men paid?” he asked. The answer was, “No, not one of them.” “Well,” he said to his subordinate, “we will begin with them. Make them pay first, and we will see what we will do afterwards.” His host, who was foremost amongst those thus alluded to, heard this unwelcome order, but it did not diminish his courtesy. On the contrary, knowing that his guest would by this time be tired, he closed the shutters of the room for him and begged him to refresh himself with a siesta. The guest gladly stretched himself out on a low divan, and before long sleep was stealing over him. Suddenly a slight noise startled him. He opened his eyes, and soon, in spite of the darkness, he became conscious that some human figure was present. He saw at last that it was a female. He concluded that she was there by mistake, and he gave a slight cough as a hint that the room was occupied. Instead of retiring, however, the apparition glided towards him, stood at the side of the divan, and in silence bent slightly over him. He raised himself on his elbow. As he did so the figure let fall her yashmak and disclosed to his gaze a beautiful Turkish girl, who in another moment he saw was his host’s daughter. He stared at her, speechless with astonishment. In answer she fixed her eyes on him, and he read a meaning in them—no matter what it was—which no well-conducted father, whether Christian or Turk, would approve of. For a second or two he was almost stupefied; then, as if by inspiration, a sense of the truth came to him. He suddenly sprang up, he threw the doors open, and there outside were all the chief Turks of the village, waiting for a sign from the girl that the collector of taxes had committed himself. Had the plot succeeded, as Colonel Falkland observed, needless to say that the taxes of those Turks would have been light.

This kind of discourse carried us far into the evening, and a few days later the thread of it, which was now broken by bed-time, was taken up, not by Colonel Falkland, but by Mr. Matthews, who, true to his word, went again with me to look for the marble. As to the marble, the result of our researches was disappointing, and I came to the conclusion that it was worth no further trouble; but on the way back such a trifle as the collapse of my whole practical expectations was quite put out of my mind by the series of stories that were told me. I can only repeat—indeed I can only recollect—a few, for even the best of stories often fade from the memory almost as quickly as happiness fades from life. It is true that in the *motif* of them there was a certain amount of sameness; but so there is in most of Boccaccio’s tales and in every French novel that reaches a tenth edition. In fact what a breach of the seventh commandment is to these, some attempt at evading the taxes was to the others.

Mr. Matthews, being connected with the assessment of taxes himself, was naturally on familiar ground. Two of his principal heroes were prelates. At the beginning of the British occupation the Archbishop of Nicosia came to the authorities and inquired with perfect gravity if it really were possible that he would be expected to pay his taxes. The answer, of course, was “Yes.” “Very well,” said the Archbishop, in a tone of obstinate meekness, “then you expect something of me that I am quite unable to do.” Asked what he meant, he replied "I mean simply this: that my lands are assessed at four times their actual value." "Indeed," said the authorities. "If that is the case we will have your lands revalued. But we have gone by the assessment left us by the late Government, to which it appears you have never taken exception. Can you kindly explain this to us?" "Heh?" said the Archbishop; "but that is explained easily." The Turks, it appears, had assessed him at this really exorbitant figure, with his own consent, but on this distinct understanding: he was never to pay a penny. Then, when any of the Greek peasantry grumbled, the officials would be able to say, "Look at your good Archbishop: what are your burdens to his? And yet he never makes a murmur."

If the Government, however, has trouble in getting the taxes out of the bishops, the bishops in their turn have trouble in getting their dues out of their flocks. "Ah," said one of them one day to Mr. Matthews, "dreadful, dreadful people in the village of Alitsópalo! They will pay me nothing! As soon as ever my collector goes to them all the Christians at once pretend to be Turks. The first cottage he enters, the owner, when asked his name, declares that he is Mohammed and his wife over there is Fatima; whilst the collector knows, though at the moment he may not be able to prove it, that this one is really George and the other is really Anna. Ah!" said the bishop, "dreadful, dreadful people!"

But this piece of ingenuity is crude and simple when compared with others which at times are resorted to for a similar purpose. In one town Mr. Matthews found that the amount of unpaid taxes was exceptionally and inexplicably large; and of these arrears he was told that the larger part was irrecoverable, and that he need not therefore trouble his head about them. The mystery was inquired into, and the names of the defaulters were produced. Then came to light this singular fact: all these men were aliens, and therefore were exempt from taxation. How, then did it happen that they had been assessed at all? The answer was this: a certain gross sum was due from the town to the Government, and the townspeople, having engaged to pay this, were allowed to distribute the burden amongst themselves as they pleased. The lion's share had accordingly been at once laid on the aliens, who readily fell in with a plan from which they could not possibly suffer; and in this pleasant way the liabilities of the natives had been halved.

Another town distinguished itself as follows. The inhabitants were desired by the Government to send in their own valuation of the house property that was to be taxed. A statement was accordingly presented duly to the commissioner. He looked at the total with astonishment. It was only £3000. He desired that the assessors should be sent for; and when they came he asked them if they were satisfied that their valuation was really correct. They said, "We certainly are. If it errs at all it errs by being a little too high." "Well," said the commissioner, "the matter is of some importance. May I ask if you are prepared to sign a paper to this effect?" The assessors drew themselves up with an air of virtuous hauteur. "Sir," they replied, "on serious occasions like the present, when we deliberately say a thing, we are naturally ready to sign it." "Then in that case," said the commissioner quietly, again casting his eye over the list of figures before him, "I shall, under powers given me by the Government, take over from you, for the purpose of public improvements, a hundred of these houses; and I will do so at your own valuation, which you cannot complain of, as you have just told me that it is high rather than otherwise. Here is the paper, gentlemen. Have the goodness to sign it." The assessors started. For a moment they were utterly silent. Then came a shuffling of feet, an interlude of hemming and hawing, and then stuttered excuses. "Well," said the commissioner blandly, "if you are not quite sure about the matter take a day to think it over. Come back to-morrow, and then you shall tell me the sum that will really satisfy you." The assessment by next day had risen from £3000 to £7000.

Some readers, perhaps, may think these anecdotes trivial. My own view is that they throw a great deal more light on that least trivial of subjects, the corporate character of the people, than volumes of scientific speculation on the future of man and of democracy. At all events here is one anecdote more, and it certainly can be called trivial by nobody. It is, indeed, hardly an anecdote; it is rather a piece of important constitutional history, which shows how democracy in Cyprus was within an inch of destruction, and how it saved itself.

The policy of the Cyprian patriots has been, from the beginning of the chapter, at once consistent and simple. It has been to oppose every scheme or suggestion, no matter what, that originated with the British authorities. The authorities for a long time had borne this treatment with patience, when a measure was laid by them before the Council which was not only so obviously but also so urgently necessary that no rational man could have two opinions about it. When, therefore, the patriots, utterly undaunted, proceeded to oppose it, just as they had opposed the others, the Governor's patience fairly gave way at last, and he told them plainly that if this sort of thing continued he should be obliged to appeal to her Majesty to reconsider the constitution. The patriots were staggered; they could hardly believe their ears. They were like dreaming somnambulists, marching to imaginary conquests, who had been suddenly wakened by coming into collision with a wall. To reconsider the constitution they knew could mean only to abolish it. They saw, therefore, that in this case there was nothing for them to do but to drop their opposition with as good a grace as possible. But how was this to be done with any grace at all? That was the question. They could not make themselves ridiculous in the eyes of their chief supporters by voting for a measure which they had been calling abominable yesterday. They accordingly hit at last on the following plan. When the day came on which the fate of the measure was to be decided, a number of those who opposed it were to keep away from the Council, just sufficient to allow of its being carried by a majority of one, the rest of the party declaiming against it as formerly. Everything was settled; but on the morning of the eventful day the patriots discovered that somehow they were still one too many. It was necessary, therefore, that one more of them should absent himself. Their choice fell on a gentleman whose name, if I recollect rightly, was Pierides, and he was told to suggest some pretext by which his absence might be accounted for. "Come," they said, "you can easily pretend that you are ill." "No, no," he said; "that will never satisfy my supporters. I live in Nicosia and I am known to be in robust health." "I have it," said some one. "Urgent business summons you, and in half an hour's time you must be on your way to Larnaca." This suggestion met with universal approval, Mr. Pierides himself being as well satisfied with it as anybody. But presently recollecting himself, "Bah, my friends!" he exclaimed, "you have forgotten one thing; you have forgotten the expense of travelling there and back. The double fare by the diligence will come to full five shillings. Do you expect me to pay that out of my own private pocket? Never. I go for the sake of my party, and my party must pay it for me." At this the other patriots looked extremely blank. "Very well," said Mr. Pierides calmly, "if you will not pay for me I remain, and my country must take the consequences." Awed by so much firmness, the others at last gave in. Mr. Pierides was given the sum required. He went for the day to Larnaca. In his absence the measure was carried; and he thus stands alone in the annals of the popular cause as a hero who engaged to save, and who did save, a democracy, for no other reward than the payment of his own expenses.

Stories tale a colouring from the scenes amongst which one hears them. These I heard as, for a second time at twilight, we were driving home from the spurs of Pentedactylon and were speeding across the plain towards the walls and minarets of Nicosia. The last time I had done this I had been listening to the romance of the past. Now, with equal entertainment, I had been listening to the comedy of the present; and this, though many of its details were modern and prosaic enough, and indeed called to mind the paragraphs of our own newspapers, was yet for the most part so naïve and so whimsical that, under the influence of surrounding associations, it seemed to become insensibly part of the romance itself. If it suggested our newspapers it suggested them only as a certain bank of clouds, which came floating over the mountains, suggested to my eye a phalanx of Irish members. For a moment I thought I saw the features of Dr. Tanner, about to provoke the censure of some unseen Speaker in the firmament; but just as he seemed on the point of calling the stars "liars" the noiseless air transformed him into a dignified, silent Turk, whilst the body of his supporters, all prepared to cheer him, softly melted together into a single monstrous griffin. Then up from behind the mountains, closely following after them, came a giraffe and a camel, with necks as tall as steeples and heads like cotton-wool, dipped in the light of evening; and the whole aërial medley slowly floated and vanished into the darkening depths of the sky, at the edge of which the sunset was burning. And thus the politicians of contemporary Cyprus, instead of breaking the charm or disturbing the associations of their ancient Oriental island, merely added to them a new element of unreality. Their antics and tricks seemed to me, as I heard of them, to harmonise completely with the dream-like evening that then surrounded me. I remember its aspect still. The dome of the sky above was a transparent Prussian blue; lower down in the east it was clear like alabaster. One by one the golden points of the stars began to show themselves suddenly, as if they were being lighted. In the west the sunset at first was a brilliant orange; then this darkened into a deep stain of crimson, and against it black from the plain rose clusters of far-off palm trees.

CHAPTER XII

THE ETERNAL TRAGEDY

I was sorry to disturb the placidity of my life at Nicosia by even a thought of leaving it; but, as there were other places which I was fully determined to visit, I had already settled with myself what these places should be. Three of them, so I found, lay not very far apart—the town and castle of Kyrenia, the mountain castle of St. Hilarion, and the mediaeval monastery of Bella Pais, which report said was wonderful. Accordingly, in the course of the next few days, Colonel Falkland, to whom I explained my wishes, procured for me an invitation to stay with one of the district judges, Mr. St. John, who lived within easy distance of all the three places I have mentioned. Mr. St. John's official duties would be shortly calling him from home, so he begged that, if I came, I would come as soon as possible. I had not expected quite so much hurry in the matter; but, as hurry was necessary, it was arranged by an exchange of telegrams that I should go to him as soon as I could get a carriage to take me.

Meanwhile, in the single day that intervened, I underwent an experience entirely new and unexpected. I came down to breakfast, idly thinking over the stories which I have been just confiding to the reader. Little did I know, whilst I was smiling at the comedy of the island, that I was going in an hour or two to be introduced to its tragedy.

There was an old building in Nicosia which had once been a caravanserai, and which some one told me, the Turks had used as a prison. I had several times been struck by its picturesque appearance, by its external arcades, by its deep and shadowy gate, and by its gray mouldering walls. Mrs. Falkland this morning greeted me with the pleasant intelligence that a certain Captain O'Flanagan, who occupied some post of authority, had promised to come at eleven o'clock to fetch us and show us over it, as it still was Government property. The Captain arrived duly—a tall, handsome Irishman, buoyant and almost bounding with the proverbial spirits of his nation. I was somehow disappointed to learn from this sprightly gentleman that the building was a prison still, and that a body of police were quartered in it. The rascality of the natives, so far as I had heard of them, was, it is true, almost as idyllic as innocence; so I had no fear of being introduced to an Oriental Newgate: but the sight of a sergeant and three or four subordinates, whom we found standing under the arch to receive us, quite dispelled my prospect of rambling over the precincts as I pleased. There was a good deal of military saluting, and then an unlocking of gates, and we passed into an open court, even more picturesque than I had anticipated. It was surrounded by two stories of cloisters, with the usual pointed arches, and in the middle was a miniature mosque with a cupola. The upper cloisters were reached by several graceful staircases; against the wall of the mosque was a fountain, gray with age; and quaint stone shoots for discharging the rain water protruded all round from the top of the walls like cannon. The ground-floor on one side was occupied by vaulted stables opening into the external arcades, which had originally caught my attention.

The imagination peopled the place with antique Oriental travellers; but I had soon seen enough of it, and I thought we were all departing when I found that, besides the prison, we were going to be shown the prisoners. I had myself no wish whatever to see them, but the others were more curious; and Captain O'Flanagan, whose hilarity rose with the occasion, seemed as anxious to show them to us as if they were pet monkeys.

Accordingly a gate was unlocked at the foot of one of the staircases, and we mounted to the upper cloisters. I had expected to find a few poor creatures in corners, far apart from each other and looking more like hermits than prisoners. To my astonishment the cloisters, from end to end, were crowded. Rows and groups of human beings, with the warm sunlight falling on them, were standing or sitting, engaged in various occupations. Some were boot-making, some were rope-making, some were sewing soldiers' trousers. They were of all ages, from the age of gray hairs to boyhood; and the chief effect they produced on me, as I watched them quietly at their work, was wonder that such harmless-looking people should be in prison at all.

I lost no time in inquiring what were their offenses. As to four men and two youths in succession, I received the same answer, "Sheep-stealing." That was just as it should be. It was a pastoral and picturesque offense; and I was glad to think that they were expiating here in the sunlight instead of in their cells, whose dark, grated apertures were gaping just behind them like the cages of wild animals.

We had advanced some way, and I had been standing still for a moment to watch a wistful-eyed boy—a little fellow of fourteen—who was working diligently with a sewing-machine, when, turning to continue our progress, I saw something move in the gloom of the cell close to me. I looked in through the bars; but in a second I withdrew my eyes, for they had encountered those of a miserable human being. I called to Captain O'Flanagan, who was in the middle of an Irish witticism, as, with another of our party, he was peering into the cell adjoining, and asked him of what the man I had just seen was guilty. He consulted a scrap of paper posted against the wall with the prisoner's name and offence on it, and placidly said, "Murder." We passed on, and I now began to realise that half of these cells, which I had thought empty, were tenanted; and we were constantly invited to pause before this one or that one, exactly as if we were being taken round a menagerie. Some of the forms within looked hardened and desperate enough, and there was a certain grim satisfaction in seeing that the iron had closed on them; but for the most part it seemed to me, as I glanced reluctantly into the shadow, that their aspect betokened a humble, lamentable resignation, as if some weight had fallen on them, they knew not how nor whence, and they could only bear it with the amazement of dumb animals. At these poor creatures I was unable to look steadily. One instinctively turned away from them with the reverence due to sorrow. And yet from time to time I could not help inquiring what this man or what that man had done to bring him here. I could hardly believe my ears when my questions, one after the other, with a sinister sameness, met with the answer, "Murder." Here and there was somebody who had only robbed with violence; in one cell was a forger, and in another was a veteran pirate; but murder seemed to preponderate over every other crime. I expressed my surprise at this to the sergeant, an intelligent Englishman. He answered, shrugging his shoulders, "I saw you, sir, stop just now to look at a little boy. That's one of our specimens! He's here for murder too!" "That boy!" I exclaimed. "I suppose it was an accident that took place in a quarrel?" "Not a bit of it," said the sergeant. "He and a friend of his, of the same age as himself, had some grudge against another boy. They waited for days and days, till that boy was alone, and they strangled him with a couple of boot-laces, which they had knitted together for the purpose." As I listened to all this, whilst we slowly made our progress, all the air seemed to grow sickly round me, and to come to my nostrils tainted with blood and sorrow. The prisoners at work in the sunlight were most of them tolerable objects; but these black cells, with the guilty eyes within, which one felt, without looking at them, were gleaming at one out of the shadow—the sense that these were close to us became soon intolerably painful. I drew a long breath when I found myself once again in the street; and I was glad to learn, since it seemed we were to make a morning of it, that the rest of our time was to be given up to the Konak.

As I passed again through its silent vaulted guard-rooms, as I again looked at the beauty of the crumbling window over them, and caught through a broken arch a breath of the hiding violets, I was conscious of an effect like that felt by the nerves when something cool is laid on a head that is physically aching. I mentioned to Captain O'Flanagan that I had seen the place before. "Ah!" he said, "but you couldn't have seen half of it." I at once found that this was true; for whilst he was in the act of speaking we were being introduced to a scene that was certainly quite new to me. It was a small, irregular yard, surrounded by mean outhouses, much like the yard of a dirty farm-house in England. There was a pump in the middle of it; on the ground were some earthenware basins; here and there was a heap of kitchen refuse, and our noses were soon saluted by an odour of warm cooking. At the sound of our voices a door presently opened, and a woman emerged, whose proportions were those of a female Falstaff. With a rolling gait she advanced a few paces towards us, and then, perceiving Captain O'Flanagan and the sergeant, she turned round and preceded us into a kind of kitchen. Through this we passed into a whitewashed passage; the female Falstaff opened a door at the end of it, and we found ourselves in a bare room, with windows high up in the walls, confronted by a party of fourteen or fifteen women. I asked some one near me what these women were doing here. "Don't you know?" was the answer. "They are some of the female prisoners."

The horrors of the day, then, were not ended yet. We had left one prison merely to enter another. I faced the situation, however, and examined the faces before me. A part were young, but the larger part seemed old—wrinkled, and dejected, and suggesting nothing but compassion—all but one; amongst them was one exception. This was the face of a hideous, blear-eyed crone, who was almost bent double, and, with hands pressed against her stomach, peered up at us, showing her red eyelids, with an expression of cringing wickedness. Never in my life had I seen a face at once so miserable and so evil. "And what," I asked, "has she done?" I anticipated the answer. It was the old story, "Murder." But there was more to follow. This old woman, I learned, had caused the death, not of her victim only, but of two other men besides. She had hired three to assist her in her deliberate deed, and two of them had been hanged, whilst the sentence of the third had been commuted. The old woman's sentence had been commuted also—perhaps in consideration of her great age and feebleness—but if justice in this case demanded the extreme penalty the debt had been paid practically not once, but many times. At the beginning of her imprisonment the old woman had a fever; and in her delirious sleep she was continually waking up, clutching her wizened throat, and imagining that the rope was round it. Turning away from her, I saw amongst the medley of criminal faces, a little creature looking at us with soft coal-black eyes. This was a baby that had been lately born in the prison. It lay in its mother's arms, surrounded by squalor, and by calamity; but already its small nails had been made pink with henna, and a rude care had darkened it under its eyes with kohol. Were all the seeds of the full-grown evil near it, sleeping, ready to sprout in this half-conscious seedling?

There was one experience more, and the nightmare of the morning was ended. From this prison of criminals we were taken to an adjoining building; and there, in a double row of sunless, silent cells, we were shown the lunatics. There were not many of them. One and all they were old. Each was alone, and if they had not moved occasionally they might almost have passed for parts of the dilapidated walls confining them. I could not learn anything about the past lives of any of them, but, judging from their battered aspect, all of them must have long been familiar with some form of misfortune. If this were the case, for one thing they were to be congratulated on their present condition; for madness had taught them what sanity could not teach them—to smile.

At luncheon Colonel Falkland questioned me as to what I had seen. I was glad to thrust away from me the oppressive feelings that had been caused by it, and get about one or two points a little practical information. I remarked on the apathy with which the prisoners, those even in the cells, seemed to bear their confinement. "Yes," said Colonel Falkland, "and some of them—though not all—go to the gallows with as little apparent feeling. As for the mere confinement, so long as it is not solitary, I doubt if they mind that. They like doing nothing, and they are able to talk with their companions. Solitude, without tobacco, is the thing that they really dread. I suppose," he added, "that of the prisoners you saw to-day, not more than one or two, even if any, were solitary?" That was true; and I asked why, if such was their feeling, the worst of them were not given the only punishment they could appreciate. Colonel Falkland said that this was at present impracticable, for the simple reason that the prison did not admit of it. Packed as the prisoners were, even now there was hardly room for them, and the Government had not a penny with which to enlarge the building. "But why," I asked, "need they all be sent to Nicosia? Are there no old prisons in the other parts of the island? And does Cyprus, with its handful of 160,000 inhabitants, really contribute the whole throng I have been looking at?" "Without a doubt," said Colonel Falkland, "there are other prisons in Cyprus—a prison in every district; but each of these is just as crowded as this. You ask if all the prisoners you have seen come from Cyprus. Every one of them comes from the single district of Nicosia."

Ever since that morning a veil had been drawn across the sun for me; and now, as I listened, the day grew darker still. One of my Cyprian dreams—of my happy dreams—had been broken: and it was a dream which till today I had always taken for a reality. I had imagined that, in spite of their petty, bizarre rascalities, these islanders knew little of the more monstrous horrors of life. I had taken pleasure in noticing the honest faces of the peasantry, and their frank smiles, when one exchanged greetings with them on the road. I had heard much of their readiness to offer hospitality or help to strangers, and of the firm but gentle pride with which they always refused any payment for it. I now learned that in this island of Cyprus there was more crime, in proportion to the number of its inhabitants, than in any other known country in the world.

I asked from what classes the criminals mostly came, in especial the murderers, and how the murders arose. From what I was told I derived a little comfort. In the towns the Turkish murders nearly always originate in some ordinary fit of sombre but sudden passion, and the Greek murders in some half-drunken brawl. A number of these last have taken place at weddings. Wine has flowed; quarreling has risen out of laughter; knives have flashed, and in a second or two one knife has been red. In the country districts the cause has generally some connection with sheep-stealing, or disputes about boundaries and water rights, or matters equally simple. I saw, however, that this explained a part of the case only. Blood was shed in ways that left darker stains than these. One father whose son had been sent to prison for stealing considered that the lad had brought disgrace on his family, and deliberately murdered him on the day he was set free. I had already seen a boy and an old woman whose crimes had been as cold-blooded and premeditated as crimes could be; and now Colonel Falkland told me that at this moment at Kyrenia three men were under sentence of death for a murder of which the only motive was robbery, and which had been planned for days and had been resolved on for weeks beforehand.

And yet, even among these dark clouds, a touch of whimsical simplicity stole like a faint thread of light, and relieved my mind by at last justifying a laugh. One of the three men whom I have just mentioned fled, after the murder, to the hut of a lonely shepherd, and begged to be kept there in hiding. The shepherd, who had only a slight acquaintance with him, asked why he wished to be hidden. On this the murderer, more like a child than a man, explained everything in the most naïve manner possible. The shepherd looked grave. He said that this was a serious matter, and that under the circumstances his protection would have to be paid for. The murderer replied that the booty had not yet been divided. "I have no money," he said, "but save me, and I will steal a sheep for you.

With this anecdote Colonel Falkland left me. He went to his office, and I sat in the garden alone, feeling as if the burden of life, which I thought I had left in England, had again laid its hands on me, like a bailiff on an absconding debtor. This mere dejection, however, which was after all useless, in time gave way to reflections that were more profitable. I thought of our modern Radicals, of our sentimental believers in the natural goodness of man, and of what a lesson these people might learn from Cyprus. Here were no wicked plutocrats, no hereditary aristocracy. The merchant princes and the nobles of the Middle Ages had gone. They had not left even the memory of their names behind, and modern times had produced no class to replace them. The larger part of the population owned the larger part of the soil. They worked by themselves and for themselves. They had no example except their own to corrupt them, and no oppression except that of the necessary tax-gatherer. They lived, in fact, under the Radical's ideal conditions; and yet crimes, which included crimes of the most brutal and degraded character, occurred amongst them with a frequency not to be matched in any country of aristocratic and capitalistic Europe. Surely this in itself is enough to show how false, or at best how insufficient, is the theory, that the wickedness of the many is caused by the artificial oppressions of the few.

If a man wishes to ensure the bad opinion of others, his best course probably is to be honest about himself. At the risk of achieving this result, though I do not profess to be anxious for it, I am going to indulge in a piece of honesty here. I am going to confess that the foregoing obvious moral, being at the expense of people with whom I specially disagree, if it did not exactly reconcile me to the miserable facts that suggested it, at least made me look at them in a less lugubrious light. In the middle of this mood a slight sound disturbed me. I looked round, and there—with her feet on a bed of violets—was poor Metaphora, blowing her nose in her petticoat.

Poor Metaphora! She seemed to reconcile me to everything. She again supplied us at dinner with unfailing amusement, and afterwards Colonel Falkland, when we were smoking our cigarettes together, asked me if I ever had heard this strange creature's history. I had not, and so he told it to me. "Metaphora was once in prison," he said. "Metaphora was tried for murder. Yes," he went on, "I can see what I say surprises you. What happened was this. Some years ago, just before we came here, she—she was hardly fifteen—was seduced by a Turkish official. She had twins, and both of the twins were murdered. She was accused of the crime and tried for it, but medical evidence showed her to have been at the time so weak that she could not have committed it—it was a physical impossibility. The real criminal was most probably her mother. Anyhow, the event for the time—and I am sure it is no wonder—quite deranged the poor girl's faculties, and to this day she has never quite recovered them. So the other night," he added, "when Mrs. Falkland called her half-witted, what she said had more truth in it than perhaps at the time you thought."

This was enough, and more than enough, to make the morbid clouds of dejection, which had only partially lifted, once more descend on me. "And so," I said to myself, "this delightful city of Nicosia—this city of dreams and peace—is haunted by all the plagues and all the sorrows of London, and the lightest and silliest laughter to which one goes for refuge has its hidden roots in an unnatural pool of blood." As I went to bed, and for some hours tried vainly to sleep, the air seemed heavy and oppressive as if charged with thunder, and I was pleased to think that on the following day I was going to escape to new, even if not very distant, scenes.

CHAPTER XIX
"VELUT UMBRA"

That evening at dinner I made a very pleasant acquaintance in the person of Mr. Guillaume, a distinguished naturalist and traveller. He had contrived to find in Varoshia bedrooms for himself and his servant, but so far as meals went he was the guest of Captain Scott. Excepting myself he was the only stranger in Cyprus who was thus at a loose end, as it were, and not on some professional duty. What castles and ruins were to me birds and beasts were to him; but he had no objections to taking a castle by the way, so when I told him what were my next day's plans he offered me his companionship, which I very gladly accepted.

My next day's plans were these: I have already mentioned that I had heard of another castle, which I had wished to see during my visit to Captain Scott. The name of this castle was Aya Napa, and Mr. Matthews had described it to me as the best specimen he knew of a country seat of a mediaeval Cyprian noble, in which the feudal fortress had softened into an Oriental pleasure-house. Its original lords, in common with the whole Western *noblesse*, had long since wholly disappeared out of the island. Since then the building had been a monastery; at the present moment it was a farm; and though some parts of it were gone, much of it was in good preservation. Such was the information I was able to give to Mr. Guillaume when, at the hour appointed, our mules—we were to ride on mules—assembled at Captain Scott's door, and thrilled the street with excitement. We had two muleteers, two servants, and a *zaptieh*, or mounted *gendarme*, whom Captain Scott sent with us. I forget why or how it was supposed he might be of use to us, but he at all events gave our cavalcade such an air of dignity that the street boys cheered us as we started as if we had been a coach and four.

Our road lay over a perfectly flat country, some of which was grassy like an English common, some ploughed like fields in Essex or Lincolnshire, and some a waste covered with bog-myrtle and boulders. The first special feature that caught my eye in the landscape was the presence of several churches, evidently long abandoned, standing on the plain amidst the plough-land, with no habitation near them. There were three of them in a single field, as lonely as three crows. I took them to be one of the many indications remaining, of how densely the country in former times was populated. By and by we passed by a large lake—large at least in proportion to anything I expected to come across.

It was several miles in length. A fringe of reeds was round it, and water birds flew and flitted over its smooth surface. Just beyond this we passed through a mud-built village, called Paralimni, or in plain English Lakeside. One thing made it peculiar: it was a village of dyers and the only dye used was black, or an inky purple. We saw the liquid simmering in smoky caldrons at cottage doors, over fires on the bare ground; blue-black washings meandered in streams along the gutters, and dyed material hung drying over garden walls and over currant bushes. After this we met nothing but open country, on which, like breath on a glass, spring was breathing a faint mist of greenness.

The last two miles of our ride were down a gentle stone-strewn slope, with the sea in front of us, fleeted by low gray rocks. At the lower edge of the slope, between it and the sea, was a straggling village, built on a level belt of land, and at one end of it was a grove of sycamore-figs and olives. The *zaptieh*, who preceded us, trotted on towards this, and presently disappeared behind a ridge of rocks and a cottage. We followed in his track, and as soon as we had surmounted the ridge the castle of Aya Napa, before completely invisible, was straight in front of us, not thirty yards away.

It was a square building, surrounding a courtyard. It had been originally two stories in height, but the second story remained over the entrance only. It was pierced externally on the ground-floor with small square-headed windows about eighteen inches in width, and also with a line of loop-holes. The upper windows were of a very different character, the two that remained having graceful pointed arches, and their height and width being nine feet by five. The entrance was much like the entrance of an ordinary mediaeval castle—a vaulted passage fronted by a ponderous archway, which was still ornamented with the arms of its original owner. Within the scene was curious. In the middle of the court, which was shady and green with orange trees, was a marble fountain, surrounded by Gothic arches and roofed over with a low stone cupola. Round two of the four sides ran cloisters with similar arches, singularly slender and graceful, enriched with mouldings and built of carefully hewn stones. On a third side were the stables, and on the fourth were two chapels. Of these chapels one was still in use, and I discovered on entering it a very singular thing. On this side of the castle was a low bank of rock, which formed a wall of some fifteen feet in height: against this rock the chapel of which I speak was built; and the chancel was formed, not out of masonry, but out of a crooked cave, which averted itself from the nave at an angle. Over both of the chapels there had once been an upper story, the floor of which must have been level with the ground outside. The fragment of the upper story which still remained over the entrance contained three rooms, reached by an external staircase. They were whitewashed and weather-tight, but had no noticeable feature—at least they had not till we ate our luncheon in one of them and they thus became part of a very agreeable memory. Beneath these rooms was a vaulted kitchen, again beneath this a place that was once a cellar; and close by, in the wall, was a shadowy conduit, bubbling and echoing with the noise of unseen waters, which discharged themselves into a trough of greenish marble, through the quaintest spout in the world—the nose of a marble pig. The boughs of the trees, as I remained looking at this object, made on the wall a wickerwork of light and shadow, and flickering in it was standing a group of girls with hideous faces, but unconsciously draped like statues, and filling pitchers that belonged to the Heroic Ages of Greece.

The rooms on the ground-floor I examined one by one. They were dark and heavily vaulted; they were now used for farming purposes. In one were some broken ploughs; in one was an old olive press; and in one I came on a milk-white Corinthian capital, with a small cavity about the size of a basin on the top of it, in which some one had just been washing the lid of a tin saucepan.

Thus making my rounds, I discovered a back gateway, on the opposite side of the court to that on which we entered. I passed through this, and found myself in the grove of trees, the rich greenness of which I had admired already from a distance. The scene was beautiful. Under the boughs the grass was the tenderest emerald; and a furlong beyond it, between the dark stems, shone the fresh levels of the sea. Presently I was conscious of a sound like the splashing of a small stream; and I saw that, just under the shadow of the castle wall, was a cistern or artificial pond, full of green reflections—reflections troubled at one spot only, where issuing from one of the walls a thread of water fell into it. As Moses brought water out of the rocks in Arabia, so one might fancy that water brought trees out of the rocks in Cyprus. By the side of this cistern stood a colossal sycamore-fig, almost a grove in itself, and neighboured by several others. As I rode away from the place, I noticed that for miles over the plain there came to the castle from somewhere a now broken aqueduct; and it cannot be doubted that when in this way the supply of water was doubled, the sycamore-figs and the olives grew over a wider area, and embowered the castle in green and silvery shadow.

It was a pleasant place to think about—this secluded feudal dwelling, with all its piquant incongruities and all its obscure associations. The count or baron, its owner, with the name of some Western family—we know how in the feudal ages his counterparts in the West lived. We know what gloom, we know what roughness of life, was found within the walls of even the largest and most important castles. But he, the Cyprian lord, in an air scented with orange-blossom, was moving luxuriously in the cool of his calm arcades, which were bright with Eastern carpets, sweet with Eastern perfumes, vivid with fountains—let the reader complete the picture. It filled and amused my mind for half of my ride back; and was only obliterated by the fact that for the last five miles of the journey it was dusk and then was dark, and I had to look where I was going.

Guillemard and Hogarth 1883

F. H. H. Guillemard and D. G. Hogarth were intrigued during their travels in Cyprus by large stone monuments of uncertain origin. They were able to investigate a number of them in the Paphos district and reported of their findings in 1883, which they published in April 14, 1888 as an article "Monoliths in the Island of Cyprus" in *The Athenaeum*, No. 3155. Guillemard wrote the major part of the article, and Hogarth appended the note at the end. Hogarth's book *Devia Cypria* concerning the archaeology of Cyprus in the late 19th century is widely available and not included in this volume.

The discovery of a number of hitherto unknown monoliths, which Mr. D. G. Hogarth and myself were fortunate enough to make before the excavations at Old Paphos had begun, is perhaps a fact of sufficient interest for publication.

Learning from Mr. Michell, Commissioner for the Limassol district, that a "perforated stone," and apparently extensive ruins, existed at a place called Anoyira, we proceeded thither on the 12th of January. The village is situated on the southern slopes of the Troödos range, about 1,800 ft. above the sea, and is close to the deep, abrupt valley of the Kostithes river. Near it we found pottery-strewn ground, marking the site of what must have been a town of some size. None of this pottery was figured, almost all of it was coarse, and we found no fragment that might not have been Roman. Opposite the west end of a ruined Byzantine church, about half a mile from the village, was the stone of which Mr. Michell had spoken—a well-hewn monolith of hard limestone rock, perforated by a hole 8 in. wide and 2 ft. 8 in. high. The stone stands 8 ft. out of the ground, is 3 ft. 2 in. broad, and is slightly rounded at the top. No one having seen the two stones at Kuklia figured in Di Cesnola's book could doubt that it was made by the same people and for this same purpose.

Inquiry of the villagers elicited the fact that there were other stones similar to this in the neighbourhood, and at the end of the fifth day of our stay we had visited and made notes of no less than eleven. Mr. Hogarth was then obliged to proceed to Nikosia. After his departure I discovered sixteen others, and as each of us has since found another—one at Cape Greco and one near Kuklia—twenty-nine stones have to be added to the list of those already known. There are also said to be four others near Anoyira, which I did not visit.

To describe individually each monolith and its surroundings would, of course, be impossible within the limits of a letter, but there are certain leading features worthy of mention. which are more or less common to all of them. Firstly, with regard to the stones themselves. The material is in every case limestone and in some is of so hard and durable a nature that, as far as regards preservation, they might have been hewn yesterday. The usual depth is about 2 ft. The extremes of breadth are 2 ft. 5 in. and 4 ft. 3 in.; but it is worthy of note that in as many as nine cases, out of twenty-three in which its accurate determination was possible, the measurement was 3 ft. 2 in. The width of the hole by which each is perforated is far less than regular, but is generally about 9 in., and its height is still more variable, for, though on the average about 2½ ft., it is in two instances as much as 4 ft. In several stones the floor of the perforation is sloped downwards, so that (its roof being level) the height-measurement of the hole is greater on one front than the other, in one case as much as 12 in. Two monoliths are imperforate, the hole only penetrating to a depth of 18 in. The stones face to every point of the compass, and an equal amount of variation exists in the quality of the workmanship. The height above the ground ranges from 6 to 10 ft.

Secondly, with regard to position. The greater number are placed on the steep slopes of the highly cultivated Kostithes valley. They stand, almost without exception, in a commanding position upon little spurs—such a position as in hilly countries is always chosen for winnowing floors. With one exception, where there is a group of three (and that of the Kuklia stones, where the two are in close proximity), they invariably occur alone. The ruins by which they are surrounded are for the most part remarkably small—a few paces, perhaps twenty or less, in their largest diameter. In those instances where they have been least disturbed it is possible to make out their original plan. The stone appears to have been placed at the corner or edge of a small platform constructed either of well-hewn masonry, or of rubble held together by coarse cement, such as it is customary to call Roman.

The two monoliths at Kuklia, which have been visited by many travellers in Cyprus, have, I believe, been regarded by almost every one as Phoenician, and by many they have been considered to be of a phallic nature. A careful examination of the Anoyira stones has, however, led me to an entirely different conclusion with regard both to their origin and use. It is in their surroundings that the key of the problem lies.

In close proximity to the platform or its remains fragments of pottery are invariably to be found. No one of them is figured, concentric, ringed or glazed. They are almost without exception of the very coarsest kind, and form portions of vessels of so large a size that they can have been used for no other purpose than storing wine or oil. A piece of the lip of a huge jar of this nature enabled me to measure the diameter of the mouth, which was 3 ft. 4 in. This was no doubt unusually large, but from 18 to 24 inches appeared a common measurement. I found none of the rude figures with conical hats so frequently met with in Cyprus, and no fragments of statuary or columns, or, indeed of anything which might support the theory of a temple site.

The most important feature, however, in what may be described, for brevity's sake, as the "properties" of these monoliths, is a circular stone, hollowed out to a depth of 5 or 6 inches at the top, and of very large size—about 6 ft. in diameter by 3 ft. in thickness. This I found on seven sites, and a smaller roller-stone of peg-top shape was also not infrequently to be met with. These are millstones, and are in every respect identical with those in use in the district at the present day for crushing the olives and the seeds of the Ceratonia (locust bean). The roller-stone is in length rather less than half the diameter of the lower millstone, and is made to revolve around the latter's centre. This is furnished with a peg which passes through a pole fixed in the smaller end of the roller-stone. The pole projects horizontally beyond the edge of the mill, sufficiently far for a couple of men to breast it capstan fashion, and thus to work it. I should mention that in every case, with one exception, these stones were in a fragmentary condition, and that it was only by collecting and piecing the fragments that the nature of the whole could be discovered. I have no doubt that those in good condition were long ago removed by the natives.

Besides these millstones there are other "properties" calling for remark. Cisterns, often lined with a blackish, fine pebble cement, frequently occur; and small conduits or gutters, which seem in some cases to lead into them, are not less common. The same may be said of certain stone vessels about 10 in. in depth, of which tolerably large fragments may sometimes be seen. Less easy of explanation is a sort of gateway formed by two massive stones from 3 to 4 ft. apart, which I found in six cases. It is quite possible that they may exist on other sites also, for the ruins were often overgrown with bush so dense and resistant that I could with difficulty force my way through it. The opposed faces of these stones have deep square holes sunk in them, and that these were intended for the reception of a heavy cross beam is evident from the fact that in one of the stones the hole is always carried out fairly to the side, and two deep up and down notches mark the place of a cross clip to keep the beam in place after its insertion. At the present day, after the olives have been crushed they are pressed by a rough screw, which works through a cross beam supported by two uprights sunk in massive stones. It is possible that the stones of which I am speaking may have been used for a like purpose. That they can ever have formed a gateway is impossible from the fact that they only stand about 3 ft. out of the ground.

From the above-mentioned and other facts, therefore, I have been led to the conclusion that these monoliths are neither Phoenician nor phallic, but rather Roman and for purposes of agriculture. The number of them, and their position on the slopes of the highly cultivated valley, far from the town, tend further to support this view. But what the exact purpose which they served may have been it is difficult to say. Possibly they formed the fulcrum of the lever of an olive press. It is certainly not too much to suppose that the co-existence in so many instances of what are without doubt oil-mills is no accidental matter.

It should be added that the Cypriotes have certain superstitions connected with these stones. Children suffering from illness are passed through the holes, and wayfarers toss a pebble on the top, auguring good fortune should it lodge there.

F. H. H. GUILLEMARD

Kuklia, March 20, 1888.

To the above statement may I add that the characteristics and surroundings of the two perforated monoliths near here, on which the "phallic" theory has been chiefly based, and around which General Cesnola constructed his Temple of Aphrodite Anadyomene, in no way militate against, but rather support Dr. Guillemard's view? The remains about them may well be those of a Roman farmstead standing in the midst of the fertile lowlands stretching to the sea; there is certainly no trace of a temple, and the situation of the remains is much further inland than Cesnola's absurd picture would lead one to suppose. The large size of the monoliths (one of them is more than 12 ft. high by 4 ft. wide) is nothing in comparison with unquestionably late monolithic columns in New Paphos, nine miles away. The other example which I found near here is quite small, and I believe that there are several others in this district. No one that I have yet seen bears the slightest resemblance to the famous sacred cones, as represented on coins of Paphos.

D. G. HOGARTH

Guillemard *et al.* 1888

Guillemard followed up with another letter on the monoliths dated August 2, 1888 and published in *The Athenaeum,* Vol. 2, No. 3172, August ll,1888.

Some few weeks ago, in the pages of the *Athenaeum,* I gave an account of a number of monoliths discovered by Mr. Hogarth and myself in Cyprus during the past winter, and hazarded an opinion as to their *raison d'être* which was rather different to that previously advanced with regard to the exactly similar stones existing as Colossi and Papho.

Of those at the latter place Prof. Sayce (*Academy,* Feb. 11th, 1888) says:—

> "The two stones, like the stones Jachin and Boaz in front of Solomon's Temple, or the upright stones in the Giant's Tower in Gozo, are

> memorials of the worship of Bethels, or sacred stones, common throughout the Semitic world, which the Phoenicians brought with them to Cyprus."

Shortly before leaving the island I found another of these monoliths in the Diorizos valley, near the village of Kithasi. Lying immediately before it, but tilted on its side, was a massive flat stone, which, as far as I can remember without my notes, must have measured about 7 ft. by 5 ft. and about 2 ft. in thickness. That it was the stone of a press was evident from the fact that a deep circular groove was cut on its surface—the depth of it increasing from the back, or part nearest the adjacent monolith, to the front, where it was carried out in a small spout which projected about 6 in. Such stones, though of smaller size, are in use at the present day.

In the course of a conversation with Col. Warren, Chief Secretary, I learnt that in a village in the northern range there exists—or did exist not long ago—a press of the same nature as those of which there is no doubt the monoliths form a part, differing only in the fact that massive timbers took the place of the perforated stone.

These curious, and at first sight puzzling monuments of a bygone age are thus the fulcra of levers of oil or wine presses, and I fear that if any one ever fell prone at Prof. Sayces's Bethels he must have been no Phoenician filled with religious fervour, but some erring Roman husbandman filled with the juice of the Cyprus grape.

F. H. H. GUILLEMARD.

C. R. Conder, Major in the Royal Engineers with experience in the Levant, added to Guillemard's observations with his own in *The Athenaeum,* Vol. 2, No. 3174, August 25, 1888.

The oil press stones to which Mr. Guillemard refers are commonly found in ruins all over Syria. They are generally distinguished by a vertical groove and a hole through the stone.

The use of *betyloi* among the Phoenicians is, on the other hand, of course undoubted. They are figured on coins of Tyre, &c., and here and there a monolith of this kind still exists, such as the *Hajr el Mansûb* and other examples in Moab. It is for the explorer, by careful examination, to distinguish in every case important from unimportant finds.

C. R. CONDER, Major R.E.

The Athenaeum, Vol. 2, No. 3177, September 15, 1888, contains a response by Captain S. Pasfield Oliver.

The interesting particulars given by Messrs. Guillemard and Hogarth respecting the origin and destination of the Cyprian monoliths at Kuklia, Cape Greco, and Anoyira may, perhaps, at first sight seem altogether to demolish the "Phallic" theories of General Cesnola and the "Bethel" hypotheses of Prof. Sayce; but on closer examination it appears to some outside observers far from impossible that such early monolithic slabs and pillars may, not infrequently, have been adapted at later periods by Greeks and Romans, not to say Venetian and Mohammedan invaders, as *fulcra* and other portions of oil-mills and wine-presses, for which uses they would readily lend themselves.

Those who have had an extended experience in the examination of rude stone monuments of all ages in many distant lands must be ever prepared to find objects which may have been sacred or monumental relics put to the commonest and basest uses, and, of all classes of ancient remains, stone pillars must always be regarded as available material to be utilized for building construction, and even for macadam. "Nothing is sacred to the sapper" (*pace* Major Conder), and doubtless the Greek or Roman vintner hesitated not to avail himself of Phoenician shrines to Ashtoret or Ishtar without a thought of puzzling investigators of the nineteenth century.

Constantly the archaeologist is confronted with cromlechs used as pigsties (the Creux des Fées, Guernsey), dolmens as stables (at Krukenho, near Carnac), and with menhirs (*passim* in the Channel Islands) broken up to mend roads with. In Finistère and the Morbihan (Erdeven), as often as not, the *calvaire* by the wayside has been sculptured from or erected on a rude Celtic megalith. At St. Martin's churchyard in Guernsey one of the gateposts is a thrice-transformed memorial of antiquity—first a pre-Celtic unhewn pillar, next incised with a Celtic hieroglyph, again sculptured by the Gauls of the Empire, and now filling an obviously useful *rôle* at the entrance of an ultra-Protestant sanctuary. What a story it could tell! Why should not some, at least, of these much-vexed (much-pressed) stones in Cyprus have undergone analogous metamorphoses?

Messrs. Guillemard and Hogarth have not made it appear quite plain whether they are also sceptical regarding the archaeological value or authenticity, as it may be called, of one conspicuous megalithic monument which, of course, has been examined by them, viz., the huge trilithon which is enshrined beneath the dome of the Sultana mosque on the south-west side of the salt lake near Larnaca. The mosque itself only dates from the sixteenth century, according to Capt. Sinclair, of the Royal Engineers, who first described this rude stone erection, which he likens to the Stonehenge blocks. He found that the mosque stood in the bed of an ancient canal which skirted the lake, and infers that the stones must have been placed *in situ* after the excavation of the channel. It is, nevertheless, open to argument whether the trilithon may have been discovered by the excavators of the canal. At all events, a likely field for exploitation is indicated by the heap of *débris* forming the embankment of the old waterway, of which it is to be hoped the Cyprus Committee have taken cognizance.

Can it be such a trilithic portal as is found represented together with the sacred cone and adjuncts of the worship of the Phoenician Venus? Or are we to be told that this massive erection was put up for a co-operative oil-mill, and that this practical machine has, by an inverse process of devolution, become in these degenerate days an object of adoration by Moslems and of discussion by Christian professors?

Of the upright acuminated pillar stones alluded to by Prof. Sayce (which have been supposed to resemble the celebrated Jachin and Boaz and allied Semitic relics of stone worship), such as those found in the Maltese ruins at Hagiar Khem and in Gozo, previous mention has been made in the *Athaeneum* at least fifteen years ago, when their connexion with similar conical pedestals in Sardinia was pointed out. Since then comparison has shown that they coincide in a remarkable manner with stones evidently intended for symbols in the Mithraea at San Clemente in Rome and near Spoleto; and the practice of almost identical rites connected therewith is to be found represented on the bronze plates of Shalmaneser's palace discovered by Mr. Rassam at Balawat, dating from the ninth century B.C.

S. PASFIELD OLIVER, Capt. late R.A.

Hogarth 1889

This selection, by W. D. Hogarth, "The Present Discontent in Cyprus," was published in *Fortnightly Review* Vol. 52, 1889.

During last year a vigorous agitation was going forward in Cyprus to promote the dispatch of a deputation which should lay before the Colonial Office, and, as the peasants hoped, before the Βασίλισσα Βικτωρία herself, the native version of the island's history since 1878. Subscriptions were collected (or rather promised) in even the poorest districts, and, chiefly through the energy of the Greek priesthood, a sum of several hundreds of pounds was guaranteed. Towards this the rich monastery of Kykko, the bishops, and the merchants in the towns contributed, but the larger proportion of nearly a thousand pounds was collected from the peasants themselves in spite of their extreme poverty and the failure of their crops in the terrible drought of 1887. Even the villages of the central plain—the Mesaoréa—and of the Carpars, which had suffered the most, scraped together considerable sums, and only the most poverty-stricken of the Paphiti were slow to help the cause.

After many difficulties and delays the members of the deputation were chosen: originally it was to have consisted of three or four private Greeks only, but in accordance with good advice the Archbishop of the island was added to the number, and, as the event has proved, his high dignity in the Orthodox Church has secured to himself and the Embassy especial attention in this country. It was also proposed to give a really national character to the venture by including among the envoys two representatives of the Moslem community; but the fact that most of the funds had been subscribed through the Church, and some personal considerations, have apparently defeated this project, and caused the small band of representatives to be wholly Christian.

A start for England was originally to have been made last summer; then it was postponed to autumn, then to winter, and it has finally taken place in the spring of this year. The timely douche administered by the authorities retarded, but did not stop it altogether, and it has now laid its burden of grievances and wrongs at the feet of the Colonial Secretary; the Archbishop has been made much of by Anglican prelates, and has received an Oxford D.D.: the rest of the deputies have resided somewhat obscurely in London, and will presently return to their own land sadder but wiser men, while the Colonial Office will doubtless pigeon-hole the whole affair.

But ought the matter to rest thus? Such an effort on the part of the peasantry cannot be quite uncalled for, and responsive even to an imperfect appeal the most enlightened country in the world (as it delights to style itself) ought to inquire into the grievances which evoked it in something more than the usual perfunctory manner. The very weakness and obscurity of this island, of which we of our own motion assumed the administration, invites our closer consideration, and should prompt our cordial action.

Neither the association of the Greek priests, nor of the pan-Hellenic agitators with the movement, ought to blind us to the amount of genuine grievance which underlies it. It is true that the former class are often identical with the latter, and pose as professional agitators, eager to seize on any and every pretext to inveigh against constituted authority, their ignorance being only to be measured by their sublime unconsciousness of its existence. A certain section (for all do not deserve this censure—far from it!) were sure to identify themselves, as they have ever done, with a movement arising from discontent. But no one who knows the villages of Cyprus will believe in their power to lead the people whither they wot not, or extract money from the hardest-fisted peasantry in the Levant, for a groundless pretext.

Pan-Hellenism is a mere newspaper cry as yet. The peasant hardly knows that Athens exists and would not contribute a piastre to promote a union with the blue and white flag. The more educated laymen and clergy recognise that, bad as their lot may be under England, it would be worse under Greece; and like Chios, Samos, and the rich islands of the Eastern Archipelago, have no wish to share the tremendous taxation, compulsory military service, and other evils which oppress the Hellenic kingdom. In spite of the Athenian propaganda which is assiduously introduced into the island, the flame of national patriotism burns very low among the Greeks; and it must not be forgotten that one-third of the whole native population is not Greek at all.

No; there is at this moment vehement feeling of discontent in Cyprus, independent of agitation, and based on real wrongs, which no one who has been much in the country districts and in contact with the peasantry can fail to perceive and appreciate. Those who knew the island in the first years of the occupation can testify that this feeling is much stronger now than then. In 1878 the Greeks welcomed us with open arms, partly on religious, partly on commercial grounds. It would be wrong to say that we were welcomed as *deliverers*, for in Cyprus (for many years at least) the Turkish rule had not been oppressive; a law, Orientally just, was fairly administered, taxation was not excessive, and acts of wanton tyranny rare; but welcomed we were with that form of gratitude which is said to consist in a lively sense of favours to come. The Turkish population was naturally apprehensive; some talked of fighting, some of emigrating to Anatolia; but the conspicuous justice and even favour with which we treated them in the early days of our rule, our assiduous care of their religious foundations and schools, and concession of ample representation in the district courts and the Legislative Council, convinced them of our *bona fides* and reconciled them to the change.

The better educated began to entertain great hopes: Cyprus was to be an important military and naval station, the centre of the Levant, the special care of the richest and most progressive nation in the world. Roads, harbours, and, perhaps, railways would be made, famines cease, and agriculture flourish. Taxation was as high or higher, than ever; but what of that with the prospect of increased wealth? And much speculation of a mild order was indulged in; land was to bought in Larnaca and Famagusta, where the harbours were to be; houses secured on the main routes: hotels projected; and vine, charub, and olive culture anticipated on a large scale, This was ten years ago! what has been done in the decade for an island which we took from no harsh masters that we might administer it for mutual advantage?

There is not a single safe harbour in Cyprus capable of accommodating anything larger than a sponge boat. Limasol and Larnaca are mere open roadsteads, as in Turkish times: a short pier has been erected at each, and a rough foreshore, but the large steamers of the Austrian Lloyd or Messageries Maritimes have to lie half-a-mile out to sea, and in very rough weather cannot call at all. The old harbours of Baffo and Kyrenia have been made fit for fishing boats, while that at Famagusta, once so famous and still of such capacity, has been left to the continued action of time and neglect. The old inner port is a marsh, the outer is still deep enough for a large ship to enter (but the latter should be well insured before the experiment is tried), and its broken moles attest the magnificence of its former lords. Time was when Famagusta ranked after Constantinople and Alexandria, and above Genoa or Venice, as third port in the Mediterranean. Its harbour was crowded with all the shipping of the Levant, and the wares of three continents were exchanged in its bazaars. Nor is it impossible that it should be once more the principal port of the Syrian Levant, if the harbour were restored to its former state. Lying on the eastern side of the island it is protected from the prevailing west winds which vex the dangerous road of Beyrout, and it has been estimated that nearly all the deposit trade of the latter might be diverted hither. The question has been considered again and again: estimates for the making of the harbour have been invited, and found to range from £80,000 up to £300,000, according as the inner port be cleared or not; but the impossibility of agreement between the naval and military authorities in England on the question of fortification seems to have resulted in a dead-lock. Cyprus has no decent outlet for its trade, and the island which lies in so matchless a position as regards Egypt, the Suez Canal, the Syrian coast, over which we once aspired to a protectorate, and Anatolia, where one day or another we shall have developments of the Russian "question" to encounter, cannot shelter a single ship of war.

On the hundreds of miles of rock coasts, fringed with reefs and shoals, there are about seven lights all told, and perhaps three out of this number are of any considerable radius. Between Famagusta and Kyrenia, a distance of nearly one hundred and fifty miles, in spite of the fact that the great peninsula of the Carpars lies right athwart the path of vessels bound from Alexandria or Port Said to the ports of Asia Minor, there is not a single light of any description. Even Cape St. Andras, with its reefs and islands, known as the "keys," running out for a mile into the sea, carries no warning to the mariner. Only in this last year has the western coast been supplied with a lighthouse, at a point where vessels from Rhodes and the west first sight the island.

Excluding short roads near the capital, there are just two properly metalled "bad-weather" roads supplied with bridges throughout and kept in repair, in all Cyprus. These are the post-road from Larnaca to Nicosia, a distance of twenty-six miles, and thirty miles of a military road from Limasol to the summer camp on Mount Troodos. True, there is a so-called road from Limasol to Larnaca; from Nicosia to Kyrenia, to Nyso, and to Famagusta; and from Famagusta up the Carpars; and from Limasol to the wine villages under Mount Troodos. Two short lengths have also been constructed from Papho, one near Delhi, and a few others. But these are as yet mere "fair-weather" roads, impasssable after heavy rains for wheeled vehicles, whereas between centres of administration like Limasol and Papho, Papho and Kyrenia or Nicosia, and Limasol and Nicosia, there is absolutely no way for wheeled vehicles whatever, and hardly even a path over which mules can travel in really bad weather. Papho can be isolated by two days' rain; the traveller from Nicosia to Limasol by the mule-path can be imprisoned for a week between the Nyso and Mouni rivers; and it must be remembered that while there is no sort of steam communication round the coasts, the prevalence of west winds makes sailing from east to west very tedious. It need hardly be added that there is no railway, nor any chance of one.

A considerable apparatus of government there is, and a large staff of officials, the latter by no means too numerous or, except in a few instances, too well paid. Little fault can be found with them; they work hard in their departments, and are a credit to the civil service of this country, and if the Cypriotes lay the blame at their door, they are entirely in the wrong. The staff has been cut down to the lowest possible number; all the head-quarter offices are undermanned, and such important departments as those of Land Registry and the Forests, have been amalgamated, not to the advantage of either in an island where, on the one hand, tenure is complicated by the religious foundations of two creeds and the native vagueness as to boundaries; and on the other, neglect has caused the destruction of almost all the forests on which climate, and therefore agriculture, so largely depend. The police force is very small and underpaid; the best of the natives cannot be attracted into it, and in wild districts like that of Papho it copes very ineffectually with a population more criminal than any in the Levant. The statistics of murder, especially that due to sheep-lifting, for the past two years are truly startling; and criminals who have been lucky enough to escape, as did a daring gentleman in October, 1887, from the door of the Papho court-house after hearing his sentence, may live for months in and about the hill villages, secure from *zaptiehs*, who cannot shoot straight, and who, if not in collusion with the delinquent have about as much idea of playing the detective as has the proverbial Dorsetshire labourer.

Thus under our enlightened rule the expenses of government in Cyprus are reduced below the minimum efficiency, and almost no money is spent on public works which would develop the island and differentiate this decade from the three centuries before it. Is the Cypriote then in the happy, if unprogressive, state of the Anatolian villager, who pays almost no taxes to a paternal administration, which, making no public works to speak of, and habitually falling short in the matter of public payment, whether they be due to men of peace like ourselves, or of war like the Russians, consults its own and its Empire's internal peace by exacting little more than is required for the private purses of its constituent members? Far from it: the Cypriote pays (or is asked to pay), whether in tithes on his crops, in locust-tax, or in other ways, about one pound English per head, an enormous rating for so incredibly poor a population; and yet, as we have seen, every department of Government is as poverty-stricken as himself, and almost nothing is done for him which a civilised administration should do for those under its care. And why? The answer is simple, and contains the gist of the bitter and genuine grievance which the envoys were to have laid before our home authorities—because this half-developed island, under an enlightened ruler, has only half of her own revenue to spend on herself, pays the other half away year by year for purposes with which she has no possible concern, and receives not one penny of contribution, direct or indirect, from her self-appointed mistress.

The details of the original scheme of occupation are too well known to need repetition here. The ninety-two thousand pounds which it was arranged that the island should pay to the Sultan as compensation for his supposed profits, have been diverted to paying a part of the interest guaranteed by England and France on the loan of 1885, but the change does not affect the island in any way, except in so far as it renders any rearrangement the more impossible for a considerable term of years to come. It rests with those responsible for the original scheme to say whether it was ever really contemplated that an island like Cyprus would continue, under our rule, to pay out unaided as much as under the Turk. It may be that Cyprus, being then intended to be a strategic *point d'appui,* and a centre of a large Levantine protectorate, was to have been subsidised by the Imperial Government: it may be that it was vaguely calculated that it would so mightily prosper and absorb so much foreign capital under our fostering care, that this payment would bear but lightly upon it. If the truth were known, the whole matter was, perhaps, arranged with that airy indifference to figures and the future which characterized the very Oriental policy of the diplomatists who negotiated the transfer of Cyprus. "Get the island first and then arrange for its future" might not have been so pernicious a principle had the foreign policy of our Government been independent of general elections; but in less than a year there was a change of Ministry, and those came into power who knew not and cared not for Cyprus. Whatever had been the original scheme of its relation to the Levant, it was now regarded as an unnecessary encumbrance, an isolated dependency, which our national prestige forbade us to relinquish, but which must be retained if possible, at no cost to the British public, and with the smallest possible trouble to ourselves. The ten thousand soldiers of the Occupation dwindled to half a battalion: the exposure of the men to the heat of a Cypriote sun under bell-tents at mid-day had caused an outbreak of fever in the first year of the Occupation, which gave what is really the healthiest and driest of Mediterranean islands a reputation for malaria. The large scale on which the original administration was conceived was reduced: their projected native regiment was never enrolled: the harbour never made, and no capital either directly or indirectly introduced into the island. In short, almost the only part of the original scheme which remained inexorably the same was this payment of £92,000 out of a total revenue of about £186,000, with nothing whatever to set against it on the other side of the account. No wonder the administration is starved; no wonder that nothing can be done to better the condition of the peasantry and put them in the way of making money. Only last year Sir James Fergusson declared again in the House of Commons that, although he was aware that the finances of Cyprus were in "an unsatisfactory state," he could at least assure his interrogator that the island cost nothing to the British tax-payer. Such a guarantee is doubtless satisfactory to our pockets, but none the less conveys a reproach which enlightened England should not be slow to observe. Because Cyprus is weak and unable to cause much commotion in the Colonial Office, are the finances to be left "in an unsatisfactory state," and a deaf ear turned to her appeals?

A further question arises, which after two bad seasons is becoming grave indeed. Little as is done by the State for the Cypriote, can he afford to pay at the present rate even for that little? Can he, in short, continue to contribute one pound per head of population? Ask the district Commissioners; they will reply in the negative, and state the amount of arrears which have accumulated in 1887 and 1888, and competent non-official opinion endorses their verdict. The rating is beyond the just capacity of an oriental peasantry dependent on the products of the soil: for an important consideration seems to have been overlooked ten years ago, namely, that seasons of drought are to be regularly looked for in Cyprus. The revenue appears to have been calculated on uniformly fair crops, in oblivion of the fact that every few years so little rain falls that, not only are the cereals ruined for that particular season, but the charubs and olives for a year or two afterwards. True, that locusts are no longer a scourge, the energy of our Government having combated them successfully: nor were they ever abundant in the west of the island; but the sheer scarcity of rain produces terrible dearth among a peasantry which continues to cultivate, after the manner of its forefathers, that which is least independent of climatic conditions. In 1887 scarcely a drop of rain fell for the first eight months; and Cyprus, in common with all the coasts of the Levant, was without food to eat. As the summer went on the distress in the Papho district was fearful, and so far from getting in its revenue the Government had to distribute seed corn among the villagers, who in most cases (and small blame to them) made it forthwith into bread. The invaluable charub-trees, which bear well only once in two seasons, were dried up by the long drought, and will not recover wholly for a year to come. In 1888 matters were better in the Papho district, but in the Carpars and the Mesaoréa the spring rains failed, and thus the great corn-growing districts of the island were ruined for the second time. The fates seem to war against the luckless island: hail in April broke the vines; sudden and tremendous rains in the first week of June washed away the grain which was lying on the threshing floors of the more productive west; and in the second week of July came a fierce scirocco under whose breath the crops of melons, gourds, and fruits perished, the half-ripened grapes withered on the stalks, and the water supply ceased throughout whole districts, such as that of the Carpars. And now the arrears of two years are hanging like a millstone round the peasants' necks, driving them to prey upon each other, and often to commit crimes simply in order to get into prison. Naturally the island finances are "in an unsatisfactory condition," and the officials scarcely know how the government is to be carried on, unless the annual payment, above mentioned, be retained in the island, or help sent from England.

No series of good seasons will enable the Cypriote peasant to pay off his arrears. In the outlying districts, especially that of Papho, he is one of the most poverty-stricken individuals in existence, living always from hand to mouth, and working out—on the rare occasions when he can get to work for wages, which never rise to a shilling a day, and often fall to about seven pence—a meagre pittance on which to feed himself, his wife, and family, without mentioning the payment of taxes, offerings to the Church, or such extras. His house is a one-roomed hovel, with walls, floor, and roof alike of mud, furnished with a rickety table or two, which serve as beds, a broken chair, a yoke, winnowing shovels, a waterpot, a few utensils, and little else but filth and fleas. The squalor of a Cypriote interior is characteristic of the people, whether Greek or Moslem: far more ignorant of comfort that the rudest Anatolians or Arabs, they slouch through life, as poor and as helpless as their forefathers two hundred years ago. The majority are small proprietors farming with very imperfect means of irrigation plots of arable land. The tithe on corn is assessed upon the threshing-floor by Government officials, natives and commonly honest. But the Cypriote complains bitterly that he must pay his quota in ready-money. In Turkish times, he maintains that in addition to the innumerable ways of evading or "squaring" an Oriental tax-collector—in addition to the remissions or postponements which an Oriental system, made for an Oriental people, allowed—every proprietor had the option of paying his tithe in kind. The collector measured off his grain, piled it in a heap, removed it, and the matter was ended without the peasant being perceptibly galled by the impost. Not so under an iron Western rule; the tax-collector is regular and inexorable, and the peasant, who never has any reserve of ready-money whatever, must either realise on a portion of his grain at a time when prices are very low, or go to the money-lender; and what becomes of him if he takes the latter alternative is not doubtful. Two years ago a Papho villager borrowed £19 from one of these sharks. At one time or another he repaid as much as £25 in cash, was sold up and still owes money! But it will be objected, what would the Administration do with the stores of grain, charubs, and so forth, which would be accumulated if tithe were taken in kind? Well, it can undoubtedly sell them better and command a wider circle of buyers than the individual peasants. Both grains and charubs find a ready acceptance in foreign markets, and the producers would gain by the elimination of the town middleman. If there is to be loss it should not fall on the needy peasantry, but, as the lesser evil, on the British Government.

Not without reason is the native population dissatisfied with our rule, and its grievances should receive sympathetic attention from us, if urged with a due recognition of those benefits which, all hampered as we are by chains of our own forging, we have endeavoured to confer on the island. Equality before the law; incorruptible, single-minded, and zealous administrators; freedom of speech, and even a representative system, we have given to the Cypriotes; we have cleansed their towns, supplied medical supervision, made their prisons all too luxurious, secured as far as possible their lives and property. Perhaps in our British zeal for liberal institutions we have somewhat neglected to adapt ourselves to the new circumstances and old customs and prejudices with which we were confronted in Cyprus. If John Bull conquers for the kingdom of God, he sometimes administers his conquests a little woodenly; we have undertaken to rule a people, the vast majority of whom are in about the same stage of development as the subjects of our first Norman kings, and have given them, Heaven help them! the blessings of the Victorian era! We have created, for example, a Representative Legislative Council, consisting of nine Greeks, three Turks, and six English officials. With what result? Turk has combined with Greek, and hardly a single salutary measure can be carried through. Of course the crown has a right of veto; but this is a small compensation for a total inability to pass anything on its own initiation. Freedom of the press, again, is much abused in the island; our system of comfortable imprisonment is no deterrent to a criminal population, conscious of no moral stigma attaching thereto, and acknowledging the influence only of fear. The introduction of the lash for all grave offences would be a great boon to the peaceable portion of the Cypriotes; and it is really a much more open question than is ever admitted in England, how far the social condition of an Eastern people is bettered by the abolition of the *corvée,* by which public works of the utmost benefit to the natives are cheaply constructed at the expense of a few hours of each peasant's leisure, which are usually spent in the village coffee-shop. We shall not prosecute our mission of civilisation the better for forgetting that we have to deal in Cyprus for the most part with Orientals, for whom Liberal institutions are as yet an anachronism, and whose character is adapted by nature and long usage not to self-government, but to being governed. We have other benefits to confer on the island before these; let us first reform the financial arrangement, and by developing industries and lightening taxation make it more easy for the peasant to live. Then may he be educated to an appreciation of those institutions which England confers sometimes, it must be confessed, with more generosity than wisdom.

Lewis 1893

In her book, *A Lady's Impressions of Cyprus in 1893,* London: Remington & Company, 1894, Elizabeth A. M. Lewis presents a balanced view of Cyprus in 1893. She refers to earlier historians, to recent travelers, and makes a circuit around the island. In the selections reproduced here she revisits the monolith controversy and makes observations about some areas and subjects not often described by other authors of this period.

[p. 88]

Descending a steep path southwards from the Keep of Colossi and crossing various irrigation streams, we reached an old ruined building, of which not much remains, and near it stands one of the pierced monoliths, called, in Cyprus, Holy Stones. The supposed use and purpose of these involves a difference of opinion between the antiquarians, as represented by Professor Sayce and Dr. Ohnefalsch Richter (whatever value may attach to the conclusions of the latter), and the modern explorers, such as Dr. Guillemard and Mr. Hogarth, as to whether they were or were not rude copies of the famous cone worshipped at Paphos.

To this matter fuller reference will presently be made, but the sight of this stone at Colossi aroused a separate train of thought of my own in connection with the Knights Templars. Paphos is called Baffo, and adoration was paid at Old Paphos to a stone called by some of the Roman historians a *meta,* or mile-stone, from its shape. Anyone who has taken an interest in the trial and condemnation of the Templars knows that they were charged with assimilating Eastern rites and superstitions, derived from the people among whom they sojourned, to a form of Christianity, and that the idol, or whatever the object was, they were accused of celebrating in their mysteries, was called by them Baffometus; and all sorts of rather far-fetched explanations of the name have been brought forward, such as the derivation from *Mahomet,* and so on. But what if it simply meant, "The Stone of Paphos?"

[Mrs. Lewis subsequently quotes extensively from Guillemard's "Monoliths in Cyprus" and concludes with his following paragraph.]

"These curious, and at first sight, puzzling monuments of a bye-gone age are thus the fulcra of levers of oil or wine presses, and I fear that if any one ever fell prone at Professor Sayce's Bethels, he must have been no Phoenician filled with religious fervour, but some erring Roman husbandman filled with the juice of the Cyprus grape."

Perhaps there may have been a little of both; the cults and the Roman may, on finding the Phoenician Holy Stone already standing, have carved his hole in it for a mechanical purpose.

I gather from what Mr. Hogarth says in *Devia Cypria* that if these were ancient oil-presses the suggested use of them is so obsolete as to have been long entirely forgotten.

With the exception of the timber press observed upon by Colonel Falkland Warren, the monolith cannot be connected with any known method of olive crushing, nor can any system be found in any countries of Syria or the Levant parallel to the method supposed, or imagined, of using a ponderous upper mill-stone suspended to one end of a massive baulk of timber, while ropes attached to the other end would pull the baulk down, thus raising the mill-stone up, to be lowered again with force upon the olive berries lying on the nether mill-stone. For this baulk a fulcrum would be supplied by the perforation of the monolith, the long, central slit allowing for a good deal of play.

This system would, they suggest, have been abandoned, and that not till Byzantine times, as a clumsy contrivance, and absolutely forgotten; while the far more ancient attributes of Aphrodite are still freshly remembered—and these being no modern superstitions, but relics of the primaeval nature worship, why should they have attached themselves so specially to the farmers' oil-stones of the early Christian ages?

For it is easier to believe that the oil-press use of the stones is too old to be remembered than that the various superstitions attached to them are "only of modern origin," as Mr. Hogarth says.

Superstitions such as these:—women and children and sick persons passing through the stone, an ancient form kept alive by us when the finger is passed through the wedding-ring: or sitting on the stone in appeal to the Great Mother, whether called Aphrodite or Astarte or by any other ante-Greek title; or betrothed by clasping hands through the slit; these are survivals of the very oldest conceptions the world has ever known, lurking yet in various odd, remote corners of the globe, as, for instance, in the Hebrides, to look westwards; and among the Cornish moor-folk, who even now believe the clasping of hands through a holed stone to constitute a valid marriage; and, looking east, do we not, to this day, find the Afridis of the Punjaub wrapping their new-born male child in a blanket, and passing him through a window, with earnest prayers that he may turn out a successful thief?

Surely one may safely challenge any assertion that such things as these have been newly-started anywhere as "modern superstitions," even if the manner in which the Cypriots crushed their olives previously to Byzantine times can scarcely be said to have been determined with much precision; for after all it is only asserted that the mill-stones accompany nineteen out of the fifty monoliths that have been discovered, while I have a strong impression of having seen many ancient disused mill-stones lying about in places where there are certainly no monoliths.

Again, who have ever heard of superstitions such as these originating in the Christian epoch? Their origin is lost in the mist of antiquity; they are older than we can dream of, and the marvel has always been that so much of them should have survived so far into this most practical and prosaic of all the ages. Remembered things are more surprising than things forgotten. Forgotten cults, forgotten industries, forgotten worthies, forgotten hopes and aspirations are all of the nature of humanity; how strong then must once have been the impression made, when traditional forms remain whose earlier import is buried in oblivion!

[p. 156]

We were introduced at Ktima to certain native delicacies, such as *Kaimak,* a kind of scalded cream of the nature of *Devonshire* cream, as we often designate the clotted cream, which, in reality the people of Cornwall indignantly lay claim to as being, by origin, Cornish only; and the idea in Cyprus is that the Phoenicians introduced it into both Cyprus and Cornwall, whither they went in quest of tin.

The we had two kinds of white cheese, much like those made of goats' milk in Corsica, and sold in somewhat similar little baskets, made of green rushes. The kind which resembled the Corsican *Broccio* must be made in the same way, of new milk boiled. It lacks, however, the peculiar aromatic flavour which is only found in Corsica, and which *Madame Mére,* Napoleon's mother strove in vain to reproduce in a *Broccio* dairy she set up in France.

It was a well-known saying of Napoleon's: "*A l'odeur seul je reconnaitrais la Corse, les yeux fermés.*" I often noticed, however, in the wild commons of Cyprus, that well-known smell of aromatic herbs; though they are not so ubiquitous as in Corsica, and myrtle, the most perfumed of all shrubs, is much less common, growing chiefly on the banks of streams and where there is water, where its vivid green contrasts richly with the duller-leaved Lentiscus and oleander.

Halva made of sesame pounded up with honey I liked very much, and also some little baked cakes of honey and sesame with rather a burnt taste. An excellent *nougat* is also made of honey and walnuts. We tasted a curious gelatinous kind of sausage made from grapes, and containing pieces of walnut. This did not meet with our approbation, but we were told the natives thought it very sustaining, and were in the habit of carrying it with them, and refreshing themselves with slices of it when they went on a journey.

A beautifully clear jelly, with delicate acid flavour, is made from the large haw of a kind of Crataegus, very much like the common hawthorn to look at, only rather larger leaved, and with a somewhat larger blossom.

The *Lakoum,* or Turkish delight, was good at Papho, but it had not in all places an equally pleasant taste, and at Nicosia was, in fact, voted by common consent to be supremely nasty.

But the viand *par excellence* at Papho was the fat little Beccaficos pickled in wine vinegar. Some of these ought to be imported into England, but I could not well manage it on this occasion.

The game season being just closed we were unable to taste the Francolin, a bird between a pheasant and a partridge in size, and reputed much better than either, which abounds in the district of Papho. We saw one later; it is nearly black, with white specks.

Papho has been celebrated from of old for its "diamonds," which are a crystal, differing from quartz, and distinguished scientifically as "analcime." Pliny distinguished between this and the ordinary crystal, and so did Etienne de Lusignan, writing in the 16th century, who says that though they are not real diamonds, the goldsmiths arrange them so well in rings that they are taken for and sold as good ones. Another writer, the Pious Pilgrim, says "they have deceived many lapidaries." The Turks at first thought they had discovered in them a great treasure, and surrounded the mountain with guards; but before long they abandoned the place in disappointment. These crystals are the colour of water. A nice specimen of them, formed on the rock, was given to me, but I am sorry to say they did not at all deceive the London lapidary to whom I showed them, and was so unkind as to say they were not worth polishing.

Some good embroidery, peculiar to this district is done at Phyti and other villages, whither messengers were despatched inviting the workers to send some in for us to inspect and purchase. They work a thick stitch in coloured cottons, and also do some very good open-work in white. Cyprus attained, in very early times, a high skill in embroidery, and is considered to be the mother country of that art in the west; and from Paphos, Laodice, daughter of the colonizing Agapenor, sent to Athene, in Arcadia her fatherland, a peplum, no doubt embroidered. This is related in a distich preserved by Pausanias. The Phoenicians probably introduced this art, among many others.

[p. 263]

At Kyrenia we kept the carriage, and having rested the horses during the day that we rode to Bella Païs, we drove the next day to Lapitho. Our host and hostess were unfortunately unable to accompany us, and one young lady was the only addition to our party; the Commissioner of Kyrenia having been unavoidably detained by some case of importance in the Courts. He put us, therefore, under the escort of a gallant zaptieh trooper, who could speak English to a certain extent, and who showed his advanced culture by addressing me as "*Madame*." He entered upon his office *con amore,* manoeuvering adroitly his mettled and fiery steed, and pioneered us successfully through the devious paths leading to all we wanted to see.

We drove along a flowery road, green with myrtles and intersected by occasional streams, and passed on our right by the sea, six miles west of Kyrenia, the ancient Dorian Lapithos, one of the nine kingdoms, where once stood a temple of Venus. The land of the ancient site is now held by an Episcopal See, and it is called Acheropiti, from the Greek convent of that name, and exhibits a grey group of remains of towers, walls, and Latin churches.

Lapithos had no celebrity outside the island, and its period of prosperity was late. It lies off the road, and the carriage could not approach it. To walk to it would have occupied too much time, and we regretted being obliged to leave it on one side. Cesnola saw there many sculptured fragments of Greek temples, in white marble, and a curious building resembling a mausoleum, but said to have been a king's palace. The remains of ancient architecture are, however, unimportant.

The name of the old city has passed over to Lapitho, an extensive village on the hill-side, where is the source of a perennial river, whose copious waters provide abundant harvests and delicious shades. It is about three miles beyond Acheropiti. We drove through its narrow, sharp-cornered streets, till the carriage became fairly entangled in an abrupt turn, and unable to advance or back out; then we alighted and walked the rest of the way to the zaptieh station.

Of this large, airy house, one room was tenanted by three of the force, an inspector, a trooper, and a private, and the other was reserved for the use of the Commissioner of Kyrenia, who is also Police Commandant. We waited here for a mule, to ride up to the fountain-head of the river, and remarked with pleasure the taste for gardening and flower-growing displayed by the men in the ground surrounding their house. Fine wall-flowers and sprays of the deepest pink peach-blossom were presented to us, nor was there anything wasteful in the latter abstraction, for the trees were crowded with bloom in this "Macaria," or Blessed Land of the ancients, and no frost was impending to hinder its development into fruit.

We went up—with the mule to ride by turns—the cosy, picturesque village to the source of the stream which transforms the whole place into an enchanted garden. Lapitho is divided into six districts, corresponding to its six Churches, and evidently teems with prosperity. Not far from the source, we came to a picturesque fern-covered aqueduct ending in an octagonal basin.

At the source itself, the stream issues from a well-built Gothic arch, forming the mouth of a cavern, within which the stream is very narrow, having on either side a flat space of rock, barely wide enough to stand upon; and on the left-hand side and down to the further end, five larger and two smaller chambers open out of it. The water runs up into each, as a narrow finger, with precisely the same level ledge on either side of it.

With the aid of the strong zaptieh, who strode from side to side of the stream, giving a hand when we staggered on the narrow, slippery slab of rock, we managed to make our way along it and into the chambers, and thoroughly to explore this unaccountable, and to me, meaningless arrangement of the recess.

Murray says that "on excavating" the chambers were found. It is difficult to understand how "excavation" comes in, with respect to a hole in the rock from which the river Lapithos has eternally flowed and which was built round at some past time, with a pointed arch to consolidate the opening and protect the head of the stream, whence

"A fountain issuing from its rocky cell
Pours down its shining water."

The view from this height, looking down upon the azure sea, framed in the "mystic floating gray of olive trees," beggars description, so perfect was the contrast of colour, so grand the crags, so fair the fleckless blue above and below; the two expanses separated only by the dividing white line of the snow-clad Caramanian mountain peaks. Some artistic word-painting powers should supply memory's fleeting grasp of it; for though without them the remembrance at first seems enough and more intense than words could make it, it passes with time, its vivid colours fade out, and we "forget because we must, and not because we would" this, among so many other once highly prized mental joys.

Higher on the hill, at a place called *Larnaca* of Lapithos, there are remains of many tombs, and here a bilingual inscription in Phoenician and Greek was found.

To visit the potteries of Lapitho, we scrambled down the village by a different track, threading endless narrow lanes and populous Lilliputian streets till we reached the ovens, probably immemorial, where pots and vases are still rudely made in the antique forms and, unlike the Famagousta pottery which is plain, are marked with the concentric brown rings and the stripes, such as may be seen in the old specimens in the British Museum.

As we filed down, a regiment of ulsters, the weather having turned chill and threatening, an old woman rushed forward on an upstairs balcony, and called in tones of high excitement to someone behind her to come and see "Kyrias." It was too late, and she had to enjoy by herself the response to her smiling greeting.

We went in to a man's house to buy pots. His kitchen was full of them, and so was a loft on the roof, which we reached by a rude external staircase. We bought as many of the quaintest specimens as we could manage to carry away: the potter lent a basket which two little boys carried down, the zaptieh exhorting them, all the way, not to break them. To receive the overflow, he produced a beautiful white handkerchief with a blue border, in which he wrapt up some of the more fragile articles.

The hill-sides were richly adorned with cyclamen and huge yellow ranunculus, growing ranker and finer here in the well-watered soil than on the rocky surface of the Nicosia plain; and the zaptieh, to whom the steep and slippery places were as nothing, soon collected a great armful of them. It struck us curiously, as we watched this lithe and active Mahommedan, tall, supple and virile, entering into the spirit of everything and showing no signs of discomfort, to think that he had had nothing to eat or drink all day and had no hope of anything till sun-down. He, for his part, no doubt saw us eat our lunch with a feeling of gracious superiority and mild toleration. What would Tommy Atkins, whom I am sorry to say I once or twice saw lying in a ditch, say to such a *régime?* Tommy would succumb long before the *régime* would have time to do him any good.

The paths continued to be very steep, tortuous, and narrow, and thickly overhung with trees whose sweeping branches constitute the chief danger in riding; and the zaptieh had dismissed the mule before we began the descent and sent it back with a boy, explaining that it would be of no further use. His real words were: "No good, mool." We found walking not very easy, as there was a good deal of water in the hollows of the lanes, and much energetic hopping from side to side was necessary, to preserve dry feet. Before we reached the zaptieh station we passed a closely shut gate leading into the rock, which we learnt was a petroleum store. It might perhaps be some ancient cave thus utilized.

After a short rest at the zaptieh quarters, where the Inspector presented us with bunches of violets, our zaptieh conducted us to the house of the Mudir of the district, a person of great importance as Turkish local Governor, second only to the Commissioner.

Following the usual wise method of the British Government in dealing with states under the Queen's suzerainty, we have not changed the existing laws of Cyprus but allow them to work themselves out in their own way; only modifying them in any direction that might interfere with the security of life and property, and freedom of contract and of religion.

The Mudir and his wife received us, the zaptieh standing by and, in a sort, doing the honours as we could none of us say a word to each other. Then ensued the usual course of bunches of violets, jam and coffee. The jam, of a dark purple colour, was the most delicious imaginable.

I was saying to the others, "What can this exquisite confection be? Mulberry?" when the zaptieh stepped up, touched the violets and pointed to the jam, and we realized that we were eating, what I had heard of but never seen, preserved violets. These large and plentiful violets which play so marked a part in social amenities are double, and much like the Neopolitan, but darker.

We hoped to have seen some silk here, knowing the Mudir was a silk grower. I knew the word for that, *Metaxa,* and the Mudir's wife produced some beautiful glossy hanks, both yellow and white, of fine quality; but she had none woven left to show us, except some of the silky white material made up into a skirt. The production of silk is steadily on the increase in the district of Kyrenia.

This visit ended, we walked out of the village and set to work picking cyclamens, with which the ground was carpeted, and were rejoined by the carriage, which had contrived to disentangle itself as soon as relieved of our embarrassing presence.

As we drove back to Kyrenia the clouds gathered blackly behind us, and we soon realized that we were having a race with the storm, which, in fact, burst forth almost immediately after we were once more safely housed.

Geddes 1896

Sir Patrick Geddes (1854-1932) started his professional life as a biologist, but eye problems caused him to switch to botany and later he became an outspoken evolutionist. His broad views of life as a whole and the integration of practical and philosophical points of view led him to develop a considerable reputation as a country and city planner. After some time in that role in Britain he visited Cyprus in that capacity for nine months in 1897, followed later by service in India from 1914 to 1932. He described his visit to the island in "Cyprus, Actual and Possible, A Study in the Eastern Question," which appeared in *The Contemporary Review,* London, Vol. 71, 1896. To Geddes the Eastern question was an agricultural question and he felt that was the most important sector to be developed in Cyprus. Much of his article not replicated here is devoted to his recommendations that Armenian exiles in Cyprus would be best served by involvement in mulberry and silkworm culture with the funds invested at the top in experts which would eventually would devolve down to support the peasant class.

Up from Larnaka, the port, to Nicosia, the central capital, the journey, most of the way, is more desolate than beautiful. Yet before hurrying on, let us pause for a moment to interpret it. This desolation is the work not of nature but of man. That sea margin of fever swamp, that dry torrent bed, these barren hill slopes, these skeleton hills, all go back for their explanation to the always wasteful and often wanton destruction of forests which has been the crime of almost every successive race. Nowhere better can we see the lamentable way in which in these once glorious countries man has turned the forces of nature to the destruction of his home. How far the desolation and decadence, so manifest in every Mediterranean country from Spain to Syria, is the fault of man, how far also a natural process, are questions hard to settle in exact proportion, and still likely to be long under debate; but there is no doubt of the co-operation of both destructive agencies . . .

Meantime a new landscape is opening. We have crossed the hills, and the vast Messaorian plain lies before us, with a noble sierra for its northern wall. A palm-oasis lightens the monotonous foreground; around it lies a group of strange little flat-topped hills, scarped away by denudation from the adjacent plateau, one capped with the remnant of a megalithic citadel, the Acropolis of an old king of Cyprus who paid his tribute to Assyria in Hezekiah's day. From a point like this we command the whole amphitheatre of Cyprus and understand almost at a glance the historic contrast of Cyprus and Crete. Why should the Cretans remain half unconquered (that is, unconquerable) from Spartan days to the present hour, while Cyprus has hardly ever even resisted its foreign masters? Obviously it is because Crete is a labyrinth of mountain citadels, almost each village having its natural hill fort—far too costly an aggregate to storm, even for the six Powers; whereas from this high centre of the Cyprus plain a small garrison has always been able to dominate the whole island, striking at will into the two isolated mountain ranges glen by glen. For its own inhabitants Crete is more defensible than Rob Roy's country; Cyprus, in the main, almost as little so as Egypt.

Before us lies Nicosia, a miniature Damascus, with its minarets and palms. At its western side, too, stands a goodly mass of eucalyptus, completely purifying the once-feverish city moat, and showing what the island might have been had Cypriote and Briton alike during the last eighteen years given more thought to planting and less to politics. The massive ramparts, the quaint labyrinthine streets, the goodly Venetian and Turkish houses, each with its glimpse of arcaded court and its gleam of golden oranges, the half-oriental bazaar, the stately cathedral-mosque, the ruined Latin churches, the quaint Byzantine ones, the spacious gardens with their innumerable palms, give an endless succession of pictures among which one might wander, or sketch, or photograph for many days. All possible excursions conveniently radiate from this central strategic point. The great south road, for instance, takes us over hill and dale to Limassol, the second seaport of the island—indeed, the first for some things—carobs and wine especially.

Riding westward through the rich plain of Limassol, as well clothed as an English park, with rounded masses of the carob-tree amid level corn-land, we come to the ancient manor and tower of Kolossi, whither the Templars retreated after their expulsion from the Holy Land, and whence they sailed to meet their doom. At a glance one sees the secret of that sorcery whereby they were said to amass the wealth which cost them so dear; it was the simple agricultural art of shrewdly choosing soil and climate, of wisely managing water supply; in a word whatever their symbolism and ritual may have been, their wealth-sorcery was that of the irrigator and farmer, of the vineyard and the olive-press . . .

Farther on, above the pretty village of Episcopi, stands the noble Acropolis of ancient Curium, its temples shattered, its hippodrome now a long ellipse of ruin amid returning natural forest, its valleys filled with tombs. Past picturesque cliff and precipice and landslip goes the winding hill-path; above the endless pistacia-scrub rise thousands of wild olives and wild carobs, each awaiting the grafter. Once amid all this wildness we find a little long-forgotten grove of ancient olives, their silvery vesture, their undying youth full of the solemn beauty of the Holy Wisdom herself. For Pallas of the olive-grove is no dead goddess, as they teach that know of her only in books. As in each of her living trees a deeper nature-lore than that which only dissects and classifies again reveals to us the living dryad, moving, breathing, light-discerning, sensitive, so a deeper economics and politics, a deeper and newer, yet older and simpler, social science—that is social wisdom—than that of our party strife begins to appear; and we see in these old fables and visions not merely ancient poetry, ancient mythology, but ancient science, ancient truth . . .

Returning to the south-western coast, the forest region suddenly ends at a day's ride west of Limassol, and a new landscape opens, that of historic Paphos, and long, bare perspectives of parallel hill slopes sweep down into the goodly plain watered by at least one perennial river. While the scholar has unearthed the massive foundations of the ruined temple, and the mediaeval antiquary mourned over knightly tower and hall in their fallen estate of loft and byre, the geologist has sometimes pointed out that the height these stand on is a well-marked raised beach, and asked whether the story of the foam-born goddess was not meant to express or at least include that of her island home . . .

Another of the great excursions of the island is eastward to Salamis and Famagusta. A little north of the ruined Graeco-Roman city stands the yet earlier Mykenian citadel; a little south of the ruined mediaeval city stands the mean modern town. So here in an hour's ride the essential procession of European history rises before us. Nor are great scenes of world-drama wanting, from Paul and Barnabas in the forum of Salamis to Othello and Desdemona in their tower. For in this strange island of tomb and temple there echo everywhere the voices of Love and Death. Nowhere better than in Famagusta can we see the stately mediaeval world with its piety and heroisms, for nowhere stand nobler churches within more gallantly defended walls. Nowhere, alas, more clear are the lapsed ideals, the corresponding material squalor of modern life, than in the ruinous hovels of the Turkish village, shrinking within the city walls, or in the sordid lanes and cafés of the modern Greek townlet spreading without.

Yet neither is dead; the old Turkish spirit lives in the strong, silent faces at the mosque; the Hellenic spirit sparkles from the children's eyes. Even the sordid modern village gains upon us. In every dirty café the arches spring light and true, as from the mediaeval workman's hands, and one sees with fresh clearness that architecture is not a function of paper plans, unrolled by those clerkly gentlemen we call architects in the west, for their drilled mechanics to copy, but that the masons themselves build like bees without architects, because they are architects, to this day the freemasons of old. There can be few more pleasing sights for any who know and care for traditional craft and individual skill. This arch-building one can see anywhere in Cyprus; but here at Varoschia is a local industry even more ancient, and more widely fascinating—the potteries. And if the forms, when reminiscent of classic shapes, be so rather as degenerations than as active survivals of the old art-spirit, let us not wholly blame the producer. We admire, or think we admire, the Greek vases from the tombs; we blame the living Greeks for not making the like; yet do we not ourselves contentedly live amid the meanest crockery of any ceramic period, at best relieved by Oriental ornaments in utter contrast to our needs and ways? Let but some museum, some educated consumer here and there give at once an outlet and an impulse to better things, and no local industry in the world would be more easy of renascence. As by these masons the House Beautiful might again be simply built, so with these potters it might again be adorned. Similarly, good metal-workers are still in the bazaars, good needlewomen likewise not far to seek, for this and that old style of Eastern embroidery still lingers among the villages, though Western "education," with its Kindergarten ornament and aniline colour, already poisons the town. Here, then, as elsewhere in Cyprus, the ways of active initiative lie open.

Yet one more excursion, this time to the northward. Across the cereal plain, we come to low barren hills, treeless and soilless, where, after too many years of Treasury delay, the present energetic forest officer has found some scanty means to make a successful beginning of afforestation, the acacia taking as kindly to these dry gorges as does the eucalyptus to its marshy levels. From these barrens the scene suddenly changes, thanks to a good spring, to the loveliest of oasis valleys, full of watercourses, and busy mills, houses and gardens, corn and trees. After an hour of stumbling and scrambling (for the good roads of Cyprus, as of so many other places, are essentially the tentacles of the town, not the arteries of the village), we reach the spring, and thence wind on by a precipitous hill-path, past the splintered giant fist of Pentedactylon, and thence to a new landscape, indeed another world, of sharper contrast than any of us had seen on two sides of a mountain range before. On the south side the narrow oasis valley up which we had climbed the landscape is practically treeless. On the north, the cypress, pine, and arbutus forest thickly clothes the heights, while the deep-gorged lower plateau slopes gently to the sea, rich and beautiful in its perennial light-grey and dark evergreen of olive and carob, stretching far as the eye can reach on either side of the little provincial capital of Kyrenia, itself a townlet and suburb grouped around a gigantic Venetian fort.

Here, then, we reach the fullest beauty of Cyprus, indeed the full beauty of the Mediterranean. The lovely plain, well-watered and well-wooded, the pleasant, prosperous-looking farms with their springs and fountains, the picturesquely perched villages on the hillsides, the noble mountain range with its peaks and cliffs, make up a panorama not to be forgotten. On one side of the slope above Kyrenia we see the glorious abbey of Bella Pais, and crowning the 3000 feet peak above the town, towers the extraordinary castle-labyrinth and turret-medley of St. Hilarion—complex as a drawing of Dürer's, fantastic in its intense light and shade as a woodcut of Doré's. Here, at any rate, there is little wonder that, to the romantic traveller, Cyprus seems an enchanted island. But our journey is not merely, nor mainly, in search of the picturesque and the romantic, though both artist and photographer are in their element; we are also a scientific party on business, that is, in search of the practical, of the miraculous; and we are in a high feather especially over one particular combination of these, the rediscovering for ourselves of the old miracle of Moses's rod. Not a divining rod, of course, for we read that he "smote" the rock, and the waters "gushed forth," which (if a re-revised reading be still admissible) means that he chipped the travertine, and so re-opened the spring.

For in these too calcareous countries the springs are constantly sealing themselves up with a crust, just like a kettle with its deposit, and so year by year they run less freely; nay, in time one little outlet after another becomes closed altogether, and thus most, it may be even all, of the water supply disappears, with corresponding shrinkage of fertility, which peasant and ruler (Turk and Briton alike) seem to have accepted hitherto in the same ignorant fatalism. At one spring a few kicks and scratches set free enough water to prove this view to all concerned, and an hour of pickaxe and crowbar gives a permanent increase of twenty or more per cent.; at another, where the crust is thick and old, hard work is wanted; at another, skilled miners and perhaps a charge of dynamite would be required. But it is safe to say there is probably not one spring, along the northern chain at least, which has ever been properly developed, or which might not be vastly and permanently improved at an expense altogether insignificant in comparison with the agricultural return. The want of Cyprus is water, peasant and official alike truly tell you; yet in no district, so far as our journey went, are the water resources even properly known, much less properly exploited. Again, even of such water as is obtained too much is either wasted for irrigation or wasted in over-irrigation; this latter often so copious as to sicken and drown the roots; to cake, and choke, and impoverish the soil. It is manifest that such an island, with its many small but various and varied sources of supply, is not to be treated by any rough and wholesale engineering application of the methods of the vast yet comparatively simpler Indian or Egyptian plains with their perennial rivers. It is rather for Cyprus to offer to larger countries a comparative microcosm of irrigation methods, in which economy and efficiency of local adaptation might readily combine—so becoming the spot where not only the Eastern, but also the young engineer for India or Egypt, the young colonist for the Cape or Australia may pause to learn his business more simply and rapidly than on the immense scale of these larger countries. Here, in fact, far more than in these great countries, one can see much within little space. And thus by cheap and simple methods we might, on the one hand, vastly improve Cyprus for the Cypriote, a much-needed service which it is full time we should undertake; and, on the other, make Cyprus an object-lesson and training-school for the East, for India and the Colonies. It is safe to predict also that this would help forward the incipient reaction towards a renewal of ancient, simple, and economic irrigation methods, away from undue dependence on gigantic and costly engineering works. This reaction is beginning, for instance, to be expressed by Californian or Dakotan irrigation engineers, who, after long dependence on mighty reservoirs and costly dams, on expensive artesian wells, have of late been re-discovering for themselves that "underflow" on which most of the simple, effective and economical irrigation of antiquity and the Middle Age was wont to depend in Cyprus and through the East.

Nor is Cyprus a potential centre and school of hydrogeology and irrigation alone, but of agriculture also, of acclimatisation as well. With finer climate and better soil than the Riviera, much might surely be done, alike again for the island itself in the first place, for the East also, for the Empire as a whole. Far away it is, no doubt, as our small island and our small European distances go; but it is well-nigh at our doors as compared with the mighty distances of Empire, and on its very main street also. For what else have we to compare within one night's run from Alexandria or Port Said? Here, too, within a single farm, lie zones of culture for which we might elsewhere have to go half round the world. Beginning with date-palm and banana, we pass to pomegranate and to orange, to mulberry and to fig, to olive and to vine, to almond and apple. With water we can grow cotton or cereals, roots or forage crops. Here, then, is a possible centre, agricultural and educational, both regional and Oriental, both Mediterranean and Colonial, which we might with little outlay develop and utilise . . .

Here in Cyprus is one such experimental field, alike for colonial development and colonial education. Here are contacts with well-nigh all the problems of nature and man, present and future, home and colonial, European and world-wide, which the world can at present show; and here, too, is that very atmosphere of ancient culture from which both our classical and religious traditions are derived . . . Our possible college might be not only of local, technical, and colonial, but of general interest and importance, a Cyprus College, where European and Eastern might conveniently and profitably meet; nay, for which there is such ample room that it might soon justify a useful existence, were it but a sanatorium alone.

Haggard 1900

[Plate 55]

Sir H. (Henry) Rider Haggard (1856–1925), a popular British novelist in the late 19th and early 20th centuries, author of *King Solomon's Mines, She,* and *Cleopatra,* made a Mediterranean trip in 1900 recorded in his book, *A Winter Pilgrimage, Being an Account of Travels through Palestine, Italy, and the Island of Cyprus, accomplished in the Year 1900,* published by Longmans, Green and Co., London, 1901.

Haggard had visited Cyprus fourteen years earlier, recorded only in "Our Position in Cyprus," an article in *Contemporary Review*, II,1887. This second trip gave him some opportunity to compare and note the changes that had occurred.

CHAPTER V

NAPLES TO LARNACA

. . . After the dull weather we had experienced between Italy and Egypt, the twenty-four hours' run of our lonely voyage to Larnaca was very pleasant, for the sun shone brightly, the wind did not blow, and the sea was blue as only the Mediterranean in its best moods knows how to be. When we got up next morning—we were provided, each of us, with a whole four-berth cabin, but the *Flora* does not boast a bath—it was to find that Cyprus was already in sight: a long, grey land with occasional mountains appearing here and there.

Onward we steamed, watching a single white-sailed bark that slid towards us across the azure sea like some dove on outstretched wings, till at length we cast anchor in the roadstead off the little port of Larnaca, a pretty town lying along the seashore. Some miles away, and to our left as we face it, rises the mountain of the Holy Cross—I think that it is, or used to be called Oros Staveros by the Greeks, and by the Latins Monte Croce, at any rate in the time of Pocock.

Felix Fabri, the German monk who made two pilgrimages to Palestine in or about the year 1480, tells how he visited this monastery and saw its relics. It will be remembered that St. Helena, the mother of Constantine the Great, who when an old woman journeyed to the Holy Land in 325 of our era, was so fortunate as to discover beneath the alleged site of the Holy Sepulchre, the veritable cross of our Lord together with that of one or both of the thieves who suffered with Him. But of this more hereafter. The cross of the good thief who, why I know not, has been named Dysma, she is said to have brought to Cyprus and established upon this mountain. Whether anything of it remains there now I cannot say, as I made no visit to the place either on this occasion or on a former journey in the island some fourteen years ago. This is what old Felix says about it. I quote here and elsewhere from the most excellent and scholarly translation of his writings by Mr. Audrey Stewart, M.A., which is unfortunately practically inaccessible to most readers, as it can only be obtained as part of the "Palestine Pilgrims' Text Society" at a minimum cost of ten guineas:—

"She"—*i.e.* St. Helena—"brought her own cross, that which had been Dysma's, entire from Jerusalem to this mount, and here she built a great convent for monks, and a church within which she placed this cross as an exceeding holy relic. She ordered a chamber or closet to be built in the wall over against the altar, and placed the cross within it; and there it stands unmoved even to this day, albeit the monastery itself has long since been overthrown, even to the ground, by the Turks and Saracens, and the monks of the Order of St. Benedict who once dwelt therein have been scattered. The position and arrangement of this cross in its place is wonderful. The cross stands in a blind window, and both its arms are let into holes made in the walls, and its foot is let into a hole made in the floor. But the holes which contain the arms of the cross and the foot of the cross are large out of all proportion, and the cross nowhere touches the wall, but is free and clear from contact with the wall on every side. The miracle which is noised abroad about the cross is that it hangs in the air without any fastening, and withal stands as firm as though it were fixed with the strongest nails or built into the wall, which nevertheless it is not, because all the three holes are very great, so that a man can put his hand into them and perceive by touch that there is no fastening there, nor yet at the back or at the head of the cross. I might indeed have searched this thing more narrowly than I did, but I feared God, and had no right to do that which I had forbidden others to do. I climbed this mount to show honour to the cross, not to try whether there was a miracle or not, or to tempt God. That this cross may be the more worthy of reverence, they have joined to it a piece of the true Cross of Christ."

Felix Fabri was easily satisfied, as a mediaeval monk should be. So much for the cross of Dysma.

Soon we were rowing ashore in the Government boat, a distance of three-quarters of a mile or so, for Larnaca is not a harbour, but an open roadstead—there are now no harbours worthy of the name in Cyprus. Landing at the pier we were at once conducted to the custom-house, and explained that we had nothing to declare.

"But have you a revolver?" asked the officer.

I answered that I had.

"Then I must trouble you to hand it over," he replied. "I will give you a receipt for it, and you can claim it when you leave the island."

I looked what I felt, astonished, but obeyed. On inquiry it appeared that the Cyprus Government has recently passed some legislation as to the importation of firearms. It would seem that murders had been somewhat frequent in the island, mostly carried out by shooting, hence the law. Whether it was intended to prevent respectable travellers who purpose journeying in the mountain districts from carrying a pistol for their own protection, is another matter. Doubtless in fact it was not; but in Cyprus they have a great respect for the letter of the law, and therefore put this somewhat unnecessary query. For instance, they have another regulation—aimed, I suppose, at the exclusion of phylloxera—against the importation of seeds or plants, which has been known to work in an unforeseen manner. Thus a year or two ago a foreign royalty, I think it was the Prince of Naples, visited the island wearing a carnation in his buttonhole. His Royal Highness must have been somewhat amazed when a custom-house official leant forward and gently but firmly removed the contraband flower.

I am told that this story is quite true, but it may be only a local satire upon the kindly providence of a patriarchal Government.

It is right to add, however, that there is not the slightest need for a traveller of the ordinary stamp to carry any defensive weapon in Cyprus. Since the English occupation of the island at any rate, now some twenty years ago, no place can be more safe. In the wildest parts of it he who behaves himself has nothing to fear from the natives, a kindly, gentle-natured race, Turk or Christian, although, as I have said, not averse to murdering each other upon occasion. But of this also more hereafter.

Having delivered up the weapon of war and been given an elaborate receipt for the same, we proceeded to our hotel accompanied by a motley collection of various blood and colour, each of them bearing a small piece of our exiguous belongings, whereof the bulk, it will be remembered, had travelled to Reggio. These folk, however, are not exorbitant in their demands and do not grumble or ask for more. Tourists have not come to Cyprus to spoil it; I never heard of an American even setting foot on the island, therefore a shilling here goes as far as five elsewhere.

The hotel at Larnaca is now I believe the only one in Cyprus. It stands within a few feet of the shore—safely enough, for the sea is tideless—is comfortable, with large, cool rooms, and absurdly cheap. I grieve to add that its proprietor cannot make it pay. No travellers visit this lovely and most interesting isle, in ancient days the garden of the whole Mediterranean, therefore there are no hotels. Once there was one at Limasol, but it failed and converted itself into a hospital. He who would journey here must either rely upon tents, which are a poor shelter before the month of April, or upon the kind and freely offered hospitality of the Government officials. Naturally this lack of accommodation frightens away tourists, which for many reasons in a poor country like Cyprus is a vast pity. Yet until the tourist comes it is idle to expect that conveniences for his reception will be provided. So this matter stands.

Where Larnaca now lies was once the ancient Citium, of which the marsh near at hand is believed to have been the harbour. Quite half of the present town, indeed, is said to be built upon the necropolis of Citium, whence comes its name, Larnaca, derived, it is supposed, from *Larnax*, an urn or a sepulchre. The town is divided into two parts, Larnaca proper and the Marina along the seashore, which is reported to have been recovered within the last few centuries from the bed of the ocean.

After luncheon we went to a house whose owner deals occasionally in curiosities. Of these and all antiquities indeed the export is forbidden except to the British Museum, private digging having been put a stop to in the island, as its inhabitants aver, in the especial interest of that institution. Here we saw a few nice things, but the price asked was impossible, £12 being demanded for a set of little glass vases which I should have valued at 40s. So we left the place, richer only by an Egyptian or Phoenician spear-head of Cyprian copper, a very excellent specimen, and walked to the upper town about a mile away to take tea with Mr. Cobham, the Commissioner.

Mr. Cobham lives in a beautiful house which he has purchased. For generations it had been the abode of the British consuls at Larnaca, but was abandoned by them many years ago. Here in a noble room he has his unique collection of ancient books written by travellers during the last five or six centuries, and others dealing with, or touching on, Cyprus and its affairs. It is from these sources that its learned author has compiled the work known as *Excerpta Cypria*, which consists of translations from their pages, a book invaluable to students, but now unhappily out of print. I considered myself fortunate in being able to purchase a set of the sheets at an advanced price in the capital, Nicosia, where it was printed.

Set upon a wall of the saloon in this house and although newly painted, dating from a century and a half or more ago, is a fine, carved example of the royal arms of

England. This very coat, as Mr. Cobham has ascertained, used to stand over the doors of the old British Consulate during the tenancy of his house by the consuls. When they left it was taken down and vanished, but within the last few years he found it in a stable in Larnaca, whence the carving was rescued, repainted by some craftsman on board an English man-of-war which visited Cyprus, and after a hundred years or so of absence, returned in triumph to its old home.

Cyprus is fortunate in possessing in Mr. Cobham an official who takes so deep an interest in her history, and spares no expense or pains in attempting its record. On the occasion of my visit he spoke to me very sadly of the vandalism which the authorities threaten to commit by the throwing down of the seaward wall, curtain-wall I think it is called, of the ancient, fortified city of Famagusta, in order, principally, that the stone and area may be made use of for the purposes of the railway, which it is proposed to construct between Famagusta and Nicosia. Of this suggested, but as yet happily unaccomplished crime, I shall have something to say on a later page.

CHAPTER VI
COLOSSI

On the day following that of our arrival in Cyprus the *Flora* reappeared from Famagusta and about noon we went on board of her to proceed to Limasol, some forty or fifty miles away, where we were engaged so stay a week or ten days. The traveller indeed is lucky when he can find a chance of making this journey in the course of an afternoon by boat, instead of spending from ten to fifteen hours to cover it in a carriage. Although Cyprus in its total area is not much, if any, larger than the two counties of Norfolk and Suffolk, locomotion is still difficult owing to the impassable nature of the ways and the steepness and frequency of the mountains. When I visited it fourteen or fifteen years ago there were no roads to speak of in the island, except one of a very indifferent character between Larnaca and Nicosia. The Turks, its former masters, never seem to make a road; they only destroy any that may exist. Now in this respect matters are much improved. The English Government, out of the pitiful sums left at its command after the extraction from the colony of every possible farthing towards the payment of the Turkish tribute, has by slow degrees constructed excellent roads between all the principal towns, with bridges over the beds of the mountain torrents. But as yet in the country districts nothing of the sort has been attempted.

With us were embarked a number of lambs, little things not more than a week or two old, bought, I suppose, for the provisioning of the ship. At this season of the year everybody in Cyprus lives upon lamb. It was melancholy to see the tiny creatures, their legs tied together, heaped one upon another in the bottoms of large baskets, whence, bleating piteously for their mothers, they were handed up and thrown upon the deck. A more satisfactory sight to my mind were one or two cane creels half filled with beautiful brown-plumaged woodcock, shot or snared by native sportsmen upon the mountain slopes.

On board the steamer, a fellow-passenger to Limasol, whither he was travelling to negotiate for the land upon which to establish a botanical garden, was Mr. Gennadius, the Director of Agriculture for the island. He told me what I had already observed at Larnaca—that the orange and citron trees in Cyprus, which on the occasion of my former visit were beautiful to behold, are to-day in danger of absolute destruction, owing to the ravages of a horrible black scale which fouls and disfigures fruit and leaves alike. (*Avnidia coceinea* or *Avnidia orantii.*)

For the last dozen years or so this blight has been increasingly prevalent, the mandarin variety of fruit alone showing any power of resisting its attacks. The proper way to treat the pest is by a number of sprayings with a mixture of from twenty to twenty-five per cent. of soft soap to eighty or seventy-five per cent. of warm water. A dressing thus prepared destroys the scale by effecting a chemical union of the alkali of the soap with the fatty matter in the organism of the parasite, or failing this stifles it by glazing it over and excluding the air necessary to its existence. Mr. Gennadius believes that if this treatment could be universally adopted, scale would disappear from Cyprus within a few years.

But here comes the difficulty. For three centuries the Cypriote has been accustomed to Turkish rule with its great pervading principle of *Kismet*. If it pleases Allah to destroy the orange-trees (in the case of the Christian peasant, read God) so let it be, he says, and shrugs his shoulders. Who am I that I should interfere with the will of Heaven by syringing? Which being translated into Anglo-Saxon means, "I can't be bothered to take the trouble." If the Director of Agriculture in person or by proxy would appear three or four times a year in the sufferer's garden with the wash ready made and a squirt and proceed to apply it, the said sufferer would look on and smoke, making no objection. Beyond this he will rarely go.

Therefore unless the blight tires of attack it begins to look as though the orange is doomed in Cyprus. This is a pity, as that fruit does very well there, and the mildew which threatened it at one time was taken at its commencement and conquered by means of powdered sulphur puffed about the trees with bellows, Government distributing the sulphur at cost price.

About three hours after leaving Larnaca the vessel passes a sloping sward clothed with young corn and carob-trees that, backed by lofty peaks of the Trooidos range, runs from a hill-top to the lip of the ocean. Here once stood Amathus, a great city of immemorial antiquity which flourished down to Roman times if not later, and ultimately, it is said, was destroyed by an earthquake. Now all that is left of it are acres of tumbled stone and a broken fragment of fortress, whether ancient or mediaeval I cannot say, against the walls of which the sea washes. It is told that here, or at some later town built upon the same site, Richard Coeur-de-Lion landed when he took Cyprus from the Emperor Isaac Comnenus.

Wonderful indeed is it for us, the children of this passing hour, to look at that grey time-worn coast and as we glide by to reflect upon the ships and men that it has seen, who from century to century came up out of the deep sea to shape its fortunes for a while. Who were the first? No one knows, but very early the fleets of Egypt were here. Then followed the Phoenicians, those English of the ancient world as they have been called, who like eagles to the carcass, gathered themselves wherever were mines to be worked or moneys to be made. They have left many tombs behind them and in the tombs works of art, some of them excellent enough. Thus before me as I write stands a bronze bull made by Phoenician hands from Cypriot copper, a well-modelled animal full of spirit, with a tail that wags pleasingly upon a balled joint.

After the Phoenicians, or with them perhaps, were Greeks of the Mycenian period. Their tombs also celebrate a glory that is departed, as the British Museum can bear witness. Next to the Greek the Persian; then the satraps of Alexander the Great; then the Ptolemies; then galleys that bore the Roman ensign which flew for many generations; then the Byzantine emperors—these for seven centuries.

After this a new flag appears, the lions of England flaunting from the ships of war of Richard the First. He took the place and sold it to Guy de Lusignan, King of Jerusalem so called, whose descendants ruled here for three centuries, till at length the island passed into the hands of the Venetian. These only held it eighty years, and after them came the most terrible fleet the Cyprian Sea has seen, that which flew the Crescent. For three centuries Cyprus groaned and withered under the dreadful rule of the Turk, till at last a few gentlemen arrived in a mail-steamer and for the second time in the history of the island ran up the flag of Britain. How long will it float there, I wonder?

It was very interesting to watch the beautiful gulls that followed the vessel off this coast, the wind blowing against them making not the slightest difference to the perfect ease of their motion. So near did they hang that I could see their quick, beady eyes glancing here and there, and the strong bills of a light pink hue. From time to time as I watched, one of them would catch sight of something eatable in the water. Then down he went and suddenly from the feathers of his underpart out shot his claws, also pink-coloured, just as though he were settling upon a tree or rock. Why, I wonder, does a gull do this when about to meet the water? To break his fall perhaps. At least I can suggest no other reason, unless in the dim past his progenitors were wont to settle upon trees and he is still unable to shake off an hereditary habit.

At length on the low mountain-hedged coast-line appeared the white houses, minarets, and scattered palms of Limasol, with its jetty stretching out into the blue waters. The town looked somewhat grown, otherwise its aspect seems much the same as when first I saw it many years ago.

So we landed, and after more custom-house formalities, marched through the crowded streets of the little town, preceded by stalwart Cypriotes bearing our belongings, to dine (in borrowed garments) with the kind friends who were awaiting us upon the pier.

Our first occupation on the following morning was to retain the services of three mules and their coal-black muleteer, doubtless the offspring of slaves imported in the Turkish days, known to us thenceforth by a corruption of his native name or designation which we crystallised into "Cabbages." For a sum of about thirty shillings a week this excellent and intelligent person placed himself and his animals at our disposal, to go whither we would and when we would.

Our first expedition was to a massive tower, or rather keep, called Colossi, which stands at a distance of about six miles from Limasol, in the midst of very fertile fields upon the Paphos road. Off we went, my nephew and myself riding our hired mules and the rest of the party upon their smart ponies, which in Cyprus are very good and cheap to buy and feed.

I have now had considerable experience of the mule as an animal to ride, and I confess that I hate him. He has advantages no doubt. Over rough ground in the course of an eight or ten hours' day he will cover as great a distance as a horse, and in the course of a week or less he will wear most horses down. Also he will live somehow where the horse would starve. But what a brute he is! To begin with, his fore-quarters are invariably weak, and feel weaker than they are. The Cypriote knows this and rides him on a native saddle, a kind of thick padded quilt so cruppered that he is able to sit far back, almost on the animal's tail indeed, as, doubtless for the same reason, the costermonger rides a donkey. To the stranger, until he grows accustomed to it, this saddle is most uncomfortable, but old residents in the island generally prefer to use it upon a long journey. Also it is dangerous to the uninitiated, since the stirrups are very short. Not being fixed they slide from side to side, suddenly lengthening themselves, let us say to the right, with any unguarded movement, which will produce a proportionate curtailment on the left and the unexpected consequence that the traveller finds himself face downwards on the ground. With a European saddle this particular accident cannot happen, also it is more comfortable for a short journey. As a set-off to this advantage, however, the rider's weight comes upon that portion of his steed which is least able to support it, namely the withers. The result is that the mule, especially if pushed out of its customary amble, sometimes falls as though it were shot, propelling him over its head.

It is a mistake to suppose, also, that these creatures are always sure-footed; many of them stumble abominably although they do not often actually fall. Never shall I forget my first mule-ride in Cyprus in the days when there were no roads. It was from Nicosia to Kyrenia, a distance of about sixteen miles over a mountain path. The muleteer into whose charge I was given was a huge man weighing at least eighteen stone, and I thought to myself that where this monster could go, certainly I could follow.

In this I was right, I did follow, but at a very considerable distance. Mr. Muleteer perched himself upon his animal, doubtless one of the best in the island, looking in his long robes for all the world like a gigantic and half-filled sack, and off we ambled. Scarcely were we clear of the town when my mule, unaccustomed, I suppose, to the weight upon his withers and the European saddle, began to stumble. I do not exaggerate when I say that he stumbled all the way to Kyrenia, keeping me absolutely damp with apprehension of sudden dives on to my head down precipitous and unpleasant places. Meanwhile Mr. Muleteer, very possibly anticipating my difficulties, had been careful to place about five hundred yards between us, a distance which he maintained throughout the journey. I yelled for assistance—in fact I wished to persuade him to exchange mules—but either he would not or he could not hear; moreover he had no knowledge of my tongue, or I of his. So we accomplished that very disagreeable journey.

* * * * *

Much of the land through which we rode to Colossi was under crops of wheat and barley, the latter now coming into ear. The cultivation struck me as generally very poor, but what can one expect in a country where they merely scratch the surface of the soil, and so far as I could see never use manure? So shallow is their ploughing that in most cases squills and other bulbous roots are not dislodged by it, but grow on among the corn, where, dotted about, also stand many carob-trees, of which the fruit, a bean, is the basis of Thorley's and other foods for cattle. On the patches of uncultivated land a great many very beautiful anemones, the harbingers of spring, were in flower, also large roots of asphodel with its stiff sword-shaped leaves. This was the flower of which the Greek poets were so fond of singing. Their wars and labours o'er, the heroes are to repose

> ". . . in the shadowy field
> Of asphodel."

In point of fact it is in my opinion an unpleasing plant, the flowers, which spring from a tall stem, being small individually and neutral-tinted. Also they have this peculiarity; if cut and set in a room, they cause the place to smell as though many cats had slept there.

A ride of about an hour brought us to Colossi. That the tower in its present shape was built or repaired in the Lusignan time is evident from the coats of arms—very beautifully cut—of the orders of the Knights Templars and St. John which still appear upon the east face of the fortress. On one of these shields, that below the other three, all the four quarters carry a fleur-de-lys and nothing else. Another, the centre of the three in the upper line, immediately beneath the crown which seems to take the place of a crest, has four crosses in the dexter quartering, and a rampant lion on the rest. I say of the three coats, but as a matter of fact there are only two, the third, which has been removed, being represented by an ugly gaping hole. It seems that some cantankerous old person who still lives in the village had a lawsuit, which he lost, as to the ownership of this tower of Colossi. In order to reassert his rights, however, he wrenched out one of the coats-of-arms and took it off to his house, where it remains. In the interest of the archaeology of the island the Government ought to insist upon its being restored, or if necessary to replace it by force. [*Haggard footnotes*: Since the above passage was written, I hear that on the death of the individual spoken of, a search was made for the missing shield. It has vanished quite away—probably by secret burial!]

The tower itself, according to my rough pacings, is a square of about fifty-seven feet internal measurement, and from sixty to seventy feet in height. It is a very massive building still in fair order, although I suppose that it has not been repaired for centuries. Now—so low are the mighty fallen—it serves only as a grain and chaff store for the surrounding farm. Its bottom storey, which is strongly vaulted, evidently was used for soldiers' quarters and dungeons. Above is a fine chamber now partitioned off, which occupies the whole square of the castle and is adorned with a noble, vaulted fireplace stamped on either side with a fleur-de-lys. The tradition is that Richard Coeur-de-Lion spent his honeymoon with Berengaria in this chamber after rescuing her *vi et armis* from the Emperor Isaac, whom he defeated in the plains below. There is another story which I have heard but am unable to trace, namely that Richard in his hurry to attack the forces of the Emperor outrode his companions, and reaching this tower of Colossi, shook his lance and galloped about it alone calling to Isaac, who was a poor creature and had not the slightest wish to accept the invitation, to come out and fight him.

A narrow winding stair of the usual Norman type, whereof the ends of the steps themselves form the central supporting column, leads to the cement roof, which is flat, as is common in Cyprus. Hence the view is very beautiful, for beneath lies a wide stretch of country, now looking its best in the green garment of springing crops, while to the right the eye is caught by a great salt lake, once a source of considerable revenue to the island.

This it might be again indeed, were it not that with the peculiar ineptitude and want of foresight which distinguished the agreement concluded by the Government of this country as to the occupation of Cyprus, we have promised the Turks not to work it in competition with other salt lakes of their own on the mainland. Loveliest of all perhaps is the blue background of the measureless, smiling sea, dotted here and there with white-sailed ships.

Projecting from this roof upon one side is a curious grating of massive stone, of which presently I guessed the use. Immediately beneath hung the portcullis of the castle, whereof the wooden rollers or pulleys are still to be seen. Doubtless this grating was designed as a place of vantage whence the defenders could let fall stones or boiling oil and water upon the heads of those who attacked the drawbridge.

Some rich man ought to buy Colossi, sweep away the filthy farm-buildings about it, and restore the tower to its original grandeur. With suitable additions it would make a delightful country-house.

Night was falling before we came home to Limasol. The last glow of sunset still lingered on the white walls and red roofs of the scattered houses, while above them here a feathery palm, and there a graceful minaret stood out against the pale green sky in which the moon shone coldly.

CHAPTER VII

A CYPRIOTE WEDDING

On Sunday we attended church in the Sergeants' room, a congregation perhaps of twelve or fifteen people. Limasol has a chapel belonging to it which was once used for the troops, but as it seems that the War Office, or the Treasury, I am not sure which, lay claim to the altar rails and benches, no service is now held there. In Cyprus as elsewhere there is such a thing as Red Tape.

After luncheon I accompanied Mr. Michell, the Commissioner, to a grand Greek wedding to which he had kindly procured me an invitation. On arriving at the house we were conducted upstairs to a large central room, out of which opened other rooms. In one of these stood the bride dressed in white, a pretty, dark-eyed girl, to whom we were introduced. By her, arrayed in evening clothes, was the bridegroom, a Greek, who is registrar of the local court, and about them their respective parents and other relatives. In the main apartment were assembled a mixed crowd of friends, guests, and onlookers. Near its centre stood a marble-topped table arranged as an altar with two tall candlesticks wreathed in orange blossoms, a cup of sacramental wine, two cakes of sacramental bread, a silver basket holding two wreaths of orange blossom with long satin streamers attached, and a copy of the Gospels beautifully bound in embossed silver.

Presently a procession of six priests entered the room, attired all of them in magnificent robes of red and blue worked with silk, gold and silver. They wore tall Eastern-looking hats very much like those affected by Parsees and had their hair arranged in a pigtail, which in some instances hung down their backs and in others was tucked up beneath the head-dress. All of them were heavily bearded.

Most of these priests were striking in appearance, with faces by no means devoid of spirituality. Indeed, studying them, it struck me that some of the Apostles might have looked like those men. The modern idea of the disciples of our Lord is derived in the main, perhaps, from pictures by artists of the Renaissance school, of large-made, brawny individuals, with wild hair and very strongly-marked countenances, quite different from the type that is prevalent in the East to-day. It is probable that these fanciful portraits have no trustworthy basis to recommend them to our conviction; that in appearance indeed the chosen twelve did not differ very widely from such men of the more intellectual stamp, as are now to be seen in Cyprus and Syria. But this is a question that could be argued indefinitely, one moreover not susceptible of proof.

Tradition, however, curiously unvarying in this instance, has assigned to the Saviour a certain type of face which, with differences and modifications, is not unlike that of at least two of the priests whom I saw at this ceremony. They looked good men, intellectual men, men who were capable of thought and work—very different, for example, in their general aspect and atmosphere to the vast majority of those priests whom the traveller sees in such a place as Florence. Still the reputation of these Greek clergy is not uncommonly malodorous. Critics say hard things of them, as the laity do of the priests in South America. Probably all these things are not true. In every land the clergyman is an individual set upon a pedestal at whom it is easy to throw dirt, and when the dirt strikes it sticks, so that all the world may see and pass by on the other side. Doubtless, however, here as elsewhere there are backsliders, and of these, after the fashion of the world, we hear more than of the good and quiet men who do their duty according to their lights and opportunities and are still.

When all the preliminaries were finished the bride and bridegroom took their places before the table-altar which I have described, and crossed themselves ceremoniously. Then the service began. It was long and impressive, consisting chiefly of prayers and passages of Scripture read or chanted by the different priests in turn, several men standing round them who were, I suppose, professionals, intoning the responses with considerable effect. At an appointed place in the ceremony a priest produced two rings with which he touched the foreheads and breasts of the contracting parties, making with them the sign of the cross. One of these rings was then put on by the bridegroom and the other, oddly enough over her glove, by the bride.

At later periods of the service the silver-covered book of the Gospels was given to the pair to kiss, and cotton-seed, emblematic apparently of fertility, like our rice, was thrown on to them from an adjoining room. Also, and this was the strangest part of the ceremony, the two wreaths that I have described were taken from the silver basket and set respectively upon the brow of the bridegroom and the veil, already wreath-crowned, of the bride, where it did not sit at all well, giving her, in fact, a somewhat bacchanalian air. The bridegroom also looked peculiar with this floral decoration perched above his spectacles, especially as its pendant satin tails were seized by six or eight of his groomsmen of all ages who, with their help—the bride being similarly escorted by her ladies—proceeded to drive the pair of them thrice round the altar-table. Indeed this part of the service, however deeply symbolical it may be, undoubtedly had a comic side. Another rite was that of the kissing by the priests of the wreaths when set upon the heads of the contracting parties, and the kissing of the hands of the priests by the bride and bridegroom.

After these wreaths had been removed the newly-married pair partook of the Communion in both kinds, biting thrice at the consecrated cake of bread that was held to their mouths, and drinking (I think) three sips of the wine. This done the elements were removed. The ceremony ended with a solemn blessing delivered by the head priest and the embracing of the bride and bridegroom by their respective relations. At this point the bride wept after the fashion of ladies in her situation throughout the world. Indeed she was moved to tears at several stages of the service.

After it was over, in company with other guests we offered our congratulations to the pair, drank wine to their healths and partook of sweetmeats. Also we inspected the nuptial chamber, which was adorned with satin pillows of a bright and beautiful blue. I am informed, but of this matter I have no personal knowledge, that the friends of the bride stuff her mattress with great ceremony, inserting in it pieces of money and other articles of value. So we bade them good-bye, and now as then I wish to both of them every excellent fortune in life . . .

Later in the afternoon of the wedding we went for a ride to the military camp, about three miles from Limasol. Once there was a regiment quartered here, but the garrison is now, I think, reduced to a single company. It would be difficult to find a healthier or more convenient site whereat to station soldiers, the place being high and the water excellent. Perhaps those empty huts will be filled again some day.

On our way back we passed through a grove of the most gigantic olive-trees that I ever saw. Those in the Garden of Gethsemane seem small compared to them. Having a rule in my pocket I dismounted and took the measure of one of these. It proved to be approximately fifty feet in circumference by sixteen in diameter at the ground, but of course was almost hollow. How old must that tree be? Taking into consideration the hard wood and slow-growing habit of the olive, I imagine that in the time of the Romans, and very possibly in those of the Ptolemies, it was already bearing fruit. Perhaps a Mycenian, or one of Alexander's legionaries, planted it, who can say? Probably, too, it will last for another three or four hundred years before, in the grip of slow decay, that end overtakes it which awaits everything earthly, not excepting the old earth herself.

One morning Mr. Mavrogordato, the Commandant of Police for the Limasol district, to whose kindness I owe many of the photographs of scenes in Cyprus which are reproduced in these pages, took us to see the ancient fortress of the town, now used as its prison. The road to this castle passes through a misused Turkish graveyard where Mr. Mavrogordato has had the happy thought to plant trees which, in that kindly air and soil, are now growing up into a welcome patch of greenery and shade. This castle is a massive building in stone belonging apparently to the Venetian period, that is, above ground, for the chapel and vaults below are Gothic. The interior is kept most scrupulously clean and whitewashed. Round the central well run galleries in two storeys, which galleries are divided into cells whereof the iron gates are secured with large and resplendent brass padlocks. I do not think that I ever saw padlocks which shone so bright. From side to side of the second storey, stretched across the deep well beneath, is an ugly-looking black balk of timber, and screwed into it are two bolts and eyes of singularly uncompromising and suggestive appearance. This is the gallows beam, so placed and arranged that the prisoners in the cells have the advantage of a daily contemplation of the last bridge of evil footsteps.

An execution from that beam, and there have been several, I believe, must create quite an excitement among the wrong-doers of Limasol . . .

On the occasion of my visit, amongst other convicts there were in the Limasol prison, contemplating the gallows-beam aforesaid, four men who were accused of the murder of a fellow-villager suspected of having poisoned their cattle. Murder is a crime of not uncommon occurrence in Cyprus, where many of the inhabitants are very poor and desirous of earning money, even in reward of the destruction of a neighbour with whom they have no quarrel. It has been proved in the course of investigation of some of these cases that the fee paid was really absurdly small, so low as ten shillings indeed, or, as one of the judges informed me, in the instance of a particularly abominable slaughter, four shillings and no more. Some of the victims suffer on account of quarrels about women, as in Mexico, where in a single village street on a Sunday morning, after the orgies of a Saturday night, I have seen as many as three dead, or at least two dead and one dying. More frequently, however, in Cyprus the victim is a downright bad character of whom a community are determined to be rid, so that in fact the murder, as in the present example, partakes of the nature of lynch-law.

After the commission of the crime its perpetrators, if suspected, hide themselves in the mountains, where they must be hunted down like wild beasts. One party of these outlaws defied arrest for quite a number of months, during which time they took several shots at the pursuing Mr. Mavrogordato. Ultimately, however, they were themselves shot, or caught and hanged.

The view from the top of the castle was perhaps even more beautiful than that of Colossi. In front, the boundless sea whereon poor Berengaria of Navarre, rolling in the roads of Limasol, suffered such dire perplexities and exercised so wise a caution. Behind, the slopes of the grey mountains with Trooidos towering above them, white-capped just now with snow. To the right the salt lake, and immediately beneath, the town dotted here and there with palms.

Just at the foot of the fortress is the Turkish quarter, for the most part nothing better than a collection of mud hovels. The population of Cyprus, it may be explained, is divided into Turks and pure Cypriots. These Turks, I suppose, are the descendants of those members of the invading Ottoman army under Mustafa which conquered Cyprus three centuries ago, who elected to remain in the island as settlers. The proportion is roughly—Turks one-third of the population, Cypriotes two-thirds. The Turks, who generally live in villages by themselves, are going down the hill rapidly, both in numbers and wealth, being poor, lazy, fatalistic, and quite unfitted to cope with their cleverer Christian compatriots. In many instances, however, they are respected and respectable members of the community, brave in person and upright in conduct. Few of them can afford more than one wife and as a rule their families seem small.

The richer and more successful class of Cypriotes have a habit of adopting Greek names, but in fact very few of them are Greeks except for so much of the Mycenian blood as may remain n their veins. Still some of them intrigue against the British Government and affect a patriotic desire for union with Greece, that even the disillusionment of the Turkish war has not quenched. These aspirations, which, in some instances at any rate, are said to be not uninfluenced by the hope of rewards and appointments when the blessed change occurs, are scarcely likely to be realised. If Cyprus is ever handed over to any one by Great Britain, it must be to its nominal suzerain the Sultan, to whom the reversion belongs. But surely, after the stories of the recent massacres of Christians, and other events connected with Turkish rule, British public opinion, exercised as it is profoundly by the existing if half-avowed alliance between this country and the evil system which the Sultan represents, could never allow of such a step. It would be monstrous to give back Christians into his keeping, and a crime to plunge Cyprus once more into the helpless, hopeless ruin, out of which under our just if sorely hampered government it is being slowly lifted.

After inspecting Mr. Mavrogordato's stud—if that be the correct expression—of homing pigeons which with characteristic energy—not too common a quality in Cyprus—he is breeding up from imported birds, we descended from the roof to the foundations of the castle. Here we visited a large vaulted place whereof the windows have been built up in some past age. Now, we see by the light of our lanterns, it is a rubbish room, and before that, as I imagine from several indications, under the Turkish regime, probably it served as a magazine for the storage of powder. In the old days, however, this place was a chapel and here it is said, upon what exact authority I know not, that Richard Coeur-de-Lion was married to Berengaria of Navarre. The only account of these nuptials that I can lay my hand on at this moment is from a contemporary chronicle of Geoffrey de Vinsauf or Vinosalvo. He, it will be observed, although writing of Limasol, or Limouzin as he calls the town, does not mention the church in which the wedding was solemnised. If there was more than one available, which is to be doubted, it seems most probable that the chapel of the fortress would have been chosen. This is what Geoffrey says:—

> " On the morrow, namely on the Sunday, which was the festival of St. Pancras, the marriage of King Richard and Berengaria, the daughter of the King of Navarre, was solemnised at Limouzin: she was a damsel of the greatest prudence and most accomplished manners, and there she was crowned queen. There were present at the ceremony the Archbishop and the Bishop of Evreux and the Bishop of Banera, and many other chiefs and nobles. The king was glorious on this happy occasion, and cheerful to all, and showed himself joyous and affable."

How strange are the vicissitudes of walls! The fortunes of the short-lived generations that inhabit them are not so variable, for these stones last longer and see more. What a contrast between this place in its present state, lumber-strewn and lit only by a few dim lamps, to that which it must have presented in the year 1191 when the warrior king, Richard, one of the most remarkable and attractive characters who occupy the long page of our English history, took to himself a wife within their circuit. It is not difficult, even to the dullest and least imaginative of the few travellers who stray to this unvisited place, to reconstruct something of that pageant of the mighty dead. The splendid figure of the king himself, clad in his shirt of mail and broidered tabard gay with the royal arms of England. The fair bride glittering in her beautiful silken garments and rich adornment of gems. The archbishop and bishops in their mitred pomp. The great lords and attendant knights arrayed in their various armour. The crowd of squires and servitors pressing about the door. The altar decked with flowers, the song of such choristers as could be found among the crews of the galleys—all the gathered splendour, rude but impressive, of perhaps the most picturesque age that is known to history.

Then these great folk, thousands of miles away from their northern home, who had labouriously travelled hither exposed to the most fearful dangers by land and sea, enduring such privations as few common soldiers would now consent to bear, not to possess themselves of goldmines or for any other thinly-veiled purposes of gain, but in the fulfillment of a great idea! And that idea—what was it? To carry out a trust which they conceived, wisely or in foolishness, to be laid upon them—the rescue of the holy places from the befouling hand of the infidel. Well, they are gone and their cause is lost, and the Moslem, supported by the realm which once they ruled, still squats in the Holy Land. Such is the irony of fate, but for my part I think that these old crusaders, and especially our hot-headed Richard of England, cruel though he was at times, as we shall see at Acre, are worthy of more sympathy than a practical age seems inclined to waste upon them. Peace to their warlike, superstitious souls!

On leaving the castle we visited an inn, in the yard of which stood scores of mules. It was an odoriferous but interesting place. Under a shed at one side of it sat about a dozen smiths at work, men who hire their stands at a yearly or monthly rent. Fixed into the ground before each of them—it must be remembered that these people sit at their work, which is all done on the cold iron without the help of fire—was a tiny anvil. On these anvils the craftsmen were employed in fashioning the great horseshoe nails of the country, or in cutting out and hammering thin, flat, iron plates which are used in the East for the shoeing of mules and donkeys. These discs that are made with only one small hole in the centre, must in many ways be prejudicial to the comfort and health of the beast, or so we should think, since they cause its frog to grow foul and rot away. The teachings of practical experience, however—for which after some study of such things I have great respect—seem to prove this kind of shoe to be best suited for use upon the stony tracks of the country. These plates are secured to the animal's hoof by six of the huge-headed nails that I have mentioned, and if properly fixed will last for several months without renewal.

The instrument used to trim the hoof before the shoe is fastened, is a marvelous tool, almost of the size of a sickle with a flat knife attached to it as large as a child's spade. Probably all these implements, especially if connected in any way with agriculture, such as the wooden hook with an iron point which they call a plough, are essentially the same as those that were familiar to the Phoenicians and the Mycenian Greeks. In the Holy Land, at any rate, as we shall see later, they have not changed since the time of our Lord.

That this was so as regards the shoeing of horses in or about the year 1430 is proved by the following passage which I take from the travels of Bertrandon de la Brocquière of Guienne, who made a pilgrimage to Palestine in 1432. He says:—

> "I bought a small horse that turned out very well. Before my departure I had him shod in Damascus; and thence as far as Bursa, which is fifty days' journey, so well do they shoe their horses that I had nothing to do with his feet, excepting one of the fore ones, which was pricked by a nail, and made him lame for three weeks. The shoes are light, thin, lengthened towards the heel, and thinner there than at the toe. They are not turned up, and have but four nail-holes, two on each side. The nails are square, with a thick and heavy head. When a shoe is wanted, and it is necessary to work it to make it fit the hoof, it is done cold, without ever putting it in the fire,

which can readily be done because it is so thin. To pare the hoof they use a pruning knife, similar to what vine-dressers trim their vines with, both on this as well as on the other side of the sea."

This description might well apply to the shoeing of animals in Cyprus and Syria to-day.

From the inn we walked to the municipal market, where we found many strange vegetables for sale, including radishes large as a full-grown carrot. Nothing smaller in the radish line seems to flourish here, and I am informed that for some occult reason it is impossible to intercept them in an intermediate stage of their development. Perhaps, like mushrooms, they spring up in a single night. I am grateful to these vegetables, however, for the sight of them made clear to me the meaning of a passage by which I have long been worried. I remember reading, I forget where, in the accounts of one of the pyramid-building Pharaohs—Chufu, I believe —that he supplied tens of thousands of bunches of radishes daily to the hundred thousand labourers who were engaged upon the works.

What puzzled me was to know how Chufu provided so enormous and perennial a supply of this vegetable. The radishes of Cyprus solve the problem. One of these would be quite enough for any two pyramid-builders. I tasted them and they struck me as stringy and flavourless. Another old friend in a new form was celery tied in bunches, but such celery! Not an inch of crisp white root about it, nothing but green and leathery head. It appears in this form because it has been grown upon the top of the ground like a cabbage. Many people have tried to persuade the intelligent Cypriote to earth up his celery, but hitherto without result. "My father grew the herb thus," he answers, "and I grow it as my father did." Doubtless the Phoenicians, ignorant of the arsenic it is said to contain, liked their celery green, or perhaps it was the Persian.

Meat and game, the former marked—so advanced is Limasol—with the municipal stamp for *octroi* purposes, are also sold here. There on one stall next to a great pile of oranges, lie half-a-dozen woodcock, brown and beautiful, and by them a brace of French partridges now just going out of season, while further on is a fine hare. On the next, hanging to hooks, are poor little lambs with their throats cut, scarcely bigger than the hare, any of them; and full-grown sheep, some not so large as my fat black-faced lambs at Easter. A little further on we came to a cobbler's shop, where we inspected the native boots. These are made of goatskin and high to the knee, with soles composed of many thicknesses of leather that must measure an inch through. Cumbersome as they seem, the experience of centuries proves these boots to be the best wear possible for the inhabitants of the mountainous districts of this stony land. On the very day of which I write I saw a Cypriote arrayed in them running over the tumbled ruins of an ancient city and through the mud patches whereby it was intersected, with no more care or inconvenience than we should experience on a tennis lawn.

CHAPTER VIII

AMATHUS

Now I have to tell of Amathus, the place we passed on our journey down the coast, to-day a stone-strewn hill covered with springing corn. Even in the far past Amathus was so ancient that no one knew with certainty of its beginnings. It is said to have been founded by the Phoenicians; at any rate in it flourished a temple to the god Melkarth, and with it a famous shrine erected in honour of Venus. The mythical hero, Theseus, according to one account, is reported to have landed here with Ariadne, the daughter of Minos, who died in child-birth in the city, although the story more generally accepted says that he abandoned her on the island of Naxos. Whatever truth there may be in all these legends—and probably it is but little—this is certain, that in its day Amathus was a great town inhabited by a prosperous and powerful people. It lies about five or six miles from Limasol and is approached by a road which runs along the sea, whence it is separated by a stretch of curious black sand which blows a good deal in high winds. On the way Mr. Mavrogordato pointed out to me an ingenious method whereby he is attempting to turn that barren belt into profitable soil. He seems to have discovered that this sand, wherein one might imagine nothing would grow, is suitable to the needs of the black wattle. At any rate the trees of that species which he planted there, although scarcely more than a year old, are now large and flourishing shrubs.

As we drew near to Amathus I perceived curious holes by the roadside, covered in for the most part with rough slabs of stone. Once these holes were tombs, rifled long ago. Then we came to the site of the town stretching down to the sea-beach, where stand the remnants of a castle which we saw from the steamer. Now it is nothing but a hillside literally sown with stones that, no doubt, once formed the foundations of the dwellings of Amathus. I say the foundations, for I believe that the houses of these ancient cities, as in the villages of Cyprus to-day, were for the most part built of green brick, or what here in Norfolk we should call clay-lump, which in the course of centuries of sun and rain has melted away into the soil. The temple, public buildings, and palaces must have been magnificent, and as I shall show presently, wonderful care was lavished upon the tombs; but the habitations of the great mass of the citizens were in all likelihood humble and temporary structures, or so I think. It is the same in Egypt, where the old inhabitants grudged neither wealth nor labour in the preparation of graves, their everlasting abode, but were content to fashion their earthly lodgings of the Nile mud that lay at hand.

Amathus must have been very strong, indeed it would be difficult to find a site better suited to defence. It is surrounded by steep natural ravines which served the purpose of moats, and surmounted by a towering rock with precipitous sides, along whose slopes the city lay. Upon this rock, says tradition, stood an impregnable citadel; indeed the site is still called "The Old Castle" by the peasants of the neighbouring village of Agia Tychenos. Now all these countless stones furnish their humble tillers with a seed-bed for wheat and barley. The inexperienced might imagine that no place could be more unsuitable for the growing of crops, but in fact this is not so, seeing that in the severe Cyprian droughts stones have the property of retaining moisture to nurture the roots which otherwise would perish.

On arriving at the foot of the hill we rode round it to visit the tombs which lie behind and beyond, taking with us a supply of candles and several peasants as guides. These sepulchres were, I believe, discovered and plundered more than twenty years ago by General Cesnola, the consul, whose splendid collection of antiquities is to be seen in America. The first we reached lay at the bottom of a deep pit now rapidly refilling with silt washed into it by the winter wet. In the surrounding rubbish we could still see traces of its violation, for here lay many fragments of ancient amphorae and of a shattered marble sarcophagus. After the rains that had fallen recently the path through the hole leading into the tomb was nothing but a pool of liquid mud through which, to win an entrance, the explorer must crawl upon his stomach, as the soil rises to within about eighteen inches of the top blocks of its square doorway. The task seemed dirty and in every way unpleasing, but I for one did not travel to Cyprus to be baffled by common, harmless mud. So I took off my coat, which in the scant state of our wardrobe I did not care to spoil, and went at it, on my hands and toes, that the rest of me might avoid the slush as much as possible.

It was a slimy and a darksome wriggle, but quite safe, in this respect differing somewhat from a journey of a like nature which I made a good many years ago. That was near Assouan in Egypt, where at the time certain new tombs had just been discovered which I was anxious to explore. These tombs were hollowed in the rock at the top of a steep slope of sand, which choked their doorways. Seeing that, as at Amathus, there was just sufficient space left beneath the head of the doorway of one of them for a man of moderate size to creep through, I made the attempt alone. Writhing forward, serpent-wise, through the sand, presently I found myself in the very grimmest place that I have ever visited. It was a cave of the size of a large room, and when my eyes grew accustomed to the faint light which crept through the hole, I saw that it was literally full of dead, so full that their bodies must once have risen almost to the roof. Moreover these dead had not been embalmed, for round me lay their clean bones by hundreds and their skulls by scores. Yet once this sepulchre was at the service of older and more distinguished occupants, as under the skeletons I found a broken mummy-case of good workmanship, and in it the body of a woman whose wrappings had decayed. She died young, since at the time of her decease she was just cutting her wisdom teeth.

As I wondered over these jumbled relics of the departed, I remembered having read that about the time of Christ, Assouan was smitten with a fearful plague which slew its inhabitants by thousands. Doubtless, I thought, here are the inhabitants, or some of them, whose bodies in such a time of pestilence it would have been impossible to embalm. So they must have brought and piled them one on another in the caves that had served as sepulchres of the richer notables among their forefathers, till all were full. I remembered also that plague germs are said to be singularly long-lived and that these might be getting hungry. With that thought I brought my examination of this interesting place to a sudden end.

Just as I was beginning my outward crawl, foolishly enough I shouted loudly to my companion whom I had left at the entrance of another sepulchre, thinking that he might help to pull me through the hole. Almost immediately afterwards I felt something weighty begin to trickle on to my back with an ever-increasing stream and in a flash understood that the reverberations of my voice had loosened the over-hanging stones already shaken and shattered by earthquakes, and that the sand was pouring down upon me from between them. Heavens! how frightened I was. Luckily one does not argue under such circumstances where, indeed, he who hesitates is lost. If I had stopped to think whether it would be best to go back or to go forward, to go quick or go slow, it is very probable that long since I should have added an alien cranium to those of that various pile. Instead I crawled forward more swiftly than ever I crawled before, notwithstanding the increasing weight upon my back, for the sand fell faster and faster, with the result that as no stone followed it to crush me, presently, somewhat exhausted, I was sitting fanning myself with a grateful heart in the dazzling sun without.

To return to Amathus and a still older tomb: this doorway beneath which we passed was also square and surmounted by four separate mouldings. Once through it, we lighted our candles to find ourselves standing in a kind of chapel, where I suppose the relatives of the dead assembled at funerals or to make offerings on the anniversaries of death. Out of this chapel opened four tombs, each of them large enough to contain several bodies. They are empty now, but their beautiful workmanship is left for us to admire. Thousands of years ago—though to look at them one might think it yesterday—the hard limestone blocks of which they are built were laid with a trueness and finish that is quite exquisite. Clearly no scamped work was allowed in old Phoenician tombs. In these graves and others close at hand, General Cesnola found many antiques of value. Indeed one of our guides, who was employed to dig for him, assisted at their ransack.

Some readers may remember a violent controversy which arose among the learned over the allegation that Cesnola unearthed the most of his more valuable antiquities in a single treasury at Curium. The said antiquities, however, being, so the critics declared, of many different styles and periods, it was found difficult to understand how they could have been discovered in one place, unless indeed Curium boasted a prehistoric British Museum with a gold-room attached. Here I may say that a few days later I visited Curium in the company of official gentlemen, who informed me that they were present when excavations were made with the object of investigating these statements. The statements, they said, were not proved.

Bearing this dispute in mind, I asked the Cypriote guide whether General Cesnola found his most important objects heaped in one place at Curium. He answered that antiquities were found here and there; that often Cesnola himself was not present when they were found, but that as they were dug up from the tombs they were collected by the workmen and taken care of, to be given over to him whenever he might come. I quote this bit of evidence for what it is worth, as in future generations, when all these burial-places have been thoroughly ransacked, the matter may become of interest because of the side-light which it throws upon ancient history.

* * * * *

These poor Phoenicians of Amathus had no such high hopes, although from time to time there were plenty in Cyprus who shared them. Yet they built their sepulchres with extraordinary expense and care, facing towards the sea as though they wished to watch the sun rise and set for ever. We break into them under the written order of the British Museum, or secretly by night, and drag their ear-rings from their ears, and their rings from their fingers, and set their staring skulls upon back shelves in dealers' dens in Limasol where once they ruled, to be sold for a shilling—skulls are cheap to-day—to the first relic-hunting traveller. Well, so it is and so it will ever be.

The next tomb we came to had a beautiful V-shaped doorway, though only the top of the inverted V was visible above the rubbish. I did not go in here, being already sufficiently plastered with mud, almost from head to foot indeed, but my companion, who is young and active, achieved the adventure. As it turned out it might very easily have been his last, for in climbing up the walls of the pit again, his foot slipped on a little piece of greasy earth and down he went backwards, dragging two Cypriotes with him in such fashion that all three of them lay in a tangled heap at the bottom of the hole. The sight was ludicrous enough, but as the older of the two guides explained to us, had it not been for his quickness and address my nephew would certainly have met with a serious accident. The man saw from the way he was falling that his head or neck must strike against a stone at the bottom of the pit, and managed to thrust his arm and thick sleeve between the two. Once my own life was saved in a very similar fashion, except that no human agency intervened. I was galloping a pony along an African road when suddenly it crossed its legs and went down as though it had been shot. In falling my head struck a stone on the road with great force, but by chance the thick cloth hat which I was wearing, being jerked from its place, interposed itself as a kind of doubled-up cushion between my temple and the stone, with the result that I escaped with slight concussion. I remember that the shock of the fall was so great that my stout buckskin braces were burst into four pieces.

That my nephew's danger was not exaggerated by the Cypriote is shown by the fact that, within the last few years, at the mouth of this or the very next tomb a German professor was killed in precisely the same way. Indeed, now that I think of it, I remember reading of his sad death in a paper. The poor gentleman, who was accompanied only by an old woman, having finished his inspection began to climb up the sides of the pit when a stone came out in his hand and he fell head first to the bottom. He only lived about five minutes and our friend, the protecting Cypriote, helped to carry away his body.

After this experience, having had enough of the interesting but dirty pursuit of "tombing," we mounted our mules and rode round the hill of the ancient city, a stone-strewn and somewhat awkward path. The streets there must have been very steep in their day and a walk up to the citadel on business, or to buy a slave or two kidnapped on the shores of Britain as a special line for the Cyprian market, excellent exercise for the fat old wine-bibbing merchants, whose scattered bones and broken drinking-cups we had just been handling yonder among the tombs.

Now the place is melancholy in its desolation. There is nothing left, nothing. It might have formed the text of one of Isaiah's prophecies, so swept of life is it and of all outward memorials of life. I could only find one remnant. On the face of a towering rock we discovered a short uncial Greek inscription which is beginning to feel the effects of weather. Our united scholarship pieced this much out of it: "Lucius Vitellius, the great conqueror, erected this from his own." Here the information comes to a full stop, for we could not make out any more. Perhaps some reader of this page may know with certainty which Lucius Vitellius is referred to and why he was engaged in conquering at Amathus. Is it perchance Lucius Vitellius, the father of the emperor who was governor in Syria, in A.D. 34? If so he might well have described himself as "the great humbug" instead of the great conqueror, as is proved by the famous story that is told of him concerning Caligula and the moon. According to Tacitus, however, he was a good governor. "I am not ignorant that he had a bad name in Rome and that many scandalous things were said of him, but in the administration of the provinces he showed the virtues of an earlier age."

I daresay that yonder crumbling screen may be the only actual monument that is left to-day of this Vitellius, his pomp, his cunning, and his flattery.

As we returned home the scene was very beautiful. In the west the sun sank gorgeously, his fan-like arrows breaking and reflecting themselves from the dense purple under-clouds that had gathered and lay low upon the horizon of the slumbering deep.

High above in the fathomless blue spaces of the Cyprian heavens, rode the great moon, now rounding to her full, her bright face marked with mountain scars. And the lights that lay on sea, sky and land, on the plain of Limasol and the mount of ruined Amathus, who shall describe them—those changeful, many-coloured lights, so delicate, so various and so solemn?

On the day after our visit to Amathus I attended the Court-house to listen to the magisterial examination of the men (whose numbers had now increased to six) whom I had seen previously in jail awaiting their trial upon a charge of murder. The court was crowded with the relatives of the accused; *zaptiehs*, or policemen; a selection of idlers from among the general public; a goodly number of Greek advocates crowded together in the front bench, and the six prisoners themselves all squeezed into a dock which was much too small for them, where they stood in a double row listening to the evidence with an indifferent air, real or affected. For the rest Mr. Mavrogordato, as I am told a veritable terror to evildoers, conducted the case for the prosecution, bringing out his points with great clearness, while the district judge, Mr. Parker, sat as a magistrate's court. The judicial functions of the legal officials in Cyprus are by the way rather curiously mixed, the same individual being able, apparently, to sit in varying executory capacities.

The case was opened by the different advocates announcing for which of the prisoners they appeared. Then Mr. Mavrogordato took up his parable and began to examine the Greek doctor through an interpreter, whose somewhat lengthy translations made the proceedings rather slow. When, after a couple of hours, we had just got to the point where he turned the body over, growing weary I went home to lunch. To this hour I cannot say whether or no those reputed murderers, or if any, which of them, still adorn the land of life, or whether under Mr. Mavrogordato's guidance, they have passed beneath that black beam which spans the central well in the old castle at Limasol. I think very possibly, however, that they were all acquitted or reprieved, for although I am certain that they, or some of them, did the deed, from the opening of the case, out of the depths of a not inconsiderable experience of such inquiries, I am convinced that every ounce of the evidence in possession of the prosecution was absolutely and solely circumstantial. Moreover, although they had dug him up again and looked for it, the missing knife-point could not be found in the vitals of the late-lamented cattle-poisoning rascal whom somebody had slain. A broken and recovered knife-point goes a long way with a jury, and its absence is equally favourable to the prisoner.

One afternoon I attended some athletic sports at Limasol. It was a general feast-day, in honour of what or of whom I grieve to say I forget, but on that occasion there were festivities everywhere. Earlier in the day I went for a ride to a village some miles distant which also was celebrating sports, that is to say a few loungers were gathered together about an open place in the hamlet, and nobody was doing any work. This I noticed, however, both in the village aforesaid, on the ground at Limasol, and from the spires of all the churches that I could see, a flag was flying. As it was a public holiday one might have expected that this flag would be English, or perhaps here and there, in deference to ancient and long-established custom, Ottoman. It was neither, it was Greek. Everywhere that not very attractive banner flaunted in the wind. I asked the reason but nobody seemed to know an answer. They suggested, however, that it had something to do with the Greek churches, and added that the upper classes of the Cypriotes who call themselves, but are not, Greeks, always flew the Greek flag.

I submit that this is not a good thing. Throughout the world and at all periods of its history the flag flown is the symbol of the authority acknowledged, or that the population wish to acknowledge. In Cyprus of course the bulk of the inhabitants are not concerned in this matter. The villagers of the remote hills and plains care little about banners, but if they see continually that of Greece displayed on every church tower and high place, and never, or rarely, that of Great Britain which rules them, they may, not unnaturally, draw their own conclusions. It is a small affair perhaps, but one, I believe, which might with advantage be attended to by the Government. Eastern peoples do not understand our system of *laissez faire* where the symbols of authority are concerned, and are apt to argue that we are afraid to show the colours which we do not fly. The Union Jack is not a banner that should be hidden away in British territory. Nor is this my own view only. It is shared by every unofficial Englishman in Cyprus, though these are few. Officials may have their opinions also, but it would not be fair to quote them.

After the sports were over I had an interesting conversation with a gentleman well acquainted with the customs of the country. He told me that few traces of the old Phoenician rites remain, except that which is still celebrated in some districts upon Whitsunday. Then, as did their forefathers thousands of years since, the villagers go down to the sea and bathe there, both sexes together. It is the ancient welcome given to Venus in the island fabled to be her chosen home, mixed up perhaps with some Christian ceremony of washing and regeneration. The bathers throw water over each other, but so far as outward appearances go, there is nothing incorrect in their conduct at these quaint and primitive celebrations.

CHAPTER IX
CURIUM

. . . Our next expedition was to the site of ancient Curium, which is said by Herodotus to have been peopled by Argives. To reach this ruined city we passed the tower of Colossi and lunched in the police-station of the beautiful and fertile village of Episcopi, a pleasant place for picnics. Thence we rode on a mile or so to the waste that once was Curium, through whole rows of tombs, every one of which are said to have been plundered by the omnivorous Cesnola. In front of us rose a steep hill upon whose face could be seen more tombs or rock chapels. Up this mount we climbed and at the summit came to the ancient city. As usual it was nothing but a tumbled heap of stones, but here the anemones grew by thousands among them and made the place most beautiful. Presently we found ourselves on the site of a temple. The great columns prostrate and broken, the fragments of shattered frieze, and the bits of mosaic flooring revealed by tearing up the sod, all told the same unmistakable story of fallen greatness and a magnificence that time, man, and earthquake have combined to desolate. A little further on we reached a spot where the ground is literally strewn with fragments of broken statues, some of them almost life-size, but the greater number small. I picked up the lower parts of two of these stone statues and put them into my—or rather the *zaptieh's* pocket. As I anticipated, they make excellent letter-weights. What a falling off is here! The effigies of the gods of old—the feet that were bedewed with tears of amorous maidens and of young men anxious to succeed in piratical expeditions, serving as the humble necessary letter-weight! Well, perhaps it is more honourable than to be broken up to fill the shovel of a Cyprian roadmaker.

By this spot is a well or pit which is said to be quite full of these broken statues. Probably they were thrown here on some occasion when the temple was sacked. Picking our path on horseback through the countless stones for two-thirds of a mile or so, we came to another and a larger temple. This was the great fane dedicated to Apollo Hylatus. A wonderful place it must have been when it stood here in its glory, peopled by its attendant priests and the crowd of worshippers flocking to its courts with gifts. The situation on that bold highland brow is superb and must be most splendid of all at dawn when the first level rays of the sunrise sweep its expanse. Doubtless the ancients placed the temple of their sun-god here that it might catch his arrows while darkness yet veiled the crowded town below, the wide, fertile plain which we call Episcopi, and the fields about the Norman tower of Colossi—compared to these old columns but a mushroom of yesternight.

It is not possible, at any rate to the uninstructed traveller with scant time at his disposal, to follow the exact configuration of this temple of Apollo and its courts, nor indeed if he knew them, would these details be of any great assistance to the imagination. Everywhere are tumbled stones, shattered pillars, some of them elegantly wreathed, overthrown altars and cavernous holes, in the depths of which underground cisterns and passages become visible. In short the cult of the worship of Apollo and his brother and sister divinities—always excepting that of Venus who is immortal—is not more ruined, neglected, and forlorn than this unvisited place, once its splendid sanctuary. Apollo was a joyous god, but evidently he had his stern side. At any rate not far away a headland runs out into the sea, and from its precipitous bluff those who had offended against his majesty—or had differences of opinion with his priests—were hurled to expiate their crimes by a terrifying death. At least so says tradition.

Leaving the temple of the lost Apollo our animals scrambled on through the stones till at last these ceased and we came to a stretch of bush-clad country. This is now one of the Government reserves kept thus to enable the timber of which the Turks denuded the island to spring up again safe from the ravages of man and beast. In such reserves goats are not allowed to graze, for of all animals these do the most damage to young timber, which they gnaw persistently until it perishes. It is not too much to say that where there are many goats no forest can arise. Cyprus in bygone ages was a densely wooded land. Strabo, writing in the first year of the Christian era, says of it:—

> "Such then is Cyprus in point of position. But in excellence it falls behind no one of the islands, for it is rich in wine and oil and uses home-grown wheat. There are mines of copper in plenty at Tamassos, in which are produced sulphate of copper and copper-rust, useful in the healing art. Eratosthenes talks of the plains as being formerly full of wood run to riot, choked in fact with undergrowth and uncultivated. The mines were here of some little service, the trees being cut down for the melting of copper and silver; and of further help was ship building, when men sailed over the sea without fear and with large fleets. But when even so they were not got under, leave was given to those who would and could cut them down to keep the land they had cleared in full possession and free of taxes."

Alas! far different is the case to-day. The Turks suffered the timber to be destroyed in all save the most inaccessible places, and the wasteful habits of the peasants who, if allowed, will cut up a whole tree to make a single sheep-trough, completed the ruin. So it came about that at last the land which used to supply Egypt with all the wood necessary to build her fleets was almost denuded save on the mountain peaks of Trooidos, with the result that the rainfall lessened alarmingly. Since its advent the British Government has done its best to remedy this state of affairs. As it has no money to spend in planting it has adopted another and perhaps on the whole a more effective method. Although the trees have vanished in Cyprus, by the wonderful preservative agency of nature their seeds remain in the soil, and if goats can be kept off the hills where forests stood, forests will again arise. Thus, although to speak of it anticipates my story a little, it was with a most real pleasure that in travelling from Nicosia to Cyrenia I saw the tops of great mountains which fourteen years ago I remembered naked as a plate, covered to-day with a thick growth of young firs that must now be fifteen or twenty feet in height. A generation hence and those mountain tops will once more bear a splendid forest. Care, however, is required which I do not think is always exercised. The new-formed forest should be thinned, as the wise woodman knows how to do, and the peasants allowed the use of the thinnings. This would prevent their destroying the trees by secretly firing the country, either from irritation and spite, or to get the benefit of the young grass which springs up afterwards.

In this particular reserve near Curium of which I speak, however, to my surprise I saw a flock of sheep and goats in the charge of a herd. On asking how this came about, Mr. Michell, the commissioner for the Limasol district, who kindly accompanied us and gave us the advantage of his knowledge and experience, told me that the owners of these animals claim ancient rights of which they cannot be dispossessed. These rights endure until the man dies, or sells his flock. They are however untransferable, nor may he add to the number of the animals which he grazes. Thus by degrees the matter mends itself.

In the midst of this bush-clad plain stands the ancient *stadium* of Curium, where according to tradition the old inhabitants of classic times celebrated their chariot races. In considering the place I was much puzzled by one detail. The course is about two hundred yards or six hundred feet long, but according to my rough pacings it never measured more than eighty-four feet at the end where the chariots must turn. I could not understand how three or four vehicles, harnessed with four horses abreast, could possibly manage to negotiate this awkward corner at full speed without more smashes than would tend to the success of the entertainment. On reflection I am convinced that chariot races were not run in this place. It has never, I think, been a hippodrome, but was intended solely for athletic games and foot-running. To this supposition its actual measurements give probability, as they tally very well with those which were common in old days.

This stadium is still singularly perfect; its walls being built of great blocks of stone which here and there, however, must have been shaken down by earthquakes, for nothing else could have disturbed masonry so solid. The visitor can see also where the spectators sat, and in the midst of that desolate scrub-covered plain it is curious to think of the shouting thousands gathered from Curium, Amathus, and perhaps Paphos, who in bygone generations hailed the victor in the games and hooted down the vanquished. Now the watching mountains above, the eternal sea beneath, and the stone-ringed area of their fierce contests remain—nothing more. All the rest is loneliness and silence. Dust they were, to dust they have returned, and only wondering memory broods about the place that knew them. These relics of a past which we can fashion forth but dimly, seem to come home with greater vividness to the mind when a traveller beholds them, as on this spot, in the heart of solitudes. Seen in the centre of cities that are still the busy haunts of men they do not impress so much.

So we turned back to Limasol, riding by another road along the headlands which overhang the ocean, and pausing, as I did now and again, to watch the wide-winged vultures sweep past us on their never-ending journeys. Very solemn they looked hanging there upon outstretched pinions between the sky and sea, as they hung when the first Phoenician galley rowed to the Cyprian shores, as they will hang till the last human atom has ceased to breathe among its immemorial plains and mountains.

CHAPTER X

LIMASOL TO ACHERITOU

. . . On the termination of our stay at Limasol, our plan was to go by sea to Paphos, forty miles away, where our mules would meet us, thence to ride to Lymni where an enterprising English syndicate is attempting to reopen the old Phoenician copper mine, and lastly by Pyrga and Lefka to the capital, Nicosia; in all about five days' hard travelling, for the most part over mountains.

As the time of departure drew near, mighty and exhausting were the preparations. Packing is always a task as laborious to the mind as to the body. But when it means thinking out what is to go on the mules, what to go to Nicosia, what to the final port of departure, what to be thrown away as too cumbersome to carry, and what must be kept with the traveller at all hazards in the very probable event of these various parcels and belongings vanishing away to be seen no more, then positive genius and genius of a peculiar sort is required to deal with the emergencies of the situation. However at last Cabbages, that is the muleteer, departed with his animals on which were laden camp-beds, kettles, pounds of tea, candles, and I know not what besides, with instructions to await our arrival at Paphos. The day passed on and it was announced that the *Flora* was once more in sight.

We went to the office and it was suggested that I should take the tickets. Now Paphos is a harbour where the voyager can only land in fine weather, whence, too, if it be not fine he is carried on to Egypt, where he must wait until the unwearying *Flora* again begins her weekly round. As it happens, in the course of my life I have had some experience of remote places where one cannot land or embark. Indeed a mishap which once I met with at one of these in a far country entailed upon me a considerable risk of being drowned, a large expenditure of cash, some anxiety of mind, and a five days' journey in a railway train. But although it is rather interesting, I will not tell that tale in these pages.

"I suppose," I said to the agent, "that we shall be able to land at Paphos?"

"Oh! I think so," he replied casually, whereon I intimated that I would wait to take the tickets till the boat came in.

In time one learns to put a very exact value on the "I think so" of a shipping agent. In this instance it assured me that there was not a chance of our visiting the temple of Venus on the morrow.

The *Flora* came in and with her my friend, Mr. Charles Christian, who was kindly going to conduct us upon our tour.

"Shall we be able to land at Paphos?" I shouted.

He shook his head. "All the agents say we can," he said, "but the captain and the boatmen say we can't."

Then resignedly I suggested that we had better give it up, since I could not face the risk of making an involuntary trip back to Egypt. Mr Christian agreed and it was given up, though with great regret, a message being dispatched to Cabbages to travel with his mules to Nicosia.

It was a true disappointment to me thus on my second visit to the island, as on my first, to be prevented from visiting the very home of Aphrodite, the place that the goddess chose to set her foot when she rose from the foam of the sea. Not that there is, as I understand, much more to be seen at either Old or New Paphos—Paleopaphos and Neopaphos; they are six or eight miles apart—than among the ruins of other ancient cities in the island. Still I wished to look upon the place where St. Paul once reasoned with Sergius Paulus, the Deputy. What a spectacle even for those ancient shores of Chittim that have witnessed so many things—the mighty Apostle before the gates of the wanton shrine of Venus, thundering denunciations at the wizard Elymas and smiting him to darkness with the sword of the wrath of God! I desired to have stood upon that road which, as Strabo tells us, "was crowded year by year with men and women votaries who journeyed to this more ancient shrine" from all the towns of Cyprus, and indeed from every city of the known world. I desired also to have seen the tumbled wrecks of the temple, that "sacred enclosure" which Perrot and Chipiez recreate so vividly and well that, as l cannot better them, I will quote their words, where

"everything spoke to the senses; the air was full of perfume, of soft and caressing sounds, the murmur of falling water, the song of the nightingale, and the voluptuous cooing of the dove mingled with the rippling notes of the flute, the instrument which sounded the call to pleasure or led the bride and bridegroom to the wedding feast. Under tents or light shelters built of branches skillfully interlaced, dwelt the slaves of the goddess, those who were called by Pindarus in the scoliast composed for Theoxenius of Corinth, the *servants of the persuasion*. These are Greek or Syrian girls, covered with jewels and dressed in rich stuffs with bright-coloured fringes. Their black and glossy tresses were twisted up in *mitras*, or scarves of brilliant colour, with natural flowers such as pinks, roses, and pomegranate blossoms hung over their foreheads. Their eyes glittered under the arch of wide eyebrows made still wider by art; the freshness of their lips and cheeks was heightened by carmine; necklaces of gold, amber and glass hung between their swelling breasts; with the pigeon, the emblem of fertility, in one hand, and a flower or myrtle-branch in the other, these women sat and waited."

But Aphrodite was against me who serve Thoth, a foreign Egyptian god with whom she had naught in common, and doubtless did not admire, since—except in Ladies' Colleges—learning does not consort with loveliness. So her shrine remains and will remain unvisited by me. I regretted also not being able to examine the copper-workings of the ancients at Lymni with the vast pit whence the ore was dug, the mountains of slag that lie around, and the tunnel hundreds of yards long which the genius and perseverance of the men of our generation have burrowed through the solid rock with a lake of water above their heads, in search of the lode which is waiting somewhere to make the fortunes of those who find it. Last of all and most of all perhaps, was I sorry not to see the beautiful stretch of mountain country which lies in this part of the island.

Yet it was well that we did not attempt the adventure travelling overland, as for a while we contemplated, for immediately thereafter it came on to rain and rained for days. Now a journey on mule back over the roadless Cyprian hills in rain is not a thing to be lightly undertaken. The paths are slippery and in places dangerous, but worst of all is the continual wet which, wrap himself as he will in macintoshes, soaks baggage and traveller. If he could dry himself and his belongings at the end of the day, this would matter little, but here comes the trouble. The fire made of wild thyme or what not that suffices to cook his food in a police-station or a tent, will not draw the moisture from his clothes or blankets. So he must sleep wet, and unless the sun shines, which in these seasons it often does not do for days together, start on wet next morning. In any country this is risky, in Cyprus it is dangerous, for here, as all residents in the land know, a soaking and a subsequent chill probably breed fever.

I may add that certain passengers, pooh-poohing doubts, went on by the *Flora* to Paphos, to find themselves in due course in Egypt, whence they returned ten days or so later. One gentleman, Mr. Mavrogordato indeed, did succeed in landing, but from another steamer. When the Paphos boatmen learned by signal or otherwise that he was on board this ship, which as I understand, having cargo to discharge, rolled off the port for days, they clad themselves in lifebelts and made an effort, with the result that ultimately he was landed, also in a lifebelt and little else. The journey, I gather, was risky, but there comes a time when most of us would rather take the chance of being drowned than after a prolonged, involuntary tour return miserable and humiliated to the place of starting.

At length came the eve of our departure from Limasol, not for Paphos, but for Famagusta via Larnaca and Acheritou. In the afternoon we went for a walk and gathered many wild flowers, and as the sun set I retook myself to stroll upon the jetty. It was a calm evening and the solemn hush which pervaded the golden sky and the sea, still heaving with recent storm, made the place lovely. Some brutal boys were trying to drown a cat, but to my delight the poor creature escaped them and scrambled along the rough planks to the shore. They followed it into the town, and I was left alone there listening to the water lapping against the piers and watching an old fisherman in a fez sitting still as a statue, his line between his fingers. He did not seem to belong to the nineteenth century. He might have lived, and doubtless in the persons of his progenitors did live, one or two or three or four thousand years ago. I smoked my cigarette and contemplated him, half expecting that presently he would draw out a brass bottle, as was the fortune of fishermen in the "Arabian Nights," and thence uncork a Jinn. But the brass bottle would not bite, or the fish either. Somehow it reminded me of another scene—a little pier that runs out into the icy waters of the North Sea at Reykiavik, whence on such an eve as this I remember seeing a boy angling for the flat fish that lie in the yellow sands. Only here in Cyprus were no eider-duck, and there in Iceland rose no minarets or palms.

I do not suppose that I shall see Limasol again, but thus while memory remains I wish ever to recall it, with its twilight stillness, its illimitable darkling ocean, its quaint eastern streets and buildings, and over all of them and the mountains beyond a glorious golden pall of sunset.

On a certain Sunday—everybody seems to travel upon the Sabbath in Cyprus—the three of us, my nephew, Mr. Christian, and myself, started in a rattle-trap carriage dragged by four scaffoldings of ponies, one of which was dead lame, for Larnaca, about forty-five miles away. There were many agitations about this departure. First of all arrived a sulky-looking Greek, who declared that the carriage could not take the luggage and refused to allow it to be loaded. This was rather gratuitous on his part, as it seems that he had no interest in the conveyance, except some possible unearned commission. Then it was doubtful whether the dead-lame horse could go at all; but after a nail had been extracted from his bleeding frog he was pronounced to be not only fit, but eager for the journey. At this season of the year it is customary in Cyprus to turn the horses and mules on to green barley for three weeks, whence they arrive fat and well-seeming. This is why all draught animals were then so hard to hire.

At length with many farewells we creaked off through the narrow streets and difficult turnings of Limasol, to find ourselves presently in the open country. Here among the springing corn I saw white thorns in bloom, though I think that their species differs slightly from our own; also many carob-trees, some of them in the warmer situations now beginning to form their pods.

Trees, by the way do not as a rule belong to the owner of the soil. If you buy a piece of land in Cyprus, it will be to find that the timber on it is the lawful possession of somebody else, with all rights and easements thereto pertaining. These must be purchased separately, a fact that makes the possession of property under the prevailing Turkish law a somewhat complicated and vexatious affair.

I noticed that at the extremity of the boughs many of these carobs, especially in the case of old specimens, were disfigured by bunches of red and rusty leaves. On inquiring the reason Mr. Christian informed me that the harm is due to the ravages of rats which live in the hollow boles and gnaw the juicy bark of the young shoots. Sometimes they destroy the entire tree, but the Cypriotes are too idle to kill them out. They prefer to lose their crop. The goats too damage everything that they can reach, and show extraordinary ingenuity in their efforts to secure the food they love. Thus with my own eyes I saw a couple of these intelligent animals reared up upon their hind-legs, their fore-feet propped together in mid air for mutual support, their bearded heads outstretched to pluck the succulent shoots above. The group thus formed would have furnished an admirable subject for a sculptor, but I have never seen it represented in any work of art, ancient or modern. Perhaps it is too difficult for easy treatment, or it may be of rare occurrence. One of the methods by which Cyprian peasants avenge injuries upon each other, is to attempt to destroy the olive-trees of an offending neighbour by cutting the bark with knives. Some of the olives which we passed upon this journey were disfigured with curious wart-like growths upon their ancient boles, which Mr. Christian informed me, as he believed, had been produced by such acts of petty malice practised perhaps hundreds of years ago. In these instances of course the trees had ultimately recovered.

The country through which we passed was on the whole very desolate. Although a good deal of the land seemed to be under cultivation of a kind, we saw few villages. These, I suppose, lay hidden behind the hills, but in truth the population is scant. Different indeed must it have been in the days of the Roman occupation. Then there were enough people in Cyprus to enable the Jews who had settled there to put two hundred and forty thousand to the sword in the course of a single revolt, that is, a hundred thousand more than the present population of the island.

After we had driven for nearly five hours and beguiled the tedium of the road by lunching in the carriage, we came to a half-way house or hovel, called Chiro-Kitia, *i.e.* Kitia of the Pigs. Although it looked somewhat dreary in the rain which fell from time to time, it was a prettily situated place, hill-surrounded, fronting a bold brown mountain which lay between it and the sea, and standing over a green and fertile bottom with olive-gardens and fig-trees through which a torrent brawled. The inn itself, if such it can be called, had a little verandah, reached by external steps, half ladder and half staircase. From this verandah we entered the guest-room, which was whitewashed and scribbled over with writings in English, Turkish, Greek, and French; with drawings also whereby long-departed travellers had solaced the weary hours of their stay. This room was stone-paved and furnished with a table, a bench, a bed, and some rush-bottomed chairs. Here the mistress of the rest-house, the mother of several pretty little girls, who were standing about in the mud ragged and bootless, presently arrived with refreshments, a sort of cream cheese that is eaten with sugar, and tiny cups of sweet Turkish coffee accompanied by glasses of water with which to wash it down.

Mr. Christian asked me how old I thought this good woman might be. I replied nearly sixty, and indeed she looked it. He said that she was about twenty-six, and that he remembered her not many years ago as a pretty girl. Since that time, however, she had presented the world with an infant regularly once a year, and her present weary, worn-out aspect was the result.

"You shouldn't have so many children," said Mr. Christian to her in Greek.

"God sends them," she answered with a sad little smile.

This poor woman, with another of her familiar troubles close at hand, was in the unhappy position of being separated from her husband, now doing "time " under the care of Mr. Mavrogordato. She told us that he had come into this misfortune on the false evidence of the keeper of a rival rest-house some few hundred yards away; the only other dwelling in the place, indeed. As to our house and the owner there was a sad, and if true, a cruel tale of how its host, he of the jail, seeking to better his fortunes had put up a mill upon a piece of land at the back of the dwelling; how the rival had waited until the mill was erected and then claimed the land, and various other oppressions and distresses which resulted in assaults, false evidence, and for one of them, a term of retirement. Mr. Christian told me that the story was accurate in the main, and added that out of such quarrels as these come most of the frequent Cyprian murders. It is quite likely that the injured man will emerge from jail only to lie up behind a wall with a loaded gun, thence in due course to return to the care of Mr. Mavrogordato steeped in the shadow of a graver charge.

The scene from the verandah, at least while it rained, was not much more cheerful than the story of our hostess. To the right lay a little patch of garden with nothing particular growing in it, surrounded by an untidy fence of dead thorns. Behind this were filthy sheds and stables, in one of which kneeled half-a-dozen angry-looking camels, great brown heaps, with legs doubled under them, showing their ugly hock joints. The saddles were on their backs but the loads lay beside them, and resting against these reposed their drivers, smoking; motley-garbed men with coloured head-dresses, half-cap, half-turban, who stared at the wretched weather in silence. In front of the house a pair of geese were waddling in the mud, while a half-starved cat crouched against the wall and mewed incessantly. Presently we had a little welcome excitement, for along the road came a Turk mounted on a donkey. He was followed by three wives also mounted on donkeys, one or two of them bearing infants, and shrouded head to foot from the vulgar gaze of the infidel, in *yashmaks* and white robes that in such chilly weather must be somewhat cheerless wear. They passed chattering and arguing, their poor beasts piled up behind the saddles with what looked like, and I believe were, feather-beds, for whatever else these people leave behind, they like to take their mattresses. Then the prospect was empty again save for the groaning camels, the geese, the thin cat, and the pretty little ragged girls who stood about and stared at nothing.

Wearying of these delights after an hour and a half or so, as the rain had stopped at length, I went for a walk along the edge of the stream which looked as though trout would flourish there, did it not dry up in summer. Here, growing among the grasses I found several beautiful flowers, ranunculi, anemones, and others that were strange to me. Also I noted our English friends, chaffinches and sparrows, looking exactly as they do at home, only somewhat paler, as is the case with almost every other bird I saw. I suppose that the hot sun bleaches them. One sparrow that I saw flying about was pure white, and the larks of which there are two varieties, crested and common, are almost dust-coloured. By the way these larks never soar like their English cousins.

At length the poor screws being rested, or a little less tired, we resumed our journey, travelling for some distance through hills. What a pity it is that it does not please the War Office to make Cyprus a half-way house for troops on their road to India, where they might grow accustomed to a warm climate without running any particular risk to health. Also there would be other advantages. The great lesson of the present war in Africa is the value of mounted infantry who can shoot, think for themselves, and ride over rough country. What a training-ground Cyprus would afford to such troops as these. There are horses and perhaps the best mules in the world in plenty; the country is wild and mountainous, and nothing would be hurt in manoeuvring men. Moreover every conceivable physical difficulty can be found here and dealt with for practice as occasion may require. There is heat, there is cold, there are droughts and rains, flooded torrents to be bridged and precipices to be climbed; forests to take cover in and plains to scout over; besides many more advantages such as would appeal to a commander anxious to educate his army to the art of war in rough countries.

Why then does not the Government always keep a garrison of say five or ten thousand mounted men manoeuvring through the length and breadth of Cyprus ? This would assist the island and produce a force that ought to be absolutely invaluable in time of war. Also, the place being so cheap, the cost would be moderate. I give the suggestion for what it is worth.

It was past nine at night when at last we crawled into Larnaca, the journey having taken three hours longer than it should have done owing to the weakness of our miserable horses. Next morning we started for Acheritou near to Famagusta, where we were to be the guests of Messrs. Christian, who are now completing their contract for the great drainage works and reservoirs which have been undertaken by the Government of Cyprus with money advanced by the British Treasury. Of these I shall have something to say in their place.

Leaving Larnaca in a high wind, for the first few miles we passed through a very grey and desolate part of the island, having the sea on our right and flat swampy lands upon our left. Striking inland we halted for a few minutes to look at a curious stone tower of the Lusignan period, in appearance not unlike a small Colossi, which raises its frowning walls among the dirty mud dwellings of a dilapidated, poverty-stricken, Turkish village. There is nothing remarkable about the building which is now tenanted only by goats and pigeons, except its age. Doubtless it was once the stronghold of some petty noble, built for refuge in times of danger. Afterwards we came to a place, Pergamos, where stood some deserted-looking huts, out of one of which ran a large rough-haired dog.

"That dog is all that is left of the Dukobortzi," was Mr. Christian's cryptic remark.

I inquired who or what the Dukobortzi might be and learned that they are a sect of vegetarian Quakers from the Caucasus distinguished from their countrymen, and indeed the rest of mankind, by various peculiarities. Thus they have no marriage ceremony, all their earnings go into a common fund, and whole families of them sleep in a single room. One of the chief articles of their faith, however, is a horror of killing. This it was that brought them into conflict with the Russian Government, who persecuted them mercilessly because, being men of peace, they refused to serve in the army. In the end the English Society of Friends exported them, settling two thousand or so in Cyprus and another three thousand in Canada. A place less suited to this purpose than Pergamos could scarcely be found in the whole island. To begin with the Dukobortzi are vegetarians, and the land being here unirrigated will only grow vegetables for about half the year. Also the climate of the locality, which is very hot, was not at all congenial to emigrants from the Caucasus with a perfect passion for overcrowding at night. So the poor people sickened rapidly and a considerable number died. Some of them went to labour at the irrigation works, but were quite unable to bear the sun. Then they tried working at night and resting during the heat, but still it did not agree with them. In the end they were helped to join their co-religionists in Canada, and now all that remains of them is the rough-haired Russian dog, which must feel very lonely. They were it seems in most respects an estimable people, gentle and kindly, but clearly this was no Promised Land for them.

Cyprus seems to be a favourite dumping-ground for philanthropists who wish to better communities that cannot flourish elsewhere. I remember that when I was last in the island some well-intentioned persons had forwarded thither a motley assortment of Whitechapel Jews, who were expected to turn their old hats into shovels and become raisers of agricultural produce upon lands that had been provided for the purpose. Needless to say they entirely refused to cultivate the said lands. The unfortunate Commissioner of the district had been placed in charge of them and never shall I forget his tale of woe. He furnished them with implements, but they would not plough; with seeds, but they declined to sow. As the charitable society in England was endowing them with six pence a head per diem, and food is cheap in Cyprus, things went on thus until the fund dried up. Then the Commissioner descended full of wrath and interviewed the head of the settlement, who met him, as he told me, clad in a tall black hat and adorned with lavender kid gloves. Much argument followed, till at last the exasperated Commissioner exclaimed—

"Well, you must either work or starve. Will you work?"

The kid-gloved representative shook his head and murmured "No."

"Will you starve?" asked the Commissioner.

Again the answer was a gentle but decided "No."

"Then what the devil will you do?" shouted the enraged official.

"We will telegraph to the Lord Mayor of London," replied the representative suavely. "In fact, sir, *we have already telegraphed*."

The end of the matter was that the members of the community dispersed to the coasts of Syria, where, when last heard of, they were understood to be doing well in more congenial lines. The Whitechapel Jew has no agricultural leanings. He prefers to till some richer field.

Leaving Pergamos we crossed an enormous stony plain that is named after it. This tract of country, there is no doubt, would grow certain classes of timber very well, and within twenty years of its planting, produce a large revenue. Unfortunately, however, the Government has no money to devote to the experiment, and private capital is wanting.

Next we came to the pretty village of Kouklia and passed the recently finished dam enclosing an area of two square miles, now for the first time filling up with water. Then we began to travel round the great basin of the Acheritou reservoir, which when finished is to include forty square miles, most of which will be under water during the winter season. It is destined to irrigate the lower part of the Messaoria plain, which comprises league upon league of some of the most fertile soil in the world. On our way we came to a stony pass in the neck of two small hills, where I noticed that every rock was scored with rude crosses. It appears that some years ago frequent complaints were received by the ecclesiastical authorities to the effect that this place was badly and persistently haunted, the ghosts being of a violent and aggressive order, given to sallying forth at night with uncanny shouts and leapings, to the great disturbance of peaceable travellers on the highway. Feeling that the thing must be dealt with, every available priest and bishop assembled, and cursed and exorcised those ghosts by all lawful and efficient means; stamping them morally flat and abolishing them so that from that day to this not one of them has been heard or seen. To make their triumph sure and lasting the holy men cut and painted these crosses upon the rock, with the result that no "troll" of dubious origin can now stop there for a moment.

At length we saw the house that the Messrs. Christian have built to live in while the works are in progress. It is splendidly placed upon a bluff overlooking the great plain, and from a distance, I know not why, has the appearance of a small ruined temple. Very glad were we to reach it about three o'clock in the afternoon, and partake of a lamb roasted whole in the Cyprian fashion, with other luxuries.

Just below this house start the six miles of massive dam that runs across the plain to form the retaining wall of the vast body of water which is to be held up. As yet this water is allowed to escape, but next winter, when the dam is completed, it will be saved and let out for purposes of irrigation. There is nothing new in the world. In the course of the building of the dam were discovered the remains of one more ancient, also running across the plain, but enclosing a smaller area; indeed its sluice is to be pressed into the service of the present generation. I examined it, and came to the conclusion that the masonry is of the Roman period. Mr. J. H. Medlicott of the Indian Irrigation Department, the very able engineer who has designed these great works and carried them out so successfully, is however of opinion that it is Venetian. Probably he is right. This at least is clear, that people in days long dead could plan and execute such enterprises as well as we do to-day. Roman or Venetian, the stone-work is admirably laid and bound together with some of the hardest and best cement that ever I saw.

The Messes. Christian, who have contracted to complete this undertaking, employ about three thousand men and women, mostly on a system of piece-work. In the evening I walked along the great dam and saw them labouring like ants there and in the trenches which are to distribute the water. They were then engaged in facing the dam with stone which is fitted together but not mortared, carrying up great blocks upon their backs and laying them in place under the direction of overseers. At first the provision of this facing stone was difficult and expensive, as the stuff had to be carted six or seven miles; indeed its cost threatened to swallow up most of the contractors' profits. Then it was, that within half a mile of the place where the material was needed, very luckily Mr. Charles Christian in the course of an evening walk discovered an outcrop of excellent stone, soft to work but with the property of hardening in water. The cutters get it out by a simple but effective system, no doubt that which has been followed by their ancestors for thousands of years. A skilled man can loosen a great number of suitable blocks in a day, apparently with ease. When I tried it, however, I found the task somewhat beyond me.

From the strong resemblance of the material I believe that this was the very stone used by the builders of the ancient dam below the house. Doubtless they discovered the quarry as Mr. Christian did, although oddly enough the natives who had lived in the neighbourhood all their lives, declared that nothing of the sort existed for miles around. It was the old case of eyes and no eyes.

I said some pages back that living in Cyprus is cheap, and of this here I had an instance. The house put up by Messes. Christian for their convenience while directing the works is spacious, two-storeyed, and capitally built of stone, with, if I remember right, a kind of mud roof laid upon rafters covered with split cane mats. Properly made and attended to, such roofs last for years. The whole cost of the building, which was quite large enough to accommodate with comfort seven or eight people and servants, was less than £300, including the large verandahs. In England it would cost at the very least a thousand, and probably a great deal more.

CHAPTER XI

FAMAGUSTA

. . . The tower, where according to ancient tradition Desdemona was actually stifled by Othello, is an odd place for picnics, yet thither on our arrival we were escorted through the ancient gates of Famagusta. Indeed the feast was spread exactly where the poor victim lived and died, that is, if over she existed beyond the echoes of romance.

In the Venetian days Famagusta, which is said to be built upon the site of the ancient Arsinoë, was a great commercial port. Now its harbour is choked and, principally because of the heat within the walls, such population as remains to the place lives about a mile away, in a new town called Varoshia. How am I to describe this beautiful mediaeval monument! An attempt to set out its details would fill chapters, so I must leave them to the fancy of the reader. The whole place is a ruin. Everywhere are the gaunt skeletons of churches, the foundation walls of long-fallen houses, and around, grim, solid, solemn, the vast circle of the rich-hued fortifications. What buildings are here! Millions of square yards of them, almost every stone, except where the Turks have cobbled, still bearing its Venetian mason's mark. Walls thirty feet thick; great citadels; sally ports; underground foundries still black with the smoke of Venetian smithies; fragments of broken armour lying about in the ancient ash-heaps; water-gates, ravelins, subterranean magazines; gun embrasures, straight and enfilading; enormous gathering-halls now used as grain-stores; tortuous, arched vaults of splendid masonry, the solid roof-stones cut upon the bend; piers running out to sea commanding the harbour mouth; every defence and work known to mediaeval warlike art. Then round them all, hewn in places through the solid rock, the mighty ditch sixty feet or more in depth. It was an impregnable stronghold this Famagusta, and in the end it fell to the power of the greatest of all generals, Hunger, and not through the batterings of Mustafa the Moslem, known as the Destroyer, and his vast army.

The Turk came and conquered, how I will describe presently, and from that hour the glory of Famagusta departed. To begin with no Christian was allowed to live within the gates. Even the visitor of distinction must not ride or drive there, but walk humbly as became a representative of a conquered faith. "Where the Turk sets his foot, there the grass will not grow," but here the saying is reversed, the grass grows everywhere amid the empty walls. Indeed barley is sown where men dwelt in thousands, and the Christian churches, some of them, were turned into baths for the comfort of the Mussulman, while the rest rotted into ruin. One of the three hundred and sixty-five of these ruined fanes—it is said that there were this number—that of St. Peter and St. Paul, a very noble and beautiful building, is now a Government grain-store, a desecration which I do not think ought to be allowed under the rule of England.

The grand Gothic cathedral wherein lie the bones of many knights and noted men of the Lusignan period, whose wealth, intelligence, and labour reared it up, is now a mosque. I am not learned enough to describe its architecture in detail, this should be left to those who understand such matters. I can only say that it is lovely. In the front are three pointed, recessed arches, the centre pierced by the doorway surmounted with exquisite carved work. Above are three windows in similar style, all of them now walled up, and above them again two ruined towers. Fixed on to one of these, that to the left of the spectator as he faces the building, is a wretched and incongruous Moslem minaret, a veritable pepper-pot. Within the place is bare and empty, with here and there a carpet, or a tawdry pulpit.

Is it right, I ask, now that the country is again in the hands of a Christian power, that this ancient shrine dedicated in the beginning to the God we worship, should be left in the hands of the followers of Mahommed? I say, and the remark applies also to the cathedral at Nicosia, that in my humble judgment this is wrong. A matter of policy, that is the answer. But has policy no limits? Would it be so very hard and dangerous for this great empire to say to those Turks who are now its subjects: "This is a Christian place which your fathers snatched with every circumstance of atrocity and violence from Christians. Take your shrines elsewhere. The land is wide and you are at liberty to set your altars where you will." It is true that they might answer: "Does it lie in your mouth to protest when you turn other buildings equally sacred in your eyes into grain-stores, and clerks sit upon their altars to take count?"

For generations the Turks have used Famagusta as a quarry, exporting most of the stone of its old buildings to Egypt. Now, it is commonly said, our Government proposes to follow their evil example, since the present railway and harbour scheme involves the destruction of the beautiful curtain-wall abutting on the sea and the use of the material it contains in the projected works. I have been assured by a competent engineer and others who can judge, that such an act of vandalism is absolutely unnecessary; that this monstrous thing will be done, if it is done, principally for the sake of the shaped stone that lies to hand. Will nobody stop it? If the Colonial Office refuses to intervene, where are the Company of Antiquaries and where is Public Opinion? Where too is the Society for the Preservation of Ancient Monuments?

Famagusta is one of the most perfect specimens of mediaeval fortification left in the world. It can never be reproduced or reborn, since the time that bred it is dead. Now in our enlightened age, when we know the value of such relics, are the remains of the old city to be wantonly destroyed before our eyes? I trust that those in authority may answer with an emphatic "No."

In itself the scheme for clearing out the ancient harbour and making of Famagusta a port connected by railway with Nicosia is good. But the haven thus reconstructed, although old Sir John Mandeville, more regardless of the truth than usual even, declares that it was one of the first harbours of the sea in the world, can never be of great importance or competent to shelter liners and men-of-war. Also I imagine that it will be incapable of defence except by sea-power. Now at Limasol it is different. There, owing to the natural configuration of the shore, a harbour where fleets might ride could be made with two entrances far apart, and having seven or eight miles of high land between it and the ocean, so that in practice nothing could touch the vessels that lay within. The necessary dredging would of course cost a good deal, although the bottom to be acted upon is soft and kindly. Perhaps the total expenditure might mount up to a million and a half, or even two millions, the price of a few battle-ships. Battle-ships are superseded in a score of years; the harbour, with proper care, would remain for centuries. We need such a place in this part of the Mediterranean. Is not the question worth the serious care of the Admiralty and the nation?

CHAPTER XII

THE SIEGE AND SALAMIS

I could see but few changes in Famagusta since I visited it fourteen years ago. Trees have grown up round the tombs where the execrable and bloody Mustafa and some of his generals lie buried; also the Commissioner, Mr. Travers, has planted other trees in portions of the moat where they do not flourish very well owing to the stony nature of the subsoil. Moreover, a large fig-tree which I remember growing in the said moat has vanished—I recall that I myself found a Cyprian woman engaged in trying to cut it down, and frightened her away. Probably when we had departed, she returned and completed the task. Lastly, when I was here before the iron cannonballs fired into the city by the Turks three centuries since, still lay strewn all about the place as they had fallen. Now they have been collected into heaps, or vanished in this way or in that. Otherwise all is the same, except that Time has thrust his finger a little deeper into the crevices of the ruined buildings.

* * * * *

Within three miles or so of Old Famagusta lie the ruins that were Salamis, formerly the famous port of the Messaoria plain, where once St. Paul and Barnabas "preached the word of God in the synagogues of the Jews." It was a town eight hundred years before Christ was born however, for a monument of Sargon the Assyrian tells of a certain king of Salamis, and until the reign of Constantine the Great when an earthquake destroyed it, it flourished more than any other Cyprian city. Now not even a house is to be found upon its vast site, and the harbour that was always full of ships, is quite silted up. Many of the stones also that made its palaces and temples, have been built into the walls and churches of Famagusta, to find often enough an ultimate home in Egypt, whither the Turks exported them.

One day we visited this place. On our left as we went our host, Mr. Percy Christian, pointed out to me a tumulus, in Cyprus a rare and notable thing. Some years ago he opened it, indeed the scar of that operation is still visible. Tunnelling through the outer earth the workmen came to a most beautiful tomb, built of huge monolithic stones fitted together with an accuracy which Mr. Christian describes as marvellous. As it proved impossible to pierce these stones, the visitors were obliged to burrow lower and force a passage through the floor. I could not, I confess, help laughing when Mr. Christian added that to his intense disgust he discovered that other antiquarians, in some past age, had attacked the sepulchre from the further side of the mound. They also had been beaten by the gigantic blocks. They also had burrowed and made their visit through the floor. Moreover, by way of souvenir they had taken with them whatever articles of value the tomb may have chanced to contain.

Even sepulchre-searching has its sorrows. I am afraid that if after those days and weeks of toil, it had been my fortune, full of glorious anticipation, to poke my head through that violated floor merely to discover in the opposite corner another hole whereby another head had once arisen, I should have said how vexed I was and with some emphasis. He who labours among the tombs should be very patient and gentle-natured—like Mr. Christian.

Almost opposite to this tumulus is a barrow-shaped building also composed of huge blocks of stone, set in an arch and enclosing a space beneath of the size of a small chapel out of which another little chamber opens. This is called the tomb of St. Katherine, why I do not know. From its general characteristics I should imagine that it is of the Mycenian period, if the Mycenians understood how to fashion an arch. The individual blocks are truly huge, and it is nothing short of marvellous that men of the primitive races were able to handle them. It seems probable that this sepulchre and that in the opposing tumulus date from the same age. Perhaps both the tombs were first built upon the level with the design of covering them in beneath mounds of earth. In this event we may conclude that the reputed burying-place of St. Katherine was never finished or occupied by any distinguished corpse. At least it is a curious and most durable monument of the past.

All this district is very rich in tombs. Near by is the village of Enkomi where Mr. Percy Christian, digging on behalf of the British Museum, recently found the Mycenian gold ornaments now to be seen in its Goldroom. These Enkomi tombs are not structurally remarkable and lie quite near the surface. Indeed they were first discovered by the accident of a plough-ox putting his hoof into one of them. At the period of their construction, however, evidently it was the habit of the people who used them as their last resting-places, to bury all his most valuable possessions with the deceased. Thus one of the graves appears to have been that of a jeweller, for in it were found solid lumps of gold sliced from cast bars of the metal, as well as fashioned trinkets.

In many instances they have been plundered in past days, although when this has happened the conscience of the ancient tomb-breakers, more sensitive than that of us moderns, generally forbade them to take everything. Thus in one tomb which Mr. Charles Christian entered, though this was not at Enkomi, he found a portion of a splendid beaker, worth £60 or £70 in weight of gold, which fragment very clearly had been wrenched from the vessel and thrown back into the grave. It is a common thing in such cases to find that all valuables have been removed except a single ear-ring, or one bead of a necklace, left among the mouldering bones to appease the spirit of the dead. Obviously these poor ghosts were not supposed to possess more intelligence than the domestic hen which, after all the rest have been removed, will continue solemnly to sit upon a single egg, even if it be of china.

In one of the Enkomi tombs Mr. Percy Christian discovered the unique ivory casket which is now in the British Museum and valued there, I understand, at thousands of pounds.

The story of its finding is curious, and shows how easily such precious treasures may be missed. The actual clearing of the tombs from loose earth and rubbish is of necessity generally left to experienced overseers. On a certain evening Mr. Christian came to the diggings and was informed by the head man that he had carefully excavated and sifted out this particular grave, finding nothing but a few bones. By an after-thought, just to satisfy himself, Mr. Christian went into the place with a light and searched. Seeing that it was as bare as the cupboard of Mother Hubbard, he was about to leave when by a second after-thought—a kind of enacted lady's postscript—he began to scrape among the stuff upon the floor. The point of his stick struck something hard and yellow which he took up idly, thinking that it was but a bit of the skull or other portion of the frame of a deceased Mycenian. As Mycenians, however, did not carve their skeletons, and as even in that light he could see that this object was carved, he continued his researches, to discover, lying just beneath the surface much disjointed by damp, the pieces of a splendid ivory casket. The method, extraordinarily ingenious, whereby he succeeded in removing all these fragments *in situ* and without injury, is too long to describe, even if I remembered its details. Suffice it to say that he poured plaster of Paris or some such composition over them, thereby recovering them in such perfect condition that the experts at home have been able to rebuild this valuable casket exactly as it was when, thousands of years ago, some Mycenian placed it in the resting-place of a beloved relative. Doubtless it was that relative's most treasured possession.

In some respects these ancients must have been curiously unselfish. Few heirs of to-day would consent to objects of enormous value—such as pictures by Titian or gold cups by Benvenuto Cellini—being interred with the bones of the progenitor or testator who had cherished them during life. Yet in the early ages this was done continually. Thus, to take one example, I saw not long ago, I think in the Naples Museum, a drinking-vase that even in its own period must have been absolutely without price, which was discovered in the tomb of one of the Roman emperors. More, a screw or nail hole has been pierced rudely through the bottom of the vase, whether to destroy its value or to fasten it to the breast-plate or furnitures of the corpse, I cannot say. In Cyprus such instances are very common.

Close by St. Katherine's tomb stands that grove which among the inhabitants of this neighbourhood is known as the "accursed trees." Those trees nobody will touch, since to carry away any portion of them for burning or other purposes, is supposed to entail sudden and terrible disaster. Indeed it is said that one bold spirit who, being short of firewood, dared to fly in the face of tradition, suffered not long ago many horrible things in consequence of his crime. Of these trees it is reported also that they have never put out any leaves in spring or summer for uncounted generations, and yet neither rot or die. Also that no other trees of the sort are known in Cyprus, which I do not believe. Certainly at first sight their appearance is very curious, for they are spectral-looking and seem to be quite dead. On careful examination; however, I solved the mystery. It is this, or so I think; the thorns grow upon very poor, shallow, and stony ground, perhaps over ruins. Nearly all their twigs are sere and brittle for they snap between the fingers, but if looked at closely it will be seen that upon the stems faint new growths can be found here and there, which at the period of our visit were just breaking into leaf like those of every other tree. Their vitality is sufficient to enable them to do this and no more, thereby saving them from actual decay. So much for the "accursed grove" and its attendant superstition.

All about this place among the ruins grow huge plants of fennel throwing up flower-stems six or eight feet high. With the roots of this herb is found a species of mushroom or fungus, which is much prized locally and considered very delicate eating. We saw a native searching for these mushrooms by the help of a long stick. As he wandered from bush to bush, his steadfast eyes fixed upon the ground, this man added a curiously lonesome and impressive note to that solemn and deserted landscape.

The walls of old Salamis, enclosing a great area of land, and even some of its gateways, can still be clearly traced. The sites of Amathus and Curium were desolate, but neither of them, to my fancy, so desolate as this, where not even a patch of barley is sown among the ruins that stretch on and on, tumbled heaps of stone, till they end in barren dunes, self-reclaimed from the sea, the place where flighting cranes pause to rest after their long journeys.

Since last I visited this dead city the Cyprus Exploration Fund has been at work here, revealing amongst other buried buildings the site of the great market, or forum, a vast place, at a guess six hundred yards or so in length by some two hundred broad. This mart was surrounded by columns of Egyptian granite; there they lie in every direction, shattered, doubtless, by the earthquake in the time of Constantine. What labour and money it must have cost to set them here. Along one side of this public ground, which in its day must have been magnificent indeed, probably beneath the shelter of the colonnade, there seems to have been a row of shops, whereof some of the name or broken advertisement boards carved on marble in Greek letters are still lying here and there. Perhaps this was the Burlington Arcade of Salamis, but oh! where are the Arcadians?

It is wonderful, in a sense it is almost terrifying, to look at this empty stone-strewn plain with its tall yellow-flowered weeds, its solitary fungus-hunter, its prostrate colonnades; its mounds that once were walls, its depressions which once were gates, its few scattered sheep and goats hungrily seeking for pasture among the coarse growth that in every clime springs up where mankind has had his home; its choked harbour, and then to close our living, physical eyes and command those of the mind to look backward through the generations.

Behold the great glittering sea alive with galleys, the hollow port filled with rude trading vessels from the coasts of Italy, Syria, Greece, and Egypt. Look down from this high spot upon the thousands of flat, cemented roofs, pierced by narrow streets roughly paved and crowded with wayfarers and citizens standing or seated about their doors. Yonder, a mile away upon the hill beyond the harbour, stands a lovely building supported and surrounded with columns of white marble, between which appear statues, also of white marble. It is the temple of Venus, and those gaily-decked folk advancing to its portals are pilgrims to her shrine. Turn, and here and here and here are other temples dedicate to other gods, all dead to-day, dead as their worshippers. And this market at our feet, it hums like a hive of bees. There law-courts are sitting; see the robed pleaders, each surrounded by a little following of anxious, eager clients. There to the south on the paved place clear of buildings, except the marble shelters for the auctioneers, two sales are in progress, one of human beings and one of beasts of burden. There again in the shadow of the colonnade is the provision mart where butlers, eunuchs, and housewives haggle loudly with peasants and fishermen. At yonder shop several young men of fashion and a white-robed woman or two with painted eyes inspect the marvellous necklace wrought by the noted jeweller named—ah! his name escapes us. He neglected to write it in his tomb whence last year Mr. Christian took this golden collar that the artist would not part with save at a price which none of those gallants or their loves could pay. Hark now to the shouting! Why do those gorgeously attired runners, followed by outriders clad in uncouth mail, push a way through the crowd beating them with their wands of office? The king—the king himself drives down the street to pass along the market towards that temple at its head, where he will make an offering because of the victory of his arms over certain enemies in the mountains. He is a splendid-looking figure, shining with gold and gems, but very sick and weary, for this king loves the rich Cyprian wine.

But such pictures are endless, let us leave them buried every one beneath the dust of ages. Our lamp is out, only the blank dull sheet is there; about us are ruins, sky and sea, with the fungus-pickers, the yellow-flowered weeds and the wandering sheep—no more.

What a sight must that have been when great Salamis fell at last, shaken down, hurled into the sea, sunk to the bowels of the earth beneath the awful sudden shock of earthquake. Those mighty columns shattered like rods of glass tell us something of the story, compared to which the burying of Pompeii under its cloak of flaming stone was but a trivial woe. But each reader must fashion it for himself My version might not please him.

Not far away from the forum or market are baths. One can still see portions of their mosaic floor, polished by the feet of many thousand bathers, and the flues that warmed the water. Further on is the site of the great reservoir with remains of the aqueduct that filled it. As one may still see to-day its waters must have been distributed along the streets by means of little marble channels at their sides, a poisonous practice that doubtless bred much sickness, since they were open to every contamination. It would be interesting to know what was the death-rate in these old places. I imagine that it would appal us.

The necropolis of Salamis, as Mr. Percy Christian informed me sadly, has never yet been discovered. He showed me, however, where he believed it to be, under certain drifted sand-heaps near the temple of Venus and the seashore, but outside the walls of the city. If so, there it will rest till the British Museum ransacks it, since private persons may dig no longer. Then what treasures will appear! The gathered wealth of forty or fifty generations of the citizens of one of the richest cities of the ancient world, or such portions of it as its owners took with them to their tombs—nothing less.

If only all the multitudes which once inhabited these walls could rise again before our eyes and in their company those of the other dead cities of Cyprus! The great Messaoria plain would be white with the sea of their faces and alive with the flash of their eyes. There would be no standing-room in Cyprus; the millions of them would overflow its shores and crowd the brow of ocean further than the sight could follow. What has become of them? Where can there be room for them—even for their ghosts? I suppose that we shall find out one day, but meanwhile the problem has a certain uncanny fascination. Perhaps the stock is really strictly limited and *we* are their ghosts. That would account for the great interest I found in Salamis, which most people, especially ladies, think a very dull place, duller even than Famagusta.

Perhaps the most interesting relic of all those at Salamis is that ruin of the fane of Cypris which is set upon a hill. There is, however, not much to be seen except broken columns of the purest white marble, and here and there the fragments of statues. But the shape of the temple can still be traced; its situation, overlooking the sea upon a rising mount where grow asphodel, anemones, and other sky-blue flowers of whose name I am ignorant, is beautiful, and the sighs of a million lovers who worshipped Venus at this altar still seem to linger in the soft and fragrant air.

When we reached home again a lady, our fellow-guest, described to me the ceremony of a Turkish wedding to which she had been invited that afternoon. I will not set down its details second-hand, but the bride, she said, was a poor little child of eleven who had to be lifted up that the company might see her in her nuptial robes and ornaments. The husband, a grown man, is reported to be an idiot. It seems strange that such iniquities, upon which I forbear to comment further, can still happen under the shadow of the British flag.

This reminds me of another Turkish ceremony. On the day that we left Famagusta, at the conclusion of our visit, for Nicosia, we halted a while to breathe our horses in the village of Kouklia, where, by the way, there is a beautiful leaking aqueduct that is covered with maidenhair fern. While I was admiring the ferns and the water that dripped among them, a Turkish funeral advanced out of the village, which at a respectful distance we took the liberty of following to the burial-ground. The corpse, accompanied by a motley crowd of mourners, relatives, sight-seers, and children, was laid uncoffined upon a rough bier that looked like a large mortar-board, and hidden from sight beneath a shroud ornamented with red and green scarves. Upon arrival at the graveyard, an unkempt place, with stones innocent of the mason's hammer marking the head and foot of each grave and serving as stands for pumpkins to dry on in the sun, the dead man was carried to a primitive bench or table made of two slabs set upright in the ground about seven feet apart, and a third laid on them crossways. Here, while a woman sitting on a little mound at a distance, set up a most wild and melancholy wail for the departed, a priest, I know not his proper appellation, stepping forward began to offer up prayers to which the audience made an occasional response. The brief service concluded, once more the body was lifted and borne round the cemetery to its grave, that seemed to be about three feet six inches in depth. Here it was robbed of its gay-coloured scarves, of which a little child took charge, and after a good deal of animated discussion, lowered into the hole in a sitting posture with the help of two linen bands that one of the company unwound from about his middle. Then while a sheet was held over the corpse, as I suppose to prevent its face from being seen, some of the mourners arranged planks and the top of an old door in the grave above it, perhaps to keep it from contact with the earth. At this point we were obliged to leave as the carriage waited, and I am therefore unable to say if there was any further ceremony before the soil was finally heaped over the mortal remains of this departed and, I trust, estimable Turk.

Then we drove on across a grey expanse relieved now and again with patches of rich green barley breaking into ear. On our right the rugged, towering points of the five-fingered mountain called Pentadactylon, stood out above the black clouds of a furious storm of wind and rain which overtook us. Still we struggled forward through its gloom, till at length the sun shone forth, and in the glow of evening we saw the walls, palms and minarets of the ancient and beautiful city of Nicosia.

CAPITAL XIII

NICOSIA AND KYRENIA

Nicosia looks little changed since first I saw it many years ago. The trees that were planted in portions of the moat by the governor of that day Sir Henry Bulwer, have grown into considerable timbers, though, by the way, those set upon the rocky soil round the wooden Government House have not flourished as I hoped they would. Also the narrow streets are somewhat cleaner and more wholesome, if any Eastern town where all household slops are thrown out into the gutters or gardens can be called wholesome; that is about all. No, not quite all, for sundry houses have arisen outside the new city, pretty dwellings with gardens round them, inhabited for the most part by officials, and the old Konak, or Turkish government office, after standing for some six hundred years, has been in great part pulled down, and is now a gaping ruin. This seems to me a very wanton and ill-judged act, for the building had many beauties which can never be seen again. Indeed on second thoughts the authorities appear to have shared this view, since when it was pressed upon them by some local antiquaries, they desisted from their destroying labours, leaving the unique gateway untouched, though, unless something is soon done to support it, not, I fear, for long. Now it is a sheltering place for wanderers, at least I found the blackest woman I ever saw, in bed there, who as I passed made earnest representations to me, in an unknown tongue, to what purpose I was unable to discover. It seemed odd to find so very black a person reposing thus in the middle of the day beneath that draughty antique portal. Otherwise all is the same; even many of the government officers remain, like myself grown somewhat older, although death and migrations to a better post have removed several familiar faces.

I think it was on the day after our arrival that we started with our hosts, Mr. and Mrs. Hart Bennett, on a visit to Kyrenia, the beautiful little seaport which lies across the northern mountains. Our plan was to drive to the foot of these mountains and thence to ride on mule-back to the wonderful old castle of Hilarion, set high upon its almost inaccessible crags. We never got there, however, for the rain stopped us. In my case this did not so much matter, for I had visited the place before, but to my nephew it was a great disappointment. The country between Nicosia and the mountains is very curious and desolate. Here the strata seem to have been tilted on edge by some fearful convulsion in the beginnings of the world, so that more than anything else they resemble long lines of military trenches of brown earth lying behind each other in numberless succession, and topped, each of them, with a parapet of rock.

On arriving at the police-station near the foot of the mountains, we halted to lunch in the company of friends who had ridden out from Kyrenia. Our meeting-place should have been Hilarion, but as I have said the rain stayed us. To climb up into the bosom of that black cloud seemed too forbidding, and had we done so the castle is sheltered by no roof beneath which we could have picnicked.

Nobody seems to know who built Hilarion or who lived there. Mr. Alexander Drummond, writing in 1754, tells us that it is said to have been fortified by one of the Lusignan queens, Charlotta, who was obliged to shelter there when a usurper called James the Bastard, as I think, her half-brother, had been established on the throne by the "Egyptian Power." Cesnola writes also that it was a stronghold of the Lusignans and used by them as a state prison. Lastly, I remember that when I was there in past years, a well-informed gentleman told me that it had once stood a siege and been captured, whereon three hundred persons, men, women, and children, were hurled from a particularly hideous height into a chasm of the mountains. I do not know if there is any foundation for this legend. At least the place, which still boasts some lovely windows and a huge cistern for the storage of soft water, is very wonderful, set as it is so high among those giddy peaks. With what infinite toil, cost, and pains must some old tyrant have reared its towers. Their style by the way is Gothic.

When the rain began to slacken I went for a walk, to look at a wood of young trees which some enterprising gentleman has planted here. They are doing well, and among them I was so fortunate as to find the bee orchis of our shores in flower. Also, as I think I have said upon a previous page, to my delight I observed that all the steep-flanked mountains round are becoming clothed again with forests of young fir.

In the afternoon, the weather now being fine, we started for Kyrenia on the mules, some of us taking a rough ride across country to visit Bella Pais—or De la Paix as it is called by Cornelius van Bruyn, who wrote about 1693, and other authors—the old Lusignan abbey which stands in the village of Lapais, to my mind the most beautiful spot in all Cyprus. I am not, however, certain that it was an abbey. Drummond (1745) questions this, saying that he supposes it to have been "the grand *commanderie* of the island owned by one of the knightly orders." He finds corroboration of his view in the name Della Pays, derived, he says, from the Italian Della Paese, though how this proves that the building was a *commanderie* I am at a loss to understand. I confess, however, to a certain curiosity as to the true designation of the ruin. De la Paix means, of the peace; de la Pays, of the country; Bella Pais, beautiful peace; Bella Paese, beautiful country. Whatever may have been the ancient form, the last and modern reading seems the most appropriate.

The building is as I remember it years ago, only somewhat more dilapidated. Certain cracks are wider, certain bits of wall have fallen, its end draws more near. This indeed must come within the next few generations unless the Government will find money to restore one of its most beautiful possessions. At present, as I assured myself by personal inquiry, it is not the will that is wanting, but the means. While the British Treasury grabs at every farthing of surplus revenue, Cyprus has no funds wherewith to preserve her ancient and mediaeval monuments.

The place cannot have changed much during the last two centuries. Indeed van Bruyn's description of it might almost pass to-day. One thing that struck him, I remember struck me also. Talking of the underground chamber or crypt, he says "one might fancy it all built five or six years ago." Even now, over two hundred years later, the masonry is extraordinarily fresh. Also he speaks of a certain very tall cypress. I think that tree, a monster of its kind, is still standing, at least it stood fourteen years ago. Owing to the circumstances under which we left the abbey, on this visit I had no time to seek out its gracious towering shape.

It is difficult to describe such a building as Bella Pais, for to give a string of measurements and architectural details serves little—out of a guide-book. Much it owes to the wonderful charm of its situation. In the solemn old refectory, a beauteous chamber, leading I think to the reader's pulpit, is a little stair in the seaward wall, and at the head of this stair a window, and out of that window a view. If I were asked to state what is the most lovely prospect of all the thousands I have studied in different parts of the world, I think I should answer—That from the little window of the refectory of the Abbey of Bella Pais in Cyprus.

Around are mountains, below lie woods and olive groves and bright patches of green corn. Beyond is the blue silent sea, and across it, far away but clearly outlined, the half-explored peaks and precipices of Karamania. I said it was difficult to describe an ancient building, but who can describe a view which so many things combine to perfect that can scarcely be defined in thought, much less in words? The thousand colours of the Eastern day drawing down to night, the bending of the cypress tops against the sky, the slow flash of the heaving ocean in the level rays of sunset, the shadows on the mighty mountain tops, the solemnity of the grey olives, the dizzy fall of the precipice, the very birds of prey that soar about it—all these are parts of that entrancing whole. But what worker in words can fit them into their proper place and proportion, giving to each its value and no more?

In this refectory they show rings in the wall where Turks stabled their horses when they took the island; also many holes at one end caused, the old native custodian swore, with bullets fired in sport by British soldiers who were quartered here at the time of the occupation. I like to think, however, that the Turk is responsible for these also, and not Mr. Atkins.

I went to look at the old chapel, not the building now used as a Greek church, which we also visited. This chapel is quite in ruins, and weeds grow rankly among the stones that doubtless hide the skeletons of the priests and Templars who once bent the knee upon them. The cloisters still remain with their charming pillared arcades and the marble sarcophagus of which all the old travellers talk. Now the quadrangle they enclose is a grove of oranges which have been planted since my last visit. In van Bruyn's day it was a garden, and some other voyager a century or so later talks of it as a barley patch. Perhaps the Templars used it as a court set out with flower-beds and fountains.

By the time that we had finished our inspection the rain set in again and night was near. For a while we waited under the shelter of the cloisters hoping that it would stop, but at length made up our minds to a soaking and started. We were not disappointed; it poured, and that is why in the gathering gloom I was unable to look out for my old friend the cypress tree. Moreover the road, or rather the track, was awful and my mule, a proud and high-stomached beast which had waxed fat on green barley, one of the laziest I ever rode. My belief is that he had been accustomed to carry baggage, not men, and baggage mules have their pace. At least being innocent of spurs I could not get him along, and to make matters worse, at every slippery or awkward place he stumbled out of sheer idleness, once very nearly falling in a mud-hole three feet deep. What between the mule, the rain, and the cold, it was, I confess, with joy that at last we dismounted at the door of our host Mr. Tyzer, the judge for the district of Kyrenia.

Before finally bidding farewell to Bella Pais there is one point which I will mention, in the hope that the matter may be looked into, that is, if I am not mistaken in my surmise. While riding through the village my companions and I observed the strangely unhealthy appearance of the children, indeed I am sure that several of these poor, hollow-eyed little creatures are, or were, not long for this world. Now as the site is so high and wholesome, I imagine that their ill looks must be accounted for in some other way. Perhaps the water is contaminated.

The sights at Kyrenia, now vastly improved from what it used to be, are the harbour and the old Venetian fortress. Also in former days there was a Phoenician rock-cut tomb with the skeleton of the occupant *in situ* and all its trimmings, such as lamps and jars of earthenware. But of this I can find no trace to-day. Everybody except myself seems to have forgotten all about him. *Sic transit gloria—cadaveris.* There are still, however, plenty of these Phoenician tombs left in the neighbourhood.

The castle is a fine building of the same type and period as the Famagusta fortifications and those of Nicosia. According to Drummond (1750) "probably the whole work was repaired by Savorniani, who in the year 1525 demolished the old works of these places and refortified them." I do not know if he is correct and am, I confess, ignorant of the fame of Savorniani, although I think I have read somewhere that he was a noted military engineer of the period. Now the place is used as a jail, a fortunate circumstance, since it makes some care of the ancient fabric necessary. Here I would suggest that at very small expense the old chapel could be restored. This is the more desirable as no church exists for the convenience of English residents.

As at Limasol the view from the flat roof of this interesting fortress is very fine, commanding as it does the rugged heights capped by the grey towers of Hilarion, the fertile plain at their foot, and the opposing coast of Asia Minor. Immediately beneath lies the little harbour upon which the Government out of its scanty resources has spent several thousand pounds. To my mind the money might have been better expended elsewhere, since this haven is exposed to the fury of the northern gales, and notwithstanding its protecting moles no vessel of more than two hundred tons can enter it, even in calm weather.

The acting Commissioner, Mr. Ongley, pointed out to me, at the base of one of the round towers against which the sea washes, a little window that to within the last year or two has been walled up. Access was gained to it by a ladder and the stones removed. Within, he said, was found a cell without visible communication with any other part of the castle, and in it the bones of a human being and those of a chicken. It is suggested that these remains belonged to some political prisoner, sent here, perhaps from Venice, to be walled up with the chicken. Of course under the circumstances he would eat the chicken, after which the rats ate him. I must add, however, that Major Chamberlayne, the Commissioner at Nicosia, who is perhaps the best authority in the island upon the mediaeval history of Cyprus, and who actually opened this dungeon, throws doubts upon the story. Myself, I do not quite believe it, for a reason which he did not mention but that appears to me to have weight. I am convinced that upon such an occasion the starving captive would not have left those bones. He would have crunched them up and swallowed them. Perhaps some corpse of which it was necessary to be rid in a time of siege was entombed here. Who can say? At least that cell possesses considerable speculative interest.

This fortress has known the shock of war, although I do not think it offered any notable resistance to the Turks after the fall of Nicosia and Famagusta. Here, in 1465, Charlotta was besieged for a whole year by her brother, James the Bastard, when she seems to have surrendered the place and fled with her husband, Louis, to Savoy.

The coasts of Karamania, which are so clearly visible from Kyrenia and lie at a distance of about thirty miles, are not often visited by travellers, whose throats the inhabitants are apt to cut. They are reported to be a paradise for sportsmen, as ibex and other large game live upon the mountain ranges. For a sum of three shillings I purchased an enormous pair of the horns of one of these wild goats which had found their way across the straits. Ibex, I am told, have a habit when alarmed of hurling themselves off precipices and landing unharmed upon their horns. In the course of some excursion of the sort the owner of my pair has snapped off the point of one of them. Nature, however, healed the fracture, but the symmetry of the horn is spoiled.

I did not enjoy this visit to Kyrenia so much as I expected, since, as is common in Cyprus, my wetting and chill on the previous day induced a touch of fever. It was mild, however, and yielded to a timely application of quinine.

So back across the mountains to Nicosia and—a Book-Tea—a form of festivity which has just reached the ancient home of Cyprus. Myself, I confess, I could have spared it, since of all varieties of intellectual exercise this is the hardest that I know.

Nicosia is a place of many amusements. Thus they play golf there on a course of nine holes. It is odd to do the round with a gentleman in a fez acting as your caddie, and to observe upon the greens—or the yellows, for they are made of sand—Turkish ladies veiled in *yashmaks* engaged in the useful tasks of brushing and weeding. What in their secret hearts do those denizens of the harem think of us, I wonder? Would not their verdict, if we could get at it, be "Mad, mad, my masters"? But English folk would celebrate book-teas and play golf or any other accustomed game upon the brink of Styx. Perhaps that is why they remain a ruling race, for to do this it is necessary to preserve the habits and traditions of the fatherland, refusing persistently to allow them to be overwhelmed by those of any surrounding people. Witness the triumphant survival of the Hebrew. But that subject is large.

The scene on this golf-course was quaint and picturesque. In front appeared the bold outline of the Kyrenia hills with rugged old Pentadactylon's five fingers pointing to a flaming stormy sky, and behind rose the palms and minarets of eastern-looking Nicosia. Between the two lay the wide plain across whose spaces from time to time wended strings of solemn camels, the head of each tied to the tail of its brother in front, or little groups of asses laden with firewood and other goods, a Cypriote seated on the last of them in a posture to be acquired only by centuries of inherited experience. The links themselves are by no means bad, though somewhat limited and extemporary. Thus the bunkers are formed of artificial banks varied by an occasional stone wall, the other hazards consisting chiefly of breaks of asphodel and rocks cropping through the apology for turf. Upon one of these rocks alas! I broke my host's best cleek.

I had long been looking forward to paying a second visit to the museum at Nicosia, which consisted in past years of a few disorderly rooms crowded with miscellaneous antiquities. Having before I left England read reviews of an important new catalogue of the Cyprus Museum, I concluded that all this was changed. The deeper proved my disappointment.

To begin with there is no custodian, so I was dependent on the kind offices of Major Chamberlayne to show me round. After long hammering we were let into the house by a girl, who said she would go upstairs and open the shutters of the rooms. On the ground floor beneath the archway, and in a kind of court, altars, remains of marble horses and chariots, tombstones, busts, unpacked crates of antiquities, some of them marked as having been forwarded years ago, were mixed in great confusion. The more precious objects were in a little chamber opening out of this archway, but it was no easy task to discover the keys which fitted the cases from which the trays had to be taken one by one and then replaced. The Cyprus share of the famous Enkomi treasures of which I have spoken we could not find anywhere. It appears indeed that these objects are still locked up in some Government safe. Throughout the whole collection the story is the same. So far as the general public and Cyprus are concerned, it is practically valueless. For this sad state of affairs, however, the Government must not be blamed. They have not a single farthing to spend upon such things as relics of the island's past history, however important and interesting these may be.

In this Cyprus collection, to my astonishment I came face to face with an old friend. Many years ago, when first I visited Famagusta, I feloniously did steal a certain cannon-ball which lay about among the ruins just where three centuries ago it had fallen from some Turkish gun. The ladies of our party followed my evil example and stole another. Both of these mementos we bore back to Government House and there, with the effrontery of hardened offenders, openly displayed them. Now it appeared that not long before a special Governmental edict had been issued against the removal of ancient cannon-balls, and it was pointed out that his Excellency could not suffer his own guests to do those very things which he had forbidden to the public. Bowing to the inevitable I thereupon surrendered my cannon-ball, but the ladies refusing to be influenced by this pure logic, managed to retain theirs, which they afterwards presented to me, so that at this moment I hold it in my hand.

What became of that cannon-ball—mine, I mean—I often wondered, and on this day so long, long afterwards, I found out. There, yes, there neglected in a dusty corner on the floor, in company with the noseless head of a Greek child and the fragments of a Phoenician pot, unhonoured and uncared for, lay the heavy missile that with so much labour I had borne away from Famagusta. There was no doubt about it, I could swear to that lump of iron in any court of law; also it was the only one in the place, and evidently had been deposited here that the authorities might be rid of it. Moreover, by a strange coincidence the very gentleman whose official duty it had been to relieve me of the stolen property in the first instance, was now at my side.

Life is full of coincidences. Who would have thought that the three of us, Major Chamberlayne, Cannon-ball, and I, would live to meet again thus strangely after so long a lapse of time and in so far off a land? Sorely, I admit, was my virtue tempted, for while my guide was mourning over something out of place in a distant corner, I might easily have transferred the ball to my coat pocket, trusting to fortune and the strength of the stitching to get it away, and unobserved. But so greatly has my moral character strengthened and improved during the last decade and a half, that actually I left it where it was, and where doubtless it will remain until some one throws it on to the museum rubbish heap.

The island of Cyprus is one of the few countries in the world that I have felt sorry to leave. Often I have thought that it would be a delightful place to live in, not in the towns, a frequenter of book-teas, but in solitude as a hermit upon some haunted hill among the shattered pillars of old cities, with vineyard slopes beneath and the sea beyond. Only I should like to be a rich hermit—to the poor that profession must be irksome—and then I would restore Bella Pais and see what the land could grow. A friend of mine did in fact turn anchorite in Cyprus, but I noticed that he always seemed to find it necessary to come home for his militia training, and when I re-visited his hermitage the other day, lo! it was desolate.

Fortunately the road from Nicosia to Limasol by which the traveller departs runs through the very dreariest districts of the island, and thereby eases the farewell. For three hours' journey, or more, on either side of it stretch bare, barren hills, worn to the grey bones, as it were, by the wash of thousands of years of rain and bleached in the fiery Cyprian sun. I daresay, however, that with care even the most unpromising of this soil would nourish certain sorts of trees, as probably it did in past ages.

Then the denudation would cease, the earth grow green, the flood waters be held up and the former and the latter rain called down, until here too, as on the Kyrenia coast, the land became a paradise.

And so farewell to Cyprus the bounteous and the beautiful.

INDEX

A

B

C

D

E

K

L

M

T

V

W

X

Y

Z

Famagosta, the Ancient Venetian Port of Cyprus.
(*The Illustrated London News*, LXXIII, p. 49)

PLATE 2

Larnaca, the Modern Port of Cyprus.
(*The Illustrated London News*, LXXIII, p. 52)

a. The "Hundred and One Houses," between Levkosia and Cerinia.
(*The Illustrated London News*, LXXIII, p. 52)

b. Ruins of the Monastery of Cozzafani.
(*The Illustrated London News*, LXXIII, p. 52)

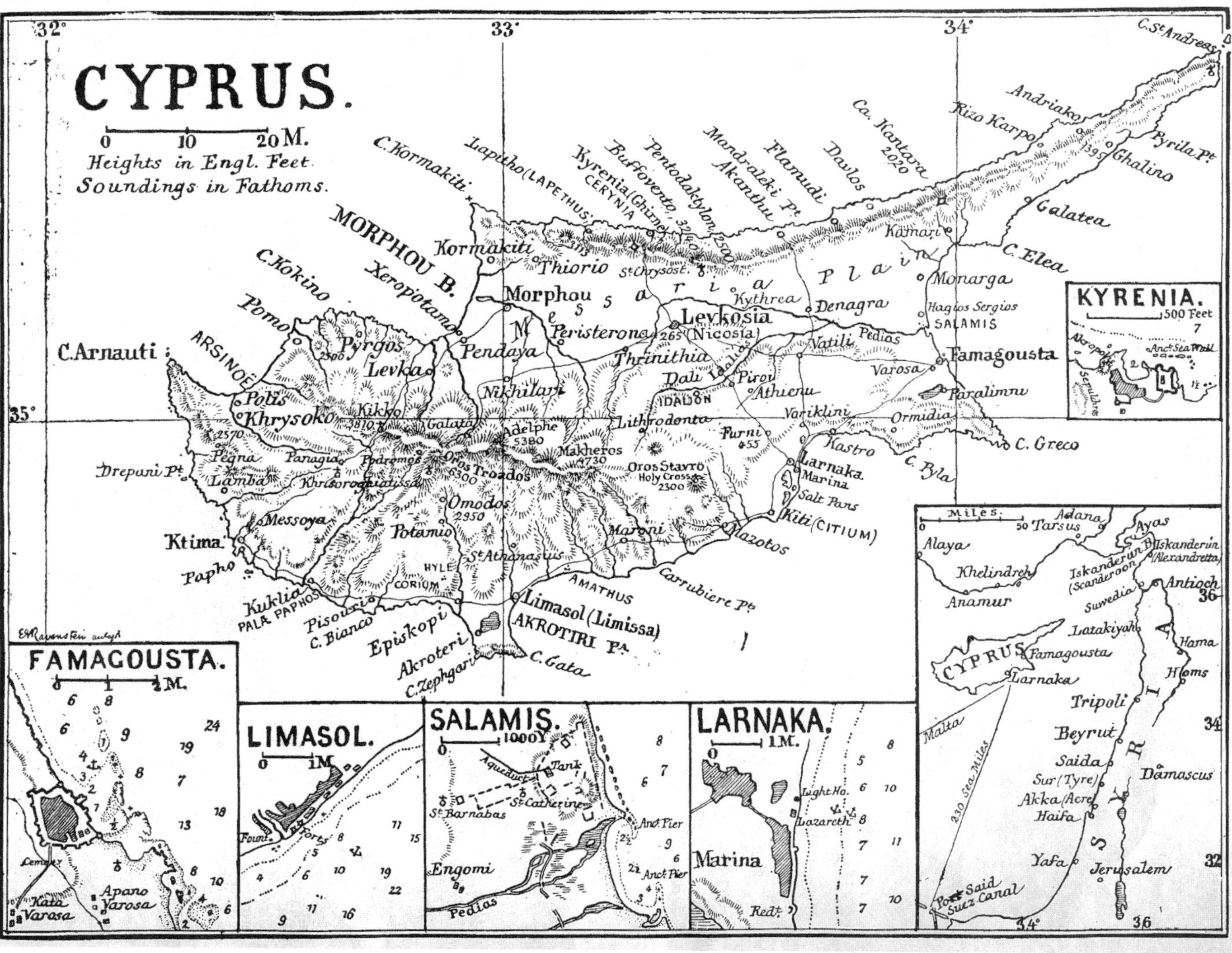

The Island of Cyprus, the Chief Towns, and the Neighbouring Coasts.
(*The Illustrated London News*, LXXIII, p. 69)

Levkosia or Nicosia, the Capital of Cyprus.
(*The Illustrated London News*, LXXIII, p. 85)

Mountain of the Holy Cross (Stravro Vouni), Cyprus: View from near Larnaca.
(*The Illustrated London News*, LXXIII, p. 89)

The Chain of Mount Olympus, Cyprus.
(*The Illustrated London News*, LXXIII, p. 101)

Hoisting the British Flag at Nicosia, the Capital of Cyprus.
(*The Illustrated London News*, LXXIII, p. 121)

Cape Kormakiti, Cyprus.
(*The Illustrated London News*, LXXIII, p. 125)

PLATE 10

Kyrenia, Cyprus.
(*The Illustrated London News*, LXXIII, p. 133)

Sketches of the British Occupation of Cyprus.
(*The Illustrated London News*, LXXIII, p. 145)

PLATE 12

The British Occupation of Cyprus: Landing-Place and Piers at Larnaca, from the House of the Duke of Edinburgh.
(*The Illustrated London News*, LXXIII, p. 148)

The British Occupation of Cyprus: Disembarking Horses in the Roadstead at Larnaca.
(*The Illustrated London News*, LXXIII, p. 149)

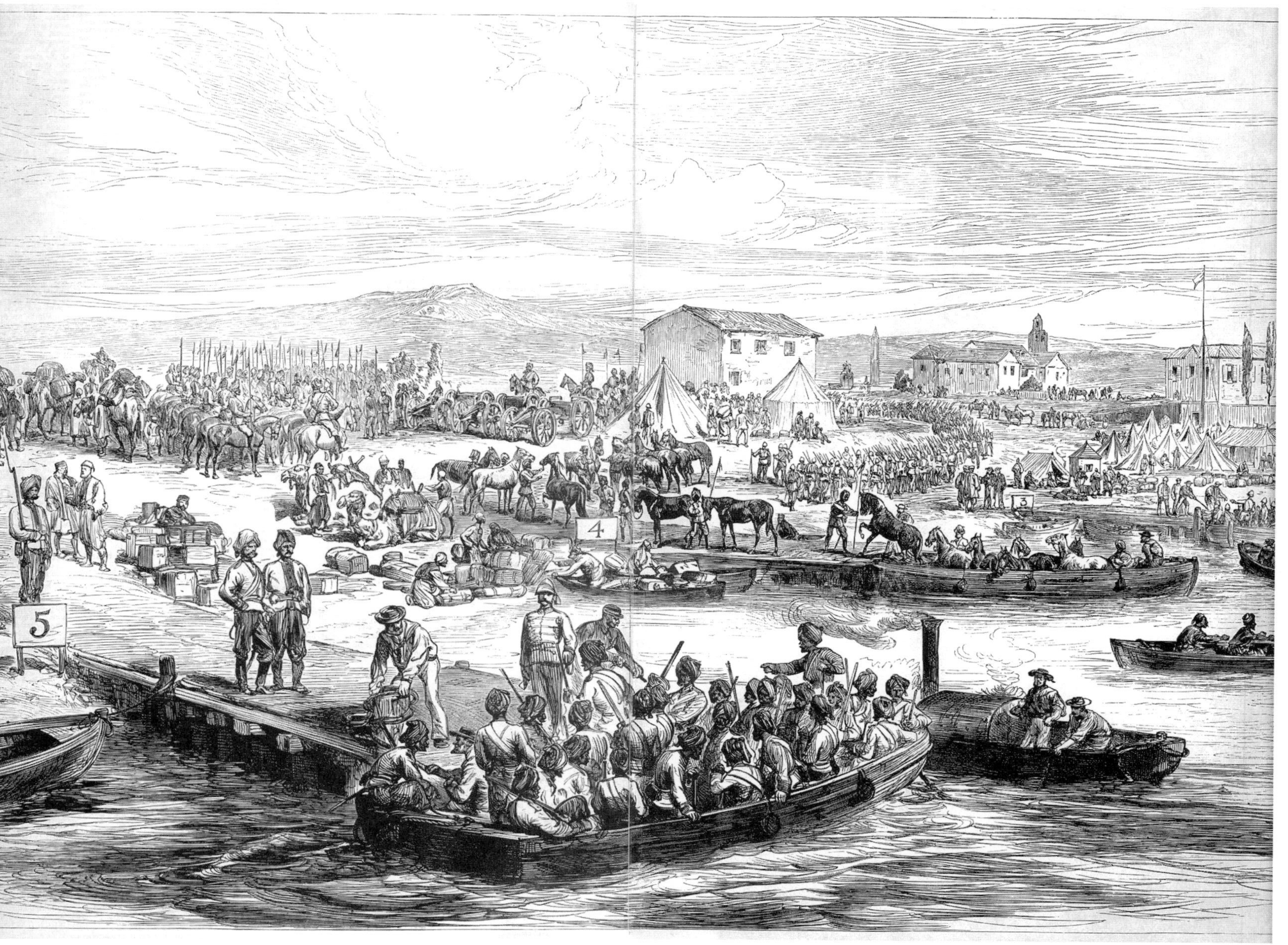

The British Occupation of Cyprus: General View of the Landing-Place at Larnaca, from the Anchorage.
(*The Illustrated London News*, LXXIII, p. 153)

North Coast View, from St. Hilarion, of the Mountain Chain of Kyrenia, Cyprus.
(The *Illustrated London News*, LXXIII, p. 157)

Waterside Café at the Marina, Larnaca, Cyprus.
(*The Illustrated London News*, LXXIII, p. 181)

The British Fleet at Larnaca, Cyprus, Saluting on the Duke of Edinburgh's Birthday.
(*The Illustrated London News*, LXXIII, p. 185)

AQUADUCT AT LARNACA.

BAZAAR AT LARNACA.

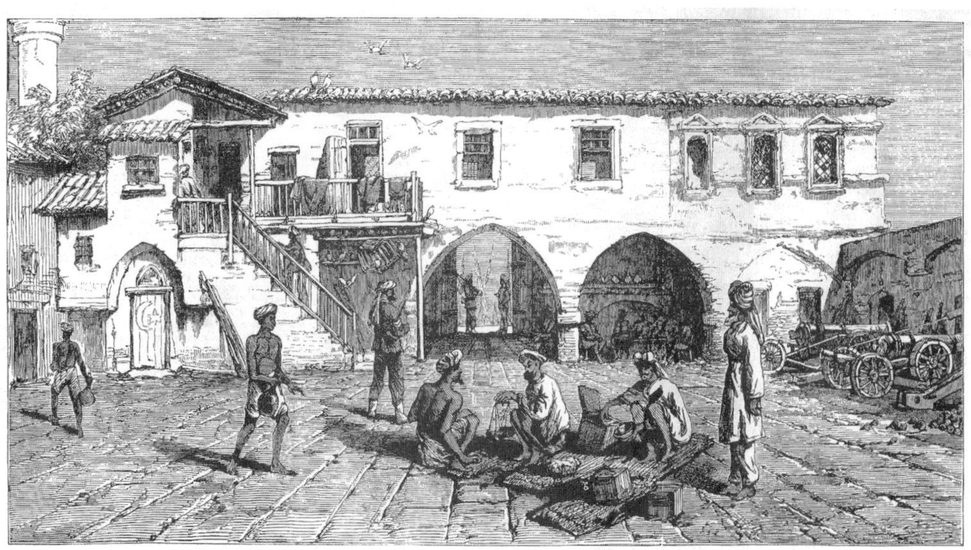

SERVING OUT RATIONS TO THE TROOPS AT LARNACA.

Sketches in Cyprus, by our Special Artist.
(*The Illustrated London News*, LXXIII, p. 200)

Sketches of Cyprus, by our Special Artist: St. Sophia, Nicosia.
(*The Illustrated London News*, LXXIII, p. 228)

WALLS OF NICOSIA, AT THE ENTRANCE FROM LARNACA.

SIR GARNET WOLSELEY'S HEAD-QUARTERS CAMP, NICOSIA.

EAST GATE, NICOSIA.

Sketches from Cyprus, by our Special Artist.
(*The Illustrated London News*, LXXIII, p. 229)

The Occupation of Cyprus: Greek Priests Blessing the Flag at Nicosia.
(*The Illustrated London News,* LXXIII, p. 276)

The Occupation of Cyprus: Prisoners from the Gaol at Nicosia escorted to Kyrenia by British and Turkish Troops.
(*The Illustrated London News*, LXXIII, p. 289)

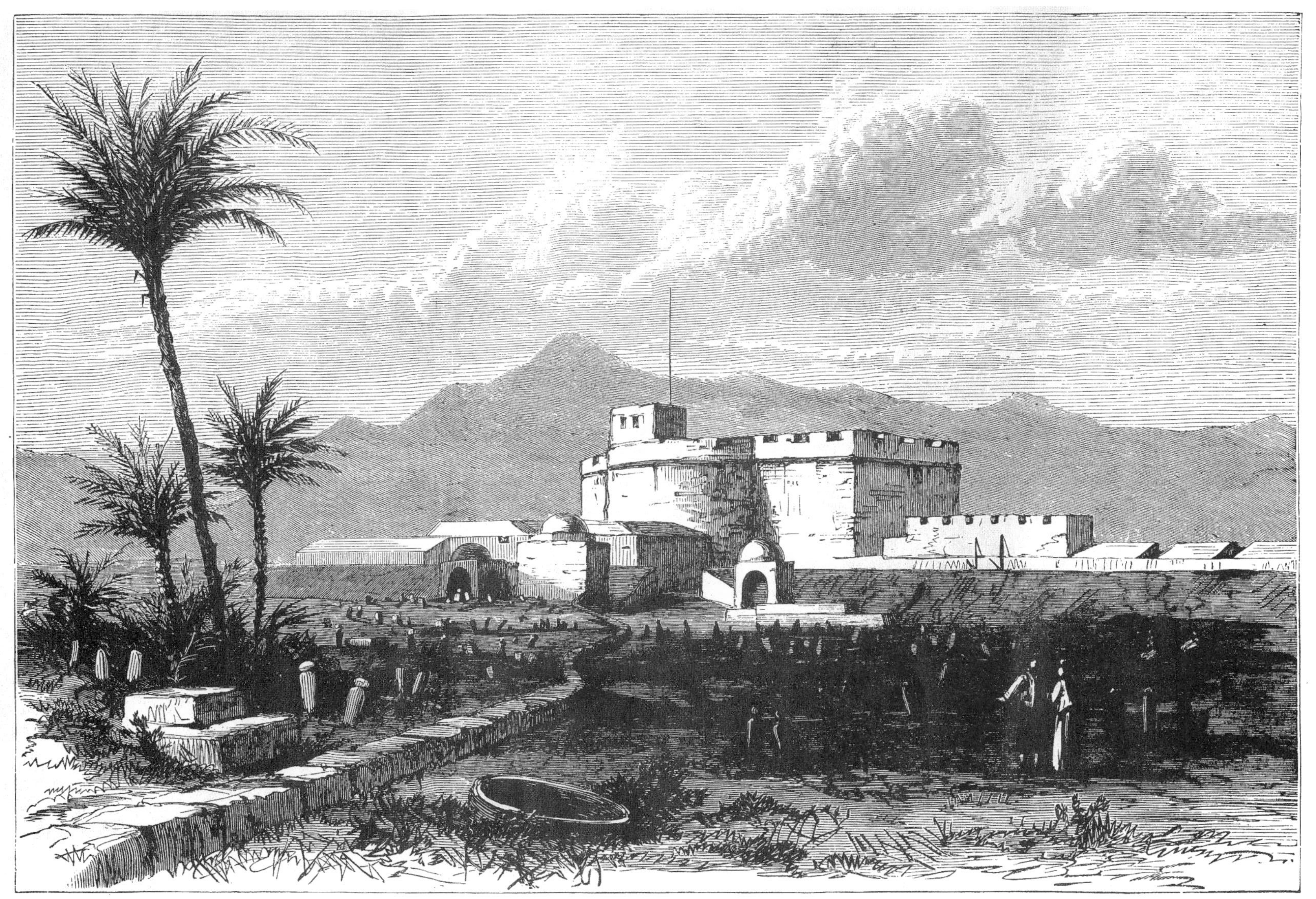

South-West Gate of Famagusta, the Old Venetian Seaport.
(*The Illustrated London News*, LXXIII, p. 292)

Château of St. Hilarion, from the Village of Tembros, North Coast.
(*The Illustrated London News*, LXXIII, p. 292)

The British Occupation of Cyprus: Landing-Place on the West Coast, near Baffo.
(*The Illustrated London News*, LXXIII, p. 296-297)

PLATE 26

The Harbour of Famagusta, Cyprus.
(*The Illustrated London News*, LXXIII, p. 312)

The Carob Harvest in Cyprus. —Gathering the Locust Beans.
(*The Illustrated London News*, LXXIII, p. 312)

a. Ancient Tomb Excavated near Larnaca, Cyprus.
(*The Illustrated London News*, LXXIII, p. 325)

b. English Tombs in Cloisters of Greek Church of St. Lazarus, Larnaca.
(*The Illustrated London News*, LXXIII, p. 325)

British Occupation of Cyprus: Triumphal Entry of Captain Swaine into Levgonico.
(*The Illustrated London News*, LXXIII, p. 344)

PLATE 30

View from the Monastery of Kantara.
(*The Illustrated London News*, LXXIII, p. 345)

Castle of Kantara.
(*The Illustrated London News*, LXXIII, p. 345)

a. Trikomo.
(*The Illustrated London News*, LXXIII, p. 352)

b. Reception of a Deputation, Trikomo.
(*The Illustrated London News*, LXXIII, p. 352)

a. Michael's House, Trikomo.
(*The Illustrated London News*, LXXIII, p. 352)

b. Cloisters of Monastery, Kantara.
(*The Illustrated London News*, LXXIII, p. 352)

PLATE 34

Cythraea, with Mount Pendedactylon.
(*The Illustrated London News*, LXXIII, p. 368)

The British Kaimakam Hearing an Assault Case at Hepta-Khumi.
(*The Illustrated London News*, LXXIII, p. 368)

a. Ancient Sepulchre in Cyprus.
(*The Illustrated London News*, LXXIII, p. 377)

b. Interior of Sepulchre, used as a Church.
(*The Illustrated London News*, LXXIII, p. 377)

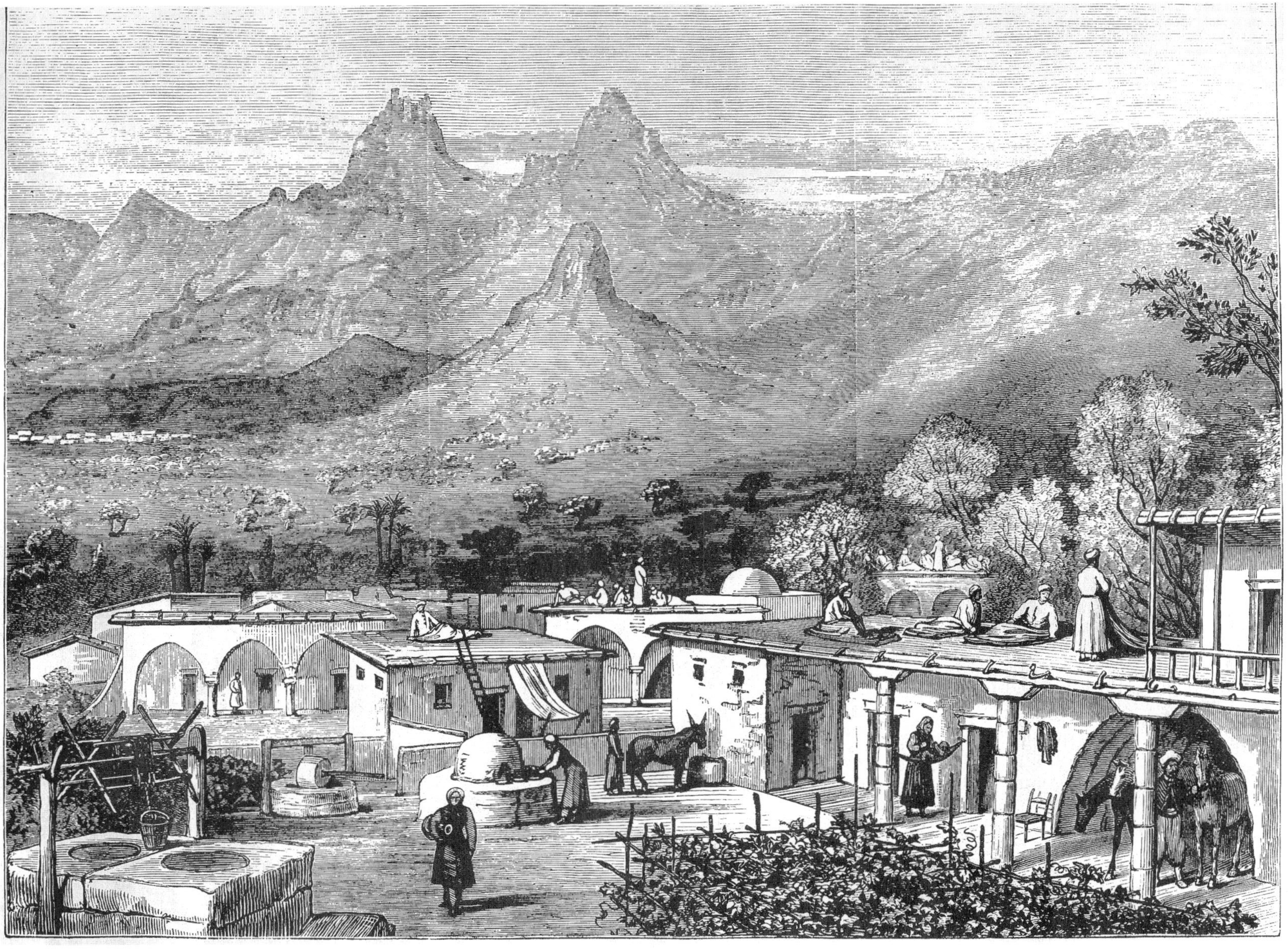

Village of Khumi Kebir, Cyprus, with Carpas Mountains.
(*The Illustrated London News*, LXXIII, p. 401)

PLATE 38

Cyprus: Sir Garnet Wolseley Holding a Reception in the Konak, Nicosia, at the Turkish Festival of Bairam.
(*The Illustrated London News*, LXXIII, p. 408)

a. Cyprus: Monastery Camp, Head-Quarters of Sir Garnet Wolseley and Staff, Nicosia.
(*The Illustrated London News*, LXXIII, p. 417)

b. Cyprus: the Site of Ancient Paphos.
(*The Illustrated London News*, LXXIII, p. 417)

PLATE 40

Photographers on Mount Olympus, Cyprus.
(*The Illustrated London News*, LXXIII, p. 432)

Summit of Mount Olympus, Cyprus.
(*The Illustrated London News*, LXXIII, p. 432)

West Front of the Cathedral of Famagusta, Cyprus.
(*The Illustrated London News*, LXXIII, P. 453)

Sketches in Cyprus: Goatherd Watering his Flock in the Plains of Paphos.
(*The Illustrated London News*, LXXIII, p. 456)

First Lord of the Admiralty and Secretary of State for War in Cyprus: the Party Leaving Nicosia.
(*The Illustrated London News*, LXXIII, p. 521)

St. Nicholas Church, Cyprus: Interior and Exterior.
(*The Illustrated London News*, LXXV, p. 348)

1. Head-Quarters Tents of Major-General Biddulph, C.B., High Commissioner, and Staff.
2. Camp of 20th Regiment, Tents of Paymaster and Post-Office. 3. Roman Catholic Chapel Tent. 4. Priest's Tent.
5. Royal Engineers' Camp. 6. Photographers' Studio and Tents. 7. Theatre of 20th Regiment. 8. Band of Royal Engineers.

Summer Encampment of the British Government of Cyprus.
(*The Illustrated London News*, LXXV, p. 363)

Interior of the Greek Church at the Monastery of St. Lazarus, Larnaca, Cyprus.
(*The Illustrated London News*, LXXV, p. 473)

a. Headquarters, Nicosia.
(Brassey, Frontispiece)

Port Papho.

b. Port Papho.
(Brassey, p. 250)

c. Mounting the 'Minotaur.'
(Brassey, p. 252)

a. Larnaka.
(Brassey, p. 261)

b. "Will they ever hear?"
(Brassey, p. 264)

c. Asking for a Pilot.
(Brassey, p. 265)

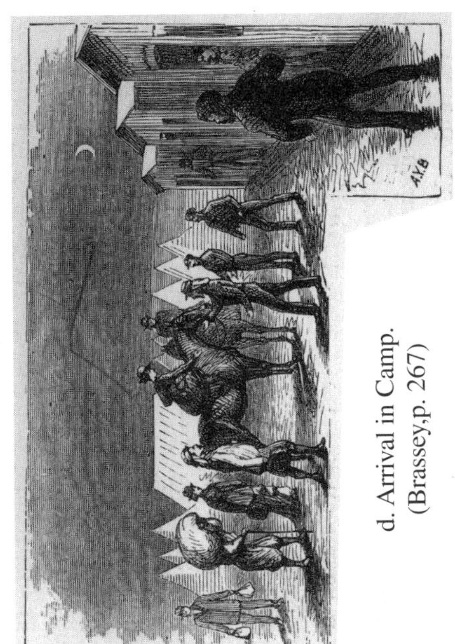

d. Arrival in Camp.
(Brassey,p. 267)

PLATE 50

a. Ruins of Famagousta.
(Brassey, p. 284)

b. Ancient Guns.
(Brassey, p. 287)

c. Kyrenia.
(Brassey, facing p. 290)

a. Convent of La Pais.
(Brassey, facing p. 292)

b. Meeting Sir Garnet Wolseley.
(Brassey, facing p. 296)

a. Kind Attentions.
(Brassey, p. 299)

b. House in Nicosia.
(Dixon, Frontispiece)

a. Our Travelling Party.
(Smith, Frontispiece)

b. Church of St. Sophia, Nicosia.
(Smith, facing p. 153)

a. Ruined Monastery at Bellapais.
(Smith, facing p. 158)

b. Courtyard of Monastery at Kykko.
(Smith, facing p. 190)

a. Among the Ruins at Famagusta.
(Mallock, Frontispiece)

b. Cyprian Boot-Shop.
(Haggard, facing p. 91)

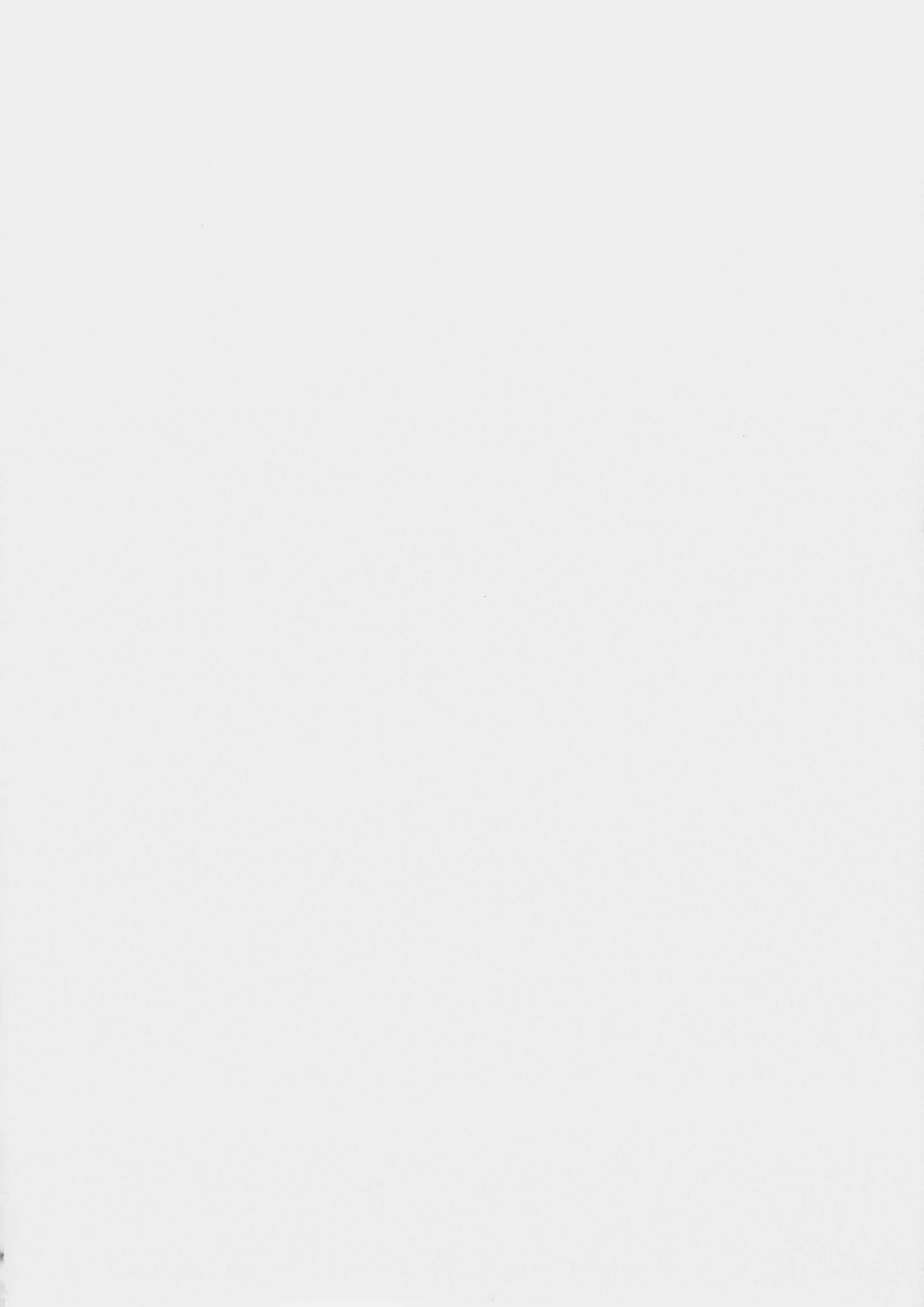

ISBN: 0-9651704-6-